ENCYCLOPEDIA OF AMERICAN CIVIL RIGHTS AND LIBERTIES

ENCYCLOPEDIA OF AMERICAN CIVIL RIGHTS AND LIBERTIES

Volume 1: A-G

Edited by
Otis H. Stephens, Jr.
John M. Scheb II
Kara E. Stooksbury

GREENWOOD PRESS
Westport, Connecticut • London

Library of Congress Cataloging-in-Publication Data

Encyclopedia of American civil rights and liberties / edited by Otis H. Stephens, Jr., John M. Scheb II, Kara E. Stooksbury.

  p. cm.

 Includes bibliographical references and index.

 ISBN 0-313-32758-0 (set : alk. paper) — ISBN 0-313-32759-9 (v. 1 : alk. paper) — ISBN 0-313-32760-2 (v. 2 : alk. paper)— ISBN 0-313-32761-0 (v. 3 : alk. paper)

 1. Civil rights—United States—Cases. 2. Civil rights—United States—Encyclopedias. 1. Stephens, Otis H., 1936– II. Scheb, John M., 1955– III. Stooksbury, Kara Elizabeth, 1969–
KF4748.E53 2006
342.7308'5—dc22   2006012037

British Library Cataloguing in Publication Data is available.

This book is included in the African American Experience database from Greenwood Electronic Media. For more Information, visit: www.africanamericanexperience.com.

Library of Congress Catalog Card Number: 2006012037
ISBN: 0–313–32758–0 (set)
     0–313–32759–9 (vol. 1)
     0–313–32760–2 (vol. 2)
     0–313–32761–0 (vol. 3)
First published in 2006

Greenwood Press, 88 Post Road West, Westport, CT 06881
An imprint of Greenwood Publishing Group, Inc.
www.greenwood.com

Printed in the United States of America

The paper used in this book complies with the Permanent Paper Standard issued by the National Information Standards Organization (Z39.48–1984).

10 9 8 7 6 5 4 3 2 1

Dedicated, with love, to our parents:

Otis H., Sr, and Margaret F. Stephens

John M., I, and Mary B. Scheb

Kyle and Betty Stooksbury

CONTENTS

LIST OF ENTRIES

GUIDE TO RELATED TOPICS

Civil Rights

Constitutional Provisions

Court Decisions

Dworkin, Andrea
Dworkin, Ronald
Evers, Medgar
Fortas, Abe
Frank, Leo
Frankfurter, Felix
Ginsburg, Ruth Bader
Goldberg, Arthur
Hand, Learned
Harlan, John Marshall
Harlan, John Marshall, II
Hart, H.L.A.
Hobbes, Thomas
Holmes, Oliver Wendell, Jr.
Jackson, Jesse
Jackson, Robert H.
Jefferson, Thomas
Kennedy, Anthony
Kennedy, Robert F.
King, Martin Luther, Jr.
King, Rodney
Kuntsler, William
Lincoln, Abraham
Locke, John
Machiavelli, Niccolò
Madison, James
Malcolm X
Marshall, John
Marshall, Thurgood
McCarthy, Joseph R.
McReynolds, James Clark
Meese, Edwin, III
Meredith, James
O'Connor, Sandra Day
Paine, Thomas
Parks, Rosa
Plato
Powell, Lewis F., Jr.
Rawls, John
Reed, Stanley F.
Rehnquist, William H.
Reno, Janet
Roosevelt, Eleanor
Roosevelt, Franklin D.
Rousseau, Jean-Jacques

Scalia, Antonin
Sharpton, Alfred Charles
Socrates
Souter, David H.
Stanton, Elizabeth Cady
Stevens, John Paul
Stewart, Potter
Stone, Harlan Fiske
Story, Joseph
Taft, William Howard
Taney, Roger B.
Thomas, Clarence
Thoreau, Henry David
Truth, Sojourner
Vinson, Fred M.
Waite, Morrison Remick
Warren, Earl
Washington, Booker T.
White, Byron R.
Zenger, John Peter

Key Concepts

Contempt, Power of
Fundamental Rights
Harmless Error, Doctrine of
Interpretivism
Judicial Activism
Judicial Restraint
Living Constitution
Original Intent, Doctrine of
Rational Basis Test
State Action Doctrine
Strict Scrutiny
Unconstitutional as Applied
Warren Court
Citizenship
Civil Disobedience
Conservatism
Democracy, Constitutional
Democracy, Representative
Diversity
Equity
Hate Crimes
In Loco Parentis

American Nazi Party
Americans United for Separation of Church
    and State
Anti-Defamation League
Center for Individual Rights
Church of Jesus Christ of Latter-day Saints
Communist Party USA
Concerned Women of America
Congress of Racial Equality
Congressional Women's Caucus
Human Rights Watch
Jehovah's Witnesses
John Birch Society
Ku Klux Klan
Motion Picture Association of America
National Association for the Advancement of
    Colored People
Nation of Islam
National Abortion Rights Action League
National Organization for Women
National Right to Life Committee
Native American Church
Operation Rescue
People for Ethical Treatment of Animals
People for the American Way
Planned Parenthood
Quakers
Reporters Committee for Freedom of the Press
Seventh-Day Adventists
Southern Baptist Convention
Southern Christian Leadership Conference
Southern Poverty Law Center
Student Nonviolent Coordinating Committee
Student Press Law Center
Students for a Democratic Society
Unitarian Universalism

Privacy, Reproductive and Family Rights

Abortion, Public Funding of
Abortion, Right to
Adoption
Die, Right to
Drugs, Private Use of
Griswold v. Connecticut

Lawrence v. Texas
Living Will
Loving v. Virginia
Medical Treatment, Right to Refuse
Meyer v. Nebraska
Parental Rights
Pierce v. Society of Sisters
Poe v. Ullman
Privacy, Constitutional Right of
Privacy, Informational
Privacy, Invasion of
Pro-choice Position
Pro-life Movement
Pro-life Position
Reproductive Freedom
Roe v. Wade
Seat Belt Laws
Sterilization, Compulsory
Substituted Judgment, Doctrine of
Suicide, Doctor-Assisted
Surrogate Motherhood

Religious Freedom

Abington School District v. Schempp
Americans United for Separation of Church
    and State
Bob Jones University v. United States
Cantwell v. Connecticut
Church of Jesus Christ of Latter-Day Saints
Conscience, Freedom of
*Employment Division, Department of Human
    Resources of Oregon v. Smith*
Establishment Clause
Everson v. Board of Education
Evolution/Creationism Controversy
First Amendment
Free Exercise Clause
Freedom from Religion Foundation
Jehovah's Witnesses
Lemon v. Kurtzman
"Memorial and Remonstrance"
Moment of Silence Laws
Nation of Islam
Religion, Freedom of

LIST OF PRIMARY DOCUMENTS

PREFACE

The *Encyclopedia of American Civil Rights and Liberties* is designed as a reference tool for students, teachers, scholars, and citizens interested in the broad subject of civil rights and liberties. Covering topics ranging from abortion to zoning, the *Encyclopedia* provides current, comprehensive, and sophisticated coverage of *both* civil rights and liberties in the United States. No other volume currently available covers both these topics in such a detailed yet readable manner. The term "civil rights" refers to the issues that arise from the democratic commitment to equality. In the United States, civil rights protections stem both from constitutional guarantees of equal protection of the laws and antidiscrimination legislation enacted by Congress, state legislatures, and local governments. "Civil liberties," on the other hand, denotes the numerous disputes pitting claims of individual freedom against assertions of governmental power. In large part, these claims are based on provisions of the United States Constitution and the state constitutions. Most noteworthy among these provisions are the Bill of Rights of the United States Constitution and similar enumerations of rights found in state constitutions. This encyclopedia encompasses both the civil rights and civil liberties dimensions. Although these are distinctive fields of law and policy, they are closely interrelated and equally important in reflecting the core values of a democratic society.

The *Encyclopedia*'s 627 alphabetically arranged entries include articles on major historical developments and social movements, such as the feminist and civil rights movements, and important legislation, such as the USA PATRIOT Act of 2001; the Espionage Act of 1917; and the seven Civil Rights Acts, ranging from the first such statute passed in 1866 to the last enacted in 1988. Other entries cover landmark Supreme Court decisions, such as *Plessy v. Feguson* (1896), *Wisconsin v. Yoder* (1972), and *Hustler Magazine v. Falwell* (1988); influential individuals, such as Rosa Parks and John Peter Zenger; groundbreaking justices of the U.S. Supreme Court, such as Benjamin Cardozo and Louis D. Brandeis; key constitutional provisions, such as the cruel and unusual punishments clause and the establishment clause; relevant groups and organizations, such as the National Right to Life Committee and the Nation of Islam; important government departments and agencies, such as the Department of Homeland Security and the Equal Employment Opportunity Commission; controversial issues, such as school prayer, smoking bans, and flag burning; and crucial legal and philosophical concepts and doctrines, such as judicial immunity and the fruit of the poisonous tree doctrine. In addition, the *Encyclopedia* contains the text of a set of original documents that have figured prominently in the development of civil rights and liberties in the Anglo-American legal and political traditions. These documents include the Mayflower Compact, Abraham Lincoln's first inaugural address, Martin Luther King's "Letter from a Birmingham Jail," the English Petition of Right of 1628, and the Universal Declaration of Human Rights of 1948.

Contributors to the *Encyclopedia* include scholars from diverse fields of study, including law, history, philosophy, political science, sociology, and related disciplines in the social sciences and humanities, as well as judges and practitioners of the law. Although the entries reflect the diversity of our contributors, as editors we have endeavored to make each article accessible to an educated lay audience by minimizing legal and academic jargon. And because issues of rights and liberties are matters over which reasonable and conscientious people can and will disagree, we have insisted that contributors avoid polemics and provide fair and balanced coverage of their respective topics.

With few exceptions, the entries conclude with a bibliography listing books, articles, or Web sites that were used in the preparation of the entry or where additional useful information can be found. Each entry also contains a "see also" line listing cross-references to related entries elsewhere in the *Encyclopedia*. To assist readers in navigating through the entries, we have included a guide to related topics, which breaks the entries down into broad categories and will allow readers to quickly and easily trace all relevant entries relating to Supreme Court justices, civil rights, or religious issues. Finally, the *Encyclopedia* contains a general bibliography listing numerous works that have contributed significantly to scholarship in the civil rights and liberties fields, as well as a comprehensive table of cases listing all the judicial decisions cited throughout the *Encyclopedia*.

Otis H. Stephens, Jr., John M. Scheb II, and Kara E. Stooksbury

ACKNOWLEDGMENTS

During the preparation of this compendium, we have received strong encouragement and helpful suggestions from our colleagues in the College of Law and the Department of Political Science at the University of Tennessee. Summer grants provided by the College of Law in 2004 and 2005 greatly facilitated completion of the project.

We have also been assisted by a great number of people, including all our contributors, many of whom reviewed the contributions of others. Special thanks are due to Judge John M. Scheb for his extraordinary effort in conducting research, reviewing numerous articles, and authoring many more entries than he was originally assigned. Others whose efforts surpassed the call of duty include Aaron Belville, Martin Carcieri, Mary Walker Michael R. Fitzgerald, David Folz, Lori Maxwell, Linda C. Noe, Charles Patrick, Rachel Pearsall, Chapman Rackaway, Adam Ruf, Mary Walker, and Caitlin Shockey. We also wish to thank Steven Vetrano, our editor at Greenwood Press, and John Wagner, the development editor on this project, for their patience and flexibility. Finally, we would like to thank our families and friends for putting up with our preoccupation with this project for the last three years.

We assume responsibility for all errors of commission or omission and invite readers to contact us to point out any such errors.

A

AARP. *See* American Association of Retired Persons

ABA. *See* American Bar Association

ABERNATHY, RALPH DAVID. *See* Southern Christian Leadership Conference

ABINGTON SCHOOL DISTRICT V. SCHEMPP (1963)

Abington School District v. Schempp is one of the Supreme Court decisions from the early 1960s referred to collectively as the "School Prayer Decisions." In this case Edward and Sidney Schempp, members of the Unitarian faith, brought suit in federal court to challenge the daily practice of prayer and Bible reading at Abington Senior High School in Abington Township, Pennsylvania. The practice was based in part on a state statute that required that "[a]t least ten verses from the Holy Bible shall be read, without comment, at the opening of each public school on each school day." The statute also provided that "[a]ny child shall be excused from such Bible reading, or attending such Bible reading, upon the written request of his parent or guardian."

At trial Edward Schempp testified that he considered having his children excused from participating in the challenged exercises "but decided against it for several reasons, including his belief that the children's relationships with their teachers and classmates would be adversely affected." The federal district court struck down the challenged practices and the statute requiring Bible reading, finding that "the children's attendance at Abington Senior High School [was] compulsory and that the practice of reading ten verses from the Bible [was] also compelled by law." It also found that the challenged practices were "in effect a religious observance." The court observed that the religious character of the exercises was "made all the more apparent by the fact that the Bible reading is followed immediately by a recital in unison by the pupils of the Lord's Prayer."

On direct appeal, the U.S. Supreme Court affirmed. Dividing eight-to-one, the Court held that public schools, as agencies of the state, must be "firmly committed to a position of neutrality" in matters of religion. According to the majority opinion authored by Justice Tom Clark, for a policy "to withstand the strictures of the Establishment Clause there must be a secular legislative purpose and a primary effect that neither advances nor inhibits religion." The Court concluded that the practice of public school-sponsored prayer and Bible reading violated these principles. Justice Clark observed that religious studies may be acceptable "when presented objectively as part of a secular program of education." But "religious exercises" in public schools violate the principle that government maintain "strict neutrality, neither aiding nor opposing religion."

In his lone dissent, Justice Potter Stewart characterized the challenged activities as "an attempt by the State to accommodate those differences which the existence in our society of a variety of religious beliefs makes inevitable." In Stewart's view, "the Constitution requires that such efforts be struck down only if they are proven to entail the use of the secular authority of government to coerce a preference among such beliefs." Stewart observed that the record in the case was devoid of evidence "as to whether there would exist any coercion of any kind upon a student who did not want to participate."

In its brief to the Court, the State of Pennsylvania argued that the challenged exercises served legitimate secular purposes, including teaching literature, countering materialism, and maintaining traditional values and institutions. The Court gave these arguments short shrift and did not address them in its opinion. The Court did respond, however, to the state's contention that to prohibit the challenged exercises would in effect establish a "religion of secularism" in the schools. Justice Clark agreed that "the State may not establish a 'religion of secularism' in the sense of affirmatively opposing or showing hostility to religion, thus 'preferring those who believe in no religion over those who do believe.'" But he denied that "this decision in any sense has that effect."

Coming one year after the Court's first school prayer decision, *Engel v. Vitale* (1962), the *Abington* decision had the effect of intensifying the controversy over the Court's role in this sensitive area.

See also Clark, Tom C.; Establishment Clause; *Lemon v. Kurtzman;* Religion, Official Endorsements of; School Prayer Decisions; Warren Court

John M. Scheb II and Otis H. Stephens, Jr.

ABOLITIONIST MOVEMENT

The movement to end slavery was initially a religious undertaking that originated in the mid-1700s. As the years passed, the movement's focus changed. The religious opposition gave way to proposals for colonization and ultimately abolition and emancipation, goals that were not achieved until slavery was abolished by the Thirteenth Amendment in 1865.

Slavery had been a feature of colonial life since 1619; it was not until the 1700s that several Protestant denominations protested the practice of slavery, believing it to be immoral. The Quakers, many of whom had owned slaves during the late 1600s and early 1700s, were the first to voice their objections in 1750, at which point, "Quaker opinion [had] turned decisively against slavery" (Hamm 2003, 34). Central to this effort was the work of Quaker minister John Woolman, who was influential in spreading the belief among Quakers that slavery was detrimental to slave owners and slaves alike. It harmed slave owners, as it led to laziness, violence, and exploitation. Slaves were harmed because they were denied the opportunity to be obedient to the guidance of the Inner Light.

Just prior to the Revolutionary War, many colonists compared their relationship to Great Britain as that of master and slave. And yet, "antislavery thought prior to 1763 condemned slavery without reference to the relationship between the colonists' liberty from the British government and slavery" (Davis 1996, 52). Slavery was abolished in New England and Pennsylvania by 1783. Ending slavery in the South, however, was much more difficult due to the sheer number of slaves and the fact that among white Southerners, slave owning had become a popular method of acquiring wealth and status.

When the delegates to the Constitutional Convention met in 1787, abolishing slavery was not on their agenda. "No delegate had come to Philadelphia hoping for anything so drastic as to outlaw slavery from the United States, even those who hated it most" (Bowen 1966, 204). The result was that the Constitution did not end the institution of slavery. There was a tacit agreement that the slavery issue had been settled when the states, rather than the national government, were given the authority to regulate it. This agreement was shattered in 1790 when a Quaker petition presented to Congress, signed by none other than Benjamin Franklin, suggested that the federal government had the authority to end slavery and the slave trade. When the petition ultimately failed, it established a precedent cited even 40 years later that Congress lacked the power to end slavery (Ellis 2000, 118).

Prior to the 1830s those wishing to end slavery supported plans to remove slaves either to their country of origin or to some other destination; such plans were referred to as colonization. Many of those plans required compensation for slave owners who would lose their "property." With those strings attached, ending slavery became more difficult as the slave population increased, thus making emancipation financially impractical. With the publication of *The Liberator* in 1831 William Lloyd Garrison introduced radical abolitionism into the American consciousness. Garrison and his followers were opposed to colonization plans because they violated the natural rights of slaves, as they implied inferiority and considered slaves property. In 1832 Garrison was instrumental in organizing both the New England Anti-Slavery Society and the American Anti-Slavery Society, the first organizations promoting immediate emancipation.

Garrison was steadfast in his belief that the organizations should remain politically neutral and that women should participate in the cause. This latter decision was significant, as the political activity of women in abolition would provide a foundation for the women's suffrage movement. In fact, the two causes became linked. Garrison came to believe that the Constitution was "a covenant with death and an agreement with hell." Therefore, he eschewed any belief that governmental institutions, and even religious institutions, would be useful tools in emancipation. His strategy relied upon convincing the public of the evils of slavery. In the 1840s, a splinter group, the American and Foreign Anti-Slavery Society, was formed in an attempt to influence the political process. This organization formed the Liberty Party and ran candidates for federal offices. "Although the Liberty Party was never successful at the polls, it was instrumental in forcing the major parties to address the issue of slavery" (Davis 1996, 196).

From the colonial era until the end of slavery, the Underground Railroad operated to help free slaves from bondage. The Underground Railroad was a system of routes from the South ultimately ending in Canada. There were, however, other escape routes leading into the western territories and into Mexico. Slaves seeking freedom either escaped alone or in a small group with the aid of conductors (those who led the slaves), who risked their own lives for the greater good. Perhaps the best-known conductor was Harriet Tubman, who had escaped from slavery herself and made 19 trips to secure the freedom of more than 300 slaves.

The movement as a whole was dissipating in the mid-1800s amidst numerous congressional agreements guaranteeing the continuation of slavery. The *Amistad* case, however, breathed new life into the abolitionist movement. The *Amistad* (a Spanish schooner) was transporting slaves from one Cuban port to another in 1839 (Cuba was a Spanish colony at that time) when the slaves revolted and took over the ship. Ultimately, the ship was towed to New London, Connecticut, where questions were raised concerning the jurisdiction of the United States in the matter and the applicability of international law. When the case was appealed to the United States Supreme Court, former president John Quincy Adams argued the case on behalf of the slaves. Justice Joseph Story's opinion in *United States v. The Amistad* (1841) asserted that the individuals aboard the *Amistad* were kidnapped and thus could not be considered slaves. He ordered their release, and they had the choice of remaining or returning to Africa.

Through the work of abolitionists and the publicity surrounding the *Amistad* case, by the 1840s "most Northerners were thinking about slavery, and once they thought about it, most opposed it" (Urofsky and Finkelman 2002, 317). Yet the opponents of slavery were unsuccessful in putting an end to the practice until the Civil War. They achieved success, however, in the Northern states in four general areas. First, they succeeded in eliminating slavery in those states; second, abolitionists convinced free states to emancipate any slaves brought within their jurisdiction; third, abolitionists lobbied Northern state legislatures for legal protection for free blacks to prevent them from being kidnapped as fugitive slaves;

and fourth, opponents of slavery worked to improve the conditions of free blacks, including the provision of public education, which was widely available by 1860 (Urofsky and Finkelman 2002, 317–18). Most Northerners opposed to slavery were more interested in preventing its spread, rather than involving themselves in an effort to rid the South of slavery. However, by 1850 the controversy over slavery was the most important issue facing the country.

Politicians of the era believed they had brokered an end to the slavery issue via the Compromise of 1850. Two key provisions allowed California into the union as a free state, and to placate the Southern states, a new fugitive slave law strengthened the penalties for helping slaves to escape. Rather than settling the issue, this compromise invigorated the abolitionist movement. Many abolitionists were incensed over the new fugitive slave law, viewing it as a victory for the slave states. As a result, the Underground Railroad was more active than it had ever been before. This compromise also inspired Harriet Beecher Stowe's novel *Uncle Tom's Cabin* (1852). Abolitionists also were infuriated by the Kansas-Nebraska Act of 1854, which repealed the Missouri Compromise's ban on slavery in the remaining areas of the Louisiana Purchase. Proslavery and antislavery advocates clashed; proslavery forces murdered several free-state settlers and ransacked Lawrence, Kansas. In response, the militant abolitionist John Brown and his followers led a raid at Pottawatomie, killing five men. The violence escalated across the state through the summer and fall of 1856, until the governor, with the assistance of federal troops, restored order. Unfortunately by that time, over two hundred people were dead, and two million dollars worth of property had been destroyed (Urofsky and Finkelman 2002, 387).

In 1857, the Supreme Court entered the fray over slavery through its ruling in the Dred Scott case. This case added fuel to the abolitionists' fire by holding that the Missouri Compromise constituted an arbitrary deprivation of property rights, and that African Americans, whether they were slaves or not, were not citizens of the United States.

The dramatic events of the 1850s continued, and in 1859 John Brown and 18 others took control of the federal arsenal at Harpers Ferry, Virginia. After their plans went awry and they were captured, Brown was sentenced to death and hanged. His death served to further divide the country. While Northerners deplored Brown's tactics, they believed that his views concerning slavery were correct. Southerners naturally viewed him as an enemy and a representative of Northern attempts to end slavery.

Against this background, the presidential election of 1860 was consequential. The election of Abraham Lincoln, who had argued against the expansion of slavery but conceded that slavery could continue where it already existed, set in motion a series of events beginning with the secession of several Southern states and culminating in a bloody civil war. When the dust had cleared, Lincoln's Emancipation Proclamation provided a basis for the Thirteenth Amendment, which abolished slavery. The ideal of equality under the law, however, would be a continual struggle in the United States.

See also Dred Scott Case; Emancipation Proclamation; Equality; Lincoln, Abraham; Quakers; Slavery; Story, Joseph; Thirteenth Amendment; Women's Suffrage

Bibliography

Bowen, Catherine Drinker. 1966. *Miracle at Philadelphia: The Story of the Constitutional Convention May to September 1787.* Boston: Little, Brown.

Davis, Sue. 1996. *American Political Thought: Four Hundred Years of Ideas and Ideologies.* Englewood Cliffs, NJ: Prentice Hall.

Ellis, Joseph. 2001. *Founding Brothers: The Revolutionary Generation.* New York: Alfred A. Knopf.

Hamm, Thomas D. 2003. *The Quakers in America.* New York: Columbia University Press.

Urofsky, Melvin I., and Paul Finkelman. 2002. *A March of Liberty: A Constitutional History of the United States.* Vol. 1: *From the Founding to 1890.* 2nd ed. New York: Oxford University Press.

Kara E. Stooksbury

ABORTION, PARTIAL BIRTH. *See* Abortion, Right to

ABORTION, PUBLIC FUNDING OF

In *Roe v. Wade* (1973) the Supreme Court effectively legalized abortion, holding that the constitutional right of privacy "is broad enough to encompass a woman's decision … to terminate her pregnancy." Yet four years later, in *Maher v. Roe* (1977), the Court upheld a Connecticut welfare regulation that denied Medicaid funds to defray the costs of abortions, unless attending physicians certified the abortions as "medically necessary." The Court found that the denial of Medicaid benefits to poor women seeking elective abortions neither discriminated against a "suspect class" of persons nor unduly burdened the exercise of fundamental rights. Therefore, the restriction was permissible under both the Equal Protection and Due Process Clauses of the Fourteenth Amendment.

In the same year, Congress enacted the Hyde Amendment (named for Representative Henry Hyde, R-Ill., who introduced the legislation), forbidding the use of Medicaid and other federal resources to support abortions, except in cases where the continuation of a pregnancy endangered a woman's life. Over the years, the terms of the restriction have varied, but Congress has continued to enact the Hyde Amendment as part of the annual budget process. In 1978, the law was liberalized somewhat to allow for federal funding of abortions in cases of rape or incest, but those exceptions were eliminated in 1981 under the Reagan Administration. During the Clinton Administration, the rape and incest exceptions were reinstated. The current version of the Hyde Amendment, which dates from 1997, allows funding for abortions in cases of rape, incest, and endangerment where the woman's life is threatened by "a physical disorder, physical injury, or physical illness, including a life-endangering physical condition caused by or arising from the pregnancy itself'" (Boonstra and Sonfield 2000, 8).

In the public policy sphere, critics have attacked the Hyde Amendment on two primary fronts. First, critics charge that it creates a double standard for wealthy and poor women in that it creates, as presidential candidate Al Gore noted in 2000, "an inequitable result" by denying poor women "the practical ability" to exercise the constitutional right to choose, whereas a woman who has sufficient funds to pay for an abortion has no practical inhibition in seeking an abortion if one is desired (Boonstra and Sonfield 2000, 8). Second, opponents critics argue that the Hyde Amendment has resulted in higher health care and welfare costs to taxpayers. Because it takes longer for poor women to gather the funds necessary to pay for an abortion, the Hyde Amendment has led to more abortions being performed later in pregnancy. Abortions performed later are more subject to complications; thus they are more costly than abortions performed early in pregnancy. And because the Hyde Amendment has made it impossible for some poor women to obtain abortions altogether, it has increased the birth rate among women who are dependent on the welfare system.

As a constitutional matter, the foregoing arguments may or may not be relevant, depending on one's approach to constitutional interpretation. Certainly those who view the Equal Protection Clause of the Fourteenth Amendment (and the implicit equal protection component of the Fifth Amendment) broadly are troubled by the denial of public funding in the abortion area. They would argue that the Hyde Amendment impermissibly denies a class of citizens the right to choose abortion and thus makes *Roe v. Wade* essentially inoperative for them. But in *Harris v. McRae* (1980), a sharply divided Supreme Court rejected this argument and upheld the Hyde Amendment. Writing for the majority, Justice Potter Stewart concluded,

It simply does not follow that a woman's freedom of choice carries with it a constitutional entitlement to the financial resources to avail herself of the full range of protected choices…. Although government may not place obstacles in the path of a woman's exercise of her freedom of choice, it need not remove those not of its own creation. Indigency falls in the latter category.

Stewart suggested that the Hyde Amendment might not be wise social policy but distinguished the policy issue from the constitutional inquiry:

It is not the mission of this Court or any other to decide whether the balance of competing interests reflected in the Hyde Amendment is wise social policy. If that were our mission, not every Justice who has subscribed to the judgment of the Court today could have done so. But we cannot, in the name of the Constitution, overturn duly enacted statutes simply "because they may be unwise, improvident, or out of harmony with a particular school of thought." … Rather, "when an issue involves policy choices as sensitive as those implicated [here] … , the appropriate forum for their resolution in a democracy is the legislature."

In dissent, Justice William J. Brennan argued that the decision was inconsistent with Roe v. Wade and subsequent decisions recognizing a woman's constitutional right to abortion:

The proposition for which these cases stand … is not that the State is under an affirmative obligation to ensure access to abortions for all who may desire them; it is that the State must refrain from wielding its enormous power and influence in a manner that might burden the pregnant woman's freedom to choose whether to have an abortion.

The Hyde Amendment restricts only federal funding of abortions, leaving states to decide whether to impose restrictions on the use of state funds. Today, most states follow the Hyde Amendment approach, prohibiting the use of state funds for elective abortions. As of 2001, however, a significant minority of states (19) allowed funds to be used for abortions deemed "medically necessary," a far broader category than that permitted by the Hyde Amendment. Four of these states (Hawaii, Maryland, New York, and Washington) adopted the more liberal policy through legislative action. In the remaining 15 states, courts have imposed these policies based on interpretation of their respective state constitutions (Nash 2001, 13).

See also Abortion, Right to; Brennan, William J., Jr.; Due Process Clauses; Equal Protection Clause; Equal Protection Jurisprudence; Federalism and Civil Rights and Liberties; Fifth Amendment; Fourteenth Amendment; Privacy, Constitutional Right of; Stewart, Potter

Bibliography

Boonstra, Heather, and Adam Sonfield. 2000. "Rights without Access: Revisiting Public Funding of Abortion for Poor Women." *Guttmacher Report on Public Policy* 3 (2): 8.

Nash, Elizabeth. 2001. "Public Funding of Abortion for Poor Women: Where Things Stand." *Guttmacher Report on Public Policy* 4 (1):13.

Sollom, Terry, Rachel Benson Gold, and Rebekah Saul. 1996. "Public Funding for Contraceptive, Sterilization and Abortion Services, 1994." *Family Planning Perspectives* 28 (4):166–73.

Otis H. Stephens, Jr., and John M. Scheb II

ABORTION, RIGHT TO

Since 1973, when the United States Supreme Court announced that the constitutional right to privacy included a woman's right to terminate her pregnancy, the Court has played an important role in determining the parameters of abortion rights. In cases decided over the next three decades, the Court eroded the right to choose but has stopped short of eliminating it entirely.

During the 1960s there were dramatic changes in popular attitudes regarding sexual mores. The sexual revolution had a profound effect on American society and provided the context for the Supreme Court's landmark ruling regarding sexual privacy. In *Griswold v. Connecticut* (1965), the Court struck down a Connecticut law prohibiting the use of contraceptives by married couples and held that the Constitution contained an implied right to privacy. A few years later, the Court struck down a Massachusetts law prohibiting the distribution of contraceptive devices or materials to single persons. Speaking for the majority in Eisenstadt v. Baird (1972), Justice William J. Brennan announced that the right to privacy was not just limited to married couples but belonged to single people as well.

The change in societal attitudes also affected the issue of abortion. Between 1967 and 1970, twelve states enacted abortion reform legislation. Although the laws differed, most permitted abortions for victims of rape or incest, cases of severe fetal deformity, or when the woman's life or health was threatened.

By 1973, although a number of states offered women somewhat easier access to abortion, some, such as Texas, still banned all abortions except to save the woman's life. The Texas law was challenged in *Roe v. Wade* (1973), which forced the Supreme Court to decide whether it violated the woman's constitutional right to privacy. Women's rights groups achieved a major victory when the Supreme Court declared that the constitutional right to privacy guaranteed a woman's choice to have an abortion. The Court warned though that the right was not absolute; its parameters must be determined by balancing the woman's control over her body with the state's interest in regulating the abortion procedure. Speaking for a seven-to-two majority, Justice Harry Blackmun asserted that the right to privacy encompassed a woman's right to terminate a pregnancy. But the Court placed some restrictions on this right, emphasizing that it must be balanced against the state's interest in the life and health of the woman and her fetus. The Court crafted a compromise, creating a trimester framework in which the state's interest was weighed against that of the woman during each stage of the pregnancy. This established the principle that abortion regulations must vary with the stage, or trimester, of pregnancy; in each trimester, the state must justify its abortion law by showing it has a compelling reason for the regulation.

Because abortion carries almost no medical risk when performed in the first three months of pregnancy, the Court found the state had no compelling reason to regulate the procedure beyond requiring the physician to be licensed. During the second trimester, the state may impose reasonable health regulations to further its interest in the woman's health. In the third trimester, abortions may be prohibited entirely unless it is necessary for the woman's health or life. Based on this standard, the Texas abortion law was declared unconstitutional. In a companion case, *Doe v. Bolton* (1973), the Court struck down a Georgia statute that restricted a woman's access to abortion. In that case, in addition to the woman's desire for an abortion, the statute required approval from a hospital abortion committee, two physicians, and further mandated that the procedure be performed in an accredited hospital.

Shortly after *Roe v. Wade* was decided, states began to impose restrictions on a minor woman's access to abortion, initially by requiring the consent of one or both parents. In a series of cases beginning in 1976, the Court was asked to decide whether a young woman's right to privacy was equal to that of an adult. In determining the parameters of a minor's right to terminate her pregnancy, the Court balanced the young woman's right to choose abortion against the parents' interest in their child and in the integrity of their family as well as the state's interest in regulating the health of the young woman.

Planned Parenthood of Central Missouri v. Danforth (1976) arose from a challenge to a Missouri law requiring an unmarried woman under 18 to obtain her parent or guardian's written consent; and for a married woman, her husband's consent. Known as a blanket veto, this law removed the decision from the woman, giving it to her parents or husband instead. The Court struck down both consent provisions, reiterating that the abortion decision must be between the woman and her physician. The state was constitutionally barred from granting a third party an absolute veto over this decision. Although the Court recognized that the parents had a role to play in the decision, their daughter's right to privacy trumped this role.

With the blanket veto forbidden, states began to insert judicial bypass procedures into their consent laws. For the most part, they allowed minors who were unable to secure their parent's consent (or were unwilling to ask) to go before a judge to obtain consent. Under most bypass procedures, the teenager had to prove that she was sufficiently mature to make her own decision or that an abortion was in her "best interests."

The case that best clarified the Court's view on the judicial bypass process was *Bellotti v. Baird* (1979). This case involved a challenge to a 1974 Massachusetts law requiring parental consent for unmarried minors under 18. If the parent refused consent, a judge could hold a hearing and supply the necessary permission. If one parent had died or deserted the family, the other's consent was sufficient. The law specified criminal penalties for physicians who performed abortions without the requisite consent.

The Court's ruling was sharply divided. Although there was only one dissent, there was also no majority opinion for the Court. Justice Lewis Powell, writing for a plurality of four, recognized the state's important interest in furthering the role of parents in raising their children. However, he believed that the state must acknowledge the minor's right to privacy by creating an alternate method for obtaining consent. It must allow a young woman to demonstrate she is mature enough to make an abortion decision on her own *or* that an abortion is in her best interests. Justice Powell articulated three criteria that became the standard for determining a proper judicial bypass procedure: a minor to show either that she is mature enough to decide to have an abortion or, if she is not, that an abortion would be in her best interests; the bypass must ensure her anonymity; and it must allow expedited appeals.

Other states adopted notice laws requiring physicians and hospitals to notify the parents if their teenage daughter sought an abortion. The first case to challenge the constitutionality of a notice law was *H. L. v. Matheson* (1981), in which a Utah statute required a physician to notify the parents or guardian before performing an abortion on a teenager; the law did not provide for a judicial bypass procedure.

The statute was challenged by a 15-year-old pregnant and unmarried teenager living at home with her parents. Based on the fact that she was an "immature and dependent minor," the Court upheld the law and did not require the state to provide a bypass procedure. Writing for a six-to-three majority, Chief Justice Warren E. Burger stated that the Court was satisfied that the Utah law, unlike the Missouri regulation in *Planned Parenthood of Central Missouri v. Danforth*, did not give the parents a veto over the decision, nor did it attempt to discourage the minor from seeking the abortion. Rather, the law advanced the state's interest in promoting the family unit and protecting the teenager from harm.

The next abortion rights case arose from a challenge to an ordinance regulating abortion enacted by the city of Akron, Ohio. Perhaps the most important provision of the ordinance was the one requiring all abortions after the first trimester to be performed in hospitals rather than in clinics or physicians' offices. It also required physicians to obtain a woman's written consent and wait 24 hours after obtaining the consent before performing the abortion. To ensure that her consent was "informed," the physician was told to present information to her about the characteristics of her unborn child and to warn her of the possibility of serious physical, psychological, and emotional damage.

Justice Powell announced the six-to-three opinion for the Court in *Akron v. Akron Center for Reproductive Health* (1983). Substantially reaffirming *Roe v. Wade*, the ruling struck down the requirement that the abortion must be performed in a hospital because it created a "significant obstacle" to a woman wanting an abortion. The city had defended the law as a reasonable health measure, but Justice Powell stated that it was unconstitutional because it did not further the state's interest in the woman's health. The Court also found that the 24-hour waiting period led to scheduling delays that increased a woman's risk and did not further a legitimate state interest. Finally, the Court depicted the information presented by the physician to obtain informed consent as "a parade of horribles" that was intended to influence her to reject an abortion.

Justice Sandra Day O'Connor disagreed with the majority, using her dissent to criticize the trimester approach. She argued that it was inappropriate to divide the state's interests into trimesters because the state had a compelling interest in maternal health and the fetus throughout the woman's pregnancy. Justice O'Connor urged the Court to limit itself to one question only in deciding these cases: was the regulation "unduly burdensome" on a pregnant woman's right to abortion? She concluded that none of the provisions of the Akron ordinance were unduly burdensome.

In a companion case, *Planned Parenthood v. Ashcroft* (1983), the Court upheld a parental consent statute because the law allowed a minor the option of seeking judicial intervention prior to parental consent. The Court also upheld other requirements, including the presence of a second physician during a late-term abortion because it furthered the state's interest in protecting viable fetuses, and pathology reports because they furthered that state's interest in health. The Court invalidated the requirement that a second-trimester abortion be performed in a hospital on the basis of *Akron*.

In 1982, Pennsylvania enacted an Abortion Control Act that was similar to the Akron ordinance. It contained a number of regulations, including an informed consent requirement and a 24-hour waiting period. In *Thornburgh v. American College of Obstetricians and Gynecologists* (1986), the five-to-four opinion again invalidated the informed consent requirement that required a physician to describe the physical characteristics of the fetus, among other things, to the woman, after which 24 hours must elapse before the woman could legally give consent. The Court found that, like the "parade of horribles" in *Akron*, the informed consent provision of the Pennsylvania law was intended to discourage women from having abortions rather than simply provide them with information. Because a good deal of this information did not relate to consent, it served "no legitimate state interest." The Court concluded that the provisions were intended to prevent women from exercising choice rather than aiding them in making choices.

Webster v. Reproductive Health Services (1989) sparked renewed interest in the abortion debate by raising serious doubts about the future of *Roe v. Wade*. The case centered on a number of provisions in a 1986 Missouri abortion law, including a preamble that declared that life began at conception, a ban on abortions at public hospitals, and a test to determine fetal viability.

The preamble to the Missouri law stated that human life "begins at conception" and that the state had an interest in an unborn child's "life, health, and well-being." The state justified this provision by arguing it simply extended the protections of tort, property, and criminal law to the fetus and that it had no effect on abortion policy because it specified that it must be interpreted in a manner consistent with past Supreme Court decisions. Chief Justice William H. Rehnquist's plurality opinion for himself and Justices Byron White and Anthony Kennedy declined to resolve this issue, ruling that the Court did not have to decide on the constitutionality of the preamble because it did not regulate abortion; rather, it was merely expressing the state's legitimate preference for childbirth over abortion.

The law barred physicians from performing abortions at the Truman Medical Center in Kansas City, Missouri, which performed 97 percent of all Missouri hospital abortions at 16 weeks or later. Although it was a private hospital, and no public funds were spent on abortions performed there. It was considered a "public facility" because it was on state-leased land. The plurality also approved the ban on abortions at Truman Hospital on the grounds that if states preferred childbirth to abortion, they were permitted to ban abortions at their public hospitals. The justices found that the law did not erect a barrier to abortion because women were placed in the same position as if the city had chosen not to operate a public hospital at all.

The most significant part of the law was the fetal testing section, because it appeared to implicate the trimester framework established in *Roe v. Wade*. This section required that if physicians believed a woman was at least 20 weeks pregnant, before performing an abortion on her, they must first do a series of tests to determine whether the fetus was viable. The lower court ruled that because these tests were costly and potentially dangerous to the woman and the fetus, the provision was unconstitutional.

Chief Justice Rehnquist and the other two members of the plurality upheld the law, interpreting it to require physicians to perform the tests only when they believed they would help to determine viability, not in all cases. He acknowledged that the Missouri law was inconsistent with *Roe v. Wade* by allowing viability tests during the second trimester. But instead of overruling the 1973 decision, the Rehnquist plurality attempted to resolve the conflict between *Roe v. Wade* and the Missouri law by abandoning the rigid trimester framework. It approved the fetal test provision as a permissible method for the state to further its interest in protecting fetal life, which, in their view, was not simply limited to the third trimester. Conceding that it would allow government regulation of abortion that would have been forbidden under *Roe v. Wade*, Chief Justice Rehnquist seemed to invite legislatures to pass laws challenging that ruling and indicated that he believed the trimester framework adopted in *Roe v. Wade* should be modified in future cases.

Justice O'Connor agreed with the plurality's interpretation of the fetal viability section, believing that the tests did not impose an undue burden on a woman's abortion right. She felt that this section was consistent with *Roe v. Wade*, and she was not persuaded that the Court was required to reexamine its 1973 ruling. When it was faced with that need, she emphasized, it must do so "carefully." Justice Antonin Scalia agreed with the plurality on upholding the abortion restrictions but expressed disappointment that the Court did not overrule *Roe v. Wade*. He criticized the plurality for refusing to forthrightly address the constitutionality of abortion.

Justice Blackmun's dissent defended the trimester approach that the Court had created almost 20 years ago. In his view, it remained the most effective and reasonable way to balance the state's interest in regulation and the woman's interest in privacy.

During the 1980s, state legislatures enacted a variety of parental involvement laws, requiring either notice or consent to one or both parents when a minor sought an abortion; most included a judicial bypass procedure. On June 26, 1990, in *Hodgson v. Minnesota* (1990) the Supreme Court addressed the issue on review of a 1981 Minnesota law with two major parental notice provisions. Subdivision 2 required a physician to notify both parents before performing an abortion and to wait 48 hours after the notification before performing the abortion. Subdivision 6 of the law specified that a judicial bypass procedure would take effect if Subdivision 2 were declared unconstitutional. The bypass allowed the young woman to go before a judge to demonstrate that she was sufficiently mature to make the abortion decision herself or that an abortion without notice would be in her best interests.

Five members of the Supreme Court found Subdivision 2 unconstitutional because it was not reasonably related to a legitimate state interest. A different five-justice majority sustained Subdivision 6 and inserted a judicial bypass provision into the law. Therefore, the Minnesota notice law, including the 48-hour waiting period, was declared constitutional. Four of these justices would have found the law constitutional with or without the bypass provision.

Speaking for the Court on Subdivision 2, Justice John Paul Stevens distinguished between this case and earlier cases addressing the constitutionality of a notice or consent requirement. None of those cases, he said, revolved around the question of a consent or notice requirement applying to both parents. Justice Stevens rejected the view that the two-parent notice advanced the state's interests in the teenager, the parent, or the family. The state could simply order that one parent be notified and leave it up to that parent to decide whether to notify the other or whether the notice would harm the teenager. He responded to the state's argument that the family functions best if both parents are involved in a teenager's abortion decision by saying that the state could not attempt to mold the family into its idealized view of what it should be. In her opinion on the constitutionality of Subdivision 6, Justice O'Connor maintained that the bypass procedure alleviated any concern about the rigidity of the two-parent notification requirement.

In 1992, after a three-year hiatus in which no major abortion decision was announced, the

Court issued its ruling in *Planned Parenthood of Southeastern Pennsylvania v. Casey* (1992). The case addressed the 1982 Pennsylvania Abortion Control Act, amended in 1988 and 1989. Under the heading of informed consent, the law required a physician to inform a woman of the risks of abortion and wait at least 24 hours before performing the procedure. It also required married women, under most circumstances, to present signed statements that they had notified their husbands about their intention to have an abortion.

The Court issued a lengthy and complex ruling on June 29, 1992. The opinion indicated that a new consensus had formed with Justices O'Connor and Kennedy and Justice David Souter jointly authoring a plurality opinion that retained "the essential holding" of the Court's landmark 1973 opinion, *Roe v. Wade*. The joint opinion outlined three elements it considered essential to *Roe v. Wade*. First, the woman had a right to have an abortion before the fetus is viable without "undue interference" from the state. Second, the state could restrict abortions after the fetus was viable as long as it allowed an exception for her life or health. Third, the state's interest in the life of the woman and the fetus began at the start of the pregnancy, not merely at the point at which the fetus was viable. The authors of the joint opinion stressed that the Court's commitment to individual liberty, in conjunction with the constraints of its earlier decisions and the rule of law, convinced them to reaffirm *Roe v. Wade*.

In light of these considerations, and in an attempt to balance the woman's constitutional right to abortion with a state's interest in prenatal life throughout the pregnancy, the Court drew a line at viability. Abandoning the trimester framework, which it did not consider "essential" to its ruling in *Roe v. Wade*, the Court replaced the three trimesters with two stages of pregnancy: pre- and post-viability. Before viability, a state could enact laws to ensure that the abortion decision was "thoughtful and informed," but it was not permitted to prohibit abortions outright or even to restrict them unduly.

The opinion explained that because of its legitimate interest in protecting potential life, the state did not have to remove itself from the abortion decision throughout the pregnancy; it was only forbidden to enact abortion regulations during the previability stage that imposed an "undue burden" on the woman's choice. It specified that a woman with a previable fetus would be unduly burdened if the state placed "a substantial obstacle" in her path. Thus, states were no longer required to have compelling reasons to restrict a woman's access to abortion as long as they did not impose an undue burden on her choice. Once the fetus was viable, states were permitted to regulate or proscribe abortions entirely as long as reasonable health exceptions were in place; that is, as long as the laws exempted women whose life or health was at risk.

Given these principles, the Court accepted the lower court's judgment on the regulations in the Pennsylvania statute. Under the standards it had just announced, the holdings in *Akron v. Akron Center for Reproductive Health and Thornburgh v. American College of Obstetricians and Gynecologists* on the 24-hour delay, and the informed consent provisions were overruled. With respect to the former, although the Court noted that the 24-hour waiting period might be a burden on some women, especially those having to travel long distances, in the end, it felt that the provision was not unduly burdensome.

However, the Court did not uphold the Pennsylvania law in its entirety. It held that the requirement that a woman notify her husband of her intention to have an abortion was unconstitutional. In light of concern for spousal abuse and battery as well as marital rape and other forms of domestic violence, the opinion concluded that most women informed their husbands of their intent to have an abortion and those who did not likely had a good reason for not wishing to do so. Because the spousal notification requirement had the effect of creating a veto power over some women's abortion decisions, it created a "substantial obstacle" and was unconstitutional.

In the end, *Planned Parenthood of Southeastern Pennsylvania v. Casey* allowed states greater leeway in regulating abortion, but the Court still permitted women to retain their right to terminate a pregnancy before the fetus was viable. Clearly, the states could not revert back to their pre-1973 abortion laws and prohibit abortions entirely except to save the woman's life.

The most recent controversy over abortion rights concerns a method known as intact dilation and extraction (D&X), a variation of the procedure known as dilation and evacuation (D&E), which is performed during the second and third trimesters of a pregnancy. For more than five years, the legal and political battles over the method known as "late-term abortion" by abortion-rights supporters and "partial birth" abortion by opponents of abortion rights raged, encompassing the courts, Congress, and the executive branch.

Although President Bill Clinton's veto prevented the federal government from enacting a law restricting such abortions, more than half the states did, including Nebraska. A Nebraska physician challenged the state's law that subjected physicians to felony charges for performing such procedures, including up to 20 years in prison, a $25,000 fine, or both. The physician argued that because the D&X is often the safest method of abortion for women under certain circumstances, the law imposed an undue burden on women seeking an abortion. Additionally, he claimed that the law was unconstitutionally vague because it contained definitions that were subject to misinterpretation.

In assessing the constitutionality of the Nebraska law in *Stenberg v. Carhart* (2000), the Supreme Court focused on two issues: first, the absence of an exception to preserve the health of the woman; and second, the burden on her ability to obtain an abortion. In announcing the opinion for the five-to-four majority, Justice Stephen Breyer identified three principles upon which the Court based its decision: First, a woman had a right to terminate her pregnancy before viability; Second, a state could not place an undue burden on a woman's right to

terminate her pregnancy before viability; And third, after viability, the state could regulate and even prohibit abortion unless an abortion was necessary to preserve the life or health of the woman.

Justice Breyer cited two factors that persuaded the Court that the Nebraska law was unconstitutional. First, he noted that the law does not contain an exception for the health of the mother. Moreover, it imposed an undue burden on a woman's ability to opt for a D&E abortion. He stressed that the state's interest in a fetus after viability, although it was not subject to the undue burden test, must nevertheless consider the life and health of the woman. Additionally, the Nebraska law was not restricted to third-trimester abortions only. Because it also encompassed abortions performed in the second trimester, when the state has a lesser interest in potential life, the law must contain a health exception. Furthermore, he said, the law was directed at a specific type of abortion procedure, and the Court has repeatedly held that the state may not subject the woman to greater health risks by regulating the method of abortion. He rejected the state's contention that outlawing this procedure would not create any risks for the woman because other methods were available, saying it was simply not supported by the medical testimony in the record; there were situations in which the D&X procedure was the safest one for the woman.

The second consideration centered on the relationship of the two abortion procedures. The state conceded that the statute would place an undue burden on the woman's right to abortion if it applied to the D&E as well as the D&X procedure. Reiterating the findings of the lower court, Justice Breyer held that the statute did not distinguish between the two procedures and was so broadly written that it encompassed both. Whether the state intended to ban the D&X was not the issue, he maintained; the issue was whether the law only reached the D&X or also reached other types of procedures, notably the D&E. In the Court's view, it was applicable to both.

Justice Stevens's concurring opinion was brief. He questioned how the state could legitimately prevent physicians from performing a procedure that was the safest for women who chose to exercise their right to abortion. Similarly, Justice Ruth Bader Ginsburg's concurring opinion questioned the motives of the legislators, who, she believed, were using the law to weaken settled abortion rights. Justice O'Connor concurred as well, agreeing that a health exception was required; but she believed that the state could have limited the statute to only D&X abortions as other states had done. If it had, and if it had included a health exception, she believed the Court would have faced a different issue and might have decided the matter differently.

Justices Rehnquist, Scalia, Kennedy, and Thomas dissented, arguing that the majority had expanded the right to abortion beyond the principles articulated in *Planned Parenthood of Southeastern Pennsylvania v. Casey*. They expressed concern that the Court had entirely negated the state's ability to regulate abortion in the future. Justice Kennedy's dissent, coupled with Justice O'Connor's care in pointing out that a different statute with a health exception would likely have been acceptable to her, suggests that the Court will revisit this issue again, as both justices were part of the joint opinion in *Casey*.

In 2003, Congress enacted a statute aimed at prohibiting D&X abortions. Called the Partial-Birth Abortion Ban Act of 2003, it was similar to the Nebraska law struck down in *Stenberg v. Carhart*. Signed by the president on November 5, 2003, the law was immediately challenged in federal district courts in New York, California, and Nebraska, and in all three cases the courts declared the statute unconstitutional. Most observers expect this issue to be ultimately decided by the Supreme Court.

A recent trend involving abortion rights has developed at the state level. After the Court's ruling in *Casey* allowed for more limitations on abortion rights, several state supreme courts have considered whether their state constitutions provide broader abortion rights protection than the federal Constitution. In a number of instances, abortion rights have received more protection. In *American Academy of Pediatrics v. Lungren* (1997), the California Supreme Court struck down a parental consent statute because it violated the explicit right to privacy in the California Constitution. The New Jersey Supreme Court also expanded abortion rights in *Planned Parenthood v. Farmer* (2000) by invalidating a parental notification requirement on the basis of the equal protection provision of the state constitution. In *Planned Parenthood v. Sundquist* (2000), the Tennessee Supreme Court held that abortion was a fundamental right in Tennessee on the basis of the implied right to privacy guaranteed in the Tennessee Constitution and thus invalidated restrictions on abortion. There have also been instances where state supreme courts have been less inclined to engage in state constitutional development and more inclined to follow federal precedent when evaluating post-*Casey* abortion restrictions. These developments indicate that the controversy begun in *Roe v. Wade* has yet to diminish.

See also Abortion, Public Finding of; Blackmun, Harry A.; Brennan, William J., Jr.; Burger, Warren E.; Catholicism and Anti-Catholicism; Due Process, Substantive; Feminist Movement; Freedom of Access to Clinic Entrances Act; Ginsburg, Ruth Bader; *Griswold v. Connecticut*; Kennedy, Anthony; National Abortion Rights Action League; National Right to Life Committee; O'Connor, Sandra Day; Operation Rescue; Parental Rights; Planned Parenthood; Powell, Lewis F., Jr.; Rehnquist, William H.; Reproductive Freedom; *Roe v. Wade*; Scalia, Antonin; Thomas, Clarence; White, Byron R.

Bibliography

Bowers, James R. 1994. *Pro-choice and Anti-abortion*. Westport, CT: Praeger.

Faux, Marian. 1998. *Roe v. Wade*. New York: Mentor Books.

Mezey, Susan Gluck. 2003. *Elusive Equality: Women's Rights, Public Policy, and the Law*. Boulder, CO: Lynne Rienner.

Redman, Hyman, Betty Sarvis, and Joy Walker Bonar. 1987. *The Abortion Question.* New York: Columbia University Press.

Susan Gluck Mezey

ACADEMIC FREEDOM

Justice Lewis Powell stated the constitutional status of academic freedom in his opinion in *Regents of University of California v. Bakke* (1978): "Academic freedom, though not a specifically enumerated constitutional right, long has been viewed as a special concern of the First Amendment." In opinions beginning more than 50 years ago, justices of the United States Supreme Court have discussed the meaning of the concept, the particular constitutional interests it raises, and the conditions necessary for it to exist. The Court has addressed academic freedom as freedom of teachers and students as well as institutional autonomy in decision making. Since the Court has generally decided cases in which academic freedom is discussed on other grounds, however, it is in dicta that its pronouncements about academic freedom are often located. (See, e.g., Rabban 1990; Van Alstyne 1975.)

The term "academic freedom" was first used in U.S. Supreme Court opinions in cases arising in a time of national concern about communist subversion, and these early opinions laid foundations that the Court continues to use. In his dissent in *Adler v. Board of Education of the City of New York* (1952), Justice William O. Douglas became the first justice to use the term "academic freedom" when developing the position that while the constitutional right to "freedom of thought and expression" applies to everyone, "none needs it more than the teacher." Central to this analysis was the effect on academic freedom when teachers' associational rights and their speech in the classroom were stifled.

It was in *Sweezy v. New Hampshire* (1957) that the Court first brought academic freedom within First Amendment protection. (See, e.g., Rabban 1990, 236.) Sweezy had been held in contempt for refusing to answer a number of questions during legislative investigative hearings conducted under the state's Subversive Activities Act. These inquiries concerned the contents of an address that Sweezy delivered to a university class as an invited lecturer. The plurality opinion framed the central issue in terms of Fourteenth Amendment due process rights and found them to have been violated. The plurality also found violations of constitutional "liberties" of academic freedom as well as political expression and stated in dicta that they were unable to envision "any circumstance wherein a state interest would justify infringement of [these] rights." In a seven-sentence paragraph, the plurality explained "[t]he essentiality of freedom" within universities and concluded that "[t]eachers and students must always remain free to inquire, to study and to evaluate, to gain new maturity and understanding; otherwise our civilization will stagnate and die." Justice Felix Frankfurter's concurring opinion, which marked what Justice Clarence Thomas later called the beginning of academic freedom's "constitutionalization" (*Grutter v. Bollinger*, 2003), explained that the good of society requires "the pursuit of understanding [to be] as unfettered as possible" and that the meaning of "the dependence of a free society on free universities [is] the exclusion of governmental intervention in the intellectual life of a university." In what became a foundation for later considerations of the environment essential for the freedom of inquiry, Justice Frankfurter quoted a statement from scholars in South Africa that identified "the four essential freedoms" of a university—to determine for itself on academic grounds who may teach, what may be taught, how it shall be taught, and who may be admitted to study.

In *Barenblatt v. United States* (1959), five members of the Court affirmed a former college teacher's contempt of Congress conviction for refusal to answer questions of a House Un-American Activities Subcommittee investigating communism in education. In stating the principles to be applied, Justice John M. Harlan wrote for the majority that "broadly viewed, inquiries cannot be made into the teaching that is pursued in any of our educational institutions" and referred to "academic teaching-freedom and its corollary learning-freedom" as a "constitutionally protected domain." They did not, however, interpret this to mean that the status of being a teacher in and of itself prevented questioning by Congress. The majority found the case distinguishable from *Sweezy* and that there was no intent to control the content of teaching in universities.

In *Shelton v. Tucker* (1960), the Court invalidated as unconstitutionally overbroad an Arkansas law requiring teachers in its state schools and colleges, as a requirement for employment, to submit annual lists of all organizations in which they held membership or to which they had contributed regularly during the previous five-year period. The majority opinion recognized that the law diminished associational rights of teachers. Drawing support in part from the plurality's statement in *Sweezy*, the majority stated that "[t]he vigilant protection of constitutional freedoms is nowhere more vital than in the community of American schools."

In three subsequent cases, the Court invalidated on grounds of vagueness loyalty oaths as a condition of employment for faculty at state universities (*Baggett v. Bullitt*, 1964; *Keyishian v. Board of Regents of the University of the State of New York*, 1967; and *Whitehill v. Elkins*, 1967). *Keyishian* included the Court's most extensive statements regarding academic freedom. Writing for a five-member majority, Justice William Brennan stated, "Our Nation is deeply committed to safeguarding academic freedom, which is of transcendent value to all of us and not merely to the teachers concerned. That freedom is therefore a special concern of the First Amendment, which does not tolerate laws that cast a pall of orthodoxy over the classroom." Classrooms were characterized as a "marketplace of ideas," with the future of the country dependent on leaders with such training. The opinion also quoted in full the paragraph from the *Sweezy* plurality explaining that freedom is essential in universities. That full paragraph again appeared in Justice Douglas's opinion for a six-member majority in *Whitehill v. Elkins*. Addressing the First Amendment issue, Douglas concluded that the law's surveillance of teachers

was "hostile to academic freedom." By 1967 academic freedom had been linked to the First Amendment, with *Sweezy* and *Keyishian* providing foundations for the Court's subsequent considerations of that freedom.

Since 1967 the Court has discussed academic freedom in a variety of contexts while continuing a general trend of basing decisions on other issues. This was the case when the Court used the religion clauses of the First Amendment as the basis for declaring two laws that affected academic freedom in the classroom to be unconstitutional—a state law that barred the teaching of the theory of evolution in its public educational institutions in *Epperson v. Arkansas* (1968), and one that prohibited public schools from including instruction in the theory of evolution unless "creation science" was also taught in *Edwards v. Aguillard* (1987).

In two cases, the Court articulated the outer limits of constitutional protection in the field of academic freedom. In *Minnesota State Board for Community Colleges v. Knight* (1984), the majority opinion stated that "there is no constitutional right to participate in academic governance," although faculty have free speech and associational rights under the First Amendment. In a unanimous opinion in *University of Pennsylvania v. Equal Employment Opportunity Commission* (1990), the Court declined "to recognize an expanded right of academic freedom to protect confidential peer review materials from disclosure" during an EEOC investigation of a complaint that denial of tenure was a result of discrimination prohibited under Title VII of the 1964 Civil Rights Act. The Court reaffirmed, instead, its "principle of respect for *legitimate* academic decisionmaking."

The Court has addressed academic freedom in terms of selecting the student body within cases that focused on Fourteenth Amendment rights. In *Regents of University of California v. Bakke* (1978), a case challenging a medical school's minority admissions program, Justice Powell found only one of the four asserted purposes of the admissions program to be compelling and constitutional—that of diversity in the student body. Reasoning from *Sweezy* and *Keyishian* on academic freedom, he concluded that universities require "wide discretion" in admissions decisions, although they may not disregard constitutional protections of individual rights. In *Regents of the University of Michigan v. Ewing* (1985), the Court held that a student's due process rights had not been violated in his dismissal from a joint undergraduate–medical school program. It cited academic freedom as one factor constraining the scope of substantive review of academic decisions by courts. In *Grutter v. Bollinger* (2003), a state law school's admissions process, in which race was a factor, was upheld against an equal protection challenge. The majority opinion endorsed Justice Powell's position in *Bakke* on diversity and characterized his opinion as "invok[ing] our cases recognizing a constitutional dimension, grounded in the First Amendment, of educational autonomy: 'The freedom of a university to make its own judgments as to education includes the selection of its student body.'"

To date, the Court has brought academic freedom under the First Amendment as "a special concern," but it has not interpreted academic freedom to be a separate constitutional right as it has, for example, the freedom of association (Van Alstyne 1975, 64–65, 67) or the right of privacy (Emerson 1970, 610). Numerous questions related to constitutional protection of academic freedom remain to be clarified or decided by the Court. (See, e.g., Rabban 2000.)

See also Affirmative Action; Brennan; William J., Jr.; Civil Rights Act of 1964; Douglas, William O.; Evolution/Creationism Controversy; First Amendment; Fourteenth Amendment; Frankfurter, *Felix*; Free Marketplace of Ideas; Harlan, John Marshall, II; House Un-American Activities Committee; Overbreadth, Doctrine of; Powell, Lewis F., Jr.; Public Employees, Constitutional Rights of; Thomas, Clarence; Vagueness Doctrine

Bibliography

Emerson, Thomas I. 1970. *The System of Freedom of Expression*. New York: Random House.

Metzger, Walter P. 1988. "Profession and Constitution: Two Definitions of Academic Freedom in America." *Texas Law Review* 66: 1265–322.

Rabban, David M. 1990. "A Functional Analysis of 'Individual' and 'Institutional' Academic Freedom under the First Amendment." *Law and Contemporary Problems* 53 (3): 227–301.

———. 2000. "Academic Freedom." In *Encyclopedia of the American Constitution*, ed. Leonard W. Levy and Kenneth L. Karst. 2nd ed. Vol. 1. New York: Macmillan Reference USA.

Van Alstyne, William W. 1975. "The Specific Theory of Academic Freedom and the General Issue of Civil Liberty." In *The Concept of Academic Freedom*, ed. Edmund L. Pincoffs. Austin: University of Texas Press.

———. 1990. "Academic Freedom and the First Amendment in the Supreme Court of the United States: An Unhurried Historical Review." *Law and Contemporary Problems* 53 (3): 79–154.

Norma Cox Cook

ACCUSED, RIGHTS OF THE

In the United States, the government must perform the crucial function of crime control while respecting the constitutional rights of individuals. Many of the legal protections of persons suspected, accused, or convicted of crimes are enshrined in the Bill of Rights, particularly the Fourth, Fifth, Sixth, and Eighth amendments. Collectively, these provisions were designed to prevent government from subjecting individuals to arbitrary arrest, prosecution, and punishment. As Justice John P. Stevens recognized in his dissenting opinion in *United States v. Leon* (1984), "In a just society those who govern, as well as those who are governed, must obey the law."

The Fourth Amendment forbids unreasonable searches and seizures and provides that search warrants are to be issued only when there is probable cause to believe that a search of a particular place will produce specific evidence of crime. Subject to certain exceptions, evidence obtained by police in violation of the Fourth Amendment is not admissible at trial. In *Weeks v. United States* (1914), the Supreme Court recognized that if illegally obtained evidence can be "used in evidence against a citizen accused of an offense, the protection of the Fourth Amendment, declaring his right to be secure against such searches and seizures, is of no value, and … might as well be stricken from the Constitution." The federal exclusionary rule thus adopted in *Weeks* was applied to the state courts in the 1961 decision of *Mapp v. Ohio*.

The Fifth Amendment contains a number of important provisions involving the rights of persons accused of crime. It requires the federal government to obtain an indictment from a grand jury before trying someone for a major crime. It also prohibits "double jeopardy," that is, being tried twice for the same offense. Writing for the Supreme Court in *Green v. United States* (1957), Justice Hugo L. Black stated the rationale behind this prohibition, observing that "the State with all its resources and power should not be allowed to make repeated attempts to convict an individual for an alleged offense, thereby subjecting him to embarrassment, expense and ordeal and compelling him to live in a continuing state of anxiety and insecurity, as well as enhancing the possibility that even though innocent he may be found guilty."

Additionally, the Fifth Amendment protects persons against compulsory self-incrimination, which is what is commonly meant by the phrase "taking the Fifth." The Supreme Court has interpreted this protection as conferring on the accused the "right to remain silent," not only in court but during police interrogation as well. In *Miranda v. Arizona* (1966), the Supreme Court observed that the protection against compulsory self-incrimination "serves to protect persons in all settings in which their freedom of action is curtailed in any significant way from being compelled to incriminate themselves." The Court noted that "without proper safeguards the process of in-custody interrogation of persons suspected or accused of crime contains inherently compelling pressures which work to undermine the individual's will to resist and to compel him to speak where he would not otherwise do so freely." To effectuate the protection against compulsory

self-incrimination, the Court held that before interrogating a suspect in custody, police officers must advise him or her of the right to remain silent and the right to have an attorney present during questioning. In most cases, the failure to provide these *Miranda* warnings means that any confession obtained from the suspect cannot be used as evidence against him or her.

Finally, the Fifth Amendment prohibits the federal government from depriving persons of life, liberty, or property without due process of law. A virtually identical clause is found in the Fourteenth Amendment, which applies specifically to the states. The Due Process Clauses both have implications for criminal cases. Most importantly, due process requires that defendants be presumed innocent and that the prosecution carry the burden of proving guilt beyond a reasonable doubt. In *Coffin v. United States* (1895), the Supreme Court stated that the "presumption of innocence in favor of the accused is the undoubted law, axiomatic and elementary, and its enforcement lies at the foundation of the administration of our criminal law." And in *In re Winship* (1971), the Court held that due process "protects the accused against conviction except upon proof beyond a reasonable doubt of every fact necessary to constitute the crime with which he is charged."

The Sixth Amendment is concerned exclusively with the rights of the accused. It requires, among other things, that people accused of crimes be provided a "speedy and public trial, by an impartial jury." Trial by jury dates from the thirteenth century and remains the hallmark of the Anglo-American system of justice. The Supreme Court has repeatedly stressed the right to a fair trial. In Chambers v. Florida (1940), the Court insisted that "no man's life, liberty or property be forfeited as criminal punishment for violation of that law until there ha[s] been a charge fairly made and fairly tried in a public tribunal free of prejudice, passion, excitement and tyrannical power." As means of ensuring a fair trial, the Sixth Amendment also grants defendants the right to confront, or cross-examine, witnesses for the prosecution and the right to have "compulsory process" (the power of subpoena) to require favorable witnesses to appear in court.

Most significantly, considering the incredible complexity of the criminal law, the Sixth Amendment guarantees that accused persons have the "Assistance of Counsel" for their defense. In *Gideon v. Wainwright* (1963), the Supreme Court held that because the right to counsel is crucial to a fair trial, defendants who are unable to afford private counsel must be afforded counsel at public expense. In *Strickland v. Washington* (1984), the Court said that the "Sixth Amendment recognizes the right to the assistance of counsel because it envisions counsel's playing a role that is critical to the ability of the adversarial system to produce just results." Thus, the right to counsel is more than the right to have an attorney standing at one's side—it means the right to reasonably effective representation.

The Eighth Amendment protects persons accused of crimes from being required to post excessive bail to secure pretrial release. In *Stack v. Boyle* (1951), the Supreme Court held that setting bail at a figure higher than that reasonably calculated to ensure the appearance of the accused in court is excessive under the Eighth Amendment. The Eighth Amendment also forbids courts from imposing excessive fines or cruel or unusual punishments on persons convicted of crimes. Historically, the Cruel and Unusual Punishments Clause has been used to challenge torture and other forms of corporal punishment. More recently, it has served as a means of challenging the death penalty in its various forms.

Most Bill of Rights provisions pertaining to criminal justice have been incorporated into the Due Process Clause of the Fourteenth Amendment, thereby making them applicable to the states as well as the national government. Not only can these provisions be invoked by defendants in state criminal courts, they can be used by state prisoners seeking federal court review of their convictions via the writ of habeas corpus. Of course, state constitutions contain their own enumerations of the rights of the accused, and in some instances state courts provide greater protection to criminal defendants than does the U.S. Constitution as interpreted by the Supreme Court.

It is the responsibility of courts of law to apply and enforce these protections, a responsibility that often engenders little public support. Again, to quote Justice Stevens's dissenting opinion in *United States v. Leon* (1984), courts could "facilitate the process of administering justice to those who violate criminal laws by ignoring … the entire Bill of Rights—but it is the very purpose of the Bill of Rights to identify values that may not be sacrificed to expediency." In a similar vein, Justice Arthur Goldberg, writing for the Court in *Escobedo v. Illinois* (1964), observed: "If the exercise of constitutional rights will thwart the effectiveness of a system of law enforcement, then there is something very wrong with that system."

See also Adversary System of Justice; Bail, Right to; Bill of Rights (American); Bill of Rights, Incorporation of; Black, Hugo L.; Common-Law Background of American Civil Rights and Liberties; Compulsory Process; Confrontation, Right of; Counsel, Ineffective Assistance of; Counsel, Right to; Critical Pretrial Stages; Cruel and Unusual Punishments Clause; Double Jeopardy, Prohibition of; Due Process, Procedural; Due Process Clauses; Eighth Amendment; Excessive Bail, Prohibition of; Excessive Fines, Prohibition of; Fifth Amendment; Fourteenth Amendment; Fourth Amendment; Fourth Amendment Exclusionary Rule; *Gideon v. Wainwright*; Goldberg, Arthur; Habeas Corpus; Habeas Corpus, Federal; Interrogation and Confessions; Jury, Trial by; *Mapp v. Ohio; Miranda v. Arizona*; Presumption of Innocence; Public Trial, Right to a; Reasonable Doubt Standard; Self-Incrimination Clause; Sixth Amendment; Speedy Trial, Right to; Stevens, John Paul; Warren Court

Bibliography

Scheb, John M., and John M. Scheb II. 2006. *Criminal Procedure.* Belmont, CA: Thomson/Wadsworth.

John M. Scheb II and Otis H. Stephens, Jr.

ACLU. *See* American Civil Liberties Union

ADAMS, JOHN. *See* Alien and Sedition Acts; Marshall, John

ADL. *See* Anti-Defamation League

ADMINISTRATIVE SEARCHES

In monitoring regulatory compliance of businesses and industries, administrative agencies routinely make inspections, searches, and seizures. Initially, the U.S. Supreme Court took the position that such searches were not subject to the requirements of the Fourth Amendment. Although that view has long since been abandoned, courts continue to be more permissive toward administrative searches directed at business and industry than toward law enforcement searches directed at private individuals or their residences.

In 1959, the Supreme Court found no violation of the Fourth Amendment when administrative searches were conducted without notice and without search warrants. In *Frank v. Maryland* (1959), the Court upheld the conviction of a Baltimore man who refused to allow a city health inspector looking for evidence of rat infestation to enter and inspect his home without a warrant. In his opinion for the Court sustaining the constitutionality of this ordinance, Justice William Brennan recognized that "the power to inspect dwelling places … is of indispensable importance to the maintenance of community health; a power that would be greatly hobbled by the blanket requirement of the safeguards necessary for a search of evidence of criminal acts."

The *Frank* decision suggested that administrative searches were outside the prohibitions of the Fourth Amendment. In dissent, Justice William O. Douglas insisted, "The Court misreads history when it relates the Fourth Amendment primarily to searches for evidence to be used in criminal prosecutions." In Douglas's view, the decision of the Court "greatly dilutes the right of privacy which every homeowner had the right to believe was part of our American heritage."

The Supreme Court's *Frank* decision assumed a fundamental difference between administrative inspections and searches for evidence of crime.

However, administrative inspections can lead to criminal charges or serve as a pretext for the gathering of information to assist criminal investigations. In *Camara v. Municipal Court* (1967), the Supreme Court recognized this and overruled *Frank v. Maryland*. The Court held that, as a general rule, warrants must be obtained to permit administrative searches of private residences. Writing for the Court, Justice Byron White observed that administrative searches "are significant intrusions upon the interests protected by the Fourth Amendment" and that "the reasons put forth in *Frank v. Maryland* and in other cases for upholding these warrantless searches are insufficient to justify so substantial a weakening of the Fourth Amendment's protections."

In *See v. City of Seattle* (1967), the Court extended the Camara ruling to commercial establishments. In *See*, a Seattle businessman was convicted of a misdemeanor for refusing to allow a fire inspector to enter his locked warehouse without a warrant. Entry to the warehouse was requested as part of a routine citywide program to achieve compliance with fire regulations. Again, Justice White spoke for the Court, noting, "The businessman, like the occupant of a residence, has a constitutional right to go about his business free from unreasonable official entries upon his private commercial property."

Some commentators interpreted the *Camara* and *See* decisions as requiring that administrative searches should be subject to the same Fourth Amendment requirements that apply to criminal searches. In 1970, the Supreme Court invalidated that interpretation when it decided *Colonnade Corporation v. United States* (1970). At issue there was whether agents of the federal Bureau of Alcohol, Tobacco and Firearms (ATF) needed a warrant before inspecting an establishment they had probable cause to believe was serving liquor from refilled bottles in violation of federal law. The Court held that "Congress has broad authority to fashion standards of reasonableness for searches and seizures" with respect to an industry "long subject to close supervision and inspection."

The Court amplified its *Colonnade* decision in *Biswell v. United States* (1972). In that case an ATF agent conducted a surprise warrantless inspection of a pawnshop that was federally licensed to sell guns for sporting use. The agent located and seized two sawed-off rifles that the proprietor was not licensed to possess. In reversing a lower court decision invalidating the seizure, the Court observed that "regulation of the interstate traffic in firearms is not as deeply rooted in history as is governmental control of the liquor industry, but close scrutiny of this traffic is undeniably of central importance to federal efforts to prevent violent crime and to assist the States in regulating the firearms traffic within their borders." The Court concluded that "if the law is to be properly enforced and inspection made effective, inspections without warrant must be deemed reasonable official conduct under the Fourth Amendment."

Under the *Colonnade* and *Biswell* decisions, the Fourth Amendment imposes only a general standard of *reasonableness* with respect to searches and inspections of closely regulated industries. The doctrine assumes that businesses that choose to operate in such fields knowingly subject themselves to pervasive regulation and therefore have minimal expectations of privacy. The obvious question left open by these decisions is: What constitutes a "closely regulated industry"?

In *Marshall v. Barlow's* (1978), the Supreme Court struck down a provision of the Occupational Health and Safety Act of 1970 that permitted federal officials to conduct warrantless searches of the workplace. The court determined that the mere fact that a business is involved in interstate commerce and is therefore subject to a variety of federal regulations does not make it a "closely regulated industry." Had the Court ruled otherwise, virtually every business in America could be so classified. In *Barlow's* the Court said that agents inspecting establishments not covered by the *Colonnade-Biswell* exception must first obtain administrative search warrants, but the Court was careful to point out that to obtain such warrants, inspectors do not have to meet the standards of probable cause that govern the issuance of search warrants in criminal investigations.

In the 1980s, a more conservative Supreme Court appeared to back away from the strict scrutiny of regulatory searches suggested by the *Barlow's* decision. In *Donovan v. Dewey* (1981), the Court refused to invalidate a provision of the Federal Mine Safety and Health Act of 1977 that allowed the Department of Labor to conduct warrantless inspections of mines on a regular basis. Emphasizing the "certainty and regularity" of the inspection regime, the Court held that the Fourth Amendment warrant requirement was inapplicable. "Under these circumstances," observed Justice Thurgood Marshall, "it is difficult to see what additional protection a warrant requirement would provide."

In *New York v. Burger* (1987), in upholding a warrantless inspection of a junkyard by state officials, the Court articulated a framework for determining the legality of warrantless inspections authorized by state laws. Writing for the Court, *Justice Harry Blackmun* concluded that such inspections should be upheld as long as three conditions are met:

First, there must be a "substantial" government interest that informs the regulatory scheme pursuant to which the inspection is made.... Second, the warrantless inspections must be "necessary to further [the] regulatory scheme." ... Finally, "the statute's inspection program, in terms of the certainty and regularity of its application, [must] provid[e] a constitutionally adequate substitute for a warrant."

Because this framework allows agencies considerable latitude in conducting warrantless inspections of regulated industries, it has been criticized by commentators sensitive to Fourth Amendment values. In his dissenting opinion in *Burger*, Justice Brennan, whose views in the area had changed dramatically in the 30 years since he wrote *Frank v. Maryland*, claimed that

The implications of the Court's opinion, if realized, will virtually eliminate Fourth Amendment protection of commercial entities in the context of administrative searches. No State may require, as a condition of doing business, a blanket submission to warrantless searches for any purpose.

As with other constitutional rights, state courts may grant greater protection to businesses and industries under their respective state constitutions. In this area, state courts have generally followed the approach taken by the U.S. Supreme Court in *New York v. Burger*, but state appellate courts have made differing judgments as to when there is a sufficient governmental interest to justify dispensing with normal warrant requirements. Thus, Justice Brennan's dire warning has not been fully borne out in practice.

See also Blackmun, Harry A.; Brennan, William J., Jr.; Douglas, William O.; Fourth Amendment; Marshall, Thurgood; Privacy, Reasonable Expectations of; Probable Cause; Search Warrants; Warrantless Searches; White, Byron R.

Bibliography

Scheb, John M., and John M. Scheb II. 2005. *Law and the Administrative Process*. Belmont, CA: Thomson/ Wadsworth.

John M. Scheb II and Otis H. Stephens, Jr.

ADOPTION

Adoption is a means of creating family with the use of laws and a court order. Adoption legally creates binding ties where no biological tie may have previously existed. When an adoption is completed, an adoptee becomes a legal family member with full rights of inheritance, identical to the rights of a biological child. The adoptive parents acquire the full-blown rights to and responsibilities for the child. The court finalization occurs months after the child has been placed in the adoptive home, at least three months in New York, and a minimum of six months in New Hampshire.

There must be a generational age difference between the child and the adoptive parent(s). One may not adopt a peer. In *Matter of Adoption of Robert Paul P.* (1984), a gay couple who sought to create familial ties via adoption was denied judicial approval because there was not a generational age difference.

Married couples make up the majority of adoptive parents. However, single adults may, and do, adopt children every year. Most states recognize gay and lesbian couples and unmarried heterosexual couples as fit adoptive parents also. The state of Florida does not allow openly gay couples to adopt. Although the majority of adoptees are infants, there are also thousands of children in foster care who are available for adoption.

Today's adoptions are governed by the "best interests of the child" standard. This means that the court will determine if the adoption is in the child's best interests. A home study and extensive investigation into the family's background, including fingerprinting and criminal background checks, will be provided to the court. As one might imagine, the adoption is usually viewed as "in the child's best interests."

"Best interests" is remarkably different from the standard of the early twentieth century. The focus of adoption, then, was to provide "normalcy" for a childless couple. Children were viewed almost as property. Children were given freely to an infertile couple. Today's focus is on the child, not on the adoptive parents' need for normalcy.

In recent years, there has been a marked increase in the number of single parents and gay and lesbian couples who have sought to adopt children. Because judicial approval of adoptions is now based on the best interest standard, courts today do not automatically exclude single persons or gay and lesbian couples from adopting children.

There are important differences between domestic and international adoptions. Domestic adoptions involve children born in the United States. Domestic adoptions have no schedules; they usually take a year or more to complete. They are emotional roller coasters with any number of fits and starts. An international adoption, or the adoption of a child from another country, may be more structured and scheduled. Should one adopt a South Korean infant, one may rely on the approximate date projected by the agency for the child's arrival in the United States.

In 1991 China opened its doors to adoption by foreigners. Some countries, like China, require adoption finalization before the child leaves the country. Many adoptive parents readopt these children once they return to the United States. The main purpose for the readoption process, which mirrors the adoption finalization process, is to obtain an American birth certificate for the child.

Adoption was once a process cloaked in secrecy. Often the birth mother was not even allowed a glimpse of her newborn baby. She certainly was given no information on the infant's life after birth. Today we have open and closed adoption. A closed adoption maintains the privacy of all parties. Some information, such as medical history, may be shared, but no information that might allow the parties to identify each other is exchanged. Some adoptive parents wish to have a closed adoption because they fear that the birth parent(s) might seek to vacate the adoption in the future.

Open adoptions afford contact between the adoptive and birth parents. The parties may exchange letters and photos, they may meet face-to-face, the adoptive parent(s) may be present at the birth, or they may even choose to live together for the last month or two of the pregnancy. The adoption process is as "open" as the parties choose to make it. Open adoptions have gained popularity over the last 20 years. The birth parents choose an adoptive parent or couple, based on resumes supplied with photos and heartrending essays provided by an adoption agency or by the adoptive candidates themselves. There are a number of adoption Web sites where resumes may be viewed.

The most famous case in which a child was returned to her birth parents, at age two and a half, was the Baby Jessica case, *In re B.G.C.* (1992). In that case, a birth mother and the man she named as the birth father voluntarily terminated their parental ties to the baby soon after her birth. After a short time, the birth mother admitted that another man, Dan Schmidt, was actually the birth father. Mr. Schmidt had not terminated his rights. A legal battle ensued between the birth parents in Iowa and the adoptive parents in Michigan. In the glare of the media, after two years of litigation, Baby Jessica was returned to her birth parents.

All adoption costs, that is, all birth parents' costs that are incident to the pregnancy, are borne by the adoptive parents, including home studies, legal fees for all attorneys involved, agency application and matching fees, travel costs, and all uninsured medical costs. State laws have been carefully drafted, and are carefully followed, in that regard. The birth parents may not profit from this process on the ground that, if a profit were realized, the adopted child would be reduced to property. The cost of an adoption may run from $5,000 to $30,000. Most domestic and international adoptions average around $20,000.

Adoption is an alternative means of creating a family. In our litigious society, we have had to legislate many rules to protect the vulnerable parties in this process. When the process works as it should, adoption is a life affirming experience.

See also Parental Rights; Privacy, Constitutional Right of; Reproductive Freedom; Sexual Orientation, Discrimination Based on

Bibliography

Doherty, A. L. 2000. "Foster Care and Adoption: A Look at Open Adoption." *Journal of Contemporary Legal Issues* 11:591–98.

Ramsey, S. H. and D. E. Abrams. 2003. *Children and the Law in a Nutshell*. 2nd ed. St. Paul, MN: Thomson/West.

Wiedenhoeft, C. L. 2000. "Should Race Be Considered in the Adoption of a Child?" *Journal of Contemporary Legal Issues* 11:600–606.

Margaret Ryniker

ADVERSARY SYSTEM OF JUSTICE

The adversary system of justice is the method used in the United States to seek out the truth and resolve disputes in courts of law. Its goal is to seek justice for the participants. In the adversarial system, lawyers represent competing parties' interests before a judge, who serves as an impartial referee. In criminal and certain classes of civil cases, a jury of one's peers determines the facts in controversy.

In the adversary system each litigant is entitled to be represented by trained legal counsel, who is ethically bound to vigorously present evidence and arguments to support his or her client's position.

Except in bench trials (where there is no jury) and in equity cases (where the judge, known as a chancellor, dispenses remedial justice), the jury weighs the merits of issues after hearing the lawyers forcefully present opposing viewpoints. The judge, of course, always determines the law applicable to each case.

Colonial America adopted the English concept that justice was to be achieved through law and adopted the adversary trial system that developed rather late in the history of the common law (Langbein 2003). The American colonies, and later the new states, adopted the adversary system along with the substantive principles of the common law. In fact, many attributes of the adversarial system of justice became enshrined in the Bill of Rights to the United States Constitution, including the right to confront one's accusers, the right to counsel, and the right to a public trial by a jury of one's peers.

The adversary system prevails in many countries originally colonized by the British. It contrasts with the inquisitorial system, a nonadversarial system of justice common to much of the world. In an inquisitorial system, investigation and presentation of evidence at trial are the function of a judge, who serves both as a fact finder and judge of the law. The production of evidence rests on the judge's ability and initiative to thoroughly develop the facts in search of the truth. Lawyers are relegated to a less pivotal role and are generally permitted to interview witnesses only after a judge's investigation. In contrast, in the adversarial model it is the parties' zealous advocates, in theory, who are motivated to seek out all evidence that might favor their clients and effectively present their clients' positions to the judge or jury.

The adversarial system of criminal justice places a premium on effective advocacy by lawyers, where the discovery and presentation of evidence on behalf of the government and the defendant often requires extended investigation, interviews, and research. Federal prosecutors are appointed, and in the states lawyers are either elected or appointed to prosecute persons accused of crimes. The U.S. Constitution and the constitutions of the 50 states bear the hallmarks of the common-law system of adversarial justice. The Sixth Amendment entitles an accused "to a speedy and public trial, by an impartial jury, … and to be informed of the nature and cause of the accusation; to be confronted with the witnesses against him; to have compulsory process for obtaining witnesses in his favor, and to have the assistance of counsel for his defence." But it was not until 1963 that the U.S. Supreme Court in *Gideon v. Wainwright* mandated that counsel be appointed to represent indigent defendants accused of felonies, a ruling later extended to those accused of misdemeanors who face jail terms. The Court's observation in *Gideon*, "The right of one charged with crime to counsel may not be deemed fundamental and essential to fair trials in some countries, but it is in ours," is an explicit recognition of the role of the adversary system of criminal justice in America.

The adversary system of justice in the United States applies in civil as well as criminal cases. The Seventh Amendment to the U.S. Constitution recognizes the adversary system of justice by providing the right to a jury trial in most suits at common law. Legal procedures and rules of evidence are complex. Resolution of issues in civil disputes often depends on diligent discovery and effective presentation of facts before a judge or jury. Therefore, except in cases involving small claims, it is highly desirable, if not essential, for litigants to be represented by counsel. The adversary system, in theory, motivates lawyers who represent parties to discover and effectively present oral and documentary evidence in support of their clients' positions. Increasingly, parties in civil disputes employ experts in various technical fields to testify.

Although firmly established in the American legal culture, the adversary system is not without its critics. Roscoe Pound, who was dean of the Harvard Law School from 1916 to 1936, referred to the adversary model as "the sporting theory of justice" and believed that it contributed to popular dissatisfaction with the administration of justice (see Pound 1937). Echoing Pound's sentiments, Kevin Burke has argued that the adversary system:

leads the most conscientious judge to feel that he or she is merely to decide the contest, as attorneys present it, according to the rules of the game, and not to search independently for truth and justice. It leads attorneys to forget that they are officers of the court and to deal with the rules of law and procedure exactly as the professional football coach deals with the rules of the sport. (Burke 2003, 5)

A number of modern developments in the American legal system have moved away from the adversary model. A notable example is the juvenile justice system. From their inception in the late nineteenth century, juvenile courts emphasized rehabilitation for juveniles charged with crimes and such status offenses as truancy, and their guilt or innocence was adjudicated on a nonadversarial basis. Often without adhering to the basic constitutional protections afforded adults, courts ordered juveniles to be confined in institutions until they reached their majority. As the abuses became widespread, the U.S. Supreme Court intervened and handed down its landmark decision in *In re Gault* (1967). That decision requires juvenile courts to adhere to the basic constitutional protections in the adversarial system of justice afforded adults. The Court, however, did not go so far as to award jury trials to juvenile offenders.

The widespread practice of plea bargaining and the more recent emphasis on pretrial diversionary programs can be seen as a rejection of the adversarial approach to criminal justice in favor of a more cooperative and negotiative model. The recent establishment of drug courts is another example where nonadversarial procedures are proving productive. Many observers point to the negative impact of adversarial proceedings in family law. And considerable support is building for the view that disputes in domestic relations cases can be more effectively handled through nonadversarial collaborative procedures, which tend to be less destructive of interpersonal relationships than resolution of disputes on an adversarial basis. In other areas, courts have recognized that the character of adversarial proceedings must be tempered by input from neutral parties. For example, courts often appoint independent medical examiners to testify in tort suits seeking damages for personal injuries. Finally, there is increased emphasis on resolution of disputes through less formal methods, for example, arbitration and mediation.

Unlike the common law, in which judges "discovered" the law and developed the adversarial model, modern American law has become increasingly laden with legislatively enacted statutes and administrative regulations, often based on contemporary economic and sociological principles.

Despite the costs and delays in the adversary system and the availability of alternate methods of dispute resolution, where a contest must be resolved by litigation, the adversary system provides the greatest incentives to assure disclosure of relevant facts essential to arrive at the truth of contested issues. Thus, the adversary system of justice has become the crown jewel of the American legal system.

See also Accused, Rights of the; Bench Trial; Bill of Rights (American); Common-Law Background of American Civil Rights and Liberties; Compulsory Process; Confrontation, Right of; Counsel, Right to; *Gideon v. Wainwright*; Gault, In re; Jury, Trial by; Juvenile Justice; Public Trial, Right to a; Sixth Amendment

Bibliography

Burke, Kevin S. 2003. "A Court and a Judiciary That Is as Good as Its Promise." *Court Review* 40 (2): 4–6.

Langbein, John H. 2003. *The Origins of Adversary Criminal Trial*. Oxford: Oxford University Press.

Pound, Roscoe. 1937. "The Causes of Popular Dissatisfaction with the Administration of Justice." *Journal of American Judicature Society* 20 (1):178–87.

Hon. John M. Scheb

AFFIRMATIVE ACTION

"Affirmative action" is a term traceable to Executive Order 10925, issued by President John F. Kennedy in 1961, which required that contractors doing business with the federal government "take affirmative action to ensure that applicants are employed, and employees are treated during their employment, without regard to their race, creed, color, or national origin." More recently, the U.S. Commission on Civil Rights has defined affirmative action as "any measure, beyond simple termination of discriminatory practice, which permits the consideration of race, national origin, sex, or disability, along with other criteria, and which is adopted to provide opportunities to a class of qualified individuals who have either historically or actually been denied those opportunities, and to prevent the recurrence of such discrimination in the future."

As these references suggest, the meaning of affirmative action has shifted considerably since its first appearance. While once denoting vigorous enforcement of race and gender nondiscrimination, affirmative action now encompasses a large range of practices and rationales affecting various groups. It is embodied in private sector policy as well as in legislation, executive orders, and court decisions at the federal, state and local levels. It cannot simply be equated with civil rights, since there is no "right" to affirmative action. Moreover, even authoritative attempts to define the term are often so vague as to be useless: Does "qualified" mean minimally qualified or best qualified? Does "opportunity" mean the chance to apply and be fairly considered for a resource like a job, or the job itself? Is historical discrimination against a racial group a sufficient justification for affirmative action? In this light, it is no surprise that courts have invalidated attempts in recent years to place the term "affirmative action" on ballot initiatives in California and Texas. They have held that this term is simply too vague as a matter of law for something as important as the amendment of a state constitution or city charter by popular vote.

A full treatment of affirmative action would require far more space than this brief introduction allows. We are necessarily limited to a cursory analytical presentation, clarifying key concepts and distinctions.

At the outset, the legal and policy domains of affirmative action must be distinguished. Affirmative action might be a rational, yet illegal, policy, or it might be a legal, yet unwise, policy. This tension often arises in private sector affirmative action, which is governed by statutory law like Title VII of the 1964 Civil Rights Act. In *United Steelworkers v. Weber* (1979) and *Johnson v. State Transportation Agency* (1987), the Supreme Court upheld private affirmative action against Title VII challenge, though only under very narrow and extreme circumstances.

Secondly, within the domain of law, source of law must be recognized. We often think of affirmative action in statutory or administrative terms, as in Title VII, EEOC regulations, and their state counterparts. Yet it also finds legal expression in executive orders (e.g., Kennedy's EO 10925 and Governor Jeb Bush's One Florida Initiative) and constitutional limitations (e.g., the Equal Protection Clause of the Fourteenth Amendment and Proposition 209, now Art. I, sec. 31 of the California Constitution). The key significance of source of law concerns the relative stability of affirmative action. Political variables aside, an executive order is less stable than legislation, since it is rescindable with a stroke of the governor's pen, and legislation is less stable than constitutional amendment. While the latter can be overturned only by another constitutional amendment, the former can be struck down under an existing constitutional provision. Here we deal with public sector affirmative action, which the Court has both upheld against Equal Protection challenge (e.g., *University of California Regents v. Bakke*, 1978; *Metro Broadcasting v. FCC*, 1990; and *Grutter v. Bollinger*, 2003) and struck down (e.g., *City of Richmond v. Croson*, 1989; *Adarand Constructors v. Pena*, 1995; and *Gratz v. Bollinger*, 2003).

The question thus arises as to what factors are relevant in determining whether affirmative action is (1) good policy, (2) legal, or (3) constitutional. At least four distinctions are relevant here: (1) the ends, (2) the means, (3) the contexts of affirmative action, and 4) the race and gender groups to be favored and disfavored. These distinctions can be illustrated in part by *Gratz* and *Grutter*, the recent University of Michigan cases, widely viewed as the Supreme Court's most important civil rights rulings in a generation.

The ends of affirmative action are the goals or purposes it is designed to achieve. Several such ends have been advocated over the years, for example, the need for minority role models in education, "operational need" in law enforcement and corrections, and restitution/compensation to historically disadvantaged groups. For constitutional purposes, however, the two most significant ends are remedying discrimination and promoting diversity. The Court has consistently held the first to be a compelling interest, yet it has long distinguished between general societal discrimination and "identified" discrimination (i.e., that by a particular governmental unit), holding since *Bakke* that only remedying the latter is compelling. As for promoting diversity, Justice Lewis Powell alone held this rationale to be compelling in *Bakke*. While this was expanded to a majority ruling in *Grutter*, the Court was careful to restrict it to the context of student body diversity at public universities.

The means, or forms, of affirmative action are the practices and procedures by which institutions seek to advance the ends of affirmative action. Means can be arranged on a continuum from weak to strong, or in Mills's terminology, "soft" to "hard" (1994). Relatively weak forms of affirmative action are those used prior to the point of competition, that is, prior to the point at which it is decided who will receive the benefits for which they have applied. These include practices like outreach and aggressive recruiting, which seek to increase the pool of candidates from targeted groups who can learn about, apply, and be considered for public or private sector resources. When properly conducted, such methods raise no legal or constitutional problems: not only are they used prior to the point of competition, but they are defensible in policy and theoretical terms since they help maximize the efficiency of

the admissions, labor, and contracting markets and are thus consistent with the classical liberal values displayed throughout the Constitution.

At the same time, as noted by Peter Schuck (2003), outreach and aggressive recruiting are neither cost free nor neutral. In practice, they can easily function like preferences, a stronger form of affirmative action in which race and gender play a role at the point of competition. Schuck uses the terms "affirmative action" and "preferences" interchangeably, and they are the focus of present controversy and practice for three reasons. First, preferences were upheld in *Bakke* and *Grutter*. Second, the term "preferences" has been used in recent successful ballot measures like Proposition 209 and Initiative 200. As such, they embody current policy in some states. Third, though preferences are used at the point of competition, they are flexible in theory and sometimes in practice, race or gender being just one factor among many in the decisional process. When so used, they arguably accommodate the conflicting interests and principles at stake in a fair and equitable way.

Outreach and aggressive recruiting can operate in effect as preferences, and preferences can function like quotas. Quotas are the strongest form of affirmative action, as they involve the assignment of a minimum number or percentage of benefits solely to members of specific racial or gender groups. While successful bidders on public contracts can be required to document good faith efforts to allocate a portion of subcontracts to suitable minority- or female-owned businesses, quotas were ruled unconstitutional in *Bakke*. In *Grutter*, the dissenters argued that the University of Michigan Law School's actual admissions numbers showed that its imperative of enrolling a "critical mass" of three races amounted in effect to a minimum and thus a quota, thus rendering the decision vulnerable to reversal on this basis.

Context refers to sphere of activity, like employment or university admissions. While these contexts exist within both the private and public sectors, the latter also includes such contexts as public contracting, law enforcement, corrections, the military, electoral districting, and the FCC's grant of broadcasting licenses. Each of these presents unique if overlapping sets of interests and principles at stake in their resolution.

To illustrate, it is clear that in both employment and university admissions, race and gender preferences can make a significant difference between an individual's success or failure in securing the resources he or she seeks. In both contexts, preferences are distinct from forms of redistribution like taxation, in which burdens are minimized and widely diffused (a few extra dollars to everyone who is employed) rather than maximized and concentrated on a small minority, which thus bears the full cost of the program. At the same time, preferences are less defensible in employment than in admissions for at least two reasons. First, in pedagogical terms, race preferences in admissions unite young people of different backgrounds in a joint learning project, uniquely capturing the benefits of diversity. Second, in economic terms, the university applicant is a buyer, while the applicant for employment or public contracts is a seller, and though markets vary widely, buyers nearly always have more choices than do sellers. Those seeking to spend money, that is, generally have more options than those seeking to earn it, and this is certainly true in the case of selective university admissions. At this level of competition, there is always another program to which those rejected from their first choice will be accepted, and where they can receive a good education and thus the chance to excel in life.

Finally, the groups to be favored and disfavored by affirmative action vary from the poor or African Americans alone to everyone but rich white males. Although advocacy of affirmative action for other groups based solely on the experience of blacks is practically routine, the various groups are not identically situated, rendering much of this advocacy irrelevant and unconvincing. Though Justice Powell in *Bakke* had clarified that there is no compelling interest in simple racial diversity, *Grutter* simply deferred to the University of Michigan's judgment

that three races in particular offer diversity, avoiding this dimension of the problem. This leaves the suspicion that the real rationale for Michigan's preferences was understood not to be diversity, but rather compensation and remediation, especially given the emphasis in Justice Ginsburg's concurrence on the persistence of racial discrimination and her failure even to mention diversity. In order to avoid such problems, observers like Schuck (2003), Bok and Bowen (1997), Loury (2002), and Glazer (1998) have concluded that a plausible and coherent case for affirmative action requires that it be limited to one group, namely African Americans.

Given *Grutter's* weaknesses, then, and the possibility that in the current climate of national judicial politics only a centrist like Justice Powell could be confirmed to replace the next retiring member of the *Grutter* majority, this case could be reversed within a few years, with the battle over affirmative action continuing indefinitely.

See also Busing Controversy; Civil Rights; Civil Rights Act of 1964; Civil Rights Movement; Diversity; Employment Discrimination; Equal Employment Opportunity Commission (EEOC); Equality; Equal Protection Clause; Equal Protection Jurisprudence; Fourteenth Amendment; Gender-Based Discrimination; Group Rights; Powell, Lewis F.; U.S. Civil Rights Commission

Bibliography

Bok, Derek, and William Bowen. 1997. *The Shape of the River*. Princeton, NJ: Princeton University Press.

Carcieri, Martin. 1999. "Operational Need, Political Reality, and Liberal Democracy: Two Suggested Amendments to Proposition 209-Based Reforms." *Seton Hall Constitutional Law Journal* 9:459–503.

———. 2002. "The Sixth Circuit and *Grutter v. Bollinger*: Diversity and Distortion." *Texas Review of Law and Politics* 7:127–52.

Curry, George. 1996. *The Affirmative Action Debate*. New York: Addison-Wesley.

Glazer, Nathan. 1998. "In Defense of Preference." *New Republic*, 6 April, 18.

Loury, Glenn. 2002. *The Anatomy of Racial Inequality*. Cambridge, MA: Harvard University Press.

Mills, Nicolaus. 1994. *Debating Affirmative Action*. New York: Dell Publishing.

Schuck, Peter. 2003. "Affirmative Action: Defining and Certifying Diversity." In *Diversity in America*. Cambridge, MA: Harvard University Press.

Martin Carcieri

AGE DISCRIMINATION

The Age Discrimination in Employment Act of 1967 (ADEA) protects individuals who are 40 years of age or older from employment discrimination by private employers except where age is a reasonable occupational qualification. Thus, ADEA prohibits employers from engaging in arbitrary age discrimination in the hiring, promotion, or discharge of employees except where age is a realistic qualification necessary to the normal operations of the particular business. ADEA was modeled on Title VII of the Civil Rights Act of 1964, which prohibits discrimination in the area of employment based on sex, race, color, and religion. As established in 1967, the Act only covered workers between the ages of 40 and 65. However, in 1974 Congress amended the ADEA and extended the age to 70 and included employees in the public sector as well.

The first issue addressed by the courts was in relation to state and local public employees and regulation by the federal government in response to the ADEA. In *E.E.O.C. v. Wyoming* (1983), suit was brought on the basis of the statutory policy of Wyoming requiring retirement of game wardens at the age of 55. The state of Wyoming contended that the ADEA overreached its limitations by infringing upon powers reserved to the states by the Tenth Amendment. The Supreme Court held that if the state can demostrate that age is a "bona fide occupational qualification" then regulations posed by the Act would not affect the current policy. Also, the ADEA did not limit or restrict the state's ability to assess its employees on an individual basis through other means such as medical evaluations and job performance testing. Irrespective of the Tenth Amendment claim, the Court recognized that coverage of the ADEA was constitutional based on the exercise of congressional power to regulate interstate commerce.

The precedent established was on the basis of case-by-case evaluations regarding more than chronological age. An employer may establish mandatory retirement ages below 70 where the employer can demonstrate that age is a qualification necessary to the normal operations of the employer's business. Mandatory retirement below the age of 70 is common in the area of public safety, where daily activities involve a certain degree of physical fitness and it is recognized that muscular strength tends to deteriorate with age. However, supervisory roles are not subject to careful scrutiny because the day-to-day activities differ and require less physical exertion. Thus, challenges made on behalf of the ADEA are made and evaluated on a case-by-case basis. *Gregory v. Ashcroft* (1991) utilized the "rational basis" test in relation to Missouri's state constitutional provision requiring public officials to retire at age 70. The state's law was determined to have a rational basis given the undeniable effects of aging and the limited utility in removing judges from office through judicial elections and impeachment.

The Equal Employment Opportunity Commission (EEOC), created by the Civil Rights Act of 1964, became an important enforcement agency for ADEA. In *Gilmer v. Interstate/Johnson Lane Corporation* (1991) the Supreme Court held that the ADEA and the Federal Arbitration Act permit compulsory arbitration of employee disputes over dismissals involving age discrimination as required under an employment agreement. Employees who accuse their employers of age discrimination under the ADEA may bring suits in federal courts after state agencies have dismissed their complaints and without further appeals in state courts, according to *Astoria Federal Savings and Loan v. Solimino* (1991).

Employers may refuse to hire someone because he or she is too young, but refusing to hire someone because he or she is too old (over 40) is illegal. Employers may offer special early retirement incentives in an effort to downsize to employees who agree to take early retirement. This is not considered age discrimination as long as the employers are not trying to phase out older workers simply because of their age. The same holds true for employers trying to replace individuals who are making higher wages due to seniority compared to younger workers, who generally make less. It is not illegal for employers to replace older workers with younger ones if monetary concerns are justified. It is illegal if employers are actually trying to replace older workers with younger ones, and monetary concerns are the façade in which this goal is met. Age discrimination laws exist to ensure individuals are not mistreated on the basis of age alone. Older workers have experience and working knowledge of past organizational structures as well as the present and therefore are aware of what practices are beneficial for the companies as well as detrimental. It is this type of knowledge that employers should value, and in doing so they should also value older workers.

See also Civil Rights Act of 1964; Employment Discrimination; Equal Employment Opportunity Commission

Bibliography

Gregory, Raymond. 2001. *Age Discrimination in the American Workplace: Old at a Young Age.* New Brunswick, NJ: Rutgers University Press.

Kalet, Joseph. 1990. *Age Discrimination in Employment Law.* 2nd ed. Washington, DC: Bureau of National Affairs.

Segrave, Kerry. 2001. *Age Discrimination by Employers.* Jefferson, NC: McFarland.

Kimberly Gill

AGE DISCRIMINATION AND EMPLOYMENT ACT. *See* Age Discrimination; Employment Discrimination

ALDEN V. MAINE (1999)

A group of probation officers filed suit in the U.S. District Court alleging that the State of Maine had violated the overtime provisions of the Fair Labor Standards Act. While the suit was pending in the district court, the Supreme Court decided *Seminole Tribe of Florida v. Florida* (1996), which held that Congress lacks power under Article I of the Constitution to abrogate the states' sovereign immunity from suits commenced or prosecuted in the federal courts. On that basis, the district court dismissed the lawsuit, and the U.S. Court of Appeals for the First Circuit affirmed (see *Mills v. Maine*, 1997).

The plaintiffs then filed their complaint in a Maine state court. That court dismissed the suit on the basis of the state's sovereign immunity, and the Maine Supreme Judicial Court upheld the dismissal. Noting a conflict between that decision and a ruling by the Arkansas Supreme Court, the U.S. Supreme Court took the case on certiorari. Dividing five-to-four, the Supreme Court affirmed the decision of the Maine Supreme Judicial Court, holding that "the powers delegated to Congress under Article I of the United States Constitution do not include the power to subject nonconsenting States to private suits for damages in state courts." Writing the majority opinion, Justice Anthony Kennedy characterized the decision as consistent with the Framers' belief that "freedom is enhanced by the creation of two governments, not one." Kennedy accused the four dissenting justices of believing "that the Congress may circumvent the federal design by regulating the States directly when it pleases to do so, including by a proxy in which individual citizens are authorized to levy upon the state treasuries absent the States' consent to jurisdiction."

Justice David Souter, speaking for the dissenters, insisted that "the Court's argument that state court sovereign immunity on federal questions is inherent in the very concept of federal structure is demonstrably mistaken." Likening the Court's decision to the economic due process of a bygone era, Souter concluded, "I expect the Court's late essay into immunity doctrine will prove the equal of its earlier experiment in laissez-faire, the one being as unrealistic as the other, as indefensible, and probably as fleeting."

See also Eleventh Amendment; Federalism and Civil Rights and Liberties; Kennedy, Anthony; Rehnquist Court; Souter, David H.; Sovereign Immunity

John M. Scheb II and Otis H. Stephens, Jr.

ALIEN AND SEDITION ACTS (1798)

The Alien and Sedition Acts were comprised of four statutes enacted by the Federalist-controlled Congress and signed by President John Adams in 1798. The nature of these statutes and the controversy they produced are better understood within the context of the foreign and domestic political environment of the time. In 1798, strong anti-French feeling swept across the nation in response to French demands on the American government and insults to American envoys sent to Paris. The international situation was tense as the United States prepared for war by raising an army and expanding its navy. There were fears that aliens sympathetic to France were spies, and there simultaneously existed bitter and highly divisive partisan differences over both foreign and domestic policies. Federalist fears of excessive popular government clashed with Jeffersonian Republicans' sympathies for the aspirations of the common man. Federalists sought political stability and security, especially in regard to property rights. Led by Vice President Thomas Jefferson, Republicans tended to sympathize with the French Revolution, while Federalists saw the idea behind the revolution as endangering civil government and social order. Accordingly, Federalists sought to label Jeffersonian opposition to President Adams's foreign policy as seditious and almost traitorous. This partisan warfare fueled intemperate and insulting rhetoric on both sides, culminating in passage of the Alien and Sedition Acts of 1798 by the Federalist Congress. President Adams neither asked for nor opposed passage of these laws. He signed them into law, however, as necessary war measures.

Three of the four statutes in 1798 concerned the status of aliens. The Naturalization Act extended the time for aliens to become citizens from 5 to 14 years. The Alien Enemies Act provided for the arrest and removal of "dangerous" aliens during an official state of war. The president was authorized to decide which citizens of a hostile nation were dangerous and which citizens, therefore, were subject to removal from the country. To this day, the statute remains the basis for treatment of enemy aliens during times of war. The third statute, the Alien Friends Law, made every foreigner residing in the United States subject to arrest and deportation during either war or peacetime. The president was given the power to determine which aliens were dangerous to the peace and safety of the United States. An alien ordered to leave the country could present evidence to the president that no danger would result from his continuing to reside in the United States, but ultimately the president's decision was final. The Alien Friends Law was limited to two years (the period of crises in relations between the United States and France), but no alien was ever deported under it.

The fourth statute, the Sedition Act of 1798, declared it unlawful to "combine or conspire together, with intent to oppose any measure or measures of the government of the United States … or to impede the operation of any law of the United States…. If any person shall write, print, utter or publish … with intent to defame the said government, or either house of Congress, or the President; or to bring them … into contempt or disrepute … or to stir up sedition against the United States … or to excite any unlawful combinations for opposing or resisting any law or the United States or any act of the President … or to aid, encourage, or abet any hostile designs of any foreign nation against the United States." Depending on the nature of the specific violation, persons convicted under the statute could be fined up to $5,000 and imprisoned for up to five years. In using the language of "intent," the sedition law went beyond normal restrictions on the use of force against the government. Verbal and written opposition to government actions that had a tendency to undermine government authority was targeted by the sedition law.

Vice President Jefferson condemned the sedition law as an assault on freedom of speech and press under the Constitution. For Jefferson and his partisan followers, the Alien and Sedition Acts were "palpably in the teeth of the Constitution." He characterized the period of passage of these acts as "a reign of witches." Federalists justified the sedition statute as a war measure needed to protect national security, yet it was more probably intended to silence a Republican press whose invectives were aimed at the Federalist party and the Adams administration. Under a provision in the law, the sedition law automatically expired in March 1801. During its life there were 17 prosecutions, and 10 people convicted. Despite the small numbers, the act and its companion alien legislation produced vigorous opposition and resulted in the Virginia and Kentucky Resolutions of 1798.

The Virginia and Kentucky resolutions were secretly authored by James Madison and Thomas Jefferson. Jefferson's Kentucky resolution declared that national authority under the United States Constitution rested on a compact among the states that had delegated limited powers to the national government. Each state could make its own judgment as to whether national power had been exceeded and take appropriate action. Kentucky, while asserting its loyalty to the concept of union, declared the Alien and Sedition Acts "void and of no force" as a violation under the Constitution.

Virginia's resolution, written by James Madison, also asserted loyalty to the idea of union but asserted the right of the state to "interpose" itself against national government acts that "are not granted by the compact." The legislatures of Virginia and Kentucky requested other states to join in condemning the Alien and Sedition Acts, but no other state acceded to that request.

The Alien and Sedition Acts mark the first major debate under the Constitution's First Amendment concerning the proper balance between the freedoms of speech and press and claims regarding the need to protect national security. Although the boundaries have shifted over time, sometimes favoring security and at other times free expression, the issue remains a significant part of the American constitutional dialogue. Not until 1918 did Congress enact another sedition law, a wartime measure that was repealed in 1921. Also, in 1940 a peacetime sedition statute called the Alien Registration Act, known generally as the Smith

Act, was passed. The Alien and Sedition Acts remain a source of contention between those concerned primarily with individual freedoms and those concerned primarily with national security.

See also First Amendment; Jefferson, Thomas; Madison, James; Press, Freedom of the; Sedition; Smith Act; Speech, Freedom of; Kentucky and Virginia Resolutions

Bibliography

Levy, Leonard. 1960. *Legacy of Suppression: Freedom of Speech and Press in Early American History.* Cambridge, MA: Harvard University Press.
Miller, John C. 1951. *Crisis in Freedom: The Alien and Sedition Acts.* Boston: Little, Brown.
Thomas D. Ungs

ALIENAGE, DISCRIMINATION BASED ON.
See Immigrants and Aliens, Rights of

ALIEN REGISTRATION ACT OF 1940. *See* Smith Act

ALIENS. *See* Alien and Sedition Acts; Immigrants and Aliens, Rights of

ALLOCUTION, RIGHT OF. *See* Sentencing Hearing

AMERICAN ASSOCIATION OF RETIRED PERSONS (AARP)

The American Association of Retired Persons (AARP) consists of three major arms: AARP; AARP Services, Incorporated (ASI); and the AARP Foundation. Based in Washington, D.C., AARP advocates in the nation's Capitol, in state houses, and in the courts on behalf of AARP members and their families. AARP is a nonprofit membership organization for persons 50 years of age and older. The organization was founded in 1958 by retired California educator Dr. Ethel Percy Andrus. Today the organization represents over 35 million members. The organization focuses its efforts and resources on health and wellness, economic security and work, long-term care and independent living, and personal enrichment for the 50-plus population in all 50 states, the District of Columbia, and the U.S. Virgin Islands. The organization reaches out internationally through its Office of International Affairs. It works with governmental and nongovernmental organizations to address worldwide aging concerns.

The organization advocates specifically for long-term solvency of Social Security, pension protection, prescription drug coverage in Medicare, patient protections in managed and long-term care, and other protections for older consumers. The organization fights against age discrimination and predatory home-loan lending. AARP Services, Incorporated, is a wholly owned subsidiary of AARP. ASI manages products and services for members, including health and life insurance, prescription discounts, and travel discounts. Finally, the AARP Foundation, the charity of the organization, manages grants, engages in litigation, awards grants for research in aging, and conducts educational programs on financial security and coping with chronic health conditions.

AARP sets its policy agenda through information gathered from telephone calls, town meetings, letters, surveys, and member polls. Also in keeping with the times, AARP facilitates an Internet blog (discussion board) for its membership population. The organization's National Legislative Council makes policy recommendations based on input from members, experts and elected official officials. The council presents its recommendations to the 21 members of the Board of Directors. The Legislative Council; Board of Directors; National Officers; field directors; state presidents; and legislative, program, and chapter leaders are all volunteers (AARP 2003).

AARP's top three revenue sources in 2001 were membership dues (28%), income from AARP health-care options (17%), and royalties (14%). AARP's top three expense categories for the same year were publications (25%), programs and field services (19%), and facilities and headquarters administration (16%) (AARP 2001).

AARP represents workers and retirees, people living alone or with families, and people of various financial means. Nearly a third of AARP members are under 60, 46 percent are age 60 to 74, and 21 percent are 75 and older.

AARP publishes a monthly magazine, *AARP: The Magazine*, a monthly newspaper, the *AARP Bulletin*, and a quarterly newspaper, *Segunda Juventud*, and maintains a Web site at www.aarp.org. The organization also produces two national radio network series, *Prime Time* and *Mature Focus*. In addition, AARP compiles organizational expertise, research, and members' concerns and interests in its annual publication of *The Policy Book: AARP Policies*. The organization operates its own research center. The AARP's Research Center Digest offers research results and policy insight to members and nonmembers.

Researchers may obtain copies of the organization's annual report and archived copies of *AARP: The Magazine* on the AARP Web site or by contacting the organization.

See also Interest Groups

Bibliography

AARP. 2001. *Annual Report*. Washington, DC: AARP Foundation.

———. 2003. *Fact Sheet and Background Information*. Washington, DC: Author.

———. 2005–2006. www.aarp.org (accessed 15 March, 2006).

Kimberly L. Douglass

AMERICAN BAR ASSOCIATION (ABA)

The American Bar Association (ABA) is voluntary professional association whose membership consists of practicing lawyers, judges, court administrators, law teachers, public service lawyers, and law students as well as nonpracticing lawyers who serve as business executives and government officials. Its stated mission is "to be the national representative of the legal profession, serving the public and the profession by promoting justice, professional excellence, and respect for the law." While it does not have the power to discipline lawyers, it develops model rules and ethics guidelines.

The ABA was founded in 1878, in Saratoga Springs, New York. At that time, most lawyers were solo practitioners trained through apprenticeship. With the growing complexity of society and our legal system, today's lawyers are highly educated and frequently specialize. ABA membership is open to lawyers in good standing before the bar of any state or territory of the United States. Individuals who are not admitted to practice but who have an interest in the work of the ABA are eligible to join as associates. In 2005, ABA's membership of over 400,000 included more than 350,000 lawyers, representing about half of all lawyers in the United States.

The ABA is headquartered in Chicago, Illinois, and has an office in Washington, D.C. The House of Delegates, its policy-making body, includes delegates from state and local bar associations. A board of governors speaks for the ABA, consistent with previous action of the House of Delegates, when the House is not in session. Elected officers are the president, president-elect, chair of the House of Delegates, secretary, and treasurer. An executive director heads a professional staff of more than 750 employees.

The ABA functions through numerous sections, divisions, and forums (for example, criminal justice, litigation, real property, probate, and trust) and numerous commissions, committees, and other entities (for example, Human Rights Commission, Racial and Ethnic Justice Council). Its professional publications include magazines, journals, newsletters, and books. The ABA's Web site, from which much of the information in this article was obtained, is at www.abanet.org.

See also Interest Groups

Hon. John M. Scheb

AMERICAN BOOKSELLERS V. HUDNUT (1985)

Feminists have attacked pornography for the way in which it degrades and objectifies women (see Cornell 2000; Strossen 2000). In the early 1980s, noted feminists Andrea Dworkin and Catherine

MacKinnon called for legislation defining pornography as a form of sex discrimination remediable through civil litigation. In April 1982, the city of Indianapolis adopted such an ordinance. Defining pornography as the "sexually explicit subordination of women, graphically depicted, whether in pictures or in words," the ordinance banned pornography within the city and permitted women to sue producers, distributors, and/or sellers of pornography for damages and injunctive relief.

The ordinance was immediately challenged on First Amendment grounds and was declared unconstitutional by a federal district court. In her opinion in *American Booksellers v. Hudnut* (1984), Judge Sarah Evans Barker observed that "women generally have the capacity to protect themselves from participating in and being personally victimized by pornography, which makes the State's interest in safeguarding the physical and psychological well-being of women ... not so compelling as to sacrifice the guarantees of the First Amendment."

On appeal, the U.S. Court of Appeals for the Seventh Circuit sustained Judge Barker's ruling. Writing for the unanimous court, Judge Frank Easterbrook noted that the "ordinance establishes an 'approved' view of women, of how they may react to sexual encounters, of how the sexes may relate to each other." Easterbrook concluded that under the Constitution the government "may not ordain preferred viewpoints in this way" and that the First Amendment "forbids the state to declare one perspective right and silence opponents."

The Supreme Court affirmed the 7th Circuit without comment, thus effectively curtailing the movement to legally define pornography as a civil rights issue. However, the debate over pornography and its effect on women continues.

See also Dworkin, Andrea, Feminist Movement; First Amendment; Gender-Based Discrimination; Obscenity and Pornography; Speech, Freedom of

Bibliography

Cornell, Drucilla, ed. 2000. *Feminism and Pornography*. Oxford: Oxford University Press.

Strossen, Nadine. 2000. *Defending Pornography: Free Speech, Sex, and the Fight for Women's Rights.* New York: New York University Press.

John M. Scheb II and Otis H. Stephens, Jr.

AMERICAN CIVIL LIBERTIES UNION (ACLU)

The American Civil Liberties Union (ACLU) is one of the oldest and best-known interest groups in the United States. The group was founded in 1920 by Roger Nash Baldwin, Crystal Eastman, and Albert DeSilver, rabble-rousing antiwar activists who believed that the federal government had overstepped its bounds during World War I by prosecuting conscientious objectors under the Espionage Act of 1917 and the Sedition Act of 1918.

According to its Web site (www.aclu.org), the ACLU's stated purpose is to "defend and preserve the individual rights and liberties guaranteed to every person in this country by the Constitution and laws of the United States." The ACLU is a federated organization that works through both its national headquarters in New York and numerous local affiliates. It is an exceedingly variegated organization that lobbies all three levels and branches of government and tackles a large assortment of civil liberties and civil rights issues. The ACLU is generally considered a liberal organization due to its unwavering support for abortion rights, freedom of expression, affirmative action, gay rights, the rights of the accused, prisoners' rights, and strict separation of church and state. Indeed, conservative commentators often characterize the ACLU as being "far left" or even anti-American (see, e.g., Sears and Osten 2005). Nonetheless, the ACLU often comes to the defense of conservatives and conservative causes. For example, in 2004 the group sided with Rush Limbaugh and argued that the government had violated his rights when Florida officials gained access to his medical records. Similarly, in the 1990s, the group sided with the tobacco industry when governments throughout the United States sought to prohibit or limit tobacco advertising.

Though the ACLU actively engages in legislative and executive branch lobbying, its bailiwick clearly is litigation. The ACLU influences judicial policy making primarily by filing amicus curiae briefs, but it also supports litigants and, occasionally, is itself a party to litigation. The ACLU has been involved in some of the biggest cases in all of American law. For example, in 1925 it was the ACLU that convinced John Scopes to violate the state of Tennessee's law against teaching evolution, and it was the ACLU that paid Scopes's legal bills. In *Brown v. Board of Education* (1954), the ACLU filed an amicus brief on behalf of the winning side in the case and continued its war on segregation throughout the 1950s and 1960s. In the 1990s, the ACLU successfully challenged the Communications Decency Act, which restricted sexually oriented material on the Internet (*Reno v. ACLU*, 1997). More recently, the ACLU has worked tirelessly to challenge portions of the USA PATRIOT Act that expand the government's powers in the areas of eavesdropping and surveillance. According to information on its Web site, the ACLU is involved in more than 6,000 cases per year.

Needless to say, the ACLU is a very controversial organization. The group consistently tackles hot-button issues that inspire passion and zeal and often takes stands that infuriate large segments of the population. Perhaps the position that has most inflamed the ACLU's critics is its stance on separation of church and state. The ACLU maintains that religious freedom can be maintained only through the broadest interpretation of the Establishment Clause of the First Amendment. Thus, the ACLU has been involved in cases seeking not only to ban prayer from public schools, public meetings, and so forth, but to remove public displays of the Ten Commandments and other religious symbols, and even to strike the phrase "under God" from the Pledge of Allegiance. To some of its conservative critics, the ACLU's mission is the moral degradation of the country. The ACLU maintains that it is only seeking to further that most American of values: liberty.

See also Abortion, Right to; Accused, Rights of the; Affirmative Action; American Nazi Party; *Brown v.*

Board of Education; Conscientious Objection to Military Service; Conservatism; Electronic Surveillance; Espionage Act of 1917; Establishment Clause; Evolution/Creationism Controversy; First Amendment; Gay Rights Movement; Interest Groups; Liberalism; Prisoners' Rights; Privacy, Constitutional Right of; Privacy, Informational; *Reno v. American Civil Liberties Union*; Segregation in Public Education; Separation of Church and State; Sexual Orientation, Discrimination Based on; Speech, Freedom of; Ten Commandments, Public Display of the; USA PATRIOT Act

Bibliography

Krannawitter, Thomas L. 2005. *A Nation Under God? The ACLU and Religion in American Politics*. Lanham, MD: Rowman & Littlefield.

Sears, Alan, and Craig Osten. 2005. *The ACLU vs. America: Exposing the Agenda to Redefine Moral Values*. Nashville, TN: Broadman & Holman.

Walker, Samuel. 1999. *In Defense of American Liberties: A History of the ACLU*. 2nd ed. Carbondale: Southern Illinois University Press.

Anthony J. Nownes

AMERICAN COUNCIL OF THE BLIND. *See* Disability Rights Organizations

AMERICAN INDIAN RELIGIOUS FREEDOM ACT AMENDMENTS OF 1994. *See* Native American Church

AMERICAN NAZI PARTY

The American Nazi Party is one of five political parties subscribing to Nazi ideology presently in the United States. The other four are the National Alliance, the National Socialist Movement, the National Socialist White People's Party, and the Nationalist Workers Party. Its founder and leader, George Lincoln Rockwell, formed the American Nazi Party in October of 1959 from another group, the World Union of Free Enterprise National Socialists (WUFENS). As stated on the party's Web site (www.americannaziparty. com), the American Nazi Party is a "political-

educational association committed to bringing American National Socialism ... out of the past activities of organization and indoctrination and into the 21st Century."

According to the American Nazi Party, National Socialism addresses various issues, including a healthy environment, children's welfare, and freedom of belief without fear of system persecution. However, "the two main tenants of National Socialism embody the Struggle for Aryan Racial survival, and Social Justice for White Working Class people throughout our land" (www. americannaziparty.com). These self-proclaimed Aryan Revolutionaries claim to have taken a new direction. The party no longer uses such symbols as military rank and uniforms, and it no longer engages in publicly exposing comrades to undue publicity through pointless and dangerous rallies or marches. Instead, the party now stresses small cells and individual activism as the path for which to build its movement.

The origins of the American Nazi Party and all other Nazi movements in the United States can be traced back to the 1920s with the establishment of the National Socialist German Workers Party and the Teutonia. These groups combined in the early 1930s to become the Friends of the New Germany, which changed its name in 1936 to the German-American Bund (Canedy 1990). Beginning in 1939, Nazism's divisive racial rhetoric, coupled with German aggression in Europe and the advent of World War II, caused American support for the German-American Bund to wane. Following the bombing of Pearl Harbor by the Japanese and the entry of the United States into World War II, the Bund disbanded. After World War II, Nazism lay dormant in the United States for two decades. It was revived during the time of the civil rights movement under the leadership of George Lincoln Rockwell in the late 1950s.

Rockwell had attended Brown University but dropped out in March of 1941 to join the U.S. Navy. He was commissioned as a naval aviator and saw action in the Atlantic and Pacific theaters.

In September of 1945, Rockwell, as a lieutenant commander in the Naval Reserve, returned to civilian life and went into advertising (at which he excelled). Ever a virulent anti-communist, Rockwell was a supporter of Senator Joseph McCarthy and his investigations into communist activities in the United States. Following the demise of McCarthyism, a disenchanted Rockwell read Adolph Hitler's manifesto *Mein Kampf*. Rockwell had an epiphany that Hitler was the way and the truth, and that the real enemies of America were atheists, communists, and "race-mixers." He formed the American Nazi Party, popularized the term "white power," and called his bodyguards "stormtroopers." Rockwell and the American Nazi Party were also among the first to publicly deny that the Holocaust occurred, calling it historical revisionism made up by the Jews (Schmaltz 1999).

The civil rights movement of the 1960s became the rallying point that led to a resurgence of Nazism in the United States. Rockwell, as leader of the American Nazi Party, called for African Americans to be targeted with the same passion as Jewish Americans. In 1966 Rockwell followed Dr. Martin Luther King, Jr., during King's Open Housing Marches in Chicago. Rockwell was there to confront King. Rockwell and the American Nazi Party gained some public support for being against the civil rights movement, since quite a few white Americans who believed in segregation felt that George Lincoln Rockwell was one of the few political figures who spoke for them. Rockwell's growing support led him to decide to run for U.S. president in 1967. However, on August 25, 1967, a fellow American Nazi who had been in a doctrinal dispute with Rockwell regarding basic Nazi beliefs gunned down the American Nazi leader (Schmaltz 1999).

The American Nazi Party floundered after Rockwell's death for a few years until 1970, when Frank Collin reorganized the American Nazi Party into the National Socialist Party of America. Collin considered himself a follower of Rockwell and in 1978 announced his intentions to organize a march in Skokie, Illinois, a community where many survivors of Nazi concentration camps lived. Collin's request for a permit to march in Skokie was denied, so the Nazis turned to the United States legal system to protect their rights. An American Civil Liberties Union (ACLU) lawyer, David Goldberger, defended the Nazis' right to march by protecting their First Amendment Rights. In *National Socialist Party v. Skokie* (1977) the U.S. Supreme Court ruled that the state courts must "provide … immediate appellate review" to determine whether the injunction barring the march violated Collin's First Amendment rights. The Justice Department then talked to the Nazis and the ACLU, and the controversy was avoided. Collin and the National Socialist Party of America accepted alternative permits for marches at some public parks in the city of Chicago, so the march on Skokie was cancelled. In 1979, Collin's followers removed him as leader of the Nationalist Socialist Party. America's cherished right to free speech had been challenged by a threatened community and ironically was protected by a Nazi agitator working with a Jewish lawyer.

American Nazis again challenged America's right to free speech, pushing the boundary between speech and action. However, this time the American Nazi Party was no longer the organization responsible. William Pierce, a former comrade of George Lincoln Rockwell, believed that the Jews ruled the world through the mass media, and in 1978 he wrote *The Turner Diaries*, a fiction book that Pierce wrote under the pseudonym Andrew MacDonald. The book promoted violence against Jews and became a must read among the militant neo-Nazi movements and a motivational piece for radical action. The book led to neo-Nazis, Klan members, and white supremacists forming groups such as the Order and the Aryan Nation, and it was influential in its call for action against the U.S. government.

See also American Civil Liberties Union; Civil Rights Movement; Communist Party USA; First Amendment; Hate Crimes; Hate Speech; King, Martin Luther, Jr.; Ku Klux Klan; McCarthy, Joseph R.; Speech, Freedom of; Symbolic Speech; U.S. Department of Justice

Bibliography

Canedy, Susan. 1990. *America's Nazis: A Democratic Dilemma: A History of the German American Bund.* Menlo Park, CA: Markgraf.

Schmaltz, William H. 1999. *Hate: George Lincoln Rockwell and the American Nazi Party.* Washington, DC: Batsford Brassey.

Troy Goodale

AMERICANS UNITED FOR SEPARATION OF CHURCH AND STATE

Americans United for Separation of Church and State was founded by religious, political, and educational leaders in 1947 to advance the cause of religious liberty. Based in Washington, D.C., Americans United has chapters located in all 50 states. Its current executive director is the Rev. Barry W. Lynn, who is an ordained minister with the United Church of Christ. As chief spokesperson for Americans United, Lynn makes numerous appearances in the media to promote the idea of a strict separation of church and state.

As stated on the organization's Web site (www. au.org), Americans United seeks to "educate Americans about the importance of church-state separation in safeguarding religious freedom." In a brochure entitled "Is America a Christian Nation?" Americans United insists, "Only the principle of church-state separation can protect America's incredible degree of religious freedom. The individual rights and diversity we enjoy cannot be maintained if the government promotes Christianity or if our government takes on the trappings of a 'faith-based' state."

In recent years, Americans United has concentrated on attacking what it perceives to be the endorsement of religion by public schools and other governmental institutions. Thus, it has opposed prayers of any kind at government-sponsored events, the posting of the Ten Commandments in public buildings, and even the inscription "In God We Trust" on the nation's currency.

Americans United has been particularly active in litigation in the Establishment Clause area, filing suits in both federal and state courts and sub-

mitting amicus curiae briefs in cases filed by other plaintiffs. The organization won an important victory in *Santa Fe Independent School District v. Doe* (2000), where the U.S. Supreme Court struck down a policy that allowed for student-led prayer at public high school football games. Americans United advised counsel and filed an amicus brief in this case.

In 2004, Americans United filed an amicus brief in *Elk Grove Unified School District v. Newdow,* a case challenging the constitutionality of students reciting the phrase "Under God" in the Pledge of Allegiance, which is a common practice in public school systems. According to the brief, the practice "violates the Establishment Clause both because it communicates to schoolchildren a forbidden message of government endorsement of religion and because … [it] pressures school children to profess religious beliefs and affirm religious ideals." The Supreme Court dismissed the case, finding that the plaintiff lacked standing to sue.

Americans United also opposes "school choice" programs, wherein parents receive vouchers to send their children to any accredited school, even religious ones. The organization asserts that vouchers force taxpayers to promote religious institutions and religious opinions they may not share. Moreover, Americans United has opposed the faith-based initiatives promoted by the Bush Administration under which religious organizations receive federal funds to deliver social services. In the view of Americans United, such initiatives amount to nothing more than taxpayer-supported religious ministries.

In 2004, Americans United entered the debate over gay marriage, opposing President Bush's call for a constitutional amendment to limit marriage to heterosexual couples. The organization viewed the proposed amendment as a denial of fundamental rights to nontraditional families based on religious bias.

See also Conscience, Freedom of; Establishment Clause; Freedom from Religion Foundation; Moment of Silence Laws; Religion, Freedom of;

Religion, Official Endorsements of; Religious Displays on Public Property; Religious Schools, Government Aid to; School Choice Programs; School Prayer Decisions; Separation of Church and State; Tax Exemptions for Religious Organizations; Ten Commandments, Public Display of the

Ann M. Bennett

AMERICANS WITH DISABILITIES ACT (ADA).
See Disabilities, Rights of Persons with; Disability Rights Organizations

AMISTAD INCIDENT. *See* Abolitionist Movement

ANIMAL CRUELTY LAWS. *See* Animal Rights

ANIMAL RIGHTS

Today there are a number of interest groups advocating the cause of animal rights. By far the largest and best-known such group is People for the Ethical Treatment of Animals (PETA), which boasts more than 850,000 members worldwide. Founded in 1980, PETA is dedicated to establishing and protecting the rights of all animals.

At the present time, animals do not have rights as such under American law. Nevertheless they can be and in many instances are protected by law. Endangered and threatened species are protected by various federal and state laws, most notably the Endangered Species Act (ESA). Although enforcement is largely through civil penalties, criminal liability is imposed against any person who knowingly violates regulations promulgated under the ESA. States also have laws restricting the hunting of species that are not endangered or threatened. And every state has some sort of animal cruelty statute making it a crime to torture, abuse or intentionally injure an animal or to abandon or neglect an animal in one's custody. Many states also prohibit cockfighting, dog fighting and other forms of animal fighting.

For PETA and most animal rights activists, such protections are not good enough. They believe that animals should not be used for medical research, clothing, or even food. According to the organization's Web site, "PETA operates under the simple principle that animals are not ours to eat, wear, experiment on, or use for entertainment" (see www.peta.org/about). The site also claims that "PETA's street-theater style demonstrations, bold ads, and hard-hitting undercover investigations have grabbed the public's attention and started people thinking about the cruelty that animals endure on factory farms and fur farms, in laboratories and circuses" (see www.peta25.com).

While it is certainly true that public attitudes on issues of animal welfare have changed markedly in recent years, and that PETA's activities have played a role in these changing attitudes, few Americans are ready to embrace vegetarianism or sign on to the animal rights agenda. Indeed, billions of animals are slaughtered each year in the United States to provide food for a carnivorous culture. On the other hand, were everyday Americans to witness the mass slaughter of cows, pigs, and chickens, the number of vegetarians and animal rights sympathizers would likely increase dramatically.

See also Interest Groups

Bibliography
People for the Ethical Treatment of Animals. "About PETA." www.peta.org/about (accessed 15 March 2006).
———. "Twenty-five Years of Establishing and Protecting the Rights of All Animals." www.peta25.com (accessed 15 March 2006).
Sunstein, Cass R., and Martha Craven Nussbaum, eds. 2004. *Animal Rights: Current Debates and New Directions.* New York: Oxford University Press.

John M. Scheb II and Otis H. Stephens, Jr.

ANTHONY, SUSAN B. (1820–1906)

Susan B. Anthony is both a triumphant and tragic figure in American history. Her indomitable will drove the suffrage movement, culminating triumphantly with the passage of the Nineteenth Amendment, which guaranteed the voting rights of women. Her single-minded pursuit of this goal generated rifts and compromises along the way. She engaged in politics according to her motto:

Failure Is Impossible. Of course, failure is neither one dimensional nor black and white. Anthony was, as one of her biographers characterized her, a "singular feminist."

Susan B. Anthony was born in Adams, Massachusetts, on February 15, 1820, to Daniel and Lucy (Read) Anthony, the second of eight children in a strict Quaker family. Her niece, Lucy E. Anthony, described the social reality into which her aunt was born:

Woman was ruled by a government and a law in which she had no voice.... None of the colleges or universities admitted women students. She was barred from nearly all profitable employments .... If she was married any wages she might earn were not hers, but must be handed by the employer to her husband, who was in every way her master, the law even giving him the power to chastise or punish her.... Man endeavored in every way possible to destroy woman's confidence in her powers, to lessen her self-respect and to make her willing to lead a dependent, subservient life.

Anthony's life experiences, however, instilled a different vision of a woman's position. Initially a school teacher, she later became a world-renowned activist and lecturer. Three main causes engaged her resolute intelligence, energy, and attention: temperance, abolition, and women's suffrage. Of these, women's suffrage took precedence. In 1853, the New York State Legislature rebuffed Anthony and Elizabeth Cady Stanton's petition to limit the sale of liquor because most of the signatures were those of women and children. This response convinced the duo that social reform benefiting women would only happen when women gained political and economic power. Anthony and Stanton became life-long compatriots—usually allies, always friends. They founded a newspaper, the *Revolution*, in 1868, the masthead of which proclaimed: "Men their rights, and nothing more; women, their rights, and nothing less."

Over the next three decades, Anthony and Stanton worked tirelessly to advance the cause of women's rights. They organized the National Woman Suffrage Association (NWSA) in 1869 and argued that the recently ratified Fourteenth Amendment's Privileges or Immunities Clause, which prohibited a state from abridging the privileges and immunities of U.S. citizens, guaranteed suffrage. Their argument was that since women were citizens, they had the right to vote. In order to demonstrate this point, Anthony and 15 associates persuaded the registrar in Rochester, New York, to let them vote. As a result, the election officials and the suffragists were arrested and taken to jail. Anthony wanted to remain in jail for the sake of publicity, but her attorney posted bail on her behalf. In June 1873, her case went to trial, and she was convicted of illegally voting. The judge ordered her to pay a fine of $100 and the costs of prosecution. This fine, however, was not enforced. Two years after her conviction, the U.S. Supreme Court held that the Privileges or Immunities Clause did not confer voting rights in *Minor v. Happersett* (1875). In the face of this judicial defeat, the NWSA reverted to their legislative strategy in an attempt to secure voting rights for women.

The American Woman Suffrage Association, a rival organization founded by Lucy Stone in 1869, also fought for suffrage. For 20 years the struggle for women's rights was frustrated by a schism between these two organizations. In 1890 the two groups merged in the National American Woman Suffrage Association (NAWSA). Anthony became its second president in 1892, succeeding her friend Stanton in that position. The NAWSA mission focused primarily on gaining the vote. Its character and tactics were considerably more conservative than those of the former NWSA. Core elements of NAWSA membership consisted of temperance supporters, club women, and Southerners. A key NAWSA argument in support of woman suffrage was that native-born, white, middle-class mothers had the capacity as voters to purify American politics.

Susan B. Anthony died on March 13, 1906. While she did not live to see ratification of the Nineteenth Amendment on August 18, 1920, she clearly made it possible. In life, her organizational skills, persuasive oratory, and unswerving collaborative work facilitated an effective social movement. In death, she became a rallying symbol. In the end, her advocacy of a national strategy demanding a federal constitutional amendment carried the day.

See also Fourteenth Amendment; Nineteenth Amendment; Privileges or Immunities Clause; Women's Suffrage

Bibliography

Barry, Kathleen. 1988. *Susan B. Anthony: A Biography of a Singular Feminist.* New York: New York University Press.

Flexner, Eleanor. 1974. *Century of Struggle.* New York: Atheneum.

Kraditor, Aileen S. 1981. *The Ideas of the Woman Suffrage Movement, 1890–1920.* New York: W. W. Norton.

James C. Foster

ANTI-CATHOLICISM. *See* Catholicism and Anti-Catholicism

ANTI-DEFAMATION LEAGUE (ADL)

The Anti-Defamation League (ADL) was founded in Chicago in 1913 by 15 members of the Independent Order of B'nai Brith. The group was led by Samuel Livingston, a young lawyer who was disturbed by events surrounding the murder trial of Leo Frank. Frank was an Atlanta Jew who had been convicted, probably wrongfully, of the murder of a young white woman. Frank, who had been a local leader of B'nai Brith, was subsequently lynched by a group that would later become part of the revitalized Ku Klux Klan. The ADL's charter, written in October 1913, reads in part: "The immediate object of the League is to stop, by appeals to reason and conscience and, if necessary, by appeals to law, the defamation of the Jewish people. Its ultimate purpose is to secure justice and fair treatment to all citizens alike and to put an end forever to unjust and unfair discrimination against and ridicule of any sect or body of citizens."

A number of Jewish organizations proliferated in the late nineteenth and early twentieth centuries (Diner 2004, 113–14), each taking a particular approach to the problems of Jews. The ADL's initial efforts were largely devoted to drawing public attention to offensive anti-Semitic images and ideas in the media and to protesting anti-Semitic policies in housing and education. In the first half of the twentieth century, the ADL called for a repudiation of the practice of quotas limiting the number of Jews admitted to educational institutions and used clever ruses to expose discrimination at "exclusive" resorts.

As the century progressed, the group's focus widened. During the thirties and forties, the ADL lobbied Congress for the lifting of immigration restrictions against Jews attempting to flee Europe (Diner 2004, 214). During the sixties, the ADL and other Jewish organizations participated in the Civil Rights Movement (Diner 2004, 268). However, the subsequent controversy surrounding affirmative action saw something of a rift between Jewish organizations like the ADL, which sided with white plaintiffs in education-related affirmative action cases in the 1970s, and other minority groups.

The ADL has attempted to influence public policy in a number of ways. The organization has filed amicus curiae briefs with the U.S. Supreme Court in cases involving race relations, such as *Brown v. Board of Education* (1954), and the separation of church and state, such as *Engel v. Vitale* (1962), which held prayer in public schools to be unconstitutional. Reports published by the ADL are for many in public life a primary source of information about anti-Semitism in America, and the ADL has drafted legislation designed to combat Klan-like activities, which it promotes to local and state governments.

Politically, the ADL is somewhat associated with the left, although it went to some pains to distance itself from Communism during the McCarthy era (Diner 2004, 279). Its current chief political goal is the promotion of the welfare of Israel, and the organization continues its program of combating anti-Semitism. Criticism of the ADL tends toward the suggestion that the group is too hasty to accuse others of anti-Semitism, but the organization is largely considered to be mainstream.

See also Affirmative Action; *Brown v. Board of Education*; Civil Rights Movement; Discrimination; Frank, Leo; Hate Crimes; Housing, Discrimination in; Ku Klux Klan; McCarthy, Joseph R.; Restrictive Covenants

Bibliography

Diner, Hasia R. 2004. *The Jews of the United States: 1654 to 2000.* Berkeley and Los Angeles: University of California Press.

Kara E. Stooksbury

ANTISMOKING LEGISLATION

For decades, states have imposed minimum age requirements for smoking and sponsored programs to reduce smoking by minors. In the 1980s, as the hazards of smoking and the danger of second-hand smoke became widely recognized, states and municipalities across the nation began to require workplaces and places of public accommodation to reserve areas within their facilities for nonsmokers. In the 1990s, increasing social disapproval of smoking and the flurry of lawsuits against the tobacco industry prompted state and local governments to restrict smoking in public buildings and places of public accommodation and transportation. Today most states and many communities have laws restricting smoking in public places; several have laws restricting smoking in private workplaces as well. Some states have even enacted statutes prohibiting smoking altogether in restaurants, workplaces, hospitals, airports, and, in some cases, bars and nightclubs. For example, in 2003 the New York legislature enacted a comprehensive antismoking law prohibiting smoking in places of employment, indoor areas of bars and restaurants, subways, and numerous other enclosed areas. This controversial statute is enforced through administrative fines, not criminal penalties.

Proponents of antismoking laws contend that state and local governments are fully justified in exercising their police powers to combat a serious threat to the public health. But many smokers resent laws that they see as infringements on their freedom and often assert that their decision to smoke is no one else's business. "Smokers' rights" groups have even been formed to fight increasingly restrictive antismoking laws. One such group, Smokers United (on the Web at http://come.to/SmokersInfo), rallies support with the slogan, "If we don't get organized, we can kiss our 'butts' goodbye!"

Sullum argues that antismoking forces have exaggerated the effects of secondhand smoke. Believing that smokers really only pose a danger to themselves, and that adults have the right to make their own choices, Sullum characterizes the recent antismoking laws as "the tyranny of public health" (Sullum 1998).

Because the courts tend to defer to legislative findings regarding the public health, they have generally held antismoking laws to be constitutionally permissible. At present, how far state and local governments choose to go in this area appears to be a political issue, not a constitutional one.

See also Interest Groups; Liberty; Police Power

Bibliography

McLintock, Barbara. 2004. *Smoke-Free: How One City Successfully Banned Smoking in All Indoor Public Places.* Vancouver: Granville Island.

Sullum, Jacob. 1998. *For Your Own Good: The Antismoking Crusade and the Tyranny of Public Health.* New York: Free Press.

John M. Scheb II and Otis H. Stephens, Jr.

APPEAL, RIGHT OF

Broadly speaking, the term "appeal" refers to the opportunities afforded to losing litigants to obtain judicial review of adverse decisions by lower courts or administrative agencies. The purposes of appellate review are to ensure that lower courts and administrative agencies have correctly applied the law, have followed proper procedures in adjudicating a case, and have afforded the party seeking review all rights to which he or she is entitled under applicable constitutional and statutory provisions. Error correction is the core function of appellate courts and is crucial to the preservation of rights and the prevention of arbitrary and capricious decisions by administrators and trial judges.

The principal forms of appellate review are the appeal of right and discretionary review. An appeal of right occurs when a losing litigant exercises a right to demand that a higher judicial authority review an adverse judgment of a lower tribunal. The right to take such an appeal is not conferred by the federal or state constitutions, but rather by statutes enacted by Congress and by state legislatures. In *McKane v. Durston* (1894) the Supreme Court held that the U.S. Constitution provides no right to appeal from a criminal conviction. However, Congress has provided that criminal defendants who plead not guilty and who are convicted at trial have the right to have their convictions and/or sentences reviewed by the U.S. Courts of Appeals. Even defendants who plead guilty in federal court may appeal their sentences when trial judges depart from sentencing guidelines. The prosecution, however, may not appeal from the acquittal of the defendant, but it may appeal from certain pretrial rulings that adversely affect its case as well as from departures from the sentencing guidelines. State legislatures have provided similar rights that allow defendants to appeal in state criminal cases. States that have adopted sentencing guidelines usually provide for appeals on a basis similar to that of federal courts. In civil cases in both federal and state courts, the losing party at trial has the right to one appeal to a higher judicial tribunal.

Discretionary review comes into play once the appeal by right is concluded. Typically, the losing party in the intermediate appellate court files a petition for certiorari in the U.S. Supreme Court or a state court of last resort. Assuming that the issue presented is within the higher court's jurisdiction, the higher court may grant review at its discretion. In the U.S. Supreme Court, decisions to grant certiorari are based on the Rule of Four, which means that at least four of the Court's justices must vote to take the case before the Court will grant certiorari. Each year the Supreme Court receives thousands of "cert" petitions but typically grants review in fewer than 100 cases. State courts of last resort typically have the power of discretionary review as well, although they do not receive nearly as many petitions seeking to invoke that jurisdiction.

In most instances, the party taking the appeal (the appellant) and the party against whom the appeal is being taken (the appellee) have the right to submit briefs to the appellate court. Briefs are documents containing legal arguments and citations of relevant constitutional and statutory provisions and court decisions assembled for the purpose of persuading the appellate court of the merits of one party's position in the case. With the approval of the appellate tribunal, other interested parties sometimes file amicus curiae briefs in support of one side's position in the case. Often the reviewing court will conduct an oral argument, a public hearing in which counsel for both sides appear before the bench to make oral statements and, more importantly, answer questions posed to them by the judges.

Appeals are decided based on the record of the lower court or agency proceeding, which is sent up to the appellate court. Appellate decisions are also based upon review of the briefs and, where applicable, oral arguments presented on behalf of the parties. Appellate courts generally confine their review of lower court decisions and agency rulings to specific assignments of error asserted by the party taking the appeal or seeking discretionary review. Appellate courts do not sit for the purpose of taking new evidence and normally operate with a strong presumption that the lower court or agency made correct factual determinations. To reverse the judgment under review and remand the case to the lower court or administrative agency, the appellate court must determine that a reversible error was committed. Although specific standards vary among jurisdictions, appellate courts follow the principle that reversal is required only when substantial (as opposed to merely technical) errors have been committed by lower courts or agencies.

Unlike most trials, the decisions of appellate courts are rendered by panels of judges who must interact with one another in the process of deciding the case. Typically, appellate court decisions are accompanied by written opinions that explain and justify the court's judgment and give directions to the lower tribunal for further disposition of the case. In some instances judges who participate in but disagree with particular decisions will write dissenting opinions in which they explain the basis for their disagreement. The published opinions of appellate courts constitute what is known as the decisional law, which guides lawyers and judges in formulating arguments and opinions in other cases. In addition to its function of correcting errors committed by trial courts and administrative agencies, the appeals process also serves the important function of shaping legal doctrines in common law, statutory law, and constitutional law. Ultimately, the right of appeal is crucial to the fair and regular administration of justice, the development of the law, and the preservation of individual rights and liberties.

See also Accused, Rights of the; Appeal of Right

John M. Scheb II and Otis H. Stephens, Jr.

APPEAL OF RIGHT

An appeal of right enables a party to challenge a final order or judgment of a lower tribunal without seeking permission of any authority. Appeals of right may be invoked to challenge final judgments and orders of lower tribunals in criminal, civil, and administrative adjudications. A party must take an appeal by filing a notice of appeal within the time and in the manner specified by statute or court rule. The party taking the appeal is called the appellant; the party against whom the appeal is taken is known as the appellee. Appeals of right in federal cases are heard by U.S. Courts of Appeals (circuit courts). In the state courts, intermediate appellate courts typically hear appeals of right. In states lacking an intermediate tier of appellate courts, appeals of right are heard by the state courts of last resort. The procedural aspects of appeals are governed by rules of procedure adopted by federal and state courts.

In criminal cases, defendants who are convicted and sentenced after entering a plea of not guilty are entitled under federal and state law to one appeal to a higher court as a matter of right. In many jurisdictions, a defendant who pleads guilty as part of a plea bargain can preserve the right to appeal a specific point of law, such as a trial court's ruling against the defendant on a motion to suppress evidence arguably obtained in violation of the defendant's constitutional rights. Criminal defendants are generally not allowed to appeal interim orders but are allowed to challenge rulings made during pretrial, trial, and post-trial proceedings when appealing a final judgment.

In *McKane v. Durston* (1894), the U.S. Supreme Court held that the federal Constitution does not afford a criminal defendant the right to appeal a conviction. In light of modern courts' expansive interpretations of the Due Process Clauses of the Fifth and Fourteenth amendments, one could plausibly argue that the right to appeal is implicit in the concept of due process and is therefore an implied constitutional right. The issue is moot, however, because of the federal and state laws allowing criminal defendants to appeal their convictions.

While it may appeal specified adverse pretrial rulings, the prosecution is denied the right to appeal a defendant's acquittal. In *United States v. Sanges* (1892), the Supreme Court held that to allow the government to appeal an acquittal would violate the defendant's rights under the Double Jeopardy Clause of the Fifth Amendment, which prohibits a defendant who has been acquitted from being tried again for the same offense.

In civil cases, a losing party at a hearing or trial has the right to appeal the court's final judgment to a higher court. Although the so-called final judgment rule in federal and state courts usually confines the right to appeal to final orders and judgments, exceptions permit appeals of certain orders. As with all appeals, the appellant must conform to all procedural requirements provided in relevant statutes and court rules. In reviewing the judgment of the trial court, the appellate court will focus on particular assignments of error, that is, claims by the appellant that the trial court erred in its procedures, rulings on motions, or interpretations of the law.

Congress and the state legislatures have also provided for appeals of right from final adjudications by administrative agencies. Before taking an appeal, however, an appellant must first exhaust all avenues of relief available within the administrative agency.

See also Accused, Rights of the; Appeal, Right of; Double Jeopardy, Prohibition of; Due Process Clauses; Fifth Amendment; Fourteenth Amendment; United States Courts of Appeals

John M. Scheb II and Otis H. Stephens, Jr.

AQUINAS, THOMAS. *See* Natural Law and Natural Rights

"AREOPAGITICA" (1644)

"Areopagitica" was an address written in 1644 to be delivered to Parliament by the English poet and essayist John Milton (1608–1674) and is a key document in the development of free expression in the Anglo-American tradition. Its full title was "Areopagitica; a Speech of Mr. John Milton for the Liberty of Unlicensed Printing to the Parliament of England." The title evoked a speech in the spirit of the oration of Isocrates at the Areopagus, a hill where the highest judicial court of Athens met.

On November 24, 1644, Milton published "Areopagitica." Milton, vexed by his marriage to a young woman who humiliated him by returning home to her parents, had written two pamphlets—one unlicensed, one properly entered on the rolls of the Stationers Company—in 1643 and 1644. These pamphlets drew the ire of the Westminster Assembly of the Anglican Church and of Parliament. The Committee on Printing noted Milton's objectionable pamphlets, but no prosecution occurred (Siebert 1953, 195–96).

Knowing full well that prosecuted printers suffered imprisonment and branding, Milton, wishing that his divorce reform arguments could be freely circulated, wrote "Areopagitica," in which he argued against the very process of licensing. "And though all the winds of doctrine," Milton wrote, "were let loose to play upon the earth, so Truth be

in the field, we do her injuriously by licencing and prohibiting to misdoubt her strength. Let her and falsehood grapple, who ever knew her put to the worse, in a free and open encounter."

Milton's free expression theory was posited on the search for truth and argued that to find truth, one must hear opposing arguments. Truth is more likely to emerge from free discussion of ideas than from repression or authoritarian selection. Milton, a seventeenth-century Puritan, often is referred to as the author of the free marketplace of ideas. Perhaps he was, but the actual "marketplace" terminology came from U.S. Supreme Court Justice Oliver Wendell Holmes, Jr., as he dissented in 1919 in *Abrams v. United States*. In *Abrams*, the Court upheld the Espionage Act conviction of a man who was not protesting the World War I effort against Germany but who denounced President Woodrow Wilson and the "plutocratic gang in Washington" for working with other nations to send an expeditionary force into Russia. Abrams called upon munitions workers to strike so the bullets they made could not be used against Russians.

There was no evidence that Abrams's words had any harmful effects, but the Court upheld his 20-year jail sentence. In dissent, Justice Holmes wrote: "But when men have realized that time has upset many fighting faiths, they may come to believe even more than they believe the very foundations of their own beliefs that the ultimate good desired is better reached by free trade in ideas—that the best test of truth is the power of the thought to get itself accepted in the competition of the market." Holmes declared that this is the theory of the United States Constitution.

Miltonian ideas—often called the diversity principle, may be found in a number of the most important Supreme Court decisions interpreting the First Amendment to the Constitution. A 1945 challenge to the application of federal antitrust statutes to the newspaper industry was halted by a majority opinion written by Justice Hugo L. Black in *Associated Press v. United States*. Black declared that the First Amendment "does not sanction repression of that freedom by private interests." Concurring, Justice Felix Frankfurter quoted words written earlier in that case by U.S. District Court Judge Learned Hand. Judge Hand filtered Miltonian ideas through a First Amendment lens: "[T]he First Amendment presupposes that right conclusions are more likely to be gathered out of a multitude of tongues than through any kind of authoritative selection. To many this is, and always will be folly, but upon it we have staked our all."

Miltonian ideas were present in a 1997 U.S. Supreme Court decision that rendered unconstitutional the Communications Decency Act (CDA) portion of the Telecommunications Act of 1996. In *Reno v. American Civil Liberties Union* (1997), the Court contradicted Department of Justice contentions that even if minors were protected by the exclusion of "indecency" from the Internet, more adults would go online. The Court noted the dramatic expansion of "this new marketplace of ideas," concluding: "[W]e assume that governmental regulation of the content of speech is more likely to interfere with the free exchange of ideas than to encourage it."

In *American Civil Liberties Union v. Reno* (1999), U.S. District Court Judge Lowell P. Reed turned to the marketplace of ideas philosophy in restraining enforcement of the Child Online Protection Act (COPA). Judge Reed wrote that free expression theory holds that if speech, "even unconventional speech that some find lacking in substance or offensive, is allowed to compete unrestricted in the marketplace of ideas, truth will be discovered." In the medium of cyberspace, Judge Reed wrote, "anyone can build a soap box out of web pages and speak her mind in the virtual village green to an audience larger and more diverse than any the Framers could have imagined."

The marketplace of ideas argument in American courts goes far beyond Milton's phrase "let the winds of doctrine blow free." Milton argued for allowing ideas to conflict in a search for truth but would not allow the expression of ideas he believed to be false and pernicious. Strongly anti-Catholic,

he denounced "popery" and other ideas he believed impious or evil. Ironically, Milton, whose arguments against censorship are the foundation stone for First Amendment/free expression theory in the United States, was employed as a licenser under Cromwell in 1751 (Siebert 1953, 196). Whatever his limitations in this context, the mighty words of Milton's "Areopagitica" remain a key component of modern free expression theory.

See also Black, Hugo L.; First Amendment; Free Marketplace of Ideas; Holmes, Oliver Wendell, Jr.; Press, Freedom of the; Prior Restraint, Doctrine of; *Reno v. American Civil Liberties Union*

Bibliography

Milton, John. 2003. "Areopagitica." In *Complete Poetry and Selected Prose of John Milton*, 677–724. New York: Random House.

Siebert, Fredrick Seaton. 1953. *Freedom of the Press in England, 1476–1776*. Urbana: University of Illinois Press.

Dwight L. Teeter, Jr.

ARISTOTLE (384–322 B.C.)

Aristotle was a Greek philosopher, student of Plato, and teacher of Alexander the Great. Along with Plato, Aristotle laid the foundation of the Western intellectual tradition in several disciplines. These include politics, in which he is the father of classical republicanism. Whereas Plato was a rationalist and mathematician who used the dialogue as his instructional vehicle, Aristotle was a scientist, historian, and logician who employed the analytical treatise.

In *Politics*, Aristotle described democracy, oligarchy, and monarchy in various forms based on his study of 158 constitutions. His most complete statement on liberty appears in his discussion of democracy in Book VI, Chapter 2, of *Politics*. In contrast to Plato, Aristotle thought democracy was a viable if not ideal constitution. His preference was for what he called polity, a mix of democracy and oligarchy, with a strong middle class to stabilize the perennial conflict between rich and poor. While democracy's conception of justice is equality, Aristotle wrote that its goal is liberty, which he divided into political and civil liberty.

Political liberty consists in ruling and being ruled in turn. It corresponds to what later thinkers have called positive liberty, "freedom to," and consists of both the freedom to have a voice in the laws that will govern one's community, and the character and self-mastery to obey laws enacted by others. Influenced by Aristotle, Rousseau referred to the freedom to live by a rational rule set either by oneself or the community.

Civil liberty is the freedom to live as one likes. It corresponds roughly to the modern notion of negative liberty, "freedom from," or privacy in the broad sense. Aristotle warned that in extreme democracies, in which the will of the people is superior to the rule of law, there is an exaggerated view, "a false conception of liberty…. To live as one likes … is a mean conception of liberty. [By contrast, to] live by the rule of the constitution ought not to be regarded as slavery, but rather as salvation."

The two species of liberty, it bears noting, are logically and chronologically related. In the first instance, a citizen would hope to enjoy civil liberty under rational laws that secure the same protection for his political equals. If that is not the case, however, he would eventually have the chance to exercise political liberty by taking his turn as a legislator and trying to correct those laws he considers oppressive.

Aristotle thus valued liberty, but two points must be underscored. First, for Aristotle, liberty is not universal either in existence or in scope. Who is free, and to what degree, is a matter of status. Given Aristotle's theory of natural slavery, thus, liberty is only for nonslaves. As he wrote, "just as some are by nature free, so others are by nature slaves, and for these latter the condition of slavery is both beneficial and just." Even among nonslaves, moreover, the proportion of those within the polis possessing the fullest measure of liberty depends on whether it is constituted as a democracy or an oligarchy: under a democracy many will enjoy the full scope of liberty, while under an oligarchy, only a few will enjoy that opportunity.

Second, liberty for Aristotle is not the goal of social and political activity. Like education, property, and politics itself, political and civil liberty are means to achieving the ultimate goal of human life. The Greeks called this goal *arete*, which translates roughly as excellence or virtue (both moral and intellectual), the achievement of which Aristotle considered true happiness. While civil liberty is necessary, it is not sufficient for what is most important in life. It is an instrumental, contingent good, which can be misused if not deployed with moderation. As suggested, the failure to distinguish liberty from license undermines a good civic education, which subject is also treated at length in the *Politics*.

While he valued liberty, then, Aristotle would have been critical of the American regime of civil rights and liberties. On one hand, to be sure, he would agree that even where liberty prevails, there must be exceptions in the public interest. In our law, examples would include the exceptions to First Amendment protection for defamation, obscenity, incitement to imminent violence, and national security. Moreover, Aristotle would recognize the presumptive right, consistent with an equal right for one's political equals, against arbitrary harassment by law enforcement. Otherwise, the polis would be an undesirable place to live. At the same time, Aristotle would have seriously questioned the ultimate substance of American civil rights and liberties. As a classical republican and conservative, he would have rejected the key liberal principle of government neutrality in matters of the good life. Like Plato, and unlike Machiavelli and liberalism, Aristotle saw morality as fundamentally linked to law and politics, not separate from them. This is precisely why he and Plato attacked the Sophists— they provided the means to political power without serious inquiry into the ends for which it should be used. Though in the long run Americans have opted for liberal democracy, Aristotle would have identified many of our collective problems as stemming from a misconception of the proper role of liberty in human life.

See also Constitutional Democracy; Equality; First Amendment; Liberty; Machiavelli, Niccolo; Plato; Representative Democracy; Rousseau, Jean-Jacques; Slavery; Socrates

Bibliography

Aristotle. 1958. *Politics*, ed. Ernest Barker. New York: Oxford University Press.

Carcieri, Martin. 2002. *Democracy and Education in Classical Athens and the American Founding.* New York: Peter Lang.

Constant, Benjamin. 1819. "The Liberty of the Ancients Compared with That of the Moderns." In *Political Writings*, ed. and trans. Biancamaria Fontana. New York: Cambridge University Press, 1986.

Martin Carcieri

ARMS, RIGHT TO KEEP AND BEAR

The Second Amendment to the United States Constitution reads: "A well regulated Militia, being necessary to the security of a free State, the right of the people to keep and bear Arms, shall not be infringed." Though its meaning was uncontroversial for the first century of the nation's existence, the nature and extent of Second Amendment protections have been quite controversial in recent decades. That is because efforts at significant gun control only began in the second half of the twentieth century.

The core Second Amendment debate revolves around two questions: (1) Does the Second Amendment protect an individual right, or merely a "collective right" of the states to have militias? and (2) If there is an individual right, does that right apply only against the federal government, or is it incorporated against the states via the Fourteenth Amendment? Scholarly and judicial opinion are mixed.

The Individual Right

Supporters of an individual right to arms make several arguments in support of their position. First, the term "right of the people" is used elsewhere in the Bill of Rights to describe clearly individual rights. Second, before the Bill of Rights was broken out separately, James Madison planned to interlineate the amendments with the text of the original Constitution, and the Second Amendment was placed with other, obviously individual, rights. Third, the Second Amendment grew out of a historical right to arms: Under the English Bill of Rights, free Englishmen had possessed the individual right to arms, and many state constitutions also stood clearly for an individual right.

By 2000, there was broad agreement among scholars that the Second Amendment did protect the right of citizens to own guns, though the precise scope of that protection was subject to dispute. Scholars also agreed that the right to arms was subject to reasonable restrictions intended to keep guns out of the hands of criminals and the insane, as long as the restrictions were not simply camouflaged efforts to ban guns. Adherents to this view included such noted scholars as Laurence Tribe, William Van Alstyne, and Akhil Amar. Whether such a right should apply as against the states via the Fourteenth Amendment's doctrine of incorporation is more contentious.

The Collective Right

On the other hand, an alternative theory holds that the Second Amendment protects merely a right of state governments to maintain state militias without interference by the federal government. Under this theory, the only proper plaintiffs would be state governments, and there would be no individual right that could be asserted. The Second Amendment is merely a guarantee of state independence, somewhat akin to the Tenth Amendment.

The Cases

The lower court cases tend generally to support the collective right theory, though the Fifth Circuit, in the case of *United States v. Emerson* (1999), recently endorsed the individual rights theory. The only U.S. Supreme Court case to specifically address the Second Amendment in the twentieth century was *United States v. Miller* (1939), a case that is claimed in support of both sides of the argument, but that in fact offers only limited guidance on the extent of the Second Amendment's protections.

State Constitutional Rights

A majority of state constitutions contain protections for the right to keep and bear arms. Unlike the Second Amendment, these provisions clearly create individual rights against the state, rather than a state right against the federal government, as state constitutions are powerless to grant rights against the federal government.

The scope of these rights, and of their interpretation by state courts, varies from jurisdiction to jurisdiction, with some states offering considerably stronger protections than others. States generally distinguish between the rights to "keep" and "bear" arms, which relate to ownership and ancillary activities such as practicing shooting and purchasing ammunition, and the "carrying" or "wearing" of firearms, which generally receives considerably less protection.

An International Right to Arms?

Some gun-rights activists have argued that the right to arms should be regarded as an emerging international human right. Prevention of genocide, they argue, is an overwhelming goal of international human rights law, and history demonstrates both that armed populaces are less likely to be slaughtered by governments and that international institutions such as the United Nations (which failed to stop slaughter in Cambodia, Rwanda, and Yugoslavia) are not to be relied upon. Though this view has some academic support, it is not widely held at present.

Gun-Control Efforts

The rise of gun-control advocacy and a narrower view of the right to keep and bear arms correlate historically with the growth of immigration and Prohibition-related organized crime in the early part of the twentieth century. State and federal efforts in the gun-control arena became particularly prominent in the wake of the riots and assassinations of the 1960s, and various restrictions on the

possession and use of firearms were enacted by Congress and the state legislatures. John Hinckley's failed attempt to assassinate President Ronald Reagan in 1981 provided impetus for the Brady Handgun Violence Prevention Act, enacted by Congress in 1994. In the late 1990s after a rash of shootings in schools, advocates of gun control called for even stricter measures. Opponents of gun control, most notably the National Rifle Association, have worked hard to counter these efforts. In recent years, public support for gun control has waned, likely presaging a less sympathetic stance toward gun-control efforts from legislatures and courts.

See also Bill of Rights (English); Bill of Rights, Incorporation of; Fourteenth Amendment; International Law; Madison, James; States' Rights, Doctrine of; Tenth Amendment

Bibliography

Cottrol, Robert. 1994. *Gun Control and the Constitution: Sources and Explorations on the Second Amendment.* New York: Garland.

Henigan, Dennis. 1991. "Arms, Anarchy and the Second Amendment." *Valparaiso Law Review* 26:107–29.

McClurg, Andrew, David Kopel, and Brannon Denning. 2002. *Gun Control and Gun Rights: A Reader and Guide.* New York: New York University Press.

Polsby, Daniel, and Don Kates, Jr. 1997. "Of Holocausts and Gun Control." *Washington University Law Quarterly* 75 (3):1237–75.

Reynolds, Glenn Harlan. 1995. "A Critical Guide to the Second Amendment." *Tennessee Law Review* 62 (3): 461–511.

Van Alstyne, William W. 1994. "The Second Amendment and the Personal Right to Arms." *Duke Law Journal* 43 (6): 1236–5.

Glenn Harlan Reynolds

ARRAIGNMENT

An arraignment is a proceeding in a criminal case in which the accused appears before the trial court and enters a plea to the charges brought by the prosecutor. Normally the arraignment is the defendant's first appearance before the trial court. It is not to be confused with the initial appearance in court, which is often made for the purpose of formally advising the defendant of the charges and to determine whether he or she should be released while the case is in process.

At the arraignment the charges are read to the defendant, whereupon he or she is required to enter a plea. If the accused pleads not guilty at the arraignment, the case is scheduled for trial. However, in most jurisdictions, more than 90 percent of felony suspects arraigned plead guilty or no contest, usually as the result of plea bargaining. If the defendant pleads not guilty or no contest, the judge must determine that the plea has been entered "knowingly and intelligently," in keeping with the Supreme Court's 1969 ruling in *Boykin v. Alabama.* The purpose of this requirement is to ensure that the defendant has not been misled or coerced during the plea bargaining process. If the judge determines that a guilty or no contest plea has been entered knowingly and intelligently, the judge will normally find the defendant guilty and schedule a sentencing hearing.

See also Accused, Rights of the; Critical Pretrial Stages; Initial Appearance in Criminal Cases; Plea Bargaining; Pleas in Criminal Cases; Pretrial Detention; Sentencing Hearing

John M. Scheb II and Otis H. Stephens, Jr.

ARREST, CONSTITUTIONAL LIMITS ON

An arrest is a deprivation of a person's liberty by someone with legal authority. In the contemporary criminal justice system, an arrest usually occurs when police take an individual into custody and charge that person with the commission of a crime. There are two categories of arrest: an arrest based on a warrant and a warrantless arrest. Generally, an arrest is made by a law enforcement officer, although there are some situations in which a private citizen can make an arrest when a felony is committed in the citizen's presence.

Because it is a "seizure" an arrest is subject to the probable cause and warrant requirements of

the Fourth Amendment to the U.S. Constitution, although there are exceptions to the latter. Although not easy to define probable cause, it exists where the facts and circumstances within the officer's knowledge are sufficient to warrant a reasonable person believing that a particular crime had been or was being committed by a particular party (see *Carroll v. United States,* 1925). Police can establish probable cause without personally observing the commission of a crime as long as they have sufficient information to conclude that the suspect probably committed it. Officers often obtain their information from crime victims, eyewitnesses, official reports, and confidential or even anonymous informants. The overwhelming majority of arrests are warrantless arrests made by law enforcement officers. Many of these involve street crimes where arrests are made on the scene.

An officer generally has the discretion to issue a summons or citation to a person who has committed a misdemeanor in the officer's presence. If an accused fails to respond by appearing in court as directed or by paying a prescribed fine by a date certain, the court will issue an arrest warrant, sometimes termed a bench warrant. An arrest warrant is routine in cases where an arrest is to be made based on an indictment by a grand jury. When a grand jury issues an indictment or a prosecutor files an accusatorial document known as information, the court issues a capias, a document directing the arrest of the defendant. In such cases, suspects are often not aware that they are under investigation, and police officers have ample time to obtain an arrest warrant without fear that suspects will flee. Although arrests for white-collar crimes usually follow an indictment or information, the great majority of arrests are not made pursuant to secret investigations but are made by police officers who observe a criminal act, respond to a complaint filed by a crime victim, or have probable cause to arrest after completing an investigation. In such cases it is often unnecessary for police to obtain an arrest warrant, but it is always essential that they have probable cause to make the arrest.

As with warrantless searches and seizures, the Supreme Court has approved warrantless arrests (1) where crimes are committed in plain view of police officers or (2) where officers possess probable cause to make an arrest, but exigent circumstances prohibit them from obtaining a warrant. Absent plain view or compelling exigencies, the need to obtain an arrest warrant is unclear. Although it makes sense for police officers to obtain arrest warrants when possible, it is not always feasible to do so.

In *United States v. Watson* (1976), the Supreme Court upheld the authority of police officers to make warrantless arrests in public, assuming they have probable cause to do so. More problematic are warrantless arrests involving forcible entry of a dwelling. In *Payton v. New York* (1980), the Court invalidated a warrantless, nonconsensual entry into a suspect's home to make a routine felony arrest, ruling that this violates the Fourth Amendment. However, courts are generally inclined to uphold warrantless entries into homes for the purpose of arrest if the following conditions are met:

1. There is probable cause to arrest the suspect.
2. The police have good reason to believe the suspect is on the premises.
3. There is good reason to believe the suspect is armed and dangerous.
4. There is a strong probability that the suspect will escape or evidence will be destroyed if the suspect is not soon apprehended.
5. The entry can be effected peaceably.
6. The offense under investigation is a serious felony.

Although the Supreme Court has recognized the practical necessity of permitting police to make warrantless arrests, it has stressed the need for immediate ex post facto judicial review of detention of a suspect. Writing for the Court in *Gerstein v. Pugh* (1975), Justice Potter Stewart observed that "once the suspect is in custody … the reasons that justify dispensing with the magistrate's neutral judgment evaporate." When a suspect is in custody pursuant to a warrantless arrest, "the detached judgment of a neutral magistrate is essential if the Fourth Amendment is to furnish meaningful protection from unfounded interference with liberty." In *County of Riverside v. McLaughlin* (1991), the Supreme Court ruled that if an arrested person is brought before a magistrate within 48 hours, the requirements of the Fourth Amendment are satisfied.

Because suspects frequently resist attempts to take them into custody, police officers often must use force in making arrests. Sometimes, the use of force by police is challenged in civil suits for damages. Typically, in such cases, the courts have said that in making a lawful arrest, police officers may use such force as is "necessary to effect the arrest and prevent the escape of the suspect. Generally, a police officer has less discretion to use force in apprehending suspected misdemeanants than suspected felons. Most states have statutes providing that police officers have the right to require bystanders to assist them in making arrests. Nearly every state has a law governing the use of force by police attempting to make arrests.

In *Tennessee v. Garner* (1985) the Supreme Court struck down a statute that permitted police to use deadly force against fleeing suspects even when there was no threat to the safety of the officer or the public. This ruling effectively narrowed the discretion of police officers in using force to make arrests and broadened the possibility for civil actions against police for using excessive force.

In most states, a police officer is vested with discretion to make an arrest or issue a citation to a person who commits a minor traffic violation. Generally, police exercise their discretion by giving the motorist a ticket, yet there is little judicial guidance for the proper action to be taken in such situations. In *Atwater v. City of Lago Vista* (2001), in a five-to-four decision, the Supreme Court ruled that as long as there is probable cause, the Fourth Amendment does not forbid a warrantless arrest for a minor offense. In this case the police arrested Ms. Atwater for a seat belt violation that was punishable only by fine. In attempting to establish a bright-line rule to guide the police, the Court allowed custodial arrests for fine-only misdemeanors. But four justices dissented, characterizing Atwater's arrest for not wearing a seat belt as a "pointless indignity."

State courts can interpret their state constitution to provide more protection than the federal Constitution as interpreted in the *Atwater* decision. Perhaps a more feasible solution is for state legislatures to provide that misdemeanor offenses are subject to ticketing under a cite-and-release statute, which creates a presumptive right to be cited and released for the commission of a misdemeanor. Such a standard ordinarily requires an officer to issue a citation for misdemeanor offenses, unless the officer can show a legitimate reason to necessitate a full custodial arrest.

Once an arrest has taken place, police generally search the arrestee for weapons or contraband. Following this, the arrestee is taken to a police station and booked. At this point, police record details of the arrest and usually photograph and fingerprint the arrestee. Regardless of whether the arrest was based on a warrant, the arrestee must be brought promptly before a judge or magistrate for an initial appearance. Although this is not a federal constitutional right in instances where arrests are made pursuant to warrants, all states now have rules that require the police to promptly bring an arrestee before a magistrate.

See also Dogs, Use of by Police; Force, Use of by Law Enforcement; Fourth Amendment; Hot Pursuit, Doctrine of; Initial Appearance in Criminal Cases; Interrogation and Confessions; *Miranda v. Arizona*; Roadblocks and Sobriety Checkpoints; Search Incident to a Lawful Arrest; Stop and Frisk

Bibliography

Clancy, Thomas K. 2003. "What Constitutes an 'Arrest' within the Meaning of the Fourth Amendment?" *Villanova Law Review* 48:129–94.

Katz, Jason M. 2003. "*Atwater v. City of Lago Vista:* Buckle-Up or Get Locked-Up: Warrantless Arrests for Fine-Only Misdemeanors under the Fourth Amendment." *Akron Law Review* 36:491–544.

Scheb, John M., and John M. Scheb II. 2005. *Criminal Law and Procedure.* 5th ed. Belmont, CA: Thomson/Wadsworth.

Hon. John M. Scheb and John M. Scheb II

ARREST WARRANT. *See* Arrest, Constitutional Limits on

ARTICLES OF CONFEDERATION

The Articles of Confederation is the name of the constitution that the American colonists first adopted after declaring their independence from Britain. It was composed by members of the Second Continental Congress, who assembled in Philadelphia in May 1775 to deal with the continuing crisis. Formulating this government initially took a backseat to declaring independence and seeking foreign allies to prosecute the war. The Articles were largely drafted by Pennsylvania's John Dickinson in June 1776, debated and modified in Congress the next year, and proposed to the states in November 1777. The plan did not officially go into effect until ratified by the last state (Maryland, which was waiting until other states gave up western land claims) in March 1781, and it largely remained in effect, albeit not always particularly effectively, until the implementation of the current Constitution in 1789.

The Articles of Confederation created a confederal government, dividing power between a national congress and the states, which wielded primary power. In some ways the government under the Articles was more akin to a treaty than to a modern federal government, like that of the United States today, where the national government exercises a long list of enumerated powers and implied powers that flow from them. Indeed, although calling itself "The "United States of America" (Article I), the government under the Articles also referred to itself as "a firm league of friendship" (Article III). The most significant provision in the Articles of Confederation was Article II, added largely at the insistence of North Carolina's Thomas Burke, which stated that "[e]ach state retains its sovereignty, freedom, and independence, and over Power, Jurisdiction and right, which is not by this confederation expressly delegated to the United States, in Congress assembled." Article III indicated that the states were uniting in part to provide for "the security of their Liberties," but the

Articles largely secured states' rights, leaving them to protect individual liberties. Article IV did anticipate the idea of enhanced national citizenship by providing that "free inhabitants" (an indication that the government did nothing to ameliorate slavery) would be "entitled to all privileges and immunities of free citizens in the several states" including rights of travel and commerce.

The primary governmental structure under the Articles was a unicameral Congress in which states were represented equally by two to seven delegates, who were chosen by state legislatures and restrained from serving more than three out of any six years. Members were granted "freedom of speech and debate" within Congress (Article V). On most key matters involving finances and foreign affairs, 9 of the 13 states had to agree. Congressional committees provided what executive authority existed, and there was no independent system of courts. Congressional powers were fairly restricted. As a confederal system, the national government requisitioned states for tax revenues and for troops. States often proved unable and/or unwilling to respond as generously as Congress thought they should. Article XIII provided that amendments would have to be proposed by Congress and unanimously approved by the state legislatures.

The government under the Articles of Confederation succeeded in winning the war against Britain, but it often responded slowly to requests from the troops. Revenue was inadequate, states coined their own money, and, with Congress lacking control of interstate commerce, states began levying duties on goods from other states, destroying the potential benefits of a single nationwide market. On more than one occasion, amendments granting increased powers to Congress failed as a result of the opposition of a single state.

Delegations from five states met at the Annapolis Convention in September of 1786 to deal with problems of commerce under the Articles. This Convention in turn issued a call for the Constitutional Convention that met in Philadelphia in the summer of 1787 and drew up a new plan of govern-

ment. The inability of the Articles to deal promptly with a Massachusetts taxpayer disturbance known as Shays' Rebellion in the winter of 1786–1787 had helped convince some previously reluctant states to send delegates. During the Convention, members of the Confederation Congress successfully adopted the Northwest Ordinance of 1787, providing for government in the former Northwest Territories and prohibiting slavery there—albeit, some scholars believe, in exchange for permitting it elsewhere.

Most delegates to the Convention were convinced that the national government under the Articles of Confederation was inadequate. Some delegates were especially concerned about abuses of property rights that they observed in the states that printed deflated currency and required that it be accepted in payment of debts. James Madison argued in Federalist No. 10, that a central government, embracing a large land area, would encompass a wider variety of factions, thus making it unlikely that any one would be able to dominate and deny rights to others. Madison, and other proponents of the Virginia Plan, also thought that equal representation within Congress was unfair to the more populous states, but they ultimately secured proportional representation in only one of the two houses of Congress they created. In proposing a stronger government, the delegates thought it desirable both to add an executive and judicial branch to balance the powers of the new Congress. In addition to retaining some of the restrictions within the Articles on individual states, the new constitution specifically forbade them from impairing the obligation of contracts.

The delegates to the Constitutional Convention ultimately decided to bypass the amending provisions of the Articles of Confederation by providing that the new government would go into effect when ratified by special conventions in nine or more of the states. The Congress under the Articles of Confederation passed this resolution along to the states without comment, therefore effectively participating in its own demise. A Bill of Rights (the first 10 amendments) specifically limiting the powers of the national government emerged from debates over ratification of the new document. Generally regarded today more for its failures than for its accomplishments, the Articles of Confederation proved to be an important laboratory that pointed to the need for a stronger government.

See also Bill of Rights (American); Madison, James; Speech, Freedom of; States' Rights, Doctrine of; United States Constitution

Bibliography

Dougherty, Keith L. 2001. *Collective Action under the Articles of Confederation*. Cambridge: Cambridge University Press.

Jensen, Merrill. 1966. *The Articles of Confederation*. Madison: University of Wisconsin Press.

Rakove, Jack N. 1979. *The Beginnings of National Politics: An Interpretative History of the Continental Congress*. New York: Alfred A. Knopf.

Solberg, Winton, ed. 1958. *The Federal Convention and the Formation of the Union of the American States*. Indianapolis, IN: Bobbs-Merrill.

Vile, John R. 2005. *The Constitutional Convention of 1787: An Encyclopedia of America's Founding*. 2 vols. Santa Barbara, CA: ABC-CLIO.

John R. Vile

ASHCROFT, JOHN D. (1942–)

John David Ashcroft was born on May 9, 1942, in Chicago, Illinois. During John's childhood, the family moved to Springfield, Missouri, to be near the headquarters of the Assembly of God Church, in which his father was a pastor. Ashcroft graduated from Yale University in 1964 and then earned a law degree from the University of Chicago in 1967. He practiced law for several years and taught business law at Southwest Missouri State University before entering public service. In 1972 Ashcroft ran for a seat in the U.S. House of Representatives but was defeated. A year later he held his first public office as Missouri Auditor and later was elected to two terms as the attorney general of Missouri, serving from 1976 to 1985. Ashcroft was governor of Missouri from 1985 to 1993. In 1994, he was elected to the U.S. Senate as part of the Republican sweep

of the midterm elections that year. Ashcroft's bid for reelection failed despite his opponent's death in an airplane crash just prior to the election; he lost by a margin of 51 percent to 49 percent. He was nominated by President George W. Bush to be the U.S. Attorney General on December 22, 2000. He held that post until February 3, 2005, when Alberto Gonzales was sworn in as his successor.

Throughout his career in public service, Ashcroft has been involved in issues pertaining to civil liberties and civil rights. As Missouri's Attorney General, Ashcroft was charged with enforcing a state law that imposed limitations on abortion rights. Ashcroft argued the state's position in upholding the law before the U.S. Supreme Court in Planned Parenthood of Central Missouri v. Ashcroft (1983). The Court's ruling upheld a parental consent provision for minors but struck down a provision requiring hospitalization for second-trimester abortions. Abortion was also an issue with which Ashcroft dealt as governor. He pressed for stricter limitations on abortions, which were upheld by the Supreme Court in Webster v. Reproductive Services (1989). As a senator, Ashcroft was a consistent foe of legalized abortion and opposed President Clinton's nominee, Dr. David Satcher, for Surgeon General due to his support for abortion rights; Satcher, however, was confirmed by a large majority. Ashcroft also proposed constitutional amendments to prohibit abortion, even in cases of rape or incest. His voting record on other issues was also conservative. He supported capital punishment and the right to keep and bear arms and was opposed to affirmative action, gay rights, workplace discrimination laws, and hate crimes legislation. Ashcroft received a great deal of criticism for blocking the nomination of an African American judge, Ronnie White, for a federal judgeship.

Ashcroft's staunchly conservative record led to a particularly contentious Senate confirmation debate when he was nominated as Attorney General in 2000; he was ultimately confirmed by a vote of 58 to 42. As Attorney General, Ashcroft limited federal prosecutors' ability to plea bargain and was insistent that federal prosecutors should seek the death penalty whenever possible. He also issued the so-called Ashcroft Directive, which claimed that physician-assisted suicide, as allowed by Oregon's Death with Dignity Act, served no legitimate medical purpose, and that physicians who prescribed lethal amounts of medication to their terminally ill patients were in violation of the Controlled Substances Act of 1970 and should be punished. Two federal courts ruled against Ashcroft, who in turn appealed to the U.S. Supreme Court, which was expected to make a ruling during the 2005–2006 term.

The issue that defined Ashcroft's tenure as Attorney General was the government's response to the September 11, 2001, terrorist attacks on the United States. Ashcroft was a zealous proponent of the controversial USA PATRIOT Act, which expanded the power of law enforcement and, according to its many critics, seriously threatened civil liberties. After he left office, Ashcroft stated that he would have "liked to do a better job of explaining the Patriot Act so that it would not have been the subject of so much misinformation and mistake and controversy" (Blum 2005).

Ashcroft's religious convictions were central to the positions he held during his career in public service. Indeed, he believed that "God is the author of liberty, and that's why I really believe that freedom sourced in the eternal creator is not something that can be the subject of arbitrary regulation by the government" (Blum 2005). In 2005, Ashcroft accepted a teaching position at Regent University, a university founded by evangelist Pat Robertson.

See also Affirmative Action; Abortion, Right to; Arms, Right to Keep and Bear; Conservatism; Death Penalty and the Supreme Court; Doctor-Assisted Suicide; Employment Discrimination; Gay Rights Movement; Hate Crimes; Liberty; Religious Right; Terrorism, War on; USA PATRIOT Act

Bibliography

"Attorney General of the United States." www.white-house.gov/government/ashcroft-bio.html (accessed 29 October 2005).

Blum, Vanessa. 2005. "John Ashcroft's Closing Number." Lexis-Nexis Academic Database (accessed 27 October 2005).

"John Ashcroft: Newsmaker Profile." Facts On File World News Digest @FACTS.com Database (accessed 27 October 2005).

Kara E. Stooksbury

ASSEMBLY, FREEDOM OF

The First Amendment to the United States Constitution bars Congress from "abridging … the right of the people peaceably to assemble." Although this provision has been less extensively litigated than other clauses of the First Amendment, the Supreme Court has recognized that the right of peaceable assembly is "cognate to those of free speech and free press and is equally fundamental … [I]t is one that cannot be denied without violating those fundamental principles of liberty and justice which lie at the base of all civil and political institutions" (*DeJonge v. Oregon*, 1937). In short, the right of assembly protects the rights of individuals to join with one another in either private or public spaces for lawful purposes.

The right to assemble peaceably is linked with another First Amendment freedom, that of the right to "petition the Government for a redress of grievances." The framers' intent behind the granting of rights of assembly and petition was to protect the liberty of *individuals* in joining together with one another to curtail majoritarian excess and to allow them to petition the government for alteration of policy. At a very minimum, this clause forbids the government from prohibiting or interfering with peaceable assemblies of individuals and allows individuals to make their claims heard by any and all departments and branches of government.

The scope of the right of assembly was first tested in *United States v. Cruikshank* (1876). At issue was the application of the Civil Rights Act of 1870, which made it a felony "if two or more persons shall band or conspire together, or go in disguise upon the public highway, or upon the premises of another, with intent to injure, oppress, threaten, or intimidate any citizen, with intent to prevent or hinder his free exercise and enjoyment of any right or privilege granted or secured to him by the constitution or laws of the United States." Though the Court did not find the Enforcement Act violated in *Cruikshank*, the Court explained that the right of assembly and petition of grievances is a fundamental aspect of national citizenship and that the very notion of a republican government "implies a right on the part of its citizens to meet peaceably for consultation in respect to public affairs and to petition for a redress of grievances." The Court, however, refrained from extending freedom of assembly to the states through the Fourteenth Amendment.

The freedom of assembly was formally made applicable to the states through the Due Process Clause of the Fourteenth Amendment in *DeJonge v. Oregon* (1937). Dirk DeJonge was arrested under Oregon's Criminal Syndicalism law for speaking at a meeting in Multnomah County called under the auspices of the Communist Party and advocating support of local Party activities. On appeal to the U.S. Supreme Court, DeJonge successfully argued that the meetings he attended were public and were for lawful purposes. The Supreme Court overturned DeJonge's conviction and, in so doing, declared the freedom of assembly as a right "that cannot be denied without violating those fundamental principles of liberty and justice which lie at the base of all civil and political institutions—principles that the Fourteenth Amendment embodies in the general terms of its due process clause."

Though incorporated in 1937, the scope of the freedom of assembly was briefly debated two years later. In *Hague v. CIO* (1939), the Supreme Court struck down a Jersey City ordinance that gave public officials unfettered authority to either allow or reject a request to have a public assembly on public property. Three justices found protection against state infringement of the freedom of assembly in the Privileges or Immunities Clause of the Fourteenth Amendment, while two justices were content in maintaining protection of assembly and petition rights through the due process clause, which would

cover both citizens and aliens. The privileges or immunities approach to the freedom of assembly never received majority support from the Court.

Though freedom of assembly protects peaceful protests, the Court has extended protection to assemblies where violence was a strong possibility. For example, in *National Socialist Party v. Village of Skokie* (1977), the Supreme Court upheld the right of the National Socialist Party, with swastikas and all, to march in a town heavily populated by Holocaust survivors. The Court has repeatedly recognized that governments may not discriminate against particular viewpoints when issuing permits to assemble.

Courts are in agreement that the right to assemble is a fundamental freedom. Therefore, litigation in freedom of assembly cases centers not on whether any level of government in the United States can take away the freedom of assembly but rather on the degree to which the government can put time, place, and manner restrictions on various assemblies. Governments are allowed to impose permit fees as long as the fees are not discriminatory toward a particular viewpoint. Governmental interests in public safety and the prevention of riots are sufficient grounds for imposing restrictions on the time, place, and manner of organizational activities. Even as courts debate the merit and scope of various time, place, and manner regulations, the central thrust of the freedom of assembly is clear—governments may never breach the right of groups to assemble merely because of the content of their speech.

See also Bill of Rights (American); Bill of Rights, Incorporation of; Civil Rights Act of 1870; Criminal Syndicalism; Due Process Clauses; First Amendment; Fourteenth Amendment; Petition, Right of; Privileges or Immunities Clause; Public Forum; Speech, Freedom of; Time, Place, and Manner Restrictions

Bibliography

Rohde, Stephen F. 2005. *Freedom of Assembly*. New York: Facts on File.

Kyle Kreider

ASSET FORFEITURE

Federal law provides for the forfeiture of real estate and personal property employed in drug trafficking and other criminal activities, including counterfeiting, mail and wire fraud, forgery, money laundering, and carjacking. Although states have their own forfeiture laws, most forfeitures are effected under federal law. In 1984, federal law enforcement agencies began a program known as Equitable Sharing, under which local or state police who seize property under federal law share in the proceeds when the forfeited assets are sold at auction.

Although asset forfeiture is associated primarily with the "war on drugs," is has ancient legal roots and was well established under the English common law. Throughout its history, the United States government has had the power of forfeiture. Early laws allowed for the forfeiture of property used in piracy and customs offenses as well as forfeitures of vessels and Confederate property during the Civil War.

Forfeiture can be either criminal or civil. In a criminal forfeiture, an individual convicted of a crime is made to forfeit assets as part of the sentence. In a civil forfeiture the defendant is the property itself (an in rem action), as opposed to an individual (an in personam action). An example of such an action is *United States v. Ten Thousand Seven Hundred Dollars and No Cents ($10,700) in United States Currency (2001)*. In *United States v. Ursery* (1996), the Court ruled that "*in rem* civil forfeitures are neither 'punishment' nor criminal for purposes of the Double Jeopardy Clause." However, in rem forfeitures are subject to abuse and have been extremely controversial, leading the courts to impose safeguards to protect property rights.

In *United States v. A Parcel of Land* (1993), the Supreme Court held that a person's lack of knowledge that a real estate purchase was made with the proceeds from drug trafficking constitutes a defense to forfeiture under federal law. In *Austin v. United States* (1993) the Court held that in rem forfeitures are subject to the Excessive Fines Clause of the Eighth Amendment. Subsequently, in *United States v. Baj* (1998), the Court stated that "the question of whether a fine is constitutionally excessive calls for the application of a constitutional standard to the facts of a particular case, and in this context de novo review of that question is appropriate."

Another type of civil forfeiture involves the use of state tax laws, such as Texas's tax on controlled substances. According to the statue, "A tax is imposed on the possession, purchase, acquisition, importation, manufacture, or production by a dealer of a taxable substance on which a tax has not previously been paid under this chapter." Under the Texas statue, a dealer, who is defined as "a person who in violation of the law of this state imports into this state or manufactures, produces, acquires, or possesses in this state," is required to immediately pay the taxes due on the controlled substance. To promote compliance the law stipulates that information provided by the "Dealer" paying the tax is confidential and prohibits the use of the information provided from being used in prosecution, unless the information regarding possession of the controlled substance was obtained independently. The purpose of such statutes is simple: by requiring a tax on the controlled substance, the law subjects persons possessing a substance on which the tax has not been paid to civil prosecution for delinquent taxes. Under most state statutes, collection of these delinquent taxes allows for forfeiture of property required for satisfying the tax bill.

While forfeiture is effective against individual drug traffickers, it appears to have had little effect on the overall demand for drugs in the United States. This demand continues to fuel a multibillion-dollar-a-year business, which views forfeiture as part of the cost of doing business.

See also Common-Law Background of American Civil Rights and Liberties; Double Jeopardy, Prohibition of; Drugs, War on; Due Process, Procedural; Eighth Amendment; Excessive Fines, Prohibition of; Property Rights

Bibliography

Franze, Anthony J. 1994. "Casualties of War? Drugs, Civil Forfeiture, and the Plight of the 'Innocent Owner.'" *Notre Dame Law Review* 70: 369.

Leach, Arthur W., and John G. Malcolm. 1994. "Criminal Forfeiture: An Appropriate Solution to the Civil Forfeiture Debate." *Georgia State University Law Review* 10: 241.

Fermin De La Torre

ASSIZE OF CLARENDON (1166)

The Assize of Clarendon was a set of ordinances promulgated by King Henry II of England in 1164 to reform the existing system of criminal justice. The principal reforms instituted by the assize were the establishment of the grand jury system and the elimination of trial by compurgation. The grand jury, not to be confused with the petit (trial) jury, is assembled to determine whether there is an evidentiary basis for a criminal charge. By establishing the grand jury system, the Assize of Clarendon sought to check the power of local magnates, who often controlled the courts.

In a trial by compurgation, a defendant who had denied guilt under oath attempted to recruit a body of men to attest to his or her honor. The Assize of Clarendon abolished compurgation in cases brought by the grand jury. However, once indicted by the grand jury, the defendant remained subject to trial by ordeal, in which the defendant was tortured by fire or water. In the medieval mind, if the defendant survived the ordeal, God had intervened to prove the defendant's innocence before the law. Trial by jury would not come into being until after Magna Carta (1215). Still, the Assize of Clarendon marked a major milestone in the development of the Anglo-American system of justice.

See also Accused, Rights of the; Common-Law Background of American Civil Rights and Liberties; Grand Jury; Jury, Trial by; Magna Carta

John M. Scheb II

ASSOCIATION, FREEDOM OF

Freedom of association is the right to associate with other persons for lawful purposes without undue governmental interference. This right has long been regarded as an essential characteristic of a free society. Freedom of association has both instrumental and inherent value. On one hand, "organized association is increasingly essential for the effective use of free speech in the United States" (Guttman 1998, 3). Unless one is rich, enjoys some celebrity status, or has exceptional access to the mass media, it is very difficult to express one's views publicly without joining an organization of like-minded people. On the other hand, the freedom to associate with others "is also valuable for the many qualities of human life that the diverse activities of association routinely entail" (Guttman 1998, 3).

Although the United States Constitution makes no explicit reference to freedom of association, the Supreme Court has long recognized freedom of association as an implicit constitutional right. At the outset it must be recognized that freedom of association is a multifaceted concept, inasmuch as one can associate with others in a variety of ways and for a variety of purposes. The Supreme Court has identified various constitutional provisions as sources of protection for different forms of association, and some associational freedoms are given more protections than others. Certainly the right to associate for religious purposes is implied by the Free Exercise of Religion Clause of the First Amendment and, accordingly, is highly protected.

Intimate associations, such as those between husband and wife or parent and child, fall within the scope of the constitutional right of privacy articulated in *Griswold v. Connecticut* (1965) and its progeny. Because the right to privacy has been recognized as a "fundamental right" by the courts, any governmental interference with such associations is subject to strict judicial scrutiny. On the other hand, economic associations, like property rights in general, are typically afforded less constitutional protection under modern doctrine.

Freedom of Association and the First Amendment

While all the aforementioned forms of association are constitutionally significant, the term "freedom of association" has been developed by courts primarily in the context of political association.

The term was first coined by the Supreme Court in *National Association for the Advancement of Colored People v. Alabama* (1958), in which the Court struck down the state's effort to force the NAACP to reveal its membership. Writing for the Court, Justice John M. Harlan (the younger) opined:

Effective advocacy of both public and private points of view, particularly controversial ones, is undeniably enhanced by group association, as this Court has more than once recognized by remarking upon the close nexus between the freedoms of speech and assembly…. It is beyond debate that freedom to engage in association for the advancement of beliefs and ideas is an inseparable aspect of the "liberty" assured by the Due Process Clause of the Fourteenth Amendment, which embraces freedom of speech…. Of course, it is immaterial whether the beliefs sought to be advanced by association pertain to political, economic, religious or cultural matters, and state action which may have the effect of curtailing the freedom to associate is subject to the closest scrutiny.

Given the context from which the case arose—the epic civil rights struggle that began in the 1950s—it is not difficult to perceive why the Supreme Court viewed Alabama's effort to obtain the NAACP's membership list as an attempt to deter citizens from exercising their implicit constitutional right to participate in that organization. In ruling for the NAACP, however, the Court had to distinguish its 1928 decision in *Bryant v. Zimmerman*, where the Court upheld a New York law under which the Ku Klux Klan was forced to disclose its membership list. In *Bryant*, the Court justified the state's action by stressing the violent and unlawful tactics of the Klan. In *NAACP v. Alabama*, the Court stressed the fact that the NAACP used lawful means in seeking its political objectives.

Since 1958, *NAACP v. Alabama* has been cited in more than 150 Supreme Court decisions and the notion of an implicit freedom of association has come to be firmly established in the Court's First Amendment jurisprudence. Writing for the Supreme Court in *Roberts v. United States Jaycees* (1984), Justice William Brennan observed that "implicit in the right to engage in activities protected by the First Amendment" is "a corresponding right to associate with others in pursuit of a wide variety of political, social, economic, educational, religious, and cultural ends." Given its close connection to the rights enumerated in the First Amendment, freedom of association is a fundamental right, which means that it cannot be infringed upon except where necessary to achieve a compelling governmental interest. Moreover, any governmental interference with this right is subject to strict scrutiny by the courts, which means that the government bears a heavy burden of persuasion in seeking to justify its action.

Freedom of Association versus National Security Concerns

Despite its fundamental character, freedom of association is not absolute. Thus, in *Scales v. United States* (1961), the Supreme Court upheld Section 2 of the Smith Act, which impinged on freedom of association by making it a crime merely to belong to the Communist Party or any organization committed to the violent overthrow of the United States government. The Court rescued the constitutionality of this controversial statutory provision by interpreting it narrowly so as to apply only to "active" members of the Party who harbored the specific intent to overthrow the government. Four members of the Court (Chief Justice Earl Warren and Justices William O. Douglas, Hugo Black, and William Brennan) dissented, claiming that the majority had effectively legalized guilt by association.

Five years after the *Scales* decision, the Court in *Elfbrandt v. Russell* (1966) struck down an Arizona law under which state employees could be discharged merely on the basis of membership in the Communist Party or other organizations committed to the violent overthrow of the government. In his opinion for the Court, Justice William O. Douglas noted that the law "threatens the cherished freedom of association protected by the First Amendment" and "rests on the doctrine of 'guilt by association' which has no place here." Invoking the doctrine of overbreadth, the Court invalidated the statute on its face. Similarly, in *Keyishian v. Board of Regents* (1967), the Court struck down a New York law and associated regulations that required professors in state colleges and universities to certify that they were not members of the Communist Party. Likewise, in *United States v. Robel* (1967), the Court invalidated a provision of the Subversive Activities Control Act of 1950, a federal law prohibiting members of "Communist-action organizations" to work in defense facilities. Chief Justice Warren spoke for the Court in *Robel*, saying, "It is precisely because that statute sweeps indiscriminately across all types of association with Communist-action groups, without regard to the quality and degree of membership, that it runs afoul of the First Amendment."

With the decline of the "Communist menace," litigation pitting freedom of association against national security concerns also subsided. However, given the nation's current "war on terrorism," it is not difficult to imagine such controversies again confronting the courts. Under Section 411 of the USA PATRIOT Act of 2001, noncitizens who pay membership dues or provide material support to groups classified by the Secretary of State as terrorist organizations are subject to deportation. Critics of this measure argue that it violates freedom of association to the extent that persons who are unaware of or unsympathetic to a group's terrorist proclivities are deemed guilty merely by the fact of their association.

Freedom of Association and Discrimination by Nongovernmental Organizations

In recent years, a number of state and local governments have used their legislative powers to promote greater integration of women and minorities into the economic and cultural mainstream. Laws prohibiting discrimination by places of public accommodation have been used to force civic groups and social clubs to extend membership to women and minorities. Such efforts are often challenged on First Amendment grounds, with opponents arguing that freedom of association necessarily entails the right to exclude others.

In *Roberts v. United States Jaycees* (1984), the Supreme Court found that the societal interest in eradicating sex discrimination was sufficiently compelling to allow a state to require local chapters of the Jaycees to admit women. Acting on the basis of a state statute prohibiting sex discrimination by places of public accommodation, the Minnesota Human Rights Commission determined that chapters of the Jaycees were public accommodations and therefore could not deny membership to women. The Jaycees challenged the order as an infringement of their First Amendment freedoms of speech and association. Although the Jaycees were unsuccessful in the federal district court, the Eighth Circuit Court of Appeals held that Minnesota's action constituted a "direct and substantial" interference with the Jaycees' First Amendment rights and that the state's interest in eradicating sex discrimination was not sufficiently compelling in this context to justify that interference. In a unanimous decision, the Supreme Court reversed. Justice Brennan's opinion for the Court acknowledged a political dimension to the Jaycees' activities but nevertheless held that the organization's freedom of association must give way to the superior state interest in abolishing sex discrimination.

In *Board of Directors of Rotary International v. Rotary Club of Duarte* (1987), the Court extended its decision in the *Jaycees* case to encompass the Rotary Club as well. Justice Lewis Powell's opinion for the unanimous Court acknowledged the validity of Rotary International's constitutional claims but concluded that state infringement of Rotary members' right of expressive association was justified by "the State's compelling interest in eliminating discrimination against women."

The year after the Rotary club decision, the Supreme Court upheld a New York City ordinance requiring large all-male social clubs to admit women. Like the *Rotary* and *Jaycees* decisions, the Court's decision in *New York State Club Association v. New York City* (1988) was unanimous. Justice Byron White, writing for the Court, concluded that the challenged ordinance

does not affect "in any significant way" the ability of individuals to form associations that will advocate public or private viewpoints.... It does not require the clubs "to abandon or alter" any activities that are protected by the First Amendment.... Instead, the Law merely prevents an association from using race, sex, and the other specified characteristics as shorthand measures in place of what the city considers to be more legitimate criteria for determining membership.

The Court's decisions dealing with civic and social clubs suggest that freedom of association in that context must give way to society's compelling interest in eradicating discrimination. While civil rights activists and liberal commentators praised such decisions as progressive, libertarians and conservatives condemned what they perceived as the victory of "social engineering" over freedom.

Freedom of Association versus Gay Rights

In the 1990s the context of the debate over freedom of association versus governmental efforts to combat discrimination shifted from gender equality to gay rights. In this context, the Supreme Court's perspective was markedly different, at least in two important cases decided in the 1995–2000 period. In *Hurley v. Irish-American Gay, Lesbian and Bisexual Group of Boston* (1995), the Court held that the state of Massachusetts could not force a private organization to include a gay-rights group in its annual St. Patrick's Day parade. The Massachusetts Supreme Court had ruled against the South Boston Allied War Veterans Council, which organized the parade and refused to permit gay-rights groups to participate. The state supreme court held that gay-rights groups could not be excluded under Massachusetts' long-standing and broadly construed public accommodations statute. The Supreme Court reversed the ruling, holding that the state could not compel the parade's organizers to promote a message of which they disapproved. Writing for a unanimous Court, Justice David Souter insisted that the decision "rests not on any particular view about the Council's message but on the Nation's commitment to protect freedom of speech." The decision stressed the expressive aspect of freedom of association—the right of like-minded people to associate for the purpose of propagating shared values and beliefs.

In *Boy Scouts of America v. Dale* (2000), the Court addressed a much more controversial question involving freedom of association and gay rights.

James Dale was dismissed from his position as assistant scoutmaster when Scout leaders learned that he was homosexual. Dale successfully sued the Boy Scouts in the New Jersey courts, which ultimately ruled that the Scouts were in violation of a state statute prohibiting places of public accommodation from discriminating on the basis of sexual orientation. A sharply divided Supreme Court reversed, holding that the Boy Scouts' freedom of association trumped the state's interest in advancing the cause of gay rights. In his majority opinion, Chief Justice William Rehnquist asserted that "public or judicial disapproval of a tenet of an organization's expression does not justify the State's effort to compel the organization to accept members where such acceptance would derogate from the organization's expressive message." Writing for the four dissenters, Justice John Paul Stevens retorted that it was "farfetched to assert that Dale's open declaration of his homosexuality, reported in a local newspaper, will effectively force BSA to send a message to anyone simply because it allows Dale to be an Assistant Scoutmaster." Critics of the Dale decision argued that the Court was placing its imprimatur on bigotry. But many in the private not-for-profit sector applauded the Court for protecting a private organization from government control.

Freedom of Association and Political Parties

In *Kusper v. Pontikes* (1973), the Supreme Court recognized that the "right to associate with the political party of one's choice is an integral part of … constitutional freedom." Yet political parties present unique problems with respect to rights of association. Historically, parties were regarded as private organizations that were free to exclude anyone for any reason. That changed when the Supreme Court decided *Smith v. Allwright* in 1944. In that landmark case, the Court invalidated the so-called white primary, an arrangement under which the Democratic Party in Southern states prohibited African Americans from affiliating with the Party or running for office as Democrats. In the heavily Democratic South of the 1940s, this restriction had the effect of denying African Americans meaningful opportunities to participate in the political system. The Supreme Court found that the party machinery was so intertwined with state and local government that the Party's restrictions against African Americans amounted to state action in violation of the Fifteenth Amendment. Writing for the Court, Justice Stanley Reed declared that

The privilege of membership in a party may be … no concern of a state. But when, as here, that privilege is also the essential qualification for voting in a primary to select nominees for a general election, the state makes the action of the party the action of the state.

To what extent did *Smith v. Allwright* convert political parties into quasi-governmental entities devoid of power to control their membership? Political parties in the United States are loose-knit collections of like-minded voters; Democrats and Republicans do not carry membership cards. But a number of states have electoral systems in which voting in each party's primary elections is limited to citizens who have declared their affiliation with that party when registering to vote. Such closed primaries have fallen out of favor in recent years, and most state parties have changed their rules to create open primaries. But can such a change be accomplished by the state legislature against the wishes of the party faithful?

In 1996, California voters approved Proposition 198, which converted California's closed primary elections into open primaries. In *California Democratic Party v. Jones* (2000) the Supreme Court invalidated the new law. Writing for a majority of seven, Justice Antonin Scalia opined that

Proposition 198 forces [parties] to adulterate their candidate-selection process—the "basic function of a political party" … by opening it up to persons wholly unaffiliated with the party. Such forced association has the likely outcome—indeed, in this case the intended outcome—of changing the parties' message. We can think of no heavier burden on a political party's associational freedom.

Justice John P. Stevens dissented, arguing that "the First Amendment does not mandate that a putatively private association be granted the power to dictate the organizational structure of state-run, state-financed primary elections."

In the four decades since the courts first recognized it as an implicit constitutional right, freedom of association has become well established in constitutional law. But like other constitutional rights that have been declared to be "fundamental," freedom of association can be limited when necessary to achieve compelling governmental interests. Of course, what constitutes a compelling governmental interest is subject to varying interpretation. Nevertheless, the compelling governmental interest test is a formidable barrier against state restrictions on freedom of association. As long as the state must carry such a heavy burden of persuasion, this freedom, like the freedoms of speech and assembly, is likely to receive maximum judicial protection.

See also Academic Freedom; Assembly, Freedom of; Black, Hugo L.; *Boy Scouts of America v. Dale*; Brennan, William J., Jr.; Communist Party USA; Discrimination by Private Actors; Douglas, William O.; Due Process Clauses; Fifteenth Amendment; First Amendment; Fourteenth Amendment; Free Exercise Clause; Fundamental Rights; Gay Rights Movement; Gender-Based Discrimination; *Griswold v. Connecticut*; Harlan, John Marshall, II; Ku Klux Klan; National Association for the Advancement of Colored People; *National Association for the Advancement of Colored People v. Alabama*; Powell, Lewis F., Jr.; Public Accommodation, Places of; Reed, Stanley F.; Rehnquist, William H., Religion, Freedom of; Scalia, Antonin; Sexual Orientation, Discrimination Based on; Smith Act; Souter, David H.; Speech, Freedom of; Stevens, John Paul; Strict Scrutiny; USA PATRIOT Act; Warren, Earl; White Byron R.; White Primary

Bibliography

Guttman, Amy. 1998. *Freedom of Association*. Princeton, NJ: Princeton University Press.

John M. Scheb II and Otis H. Stephens, Jr.

ASYLUM, RIGHT TO

In general, asylum is an immigration protection that allows a citizen of another country to be sheltered from return to his or her nation of citizenship if he or she fears actual or potential harm in that country. The law describes this type of harm as "persecution." More will be said about that word below.

In the United States, the right to asylum is established by Congress and granted to noncitizens only after an application process that includes federal governmental review and approval. The concept of asylum in the immigration laws of the United States is defined in the Immigration and Nationality Act, 8 U.S.C. §§ 1101–1537, as amended. This law is commonly referred to as the Immigration Act or the INA. The basic U.S. law governing asylum is found in Section 208 of the Immigration Act, 8 U.S.C. § 1158 (2000). Related regulations are set forth in Title VIII of the Code of Federal Regulations, including part 208, entitled Procedures for Asylum and Withholding of Removal.

Congress enacted the first U.S. asylum law in 1980, basing its content on existing international law. Although the basic 1980 law still exists as part of the Immigration Act, specific provisions have been changed a number of times over the years. Not surprisingly, changes in asylum law resulted from the attacks of September 11, 2001. Until 2002, the U.S. Department of Justice administered, interpreted, enforced, and conducted rule making under the Immigration Act, including its asylum provisions. As a result of the passage of the Homeland Security Act of 2002, the U.S. Secretary of Homeland Security now administers and enforces the asylum laws and regulations. The current system of immigration regulation is complex, with authority divided among three principal bureaus: Homeland Security, the State Department, and the Department of Justice.

Not every noncitizen who fears potential harm in his or her country of citizenship can apply for or receive asylum in the United States. People who want to apply for asylum must be in or at a port of entry into the United States when they apply. Also, a foreign national must usually apply for asylum within one year after arrival in the United States. Moreover, applicants are ineligible for asylum who have: (1) engaged in certain activities connected to terrorism; (2) mistreated others on account of their race, religion, nationality, membership in a social group, or political opinion; (3) been convicted of a particularly serious crime or committed a serious nonpolitical crime outside the United States; or (4) firmly resettled themselves in a third country. Asylum relief is also denied to applicants who (1) have earlier applied for and been denied asylum (unless their circumstances have changed); (2) pose a danger to the United States; or (3) are representatives or members of a foreign terrorist organization or a similar political, social, or other kind of group. Finally, an asylum applicant who may be removed to and receive immigration protection from a third country may be denied asylum in the United States.

There are two main ways for someone to apply for asylum: affirmatively and defensively. Each way involves a different review and decision-making process. A person who is not already appearing before an appropriate immigration judge files an affirmative asylum application with a regional service center of the U.S. Citizenship and Immigration Services of Homeland Security. An Asylum Officer from this center reviews the application and interviews the applicant. The interview is intended to be nonadversarial. The role of the Asylum Officer is to hear the applicant's story and ask him or her related questions before making a determination as to whether the applicant should be granted asylum. No one presents formal arguments against the application during the interview, but the Asylum Officer does send the file to the State Department for review and comment. Applications that are not granted by the Asylum Officer are referred to an immigration judge.

A person who is in court before an immigration judge at the time he or she first makes an asylum claim files a defensive asylum application with the immigration judge as an argument against removal from the United States. The immigration judge reviews and makes a decision on the asylum application as part of the adversarial immigration court proceedings. The government has the opportunity to argue and present evidence against the asylum application to the immigration judge.

The immigration court system that hears asylum claims and appeals has two levels, both of which are part of the Executive Office for Immigration Review. Regardless of how they start, asylum cases that enter the system first are heard by an immigration judge. Asylum decisions made by these administrative judges may be reviewed by the Board of Immigration Appeals, the highest level of immigration court that can decide asylum claims. The U.S. federal courts then have the power to review decisions of the Board of Immigration Appeals.

To qualify for asylum under the Immigration Act under either application method, a person first must prove that he or she is a refugee. Once this proof is established, the U.S. Attorney General has the option of granting the applicant asylum in the United States. The exercise of judgment by the Attorney General involves a review of the facts of the case and fairness considerations, including, for example, whether the applicant has close family ties in the United States, and is subject to certain requirements. In *Matter of Pula* (1987), the Board of Immigration Appeals indicated that the Attorney General's role involves consideration of "the totality of the circumstances" and must weigh the danger of harm to the applicant against any matters that may work against the applicant. In general, however, the risk of harm to the applicant outweighs most other considerations.

The Attorney General's ability to grant or deny a refugee's asylum application in his or her discretion makes the asylum application process uncertain. However, the process of proving refugee status is also difficult and uncertain. The Immigration Act says that a person is a refugee if he or she "is outside any country of such person's nationality or, in the case of a person having no nationality, is outside any country in which such person last habitually resided, and who is unable or unwill-

ing to return to, and is unable or unwilling to avail himself or herself of the protection of, that country because of persecution or a well-founded fear of persecution on account of race, religion, nationality, membership in a particular social group, or political opinion."

Therefore, to be considered a refugee under U.S. law, a person must prove either past persecution or a well-founded fear of persecution on account of one of the five specified grounds. Neither the Immigration Act nor related regulations, however, define the key terms that are used in this definition: "persecution," "well-founded fear of persecution," and "membership in a particular social group." Nevertheless, federal and administrative court cases and other forms of guidance help to show what these three important terms mean.

"Persecution," as that term is used in the Immigration Act refugee definition, has been characterized in a number of ways. Definitions of persecution (as used in determining refugee status) predate U.S. asylum law, as described by the Board of Immigration Appeals in *Matter of Acosta* (1985). Under the definition cited in this case, persecution includes "a threat to the life or freedom of, or the infliction of suffering or harm upon, those who differ in a way regarded as offensive" The *Acosta* court went on to note that "[i]t also could consist of economic deprivation or restrictions so severe that they constitute a threat to an individual's life or freedom."

Internal guidelines used by asylum officers in the U.S. Citizenship and Immigration Service also include working definitions of persecution. Under those guidelines, persecution is defined as "a serious threat to life or freedom on account of race, religion, nationality, membership in a particular social group, or political opinion." The guidelines also note that persecution may exist as a result of "arbitrary interference with a person's privacy, family, home or correspondence; ... [or] enforced social or civil inactivity." In addition, the guidelines advise that "serious violations of basic human rights can constitute acts of persecution."

Despite judicial and regulatory guidance, however, the meaning of persecution in U.S. asylum law continues to be confused and confusing. Although international law often is helpful in giving substantive content to ill-defined concepts in U.S. immigration law, little guidance as to the meaning of the term "persecution" exists under international law. For example, the United Nations High Commissioner for Refugees notes that "[t]here is no universally accepted definition of 'persecution' and various attempts to formulate such a definition have met with little success." Accordingly, to find the best, most current definition, an applicant is well advised to check existing court decisions made by the Board of Immigration Appeals and the United States Court of Appeals for the circuit in which a particular case is being or likely would be decided.

The term "well-founded fear of persecution," as used in the Immigration Act, also has an unclear definition. At the outset, there are at least two important things to note about the phrase "well-founded fear of persecution." First, it is *not* essential that a person applying for asylum establish a well-founded fear of persecution. An applicant may prove past persecution, and that alone is enough to establish refugee status under applicable law and regulations. Moreover, where an applicant establishes past persecution, the applicant still may, and often does, argue that he or she also has a well-founded fear of future persecution. Once a person applying for asylum has proven past persecution, it is presumed that the applicant has a well-founded fear of persecution. Second, the establishment of a well-founded fear of persecution depends in part on the applicable definition of the term "persecution," which involves, as noted above, a case-by-case, fact-based analysis and decision based on varied, unclear legal standards. Accordingly, there is a significant amount of uncertainty in defining what constitutes a well-founded fear of persecution. However, the uncertainty extends far beyond the meaning of "persecution" and into the meaning of the phrase "well-founded fear."

In *INS v. Cardoza-Fonseca* (1987), the U.S. Supreme Court found that proving a well-founded fear of persecution does not require the applicant to "prove that it is more likely than not that he or she will be persecuted in his or her home country." The Court relied to some extent on existing international guidance in ruling on the meaning of "well-founded fear of persecution." Specifically, the Court relies upon guidance provided by the International Refugee Organization, the Ad Hoc Committee on Statelessness and Related Problems of the United Nations Economic and Social Council, and the United Nations High Commissioner for Refugees in support of its conclusions. As summarized by Goldberg (1993), "[t]he individual must subjectively fear, and that fear must be grounded in objective reality."

Certain decisions of the Board of Immigration Appeals are also important to an understanding of what it means for a person to have a well-founded fear of persecution. The Board of Immigration Appeals has identified four elements that a person applying for asylum must establish. These elements are (1) the applicant's possession of "a belief or a characteristic the persecutor seeks to overcome in others by means of punishment of some sort;" (2) the persecutor's awareness, or ability to become aware, of the applicant's possession of that belief or characteristic; (3) the persecutor's ability to punish the applicant; and (4) the persecutor's inclination to punish the applicant. The Board of Immigration Appeals also has stated that a person applying for asylum can establish a well-founded fear of persecution if he or she shows that a reasonable person in his or her circumstances would fear persecution.

As is true for "persecution" and "well-founded fear of persecution," there is no clear definition of what it means to have "membership in a particular social group." In *Matter of Acosta*, the Board of Immigration Appeals takes a relatively narrow view of the characteristics that constitute a particular social group, finding that persecution on this basis includes "persecution that is directed toward an individual who is a member of a group of persons all of whom share a common, immutable characteristic." The Board of Immigration Appeals goes on to say that "whatever the common characteristic that defines the group, it must be one that the members of the group either cannot change, or should not be required to change because it is fundamental to their individual identities or consciences."

In spite of the Board of Immigration Appeals' decision in *Matter of Acosta*, federal courts generally acknowledge that the idea of what it means to be a member of a "particular social group" for purposes of U.S. asylum and refugee law is relatively broad—broader than that of the other four enumerated bases for asylum protection under the Immigration Act. For example, the United States Court of Appeals for the Ninth Circuit has stated that members of a particular social group are closely affiliated with each other and motivated by some common desire or pursuit. The court also cautions, however, that "[t]he statutory words 'particular' and 'social' which modify 'group' ... indicate that the term does not encompass every broadly defined segment of a population, even if a certain demographic division does have some statistical relevance."

The same court later made it clear that its definition of "particular social group" is intended to include rather than displace the Board of Immigration Appeals' definition in *Matter of Acosta*, stating that "a 'particular social group' is one united by a voluntary association, including a former association, *or* by an innate characteristic that is so fundamental to the identities or consciences of its members that members either cannot or should not be required to change it." The United States Court of Appeals for the Second Circuit had earlier expressed similarly broad definitions of the term "particular social group," and underlying international law also supports a broad definition.

Unfortunately, however, it is impossible to say with any certainty what it means to be a member of a "particular social group." Accordingly, establishing "membership in a particular social group" as the basis for an asylum claim remains a challenge. When added to the uncertainties associated with the definitions of "persecution" and "well-founded fear of persecution," asylum claims based on membership in a particular social group remain among the most difficult to prove.

See also Citizenship and Immigration Services, Bureau of; Homeland Security, Department of; Immigrants and Aliens, Rights of; International Law; United States Courts of Appeals; U.S. Department of Justice

Bibliography

Asylum Branch, Office of General Counsel. 1991. *Immigration and Naturalization Services, Basic Law Manual: Asylum, Summary and Overview Concerning Asylum Law.*

Goldberg, Pamela. 1993. "Anyplace but Home: Asylum in the United States for Women Fleeing Intimate Violence." *Cornell International Law Journal* 26:565–604.

Office of the U.N. High Commissioner for Refugees. 1979. *Handbook on Procedures and Criteria for Determining Refugee Status under the 1951 Convention and 1967 Protocol relating to the Status of Refugees.* U.N. Doc. HCR/PRO/4.

U.S. Citizenship and Immigration Services. 2003. *Obtaining Asylum in the United States: Two Paths to Asylum.* http://uscis.gov/graphics/services/asylum/paths.htm.

Joan MacLeod Heminway and Amy M. Lighter

AT-LARGE ELECTIONS

There are two general ways to apportion elected seats in any politically representative body. One is a single-member district (SMD), where a plurality or majority vote winner wins the sole seat. Usually single-member districts are subdivided geographically so that different communities or areas combine together to send all the representatives to the body. Another allocation plan is a multimember district or at-large district, where the entire geographic area represented by the body elects a number of members based on various formulae or criteria. The U.S. is dominated by single-member districts, although in the rest of the world (particularly parliamentary regimes with proportional representation among parties) multimember districts are the norm. Political culture may explain part of the American affection for SMDs, but voting equality and civil rights explain more.

American judicial history reveals a number of instances of manipulating electoral laws to disenfranchise groups, particularly African Americans. In *Gomillion v. Lightfoot* (1960), the Supreme Court ruled that Tuskegee, Alabama's 28-sided electoral district disenfranchised African American voters and therefore was afoul of the Fifteenth Amendment's protection of voting rights. Twenty years later, the court would rule that an at-large district in Mobile, Alabama, was not a violation of the Fifteenth Amendment. In *Mobile v. Bolden* (1980) citizens of the Alabama community sued, claiming that the three-member at-large district, which elected the city commission, unfairly diluted the strength of African American voting in Mobile. The Court found that black citizens could register and vote without hindrance and therefore reversed a lower court decision that focused on the low number of African American-elected members of the commission. The Court set a standard that only intentionally diluted black voting power.

In light of the *Mobile* case, Congress amended the Voting Rights Act of 1965 in 1982, adding Section 2, which allowed African Americans to challenge any practice that (intentionally or not) resulted in dilution of black voting power. At the same time that Congress was adding its amendments, North Carolina's General Assembly was redrawing its postcensus district boundaries. The plan, which was implemented for the 1984 electoral cycle, included a mix of at-large and single-member districts. Based on the 1982 amendments, African American citizens of North Carolina sued for relief on the effects of vote dilution alone. The case, *Thornburgh v. Gingles* (1986), set forth a test to determine if an at-large district indeed diluted the voting power of a minority group. Racial fairness, according to the *Gingles* case, comprises three factors: (1) The minority group must demonstrate its numerical and geographic size to constitute a major-

ity population in a single-member district; (2) The minority group must be politically cohesive; and (3) Opposing majority populations must render the minority group's probability of electing a candidate to almost zero. *Gingles* set a standard of scrutiny so high that almost any at-large district would be shown to dilute minority voting rights, effectively rendering the use of such districts moot.

The *Gingles* standard was applied again in 1985, when the system in Bleckley County, Georgia, was challenged by African American voters. Bleckley County had long used a single commissioner for its representation but proposed a five-member commission (elected in SMDs) and a single presiding commissioner elected at large. Voters in the community rejected the proposal, and black citizens sued, claiming the single-commissioner system diluted African American voting authority in the county. In *Holder v. Hall* (1994), the U.S. Supreme Court rejected their claim that size mattered, ruling that a single-member commission in and of itself was not racially discriminatory. In effect, the Court was inviting at-large districts to be considered again, though to this point no further challenges have presented themselves to the Supreme Court.

The ideal principle of one person, one vote, recognized by the Supreme Court in *Reynolds v. Sims* (1964) and the other reapportionment cases is a particularly difficult one to implement. Any alteration of electoral rules seeks to benefit one group at the expense of another, throwing the fairness and equity of *any* voting plan into question. As Kenneth Arrow's general possibility theorem posits, there is no one optimal way to translate preferences into votes. The Supreme Court has established the *Gingles* test as a method for making the best of a difficult situation, but the end result is still the virtual banishment of the at-large district from American political life.

See also Fifteenth Amendment; Reapportionment; Reynolds v. Sims; Vote, Right to; Voting Rights Act of 1965

Bibliography

Keyssar, Alexander. 2000. *The Right to Vote.* New York: Basic Books

Spaeth, Harold J., and Jeffrey Segal. 1999. *Majority Rule or Minority Will?* Cambridge: Cambridge University Press.

Chapman Rackaway

ATTORNEY GENERAL. *See* U.S. Department of Justice

AUTOMOBILE STOPS AND SEARCHES

The Fourth Amendment prohibits "unreasonable searches and seizures." Although the Amendment states a strong preference for search warrants, courts have long recognized the validity of certain types of warrantless searches. Under the so-called automobile exception, police who have probable cause to believe a motor vehicle contains contraband or evidence of crime may stop and search that vehicle without first obtaining a warrant. In his majority opinion in *Carroll v. United States* (1925), Chief Justice William Howard Taft wrote that

the guaranty of freedom from unreasonable searches and seizures by the Fourth Amendment has been construed, practically since the beginning of the government, as recognizing a necessary difference between a search of a store, dwelling house, or other structure in respect of which a proper official warrant readily may be obtained and a search of a ship, motor boat, wagon, or automobile for contraband goods, where it is not practicable to secure a warrant, because the vehicle can be quickly moved out of the locality or jurisdiction in which the warrant must be sought.

In *Dyke v. Taylor Implement Company* (1968), Justice Byron White's opinion for the Court stated the doctrine more succinctly: "Automobiles, because of their mobility, may be searched without a warrant upon facts not justifying a warrantless search of a residence or office."

The automobile exception applies not only to cars but to all vehicles moving along the public roadways. Thus, in *California v. Carney* (1985) the

Supreme Court held that motor homes being used on the road and not in a place regularly used as a residence are subject to the automobile exception.

In *Chambers v. Maroney* (1970), the Supreme Court held that once begun under exigent circumstances, a warrantless search of an automobile may continue after the vehicle has been taken to the police station. And in *United States v. Ross* (1982), the Court held that a police officer having probable cause to believe that evidence of crime is concealed within an automobile may conduct a search as broad as one that could be authorized by a search warrant. This ruling effectively allows police officers to search closed containers found during an automobile search without first having to obtain a warrant, even if those containers are locked in the trunk or otherwise sequestered.

In *United States v. Johns* (1985), the Supreme Court upheld the warrantless search of plastic containers seized during an automobile search, even though the police had waited several days before opening the containers. The Court reasoned that since police legitimately seized the containers during the original search of the automobile, no reasonable expectation of privacy could be maintained once the containers came under police control. The search of the containers, which produced a substantial quantity of marijuana, was therefore not unreasonable simply because it was delayed for several days.

In 1999 the Supreme Court extended the automobile exception by ruling in *Wyoming v. Houghton* that police officers who have probable cause to search a vehicle may search the belongings of passengers who are capable of concealing objects of the search. The case began in 1998 when a Wyoming highway patrol officer stopped a speeding car. While speaking to the driver, the officer noticed a syringe in the driver's pocket. When questioned about it, the driver admitted using the syringe to inject illegal drugs. Thus having probable cause to search the car, the officer then opened a passenger's purse on the backseat and found contraband. The Wyoming Supreme Court ruled that the search was not within the permissible scope of search of the vehicle. Dividing six-to-three, the U.S. Supreme Court reversed. In an opinion by Justice Antonin Scalia, the Court justified the search on the following grounds:

Whereas the passenger's privacy expectations are … considerably diminished, the governmental interests at stake are substantial. Effective law enforcement would be appreciably impaired without the ability to search a passenger's personal belongings when there is reason to believe contraband or evidence of criminal wrongdoing is hidden in the car. As in all car-search cases, the "ready mobility" of an automobile creates a risk that the evidence or contraband will be permanently lost while a warrant is obtained…. In addition, a car passenger … will often be engaged in a common enterprise with the driver, and have the same interest in concealing the fruits or the evidence of their wrongdoing.

It is important to note that police may, without a warrant, stop an automobile and temporarily detain the driver as long as they have probable cause to believe that criminal activity is taking place or that traffic laws or automobile regulations are being violated. Sometimes when police stop a vehicle for a traffic violation, evidence of unrelated criminal activity comes into plain view. Such was the case in *Whren v. United States* (1996), when officers patrolling an area of known drug activity stopped a truck for a routine traffic violation. Upon approaching the vehicle, an officer observed a passenger holding plastic bags containing what appeared to be crack cocaine. The driver and the passenger were arrested, and several types of illegal drugs were found in the truck. The Supreme Court upheld the search and seizure, saying that "the decision to stop an automobile is reasonable where the

police have probable cause to believe that a traffic violation has occurred."

Finally, it must be pointed out that the courts have gone so far as to allow brief warrantless stops of automobiles even in the absence of probable cause, assuming there is "reasonable suspicion" that criminal activity is afoot. In conducting "investigatory stops," police may require a driver to exit the vehicle and produce a driver's license and proof of registration. During the course of this brief encounter, police may develop probable cause to arrest the driver and/or search the automobile. In *Michigan v. Long* (1983) the Supreme Court held that when police stop an automobile based on reasonable suspicion, they may search the passenger compartment for weapons, assuming they have reason to believe that a suspect is dangerous. The search, however, must be limited to those areas in which a weapon may be placed or hidden.

See also Accused, Rights of the; Fourth Amendment; Fourth Amendment Exclusionary Rule; Inventory Searches; *Mapp v. Ohio*; Plain View Doctrine; Privacy, Reasonable Expectations of; Probable Cause; Roadblocks and Sobriety Checkpoints; Scalia, Antonin; Search Warrants; Taft, William Howard; Warrantless Searches

Bibliography

Scheb, John M., and John M. Scheb II. 2006. *Criminal Procedure*. Belmont, CA: Thomson/Wadsworth.

Stephens, Otis H., Jr., and Richard A. Glenn. 2006. *Unreasonable Searches and Seizures: Rights and Liberties under the Law*. Santa Barbara, CA: ABC-CLIO.

John M. Scheb II and Otis H. Stephens, Jr.

B

BAD TENDENCY TEST

Rooted in English common law, the "bad tendency" test held that expression tending to corrupt public morals, incite people to commit crimes, or otherwise threaten the public welfare does not merit the protection of the First Amendment. This notion was implicitly rejected by the Supreme Court in *Schenck v. United States* (1919), where the Court held that speech is entitled to constitutional protection unless it constitutes "a clear and present danger that [it] will bring about the substantive evils that Congress has a right to prevent." The bad tendency test would resurface that same year, however, in *Abrams v. United States* (1919). In *Abrams,* the Supreme Court upheld the conviction of a self-styled "anarchist-Socialist" for distributing leaflets in New York City urging workers to resist American intervention in Russia against the newly formed Bolshevik government. For Justice John H. Clarke, who wrote the majority opinion, it was quite sufficient that Abrams had advocated a general strike "in the greatest port of our land" for the purpose of "curtailing the production of ordnance and munitions necessary and essential to the prosecution of the war." In effect, the Court had reverted to the bad tendency test, according little importance to free speech and stressing the fact that Abrams's circular might in some way hinder America's efforts in World War I.

In a powerful dissenting opinion, Justice Oliver Wendell Holmes, Jr., joined by Justice Louis D. Brandeis, argued that the proper standard was the "clear and present danger" test articulated in *Schenck,* and by that standard, Abrams's activities were protected by the First Amendment. In one of his more widely quoted opinions, Holmes insisted that "we should be eternally vigilant against attempts to check the expression of opinions that we loathe and believe to be fraught with death, unless they so imminently threaten immediate interference with the lawful and pressing purposes of the law that an immediate check is required to save the country."

Through the 1920s, the Supreme Court continued to adhere to the bad tendency test, while Holmes and Brandeis continued to espouse the clear and present danger doctrine as a rationale in support of freedom of expression and association. In *Gitlow v. New York* (1925), the Court upheld a conviction under New York's Criminal Anarchy Act, which prohibited advocacy of the overthrow of government "by force or violence." Prior to this decision, the Court had addressed issues of freedom of expression arising from the states strictly on the basis of the Due Process Clause of the Fourteenth Amendment, without specific reference to the First Amendment. In the *Gitlow* case, however, Justice Edward T. Sanford, writing for the majority, stated without elaboration: "For present purposes we may and do assume that freedom of speech and of the press—which are protected by the First Amendment from abridgment by Congress—are among the fundamental personal rights and 'liberties' protected by the Due Process Clause of the Fourteenth Amendment from impairment by the states." Nevertheless, the Court affirmed the conviction of Benjamin Gitlow, whose "Left Wing Manifesto" called for the destruction of established government and its replacement by a "revolutionary dictatorship of the proletariat." In sustaining the conviction, Justice Sanford stated the essence of the bad tendency test: "That a state, in the exercise of its police power, may punish those who abuse [freedom of speech and press] by utterances inimical to the public welfare, tending to corrupt public morals, incite to crime, or disturb the public peace, is not open to question."

Again, Justices Holmes and Brandeis dissented. They could find no clear and present danger in an effort "to overthrow the government by force on the part of the admittedly small minority who shared the defendant's views." To the contention that the "Left Wing Manifesto" was an incitement, Holmes replied:

Every idea is an incitement. It offers itself for belief and if believed it is acted on unless some other belief outweighs it or some failure of energy stifles the movement at its birth. The only difference between the expression of an opinion and an incitement in the narrower sense is the speaker's enthusiasm for the result. Eloquence may set fire to reason. But whatever may be thought of the redundant discourse before us it had no chance of starting a present conflagration. If in the long run the beliefs expressed in proletarian dictatorship are destined to be accepted by the dominant forces of the community, the only meaning of free speech is that they should be given their chance and have their way.

In *Whitney v. California* (1927), the Court, speaking again through Justice Sanford, adhered to the bad tendency test in affirming a conviction under California's Criminal Syndicalism Act. In the 1930s, the Court would finally abandon the bad tendency test in favor of the clear and present danger doctrine (see *Herndon v. Lowry*, 1937). In the decades that followed, the Court began to apply the clear and present danger test not only to seditious speech but to other First Amendment issues as well.

See also Alien and Sedition Acts; Bill of Rights, Incorporation of; Brandeis, Louis D.; *Brandenburg v. Ohio*; Clear and Present Danger Doctrine; Clear and Probable Danger Doctrine; Common-Law Background of American Civil Rights and Liberties; Communist Party USA; Criminal Syndicalism; Due Process Clauses; First Amendment; First Amendment, Approaches to; Free Marketplace of Ideas; *Gitlow v. New York*; Holmes, Oliver Wendell, Jr.; *Schenck v. United States*; Speech, Freedom of

Bibliography

Bollinger, Lee. 1986. *The Tolerant Society: Freedom of Speech and Extremist Speech in America*. New York: Oxford University Press.

Kalven, Harry, Jr. 1988. *A Worthy Tradition: Freedom of Speech in America*. New York: Harper & Row.

Konefsky, Samuel J. 1956. *The Legacy of Holmes and Brandeis: A Study in the Influence of Ideas*. New York: Macmillan.

Polenberg, Richard. 1987. *Fighting Faiths: The Abrams Case, the Supreme Court and Free Speech*. New York: Viking Press.

John M. Scheb II and Otis H. Stephens, Jr.

BAIL. *See* Excessive Bail, Prohibition of

BAIL, RIGHT TO

The term "bail" refers to a sum of money posted by a person who has been arrested and charged with a crime in order to secure pretrial release pending adjudication of the charge. The posting of bail (or a bond posted by a third party in exchange for a premium) is designed to ensure that the accused will appear in court when required to do so. Failure to appear results in the forfeiture of bail as well as the issuance of a bench warrant authorizing the immediate arrest of the fugitive.

Securing pretrial release on bail provides a number of advantages to the accused beyond the obvious benefit of being free over being in custody. A defendant who is free on bail has a greater capacity to assist counsel in preparing a defense. He or she also has the ability to continue or obtain employment, to assist in meeting family responsibilities, and an opportunity to compile a record of living as a law-abiding citizen.

The issue of bail is typically dealt with shortly after arrest. In many jurisdictions, persons arrested for misdemeanors can secure immediate release from jail by posting bail according to a predetermined schedule without the need to appear in court. In felony cases, the typical procedure is for the accused to appear in court within 24 hours after arrest to be formally apprised of the charges. At that initial appearance, the court will determine whether to release the accused on bail and, if so, what the amount of the bail should be.

Court decisions repeatedly state that the government's sole interest in detaining persons accused of crimes before trial is to ensure their presence at trial. In determining whether the defendant will appear in court as required, a judge will generally consider the defendant's financial circumstances and criminal record, if any; the seriousness of the offense charged; and the defendant's family ties, employment, length of residence in the community, and local affiliations.

The Eighth Amendment to the U.S. Constitution prohibits "excessive bail" in criminal cases. All state constitutions have similar provisions. Does the prohibition of excessive bail imply the right to pretrial release on bail? Writing for the Supreme Court in *Stack v. Boyle* (1951), Chief Justice Fred M. Vinson observed, "Unless the right to bail before trial is preserved, the presumption of innocence, secured only after centuries of struggle, would lose its meaning." However, in *United States v. Salerno* (1987), the Supreme Court said that the Excessive Bail Clause "says nothing about whether bail shall be available at all." In *Salerno,* the Court upheld the federal Bail Reform Act of 1984, which permits pretrial detention in federal cases where there is "clear and convincing evidence" that the pretrial release of a defendant would pose a serious threat to public safety. Writing for the Court in *Salerno,* Chief Justice William H. Rehnquist agreed that "a primary function of bail is to safeguard the courts' role in adjudicating the guilt or innocence of defendants" but rejected "the proposition that the Eighth Amendment categorically prohibits the government from pursuing other admittedly compelling interests through the regulation of pretrial release."

Although, as currently interpreted, there is no federal constitutional right to bail, many state constitutions provide stronger protections to defendants. For example, Article I, Section 15 of the Tennessee Constitution provides "[t]hat all prisoners shall be bailable by sufficient sureties, unless for capital offences, when the proof is evident, or the presumption great." Similarly, as recognized in *Creech v. State* (1972), the Oklahoma Constitution makes all offenses other than capital crimes bailable. But even explicit constitutional provisions granting the right to bail can be overborne by judicial interpretation. For instance, in *People v. Bailey and Coyne* (1995), the Illinois Supreme Court held that the judicial branch has an inherent power to deny bail, even though the state constitution grants defendants an absolute right to bail in most criminal cases.

A convicted defendant who appeals to a higher court may apply for bail pending appeal. But at this stage, trial courts have broad discretion in whether to grant or deny bail and, if granted, in determining the amount or conditions. Generally the trial court's decision is reviewable by motion filed in an appellate court. In reviewing a trial court's decision to deny bail while an appeal is pending, appellate courts generally follow an "abuse of discretion" standard, which means that they tend to be highly deferential to trial judges.

See also Accused, Rights of the; Arrest, Constitutional Limits on; Eighth Amendment; Excessive Bail, Prohibition of; Initial Appearance in Criminal Cases; Pretrial Detention; Rehnquist, William H.; Vinson, Fred M.

Bibliography

Lester, Joseph L. 2003. "Presumed Innocent, Feared Dangerous: The Eighth Amendment's Right to Bail." *Georgetown Law Journal* 91:289.

Scheb, John M., and John M. Scheb II. 2006. *Criminal Procedure.* Belmont, CA: Thomson/Wadsworth.

Verrilli, Donald B., Jr. 1982. "The Eighth Amendment and the Right to Bail: Historical Perspectives." *Columbia Law Review* 82:328.

John M. Scheb II

BAKER MOTLEY, CONSTANCE (1921–)

Constance Baker, the daughter of immigrants from the Eastern Caribbean island of Nevis, was born on September 14, 1921, in New Haven, Connecticut. Although the population of New Haven was only two-percent African American, Baker Motley (she married Joel Motley, a real estate and insurance broker, in 1949), her parents, and four siblings lived in an integrated working-class neighborhood. A gifted student and orator, Motley joined the local chapter of the National Association for the Advancement of Colored People (NAACP) while a teenager after being denied admission to a local skating rink and public beach (Gaines 2003).

At a young age, Baker Motley aspired to become a lawyer despite her parents' inability to pay for her education. In December 1940, she met Clarence Blakeslee, owner of C. W. Blakeslee and Sons, who would eventually become her mentor and financial supporter. Baker Motley was one of the founders and president of the New Haven Negro Youth Council. The organization's main goals were to address youth unemployment and racial discrimination in employment. Blakeslee, a wealthy philanthropist who owned one of the largest and most successful road construction businesses in New England, was concerned about the plight of minorities and the poor (Baker Motley 1998, 43). After attending a Youth Council meeting, Blakeslee became fascinated by Baker Motley's oratorical ability, intelligence, and compassion. The day after the meeting, he met Baker Motley, looked at her high school record, and noticed her exceptional grades. After she told him that she was not enrolled in college because of her parents' inability to finance her education, Blakeslee offered to pay her undergraduate and law school educational expenses at Fisk University in Nashville, Tennessee; Washington

Square College at New York University; and Columbia University Law School. Constance later discovered that Blakeslee had helped several people to attend college. In 1943, she graduated from New York University with a degree in economics and earned a law degree from Columbia three years later (Gaines 2003).

For over 20 years, Constance Baker Motley worked for the New York branch of the NAACP Legal Defense and Educational Fund, which was mounting a full-scale attack on segregation and racial discrimination. While she was in law school, Thurgood Marshall had hired her as a law clerk for the Fund. She remained there as a staff member and associate for almost 20 years thereafter, won 9 of the 10 civil rights cases she argued on behalf of the fund, and was among the first women to argue cases before the U.S. Supreme Court (Gaines, 2003). As an NAACP staff attorney, Baker Motley wrote briefs in *Brown v. Board of Education* (1954) and several other landmark cases. In *Brown,* she and the other NAACP attorneys were able to convince the justices of the Supreme Court that public school segregation had a harmful effect on the ability of black children to learn. A unanimous Court held that the segregation of black and white children in schools violated the Equal Protection Clause of the Fourteenth Amendment (Baker Motley 2003, 102).

In 1961, Constance Baker Motley argued her first case before the U.S. Supreme Court. The Alabama criminal case of *Hamilton v. State of Alabama* (1961) questioned whether defendants possessed the right of counsel during arraignments. Charles Clarence Hamilton was an African American who had been sentenced to death in Alabama for "breaking and entering a dwelling at night with intent to ravish" but lacked representation during his arraignment (Baker Motley 2003, 194). After Baker Motley argued on his behalf, a unanimous Supreme Court reversed Hamilton's conviction. Also while serving as chief council of the defense fund in 1962, Baker Motley argued before an appellate court on behalf of James H. Meredith, an African American student seeking admission to the University of

Mississippi, Oxford, in *Meredith v. Fair,* 305 F.2d 341 (1962) and *Meredith v. Fair,* 298 F.2d 696 (1962) (Gaines 2003).

During the mid-1960s, she pursued a brief but outstanding political career. From 1964 to 1965, while continuing to work for the Legal Defense Fund, she became the first African American woman to serve in the New York State Senate (Gaines 2003). Six weeks after beginning the Senate term in 1965, she became the first African American woman to win an election for Manhattan Borough president (Baker Motley 2003, 206). After her appointment to the federal bench in 1966, Constance Baker Motley abandoned the political arena for the judiciary (Gaines 2003). Only four other women were federal judges in the nation at the time. After this appointment, she became the chief judge of the U.S. District Court for the Southern District of New York in 1982 and in 1986 became the senior judge for the Southern District of New York—the largest federal trial court in the United States (Gaines 2003). In 1993, Constance Baker Motley was inducted into the National Women's Hall of Fame, and she published her autobiography, *Equal Justice under the Law,* in 1998.

See also *Brown v. Board of Education;* Civil Rights Movement; Equal Protection Clause; Fourteenth Amendment; Jim Crow Laws; Marshall, Thurgood; Meredith, James; National Association for the Advancement of Colored People; *Plessy v. Ferguson;* Segregation, De Facto and De Jure

Bibliography

Baker Motley, Constance. 1998. *Equal Justice under the Law: An Autobiography.* New York: Farrar, Straus and Giroux.

Gaines, Kim. 2003. "Constance Baker Motley." www. imdiversity.com.

Sharon D. Wright Austin

BAKER V. CARR (1962)

Democratic theorists generally accept the proposition that all citizens' votes should count equally. Malapportionment of legislative districts (gross disparities in population among districts) undermines this principle. Malapportionment can occur in two ways. One is through gerrymandering, which is the intentional manipulation of district lines. The other way is through neglect—lines are not changed even though populations of districts have become unequal as the result of demographic changes. By the 1940s, urban areas in the United States were becoming seriously underrepresented in Congress and in state legislatures.

For many years, the federal courts used the so-called political questions doctrine to stay out of controversies involving the apportionment of legislative districts. Writing for a Supreme Court plurality in *Colegrove v. Green* (1946), Justice Felix Frankfurter warned of the dangers of entering the "political thicket" of reapportionment. In Frankfurter's view, the remedy for malapportionment was the ballot box. Between 1946 and 1962, groups representing urban interests tried, without much success, to secure reapportionment through the state legislatures and through the ballot box. Beginning in 1962, however, the Supreme Court produced a series of decisions on reapportionment that would permanently alter the American political landscape and draw the Court into a firestorm of criticism.

In *Baker v. Carr,* residents of Knoxville, Chattanooga, Nashville, and Memphis brought suit in federal district court to challenge the apportionment of the Tennessee legislature, which had not changed since 1901. Plaintiffs contended that the state legislature's failure to reapportion itself was, in the words of the Supreme Court, "offensive to the Fourteenth Amendment in its irrational disregard of the standard of apportionment." The district court dismissed the case on the authority of *Colegrove v. Green* (1946), saying that the issue was a "political question" rather than a judicial one.

On appeal, the Supreme Court reversed and reinstated the complaint. Writing for a seven-justive majority, Justice William Brennan held legislative malapportionment to be a "justiciable" question. This decision signaled a veritable revolution, in which federal courts directed the reapportionment of legislative districts at all levels of government, from the House of Representatives to local school boards, on the basis of one person, one vote.

See also Brennan, William J., Jr.; Fourteenth Amendment; Franfurter, Felix; Reapportionment; *Reynolds v. Sims*

Bibliography

Ball, Howard. 1971. *The Warren Court's Conceptions of Democracy: An Evaluation of the Supreme Court's Apportionment Opinions.* Madison, NJ: Fairleigh Dickinson University Press.

Cortner, Richard C. 1972. *The Apportionment Cases.* New York: W. W. Norton.

John M. Scheb II and Otis H. Stephens, Jr.

BALANCED TREATMENT ACTS. *See* Evolution/Creationism Controversy

BALANCING TEST. *See* First Amendment, Approaches to

BARRON V. BALTIMORE (1833)

There is little doubt that, at the time of its ratification in 1791, the Bill of Rights was widely perceived as imposing limitations only on the powers and actions of the national government. This is suggested by the first clause of the First Amendment, which begins, "Congress shall make no law." The Court held as much in 1833 in the case of *Barron v. Baltimore,* when it refused to permit a citizen to sue a local government for violating his property rights under the Just Compensation Clause of the Fifth Amendment.

The case stemmed from an incident in which the city of Baltimore diverted the flow of certain streams, causing silt to be deposited in front of John Barron's wharf, making it unusable. Barron brought suit in state court, claiming that because the city's action amounted to a taking of private property, he was entitled to "just compensation" under the Fifth Amendment to the U.S. Constitution. The trial court agreed and awarded Barron $4,500. After a state appellate court reversed this judgment, Barron appealed to the U.S. Supreme Court on a writ of error.

Speaking for the Court, Chief Justice John Marshall said that "the provision in the Fifth Amendment to the Constitution, declaring that private

property shall not be taken for public use without just compensation is intended solely as a limitation on the power of the United States, and is not applicable to the legislation of the states."

The adoption of the Fourteenth Amendment would ultimately alter the relationship of the Bill of Rights to the states. In a series of decisions beginning in the late nineteenth century, the Supreme Court would hold that various provisions of the Bill of Rights are incorporated within the Due Process Clause of the Fourteenth Amendment, thus making them applicable to state action.

See also Bill of Rights (American); Bill of Rights, Incorporation of; Due Process Clauses; Fifth Amendment; Fourteenth Amendment; Just Compensation Clause; Marshall, John; Property Rights; Public Use Clause; State Action Doctrine

John M. Scheb II and Otis H. Stephens, Jr.

BARRY, MARION. *See* Student Nonviolent Coordinating Committee

BCIS. *See* Bureau of Citizenship and Immigration Services

BELLOTTI V. BAIRD (1979). *See* Abortion, Right to

BENCH TRIAL

A bench trial is one in which the verdict is rendered by a judge (or in certain instances, a panel of judges) rather than by a jury. In cases in which there is no constitutional or statutory right to a jury trial, the trial is by the bench. Even in those cases in which the law affords the right to a jury trial, that right can be waived and a verdict rendered from the bench. In many jurisdictions, the failure to elect a jury trial in a timely fashion constitutes a waiver of the right to trial by jury. In such instances, trial is normally by the bench. Waiver of the right to trial by jury does not necessarily entail a right to demand a bench trial, however. In *Singer v. United States* (1965) the Supreme Court held that there is no right to bench trial under the Sixth Amendment. Writing for the Court in *Singer,* Chief Justice Earl

Warren observed, "The ability to waive a constitutional right does not ordinarily carry with it the right to insist upon the opposite of that right."

State constitutional provisions and statutes vary on the issue of a defendant's right to demand a bench trial in a criminal case. Under Article I of the New York Constitution, defendants in criminal cases have the right to choose a bench trial, except in cases where the crime is punishable by death.

In civil cases in which the right to trial by jury applies, both the plaintiff and the defendant may exercise the right to have the case decided by jury. Thus for a bench trial to take place, both parties must waive the right to trial by jury. Some courts have held that judges may deny a party's request for a jury trial if the case is so complex that a jury could not render a rational decision based upon a reasonable interpretation of the evidence.

Typically, procedures in bench trials are more streamlined than in jury trials. Obviously, the court does not have to concern itself with empanelling an impartial jury, insulating a jury from inappropriate contacts during the trial, or instructing a jury in the relevant law. In a bench trial, opening statements tend to be brief, and counsel often dispenses with closing arguments altogether. Notwithstanding the historic commitment to trial by jury, most commentators recognize that bench trials are more appropriate than jury trials in minor or highly specialized cases and in civil cases involving highly complex or technical factual issues.

See also Accused, Rights of the; Counsel, Right to; Jury, Trial by; Seventh Amendment; Sixth Amendment

John M. Scheb II and Otis H. Stephens, Jr.

BENTHAM, JEREMY (1748–1832)

Jeremy Bentham, a noted English philosopher, economist, jurist, and author, was born in London in 1748 into a wealthy Tory family. He was educated at Westminster School and Queen's College, Oxford University. Trained as a lawyer, he was called to the bar in 1767 but did not choose to follow a career as a lawyer. Rather, his training in law led him to become a sharp critic of the English legal system. His interest in law lay in advocacy of radical reforms, and his independent wealth allowed him to pursue a career as a writer. His writings proved to be highly influential and made lasting contributions to the fields of law, economics, philosophy, and government.

Bentham is regarded as the founder of utilitarianism, a philosophy that holds that happiness is the highest goal of life and that every action or policy is to be judged according to its utility in promoting human happiness. Bentham was greatly influenced by Adam Smith's *Wealth of Nations,* written in 1776. Like Smith, Bentham was an advocate of the doctrine of laissez-faire—the notion that an unregulated marketplace would produce the greatest happiness for the greatest number of people.

Bentham's authorship of *Introduction to Principles of Morals and Legislation* (1789), which would be translated into several languages, won him wide recognition in the Western world. In it Bentham posited that because people are motivated by their self-interest, "pain and pleasure are the sovereign masters governing man's conduct." Bentham argued that human behavior is based on a rational calculus—a computation of the ratio of pleasure to pain associated with any particular action. Thus Bentham held that the criminal law should impose sanctions sufficiently painful to deter crime by altering potential lawbreakers' perceptions that the benefits of crime outweigh its costs. However, Bentham also believed that punishments more severe than necessary to deter antisocial activity were irrational and barbaric. For Bentham, the certainty of punishment is more important than its severity.

Bentham was particularly active in the reform of English law and legal procedure. Like Blackstone (1723–1780), the historic codifier of English common law, Bentham believed in codification of the law. Unlike Blackstone, Bentham preferred to write his own code. He sharply criticized the common law, finding much of it lacking in rationality. He sought to demystify law by advocating a written code that would define crimes and punishments and be administered by judges on a nondiscretionary basis.

He also advocated reforms to make definite the civil law. For example, he proposed that the law of marriage be inscribed on the back of the marriage certificate. Many social and political reforms that he advocated, such as universal suffrage, the modification of laws affecting the poor to assure a minimal level of subsistence for all citizens, and his proposal to establish norms for the use of evidence in trials, have been influential in the modern development of English and American law.

In *Principles of International Law* (1798), Bentham wrote that universal peace could only be achieved by European unity, which would require a European Parliament, a free press, free trade, and abandonment of colonial empires. In one of his last major works, Bentham proposed the abolition of trade restrictions and universal suffrage, with women, as well as men, to be given the vote.

Bentham was a mentor to John Stuart Mill (1806–1873), who defended and expanded on Bentham's utilitarian ideas and became as widely recognized as his famous teacher. Due in large part to Mill, utilitarianism would become one of the major philosophical currents of the nineteenth century.

Jeremy Bentham died at age 84, but his writings have continued to influence economics, law, and public policy. As he directed in his last will and testament, Bentham's fully dressed body is preserved in University College, London, which he founded. His body is wheeled out for display on special occasions.

See also Blackstone, William; Common-Law Background of American Civil Rights and Liberties; International Law; Liberalism; Marriage, Rights Pertaining to; Press, Freedom of the

Bibliography

Atkinson, Charles Milner. 2004. *Jeremy Bentham: His Life and Work.* Honolulu, HI: University Press of the Pacific.

Hon. John M. Scheb

BENTON V. MARYLAND (1969). *See* Bill of Rights, Incorporation of; Double Jeopardy, Prohibition of

BIFURCATED TRIAL

A bifurcated trial is any trial, civil or criminal, in which some matter at issue is severed and tried in a separate subsequent proceeding. The most common examples are civil trials separated into a liability phase followed by a damages phase and criminal trials split into a guilt phase followed by a penalty phase. The jury may or may not be the same one for the two stages involved. The determination of when a bifurcated trial is appropriate is at the discretion of the trial court based on statutory requirements, a party's motion, or the court's own interest in fairness and efficiency.

In civil courts, bifurcation is widely used in divorce, patent infringement, products liability, and, increasingly, bankruptcy proceedings. The *Federal Rules of Civil Procedure* authorize use of bifurcated trials in Rule 42(b):

The court, in furtherance of convenience or to avoid prejudice, or when separate trials will be conducive to expedition and economy, may order a separate trial of any claim, cross-claim, counterclaim, or third-party claim, or of any separate issue or of any number of claims, cross-claims, counterclaims, third-party claims, or issues, always preserving inviolate the right of trial by jury as declared by the Seventh Amendment to the Constitution or as given by a statute of the United States.

The advantage is often a savings of time and money because if the party is not found liable in the first stage, damages-related witnesses and evidence need not be presented at all. Defense lawyers for corporate clients may prefer bifurcated proceedings because the size and wealth of the corporate defendant will be less likely to color the jury's decision as to the corporation's liability. So-called reverse bifurcation, in which the order of the two stages is reversed (i.e., from liability then damages, to damages first, then liability) is also becoming more common in civil litigation, particularly to help courts manage large numbers of product liability claims, such as those involving asbestos and fen-phen.

In criminal courts, a bifurcated trial is most common in cases with a potential death sentence and in cases in which the defendant pleads not guilty by reason of insanity, although some states routinely use bifurcation in noncapital, noninsanity criminal cases in order to facilitate jury-rendered sentencing determinations. When the U.S. Supreme Court upheld Georgia's death penalty statute in *Gregg v. Georgia* in 1976, it approved a system that featured a two-part guilt/penalty proceeding, which provided an individualized approach to each case. The Court ruled in *Lockett v. Ohio* (1978) that virtually any relevant "mitigating factors" may be presented in the penalty phase of the trial. Thus, during the sentencing portion of a capital case, the defense and prosecution are not bound by the rules of evidence, and information that could never be introduced during the guilt phase is now allowable. Mitigating factors evidence submitted by the defense can range from prenatal care of the defendant to family mental-health history, from defendant's school, military, and employment history to history of sexual, physical, and/or emotional abuse. Aggravating factors presented by the prosecution often include victim impact statements, nature and circumstances of the crime, past bad acts of the defendant, and expert witness predictions of "future dangerousness" of the defendant.

Bifurcated trials dealing with pleas of not guilty by reason of insanity similarly involve a first phase to prove the guilt of the defendant for the given act and a second phase to determine if the defendant meets the statutory requirements for a finding of insanity. While the intent is to avoid admission of potentially incriminating evidence regarding insanity into the case on the merits, such cases can be more complex than death-penalty sentencing questions of aggravating and mitigating factors because the requisite mens rea (culpable mental state) is a necessary element to proving criminal guilt and thus may be difficult or impossible to sever completely from the guilt stage of the trial.

Despite appearances, the Fifth Amendment protection against double jeopardy is not breached by a properly bifurcated trial because the issues in the two stages of the trial are two distinct matters, not a repeated prosecution for the same act by the defendant.

See also Death Penalty and the Supreme Court; Double Jeopardy, Prohibition of; Fifth Amendment; *Gregg v. Georgia;* Insanity Defense; Jury, Trial by; Sentencing, Eighth Amendment and; Seventh Amendment

Bibliography

Acker, James R., Robert M. Bohm, and Charles S. Lanier, eds. 2003. *America's Experiment with Capital Punishment: Reflections on the Past, Present, and Future of the Ultimate Penal Sanction.* 2nd ed. Durham, NC: Carolina Academic Press.

Wyrsch, James R. 2005. "Bifurcated Jury Trials in Non-Capital Criminal Cases." *Journal of the Missouri Bar* 61 (1): 39.

Julie A. Thomas

BILINGUAL EDUCATION

The United States has a long history of educating language-minority students. After the colonization of the Americas by the Europeans, a number of different languages were spoken in the United States. The maintenance of one's ancestral language and culture was important to many European immigrants, and as a result, many immigrant communities continued to use their native languages in various capacities, both in public and private schools. In fact, during the nineteenth century a number of states passed laws that authorized bilingual education (Ovando 2003, 4).

Even though the United States seemed to have adopted a rather tolerant view of bilingual education during the nineteenth century, the new waves of immigrants from Southern and Eastern Europe produced changes in popular attitudes toward languages other than English (Hasci 2002, 67). World War I, and the Red Scare that followed it, led to increased hostility against immigrants who were unwilling to assimilate into American culture, and many states implemented English-language requirements as a condition of voting and holding office (Leibowitz 1980, 8). Legislation that banned the use of any language other than English for teaching purposes was also common during this time period. By the end of World War I, 15 states had established English as the language for teaching

(Donegan 1996, 62). By 1923, 34 state legislatures had enacted English-only instruction in all private and public primary schools (Ovando 2003, 5).

Nebraska took this legislation a step further by prohibiting the teaching of any foreign languages in primary schools. However, in *Meyer v. Nebraska* (1923), the U.S. Supreme Court ruled that the Nebraska law violated the Fourteenth Amendment. In the Court's majority opinion, Justice James McReynolds stated, "[T]he protection of the Constitution extends to all, to those who speak other languages as well as to those born with English on the tongue."

The federal government did not begin addressing the situation of language-minority students until the 1960s. Until this point, states and individual school districts had jurisdiction over any services provided to this group of students. The Civil Rights Act of 1964, specifically Title VI, was the first federal legislation to provide the legal basis for language-minority students to argue for equal educational opportunity. Although the Civil Rights Act did not specifically address educational opportunity, it was applied to all programs receiving federal financial assistance. Thus, while language-minority students were not mentioned as a protected group, later court rulings would interpret the protection of persons based on national origin as applicable to language-minority students.

The first federal legislation to specifically address bilingual education was the Bilingual Education Act of 1968. The Civil Rights Movement had provided a new political context in which to advance the idea of improving educational opportunity for language-minority students. Although the legislation, when originally introduced, focused solely on Spanish-speaking students, a series of amendments altered the legislation to include all language-minority students. The Bilingual Education Act of 1968 provided financial assistance to local education agencies to design and implement bilingual programs to meet the needs of language-minority students. This act has been expanded and reauthorized several times since 1968, for example in 1984, 1988, and 1994.

As previously mentioned, the Civil Rights Act was applied to all programs receiving federal financial assistance, including education. Soon after its passage, the Department of Health, Education, and Welfare (HEW) began interpreting the implications of the Civil Rights Act for federally assisted educational programs. In 1968, HEW issued guidelines to school districts that interpreted the Civil Rights Act as meaning that federally assisted school systems must not deny students equal educational opportunity based on race, color, or national origin. Then, in 1970 an additional memorandum was issued to all school districts in which the population of national origin minority students exceeded five percent. The guidelines presented in this memorandum gave responsibility to the local school districts to correct any practices that were denying language-minority students an equal educational opportunity.

The landmark court case for language-minority students, *Lau v. Nichols* (1974), originated in San Francisco, California. The court action was filed by 13 non-English speaking Chinese students on behalf of the approximately 3,000 Chinese-speaking students in the San Francisco Unified School District. These students argued that due to their inability to understand the language of instruction, they were effectively being denied an education, which violated both the Equal Protection Clause of the Fourteenth Amendment and the Civil Rights Act. Both the U.S. District Court and the United States Circuit Court of Appeals for the Ninth Circuit ruled that the Civil Rights Act and Equal Protection Clause only required equal access to school facilities, not an opportunity to derive equal benefits. The case was then appealed to the U.S. Supreme Court. Although the Supreme Court did not validate the argument that the school district was in violation of the Equal Protection Clause, it ruled that the San Francisco Unified School District was in violation of the Civil Rights Act of 1964. Citing several relevant California codes and statutes that declare the mastery of English an educational goal and designate English as the basic level of instruction, in the Court's opinion,

Justice William O. Douglas stated that "[u]nder these state-imposed standards, there is no equality of treatment merely by providing students with the same facilities, textbooks, teachers, and curriculum; for students who do not understand English are effectively foreclosed from any meaningful education."

The Equal Educational Opportunities Act (EEOA) was passed only weeks after the decision in *Lau v. Nichols* and held that states could not deny equal educational opportunity to a student on the basis of national origin. However, neither *Lau v. Nichols* (1974) nor the EEOA outlined what actions school districts should take to provide language-minority students with equal educational opportunity. Further clarification of state and school district responsibilities came in later court cases and memoranda from HEW.

The first case to provide further explanation and guidance to educational agencies was *Serna v. Portales Municipal Schools* (1974), which required a school district to implement a system of bilingual instruction, hire bilingual school personnel, and revise testing procedures to assess the progress of language-minority students. In addition, a 1975 memorandum from HEW provided guidelines that outlined specific steps that school districts must take to ensure that language-minority students receive an adequate education. These guidelines became known as the Lau Remedies. While these guidelines were not actual laws and never became such, they were used to determine whether school districts were in compliance with Title VI of the Civil Rights Act.

Court cases involving the discrimination of language-minority students continued to arise throughout the 1980s. One of the most important of these cases was *Castaneda v. Pickard* (1981). The plaintiffs in this case were Mexican American children and their parents, who alleged that the Raymondville, Texas, Independent School District was "engaging in policies and practices of racial discrimination against Mexican Americans," which violated the Fourteenth Amendment, Title VI of the Civil Rights Act, the Equal Educational Opportunities Act, and several sections of the United States Code. The U.S.

Court of Appeals for the Fifth Circuit ruled in favor of the plaintiff. The most important impact of this case was the court's definition of the federal court's responsibility in cases such as these. The justices stated that the court is not responsible for recommending a particular educational theory. Instead, the court must simply determine if a theory that is supposed to address the situation of language-minority students is sound, whether a school's practices will allow the theory to be implemented effectively, and whether, once implemented, the theory actually increases students' English proficiency. This framework set an important legal precedent because it defined what steps a school district must take to serve language-minority students.

The most recent federal legislation affecting language-minority students is the No Child Left Behind Act of 2002. This legislation mandates that language-minority students be tested annually to measure English proficiency, and that language-minority students as a subgroup be required to show adequate yearly progress in all core subject areas. Under this legislation, states are given the flexibility to design their own programs to ensure that students attain English proficiency. These programs could include English-as-a-second-language instruction, bilingual education, or a number of other alternatives.

In conclusion, language-minority students have gained access to bilingual education as a result of federal legislation, including the Civil Rights Act, Bilingual Education Act, and the Equal Educational Opportunities Act, as well as judicial rulings, most notably *Lau v. Nichols*. While these measures have not forced school districts to implement bilingual education programs specifically, they have required school districts to provide services that will enable language-minority students to have equal educational opportunity. School districts have accomplished this through a number of methods, and many have chosen and continue to use bilingual education programs.

See also Civil Rights Act of 1964; Civil Rights Movement; Douglas, William O.; Fourteenth

Amendment; McReynolds, James Clark; *Meyer v. Nebraska;* Public Education, Right to

Bibliography

Donegan, Craig. 1996. "Debate Over Bilingualism." *CQ Researcher* 6:49–72.

Hasci, Timothy. 2002. *Children as Pawns: The Politics of Bilingual Education.* Cambridge, MA: Harvard University Press.

Leibowitz, Arnold. 1980. *The Bilingual Education Act: A Legislative Analysis.* Rosslyn, VA: InterAmerica Research Associates, National Clearinghouse for Bilingual Education.

Ovando, C. J. 2003. "Bilingual Education in the United States: Historical Development and Current Issues." *Bilingual Research Journal* 27 (1):1–24.

Sarah Keeton Campbell

BILL OF RIGHTS (AMERICAN, 1789)

Known collectively as the Bill of Rights, the first 10 amendments to the U.S. Constitution were adopted by the First Congress in 1789 and ratified by the states in 1791. Prior to the framing of the Bill of Rights, the Constitution contained few provisions explicitly recognizing or protecting the rights of individuals.

In *Federalist* No. 84, Alexander Hamilton argued that because the Constitution limited the powers of the newly created national government, no listing of rights was necessary. Thomas Jefferson, on the other hand, believed that an enumeration of rights was an essential element of a written charter for the new republic. In a letter to George Mason in 1787, Jefferson urged his fellow Virginian to draft a bill of rights, writing, "You must specify those liberties and put them down on paper!"

Although Hamilton's view prevailed at the Constitutional Convention of 1787, the omission of a bill of rights from the original Constitution was widely seen as a major flaw and nearly prevented the Constitution from being ratified. Ultimately, ratification would be achieved only through a gentleman's agreement in which the Federalists agreed to support the addition of a Bill of Rights to the Constitution after ratification.

Although Congress was under no legal compulsion to honor the gentlemen's agreement, most members of the First Congress in 1789 ultimately recognized that adding the Bill of Rights to the Constitution was desirable, either as an end in itself or as a means of engendering popular support for the new Constitution and government. Although expressing some initial reservations, James Madison emerged as the principal architect of the Bill of Rights in the House of Representatives. In a speech on the House floor in June 1789, Madison appealed to both the idealistic and pragmatic sentiments of his fellow members:

> It cannot be a secret to the gentlemen of this House that, not withstanding the ratification of this system of government, … there is a great number of our constituents who are dissatisfied with it, among whom are many respectable for their talents and patriotism and respectable for the jealousy they have for their liberty…. We ought not to disregard their inclination but, on principles of amity and moderation, conform to their wishes and expressly declare the great rights of mankind secured under this Constitution.

After considerable debate over Madison's proposals, Congress adopted 12 amendments in the fall of 1789 and submitted them to the states for ratification. Two of these amendments were rejected by the states, one prohibiting Congress from giving its members a pay increase that would go into effect before the next congressional election (the amendment was resurrected and finally ratified as the Twenty-seventh Amendment in 1992). The other 10 amendments were ratified in November 1791 and were added to the Constitution as the Bill of Rights.

The Bill of Rights begins with the First Amendment, which provides that "Congress shall make no law respecting an establishment of religion, or prohibiting the free exercise thereof; or abridging the freedom of speech, or of the press; or the right of the people peaceably to assemble, and to petition the Government for a redress of grievances." The phrase "Congress shall make no law" suggests that the First Amendment was intended to apply only to the national government. James Madison's original proposal called for limitations on the states as well as the federal government, but this idea was defeated by states' rights advocates in Congress. In *Barron v. Baltimore* (1833), the Supreme Court held that the entire Bill of Rights applied only to the national government. For protection from the actions of state and local governments, citizens would have to look to their state constitutions and state courts. However, 20th century judicial interpretation of the Fourteenth Amendment has resulted in the extension of most provisions of the Bill of Rights to limit actions of the state and local governments.

The First Amendment recognizes those rights that are generally considered to be essential to any democratic society—freedom of speech, freedom of the press, freedom of assembly, and the right to petition government for a redress of grievances. It also enshrines freedom of religion, long a fundamental value of American life, and protects that freedom both by guaranteeing the free exercise of religion and prohibiting the government from establishing religion.

The Second Amendment protects the "right to keep and bear arms" but also mentions the need for a "well regulated militia." Both of these phrases have figured prominently in a long-running national debate over the constitutionality of gun-control laws.

The Third Amendment provides that "[n]o Soldier shall, in time of peace be quartered in any house, without the consent of the Owner, nor in time of war, but in a manner to be prescribed by law." Reflecting a salient concern of the generation that experienced the Revolutionary War and the indignity of having British redcoats billeted in American homes, the Third Amendment has faded into relative obscurity.

In stark contrast to the Third Amendment, the Fourth Amendment, which prohibits unreasonable searches and seizures, remains a vital source of liberty and controversy, especially with regard to police efforts to ferret out crime. The protections of the Fourth Amendment have been sorely tested in recent years, as agencies at all levels of government have waged wars on illicit drugs and terrorism.

Like the Fourth Amendment, the Fifth Amendment contains important protections for persons accused or suspected of criminal wrongdoing. It provides, subject to narrow exceptions, that "[n]o person shall be held to answer for a capital, or otherwise infamous crime, unless on a presentment or indictment of a Grand Jury." The Amendment prohibits double jeopardy, or being "subject for the same offence to be twice put in jeopardy of life or limb." It also prohibits compulsory self-incrimination, that is, being "compelled in any criminal case to be a witness against" oneself. The Fifth Amendment also affords significant protection to private property rights by declaring "nor shall private property be taken for public use, without just compensation." Most fundamentally, though, the Amendment provides that no person shall "be deprived of life, liberty, or property, without due process of law." Its roots extending deep into the soil of Anglo-American law, the Due Process Clause requires that government observe appropriate legal standards and procedures in making decisions that adversely affect persons within its jurisdiction.

The Sixth Amendment deals exclusively with the rights of the criminally accused. It guarantees the right to "a speedy and public trial ... by an impartial jury," the right to "be informed of the nature and cause of the accusation," the right to confront the state's witnesses in court, the right to invoke the power of the court (compulsory process) to require the appearance of witnesses favorable to the defense, and the right "to have the Assistance of Counsel" for one's defense.

The Seventh Amendment guarantees the right to trial by jury in civil suits for damages. The Amendment was adopted by Congress with virtually no debate and did not generate any substantial controversy during the ratification process.

The Eighth Amendment prohibits excessive bail, excessive fines, and cruel and unusual punishments. Adopted primarily to outlaw torture, the Cruel and Unusual Punishments Clause has figured prominently in the long-running national debate over the death penalty.

The Ninth Amendment provides, "The enumeration in the Constitution, of certain rights, shall not be construed to deny or disparage others retained by the people." This language was included in the Bill of Rights to counter the argument that an enumeration of liberties might be seen as a complete catalog of freedoms warranting constitutional protection. While they have seldom relied solely on the Ninth Amendment, American courts have recognized a number of rights that Americans take for granted but are not specifically enumerated in the Constitution. The right to marry, to determine how one's children are to be reared, to choose one's occupation, to operate a business, and to travel freely within the country are all examples of rights that have been judicially recognized as "constitutional," despite the fact that they do not appear in the text of the Bill of Rights.

Finally, the Tenth Amendment provides that "powers not delegated to the United States by the Constitution, nor prohibited by it to the States, are reserved to the States respectively, or to the people." At first blush, the Tenth Amendment would appear to be of a very different character from the nine amendments that precede it in that those amendments deal explicitly with the rights of individuals while the Tenth Amendment recognizes the reserved powers of the states that comprise the Union. However, to the framers of the Bill of Rights, and in particular to the followers of Thomas Jefferson, states' rights and individual rights were closely linked. Jeffersonians believed that the federal government represented a greater threat to individual liberty than did the states, which were seen as closer to the people and therefore more subject to their control. Moreover, in the Jeffersonian view, the states were vulnerable to usurpation of their powers by the federal government and hence needed explicit constitutional protection.

Today, the Bill of Rights, in combination with the Fourteenth Amendment, remains the most important compendium of rights in American law. With few exceptions, the provisions of the Bill of Rights have generated substantial bodies of case law as the federal and state courts have sought to explicate the meanings of these provisions and apply them to the constantly changing controversies of the day. Writing for the Supreme Court in *West Virginia Board of Education v. Barnette* (1943), Justice Robert H. Jackson observed:

Without promise of a limiting Bill of Rights it is doubtful if our Constitution could have mustered enough strength to enable its ratification. To enforce those rights today is not to choose weak government over strong government. It is only to adhere as a means of strength to individual freedom of mind in preference to officially disciplined uniformity for which history indicates a disappointing and disastrous end.

See also *Barron v. Baltimore;* Bill of Rights, Incorporation of; Eighth Amendment; Fifth Amendment; First Amendment; Fourteenth Amendment; Fourth Amendment; Jackson, Robert H.; Jefferson, Thomas; Madison, James; Ninth Amendment; Second Amendment; Seventh Amendment; Sixth Amendment; Tenth Amendment; Third Amendment; *West Virginia Board of Education v. Barnette*

Bibliography

Amar, Akhil Reed. 2000. *The Bill of Rights: Creation and Reconstruction.* New Haven, CT: Yale University Press.

Hyneman, Charles S., and George W. Carey. 1967. *A Second Federalist: Congress Creates a Government.* New York: Appleton-Century-Crofts.

Levy, Leonard D. 1999. *Origins of the Bill of Rights.* New Haven, CT: Yale University Press.

Schwartz, Bernard. 1977. *The Great Rights of Mankind: A History of the American Bill of Rights.* New York: Oxford University Press.

John M. Scheb II and Otis H. Stephens, Jr.

BILL OF RIGHTS (ENGLISH, 1689)

The English Bill of Rights of 1689, also called the Declaration of Right, was a product of the Glorious, or Bloodless, Revolution of 1688 and marked a significant development in English constitutional history. William III's acceptance of the declaration and its passage by Parliament officially subjugated the English monarch to parliamentary law. In addition, the declaration contains some provisions protecting individual civil rights. Like Magna Carta, it remains one of the core documents of the English constitution.

The Glorious Revolution resulted from an intractable religious conflict between King James II and Parliament. The king had attempted to impose Catholicism on the now predominantly Protestant population and had, in doing so, claimed the right to nullify or suspend parliamentary legislation. Certain of widespread public support in England, William of Orange, the Dutch-born Protestant stadtholder of Holland, and a nephew and son-in-law of James, sailed to England in November 1688, intent on taking the crown. James initially attempted to resist, but his army fell apart, leaving him little choice but to flee to France.

For a few months England had no legal government. William took the helm of a provisional government and called for the election of members to an extraordinary congress that came to be known as the Convention Parliament. The problem of the vacant throne was not merely one of choosing a head of state: the traditional concept of the divine right of kings was in conflict with the nascent ideas of the superiority of Parliament, a contractual relationship between Parliament and the king, and the advisability of religious tolerance. In the end, the latter set of ideas won out in February 1689 when the Convention Parliament offered the throne to William and his English wife, Mary (James II's daughter), *after* having set out in the Declaration of Right what powers the new joint sovereigns were to enjoy.

The declaration, accepted by William and Mary, began with a list of James's abuses both against citizens and against Parliament and the law and declared illegal the suspension or invalidation by royal fiat of acts of Parliament, royal appropriation of money without parliamentary approval, the imprisonment of subjects as punishment for petitioning their government, and the maintenance of an army in peacetime without parliamentary approval.

The declaration further stated, among other things, that Protestants should have the right to bear arms; that parliamentary elections should be free; that members of Parliament should not be subject to questioning elsewhere for their statements in Parliament; that excessive bail, excessive fines, or cruel and unusual punishments should not be inflicted; and that Parliament should be held frequently. The Bill of Rights also provided for the succession of the crown in the Protestant line. After the accession of William and Mary to the throne, Parliament passed the declaration as law in October 1689.

The declaration described its own protections as covering merely "the true, ancient and indubitable rights and liberties of the people of this kingdom." The document's tone is therefore declaratory rather than inventive, and the traditional understanding of the document is that it reflected rather than changed the constitutional order. Whether or not this is accurate, it should be noted that William and Mary became sovereigns by legislative choice and were subsequently dependent on Parliament's patronage.

Both the structure and content of the English Bill of Rights somewhat foreshadow the American Declaration of Independence. Moreover, many of the provisions of the English Bill of Rights will sound familiar to students of the U.S. Constitution, including the establishment of free elections, the right to petition the government for redress of grievances, the investiture of the taxing and spending powers in the representative legislative body, the right to bear arms, the right to jury trial, the protection against excessive or cruel punishments. Some provisions of the American Bill of Rights were taken from or influenced by the Virginia Declaration of Rights of 1776 and other early state constitutional documents, the authors of which may have in turn borrowed from the English document.

The Supreme Court has not relied directly upon the English Bill of Rights in formulating statements about the rights of Americans but has referred to its history in explicating its interpretation of the provisions of the Eighth Amendment. For examples, see *Browning-Ferris Industries v. Kelco Disposal* (1989), which allowed large monetary damages in civil suits; *Gregg v. Georgia* (1976), which permitted capital punishment; and *United States v. Salerno* (1987), which interpreted the Excessive Bail Clause as not requiring bail in all cases.

See also Arms, Right to Keep and Bear; Bail, Right to; Bill of Rights (American); Catholicism and Anti-Catholicism; Common-Law Background of American Civil Rights and Liberties; Cruel and Unusual Punishments Clause; Death Penalty and the Supreme Court Declaration of Independence; Eighth Amendment; Excessive Bail, Prohibition of; Excessive Fines, Prohibition of; Free and Fair Elections; *Furman v. Georgia; Gregg v. Georgia;* Jury, Trial by; Petition, Right of

Bibliography

Hoak, Dale. 1996. "The Anglo-Dutch Revolution of 1688–89." In *The World of William and Mary: Anglo-Dutch Perspectives on the Revolution of 1688*, ed. Dale Hoak and Mordechai Feingold. Stanford, CA: Stanford University Press.

Ogg, David. 1973. "The Revolution as a Reinforcement of English Institutions." In *The Revolution of 1688 and the Birth of the English Political Nation*, ed. Gerald M. Straka. 2nd ed. Lexington, MA: D. C. Heath.

Smith, Goldwin. 1955. *A Constitutional and Legal History of England*. New York: Charles Scribner's Sons.

Rachel Pearsall

BILL OF RIGHTS, INCORPORATION OF

The political realities associated with the ratification of the Constitution defined the context leading to the adoption of the Bill of Rights. Those political realities were, and remain, embedded in the structure of federalism intrinsic to the American political system.

When the draft Constitution emerged from the Constitutional Convention, it was clear to the document's proponents that the probability of ratification was quite low. Much opposition stemmed from supporters of the Articles of Confederation, who saw in the new document a threat to state sovereignty. Opposition came, too, from those who were concerned that the proposed Constitution did not contain a Bill of Rights. This latter point was

especially problematic since declarations of rights were found in state constitutions, and opponents to the new national Constitution viewed with alarm the failure to include a Bill of Rights in a document that armed the central government with significantly more power than it had under the Articles of Confederation. States' rights advocates could draw little comfort anyway from the fact that attempts at the convention to include a Bill of Rights met with failure, and even Alexander Hamilton had argued in *Federalist* no. 84 that a Bill of Rights was both unnecessary and potentially counterproductive to the protection of the very liberties and rights that states' rights advocates had sought.

Against this backdrop, the draft Bill of Rights that James Madison introduced into the House of Representatives on June 8, 1789, were part of the political bargain struck between the largely Federalist proponents of the new Constitution and the anti-Federalists opposed to ratification. A Bill of Rights amending the Constitution would define the rights and liberties the opponents sought and would do so by ensuring certain boundaries around the powers of the new central government.

This history frames our understanding of *Barron v. Baltimore* (1833). In this landmark case, the Supreme Court ruled that it had no jurisdiction to hear John Barron's claim that Baltimore's action in making city improvements had interfered with his Fifth Amendment property rights, and specifically the prohibition that private property shall not be taken for public use without just compensation. According to Chief Justice John Marshall's opinion, both the history associated with Constitutional ratification and the language of the Bill of Rights clearly supported the principle that the amendments were intended to be a restriction only on the powers of the "general" government, not the states. Barron thus established the important precedent that the Bill of Rights only restricts the power of the national government, not the powers of the states.

There has been much debate, however, over whether the Fourteenth Amendment, ratified in 1868, was intended to alter, if not reverse, *Barron v. Baltimore,* thus making the Bill of Rights binding on state governments. Putting aside the merits of the alternative views of this history, two aspects of this debate remain clear. One is that the broad language of Section 1 of the Fourteenth Amendment explicitly restricts the powers of the states. The other is that, despite much debate over the scope of the amendment's restrictions, and the meaning of concepts such as privileges and immunities and due process, the Supreme Court has nevertheless drawn exceptions to the *Barron* doctrine by ruling in a series of decisions that many of the provisions of the Bill of Rights do restrict state action. In effect, while the Bill of Rights on their own accord still do not restrict the states, and to that extent *Barron v. Baltimore* remains a valid principle, most of the Bill of Rights have nevertheless been made binding on the states through an incremental process of incorporating them into the meaning of the liberty and due process concepts in the Fourteenth Amendment.

This evolution towards what later became known as the doctrine of selective incorporation began with a reaffirmation of *Barron* in the Slaughterhouse Cases of 1873, the first case in which the Supreme Court had an opportunity to interpret the new restrictions imposed on the states by the Fourteenth Amendment. In this ruling, the Court rejected the idea that the Fourteenth Amendment was designed to reverse *Barron* and in doing so adopted a narrow interpretation of the nature of the rights protected by the amendment's sweeping language. *Hurtado v. California* (1884), which raised the issue of whether the state had to follow the Fifth Amendment's grand jury provision when bringing indictments against criminal defendants, reaffirmed the conclusion reached in the Slaughterhouse Cases and did so despite a dissent by Justice John M. Harlan (the elder) in which he argued that the Fourteenth Amendment was intend to make all the provisions in Bill of Rights binding on the states as well as on the national government.

Thirteen years later, however, in *Chicago, Burlington and Quincy Railroad v. Chicago* (1897), the Court drew an exception to the general rule established in *Barron* when it ruled in an opinion written through Justice Harlan, who had crafted a theory of total incorporation in his *Hurtado* dissent, that the right to just compensation was an integral part of the liberty and property clauses of the Fourteenth Amendment and thus served to restrict the state in the same way that it restricted the national government.

Despite the *Chicago, Burlington and Quincy Railroad* precedent, the Court retreated to its more restrictive interpretation of the Fourteenth Amendment in *Maxwell v. Dow* (1900) concerning parallel issues raised in *Hurtado* and did so again in *Twining v. New Jersey* (1908), where it rejected the claim that the state had to abide by the Fifth Amendment self-incrimination protection afforded criminal defendants in federal courts. In each of these cases, the Court refused to extend Fifth and Sixth Amendment restrictions into the meaning of the Due Process Clause of the Fourteenth Amendment. In each case, too, Justice John Marshall Harlan was a sole dissenter arguing in favor of the doctrine of total incorporation, the theory that he had crafted in earlier in his *Hurtado* dissent.

Gitlow v. New York (1925) was the first in a series of decisions that established additional exceptions to the *Barron* principle. In *Gitlow*, the majority opinion stated that "we may and do assume that the freedom of speech and of the press—which are protected by the First Amendment from abridgement by Congress—are among the fundamental personal rights and 'liberties' protected by the due process clause of the Fourteenth Amendment from impairment by the states." That the freedom of the press was made binding on the states was confirmed in *Near v. Minnesota* (1931).

Powell v. Alabama (1932) made the Sixth Amendment right to counsel and fair trial provisions binding on the states when capital offences were involved, and *Hamilton v. Board of Regents of the University of California* (1934) made the First Amendment freedom of religion binding on the states. In 1937, *DeJonge v. Oregon* added the First Amendment freedom of assembly to the list of rights that restricted states through the language of the Fourteenth Amendment.

This evolution highlights the significance of *Palko v. Connecticut* (1937). *Palko* presented the issue of whether a criminal defendant in state court was entitled to the Fifth Amendment's protection against double jeopardy. The case also provided the Supreme Court with the opportunity to justify why certain of the provisions in the Bill of Rights, and not others, would limit the states. In rejecting Palko's appeal, the opinion of the Court ruled that only those provisions that were of the "very essence of a scheme of ordered liberty," those rights that were, in effect, fundamental to our system of justice, would be imposed on the states through the Fourteenth Amendment. In ruling that the Fifth Amendment double jeopardy provision did not meet this standard, *Palko* formalized what had been all along the de facto theory concerning the relationship among the Bill of Rights, the Fourteenth Amendment, and the states in our federal constitutional system. This formulation, the theory of selective incorporation, stated that certain rights, like those embodied in the First Amendment, reach a "different plane of social and moral value(s)," and as such required that states as well as the national government adhere to the limits that these rights impose.

Since 1937, the Court has moved far beyond the *Palko* ruling and has incorporated virtually all the provisions of the Bill of Rights into the Due Process Clause of the Fourteenth Amendment. In doing so, however, the justices have not been of one mind as to which theory would drive the process. A majority of the justices have adhered to the theory of selective incorporation that was formulated in *Palko*. Some justices have fine-tuned this approach by arguing that, while states are restricted by certain provisions of the Bill of Rights, they should have the flexibility in a federal system to determine how to administer these principles and not be obliged to follow all the details as they would be administered in federal jurisdictions.

As far back as Justice Harlan in the *Hurtado* case, some justices have adhered to the alternative theory of total incorporation. Justice Hugo Black was a twentieth-century advocate of that approach (e.g., his dissent in *Adamson v. California*, 1947).

Some justices have rejected the idea that the Bill of Rights imposes any restrictions on the states. This third theory, sometimes referred to as the case-by-case, fair trial, or due process approach, and advocated by Justices Felix Frankfurter and John M. Harlan (the younger), proposes that the Fourteenth Amendment did not alter the original understanding described in *Barron v. Baltimore* and that, in our federal system, the Fourteenth Amendment requires states to adhere to standards of due process that would be defined independent of the language in the Bill of Rights.

A fourth theory emerged in the case of *Griswold v. Connecticut* (1965). In *Griswold*, the Supreme Court found that the right of privacy, one not expressly provided for in the Bill of Rights but one implied by both the explicit rights and by the language of the Ninth Amendment, was binding on the states as well through the Fourteenth Amendment. This theory, described by some commentators as "incorporation plus," has two variations, one rooted in the theory of selective incorporation, the other founded upon the theory of total incorporation.

By 1972, the last time the Court made a provision of the Bill of Rights binding on the states (see *Argersinger v. Hamlin*, which incorporated the Sixth Amendment right to counsel in misdemeanor cases in cases where a jail sentence possible), only the Second, Third, and Seventh amendments, and the Fifth Amendment grand jury and the Eighth Amendment excessive bail and fine provisions, have not been incorporated into the meaning of the Fourteenth Amendment and thus made binding on the states.

See also Accused, Rights of the; Articles of Confederation; Assembly, Freedom of; *Barron v. Baltimore;* Bill of Rights (American); Black, Hugo L.; *Cantwell v. Connecticut; Chicago Burlington and Quincy Railroad v. Chicago;* Civil Rights Cases, The; Counsel, Right to; Double Jeopardy, Prohibition of; Due Process, Procedural; Due Process, Substantive; Due Process Clauses; *Duncan v. Louisiana;* Eighth Amendment; Establishment Clause; *Everson v. Board of Education;* Excessive Bail, Prohibition of; Excessive Fines,

Bibliography

Berger, Raoul. 1977. *Government By Judiciary: The Transformation of the Fourteenth Amendment.* Cambridge, MA: Harvard University Press.

Cortner, Richard C. 1981. *The Supreme Court and the Second Bill of Rights: The Fourteenth Amendment and the Nationalization of Civil Liberties.* Madison: University of Wisconsin Press.

Curtis, Michael Kent. 1990. *No State Shall Abridge: The Fourteenth Amendment and the Bill of Rights.* Durham, NC: Duke University Press.

Fairman, Charles. 1949. "Does the Fourteenth Amendment Incorporate the Bill of Rights? The Original Understanding." *Stanford Law Review* 2:5–139.

Burton Atkins

BILLS OF ATTAINDER

Article I, Section 9, Clause 3 of the United States Constitution prohibits Congress from enacting bills of attainder. Article I, Section 10, Clause 1 prohibits the enactment of bills of attainder by the states. The second prohibition is echoed in many state constitutions. Defending the proposed Constitution in *Federalist Paper* No. 84, Alexander Hamilton cited the provision on congressional bills of attainder, among others, as evidence that that document did include a bill of rights, contrary to the position of some of its most fervent opponents. The absence in the original Constitution of guarantees of such fundamental rights as the right to free exercise of religion and freedom of speech made Hamilton's argument unconvincing. Nevertheless, he did call attention to two provisions that were, at least potentially, important guarantees of civil rights.

In prohibiting bills of attainder, the framers of the Constitution were reacting to English common law, which allowed the enactment of such bills. A classic example is the bill of attainder authorizing the beheading of the Duke of Monmouth following his unsuccessful rebellion against King James II. English bills of attainder imposed death sentences and worked corruption of blood. That is, they denied inheritances to the survivors of anyone against whom they were directed. The term *attainder* evokes the "attaint" or stain attached to the survivors.

In *Cummings v. Missouri* and *Ex Parte Garland,* two leading cases decided on the same day in 1867, the U.S. Supreme Court differentiated the meaning of "bill of attainder" in the Constitution from its English precursors. Confining the meaning of bills of attainder to the English definition would have trivialized the significance of this specific constitutional limitation on national and state power. The Supreme Court broadened the definition by stating that "A bill of attainder is a legislative act, which inflicts punishment without a judicial trial" (*Cummings v. Missouri,* 71 U.S. 277, 323 [1867]). Under that definition, the punishment need not be death; in fact, it need not even be one that is traditionally reserved for criminals. The definition also makes clear the problems with bills of attainder. They are the fruit of political, not judicial, actions, and they are effected without traditional procedural protections. In sum, they are likely to be arbitrary and improperly motivated.

In other ways, too, the generality of the definition has caused considerable trouble for later courts. The main reason it does so is that it potentially covers a number of proper legislative functions such as the enactment of criminal laws, regulatory measures, and enacting laws that have only prospective application. Courts have dealt with that problem by devising a series of dichotomies that they have used to determine whether particular acts are bills of attainder. Among them are activity by a person or group, privilege or right, regulation or punishment, and prospective or retrospective. Finding that an act is described by the first member of the dichotomy that is used for the test usually leads to a finding that a bill is not a bill of attainder.

In *Nixon v. Administrator of General Services* (1966), the Court proposed a four-part test: (1) a traditional punishment–nontraditional punishment dichotomy, (2) an examination of the function of the punishment, (3) an analysis of Congress's motivation, and (4) a determination of the availability of less onerous alternatives.

Courts have fairly consistently held that bills of attainder have two other identifying marks. One is the designation of the persons to whom they apply. That causes a modicum of trouble because the designation can be implicit, and thus in question, as well as explicit. The other identifying characteristic is the lack of the safeguards that pertain in judicial proceedings, such as the right to the assistance of counsel. The latter characteristic is quite straightforward; for example, the record will show whether an affected party had counsel.

The availability of a fairly long list of dichotomies has scrambled the case law on bills of attainder. The inherent discomfort of courts in judging legislative procedures has also contributed to the confusion surrounding this topic. Finally, perhaps because these cases are highly politicized—due primarily to the nature of the victims targeted by bills of attainder—the reasoning in many of the cases is not convincing, and the results often seem unjust. Courts could minimize this problem by holding that the infliction of punishment by legislation in the absence of judicial proceedings constitutes a bill

of attainder if the punished action is characterized as political. Under this test, politically motivated legislative punishments would be presumptively unconstitutional. If this test had been followed in the past, a number of questionable judicial decisions might have been avoided. The prohibition of bills of attainder could thus have provided the broad protection of individual rights contemplated by the framers.

Bibliography

Rotunda, D. 2004. *Constitutional Law,* 7th ed. St. Paul, MN: Thomson West.

Jack Stark

BIVENS V. SIX UNKNOWN NAMED FEDERAL NARCOTICS AGENTS (1971)

In this landmark decision the Supreme Court held that a person whose rights under the Fourth Amendment are violated by a federal agent acting under color of his authority may bring a civil suit seeking monetary damages in federal court. This case stemmed from an illegal search and seizure conducted by six unknown federal narcotics agents on the morning of November 26, 1965. The agents, acting without a warrant, entered Bivens's apartment, arrested him, handcuffed him in front of his family, and proceeded to search the entire premises. Although no contraband was revealed by the search, Bivens was subsequently taken into custody, strip-searched, and interrogated. After a hearing on the matter, a federal judicial commissioner determined that there was no basis for the arrest and ordered that Bivens be released.

In 1967, Bivens brought a civil suit in the United States District Court for the Eastern District of New York, seeking $15,000 in damages from each of the unnamed defendants as compensation for Bivens's humiliation, embarrassment, and mental suffering. The district court dismissed the case on the grounds that it failed to state a cause of action, and the United States Court of Appeals for the Second Circuit affirmed on that basis. In 1970, the Supreme Court granted certiorari and in 1971 reversed the appellate court.

Although the Civil Rights Act of 1871, codified at 42 U.S. Code § 1983, created a federal cause of action in cases where persons acting under color of state law caused deprivations of a person's civil rights, that statute did not apply to constitutional torts committed by federal agents. Because there was no federal statute specifically authorizing suits in federal court to redress violations of constitutional rights perpetrated by federal agents, respondents in the *Bivens* case argued that a New York state court was the proper forum for this case. There, respondents argued, federal agents could be sued for the tort of invasion of privacy. In a seven-to-two decision reversing the court of appeals, the Supreme Court rejected these arguments and recognized a federal cause of action based on the Fourth Amendment. Because the court of appeals had not considered whether the agents were immune from liability because of their official position, the Court remanded the case to the Second Circuit to determine if the agents should be afforded immunity.

Speaking for the Court in *Bivens*, Justice William J. Brennan admitted that "the Fourth Amendment does not in so many words provide for its enforcement by an award of money damages for the consequences of its violation." However, quoting from the Court's decision in *Bell v. Hood* (1946), Brennan observed that "it is … well settled that where legal rights have been invaded, … federal courts may use any available remedy to make good the wrong done."

In dissent, Chief Justice Warren E. Burger chastised the Court for inventing "a damage remedy not provided for by the Constitution and not enacted by Congress." Today the *Bivens* holding is well established in constitutional law, and federal courts have applied the *Bivens* rationale to various other protections under the U.S. Constitution.

See also Brennan, William J., Jr.; Burger, Warren E.; Civil Rights Act of 1871; Fourth Amendment; Privacy, Invasion of; Search Warrants

John M. Scheb II and Otis H. Stephens, Jr.

BLACK, HUGO L. (1886–1971)

An associate justice of the United States Supreme Court for 34 years (1937–1971), and a U.S. senator before that, Hugo LaFayette Black was something of a maverick in both bodies. During the better part of his tenure on the Court, he was a vigorous defender of civil liberties. In some cases, however, he parted company with the civil libertarians and manifested a certain populism.

Black's concern for the underdog reflected his own life experiences. The youngest of the eight children of Martha and William LaFayette Black, he was born February 27, 1886, in Clay County in eastern Alabama. His father ran a general store and was also a farmer. The Blacks moved to Ashland, the county seat, and young Hugo was attracted to the courthouse and the trials held there. When he was older, he began the study of medicine to please his mother but disliked it and turned to the study of law at the University of Alabama Law School. With only two professors, it was far from the cutting edge of legal education.

Because there was insufficient legal business in Ashland, Black eventually opened a law office in Birmingham. He successfully represented many black clients. In 1914, he was elected county solicitor. In that position, he exposed and ended a brutal system in which criminal suspects were beaten with the buckle end of a belt until they confessed. Although Black was beyond draft age, he volunteered for service in the army during World War I. He was discharged with the rank of captain but never left the United States. He returned to private practice in Birmingham, representing mostly mine and factory workers. Black did well professionally but was not a part of the local establishment. In 1923, he joined the Ku Klux Klan, at that time a powerful political force in Alabama.

Black ran for the United States Senate in 1926. He appealed to the dry Protestant voters of Alabama, pitching his campaign to the "common man." The Klan, as well as the Women's Christian Temperance Union and organized labor, supported his candidacy. Black won the Democratic primary, the only race that mattered in the one-party South. A few weeks later, he attended a Klan rally and thanked them for their support. After that, he never again had any contact with the Klan.

Senator Black's first term was fairly uneventful. His second term, with Franklin D. Roosevelt in the White House, was quite different. He supported most of Roosevelt's New Deal, although he opposed the National Industrial Recovery Act, a key element of the program, calling it unconstitutional. He also supported Roosevelt's so-called Court-packing plan. In 1937, Roosevelt nominated Black to fill the first Supreme Court vacancy of his administration. When the issue of Klan membership arose, Black acknowledged his past membership but said that he had resigned before entering the Senate. He was confirmed. Once on the Court, Justice Black settled into his new role and in time became a defender of civil liberties.

Black's changing approach to civil liberties can be seen in his votes in the flag salute cases that pitted Jehovah's Witnesses against local school officials and wartime expressions of patriotism. In *Minersville School District v. Gobitis* (1940), Black joined the majority, sustaining the authority of school officials to require Jehovah's Witness children to participate in the daily salute of the American flag, although it violated their religious convictions. In *West Virginia State Board of Education v. Barnette* (1943), Black, having changed his mind, was part of the majority that overruled *Gobitis*.

Japanese Americans did not fare as well with Justice Black. He wrote the majority opinion in *Korematsu v. United States* (1944), upholding the exclusion of persons of Japanese ancestry from the West Coast. He stated that the Court lacked the expertise to second-guess the decision of military authorities that this action was necessary to maintain national security. Black never expressed any regrets about this decision.

An important aspect of Justice Black's judicial philosophy centered on the relationship of the Bill of Rights to the states. During his first year on the Court, he joined the majority opinion in *Palko v. Connecticut* (1937) that held that the Due Process Clause of the Fourteenth Amendment made binding on the states only those rights in the Bill of Rights that were implicit in the concept of ordered liberty. Ten years later, however, in *Adamson v.*

California (1947), Justice Black wrote a dissent in which he stated that his study of the history of the Fourteenth Amendment convinced him that the Due Process Clause was intended to incorporate all the guarantees of the Bill of Rights and make them binding on the states. Other justices did not adopt Black's approach but often reached the same result as he in specific cases. As a result, Black had the satisfaction of writing the majority opinion in *Gideon v. Wainwright* (1963), which required the states to fully incorporate the Sixth Amendment right to counsel by providing indigent defendants with lawyers in felony cases.

Justice Black's successful defense of the rights of his African American clients when he was a young lawyer suggests that he did not share the racial views of the Klan even in those days. In 1939, he was the only Supreme Court justice to attend Marian Anderson's concert at the Lincoln Memorial after the Daughters of the American Revolution had barred her from Constitution Hall because of her race. He supported *Brown v. Board of Education* (1954), as did every other member of the Court.

During the 1960s, Justice Black refused to support the expansion of civil rights and liberties beyond traditional constitutional parameters. He dissented in *Griswold v. Connecticut* (1965), where the Court first recognized a constitutional right of privacy. He also dissented in *Tinker v. Des Moines School District* (1969), where the Court recognized the right of public school students to engage in symbolic speech in protesting the Vietnam War. Yet throughout his tenure on the Court Black continued to be a strong advocate for First Amendment rights, for the rights of the accused, for racial equality, and for the full application of the Bill of Rights to the states.

Perhaps the most memorable opinion from Justice Black's latter years on the Court was his concurrence in *New York Times v. United States* (1971), where the Court invalidated an attempt by the Nixon Administration to enjoin publication of the infamous Pentagon Papers. In that landmark victory for freedom of the press, Justice Black wrote:

In the First Amendment the Founding Fathers gave the free press the protection it must have to fulfill its essential role in our democracy. The press was to serve the governed, not the governors. The Government's power to censor the press was abolished so that the press would remain forever free to censure the Government. The press was protected so that it could bare the secrets of government and inform the people. Only a free and unrestrained press can effectively expose deception in government. And paramount among the responsibilities of a free press is the duty to prevent any part of the government from deceiving the people and sending them off to distant lands to die of foreign fevers and foreign shot and shell.

Hugo L. Black retired from the Supreme Court in ill health on September 17, 1971, and died eight days later. Without question, he was among the most important figures on the Court during the twentieth century.

See also Accused, Rights of the; Bill of Rights, Incorporation of; Blackmun, Harry A.; *Brown v. Board of Education;* Clear and Probable Danger Doctrine; Counsel, Right to; Due Process, Substantive; Due Process Clauses; Equal Protection Jurisprudence; Establishment Clause; Excessive Fines, Prohibition of; First Amendment, Approaches to; Flag Salute Controversy; Fourteenth Amendment; *Gideon v. Wainwright; Griswold v. Connecticut;* Interrogation and Confessions; Japanese Americans, Relocation of; *Korematsu v. United States;* Ku Klux Klan; Living Constitution; New Deal; *New York Times v. United States; Palko v. Connecticut;* Privacy, Constitutional Right of; Religion, Official Endorsements of; Roosevelt, Franklin D.; School Prayer Decisions; Separation of Church and State; Sixth Amendment; *Tinker v. Des Moines Independent Community School District;*; Warren Court; *West Virginia Board of Education v. Barnette;* White Primary

Bibliography

Ball, Howard. 1975. *The Vision and the Dream of Justice Hugo L. Black.* Tuscaloosa: University of Alabama Press.

Dunne, Gerald T. 1977. *Hugo Black and the Judicial Revolution.* New York: Simon & Schuster.

Mendelson, Wallace. 1961. *Justices Black and Frankfurter: Conflict in the Court.* Chicago: University of Chicago Press.

Simon, James F. 1989. *The Antagonists: Hugo Black, Felix Frankfurter and Civil Liberties in Modern America.* New York: Simon & Schuster.

Patricia A. Behlar

BLACK CODES

"Black Codes" refers to a group of laws passed in Southern American states and municipalities shortly after the end of the Civil War. Enacted ostensibly to provide for the legal protection of the newly freed former slaves, these laws actually provided for serious deprivations of basic rights, including property rights, contractual rights, the right to keep and bear arms, and the right to move about freely. The Black Codes were passed fairly quickly after the Civil War, most in 1865 and a few following in 1866, by white legislatures. The ideological foundation for the codes arose largely out of deeply held racist beliefs, namely that blacks are lazy and will not work without physical compulsion, that they cannot care for their own children without help, that they lack sexual self-control, and that they are predisposed to commit crimes.

Mississippi's Black Code declared that blacks may only own land in cities, which "shall control same." It even required a black person to obtain a license from a town mayor to live there. Freedmen were required to provide written documentation of a home and of employment. Any employment of longer duration than one month was required to be based on an annual contract. Blacks who left jobs without permission from their employers could be forcibly returned for a bounty. Any person who assisted such a "deserter," even with the gift of a meal, was guilty of a misdemeanor.

South Carolina's Black Codes went so far as to legislate the "predestination" of black persons for agricultural work exclusively, and it imposed annual fees for any person of color working in any other industry. Texas law declared court-imposed penal labor to be contractual employment. Employers under this system held complete control over their black workers due to laws that required that a black worker receive *his employer's* permission before having guests, bartering anything, or even walking down the city street.

The Black Codes enacted by Mississippi and Louisiana required civil officers to report the names of any black children who were orphans or whose parents could not or would not care for them. The clerk of the probate court then had the duty to place these children in apprenticeships, giving preference to any individual's former owner. The Mississippi law expressly allowed masters to mete out "moderate corporeal punishment" as long as apprentices were not mistreated.

Harshest of all were the Black Code provisions regarding "vagrants." Vagrants were usually defined as any unemployed person of color or any person of color who "misspent" his or her wages or time. Thus was unemployment criminalized by the Black Codes. The punishment, not surprisingly, was forcible hire at the discretion of a judge or mayor. Mississippi also included in the definition of vagrant any white person who associated with "freedmen, Free Negroes or mulattoes, or usually associating with freedmen, free Negroes or mulattoes, on terms of equality." Alabama even included "stubborn" children in its definition of vagrants.

These harsh provisions not only subjugated former slaves but in many cases actually reduced the liberties enjoyed by free blacks in antebellum society. Thus were blacks who had previously been free and independent made more like slaves after Emancipation than before it.

The federal government sent mixed messages regarding the possible role of the newly freed citizenry in American life. In 1865, Congress passed legislation establishing the Bureau of Refugees, Freedmen, and Abandoned Lands to promote the peaceful resettlement of freed slaves. The Bureau reported to Congress about the status of blacks and racial outrages. Although the Freedmen's Bureau is sometimes credited with countermanding some of the Black Codes, it also shared the agenda of keeping peace by compelling blacks into agricultural labor. A Freedmen's Bureau circular of 1866

passed around Savannah, Georgia, contained the admonition:

To all idle and dissolute Freedmen:
You are hereby kindly exhorted to go to work at once and make contracts for the year.... We do not wish to resort to extreme measures, but we warn you that unless you procure some useful employment within three days from this date, you will promptly be arrested and proceeded against as vagrants: the chain gang will be your inevitable fate.

The Civil Rights Act of 1866 made it a federal crime to deprive a person of color born in the United States of the rights of full citizenship. Both this legislation and the Fourteenth Amendment made civil rights the responsibility of the federal government. Reconstruction saw the repeal of most Black Codes. However, the Black Codes' cousin, the Jim Crow laws, would come into being and remain in effect for almost another century.

See also Civil Rights Act of 1866; Equal Protection Clause; Fourteenth Amendment; Jim Crow Laws; Liberty; Property Rights; Radical Republicans; Reconstruction; Slavery; Thirteenth Amendment

Bibliography

Levine, Michael L. 1996. *African Americans and Civil Rights: From 1619 to the Present.* Phoenix, AZ: Oryx Press.

Wilson, Theodore Bratner. 1965. *The Black Codes of the South.* Tuscaloosa: University of Alabama Press.

Otis H. Stephens Jr. and Rachel Pearsall

BLACKMUN, HARRY A. (1908–1999)

In the wake of controversial decisions regarding rights of the accused during the Warren Court era, President Richard Nixon pledged to appoint "strict constructionists who saw their duty as interpreting law and not making law ... not super-legislators with a free hand to impose their social and political viewpoints upon the American people" (*New York Times,* November 3, 1968). When Earl Warren retired in 1969, Nixon's first appointment to the Supreme Court was Warren Burger. After losing confirmation battles over Clement Haynesworth and G. Harrold Carswell (Grossman and Wasby 1972), Nixon appointed Burger's childhood friend Harry A. Blackmun. Initially, Nixon could not have been happier with his selection. Blackmun's close voting attachment to Chief Justice Burger led him to be tagged in the press with nicknames such as "Minnesota Twin" and "hip-pocket Harry." However, the subsequent development of Blackmun's judicial philosophy saw him drift away from the views of his appointing president and long-time friend. Although largely toeing the line in criminal cases (Wasby 1988), Blackmun's legacy is most strongly felt in the expansion of the constitutional right to privacy. Forged in "the crucible of litigation," his understanding of this right also led him to greater appreciation of other civil liberties and rights claims over his tenure.

Harry Blackmun was born on November 12, 1908, in Nashville, Illinois, however, he spent most of his childhood in St. Paul, Minnesota. Blackmun was reared in a devout Methodist home and "was a quiet, serious, hardworking youth and diligent scholar" (Yarbrough 2000, 83). He earned an undergraduate degree in mathematics in 1929 and a law degree in 1932, both from Harvard University. After graduating from law school, he clerked for Judge Sanborn on the Eighth Circuit Court of Appeals. In 1934, he was hired by a firm in Minneapolis, where he specialized in tax law and estate planning. In 1950, Blackmun moved his family to Rochester, Minnesota, when he was hired as resident counsel at the Mayo Clinic. President Dwight Eisenhower appointed Blackmun to Sanborn's seat on the Eighth Circuit Court in 1959. His voting record on that court "was moderately liberal on racial civil rights issues, moderately conservative in most other civil liberties litigation, and distinctly pro-government in cases involving the claims of criminal suspects and defendants" (Yarbrough 2000, 85). He was Nixon's third nominee to fill the seat vacated by Abe Fortas and referred to himself as the "old number three" (MacKenzie 1975, 8).

Blackmun is perhaps best known for his authorship of *Roe v. Wade* (1973), in which the Court held that the right to privacy was broad enough to encompass a woman's decision to terminate her pregnancy. Blackmun once quipped that "I suppose that I'll carry *Roe* to my grave" (Jenkins 1983, 26). He was a watchful steward of that right as it came under increasing political attack during the 1980s and 1990s. Any threat to its scope was greeted by sharp rhetoric uncommon in his writings in other areas. When the Court refused to require Medicaid payment for abortions, he snapped that "the condescension that she may go elsewhere [is] disingenuous and alarming, almost reminiscent of: 'Let them eat cake'" (*Beal v. Doe*, 1977). When the Court seemed one vote away from overturning *Roe* in *Webster v. Reproductive Health Services* (1989), he warned that "a chill wind blows." He was a part of the majority that sheltered the right from the wind in *Planned Parenthood v. Casey* (1992), in which the Court reaffirmed the central holding of *Roe* but also allowed increased state limitations on abortion. In his separate opinion in *Casey*, Blackmun wrote that, "I remain steadfast in my belief that the right to reproductive choice is entitled to the full protection by the Court before *Webster*. And I fear for the darkness as four Justices anxiously await the single vote necessary to extinguish the light."

Blackmun's view of privacy evolved to extend beyond procreative concerns. His dissent in *Bowers v. Hardwick* (1986), in which the Court upheld a criminal sodomy statute applied to homosexuals, stated that constitutional protection extended to "the [people's] right to choose for themselves how to conduct their intimate relationships." He concluded by writing that "I can only hope that … the Court soon will reconsider its analysis." This hope was realized only after his death in *Lawrence v. Texas* (2003).

Privacy cases initiated an evolving "rights consciousness" in other areas of Blackmun's jurisprudence. Prompted by his parentage of modern commercial speech doctrine (*Bigelow v. Virginia*, 1975—significantly, a case dealing with restrictions on advertising abortion services), he moved from contending that "the First Amendment is, after all, only one part of an entire Constitution" (*United States v. New York Times*, 1971) to voting that flag burning was protected speech in *Texas v. Johnson* (1989). In equality cases, he authored the opinion that extended constitutional equal protection to aliens (*Graham v. Richardson,* 1971), was a strong proponent of affirmative action programs (*Regents of the University of California v. Bakke,* 1978), and looked askance at discrimination against women (*UAW v. Johnson Controls,* 1991). A moderate disciple of stare decisis on questions of religious freedom, he strove to maintain a strict rendering of the *Lemon v. Kurtzman* (1971) test and the "wall of separation" it envisioned (e.g., *Committee for Public Education v. Regan,* 1980; *Mueller v. Allen,* 1983; *Allegheny County v. ACLU,* 1989). Again, precedent governed his votes in free exercise cases as he always, and increasingly unsuccessfully, fought to require government to have a "compelling state interest" before it limited religious practice in any form (*Goldman v. Weinberger,* 1986; *Lyng v. Northwest Indian Cemetery Association,* 1988; *Employment Division, Department of Human Resources of Oregon v. Smith,* 1990). With the Republican appointees of the 1980s, his attachment to precedent in these cases increasingly put him in dissent.

In his last year on the Court, Blackmun recanted his position that capital punishment was constitutional. Moved by an increasingly acute perception of racial disparity in capital sentencing in cases such as *McCleskey v. Kemp* (1987), Blackmun announced that "I no longer shall tinker with the machinery of death" (*Callins v. James,* 1994). On this, though, he was a lone voice, as years of Republican appointments to the Court stripped away any support he may once have garnered on this issue.

Harry Blackmun's evolution from a "White Anglo-Saxon Protestant Republican Rotarian Harvard Man from the Suburbs" (Walz 1970, 61) to one of his Court's strongest defenders of individual rights confounded the intent of President Richard Nixon to dramatically alter the course of constitutional interpretation and helped to bolster a variant of Warren-style jurisprudential liberalism that fueled battles in the political arena well into the twenty-first century. Not only did this disappoint the

president who appointed him, but it cost him the extraordinarily close 60-year friendship he had previously enjoyed with the man who helped bring him to the Court, Warren E. Burger.

See also Abortion, Right to; Burger Court; Burger, Warren E.; Death Penalty and the Supreme Court; *Employment Division, Department of Human Resources of Oregon v. Smith* (1990); Free Exercise Clause; *Lawrence v. Texas;* Privacy, Constitutional Right of; Religion, Freedom of; *Roe v. Wade;* Sexual Orientation, Discrimination Based on; Warren Court; Warren, Earl

Bibliography

Grossman, Joel, and Stephen L. Wasby. 1972. "The Senate and Supreme Court Nominations: Some Reflections." *Duke Law Journal* 21: 557–91.

Jenkins, John A. 1983. "A Candid Talk with Justice Blackmun." *New York Times Magazine,* 26 February.

MacKenzie, John P. 1975. "Blackmun Charts Own Course." *Washington Post,* 13 July.

Waltz, Jon R. 1970. "The Burger Court." *New York Times Magazine,* 6 December.

Wasby, Stephen L. 1988. "Justice Harry A. Blackmun in the Burger Court." *Hamline Law Review* 11:183–245.

Yarbrough, Tinsley E. 2000. *The Burger Court: Justices, Rulings, and Legacy.* Santa Barbara, CA: ABC-Clio.

Joseph F. Kobylka

BLACK PANTHER PARTY. *See* Student Nonviolent Coordinating Committee

BLACK POWER. *See* Student Nonviolent Coordinating Committee

BLACKSTONE, WILLIAM (1723–1780)

Sir William Blackstone, a noted English legal scholar, jurist, and author, was born in London and educated at Oxford University. In 1741, he entered the Middle Temple Inn of Court, and in 1746 he was called to the bar. He did not achieve great success in the practice of law, so he left it to devote his talents to teaching. In 1758, he became a professor of law at Oxford University. Blackstone inaugurated courses in the English common law at a time when legal studies focused on Roman law. Unlike the Roman law, the English common law was unwritten law based on decisions of judges. It developed throughout England over the centuries. It began to flourish after 1215, when King John signed the Magna Carta, a document that was later to influence not only English jurisprudence but also the development of the Bill of Rights to the American Constitution. By Blackstone's time the English common law, which consisted of judicial precedents, had developed into a viable legal system. Access to the law was unavailable to laypersons, who employed barristers and solicitors to "find the law" and to render legal advice.

Blackstone believed the law should be available to everyone in readable written form. To this end he embarked on an ambitious project to restate the principles of the common law. His *Commentaries on the Laws of England,* based largely on his lectures, was published in 1765 and in later editions. Blackstone was not a philosopher of the law, but he was a scholar who possessed a marvelous capacity to organize and categorize. While Sir Henry de Bracton compiled early common-law decisions in the thirteenth century, and Sir Edward Coke, a distinguished English jurist, authored a series of *Institutes* describing property and criminal law, jurisdiction, and commentaries on the Magna Carta in 1628, Blackstone's *Commentaries* represented the first true codification of the English common law.

Blackstone's treatise made the principles of the common law accessible to laypersons, an accomplishment not universally popular with members of the English legal profession, who for centuries had prided themselves on their ability to "discover the law" by tedious research of judicial decisions. He was, however, regarded as a distinguished jurist and author in England, and in his latter years he became a judge of the common pleas courts.

In America the colonists basically followed the English common law; however, the new America did not have the institutional structure of the English legal system. Lawyers in America were quick to rely on Blackstone's *Commentaries,* which became

somewhat of a legal Bible for lawyers and judges in America. Blackstone became a popular figure in the American legal community. New American states often enacted "reception statutes," which adopted the English common law as it existed prior to July 4, 1776, to the extent it was not in conflict with the United States Constitution, the state constitution, and subsequent legislative enactments. Blackstone's *Commentaries* became an excellent source of the common law, was used to teach law, and provided a framework for development of the American common law.

Throughout its history the United States Supreme Court has frequently cited Blackstone in cases involving civil rights and liberties. For example, in *Near v. Minnesota ex rel. Olson* (1931), a landmark First Amendment decision, the Court quoted Blackstone on the meaning of freedom of the press under English common law: "The liberty of the press is indeed essential to the nature of a free state; but this consists in laying no previous restraints upon publications, and not in freedom from censure for criminal matter when published. Every freeman has an undoubted right to lay what sentiments he pleases before the public; to forbid this, is to destroy the freedom of the press; but if he publishes what is improper, mischievous or illegal, he must take the consequence of his own temerity." In *Near,* the Court held that the First Amendment incorporated the freedom against "previous restraints upon publications," as recognized by Blackstone.

Hon. John M. Scheb

BLUE LAWS. *See* Sunday Closing Laws

BOB JONES UNIVERSITY V. UNITED STATES (1983)

Founded in 1927, Bob Jones University (BJU) in Greenville, South Carolina, is the largest private liberal arts college in that state. BJU is a conservative Christian institution committed to evangelism, fundamentalism, and separation from the perceived corruption of modern society. Its mission statement proclaims that "[w]ithin the cultural and academic soil of liberal arts education, Bob Jones University exists to grow Christlike character that is Scripturally disciplined; others-serving; God-loving; Christ-proclaiming; and focused above."

The founder of the institution, Bob Jones, Sr., believed that the Bible forbids mixing of the races and strongly supported the regime of segregation in the American South. Thus, prior to 1971, BJU refused altogether to admit African Americans as students. Between 1971 and 1975, the university accepted applications from blacks as long as they were married within their own race, but it continued to deny admission to unmarried African Americans. After the U.S. Supreme Court's 1975 decision in *Runyon v. McCrary,* which prohibited racial exclusion from private schools, BJU changed its admissions policies again. Unmarried black students were permitted to enter the university, but interracial dating and marriage were strictly prohibited.

Like most other private colleges, BJU enjoyed tax-exempt status under 26 U.S.C.A. § 501(c)(3). The statute provided tax-exempt status for not-for-profit corporations "organized and operated exclusively for religious, charitable, scientific, testing for public safety, literary, or educational purposes, or to foster national or international amateur sports competition, … or for the prevention of cruelty to children or animals."

In 1970 the Internal Revenue Service (IRS) determined, based on considerations of national policy, that private schools with racially discriminatory policies toward their students were not "charitable" institutions and therefore would no longer be eligible for tax-exempt status. In 1976 the IRS revoked BJU's federal tax exemption. Not surprisingly, BJU decided to challenge the IRS in federal court. Without question, the IRS's action was consistent with the thrust of national policy on racial discrimination, but was it consistent with the language of the relevant statute? A strict reading of § 501(c)(3) would suggest otherwise. Even granting the validity of the IRS's definition of the term "charitable," the statute granted tax exemption to "religious, charitable … *or* educational" organizations (emphasis added). Under

a strict reading of the statute, an organization had to be "religious," "charitable" or "educational," but not necessarily all three. Lawyers for BJU pressed that argument in federal district court and prevailed—the court ruled that revocation of BJU's tax exemption exceeded the delegated powers of the IRS. The Fourth Circuit Court of Appeals in Richmond reversed, and BJU asked the Supreme Court to grant certiorari.

In *Bob Jones University v. United States* (1983), the Supreme Court upheld the IRS's action. In his opinion for the Court, Chief Justice Warren E. Burger glossed over the question of statutory interpretation, stressing instead the "broad authority" that Congress has invested in the IRS. Burger noted that Congress, had it disagreed with the IRS's interpretation, could have rewritten the statute to make its intentions perfectly clear. During the 13 years from the time that the IRS changed its policy to the time the Supreme Court decided the case, Congress did not act, suggesting that it acquiesced in the IRS's action. In his lone dissent, Justice William Rehnquist argued that this sort of policy change should emanate from Congress, not from the bureaucracy. In his view, the IRS had simply taken it upon itself to rewrite the law.

Bob Jones University also claimed that even if the IRS's action was valid with respect to nonreligious private schools, it could not constitutionally be applied to schools that engage in racial discrimination on the basis of religious beliefs. The Court recognized that the Free Exercise Clause of the First Amendment "provides substantial protection for lawful conduct grounded in religious belief" but also noted that government "may justify a limitation on religious liberty by showing that it is essential to accomplish an overriding governmental interest." The Court concluded that "the Government has a fundamental, overriding interest in eradicating racial discrimination in education" and that interest "substantially outweighs whatever burden denial of tax benefits places on petitioners' exercise of their religious beliefs."

The upshot of the *Bob Jones* decision was to strengthen the national commitment to eliminate racial discrimination by nongovernmental actors. Some would argue that in the case of Bob Jones University this effect was realized at the expense of religious freedom. BJU lifted its ban on interracial dating in 2000 but did not seek restoration of its federal tax exemption.

See also Free Exercise Clause; Internal Revenue Service; Religious Right; Tax Exemptions for Religious Organizations

Bibliography

Dalhouse, Mark Taylor. 1996. *An Island in the Lake of Fire: Bob Jones University, Fundamentalism, and the Separatist Movement.* Athens: University of Georgia Press.

Turner, Daniel L. 1997. *Standing without Apology: The History of Bob Jones University.* Greenville, SC: Bob Jones University Press.

John M. Scheb II and Otis H. Stephens, Jr.

BOND, JULIAN. *See* Student Nonviolent Coordinating Committee

BORDER PATROL

In 1904, the United States Immigration Service employed 75 guards to patrol the southern borders of the United States in one of its earliest attempts to prevent illegal immigration. Congress increased the number of regular officers on border patrol in 1915 by authorizing the Mounted Guard. But because this group of patrolmen was also responsible for the staffing of inspection stations, they were not always available to patrol the larger border. Without effective patrol of the areas between inspection stations, efforts to effectively control illegal immigration were sporadic at best.

When legal immigration by people of certain races was restricted with the adoption of the 1921 and 1924 Immigration Acts, illegal immigration attempts increased dramatically. Government renewed its interest in border enforcement. In an attempt to address growing border concerns and the rising number of illegal crossings, the Congress created the United States Border Patrol in 1924, charging 450 officers with the responsibility of combating illegal immigration and the illegal importation of goods, and securing the borders between inspection stations. In 1925, these responsibilities were expanded to include the coastline of the United States. The border patrol was divided into two jurisdictions in 1932. One jurisdiction was responsible for the U.S.-Canadian border. The other was in charge of the U.S.-Mexico border.

The immigration service, and thus the border patrol, was moved into the Department of Justice in 1940. As a result of the move, additional agents and personnel were assigned to the border patrol. By the end of World War II, it is estimated that more than 1,400 law enforcement agents and civilians worked in the border patrol agency.

In the 1950s, the number of illegal immigrants was growing at an alarming rate, especially along the Mexican border. Groups in affected areas complained that immigrants were responsible for violent crime and drug trafficking. In response to the growing number of complaints, the border patrol relocated units from the Canadian border to the Mexican border.

The border patrol received authorization to board suspicious vehicles to search for illegal immigrants and drugs. Additionally, illegal immigrants became subject to arrest for the first time in the history of the border patrol. The border patrol even went so far as to repatriate over 50,000 illegal Mexican immigrants by the end of the decade.

Faced with the growing threat of illicit drugs crossing into the United States, border patrol agents began tracking the movement of unauthorized transportation to and from the United States in the 1960s. Although provisions regarding the search and seizure of persons and property crossing the borders were established during the First Congress in 1789, the legality of searches away from the borders became a contentious issue for civil rights activists. Several cases came before the Supreme Court regarding this issue. In *United States v. Almeida-Sanchez* (1973) the Court ruled that a warrantless stop and search of a defendant's automobile by a traveling patrol approximately 20 miles from the border lacked probable cause and violated the Fourth Amendment. The Court also invalidated a search at a fixed checkpoint well away from the border in *United States v. Ortiz* (1975).

The work of the border patrol has been greatly facilitated by the U.S. Supreme Court's recognition of a broad exception to the warrant requirement of the Fourth Amendment as applied to searches at the border. As Chief Justice Rehnquist pointed out in *United States v. Montoya de Hernandez* (1985), "Routine searches of the persons and effects of entrants are not subject to any requirement of reasonable suspicion, probable cause, or warrant." As a result of this ruling, the border patrol expanded its checkpoint system from states that share borders with Mexico to those that share borders with Canada: Michigan, New York, Vermont, and New Hampshire. Additionally, checkpoints were allowed within a 100-mile radius of the actual border. The number of agents on both borders was dramatically increased. These actions fueled claims by civil rights activists that U.S. borders were becoming "militarized" zones.

As illegal immigration continued to increase throughout the remainder of the twentieth century, the border patrol responded by expanding its manpower and improving its technological capabilities. In 1993, for instance, Operation Hold the Line used a show of force on the Mexican border to ward off potential illegal immigrants. A similar operation was implemented in San Diego in 1994. Other efforts concentrating on the smuggling of individuals and drugs have also been implemented, including the Border Safety Initiative (1998). This proposal was meant to improve security along the Mexican border through mutual cooperation of the United States and Mexico.

Washington's interest in border issues grew as a result of the September 11, 2001, terrorist attacks. Beneath the Department of Homeland Security's umbrella, the border patrol is experiencing a transformation. While the focus of attention largely remains on illegal immigration, the border patrol also works to keep terrorists and their weapons from entering the United States. President George W. Bush laid out his vision for border security in 2002. In addition to significant budgetary increases, the number of border patrol agents was doubled on both the southern and northern borders of the United States. New technologies to track the arrival and departure of non-U.S. citizens were also implemented. In addition to its enforcement role, the border patrol has expanded its mission to include public education about the risks of illegal border crossings. Currently, the United States Border Patrol has 20 different sectors responsible for detecting, intercepting, and apprehending individuals who attempt to enter or smuggle people, drugs, and weapons into the United States illegally.

See also Border Searches; Latino Americans, Civil Rights of

Bibliography

Cornelius, Wayne A. 2001. "Death at the Border: Efficacy and Unintended Consequences of U.S. Immigration Control Policy." *Population and Development Review* 27 (4): 661–85.

Nevins, Joseph. 2002. *Operation Gatekeeper: The Rise of the "Illegal Alien" and the Making of the U.S.-Mexico Boundary.* New York: Routledge.

Stephens, Otis H., Jr., and Richard A. Glenn. 2006. *Unreasonable Searches and Seizures: Rights and Liberties under the Law.* Santa Barbara, CA: ABC-Clio.

Denise DeGarmo

BORDER SEARCHES

Travelers entering the United States are routinely subjected to searches even when they are not the targets of suspicion. The classic example is the inspection of one's personal belongings by a customs agent. In *United States v. Thirty-seven Photographs* (1971), the Supreme Court noted that "[c]ustoms officials characteristically inspect luggage and their power to do so is not questioned in this case; it is an old practice and is intimately associated with excluding illegal articles from the country." Another routine border search is one performed by an official authorized to enforce the immigration laws. As the Supreme Court recognized in *Almeida-Sanchez v. United States* (1973), "the power of the Federal Government to exclude aliens from the country ... can be effectuated by routine inspections and searches of individuals or conveyances seeking to cross our borders."

Historically, such routine border searches were not thought to raise Fourth Amendment concerns, as courts typically took the view that the Fourth Amendment's probable cause and warrant requirements applied only to domestic searches and seizures. Writing for the Supreme Court in *United States v. Ramsey* (1977), Justice William H. Rehnquist explained the historical basis for this view:

That searches made at the border, pursuant to the longstanding right of the sovereign to protect itself by stopping and examining persons and property crossing into this country, are reasonable simply by virtue of the fact that they occur at the border, should, by now, require no extended demonstration. The Congress which proposed the Bill of Rights, including the Fourth Amendment, ... had, some two months prior to that proposal, enacted the first customs statute ... [which] ... granted customs officials "full power and authority" to enter and search "any ship or vessel, in which they shall have reason to suspect any goods, wares or merchandise subject to duty shall be concealed...." ... The historical importance of the enactment of this customs statute by the same Congress which proposed the Fourth Amendment is, we think, manifest.

After reviewing the legal history of border searches, Rehnquist concluded that the "longstanding recognition that searches at our borders without probable cause and without a warrant are nonetheless 'reasonable' has a history as old as the Fourth Amendment itself." In *Ramsey*, the Court held that the border search exception applies to mail coming into the United States as well as persons and their baggage.

The courts have also held that the border search exception extends to searches conducted at established stations near the national border or other "functional equivalents" of a border search. An obvious example would be an international flight that lands at an airport in the interior of the United States. Because the airport is the port of entry, the border search exception applies there as well. There are, however, limits to this doctrine. For example, in *Almeida-Sanchez v. United States* (1973), the

Supreme Court invalidated a search conducted by the border patrol some 25 miles from the Mexican border because agents lacked probable cause to stop the vehicle that was found to be transporting contraband. In holding the search unconstitutional, the Court observed, "It was not a border search, nor can it fairly be said to have been a search conducted at the 'functional equivalent' of the border."

The more difficult problem is the nonroutine, more intrusive border search, for example, a strip search or body cavity search of a suspected drug courier. By and large, courts have required agents to have at least reasonable suspicion before subjecting a traveler to such a procedure. In *United States v. Montoya de Hernandez* (1985), the Supreme Court held that "the detention of a traveler at the border, beyond the scope of a routine customs search and inspection, is justified at its inception if customs agents ... reasonably suspect that the traveler is smuggling contraband." In justifying this holding, the Court observed that "[t]he 'reasonable suspicion' standard has been applied in a number of contexts and effects a needed balance between private and public interests when law enforcement officials must make a limited intrusion on less than probable cause." Although the Supreme Court did not say that reasonable suspicion is the appropriate standard for all nonroutine border searches, it did warn against the creation of multiple standards in this area. Thus lower courts have tended to adopt reasonable suspicion as the default standard (see Viña 2005).

It is important to note, however, that reasonable suspicion of drug smuggling does not give agents a license to abuse a suspect through unnecessarily prolonged detention under inhumane conditions or through extreme methods that "shock the conscience" (see *Rochin v. California*, 1952). Viña suggests that "medical procedures performed by nonmedical personnel" would shock the conscience of reviewing courts (Viña 2005, 15). In *Montoya de Hernandez*, the Supreme Court upheld a prolonged detention of a suspected drug smuggler entering the United States from Mexico. Customs agents detained the suspect for more than 16 hours and refused to let her leave until she had emptied her bowels. Ultimately, the suspect was transported to a hospital, where a rectal examination led to the recovery of a latex balloon containing cocaine. As the Court noted in its opinion, "over the next four days she passed 88 balloons containing a total of 528 grams of 80% pure cocaine hydrochloride." The Court acknowledged that the suspect's ordeal "was long, uncomfortable, indeed, humiliating" but insisted that "both its length and its discomfort resulted solely from the method by which she chose to smuggle illicit drugs into this country."

An innocent traveler who is subjected to an unproductive strip search or body cavity inspection will inevitably feel that his or her rights have been violated, and many have filed suit to protest such treatment. In one highly publicized case, Genevieve Saffell filed suit against a customs agent, alleging a constitutional tort by a federal official, a cause of action created by the Supreme Court in *Bivens v. Six Unknown Named Federal Narcotics Agents* (1971). Upon her return from Jamaica, Saffell was detained by customs agents at Chicago's O'Hare Airport after a drug-sniffing dog alerted agents to a piece of her luggage. Although a search of the bag failed to reveal any contraband, Saffell was taken into a private room, where she was patted down by a female agent. The pat down revealed a slight lump under Saffell's bra, whereupon she was ordered to remove the object, which turned out to be a small amount of currency. The agent then made Saffell raise her dress and pull down her underwear so that the agent could conduct a visual inspection of her genital area. An angry Saffell complied under protest, but the strip search was likewise fruitless. The federal district court ruled that the agent's conduct was permissible up to the point of the strip search but found that the inspection of her genital area was an unreasonable search.

On appeal, the U.S. Court of Appeals for the Seventh Circuit reversed, holding that the strip search was "fully justified." In its opinion in *Saffell v. Crews* (1999), the Seventh Circuit stressed the customs service's "experience with clever and devious smugglers including ways in which the body can be and is used to secrete narcotics." The court recognized that the strip search "was no doubt a very disagreeable and embarrassing experience for Saffell" but determined that the agent "was only doing her duty as she saw it in line with Customs policy and not contrary to any other known applicable legal determination." However, the court admonished customs agents to "be sensitive to their intrusive powers and not abuse and misuse those powers so as to adversely affect travelers unjustly and unnecessarily."

Amidst mounting criticism and a rising tide of litigation, the U.S. Customs Service revised its policies in 1999 to provide additional safeguards against unwarranted intrusive searches. But in the wake of the terrorist attacks of September 11, 2001, the climate of public and judicial opinion changed dramatically. In recent years, the trend has been to enhance, rather than constrain, the discretionary authority of customs agents, immigration officials, and law enforcement officers operating at the nation's borders and ports of entry.

See also *Bivens v. Six Unknown Named Federal Narcotics Agents;* Dogs, Use of by Police; Drugs, War on; Fourth Amendment; Privacy, Reasonable Expectations of; Probable Cause; Search Warrants; Stop and Frisk; Terrorism, War on; Warrantless Searches

Bibliography

Iraola, Roberto. 2003. "Terrorism, the Border, and the Fourth Amendment." *Federal Courts Law Review* 2003:1–21.

Rosenzweig, Paul S. 1985. "Functional Equivalents of the Border, Sovereignty, and the Fourth Amendment." *University of Chicago Law Review* 52:1119.

Saylor, Nathaniel. 2003. "The Untouchables: Protections from Liability for Border Searches Conducted by U.S. Customs in Light of the Passage of the Good Faith Defense in 19 U.S.C. § 482(B)." *Indiana Law Review* 37:275–302.

Scheb, John M., and John M. Scheb II. 2006. *Criminal Procedure.* Belmont, CA: Thomson/Wadsworth.

Stephens, Otis H., Jr., and Richard A. Glenn. 2006. *Unreasonable Searches and Seizures: Rights and Liberties under the Law.* Santa Barbara, CA: ABC-Clio.

Viña, Stephen R. 2005. *Protecting Our Perimeter: "Border Searches" under the Fourth Amendment.* Washington, DC: Congressional Research Service.

John M. Scheb II and Otis H. Stephens, Jr.

BORK, ROBERT H. (1927–)

Robert H. Bork was a law professor at Yale Law School from 1962 to 1975 and 1977 to 1981; from 1972 to 1977 he served in the Department of Justice in both the Richard Nixon and Gerald Ford administrations, and it was during this time that he rose to national prominence. However, he is best known as President Ronald Reagan's failed nominee to the U.S. Supreme Court. Bork's views on civil liberties and civil rights, based on his theory of constitutional interpretation, were central in the Senate's rejection of his nomination.

President Richard Nixon named Robert Bork as U.S. solicitor general in 1972. Shortly thereafter Archibald Cox was appointed as special prosecutor to investigate the Watergate scandal, which involved the burglary of the Democratic National Committee Headquarters by men with ties to President Richard Nixon. In the course of the investigation, Cox obtained a subpoena requiring Nixon to turn over audiotapes of conversations recorded in the Oval Office. On October 20, 1973, Nixon ordered Attorney General Elliot Richardson to fire Cox; Richardson resigned instead. Richardson's deputy, William Ruckelshaus, also resigned rather than fire Cox. Nixon then turned to Bork as the third-ranking Justice Department officer to carry out this firing. Describing what was referred to in the press as "the Saturday Night Massacre," the president indicated in his memoirs that although Bork may have personally opposed the order, "he was a constitutional scholar and he felt that I had the constitutional right to do so and that he therefore had the duty to carry out my orders. He said he would fire Archibald Cox" (Nixon 1978, 934). His views as a constitutional scholar ultimately led to his appointment to the United States Court of Appeals for the District of Columbia by President Ronald Reagan in 1982.

When Justice Lewis Powell announced his retirement from the U.S. Supreme Court in June 1987, President Reagan had an opportunity to significantly alter the ideological balance on the Court to be more favorable to conservative views. Powell "had played a pivotal role as the tie-breaking vote in cases determining the Court's interpretation of constitutional law on such controversial issues as abortion, criminal justice, affirmative action, and separation of church and state" (Abraham 1999, 297). As a moderate, Powell provided the crucial swing vote that favored conservative positions on some issues, and liberal positions on others. Bork, who had often been mentioned as a potential Supreme Court nominee, had amassed a judicial and scholarly record that exhibited his conservative views. Bork believes that judges should interpret the Constitution by following the framers' intent or their "original understanding" of the Constitution's provisions. Bork's position is that to promote consistency and leave policy making to the other branches of government, judges should be faithful to the historical foundations upon which the Constitution is based. He is opposed to Supreme Court rulings concerning the right to privacy, such as *Griswold v. Connecticut* (1965) and *Roe v. Wade* (1973), because there is no explicit right to privacy in the Constitution. Therefore, these matters are better left to the legislative branch. Bork believes that law should reflect the views of the populace and not the views of unelected judges (Bork 1990).

Despite a significant paper trail in judicial opinions and scholarly writings that explicated these beliefs, President Reagan, upon announcing his nomination of Bork to fill Powell's seat on July 1, 1987, characterized his nominee as "neither a conservative nor a liberal" (Abraham 1999, 297). A mere 45 minutes after Reagan's announcement, Senator Edward Kennedy, "[i]n a patent fit of gross hyperbole" (Abraham 1999, 298), stated:

Robert Bork's America is a land in which women would be forced into back alley abortions, blacks would sit at segregated lunch counters, rogue police could break down citizens' doors in midnight raids, school children could not be taught about evolution, writers and artists could be censored at the whim of government, and the doors of the federal courts would be shut on the fingers of millions of citizens for whom the judiciary is—and is often the only—protector of the individual rights that are the heart of our democracy.

The intense opposition manifested in Senator Kennedy's statement led to an unprecedented public relations campaign against Bork's nomination during the course of the confirmation hearings. Although Bork received an exceptionally well-qualified rating from the American Bar Association, he garnered sharp criticism from a wide range of political opponents of the Reagan administration. The focus was on Bork's own judicial philosophy, rather than on his overall legal qualifications for the bench. In hearings before the Senate Judiciary Committee, he was asked how he might rule in hypothetical cases on obscenity, school desegregation, and abortion rights, to which he responded with his view on the role of a judge, not possible decisions he might make as a Supreme Court justice. During the hearings, Bork did much to undermine his chance for confirmation. For instance, he responded to questions from committee members in a "scholarly, lecture-like" manner. "Moreover, Bork's personal appearance and demeanor seemed as suspect as his ideology. His devilish beard and sometimes turgid academic discourse did not endear him to wavering Senators or the public" (Abraham 1999, 298). Bork's nomination was also hindered by several political factors: the Democrats won control of the Senate in the 1986 midterm elections, Southern Democrats in the Senate feared losing African American votes if they supported Bork, and President Reagan's political standing had been damaged by the Iran-Contra scandal and concerns about the economy (Abraham 1999, 298). In sum, "Bork was the wrong person, in the wrong place, at the wrong time" (Abraham 1999, 298).

On October 23, the Senate rejected the nomination by a vote of 58 to 42. Out of this came a new verb—*to be borked*—meaning to have one's entire professional career held up to extensive public and highly partisan scrutiny leading to a clearly political defeat. In his 1990 book, Bork suggested

the episode had the potential to shape future court nominations along more ideological than purely legal lines. Since his confirmation battle, Bork authored several books and was a senior fellow at the American Enterprise Institute, a conservative think tank. More recently, he was a lecturer at the University of Richmond law school.

See also *Griswold v. Connecticut;* Judicial Restraint; Powell, Lewis F., Jr.; Privacy, Constitutional Right of; *Roe v. Wade*

Bibliography

Abraham, Henry. 1999. *Justices, Presidents, and Senators.* Lanham, MD: Rowman & Littlefield.
Bork, Robert H. 1990. *The Tempting of America: The Political Seduction of the Law.* New York: Simon & Schuster.
Nixon, Richard. 1978. *The Memoirs of Richard Nixon.* New York: Grosset & Dunlap.

James Gilchrist

BOYCOTTS

Although the word "boycott" was first coined during the 1800s by landless peasants in Ireland in a campaign against oppressive landowners, it is a tactic with a much older heritage. Boycotts are the easiest and most direct way of communicating one's dissatisfaction with a custom, policy, or law. A boycott is normally called by an organization or group of individuals who ask consumers not to buy specific products or buy from a specific company or use the services of a particular provider in order to exert economic pressure to bring about a social or political change. Specifically, boycotts are called to compel the company or organization to change its behavior, cease an activity, or to adopt a more ethical practice.

Boycotts are effective because they bring widespread economic and social disruption to commercial systems. Boycotts have long been used by the African American community as a strategy to combat legal and social injustices. Between 1900 and 1906, there were major boycotts by African Americans to protest segregated street cars in 25 Southern cities (Meier and Rudwick 1969).

Boycotts became an effective strategy used in the modern civil rights movement in major cities in Deep South states, most notably in Montgomery, Alabama; Tallahassee, Florida; Baton Rouge, Louisiana; Savannah, Georgia; and Nashville, Tennessee, during the 1950s and 1960s (Morris 1984). After boycotts were effectively used in the civil rights movement, they became part of an overarching "aggressive nonviolent strategy," which would become the centerpiece of Martin Luther King, Jr.'s campaign to gain civil rights for African Americans in the South.

Two of the most famous American boycotts were the Great Grape Boycott and the Montgomery Bus Boycott. During the Great Grape Boycott, César Chávez developed a new strategy and brought a bold new dimension to the struggle against the grape growers. In July 1968, he launched the Great Grape Boycott, a nationwide boycott against table grapes. Boycott offices were established in most major American cities, and the Great Grape Boycott gained international recognition. Soon, many consumers around the nation supported the boycott and stopped purchasing table grapes. Prominent American union leaders, statesmen, and celebrities supported the boycott.

The most famous boycott in the United States was the Montgomery Bus Boycott. Segregation was the custom of the "old South" under which African Americans would sit at the rear of all public transportation vehicles. The Montgomery Bus Boycott started on December 1, 1955, when 43-year-old Rosa Parks, who was employed as a seamstress at Montgomery Fair Department Store, refused to relinquish her seat on a Montgomery city bus. Contrary to popular belief, Parks was not the first to refuse to give up her seat and challenge the segregation laws in Montgomery. Claudette Colvin, a 15-year-old high school student, had refused to give up her seat and was arrested a few weeks earlier (Branch 1988). She did not become the lead plaintiff because she was pregnant and unmarried at the time. After the arrest of Parks, E. D. Nixon, the president of the Montgomery chapter of the National Association for the Advancement of Colored People, asked Parks to become the lead plaintiff in the lawsuit to challenge the constitutionality of Montgomery's segregated bus system. Parks was chosen because of her character and standing in the community.

In the wake of Parks's arrest, Jo Ann Robinson, a professor at Alabama State University, a historically black university located in Montgomery, began to push for a one-day boycott. Robinson was well known for her political activism because she was president of the Women's Political Council and had challenged injustices in Montgomery prior to the arrest of Parks (Branch 1988). Robinson kickstarted the Montgomery Bus Boycott by mimeographing handouts urging African Americans not to ride Montgomery city buses. She and students from Alabama State University distributed the mimeographed fliers throughout the African American community in Montgomery.

For any mass African American boycott to be successful in Montgomery, area churches would have to be major supporters. Therefore, community leaders and church leaders pooled their resources and held a meeting to gauge community support for the boycott. In a mass church meeting, leaders discussed the rationale for a full-fledged boycott. The Reverend Dr. Martin Luther King, Jr., the 26-year-old pastor at Dexter Avenue Baptist Church and the president of the Montgomery Improvement Association, emerged from this meeting as the leader of the bus boycott, and thus the civil rights movement (Baldwin, Burrow, Holmes, and Winfield 2002). King believed that if they could achieve a participation level of about 60 percent, then the boycott could be successful. The Montgomery Improvement Association and the African American community at large agreed upon a one-day boycott until the preliminary court hearing for Parks's arrest had taken place. Depending on the outcome of the court hearing, the bus boycott would be expanded indefinitely or until Montgomery's segregative transportation laws were changed.

The bus boycott proved extremely effective. The city experienced an economic crisis as African Americans chose to find alternative methods of traveling. Instead of riding buses, boycotters organized a system of carpools, with volunteer car owners carrying people to various destinations. When the city pressured local insurance companies to stop insuring cars used in the carpools, the boycott leaders arranged policies with out-of-state and overseas insurance companies.

Even with the economic crunch of the boycott, Montgomery city government officials refused to desegregate the bus system. In November of 1956, the United States Supreme Court ordered the bus system in Montgomery to integrate (*Gayle v. Browder,* 1956). Showing a collective resolve to enact change to an unjust law, African Americans remained off the buses while the case was on appeal. After some 381 days, the boycott ended on December 21, 1956. This boycott would serve as a catalyst for segregation challenges in other Southern cities (Gray 2002).

The boycott technique became an effective tool because it brought economic distress and social disruption to Southern cities deeply entrenched in the Jim Crow tradition of segregation. Boycotts gave African Americans a direct and aggressive way of confronting the ills of social injustice.

See also Civil Rights Movement; Jim Crow Laws; King, Martin Luther, Jr.; National Association for the Advancement of Colored People; Parks, Rosa

Bibliography

Baldwin, Lewis V., Rufus Burrow, Barbara Holmes, and Susan Holmes Winfield. 2002. *The Legacy of Martin Luther King, Jr.: The Boundaries of Law, Politics, and Religion.* Notre Dame, Indiana: University of Notre Dame Press.

Branch, Taylor. 1988. *Parting the Waters: America in the King Years, 1954–63.* New York: Simon & Schuster.

Gray, Fred. 2002. *Bus Ride to Justice.* Montgomery, AL: New South Press.

King, Martin Luther, Jr. 1965. "Behind the Selma March." *Saturday Review,* 3 April.

Meier, August, and Elliot Rudwick. 1969. "The Boycott Movement against Jim Crow: Street Cars in the South, 1900–1906." *Journal of American History* 5: 756–75.

Morris, Aldon. 1984. *The Origins of the Civil Rights Movement: Black Communities Organizing for Change.* New York: Free Press.

F. Erik Brooks

BOY SCOUTS OF AMERICA V. DALE (2000)

One of the most difficult problems in the field of civil rights is that of private discrimination. It has long been settled that government may forbid commercial establishments from engaging in discrimination among patrons (see, e.g., *Heart of Atlanta Motel v. United States,* 1964; *Katzenbach v. McClung,* 1964). On the other hand the First Amendment implicitly protects the freedom of association (see, e.g., *NAACP v. Alabama,* 1958) for social and political purposes. In *Roberts v. United States Jaycees* (1984), the Supreme Court recognized that "implicit in the right to engage in activities protected by the First Amendment" is "a corresponding right to associate with others in pursuit of a wide variety of political, social, economic, educational, religious, and cultural ends." Does this freedom of association imply the right *not to associate?* Can a social or political organization exclude persons a group considers undesirable for whatever reason? In this case the question was whether the Boy Scouts of America, a nongovernmental organization that is well known, long standing, and ubiquitous in the United States, could discriminate among members and leaders on the basis of sexual orientation.

James Dale, a former Eagle Scout, was dismissed from his position as an assistant scoutmaster of a New Jersey Boy Scout troop when the organization learned that Dale was openly gay. The Boy Scouts defended their action by asserting that homosexual conduct is inconsistent with the values embodied in the Scout Oath and Scout Law, especially a Scout's obligation to be "morally straight" and "clean." The Scouts asserted that the gay lifestyle is not morally straight and claimed that they did not want to promote that lifestyle.

Dale successfully sued the Boy Scouts in the New Jersey courts, which ultimately ruled that the

Boy Scouts had violated a state law prohibiting discrimination on the basis of sexual orientation by places of public accommodation. In reaching this conclusion, the New Jersey court adopted a broad definition of "place of public accommodation." According to that court's formulation, the term is not tied to a particular place, nor is it limited to commercial enterprises.

Dividing five-to-four, the U.S. Supreme Court reversed. The votes of the justices were divided along conventional ideological lines. The majority consisted of Chief Justice William H. Rehnquist and Justices Antonin Scalia, Clarence Thomas, Sandra Day O'Connor, and Anthony Kennedy. Justices John Paul Stevens, Ruth Bader Ginsburg, David Souter, and Stephen Breyer dissented.

The Court did not invalidate the New Jersey court's definition of place of public accommodation, as that was a state law question. Rather, the High Court held that the Boy Scouts' freedom of association trumped the state's interest in advancing the cause of gay rights. Writing for the majority, Chief Justice Rehnquist insisted that the Court's decision had nothing to do with the majority's view of homosexuality or the values articulated by the Boy Scouts. In Rehnquist's view, "public or judicial disapproval of a tenet of an organization's expression does not justify the State's effort to compel the organization to accept members where such acceptance would derogate from the organization's expressive message."

Writing for the four dissenters, Justice Stevens expressed dismay at the Court's decision, noting that "until today, we have never once found a claimed right to associate in the selection of members to prevail in the face of a State's antidiscrimination law." In Stevens's view, there was "no basis in the record for concluding that admission of [homosexuals] will impede the [Boy Scouts'] ability to engage in [its] protected activities or to disseminate its preferred views." Stevens asserted that prejudice against gay people would be "aggravated by the creation of a constitutional shield for a policy that is itself the product of a habitual way of thinking about strangers." He concluded by quoting Justice

Louis D. Brandeis, who once wrote that "we must be ever on our guard, lest we erect our prejudices into legal principles."

In an official statement, the national office of the Boy Scouts of America proclaimed that the decision "affirms our standing as a private association with the right to set its own standards for membership and leadership ... and allows us to continue our mission of providing character-building experiences for young people, which has been our chartered purpose since our founding." Critics of the *Dale* decision argued that it was unrealistic to view the Boy Scouts as a strictly private organization. Others argued that even if the Scouts are a private group, the compelling public interest in defeating discrimination should prevail over any First Amendment claim.

See also Association, Freedom of; Brandeis, Louis D.; Breyer, Stephen G.; Discrimination by Private Actors; First Amendment; Gay Rights Movement; Ginsburg, Ruth Bader; *Heart of Atlanta Motel v. United States; Katzenbach v. McClung;* Kennedy, Anthony; *NAACP v. Alabama;* O'Connor, Sandra Day; Public Accommodation, Places of; Rehnquist, William H.; Scalia, Antonin; Souter, David H.; Speech, Freedom of; Stevens, John Paul; Thomas, Clarence

John M. Scheb II and Otis H. Stephens, Jr.

BRANDEIS, LOUIS D. (1856–1941)

Louis D. Brandeis, the first Jewish justice appointed to the United States Supreme Court, was born in Louisville, Kentucky, on November 13, 1856. He was the youngest of four children born to German immigrants who came to America with the hope of freedom. At the age of 18, without any college training, Brandeis entered Harvard Law School, where he thrived for the next three years. After graduating at the top of his class, he briefly practiced law in St. Louis. Relocating to Boston, he formed a partnership with Samuel Warren, a classmate at Harvard and a member of a socially prominent Boston family. Brandeis and Warren quickly developed a lucrative practice, for the most part representing well-established corporate clients.

By the early 1890s Brandeis was a millionaire and no longer dependent on income from his corporate practice. He then began to devote his professional efforts to social and political reform, much to the chagrin of many of his former clients. He soon became known as the "people's attorney" for his active participation in public causes. During his years as a litigator (1878–1916), he also taught legal courses at Harvard Law School and the Massachusetts Institute of Technology, led the fight to preserve the Boston subway system, created savings bank life insurance, was involved in the New Haven Railroad fight, and led the American Zionist movement. Moreover, in *Muller v. Oregon* (1908), Brandeis filed what became known as the Brandeis brief to the United States Supreme Court, a document containing hundreds of pages of statistics supporting a state law that limited working hours for women. This new method of using empirical data to argue cases exemplified an emerging nontraditional approach to law known as sociological jurisprudence. It had a significant influence on the teaching and practice of law in the early twentieth century.

In 1916, Brandeis was appointed Associate Justice of the United States Supreme Court by President Woodrow Wilson. His nomination created a storm of controversy because of his reputation as a social reformer and because of his religion. After an intense battle lasting more than four months, during which many representatives of the legal and business establishments expressed strong opposition, Brandeis's nomination was confirmed by a Senate vote of 47–22. Brandeis continued to influence American law until his resignation in 1939.

Brandeis contributed to nearly every economic and social movement of his lifetime, including unemployment legislation, trade unionism, trust busting, women's suffrage, Progressivism, and scientific management. He is best remembered, however, for his pivotal role in the expansion of civil liberties. Brandeis believed that in a democratic society where the majority controls the legislatures, the courts have a duty to protect the civil liberties of the individual. Specifically, Brandeis valued the rights of free speech and privacy, which he believed facilitated the development of individuals into educated citizens vital to a democratic community.

Brandeis's interpretation of the First Amendment's protection of free speech was based on the concept that a free exchange of ideas is necessary to create solutions to the changing needs of society. This concept was best expressed in his own words: "In frank expression of conflicting opinions lies the greatest promise of wisdom in governmental action; and in suppression lies ordinarily the greatest peril." In *Schenck v. United States* (1919), Brandeis joined Justice Oliver Wendell Holmes's opinion written for a unanimous Court articulating the "clear and present danger" test, which prohibited speech in only those circumstances where a real danger was posed. However, Brandeis later regretted his decision in the case upholding the conviction of the Socialist Party official who was found guilty under the 1917 Espionage Act for distributing anti-draft leaflets; thus, during the next year he authored three dissents explaining his interpretation of the clear and present danger test.

His first dissent was in *Schaefer v. United States* (1920), a case affirming convictions under the Espionage Act of five men who printed articles criticizing the American war effort and the American president. Brandeis studied the articles in full and asserted that a jury "acting in calmness" could not find that the articles caused a clear and present danger to the country. Moreover, breaking with Holmes's interpretation of the test, he asserted that the right of free speech should be the same during time of peace as during time of war, especially since during a time of war a biased majority can be easily motivated by fear. In another Espionage Act case, *Pierce v. United States* (1920), Brandeis disagreed with the majority that antiwar language in distributed leaflets posed a clear and present danger but instead advocated the benefits of the free expression of ideas that promote experimentation. In *Gilbert v. Minnesota* (1920), Brandeis again disagreed with the majority's approval of a Minnesota law that essentially made the teaching of pacifism illegal. Brandeis was appalled at a law that not only violated the freedom of speech but also intruded upon the privacy of expression available in one's home. It was also in this case that Brandeis advocated applying the Bill of Rights to the states through the Due Process Clause of the Fourteenth Amendment to extend the protection of civil liberties—a process known as selective incorporation. Finally, Brandeis's most important contribution to free speech jurisprudence was his concurrence in *Whitney v. California* (1927), in which he stated that there must be a reasonable ground to believe that danger to the state is imminent before speech is suppressed; his concurrence was the basis for *Brandenburg v. Ohio* (1969), which overturned the *Whitney* decision and continues to be binding precedent.

Brandeis was also an advocate of privacy rights. In 1890, he collaborated with his law partner, Samuel Warren, in writing "The Right to Privacy," a highly influential article published in the *Harvard Law Review*. Brandeis argued that the law should protect one's private and domestic life against the use of new technology that could threaten that sacred realm. Also in the article, he first described the right of privacy as "the right to be let alone," a phrase central to right of privacy jurisprudence. Later in *Olmstead v. United States* (1928), Brandeis condemned the government's invasion of privacy and dissented from the majority's opinion that government wiretapping of telephones was constitutional. He argued that wiretapping violated the Fourth Amendment right against unreasonable searches and seizures because of its intrusive nature. Moreover, Brandeis feared that future technology would be used by the government without justification to intrude upon individual privacy and security. Brandeis's contributions to the right of privacy are the foundation for privacy requirements in many state constitutions and are an integral part of the current political debate in the United States.

Two years after his resignation from the court, Brandeis suffered a heart attack and died on October 1, 1941. Today Brandeis's Supreme Court opinions serve as a testament to his belief that the exchange of opposing ideas is essential to a healthy and ever-changing society.

See also Bill of Rights, Incorporation of; *Brandenburg v. Ohio;* Electronic Surveillance; Espionage Act of 1917; First Amendment; Fourth Amendment; Speech, Freedom of; Holmes, Oliver Wendell, Jr.; Privacy, Constitutional Right of; *Schenck v. United States*

Bibliography

Mason, Alpheus Thomas. 1946. *Brandeis: A Free Man's Life*. New York: Viking Press.
Strum, Phillipa. 1984. *Louis D. Brandeis: Justice for the People*. Cambridge, MA: Harvard University Press.
———. 1993. *Brandeis: Beyond Progressivism*. Lawrence: University Press of Kansas.
Warren, Samuel, and Louis D. Brandeis. 1890. "The Right to Privacy." *Harvard Law Review* 4:193–220.
Sara P. Burke

BRANDENBURG V. OHIO (1969)

In *Schenck v. United States* (1919), the Supreme Court held that the First Amendment does not protect utterances where there is a "clear and present danger that they will bring about the substantive evils that Congress has a right to prevent." In *Whitney v. California* (1927), the Court upheld a state law that prohibited "criminal syndicalism," essentially the crime of advocating political change through violence. In *Brandenburg v. Ohio* (1969), the Court overturned *Whitney* and struck down a similar criminal syndicalism statute. The Court also modified the clear and present danger doctrine so as to provide significantly greater protection to freedom of expression.

Brandenburg, a Ku Klux Klan leader, was convicted under Ohio's criminal syndicalism statute, fined $1,000 and sentenced to one to 10 years' imprisonment. His conviction was based on a videotape of a Klan rally that aired on local television in Cincinnati. At the rally, Brandenburg and other hooded figures, some of whom were carrying firearms, made disparaging statements about African Americans and Jews. Brandenburg also made a speech that could be construed as a generalized threat of violence, but he threatened no particular individual.

In unanimously reversing Brandenburg's conviction and striking down the statute on which it was based, the U.S. Supreme Court held that "the constitutional guarantees of free speech and free press do not permit a State to forbid or proscribe advocacy of the use of force or of law violation except where such advocacy is directed to inciting or producing imminent lawless action and is likely to incite or produce such action." Speaking through a per curiam opinion, the Court noted that the Ohio statute purported to "punish mere advocacy and to forbid … assembly with others merely to advocate the described type of action." As such, it fell "within the condemnation of the First and Fourteenth Amendments."

Since 1969, the Supreme Court has firmly adhered to the standard announced in the *Brandenburg* decision (see, for example, *Hess v. Indiana,* 1973; *Communist Party of Indiana v. Whitcomb,* 1974; and *National Association for the Advancement of Colored People v. Claiborne Hardware,* 1982). In recent years the Court has not extensively discussed the imminent lawless action standard but also has not given any indication of moving away from it. However, in the aftermath of the terrorist attacks of September 11, 2001, a number of observers expressed concern about the changing mood of the country regarding political dissent. Some questioned whether the imminent lawless action standard would survive the war on terrorism.

See also Clear and Present Danger Doctrine; Clear and Probable Danger Doctrine; Criminal Syndicalism; Hate Speech; Ku Klux Klan; *Schenck v. United States;* Speech, Freedom of

John M. Scheb II and Otis H. Stephens, Jr.

BRAWLEY, TAWANA. *See* Sharpton, Alfred Charles

BREATH TESTS. *See* DUI Field Tests and Breath Tests

BRENNAN, WILLIAM J., JR. (1906–1997)

William J. Brennan, Jr., who served almost 34 years on the United States Supreme Court

(1956–1990), was born and raised in New Jersey. Brennan was the second of eight children born to Irish immigrants. After graduating from the University of Pennsylvania and Harvard Law School, he established a private practice in New Jersey that was interrupted by military service in World War II. He eventually left private practice to serve first as a trial judge and later as an appellate court judge. Brennan, a Democrat, was elevated to the New Jersey Supreme Court by a Republican governor in 1952. President Dwight Eisenhower nominated Brennan to the U.S. Supreme Court in 1956 when Sherman Minton resigned. Brennan's appointment was said to have been an attempt by President Eisenhower to court the Catholic vote. Eisenhower had been advised that Brennan would be a moderate. Brennan's voting record, however, did not reflect the views of the president. Indeed, in one of his final press conferences, in response to a question about whether he had made any mistakes as president, Eisenhower reportedly replied, "Yes, I made two and they are both on the Supreme Court." The other "mistake" was Chief Justice Earl Warren.

Brennan was considered a judicial activist who favored the expansion of access to the courts. His constitutional philosophy has been described as libertarian dignity, and his fingerprints are all over American constitutional law. As Chief Justice Warren's trusted lieutenant, Brennan was assigned many of the most important opinions. Later, as the most senior justice on the Court, he was able to assign important cases to himself.

Brennan authored the majority opinion in *Baker v. Carr* (1962), which forced the reapportionment of legislative districts and was considered by Chief Justice Warren to be the most important decision of his tenure. Brennan authored the major landmark decision in libel law, *New York Times v. Sullivan* (1964), which expanded the reach of the First Amendment. His opinion in *Sherbert v. Verner* (1963) rewrote doctrine in free exercise of religion. Brennan wrote the opinion that protected the right of an individual to burn the flag in *Texas v. Johnson* (1989). He was criticized for his efforts to define obscenity in *Roth v. United States* (1957). Although Brennan's opinion was very protective of free expression and made it difficult to get a conviction for obscenity, Justice William O. Douglas, who would later be proven correct, warned in dissent that the attempt to define obscenity would open the door to narrower definitions when the Court's majority changed. Brennan has been considered the father of the modern First Amendment.

Brennan is also considered the godfather of new judicial federalism. As the Supreme Court turned in a more conservative direction in the 1980s, Brennan suggested that state supreme courts should look to the bills of rights in their respective state constitutions to find greater protection for civil liberties and civil rights. He made these recommendations in both his Supreme Court opinions and in scholarly articles.

Brennan was also known for his creative use of the Fourteenth Amendment to expand civil rights. He authored the decision in *Green v. New Kent County School Board* (1968), setting the standards for expediting desegregation. He also fought to have gender distinctions in the law reviewed on the basis of a strict scrutiny standard rather than the less demanding standard of intermediate scrutiny. Ultimately, he could not attract a majority to that view. Brennan was said to be the author of the controversial *Cooper v. Aaron* (1958) decision. In a per curiam decision, the Court declared that "the federal judiciary is supreme in the exposition of the law of the Constitution." This very broad claim of authority argued for judicial supremacy over the other federal branches in constitutional matters.

Brennan supported the incorporation of the Bill of Rights to the states, and his opinion in *Malloy v. Hogan* (1964) stated assertively that the provisions of the Bill of Rights applied with the same force to the states as it did to the federal government. Brennan, together with long-time ally Thurgood Marshall, came to oppose the death penalty and dissented in every capital punishment case. Brennan was known for his influence on the Court and for his work behind the scenes in building coalitions to support his positions. His work in the internal deliberation in building consensus for reproductive rights in *Roe v. Wade* (1973) was emblematic of his pivotal role.

Brennan proved to be among the most liberal and probably the most influential justice on the modern Supreme Court. Indeed, some have considered Brennan the most important figure in American politics in the second half of the twentieth century. He played a vital role in the constitutional revolution that was launched during the Warren Court. During the Burger and Rehnquist Courts, he tried to protect those precedents. Brennan was remarkably successful in attracting and building majorities despite the exodus of liberal justices. As a result of his leadership, Brennan imparted his constitutional vision to a broad coalition of his colleagues. Brennan believed in a "living Constitution." He argued that the justices had to read the Constitution as twentieth-century Americans. He dismissed as arrogance cloaked in humility the argument that justices should search for the intent of the framers of the Constitution and should make that the sole determinant of their decisions. As a result of his flexible interpretation of the Constitution, Brennan became a symbol of liberal activism and was criticized by a number of Republicans, most notably Attorney General Edwin Meese.

After serving as an associate justice on the U.S. Supreme Court for almost 34 years, William Brennan, Jr., resigned from the Court for health reasons in 1990. He died in 1997.

See also *Baker v. Carr; Bivens v. Six Unknown Named Federal Narcotics Agents;* Burger Court; *Cooper v. Aaron;* Douglas, William O.; Equal Protection Clause; Equal Protection Jurisprudence; Gender-Based Discrimination; Judicial Activism; Living Constitution; Marshall, Thurgood; Meese, Edwin, III; New Judicial Federalism; *New York Times v. Sullivan;* Obscenity and Pornography; Reapportionment; Rehnquist Court; *Roe v. Wade;* Strict Scrutiny; *Texas v. Johnson;* Warren, Earl; Warren Court

Bibliography

Eisler, Kim Isaac. 1993. *A Justice for All: William J. Brennan, Jr., and the Decisions That Transformed America.* New York: Simon & Schuster.

Irons, Peter H. 1994. *Brennan vs. Rehnquist: The Battle for the Constitution.* New York: Alfred A. Knopf.

Marion, David E. 1997. *The Jurisprudence of Justice William J. Brennan, Jr.: The Law and Politics of "Libertarian Dignity."* Lanham, MD: Rowman & Littlefield.

Richard L. Pacelle, Jr.

BREYER, STEPHEN G. (1938–)

The 108th justice of the United States Supreme Court, Stephen G. Breyer, was born on August 15, 1938, in San Francisco, California. Breyer graduated Phi Beta Kappa from Stanford University in 1959 and then attended Oxford University on a Marshall Scholarship. He returned to the United States and earned a law degree from Harvard University in 1964. Breyer's first experience at the Supreme Court was as a clerk to Justice Arthur Goldberg. Breyer has stated that Goldberg helped mold his views regarding the role of the judiciary in American society. According to Breyer, "Justice Goldberg really felt … that judges can become isolated from the people whose lives their decisions affect. I've continued to teach and to participate in the community and other activities which are important in connecting me to the world outside the courtroom" (quoted in Abraham 1999, 324).

After his clerkship, Breyer held positions in all three branches of government. In the executive branch, he worked for the Antitrust Division of the Department of Justice from 1965 to 1967 and served as a special prosecutor for the Watergate Special Prosecution Force. His legislative experience consisted of serving as counsel for the Senate Judiciary Committee. His judicial experience began in 1980 when President Jimmy Carter appointed him to the First Circuit Court of Appeals, during which time he also became a member of the U.S. Sentencing Commission. It should also be noted, in keeping with Goldberg's views of being involved in the outside world, that Breyer taught at his alma mater, Harvard Law School, from 1967 to 1980.

President Clinton initially considered Breyer for the vacancy created by the departure of Justice Byron White from the Court in 1993. However, Breyer's interview with the president did not go well; "Clinton saw Breyer as overselling himself and lacking a 'big heart'" (O'Connor and Palmer 2001, 263). That position ultimately went to Ruth Bader Ginsburg. A year later when Justice Harry Blackmun announced his retirement from the Court, Breyer again made the short list. After Breyer's advocates made their views known to the president, Clinton appointed Breyer based on his consummate professional record, his experience on the Senate Judiciary Committee, and his bipartisan backing, all of which helped assure his confirmation without a politically contentious Senate skirmish (Abraham 1999, 323). The Senate voted 87–9 to confirm him; he was sworn in on August 3, 1994.

Despite Clinton's initial reluctance to appoint him, Breyer did not give Clinton any reason to be disappointed, as Breyer helped sustain a liberal wing on the Rehnquist Court (O'Connor and Palmer 2001, 266). However, Breyer's contribution to civil liberties and civil rights has been rather minimal because most of his landmark decisions on the Court have come in the area of regulatory policy (O'Connor and Palmer 2001). Breyer's primary contribution to civil liberties came in *Stenberg v. Carhart* (2000), where Breyer authored the majority opinion invalidating Nebraska's ban on partial birth abortions because it imposed an "undue burden" on a woman seeking an abortion, thus violating the Court's precedents in *Roe v. Wade* (1973) and *Planned Parenthood v. Casey* (1992). Breyer's opinion was significant because there was uncertainty as to whether the "undue burden" standard would command a majority of the Court in abortion cases.

Despite Breyer's propensity to vote with the liberal wing of the Court, he has from time to time surprised commentators in civil liberties cases. In *Vernonia School District 47J v. Acton* (1995) and *Board of Education v. Earls* (2002), Breyer voted to uphold suspicionless drug testing of public school students involved in athletics and extracurricular activities. Additionally, his concurring opinion in *Van Orden v. Perry* (2005), a case dealing with the public display of the Ten Commandments, surprised observers. Breyer wrote that the fact that the display had been in existence for 40 years without controversy was evidence that the display's message was viewed as secular. Breyer's majority opinion in *Gray v. Maryland* (1998), however, demonstrated a commitment to civil liberties in the application of the Sixth Amendment's Confrontation Clause.

In the realm of civil rights, Breyer authored the majority opinion in *Easley v. Cromartie* (2001), a case dealing with voting rights and race-conscious redistricting. Breyer wrote that a three-judge district court panel's determination that the North Carolina legislature used race as the "predominant factor" in drawing district lines was "clearly erroneous"; therefore, there was no violation of the Equal Protection Clause. In another case impacting civil rights jurisprudence, *United States v. Lopez* (1995), Breyer launched perhaps his best-known dissent. In this case, a majority of the Court invalidated the Gun Free School Zones Act of 1990 because it was beyond the scope of congressional power under the Commerce Clause. Breyer's dissent maintained that the Court's role was to determine whether Congress believed they had the authority to enact the statute. To that end, Breyer included a 17-page appendix to his dissent, which included reports and citations that made the link between gun possession, school violence, and interstate commerce.

Breyer's philosophy of constitutional interpretation, one he has referred to as "active liberty," posits that judges should place greater emphasis on "the people's right to 'an active and constant participation in collective power'" (quoted in O'Brien 2004, 201). This theory helps explain his commitment to pragmatism in cases where he has veered from the liberal wing of the Court.

See also Abortion, Right to; Blackmun, Harry A.; Equal Protection Clause; Ginsburg, Ruth Bader; Goldberg, Arthur; Rehnquist Court; *Roe v. Wade;* Sixth Amendment; Souter, David H.; Stevens; John Paul; Ten Commandments, Public Display of; *United States v. Lopez;* U.S. Department of Justice; White, Byron R.

Bibliography

Abraham, Henry. 1999. *Justices, Presidents, and Senators.* Lanham, MD: Rowman & Littlefield.

O'Brien, David, ed. 2004. *Judges on Judging: Views from the Bench.* 2nd ed. Washington, DC: CQ Press.

O'Connor, Karen, and Barbara Palmer. 2001. "The Clinton Clones: Ginsburg, Breyer, and the Clinton Legacy." *Judicature* 84 (5): 262–73.

Kara E. Stooksbury

BROWN, H. "Rap." *See* Student Nonviolent Coordinating Committee

BROWN, JOHN. *See* Abolitionist Movement

BROWN V. BOARD OF EDUCATION (1954, 1955)

As 1950 approached, the NAACP Legal Defense Fund (LDF) had reached a crossroads in its fight to dismantle the Jim Crow laws that had produced a pervasive system of racial segregation throughout the South and many other states since the late nineteenth century. Up to that point, the LDF had won a series of decisions challenging the higher education systems of several Southern and border states. In every instance, the legal strategy was to argue, within the confines of the *Plessy v. Ferguson* (1896) separate but equal doctrine, that the facilities and/or services offered were not, in fact, equal—in some cases, they were nonexistent (e.g., *Missouri ex rel. Gaines v. Canada,* 1938). Some members of the LDF were urging a frontal attack on *Plessy.*

This approach would require confronting at least two elements underlying Justice Henry B. Brown's opinion in the *Plessy* case: first, Justice Brown had relied on an "original intent" approach by emphasizing that the same Congress that proposed the Fourteenth Amendment also supported segregated schools in the District of Columbia; second, Brown had maintained that legally enforced segregation did not imply the inferiority of the "colored" race:

We consider the underlying fallacy of the plaintiff's argument to consist in the assumption that the enforced separation of the two races stamps the colored race with a badge of inferiority. If this be so, it is not by reason of anything found in the act, but solely because the colored race chooses to put that construction upon it.

... Legislation is powerless to eradicate racial instincts, or to abolish distinctions based on physical features.... If one race be inferior to the other socially, the constitution of the United States cannot put them upon the same plane.

In addition, there was the fear that, should the LDF ask the Court to overrule *Plessy* and fail, the separate but equal precedent would be strengthened, and the cause of civil rights would suffer a severe setback. Hence, the LDF, under the leadership of Charles Houston and Thurgood Marshall, felt the need to wait until there was some sign that the Court might be open to such an appeal. That sign came in Chief Justice Fred Vinson's unanimous opinion in *Sweatt v. Painter* (1950), in which the Court set a standard of equality that would be virtually impossible to meet without abandoning the separate but equal doctrine. Going beyond such "tangible" items as physical facilities, numbers of books in the library, and the like, Vinson pointed to "those qualities which are incapable of objective measurement but which make for greatness in a law school [such as] reputation of the faculty, experience of the administration, position and influence of the alumni, standing in the community, tradition and prestige."

Marshall and his colleagues then made the fateful decision to take on Jim Crow. The argument would be that it was segregation itself that violated the Equal Protection Clause, and the only remedy would be complete desegregation. The target, moreover, would not be higher education but the public schools. It was no longer about getting individuals admitted to college; it was about fundamentally changing an entire social system. The first hurdle to overcome was finding persons who would be willing to risk their jobs and their homes—perhaps even their lives—to sign on as plaintiffs. Over the course of several months, plaintiffs were identified, and four state challenges were filed—three in federal district courts in South Carolina, Virginia, and Kansas, and one in a Delaware chancery court. A separate federal challenge to segregated public schools was filed in

the District of Columbia (D.C., governed by Congress, was not explicitly covered by the Fourteenth Amendment's language, which applies to the states, not to the federal government). The second hurdle was proof that it was the fact of segregation, not the inequality of the facilities and services, that was the constitutional violation. In this connection, the work of Columbia University sociologist Dr. Kenneth Clark was of critical importance.

Dr. Clark and his wife, Mamie, had done considerable research into the impact of segregation on the self-images of African American children, mostly ages three to seven. The Clarks' most famous studies involved presenting these children with dolls identical in every respect except their color and asking them which doll they would most want to be like. By overwhelming margins, the black children chose the white doll. It was this evidence that led Kenneth Clark to testify at trial in the South Carolina case *Briggs v. Elliott* (1951):

The essence of this detrimental effect is a confusion in the child's concept of his own self-esteem—basic feelings of inferiority, conflict, confusion in his self-image, resentment, hostility towards himself, hostility towards whites, intensification of ... a desire to resolve his basic conflict by sometimes escaping or withdrawing. (Kluger 1976)

The state had surprised the plaintiffs in the South Carolina case by acknowledging the existing inequalities and introducing a commitment by the newly elected governor to support a $75 million bond issue aimed primarily at equalizing resources in the dual system. The three-judge panel, in a 2–1 decision, held that the essential elements of *Plessy*'s separate but equal doctrine had never been overruled by the Supreme Court. Those elements included two basic principles. First, "[t]here is no denial of the equal protection of the laws in segregating children in the schools for the purposes of education, if the children of the different races are given equal facilities and opportunities." Second, the legislature has a large amount of discretion and "is at liberty to act with reference to the established usages, customs and traditions of the people, and with a view to the promotion of their comfort, and the preservation of the public peace and good order." Hence, "the social and economic interrelationship of the two races living together is a legislative problem, as yet not solved." Later the majority drew the following conclusion:

In formulating educational policy at the common school level, … the law must take into account, not merely of the matter of affording instruction to the student, but also the wishes of the parent as to the upbringing of the child and his associates in the formative period of childhood and adolescence. If public education is to have the support of the people through their legislatures, it must not go contrary to what they deem for the best interests of their children.

Following this line of reasoning, the three-judge federal panel in *Davis v. Prince Edward County, Virginia* (1952), concluded that evidence introduced by the plaintiffs on the impact of separation did not "overbalance" that of the defendants:

[T]he separation provision rests neither upon prejudice, nor caprice, nor upon any other measureless foundation. Rather the proof is that it declares one of the ways of life in Virginia. Separation of white and colored children in the public schools of Virginia has for generations been a part of the mores of her people. To have separate schools has been their use and wont.

The panel went on to cite the testimony of Colgate W. Darden, Jr., then president of the University of Virginia and formerly a state legislator and governor, that an order to desegregate the schools would likely result in whites withdrawing their support entirely and refusing to fund public education: "[I]nvoluntary elimination [of segregation] would severely lessen the interest of the people of the State in the public schools, lessen the financial support, and so injure both races." Thus, according to Darden, the legislative judgment that segregated schools were in the best interests of the people of the state must be respected so long as the state was making a good-faith commitment to equalize the facilities.

The three-judge panel in the Kansas case (*Brown v. Board of Education of Topeka*) made a similar finding: "[I]n the maintenance and operation of the schools there is no willful, intentional

or substantial discrimination … between the colored and the white schools." Of the four state challenges, only the Delaware courts came to a different conclusion (see *Belton v. Gebhart*). Finding that there was no possibility that the facilities in question could be equalized within a reasonable period of time, the chancery court concluded that the only way in which the individual right of the plaintiffs to an equal education could be achieved was to admit them immediately to the white schools.

On October 8, 1952, the United States Supreme Court granted continuances in the Kansas and South Carolina cases, noted probable jurisdiction in the Virginia case, and took judicial notice of the D.C. case (*Bolling v. Sharpe*), scheduling all for oral argument the following December. On November 24, 1952, the Court granted the defendants' petition for certiorari in the Delaware case. The importance of these cases for the Southern defendants was reflected in their choice of counsel to argue their position: 79-year-old John W. Davis, Democratic presidential nominee in 1924 and, according to Kluger, "the most accomplished and admired appellate lawyer in America" (Kluger 1976). Davis chose to argue largely on the basis of the decisions in the lower courts. He pointed out that "separate but equal" was still the law of the land and that the states were making progress toward equalizing the facilities. He also introduced some studies designed to counter the social science evidence of the plaintiffs, furthering the defendants' position that these kinds of issues should be left to legislatures, not the courts. The LDF countered with a frontal attack on *Plessy,* arguing that circumstances had changed since 1896.

The U.S. Supreme Court was aware of the magnitude of the cases. The justices appeared in no hurry to reach a decision. Discussions continued throughout the spring of 1953, and ultimately the Court agreed to seek clarification on some points. It set the cases for reargument in the fall, when it would address five questions focusing on three areas: (1) the understanding of the framers of the Fourteenth Amendment with respect to its potential impact on segregated schools, (2) the extent of the judicial power in construing the amendment to abolish segregated schools, and (3) the scope of the Court's equity powers to fashion a decree to implement such a decision.

On September 8, 1953, Chief Justice Fred Vinson, a relatively conservative Kentuckian whose position on this case was at best ambivalent, suffered a fatal heart attack. Within three weeks, President Eisenhower chose California governor and 1948 Republican vice presidential nominee Earl Warren to replace Vinson. Because Congress was in recess, Warren was able to assume office immediately under a recess appointment. He was confirmed by the Senate on March 1, 1954. Beginning with his participation in the fall reargument, Warren made it clear that he regarded segregation as morally wrong. He indicated that he was prepared to take whatever time was necessary to bring his colleagues around to a unanimous opinion overturning *Plessy*. His primary allies turned out to be Justices Frankfurter and Black, whose sharp disagreements within the Court had become legendary. Justice Frankfurter was a strong believer in judicial restraint, while Justice Black, a native of Alabama, was, on most civil rights issues, a judicial activist (Kluger 1979; Dunne 1977; Pollack 1979). In enlisting the support of these justices and ultimately achieving unanimity, Warren produced an opinion that was far reaching in theory but very limited in practice.

First, the unanimous Court agreed that the historical evidence surrounding the intent of the framers of the Fourteenth Amendment with respect to segregated schools was "inconclusive," largely because there was very little public education at the time, especially in the South. Thus, the issue would not have been paramount in any debates. The Court found that factors deemed important in earlier public school desegregation cases were no longer applicable. In addition, the Court minimized the argument that "there are findings ... that the Negro and white schools involved have been equalized, or are being equalized." The Court stated: "We must look instead to the effect of segregation itself on public education.... We must consider

public education in the light of its full development and its present place in American life throughout the nation."

Describing education as "perhaps the most important function of state and local governments," the Chief Justice pointed to its role in socializing children and preparing them for citizenship and career opportunities. Hence, "[s]uch an opportunity, where the state has undertaken to provide it, is a right which must be made available to all on equal terms." The Court then indicated that it was persuaded by the kinds of sociopsychological evidence introduced in the trial courts by the plaintiffs. What followed was perhaps the most controversial statement in Warren's opinion: "Whatever may have been the extent of psychological knowledge at the time of *Plessy v. Ferguson*, this finding is amply supported by modern authority." The accompanying footnote cited not legal authorities but social science studies, including the work of the Clarks. Then came the judgment: "In the field of public education, the doctrine of 'separate but equal' has no place." Thus the plaintiffs had been deprived of equal protection. However, the Court then put on the brakes: "Because these are class actions, because of the wide applicability of this decision, and because of the great variety of local conditions, the formulation of decrees in these cases presents problems of considerable complexity." The Court scheduled another hearing for the following fall term, inviting the parties as well as others who might have a stake in the outcome (including the attorneys general of all states that operated dual school systems) to participate in the reargument as to the best approach to implement this potentially far-reaching judgment.

In the District of Columbia case (*Bolling v. Sharpe*), the Court, relying on the Due Process Clause of the Fifth Amendment, as distinguished from the Fourteenth Amendment's Equal Protection Clause, concluded that "discrimination may be so unjustifiable as to be violative of due process." The Court went on to explain: "That term is not confined to mere freedom from bodily restraint... [but] extends to the full range of conduct which the individual is free to pursue.... Segregation in public education is not reasonably related to any proper governmental objective."

A little over a year later, Chief Justice Warren authored a brief unanimous opinion for the Court addressing the question left open by the first *Brown* opinion. The Court held that the plaintiffs had a personal stake in admission to public schools "as soon as practicable on a nondiscriminatory basis," and that "the vitality of these constitutional principles cannot be allowed to yield simply because of disagreement with them." However, it acknowledged the complexity of the task of dismantling the dual systems and the wide variety of local conditions.

Thus it was the local school boards, with the oversight of the courts that had originally heard the cases, that were being charged with implementing the decree. Those courts were ordered to "take such proceedings and enter into such orders and decrees consistent with this opinion as are necessary and proper to admit to public schools on a racially nondiscriminatory basis *with all deliberate speed* the parties to these cases" (emphasis added).

It is likely that the Court overestimated the effect of its unanimous declaration and underestimated the willingness of parts of the South to resist. Harry Ashmore, editor of the liberal *Arkansas Gazette,* was chosen by the Ford Foundation to research the likely reactions of the South to the coming desegregation order in the 1950s. Interviewing politicians, academicians, and business leaders, "Ashmore and his colleagues found a glacial unwillingness to consider the subject publicly." He said that politicians "wouldn't even discuss the goddamn thing." Even business leaders "didn't want to believe it. There was an awful lot of rationalization" (Powledge 1991). It was also relevant to consider that many of the district judges across the South were products of the very political system that had created and perpetuated Jim Crow in the first place (Peltason 1971).

This judicial view is reflected in the response of Judge Sterling Hutcheson of the Eastern District of Virginia in *Davis v. Prince Edward County* (1957). While acknowledging that ordinarily plaintiffs

denied constitutional rights would be entitled to "immediate relief," he proceeded to expound on the Court's focus on the problems of implementation:

The conflicting rights and interests of racial and national groups in this country is nothing new.... Patience, time and a sympathetic approach are imperative to accomplish a change of conditions in an orderly and peaceful manner and with a minimum of friction.

Citing a survey that noted "marked improvement in racial relationships" but also that "many firmly fixed ancient customs and manners remain," Judge Hutcheson asserted that the county, as a result of ongoing lawsuits, had formulated plans for the erection of new buildings "exclusively for Negroes, which are now concededly equal if not superior to those occupied by the white pupils."

Laying aside for the moment the probability of the schools being closed, in the present state of unrest and racial tension in the county it would be unwise to attempt to force a change of the system until the entire situation can be considered and adjustments gradually brought about. This must be accomplished by the reasonable, clear-thinking people of both races in that locality. This objective cannot be achieved quickly. It does not require the opinion of a psychologist to understand that disaffection, uneasiness and uncertainty of the adult world around them creates emotional problems for children concerned. A sudden disruption of reasonably amicable racial relations which have been laboriously built up over a period of more than three and a quarter centuries would be deplorable. At any reasonable cost, it must be avoided.

Closing the schools, he said, "would be highly and permanently injurious to children of both races."

Many minds are now engaged in seeking an equitable solution of the problem, including those of the defendants. As was said by a great statesman, "The march of the human mind is slow." It is inconceivable that any of the litigants or other persons affected would willingly see the public school system abolished or an interruption in the education of the children of the county. Either result would be disastrous to both public and private interests of the county.... It is imperative that additional time be allowed the defendants in this case, who find themselves in a position of helplessness unless the Court considers their situation from an equitable and reasonable viewpoint.

This kind of rationale was typical of the reaction of many Southern courts to the edict that "the vitality of these constitutional principles cannot be allowed to yield simply because of disagreement with them" and to the mandate that admission to schools on a racially nondiscriminatory basis be accomplished "with all deliberate speed."

See also Civil Rights Movement; Due Process Clause; Equal Protection Clause; Fifth Amendment; Fourteenth Amendment; Jim Crow Laws; Marshall, Thurgood; National Association for the Advancement of Colored People; *Plessy v. Ferguson;* Segregation in Public Education; Vinson, Fred M.; Warren, Earl; Warren Court

Bibliography

Dunne, Gerald T. 1977. *Hugo Black and the Judicial Revolution.* New York: Simon & Schuster.

Kluger, Richard. 1976. *Simple Justice.* New York: Alfred A. Knopf.

Peltason, J. W. 1971. *Fifty-eight Lonely Men: Southern Judges and School Desegregation.* Urbana: University of Illinois Press.

Pollack, Jack Harrison. 1979. *Earl Warren: The Judge Who Changed America.* Englewood Cliffs, NJ: Prentice Hall.

Powledge, Fred. 1991. *Free at Last: The Civil Rights Movement and the People Who Made It.* New York: Harper Collins.

Coleman McGinnis

BUREAU OF CITIZENSHIP AND IMMIGRATION SERVICES (BCIS)

The Bureau of Citizenship and Immigration Services (BCIS) is an independent office within the Department of Homeland Security (DHS). The main objectives of BCIS are the promotion of national security, the elimination of immigration adjudication backlogs, and the implementation of solutions for improving immigration customer services. BCIS assumed responsibility for immigration from the former Immigration and Naturalization Service (INS) when DHS was created by Congress in 2002. The Homeland Security Act of 2002 also transferred INS's immigration enforcement functions to the Directorate of Border and Transportation Security, located within DHS. Other INS responsibilities were transferred to the management directorate within DHS.

With approximately 15,000 employees and contractors, BCIS provides immigration services such as family-based petitions, employment-based petitions, asylum and refugee processing, naturalization, special status programs, and document issuance and renewal. Other specific benefits include citizenship, employment authorization, foreign student authorization, intercountry adoptions, lawful permanent residency, and replacement immigration documents.

To accomplish its mission, BCIS is organized into local offices and local area immigration-services field offices. In addition, it provides some services through the Internet. There are 33 immigration district offices that enforce immigration laws. Some applications are filed directly with district offices, where interviews are conducted, and immigration staff are on hand to answer questions, provide forms, and perform other services. The district can include part of a state, one state, or several states, and it might have suboffices providing services to a certain part of the district's jurisdiction. Most of the BCIS staff work either in an immigration district office or in a suboffice.

BCIS has four service centers that process mail, files, and data entries and consider applications for immigration services and benefits. Due to the reduced number of employees and the organizational structure of the service centers, they do not deal with walk-in applications or answer questions. Immigration district offices are supervised by three regional offices located in Burlington, Vermont (eastern region); Dallas, Texas (central region); and Laguna Niguel, California (western region). Three immigration administrative centers located in these cities provide direct services and implement administrative policy.

There are eight asylum offices dealing specifically with asylum cases. However, applicants for asylum initially send their applications to the appropriate service center, not directly to an asylum office. Application support centers provide fingerprint background verification for certain immigration services, such as applications for naturalization and for registering permanent residence. The fingerprint background check may be conducted by a designated law enforcement agency (DLEA).

Within BCIS is the new Office of Citizenship, the main objective of which is to promote the training and instruction of citizenship responsibilities for immigrants. Through different activities, the Office of Citizenship attempts to promote common civic values, to emphasize the importance of naturalization as the most important action in becoming American, and to provide educational opportunities in English, history, and civics to new citizens.

There is also an Office of Congressional Relations, which forwards necessary information about immigration to congressional offices. According to its mission statement, "the Commissioner places the highest priority on providing professional customer service to Members of Congress and their staff on issues related to congressional inquiries, concerns and oversight."

The director of the Freedom of Information Act/Privacy Act Program coordinates the responses to FOIA requests. However, requests should be sent to the specific immigration office that keeps the solicited record. A good alternative is to consult the Electronic Reading Room (ERR), which is a Web page containing frequently requested records, opinions, policy statements, and staff manuals.

BCIS is required by law to produce various reports on its activities. Many of these reports are available to the public through the BCIS Web page, located at www.immigration.gov/graphics/index.htm. Evaluations of selected programs are provided to Congress and are accessible to citizens.

See also Freedom of Information Act; Homeland Security, Department of; Immigrants and Aliens, Rights of; Privacy Act

J. Ramon Gil-Garcia

BURGER, WARREN E. (1907–1995)

Warren Earl Burger was born on September 17, 1907, in St. Paul, Minnesota, into modest circumstances. Burger's father was a railroad cargo inspector and traveling salesman, while his mother ran a traditional household rooted in her German heritage. When he was a boy, Burger delivered newspapers to help the family. He did not compile an impressive academic record in high school; however, his achievement in extracurricular activities was sufficient to warrant a scholarship offer from Princeton University. Unfortunately for Burger, the scholarship was inadequate to meet his financial needs, and he enrolled in extension courses at the University of Minnesota while working part-time jobs. Similarly, Burger sold life insurance while attending night classes at St. Paul College of Law (now the William Mitchell School of Law). He graduated in 1931 and practiced law in his native Minnesota until 1953.

A spinal condition prevented Burger from serving in World War II. After the war, he held positions related to civil rights. He was a member of the governor's interracial commission from 1948 to 1953 and was the first president of St. Paul's Council on Human Relations, an organization created to improve relations between the city police and racial minorities (Yarbrough 2000, 78). While in private practice, Burger was heavily involved in Republican politics and supported Dwight Eisenhower in the 1952 presidential election. Eisenhower appointed Burger to the position of assistant attorney general to head the Justice Department's Civil Division in 1953. After two years, Eisenhower nominated Burger to the U.S. Court of Appeals for the District of Columbia Circuit, a position Burger would hold for 13 years. As an appellate court judge, Burger developed a conservative record, especially in cases pertaining to the rights of criminal defendants.

During his run for the presidency in 1968, Richard Nixon made "law and order" a central theme of his campaign and railed against the liberal decisions of the Warren Court, especially those protecting the rights of the accused. Thus, when Earl Warren retired from the Court in 1969, Burger struck President Nixon as logical successor. On May 22, 1969, Nixon formally nominated Burger to be the fifteenth chief justice in American history. Burger faced little opposition in the Senate and was confirmed on June 9, 1969, by a vote of 74–3.

Burger will be remembered primarily for his contribution to separation of powers in decisions such as *INS v. Chadha* (1983) and *Bowsher v. Synar* (1986). He did, however, make significant contributions in the areas of civil rights and civil liberties. Burger wrote the majority opinions in *Swann v. Charlotte-Mecklenburg County Board of Education* (1971) and *Milliken v. Bradley* (1974), two of the most significant cases on school desegregation. In *Swann,* the Court offered broad guidelines to school districts in the creation of desegregation plans and, perhaps most importantly, upheld busing as a means of achieving integration. In *Milliken,* however, Burger limited busing plans that were too broad and impacted schools that had sufficiently complied with desegregation orders. In Burger's majority opinion in *Bob Jones University v. United States* (1983), he "reaffirmed the nation's commitment to equal educational opportunity" (Lamb 1991, 149) by upholding the Internal Revenue Service's decision to revoke the tax exemption of the university because it imposed a racially discriminatory admissions policy.

Burger also wrote majority opinions in two significant cases involving race and employment discrimination. In *Griggs v. Duke Power* (1971), Burger wrote for a unanimous Court that ostensibly neutral employment practices were impermissible if their effect was to maintain the effects of past racial discrimination. Burger's opinion also held that discriminatory intent did not have to be proven to implicate Title VII of the Civil Rights Act of 1964. In *Fullilove v. Klutznick* (1980), Burger upheld a section of the Public Works Employment Act of

1977, which established a 10-percent set-aside for minority business enterprises and required recipients of federal grant money to purchase services and supplies with at least 10 percent of the funds from minority-owned businesses. Yet his votes in other employment discrimination cases tended to be more conservative (see, e.g., *Albemarle Paper v. Moody,* 1975; *Franks v. Bowman Transportation,* 1976; and *United Steelworkers of America v. Weber,* 1979).

Burger wrote significant opinions in other areas of civil rights. For instance, he wrote the landmark opinion in sex discrimination but later voted not to subject sex discrimination claims to strict scrutiny. In *Reed v. Reed* (1971), Burger authored the majority opinion striking down Idaho statutes that automatically gave men preference over women in administering the estate of a deceased relative. Burger wrote that the Equal Protection Clause of the Fourteenth Amendment prohibited classifications based on archaic and overbroad generalizations about women, and that administrative convenience was not a sufficient basis to sustain the statute. However, in *Frontiero v. Richardson* (1973), Burger joined the concurring opinion of Justice Lewis Powell refusing to subject sex discrimination suits to strict scrutiny, a higher standard of review, while the Equal Rights Amendment was pending.

In another landmark decision regarding women, Burger voted with the majority in *Roe v. Wade* (1973) and the companion case, *Doe v. Bolton,* to invalidate statutes placing limitations on abortion. In his concurring opinion in *Doe,* he wrote that the Texas and Georgia statutes were too broad and that it was clear that the Court rejected the claim that the Constitution required abortion on demand. He maintained this position throughout later abortion decisions; however, this view more often placed him among dissenting justices, who wanted to protect a woman's right to choose against state regulation (see, e.g., *Planned Parenthood of Central Missouri v. Danforth,* 1976; *Thornburgh v. American College of Obstetricians and Gynecologists,* 1986).

His votes in abortion decisions were consistent with his view of the right to privacy generally. Burger dissented in *Eisenstadt v. Baird* (1972), in which the Court invalidated a law banning the sale of contraceptives to married people. In *Bowers v. Hardwick* (1986), Burger, voting with the majority, wrote in concurrence that "there is no such thing as a fundamental right to commit homosexual sodomy."

Burger was the author of important cases concerning religious freedom. Indeed, his opinions regarding the Establishment Clause constitute perhaps "his strongest First Amendment legacy" (Lamb 1991, 146). His first Establishment Clause opinion, *Walz v. Tax Commission* (1970), upheld tax exemptions for church-owned property because the purpose of the exemptions was not to aid religion. In *Lemon v. Kurtzman* (1971), Burger articulated the three-part *Lemon* test, which relied heavily on prior cases, to guide the Court's inquiry into Establishment Clause cases; the ruling erected considerable barriers to state legislatures wishing to aid parochial schools. In *Marsh v. Chambers* (1983), however, Burger upheld a Nebraska law compensating chaplains for offering prayers to open the sessions of the state legislature. His opinion provided a history lesson to establish the tradition of the practice and noted that Congress had engaged in the same activity at the same time they drafted the Establishment Clause. Burger also wrote the majority opinion in the landmark free exercise case, *Wisconsin v. Yoder* (1972), which held that individuals of the Amish faith were exempt from a compulsory school attendance law because it infringed upon their right of free exercise.

Burger's opinions concerning other First Amendment freedoms were equally important. In general, he demonstrated a propensity to uphold free press claims (Yarbrough 2000, 82). For example, he was the author of *Nebraska Press Association v. Stuart* (1976), where the Court refused to allow a trial judge to impose a gag order on the press to preserve a defendant's right to a fair trial. But he was among the dissenters in *New York Times v. United States* (1971), in which the Court refused to allow lower courts to enjoin the publication of

the infamous Pentagon Papers. And he wrote the majority opinion in *Miller v. California* (1973), which expanded governmental power to prosecute obscenity cases.

Burger's opinions in the area of criminal justice were all that President Nixon hoped they would be when he appointed Burger to the Court. His rulings on both Fourth and Fifth Amendment cases were predominantly in favor of the prosecution. Burger consistently argued (in cases such as *Bivens v. Six Unknown Named Agents of the Federal Bureau of Narcotics,* 1971) that the exclusionary rule should be abandoned and that it was the responsibility of Congress to articulate an alternative (Lamb 1991, 153). Later in his tenure, he voted to impose limitations on the exclusionary rule such as the good-faith exception and the inevitable discovery rule. A similar pattern emerged in Fifth Amendment self-incrimination cases, where Burger supported limitations on *Miranda* warnings.

During his tenure as chief justice, Burger was heavily criticized for his lack of leadership among the other justices. Indeed, during the Burger Court era, the rate of both concurring and dissenting opinions was the highest in the institution's history. Burger was also criticized for manipulating conference votes by voting with the majority so that he could either author or assign the majority opinion, which by tradition is the chief justice's prerogative. He also evinced a strong interest in judicial reform in his capacity as the head administrative official of the federal judiciary. Burger's interest even extended to beautification efforts of the Supreme Court building and grounds.

Warren Burger died on June 25, 1995, and is buried in Arlington National Cemetery alongside several justices with whom he served.

See also Abortion, Right to; Accused, Rights of the; Affirmative Action; *Bivens v. Six Unknown Named Federal Narcotics Agents; Bob Jones University v. United States;* Burger Court; Civil Rights Act of 1964; Equal Protection Clause; Equal Protection Jurisprudence; Equal Rights Amendment; Establishment Clause; Fifth Amendment; First Amendment;

Fourth Amendment; Fourth Amendment Exclusionary Rule; Gag Orders; Gay Rights Movement; Gender-Based Discrimination; Internal Revenue Service; *Lemon v. Kurtzman; Miranda v. Arizona; Miranda v. Arizona,* Exceptions to; *New York Times v. United States;* Obscenity and Pornography; Press, Freedom of the; Prior Restraint, Doctrine of; Privacy, Constitutional Right of; Religion, Freedom of; Religious Schools, Government Aid to; *Roe v. Wade;* Segregation in Public Education; Self-Incrimination Clause; Separation of Church and State; U.S. Department of Justice; Warren, Earl; Warren Court; *Wisconsin v. Yoder*

Bibliography

Abraham, Henry. 1999. *Justices, Presidents, and Senators.* Lanham, MD: Rowman & Littlefield.

Lamb, Charles M. 1991. "Chief Justice Warren E. Burger: A Conservative Chief for Conservative Times." In *The Burger Court: Political and Judicial Profiles,* ed. Charles M. Lamb and Stephen C. Halpern. Urbana: University of Illinois Press.

Yarbrough, Tinsley. 2000. *The Burger Court: Justices, Rulings, and Legacy.* Santa Barbara, CA: ABC-Clio.

Kara E. Stooksbury

BURGER COURT (1969–1986)

Richard Nixon campaigned for the presidency in 1968 claiming he would reorient the Supreme Court and make it more supportive of law and order concerns. He said that the justices he would appoint would have "experience or great knowledge in the field of criminal justice, and an understanding of the role some of the decisions of the high court have played in weakening the peace forces in our society in recent years…. They would be strict constructionists who saw their duty as interpreting law and not making law. They would see themselves as caretakers of the Constitution and servants of the people, not super-legislators with a free hand to impose their social and political viewpoints upon the American people" (*New York Times,* 3 November 1968). Included under this rhetorical umbrella was the implication that the sweeping decisions of

the Warren Court in civil liberties and rights cases would be curtailed.

As president, Nixon appointed four justices to the Supreme Court, beginning with Chief Justice Warren Burger in June 1969. Following him were Harry A. Blackmun (1970), Lewis Powell (1971), and William H. Rehnquist (1971). By replacing four Warren Court jurists in two years, Nixon should have been in a position to prompt a sea of change in constitutional interpretation and judicial decisions. However, in the words of Robert Burns, the "best laid schemes o' mice and men *gang aft a-gley.*" In the end, the Burger Court was comprised of three Warren-era holdovers and six justices appointed by Republican presidents and thus ended up looking like a more modest version of the Court it was intended to supplant.

Examining the Burger Court's corpus in areas of concern to Nixon shows both the vagaries of trying to orchestrate constitutional change through the appointment power and the persistence of Warren-style judicial decision making. In the area of criminal law, Nixon succeeded in preventing expansion of precedents he disdained. However, in areas of expression, civil rights, church-state relations, and personal autonomy, the Burger Court ended up working against Nixonian goals. Ultimately, the Burger Court ended up as "the revolution that wasn't" (Blasi 1983).

The focus of Nixon's disdain for the Court's criminal law cases was its decisions in *Mapp v. Ohio* (1961) and *Miranda v. Arizona* (1966). *Mapp* read the exclusionary rule into the Fourth Amendment and disallowed use of evidence seized illegally—without a warrant or probable cause—in trials across the nation. *Miranda* required police to apprise criminal suspects of their constitutional rights before questioning them about criminal activity. If questioning occurred without these warnings, confessions were excluded from trials. Nixon believed that these cases created a one-two punch that devastated police work and allowed "guilty men [to] walk free from hundreds of courtrooms across the country" (Simon 1973, 7).

The Burger Court tackled issues arising out of these precedents, and it did nothing to extend them. Indeed, in cases such as *Rhode Island v. Innis* (1980) and *New York v. Quarles* (1984), it narrowed the definition of what constitutes questioning, thus making *Miranda* apply to a narrower range of police practices. The Burger Court also created a public safety exception to its exclusionary effects; that is, if non-*Mirandized* questioning was needed to protect the safety of others, confessions could be introduced into trials. Similarly, it allowed illegally seized evidence to be submitted before grand juries (*United States v. Calandra,* 1974) and evidence garnered by a search stemming from a constitutionally faulty warrant to be used in trials (*United States v. Leon,* 1984). These cases, and many others of their kind, worked to check any expansion of *Mapp* and *Miranda,* but the Burger Court reversed neither precedent.

Capital punishment received more attention during the Burger era than it had from previous courts combined. Although *Furman v. Georgia* (1972), a five-to-four decision with all the Nixon appointees in dissent, struck down the death penalty nationwide, the Court reinstituted it in *Gregg v. Georgia* (1976). In many closely divided decisions after *Gregg,* the Court grappled with the procedures of capital punishment, sometimes finding for the state, other times for the convicted. However, in nationalizing litigation of capital punishment, the Court took on an unprecedented role as supervisor of executions. Here, as in other criminal law cases, Nixon won many battles, but never the constitutional war (Epstein and Kobylka 1992).

This sort of ambiguity characterized other aspects of the work of the Burger Court. In matters of speech and press, the Burger Court did little to undo the generally libertarian inclinations of its predecessor. In obscenity law, an area that did see some revision, the Court rejected the "utterly without redeeming social importance" standard of *Memoirs v. Massachusetts* (1966) in *Miller v. California* (1973) and *Paris Adult Theatre v. Slaton* (1973), but the new test offered by these cases still protected more sexually explicit speech than had

been the case prior to the Warren Court's entrance into this field, and prosecutions remained cumbersome and costly.

In other areas of expression, the Burger Court largely continued to follow the path charted by previous Courts. Symbolic speech received protection in cases such as *Cohen v. California* (1971), *Spence v. Washington* (1974), and *Wooley v. Maynard* (1977). Even in cases where it held against the speech claim (e.g., *Clark v. Community for Creative Non-Violence,* 1984), the Court adopted a very broad definition of symbolic speech. Further, despite rumblings from some of its members, the Court continued the clear and imminent danger approach to protecting utterances in politically charged contexts (*Hess v. Indiana,* 1974). Paralleling the development in criminal law, the Burger Court trimmed the application of the actual malice standard for libel prosecutions in cases such as *Gertz v. Welch* (1974) and *Dun and Bradstreet v. Greenmoss Builders* (1985), but it never questioned the application of the *New York Times v. Sullivan* (1964) test to public officials or figures. Burger's Court, though, did not solely trim the doctrine it inherited; in some areas—most notably commercial speech beginning with *Bigelow v. Virginia* (1975) and *Virginia Pharmacy Board v. Virginia Consumers Council* (1976)—it expanded the scope of expression given constitutional protection.

Inheriting an overgrown doctrinal path in church-state matters, the Burger Court sought to clear the way to some constitutional coherence. In *Wisconsin v. Yoder* (1972), it seemed to cement the compelling state interest approach of *Sherbert v. Verner* (1963) as the test for free exercise cases. *Lemon v. Kurtzman* (1971) initially seemed to suggest a synthesis between disparate elements of the Court's establishment clause doctrine by fusing the purpose, effect, and entanglement tests of various previous cases. However, the *Lemon* machete, depending on which coalition of justices wielded it, proved to cut not one, but two, paths: one pointing toward a "wall of separation" (e.g., *Committee for Public Education v. Nyquist,* 1973; *Meek v. Pittenger,* 1975; *Wolman v. Walter,* 1977), the other leading to greater governmental accommodation of religion (e.g., *Tilton v. Richardson,* 1971; *Committee for Public Education v. Regan,* 1980; *Mueller v. Allen,* 1983; *Marsh v. Chambers,* 1983; *Lynch v. Donnelly,* 1984). Although the latter run of cases seemed to suggest the demise of the wall, Burger's ability to hold the Court to this end crumbled in its 1984 term (Kobylka 1989). In *Wallace v. Jaffree* (1985), the Court struck down an Alabama moment of silence statute by a six-to-three vote; in *Grand Rapids v. Ball* (1985) and *Aguilar v. Felton* (1985), it struck down state aid to programs in private religious schools by five-to-four votes. The justices responsible for the shifting winning coalitions were Lewis Powell and Sandra Day O'Connor, and Burger was never able to guide them fully into the clearing he had envisioned.

Nixon's electoral goals relied heavily on the so-called Southern strategy—peeling Southern states out of the Democratic column in national elections. One aspect of this strategy entailed nominating Southerners to Supreme Court vacancies (he failed with Clement Haynsworth and G. Harrold Carswell but succeeded with Lewis Powell), but significant, too, was getting the Court to ease away from extending the line of cases it began with *Brown v. Board of Education* (1954). As in most other areas of the Nixonized Court's dealings, the president's success here was ambiguous. It was "his" Court—despite Burger's efforts to moderate the effects of the decisions (Schwartz 1986), such as sanctioned busing to achieve unitary school systems (*Swann v. Board of Education,* 1971; *Keyes v. School District,* 1973), extended federal civil rights statutes to private contracting (*Runyon v. McCrary,* 1976), and upheld racial preferences in education (*Regents v. Bakke,* 1978) and employment (*Steelworkers v. Weber,* 1976). Yet because of the shifting coalitions that dominated the direction of the decisions reached by Burger's Court, other cases limited the scope of the decisions noted above. For example, *Milliken v. Bradley* (1974) confined busing plans to individual school districts, *Washington v. Davis* (1976) raised the bar for a plaintiff to prove employment discrimination, and *Wygant v.*

Board of Education (1986) narrowed constitutional protection for affirmative action programs. This decisional ambivalence resulted in part from the new issues the Burger Court had to face, but it also flowed from a moderate bloc of justices—most frequently Potter Stewart, Harry Blackmun, Lewis Powell, and John Paul Stevens—whose votes were often case specific.

Although the Burger Court oscillated on issues concerning racial equality, its approach to gender discrimination was revolutionary. This process began with a seemingly modest opinion striking down a preference in favor of fathers in administering estates in *Reed v. Reed* (1971). Burger's opinion for the Court did not explicitly articulate a new level of review under the Equal Protection Clause, but it implicitly required a state to have more than a simply plausible explanation for such discrimination to be "rational" and, hence, constitutional. In *Fronterio v. Richardson* (1973), the Court again struck down a statutory preference that favored men, but this time Justices Douglas, Brennan, White, and Marshall argued that gender-based discrimination was constitutionally "suspect" and, like racial discrimination, should be reviewed under a standard of strict scrutiny. The Nixon appointees preferred the elevated rational basis approach of *Reed,* but in *Craig v. Boren* (1976) a majority of justices coalesced on a new intermediate scrutiny approach that required that legislation that discriminated on the basis of sex must "substantially further important governmental objectives." With this, the Court joined Congress in advancing gender equality.

Perhaps the most prominent area of Burger Court activism arose in matters of personal autonomy and privacy. Foremost here was *Roe v. Wade* (1973), the seven-to-two decision that held that the constitutional concept of privacy was "broad enough to encompass a woman's decision whether or not to terminate her pregnancy." Developing a trimester approach to weigh out the competing interests of the woman, her doctor, and the state, *Roe* (and its companion case *Doe v. Bolton*) created a constitutional right to abortion. Though the support for this form of the *Roe* right shrank to six-to-three with the addition of O'Connor to the Court (*Akron v. Akron Center for Reproductive Health*, 1983) and five-to-four with Burger's own defection (*Thornburgh v. American College of Obstetricians and Gynecologists*, 1986), it weathered a sustained onslaught from within and without the Court through Burger's tenure. Only on the question of public funding of abortions for indigents (*Poelker v. Doe*, 1977; *Harris v. McCrae*, 1980) did the Burger Court constrain the availability of this right. However, the Burger Court was not inclined to extend the privacy right to consensual same-sex relations, rejecting by a vote of five-to-four a claim that privacy immunized homosexuality from criminal prosecution five-to-four in *Bowers v. Hardwick* (1986). Thus, although the abortion decisions broadened the constitutional domain of privacy, the sodomy decision fenced part of it in.

In the final analysis, the Burger Court—while not as generally activist in its use of judicial power as the Warren Court—did not systematically advance the constitutional goals of the Republican presidents who appointed the majority of its justices. It nipped and tucked some of the legacy left by the Warren Court, but in no areas of general significance did it wholly reject the doctrine it inherited. Although Burger and Rehnquist were inclined to reverse and retrench, they were not able to develop the critical mass of a majority to achieve this end. Ultimately, the Burger Court is best understood as a Court lacking ideological direction as a result of its domination by more moderate jurists. With these justices as its fulcrum, the Burger Court never teetered too far right or left.

See also Abortion, Public Funding of; Abortion, Right to; Affirmative Action; Blackmun, Harry A.; Brennan, William J., Jr.; *Brown v. Board of Education;* Burger, Warren E.; Busing Controversy; *Cohen v. California;* Death Penalty and the Supreme Court; Sexual Orientation, Discrimination Based on; Draft Cards, Burning of; Fourth Amendment Exclusionary Rule; *Frontiero v. Richardson;* *Furman v. Georgia;* Gender-Based Discrimination; Good-Faith Exception; *Gregg v. Georgia; Lemon v. Kurtzman; Mapp v. Ohio;* Marshall, Thurgood; *Miranda v. Arizona; New York Times v. Sullivan;* Obscenity and Pornography; O'Connor, Sandra Day; Powell, Lewis F., Jr.; Privacy, Constitutional Right of; Rehnquist, William H.; Religion, Freedom of; Religious Displays on Public Property; *Roe v. Wade;* Stevens, John Paul; Stewart, Potter; Symbolic Speech; Warren Court; White, Byron R.; *Wisconsin v. Yoder*

Bibliography

Blasi, Vincent, ed. 1983. *The Burger Court: The Counter-Revolution That Wasn't.* New Haven, CT: Yale University Press.

Epstein, Lee, and Joseph F. Kobylka. 1992. *The Supreme Court and Legal Change.* Chapel Hill: University of North Carolina Press.

Kobylka, Joseph F. 1989. "Leadership on the Supreme Court: Chief Justice Burger and Establishment Clause Litigation." *Western Political Quarterly* 42:545–69.

Schwartz, Bernard. 1986. *Swann's Way: The School Busing Case and the Supreme Court.* New York: Oxford University Press.

Simon, James. 1973. *In His Own Image.* New York: David McKay.

Joseph F. Kobylka

BURKE, EDMUND. *See* Conservatism

BUSH V. GORE (2000)

In the most controversial use of judicial power since *Roe v. Wade* (1973), the Supreme Court in *Bush v. Gore* effectively decided the outcome of the 2000 presidential election. Due to the closeness of the election nationally, Florida's electoral votes proved to be decisive in determining the next president. Although Governor George W. Bush ostensibly won the popular vote as recorded by the voting machines, widespread problems with ballots led Democrats to argue that the results were erroneous and that a manual recount would prove Vice President Al Gore to be the winner. Litigation in the Florida courts led to decisions by that state's supreme court extending the period for a manual recount and limiting the recount to selected counties that used different procedures for conducting their recounts. At the request of candidate Bush, the U.S. Supreme Court became involved in the dispute.

In *Bush v. Gore,* the Court ruled seven-to-two that the selective manual recount ordered by the Florida Supreme Court was a violation of the Equal Protection Clause. According to the brief per curiam opinion issued by the Court, "[t]he recount mechanisms implemented in response to the decisions of the Florida Supreme Court do not satisfy the minimum requirement for non-arbitrary treatment of voters necessary to secure the fundamental right [to vote]." Justice David Souter, who concurred in this aspect of the decision, could "conceive of no legitimate state interest served by these differing treatments of the expressions of voters' fundamental rights." In Souter's view, the different procedures for conducting the manual recount appeared "wholly arbitrary." Under normal circumstances, the remedy for this constitutional violation would be to order a statewide manual recount under judicial supervision using standardized procedures. Of course, the circumstances surrounding this case were anything but normal. By a bare majority, the Court decided to halt the recount and effectively declare Bush the winner.

Exacerbating the controversy over the Court's decision was the fact that the five justices who voted to halt the recount were the court's five conservatives: Rehnquist, Scalia, Thomas, Kennedy, and O'Connor. All five had been appointed by Republican presidents, making the decision appear to many observers, including the four dissenters, to be a case of partisan loyalty trumping judicial self-restraint. Not surprisingly, Democrats across the country were outraged by the decision. Some even called for impeachment of the five Republican appointees, who constituted the Court's majority. Very few scholars came to the Court's defense. Alan M. Dershowitz (2001) accused the Court of "hijacking" the election, and Bruce Ackerman (2002) went so far as to characterize *Bush v. Gore* as a "constitutional coup."

In his dissenting opinion in *Bush v. Gore,* Justice John Paul Stevens expressed worry that the decision would undermine "the Nation's confidence in the judge as an impartial guardian of the rule of law." Five years later, it was clear that *Bush v. Gore* did not result in a dramatic loss of public confidence in the Supreme Court. Certainly, it was not a self-inflicted wound of the magnitude of the Dred Scott Case, as some observers had suggested in the immediate aftermath of the decision.

See also Dred Scott Case; Equal Protection Clause; Fourteenth Amendment; Free and Fair Elections; Fundamental Rights; Kennedy, Anthony; O'Connor, Sandra Day; Reapportionment; Rehnquist, William H.; Rehnquist Court; Scalia, Antonin; Souter, David H.; Stevens, John Paul; Thomas, Clarence

Bibliography

Ackerman, Bruce A., ed. 2002. *Bush v. Gore: The Question of Legitimacy.* New Haven, CT: Yale University Press.

Dershowitz, Alan M. 2001. *Supreme Injustice: How the High Court Hijacked Election 2000.* New York: Oxford University Press.

Issacharoff, Samuel, Pamela Karlin, and Richard Pildes. 2001. *When Elections Go Bad: The Law of Democracy and the Presidential Election of 2000.* New York: Foundation Press.

John M. Scheb II and Otis H. Stephens, Jr.

BUSING CONTROVERSY

The landmark Supreme Court ruling in *Brown v. Board* (1954) marked the end of legally sanctioned segregated public schools in the United States. In *Brown II* (1955), the Court held that schools must dismantle segregation policies "with all deliberate speed." Because many school districts and state governments were adamantly opposed to desegregation, the battle over the time line for integration was fought until 1969, when in *Alexander v. Board of Education* the Court held that integration should be undertaken "immediately." To comply with that mandate, school officials and federal district court judges instituted busing policies to achieve racially balanced schools.

The Supreme Court first dealt with the busing issue in *Swann v. Charlotte-Mecklenburg County Board of Education* (1971). In this case the Court held that school officials could impose a wide range of remedies to eliminate segregation, including busing. The school system had 84,000 students, of which approximately 29,000 were bused in the 1969–1970 school year, a number that increased by almost 13,000 after a federal district judge's ruling in February 1970 (Savage 2004, 276). In the Court's majority opinion, Chief Justice Warren Burger upheld busing as one of many appropriate tools for desegregation. Burger acknowledged that busing could be inconvenient and burdensome, "but all awkwardness and inconvenience cannot be avoided in the interim period when the remedial adjustments are being made to eliminate the dual school systems". However, busing was not without limitations. Burger stated that several factors would come into play in defining limitations on busing plans, including the health consequences of lengthy bus rides and the age of the children involved. Burger also made it clear that once desegregation had been accomplished, there was no requirement to annually adjust racial composition in the schools, a point that was reiterated in *Pasadena City Board of Education v. Spangler* (1976).

On the same day the Court issued its ruling in *Swann,* it handed down rulings in three other cases dealing with busing. It invalidated a state law prohibiting busing by school systems in *North Carolina State Board of Education v. Swann* (1971), because the law interfered with desegregation plans. In *McDaniel v. Barresi* (1971), the Court upheld a Georgia county's desegregation plan despite the fact that only African American students were bused. The Court stated that race could be a factor in developing such plans. Finally, in *Davis v. Board of School Commissioners of Mobile County* (1971), the Court remanded a case to the court of appeals so that it could reexamine a desegregation order that had not included busing.

President Nixon responded to these decisions by warning federal officials that they could either stop pressing for forced busing or find employment elsewhere. Nixon also "expressed the view that efforts to force integration in the suburbs were 'counterproductive and not in the interest of better race relations'" (Franklin 1980, 483).

Despite this sentiment, the Court extended its support of court-ordered busing even outside the South in *Keyes v. School District No. 1* (1973). In this case the Court distinguished between de jure segregation and de facto segregation; the former involves segregation imposed through state action and is unconstitutional, while the latter involves segregation due to nongovernmental factors such as residential housing patterns and is constitutionally permissible. Critics contended that Justice William Brennan's majority opinion had blurred the distinction between the two, as "energetic plaintiffs could always find evidence that a school official had done something that could be interpreted as purposefully or intentionally fostering segregation" (Urofsky and Finkelman 2002, 901). In this case, the Court ruled that a school system that had never been statutorily segregated was still unconstitutional because the school board had used race as a factor in drawing attendance zones.

Many parents and public officials expressed outrage over the Court's busing decisions. There were protests and even a riot in Boston, Massachusetts, in September 1974, when a federal judge ordered the desegregation of schools in predominantly white south Boston and heavily black Roxbury. On the first day of the plan's implementation, only 10 of the 525 white students assigned to Roxbury were present. The buses carrying 56 African American children to south Boston were stoned (Jost 2004).

Against the din of the public outcry over busing, the Supreme Court began to limit the scope of busing policies. In *Milliken v. Bradley* (1974), the Court invalidated a plan to desegregate schools in Detroit, Michigan. The plan required busing students among 54 school districts in three counties. The Court struck down this plan because not all the districts were guilty of instituting segregation policies. Burger wrote for a five-member majority that the scope of the remedy could not exceed the extent of the violation. In other words, only the segregated district could be altered to achieve integration because the Constitution only prohibited intentional discrimination; therefore, it could not be used to remedy problems that were not created by governmental action. Reaction to the case was mixed. This was the first instance since *Brown* that civil rights lawyers had lost a case, and it was thus perceived by some as a step backward in the movement toward desegregated schools. Others, however, were relieved that local control of schools would be restored (Urofsky and Finkelman 2002).

Much like other desegregation cases, the distinction between de jure and de facto segregation was at the heart of several busing cases. According to Urofsky and Finkelman, the Burger Court struck down state-sponsored or state-endorsed discrimination as energetically as the Warren Court had. However, the Burger Court was more reluctant to intrude into areas where segregation was the result of historic patterns. Moreover, the justices had difficulty agreeing on "how far the Constitution required society to go to achieve full integration" (Urofsky and Finkelman 2002, 903). For instance in both *Columbus Board of Education v. Penick* (1979) and *Dayton Board of Education v. Brinkman* (1979), the Court split five-to-four in determining that school districts that were segregated at the time of *Brown* were still practicing de jure segregation and that further integration efforts were appropriate. The dissenters argued that any racial discrepancies in education were the result of residential patterns as opposed to overt school board action and that the majority relied too strongly on pre-*Brown* circumstances.

Some communities felt as though they had been pushed too far by court-ordered busing and began to pass initiatives to scale back the practice. In two 1982 decisions, the Court dealt with voter initiatives passed in two states. In *Washington v. Seattle School District No. 1* (1982), the Court upheld a local school board's busing plan that required students

to attend any school other than the two nearest to their homes. This plan was upheld despite an initiative passed by voters to end mandatory busing unless it was judicially mandated to eliminate de jure segregation. Writing for the Court, Justice Harry Blackmun stated that Initiative 350, a 1978 voter-approved measure, was unconstitutional because it created an "impermissible racial classification" that allowed busing for nonracial reasons but banned it for racial reasons. Furthermore, according to Blackmun, a majority of citizens could not employ the machinery of government to obstruct "the path of minorities seeking equal rights, especially when such laws relied on racial classification" (Urofsky and Finkelman 2002, 901).

On the same day this decision was handed down, the Court also issued a ruling in *Crawford v. Los Angeles Board of Education* (1982). In this case, the justices considered a challenge to a California initiative that prohibited busing as a remedy for de facto segregation. State judges in California had been active in promoting busing to achieve full integration even in the absence of governmental policies requiring segregation. In response, the voters passed Proposition I, which imposed limits on the state courts' power to order busing on the same scale as federal courts. The Court held that Proposition I did not violate the Fourteenth Amendment's Equal Protection Clause. Justice Lewis Powell's majority opinion emphasized that the "simple repeal or modification of desegregation or antidiscrimination laws, without more, does not embody a presumptively invalid racial classification."

In the 1990s, the busing issue, along with desegregation more generally, was framed in the context of the extent of judicial oversight; in other words, when do judges end desegregation efforts and return control of schools to local school boards? In *Board of Education v. Dowell* (1991), the Court ruled that once a school district has attained unitary status as determined by a federal judge, it has no further duty to maintain desegregation. Desegregation orders, including busing, were thus temporary in nature. According to Chief Justice William Rehnquist's majority opinion, "dissolution of a desegregation decree after local authorities have operated in compliance with it for a reasonable period is proper." The Court followed this ruling a year later with *Freeman v. Pitts* (1992), in which it made clear that a district court may relinquish supervision of school district incrementally in the course of supervising a desegregation plan. A district court also has the authority to refuse to order any new remedies in areas where the school authorities are complying with a desegregation decree.

The trend of limiting judicial oversight of desegregation plans continued in *Missouri v. Jenkins* (1995). In this case, the Court held that a district court had exceeded its authority in requiring interdistrict remedies to intradistrict constitutional violations. The district court had ordered the creation and funding of magnet schools along with salary increases for several thousand school employees. Chief Justice Rehnquist emphasized that the district court should be concerned with restoring control of the school system to state and local authorities, not simply remedying the constitutional violation.

Some observers have been critical of these recent rulings as patterns of resegregation in school districts have emerged. As a result, civil rights advocates have put more resources into challenging state funding schemes by either filing lawsuits or lobbying state legislatures in an attempt to attain equal resources for school districts within a state (Jost 2004).

See also Blackmun, Harry A.; Brennan, William J., Jr.; *Brown v. Board;* Burger, Warren E.; Equal Protection Clause; Equal Protection Jurisprudence; Fourteenth Amendment; Little Rock Crisis; Powell, Lewis F., Jr.; Public Education, Right to; Rehnquist, William H.; Segregation, De Facto and DeJure; Segregation in Public Education

Bibliography

Franklin, John Hope. 1980. *From Slavery to Freedom: A History of Negro Americans.* 5th ed. New York: Alfred A. Knopf.

Jost, Kenneth. 2004. "School Desegregation." In *Issues for Debate in American Public Policy.* 5th ed. Washington, DC: CQ Press

Savage, David. 2004. *The Supreme Court and Individual Rights.* 4th ed. Washington, DC: CQ Press.

Urofsky, Melvin I., and Paul Finkelman. 2002. *A March for Liberty: A Constitutional History of the United States.* Vol. 2: *From 1877 to the Present.* New York: Oxford University Press.

Kara E. Stooksbury

C

CALHOUN, JOHN C. *See* States' Rights, Doctrine of

CAMPAIGN FINANCE REFORM

Ever since the end of the Civil War the federal government has attempted to regulate the flow of money into the political process. The first efforts, such as the Naval Appropriations Bill of 1867 and the 1883 Civil Service Reform Act, concentrated on protecting government workers from pressure to make contributions to the campaigns of candidates favored by their superiors. Over the course of the next century Congress made a number of efforts at regulating the growing influence of money on politics, but most attempts at regulation floundered under lax enforcement.

The modern era of campaign finance regulation began with the Federal Election Campaign Act of 1971 (FECA). By this time money was beginning to be funneled from private interests to political actors through political action committees (PACs). The FECA not only established limits on contributions but required disclosure of contributions. Other related legislation established the check-off on the federal income tax return for the public funding of presidential campaigns.

One of the major elements of the Federal Election Campaign Act was the creation of the Federal Election Commission (FEC). Its six commissioners, appointed by the president, head an agency whose purpose is to oversee the administration of election laws passed by Congress. Until the creation of the FEC, it had proven to be extremely difficult to enforce legislation.

The impact of the Watergate scandal led to a series of important amendments to FECA. The 1974 FECA amendments set the tone for regulation of federal elections for the next 30 years. Under the act, individual contributions to campaigns were limited to $1,000, and PAC contributions were capped at $5,000. This move to regulate PACs actually set the stage for a tremendous growth of the committees and their influence for decades. It encouraged contributions to parties for party-building activities rather than to individual candidate campaigns. The provisions creating public funding of presidential campaigns, including primary elections, for serious candidates represented a major attempt to free candidates from the need to raise large sums for their campaigns.

In *Buckley v. Valeo* (1976), the Supreme Court reviewed the constitutionality of the major provisions of the FECA, as amended in 1974. The Court began its opinion by noting that legal limitations on political campaign contributions and expenditures "operate in an area of the most fundamental First Amendment activities." Although the Court upheld limits on outside contributions, both from PACs and individuals, the Court struck down the limitation on a candidate's expenditures from personal funds as well as the ceiling on overall campaign expenditures. The Court concluded that these provisions placed substantial and direct restrictions on the ability of candidates to engage in political expression protected by the First Amendment. In a sense, then, *Buckley* recognized that the expenditure of funds was, at least in some contexts, a form of speech protected by the First Amendment.

While the FECA brought a new level of public scrutiny and control to the regulation of political contributions, it had a number of unintended consequences and loopholes that created as many problems as it seemed to solve. First, the act fueled explosive growth in the number and influence of political action committees. Second, it allowed what became known as soft money to circumvent much of the intent of the act by funneling large amounts of money to party-building activities that clearly were thinly disguised efforts to directly aid a candidate's campaign.

Beginning in the late 1990s, and continuing through the presidential election of 2000, the pressure for significant alterations of the act continued to grow. The effort for reform was led by senators John McCain (R) and Russ Feingold (D), but while there was a moderate consensus that the act needed updating, the consensus broke down when it came to the details of implementation. Finally, Congress passed new reform legislation known as the Bipartisan Campaign Reform Act of 2002. The new legislation put new controls on unregulated soft money contributions and raised the limits on individual contributions to candidates, as well as strengthening requirements for disclosure, and put limits on issue advertising. During the next presidential election cycle in 2004, one element of the new legislation proved to be quite controversial, that which governed the so-called 527 groups. These nonprofit groups funneled large amounts of money directly into political advertisements around the regulations. The act also left unregulated the raising of money on the Internet.

Despite major efforts at controlling the flow of big money into political campaigns, large amounts of cash, and, presumably, influence, seem to find a way to get to candidates. The ever-escalating costs

of campaigns appear to have made this flow all but inevitable. However, while the flow of money may be difficult to stem, the disclosure requirements embodied in most of the reforms, and the availability of Internet sites such as www.opensecrets.org, have certainly increased the ability of citizens to follow the money.

See also First Amendment; Free and Fair Elections; Interest Groups; Speech, Freedom of

Bibliography

Corrado, Anthony, Thomas E. Mann, and Trevor Potter, eds. 2003. *Inside the Campaign Finance Debate: Arguments from the Court Battle over BCRA.* Washington, DC: Brookings Institution.

Mann, Thomas E. 2003. "Linking Knowledge and Action: Political Science and Campaign Finance Reform." *Perspectives on Politics* 1 (1): 69–83.

Smith, Bradley A. 2001. *Unfree Speech: The Folly of Campaign Finance Reform.* Princeton, NJ: Princeton University Press.

William Lyons

CANTWELL V. CONNECTICUT (1940)

Until 1940, the Free Exercise Clause of the First Amendment applied only to the federal government. States, if their legislatures and executives were so inclined, could pass laws prohibiting the free exercise of religion. Indeed, even the federal government had a broad range of power to impinge on religious practice. In *Reynolds v. United States* (1878), the Supreme Court upheld a bigamy conviction under federal law in the Utah Territory. George Reynolds, a devout Mormon, had multiple wives, so there was no question of fact in contest here; his defense was that this practice was essential to the free exercise of his religion and constitutionally protected. A unanimous Court disagreed, stating that "polygamy has always been odious among the northern and western nations of Europe, and, until the establishment of the Mormon Church, was almost exclusively a feature of the life of Asiatic and of African people." Since the law applied to all people (not just Mormons) in the territory and did not prohibit *belief* but only *behavior*—and that behavior was reprehensible to decent folk—it did not violate the Constitution. This rule of general applicability was called into question—and the Free Exercise Clause was incorporated against state as well as federal infringement in *Cantwell v. Connecticut* (1940).

Newton Cantwell and his two sons were Jehovah's Witnesses who aggressively proselytized their faith and solicited contributions for their church. They were arrested in a predominantly Catholic neighborhood in New Haven for going door-to-door without a government-issued permit. They appealed their conviction, arguing that it violated their free exercise rights. The Supreme Court agreed unanimously, broadening the protection the Constitution provides for religious activity by applying the Free Exercise Clause to state action and holding that religiously motivated behavior is a "preferred freedom" to be generally tolerated in the United States.

This decision came down shortly after the New Deal revolution, when the Court abandoned its activist posture in protecting economic rights but noted that "there may be narrower scope for … the presumption of constitutionality when legislation appears on its face to be within a specific prohibition of the Constitution, such as those of the first ten Amendments, which are deemed equally specific when held to be embraced within the Fourteenth" (*United States v. Carolene Products*, 1938). Not only did *Cantwell* nationalize freedom of religious exercise, but as a case that fused religious concerns with those of expression (the Cantwells were exercising these rights as well), it played into the rising tide of protection the Court was giving to speech under the emerging clear and present danger doctrine (*Stromberg v. California*, 1931).

Cantwell v. Connecticut marks the dawning of the modern era of interpretation of the Free Exercise Clause (Peters 2000). Coming to the Court as it was growing increasingly sensitive to minority rights and civil liberties, *Cantwell* marks a shift toward judicial protection of religious exercise that lasted through the 1980s.

See also Church of Jesus Christ of Latter-Day Saints, Clear and Present Danger Doctrine; Bill of Rights, Incorporation of; First Amendment; Free Exercise Clause; Preferred Freedoms Doctrine; Religion, Freedom of; Jehovah's Witnesses; *Reynolds v. United States; United States v. Carolene Products* (Footnote 4)

Bibliography

Peters, Shawn Francis. 2000. *Judging Jehovah's Witnesses: Religious Persecution and the Dawn of the Rights Revolution*. Lawrence: University Press of Kansas.

Joseph F. Kobylka

CAPITAL PUNISHMENT. *See* Clemency, Executive; Cruel and Unusual Punishments Clause; Death Penalty, Crimes Punishable by the; Death Penalty and Racial Discrimination; Death Penalty and the Supreme Court; Death Penalty for Juvenile Offenders; Death-Qualified Jury

CARDOZO, BENJAMIN N. (1870–1938)

When President Herbert Hoover finally appointed him to the U.S. Supreme Court in 1932, Benjamin Nathan Cardozo was recognized as the most outstanding appellate judge in America. In addition, Cardozo's books, journal articles, and lectures had established him as a preeminent scholar in the field of jurisprudence. As a result, he was the consensus choice to fill the "scholar's seat" on the Supreme Court, occupied for the preceding 30 years by Justice Oliver Wendell Holmes, Jr.

In spite of his serious reservations, Republican President Hoover was persuaded to appoint Cardozo, a Democrat, even though two other New Yorkers, Chief Justice Hughes and Associate Justice Harlan Fiske Stone, were on the Court at the time. Moreover, Cardozo would join Justice Louis D. Brandeis as the second Jewish member of the Court.

Although Cardozo served only six years on the Supreme Court, he is consistently ranked as an outstanding justice. It is, however, generally recognized that he had even greater influence as a common-law judge. From 1914 to 1932, Cardozo served as a member of the New York Court of Appeals, the highest court in that state and, on a national level, second in prestige only to the United States Supreme Court. In 1927 he was promoted to chief judge and held this position until his appointment to the Supreme Court.

Cardozo had an engaging rhetorical and literary style that enabled him to communicate effectively not only with other members of the bench and bar but also with students, teachers, and scholars in law, political philosophy, and the social sciences. His seminal work, *The Nature of the Judicial Process,* originally delivered as the Storrs Lectures at Yale Law School in 1921, attracted immediate and widespread attention. In that book and in his later works, including *The Growth of the Law* (1924) and *The Paradoxes of Legal Science* (1928), Cardozo challenged many of the assumptions that had characterized the formalist judicial decision making of the late nineteenth and early twentieth centuries. It was unusual and refreshing for a judge to acknowledge publicly and in print the law-making function that he inevitably performed in discharging his duties. Cardozo did not hesitate in recognizing the legislative function of the judge: "I take judge-made law as one of the existing realities of life" (quoted in Hall 1947, 109). Cardozo, who is identified with the school of sociological jurisprudence, regarded the selection and balancing of choices as the most vital and at the same time the most difficult task facing the judge. In reaching a decision that requires any degree of creativity or innovation, the judge must carefully weigh a great number of factors. Custom, precedent, statute, accepted moral and ethical standards of the community, considerations of social utility, claims of stability, and claims of progress—all of these, Cardozo maintained, go into the process of adjudication.

Cardozo was born in New York on May 24, 1870. He and his twin sister, Emily, were the youngest of the six children of Albert and Rebecca Nathan Cardozo. The Nathans and Cardozos were prominent Sephardic Jewish families who had emigrated to New York in the mid-eighteenth century. Cardozo's mother died in 1879, and his older sister,

Nell, assumed responsibility for raising the younger children.

At the time of Cardozo's birth, his father was a justice of the Supreme Court of New York, a trial court of general jurisdiction. Because of Albert Cardozo's political connections to William M. "Boss" Tweed, the Association of the Bar of New York brought several charges of mal and corrupt conduct against the justice, forcing his resignation in 1874, shortly after the exposure of the notorious Tweed Ring. Albert Cardozo returned to private law practice and died in 1885 during Benjamin's first year at Columbia College.

Cardozo received his primary and secondary education from private tutors, including Horatio Alger, who, from 1883 to 1885, prepared him for the Columbia College entrance examinations. Cardozo graduated in 1889, near the top of his class, having completed a broad liberal arts course of study and earning honors in Greek, Latin, political economy, and philosophy. He then completed two years of study at Columbia Law School while simultaneously earning a masters degree in public law from the Columbia School of Political Science. During his second year in law school, he took additional graduate courses in philosophy.

Because a law degree was not required for admission to the bar, Cardozo chose not to complete the third year of law school. Instead, he gained admission to the bar in 1891 and immediately went into private practice with his older brother, Albert. Benjamin Cardozo soon mastered New York legal procedure and gained prominence in the fields of real estate law, litigation, and appellate advocacy. Recognized as a "lawyer's lawyer," he was frequently employed by other attorneys to argue their own cases before the New York Court of Appeals.

In November 1913, Cardozo was elected to the Supreme Court of New York. He took his seat on this trial court on January 5, 1914, but five weeks later was appointed by Governor Martin Glynn to complete an unexpired term on the New York Court of Appeals (the highest appellate court in New York). Cardozo was elected to his first full term in 1917. While on the court of appeals, Judge

Cardozo actively participated in the establishment of the American Law Institute (ALI) in 1923 and served for a number of years as its vice president. The purpose of the ALI was and is to provide "restatements" of the law in various fields for the benefit of judges, attorneys, law students, and the general public. In 1926 Cardozo was elected chief judge, assuming office on January 1, 1927, and remaining in this position until his appointment to the United States Supreme Court five years later.

While on the New York Court of Appeals, Cardozo wrote path breaking opinions in a number of fields, including torts, products liability, contracts, and criminal law (see, for example, *MacPherson v. Buick Motor Company,* 1916; *Palsgraf v. Long Island Railroad,* 1928; and *Wagner v. International Railway,* 1921). In 1914, the U.S. Supreme Court had adopted the federal exclusionary rule barring the admission of evidence obtained in violation of the Fourth Amendment right against unreasonable searches and seizures. Following this landmark decision, a number of state courts considered whether to apply this rule in state criminal prosecutions. It is important to note that Cardozo firmly rejected this option. In *People v. Defore* (1926), he famously articulated the dilemma posed by the exclusionary rule: "The criminal is to go free because the constable has blundered."

President Hoover nominated Cardozo to the Supreme Court on February 15, 1932. By contrast with most confirmation proceedings in recent decades, the Senate Judiciary Committee unanimously recommended approval of his nomination on February 20, and the full Senate unanimously confirmed his nomination, without a roll-call vote, on February 24. Cardozo began his service on the high bench on March 14, 1932. His active service ended as a result of a heart attack on December 10, 1937. He suffered a serious stroke in early January, retired from the Court at the end of the term in May, and died on July 9, 1938.

During less than six years of active service on the Supreme Court, Justice Cardozo wrote more than 100 opinions. Although he tended to support New Deal measures, his endorsement of President Franklin Roosevelt's sweeping economic reforms had its limits. For example, he wrote for a unanimous Court in *Hopkins Federal Savings and Loan Association v. Cleary* (1935) in holding that Congress violated the Tenth Amendment, thereby encroaching on state sovereignty, when it authorized the conversion of a state-chartered savings and loan association into a federal entity of the same kind without the consent of the state.

On the other hand, he brushed aside Tenth Amendment objections in two major decisions upholding the Social Security Act of 1935 (*Steward Machine Company v. Davis,* 1937; *Helvering v. Davis,* 1937). Cardozo fully supported the Court's decision in the so-called sick chicken case (*Schechter Poultry v. United States,* 1935) striking down the National Industrial Recovery Act as an unconstitutional delegation of congressional power to the president. In a strong concurring opinion, Cardozo characterized the National Recovery Administration as "in effect ... a roving commission to inquire into evils and upon discovery correct them.... This is delegation running riot."

In addressing constitutional questions in the field of criminal procedure, Justice Cardozo took a balanced approach. He joined the Court majority in voting to reverse the highly controversial convictions of the Scottsboro defendants in 1932 on the ground that their due process rights had been violated as a result of ineffective representation by counsel (*Powell v. Alabama*). In the landmark 1937 case of *Palko v. Connecticut,* however, Cardozo, in the final opinion of his judicial career, expressed unwillingness to incorporate the double jeopardy provision of the Fifth Amendment into the Fourteenth Amendment, thereby making it applicable to the states. In Cardozo's view, only those rights that are "of the very essence of a scheme of ordered liberty" had been "absorbed" into the Fourteenth Amendment. According to his view of "selective incorporation," the double jeopardy clause did not embody a fundamental right. This specific interpretation of the double jeopardy clause was rejected by the Warren Court in *Benton v. Maryland* (1969). On the other hand, Cardozo accorded fundamental importance to freedom of speech, regarding it as "the matrix, the indispensable condition, of nearly every other form of freedom" (*Palko v. Connecticut*, 1937). Although most of the protections of the Bill of Rights were incorporated into the Fourteenth Amendment in a series of cases from the late 1940s through the 1960s, Cardozo's selective incorporation approach has never been abandoned. It is widely regarded as his most significant contribution to constitutional development.

See also Bill of Rights (American); Bill of Rights, Incorporation of; Brandeis, Louis D.; Counsel, Right to; Double Jeopardy, Prohibition of; Fifth Amendment; Fourteenth Amendment; Fourth Amendment; Fourth Amendment Exclusionary Rule; Holmes, Oliver Wendell, Jr.; New Deal; *Palko v. Connecticut; Powell v. Alabama;* Speech, Freedom of; Stone, Harlan Fiske; Tenth Amendment; Warren Court

Bibliography

Abraham, Henry J., 1999. *Justices, Presidents, and Senators: A History of the U.S. Supreme Court Appointments from Washington to Clinton.* Lanham, MD: Rowman & Littlefield.

Hall, Margaret, ed. 1947. *Selected Writings of Benjamin Nathan Cardozo.* New York: Fallon Law Book Company.

Horwitz, Morton J. 1992. *The Transformation of American Law, 1780–1860: The Crisis of Legal Orthodoxy.* New York: Oxford University Press.

Kaufman, Andrew O. 1998. *Cardozo.* Cambridge, MA: Harvard University Press.

Polenberg, Richard. 1997. *The World of Benjamin Cardozo: Personal Values and the Judicial Process.* Cambridge, MA: Harvard University Press.

Posner, Richard L. 1990. *Cardozo: A Study in Reputation.* Chicago: University of Chicago Press.

Stephens, Otis H. 2003. "Benjamin N. Cardozo (1870–1938)." In *Great American Judges: An Encyclopedia,* ed. John Vile. Vol. 1. Santa Barbara, CA: ABC-CLIO.

Otis H. Stephens, Jr.

CARMICHAEL, STOKELY. *See* Student Nonviolent Coordinating Committee

CASTLE DOCTRINE

The castle doctrine is an ancient common-law maxim equating the home with a castle and permitting the home owner to use force to resist unlawful invasions of the home. In *Semayne v. Gresham* (1603), Sir Edward Coke opined, "The house of every one is to him as his castle and fortress, as well for his defence against injury and violence as for his repose." In his celebrated *Commentaries on the Laws of England,* Sir William Blackstone observed that "the law of England has so particular and tender a regard to the immunity of a man's house, that it stiles it his castle, and will never suffer it to be violated with impunity." James Otis alluded to the castle doctrine in a 1761 speech denouncing the infamous writs of assistance: "A man's house is his castle; and whilst he is quiet, he is as well guarded as a prince in his castle."

Although the castle doctrine has applications to contemporary civil and criminal law, in the field of civil rights and liberties its principal manifestation is the Fourth Amendment. As Thomas M. Cooley observed in 1868, "The maxim that 'every man's house is his castle' is made part of our constitutional law in the clause prohibiting unreasonable searches and seizures."

The castle doctrine has been cited in numerous Supreme Court opinions interpreting the Fourth Amendment. Two of the more notable opinions are *Payton v. New York* (1980) and *Steagald v. United States* (1981), in both of which the Court invoked the castle doctrine in striking down warrantless entries into homes. A more recent example is *Wilson v. Arkansas* (1995), where the Court cited the castle doctrine in support of its holding that the Fourth Amendment requires police to "knock and announce" before entering a home to execute a search warrant.

See also Blackstone, William; Common-Law Background of American Civil Rights and Liberties; Fourth Amendment; Search Warrants; Warrantless Searches; Writs of Assistance and General Warrants

Bibliography

Blackstone, William. 1765–1769. *Commentaries on the Laws of England.* Oxford: Clarendon Press.

Cooley, Thomas M. 1868. *A Treatise on the Constitutional Limitations Which Rest upon the Legislative Power of the States of the American Union.* Boston: Little, Brown.

John M. Scheb II and Otis H. Stephens, Jr.

CATHOLICISM AND ANTI-CATHOLICISM

Anti-Catholicism may be "America's oldest and most abiding prejudice" (Cogley and Van Allen 1986, 8). The Protestant Reformation of the sixteenth century gave rise to religious persecution and warfare in England and throughout much of Europe. Nearly all the English-speaking settlers in the American colonies were Protestants, and many of them harbored strong anti-Catholic feelings. The Catholic historian John Tracy Ellis has written that a "universal anti-Catholic bias was brought to Jamestown in 1607 and vigilantly cultivated in all the thirteen colonies from Massachusetts to Georgia" (Ellis 1969, 19). Although some of the colonies, most notably Pennsylvania, Rhode Island, and Maryland, were tolerant of Catholics and other religious minorities, most were not. In some instances, Catholic beliefs and rituals were banned altogether under the force of penal law.

The colony of Maryland was established in 1632 when King Charles I issued a royal charter to Sir George Calvert, Lord Baltimore. As a loyal Catholic, he found England increasingly inhospitable and was even refused entry to the Virginia colony when he refused to swear an oath of fidelity to the Church of England. Lord Baltimore hoped to create a haven for English-speaking Catholics in the New World, but the Maryland charter refrained from establishing Catholicism or any other faith as the official religion of the new colony. Because there were not enough Anglophone Catholics to populate a new colony, the colonial government of Maryland established a policy of tolerance toward all Christians. This was formalized by the Act of Religious Toleration of 1649, which granted freedom of religion to Christians, at least those who believed in the Holy Trinity.

From the beginning, Catholics were a minority in Maryland, but relations between Catholics and Protestants remained friendly until the Puritans, who had been driven out of Virginia, took control of the colony in the 1640s and 1650s. Anti-Catholic persecution would continue in Maryland until well into the nineteenth century, when immigration greatly increased the number of Catholics residing there.

When the first national census was taken in 1790, Catholics accounted for only about 35,000 of the nearly four million people living in the United States (Ellis 1969, 43). In many parts of the new country, anti-Catholic sentiments remained strong. Even though the right to free exercise of religion was enshrined in the Bill of Rights, Catholics were often denounced from the pulpit as enemies of the Republic. John Jay, the first chief justice of the United States, succeeded in his efforts to amend the constitution of his home state of New York to deny citizenship to foreign-born Catholics unless they renounced any allegiance to Rome.

During the 1830s and 1840s, there were numerous clashes between native-born Protestants and the Catholic minority. Churches were vandalized and sometimes burned. Even convents were attacked. The conflict was encouraged by newspapers that were virulently anti-Catholic.

By 1850 Catholics had become the country's largest single religious denomination due in large part to a wave of immigration from Ireland in the 1840s. Ten years later the number of Catholics had doubled due to immigration from Italy, Germany, Poland, and other parts of Europe (Gillis 1999, 60–61). The waves of immigration produced a nativist reaction. The Know-Nothing Party was founded in 1852, according to its charter, "to resist the insidious policy of the Church of Rome and all other foreign influence against our republican institutions" and to ensure that "none but Native American Protestant citizens" would hold public office. The party achieved considerable success, electing many of its candidates to Congress, state legislatures, and governorships in the Northeast. Know-Nothings succeeded in enacting local laws requiring the reading of the King James Bible in public schools and barring the use of public funds to support sectarian schools, a practice that had theretofore been fairly common in Northeastern cities. The more extreme Know-Nothings engaged in acts of vandalism and arson against Catholic churches and convents in cities around the country. By 1860 the party had ceased to exist. With the election of Abraham Lincoln in 1860 and the advent of the Civil War, anti-Catholic agitation subsided as Protestants and Catholics fought side by side in the Union army.

The influx of Italian immigrants after 1870 contributed to the growth of American Catholicism. By the end of the nineteenth century Catholics accounted for one-sixth of the population of the United States. After the First World War, another wave of nativism swept across America. The Ku Klux Klan, which had been dormant for decades, made a strong comeback by targeting not only African Americans but Catholics, Jews, and immigrants as well. In Oregon in 1922, the Klan supported, and voters adopted, a ballot measure requiring all students between the ages of 8 and 16 to attend only public schools. In *Pierce v. Society of Sisters* (1925), the U.S. Supreme Court invalidated this attempt to shut down the parochial schools. In a unanimous decision, the Court found that the state law "unreasonably interferes with the liberty of parents and guardians to direct the upbringing and education of children under their control."

When Al Smith ran for president in 1928, anti-Catholics circulated rumors that if Smith were elected, the Pope would take up residence in the White House. During the Great Depression and World War II, anti-Catholicism subsided considerably. After World War II, Catholics moved en masse into the mainstream of American society. They lost their identity as "foreigners" or "immigrants." Still, when John F. Kennedy ran for the presidency in 1960, the news media commonly referred to him as the "Catholic candidate." Speaking to the Houston Ministerial Association in September 1960, Kennedy asserted that "contrary to common newspaper usage, I am not the Catholic candidate

for President. I am the Democratic Party's candidate for President who happens also to be a Catholic." Kennedy's election signaled the integration of Catholicism into American culture.

Today, Catholics represent about 25 percent of the American population, making Catholicism the largest single religious denomination in the United States. The ranks of American Catholics are continuing to swell due primarily to immigration from Mexico and other parts of Latin America. Moreover, communities in the South, West, and Midwest that once were homogeneously Protestant now have growing Catholic parishes.

The historic tensions and differences between Catholics and Protestants have largely dissipated. However, there are strong tensions within the ranks of American Catholics. There are two principal dimensions to this internal conflict. One dimension involves the character of the church itself. Increasingly, American Catholics are showing their willingness to take positions contrary to those of Rome and the church hierarchy, whether the issue is birth control, ordination of women, or whether priests should be permitted to marry. In this regard one might say that American Catholics are becoming more "Protestant." Of course, there remains a substantial bloc of traditional Catholics, although probably no longer a majority, who believe that to be a good Catholic means unquestioning adherence to the pronouncements of the church. Without question, the sexual abuse scandals of recent years have caused many "good Catholics" to question the actions and positions of priests and bishops to a much greater extent.

The other dimension on which Catholics differ substantially among themselves is ideology. Just like Americans generally, American Catholics are sharply divided between liberal and conservative views of the world. Politically conservative Catholics are uncomfortable with the church's current positions with respect to war, crime, and social justice, areas in which the contemporary church has taken a decidedly liberal stance. On the other hand, politically liberal Catholics have trouble with the church's teachings on abortion, gay rights, and euthanasia, issues on which the church has maintained staunchly conservative positions. But nearly all Catholics (and non-Catholics as well) recognize that the church has played and will continue to play an important role in advancing the causes of world peace, civil rights, human dignity, and environmental stewardship.

Roman Catholicism in America is no longer homogeneous, if indeed it ever was. The American church is becoming increasingly diverse, both demographically and ideologically. Now part of the social, political, and economic mainstreams, American Catholics are becoming less distinguishable from their non-Catholic fellow citizens. With this integration, anti-Catholic sentiment has declined to its lowest ebb in the history of the Republic.

See also Abortion, Right to; Death Penalty and the Supreme Court; Gay Rights Movement; Ku Klux Klan; *Pierce v. Society of Sisters;* Religion, Freedom of; Religious Schools, Government Aid to; Right to Die; Separation of Church and State

Bibliography

Cogley, John, and Rodger Van Allen. 1986. *Catholic America.* Expanded and updated ed. Kansas City, MO: Sheed and Ward.

Dolan, Jay P. 1992. *The American Catholic Experience: A History from Colonial Times to the Present.* Notre Dame, IN: Notre Dame University Press.

Ellis, John Tracy. 1969. *American Catholicism.* 2nd ed. Chicago: University of Chicago Press.

Gillis, Chester. 1999. *Roman Catholicism in America.* New York: Columbia University Press.

McGreevy, John T. 2003. *Catholicism and American Freedom: A History.* New York: W. W. Norton.

John M. Scheb II

CATHOLIC LEAGUE FOR RELIGIOUS AND CIVIL RIGHTS. *See* Catholicism and Anti-Catholicism

CENTER FOR INDIVIDUAL RIGHTS (CIR)

The Center for Individual Rights (CIR) is a conservative interest group dedicated to promoting its vision of individual rights and liberties through litigation. The center was established by Michael McDonald and Michael Greve in 1988 and became fully operational in April of 1989. McDonald was a former Reagan administration attorney specializing in First Amendment litigation, while Greve was a conservative scholar working in the field of environmental policy; the pair met through their involvement with the Washington Legal Foundation.

The CIR's primary purpose is to defend individual liberties, including both civil and economic rights. Greve and McDonald formed the organization because they believed that the conservative public-interest law movement needed to evolve into a national movement. Previous attempts by other organizations failed because they did not handle original litigation but instead filed amicus curiae briefs, and because they lacked sufficient funding to stay operational. Liberal firms, such as the ACLU, achieved success by specializing in a particular area of law and handling original litigation in this area.

In the beginning, the CIR focused on specific areas of litigation, with civil rights and free speech being the most important. Through specialization, the CIR provides practical and knowledgeable representation in conjunction with long-term litigation. The CIR also provides free legal representation to those clients whose civil rights are threatened and who cannot afford or obtain their own representation. However, due to limited funding, the CIR handles a small number of these cases annually. Generally, the CIR chooses cases that possess the greatest potential to effect change in civil rights, religious liberty, free expression, and federalism.

The CIR began with a modest budget of $220,000 and a board of directors totaling five members. Most of the CIR's funding in its first years came from grants from conservative foundations. In the year of the CIR's founding, there was an increase in the number of conservative, libertarian, and moderate lawyers who shared the ideals of the CIR and desired to help. Many of these attorneys saw the CIR as a tool to bring about legal change and defend individual liberties in the judicial system.

Today, the organization operates with 10 full-time employees and a budget of $1.9 million. Most of the funding comes from donations by libertarian and conservative organizations. The organization's web site is located at www.cir-usa.org.

See also American Civil Liberties Union; Interest Groups

Ann M. Bennett

CHAFEE, ZECHARIAH, JR. *See* Bad Tendency Test

CHALLENGES FOR CAUSE

The right to a trial by jury is an essential component of the American justice system. In various state and federal constitutional provisions, the right is preserved, both in civil and criminal trials, with some variations. The Seventh Amendment to the United States Constitution provides, for example, that "[i]n suits at common law, where the value in controversy shall exceed twenty dollars ... the right of trial by jury shall be preserved." State constitutional counterparts also adopt the right to trial by jury in civil cases. In criminal cases, the Sixth Amendment establishes the right to a "speedy and public trial, by an impartial jury of the state and district wherein the crime shall have been committed." Its provisions have been incorporated by the Fourteenth Amendment's Due Process and Equal Protection clauses so as to make the right to a neutral jury a right in state as well as federal courts.

A neutral jury is comprised of impartial jurors. An impartial juror is a juror who is free from bias or favor toward or against any party in the trial. An impartial juror begins the trial with an impartial frame of mind and decides the trial based on the evidence admitted and the law that is to be applied. Therefore, in order to be an impartial juror, a juror must be able to follow the law as given to the jury in the court's jury instructions and abide by the juror's oath.

In order to assure that litigants receive a fair trial by an impartial jury, jurors are questioned, in a process known as voir dire, concerning their knowledge of the case or parties, potential biases, and opinions. This process enables the lawyers for the parties to attempt to uncover biases and prejudices held by the potential jurors. If a juror is deemed to be biased or prejudiced or is otherwise incapable of fairly trying the case based on the applicable law, the juror is subject to being challenged for cause, either by the court or by counsel. Challenges are a means by which the Constitution's right to an impartial jury is protected.

Some state statutes specifically define what constitutes cause for a juror challenge. Actual bias or prejudice is always sufficient cause for challenge. When a juror is challenged for cause, counsel must allege specific facts that support the challenge. The judge must then determine whether the challenge is meritorious. If the judge finds that the cause challenge should be sustained, the juror is excused from service. The juror is said to have been excused for cause.

The test for determining whether a challenged juror should be excused for cause is whether the juror's "views would prevent or substantially impair the performance of [the juror's] duties ... in accordance with [the juror's] instructions and ... oath." The standard anticipates that the juror be excused unless the juror is able to follow the instructions that are given to the jury by the judge concerning the applicable law in the case. Additionally, the standard anticipates that jurors must be excused if they cannot follow their oath, which obligates them to "well and truly try the issues joined in accordance with the law and the facts."

A juror who is actually biased or prejudiced against a party, witness, lawyer, or matter should be excused for cause unless the court is convinced that the juror can set aside the biases or prejudice and "render a verdict solely upon the evidence presented and the instructions of law given by the court." Similarly, a juror who has an interest in the outcome of a lawsuit should be excused for cause.

A juror may be challenged for cause if the juror does not meet the statutory qualifications to serve. Such statutory qualifications include age, residency, and lack of infamy, in some jurisdictions. A challenge for cause also exists, for example, when a juror is closely associated with a party or a significant witness in the lawsuit; when a juror has a financial interest in the outcome of the lawsuit; or when a juror has already formed or expressed an opinion as to what the verdict in the lawsuit should be.

The number of jurors who may be challenged for cause is not limited. If a court refuses to excuse a juror for cause when cause exists, the court has made an error affecting the party's right to a fair and impartial jury. The court's error will not result in a reversal of the verdict, however, unless the party used all other mechanisms to remove the juror, including exhausting all peremptory challenges and requesting additional ones. Even then, some appellate courts will deem the trial court's error in not excluding the juror harmless, allowing the verdict to stand.

See also Accused, Rights of the; Appeal, Right to; Common-Law Background of American Civil Rights and Liberties; Counsel, Right to; Due Process Clauses; Equal Protection Clause; Fourteenth Amendment; Harmless Error, Doctrine of; Jury, Trial by; Peremptory Challenges to Prospective Jurors; Seventh Amendment; Sixth Amendment

Bibliography

Childs, William G. 1999. "The Intersection of Peremptory Challenges, Challenges for Cause, and Harmless Error." *American Journal of Criminal Law* 27:49–80.

Pizzi, William T., and Morris B. Hoffman. 2001. "Jury Selection Errors on Appeal." *American Criminal Law Review* 38:1391–442.

Starr, V. Hale, and Mark McCormick. 2000. *Jury Selection.* 3rd ed. New York: Aspen Law and Business.

Penny White

CHÁVEZ, CÉSAR. *See* Latino Americans, Civil Rights of

CHECKS AND BALANCES, SYSTEM OF. *See* Madison, James; United States Constitution

CHICAGO, BURLINGTON AND QUINCY RAILROAD COMPANY V. CHICAGO (1897)

In *Barron v. Baltimore* (1833), the Supreme Court held that the Just Compensation Clause of the Fifth Amendment (and, by implication, the entire Bill of Rights) applied only to actions of the federal government. For protection against state and local governments, citizens should look to their respective state constitutions. The adoption of the Fourteenth Amendment, with its broad limitations on state power, created a basis for the Supreme Court to reconsider the relationship between the Bill of Rights and the states. In a series of decisions beginning with *Chicago, Burlington and Quincy Railroad Company v. Chicago* (1897), the Court developed the doctrine of incorporation. Under this doctrine, various provisions of the Bill of Rights have been held to be incorporated within the Due Process Clause of the Fourteenth Amendment and therefore made applicable to state action.

The *Chicago B&Q Railroad* case arose after the city of Chicago sought to widen Rockwell Street between West Eighteenth and West Nineteenth streets. To obtain the land necessary to widen the street, the city used its power of eminent domain, taking part of the right-of-way owned by the railroad. A state trial court awarded the railroad company a mere one dollar as just compensation for the condemned parcels of land. The railroad took the case to the U.S. Supreme Court on a writ of error. Although the Court ultimately ruled in favor of the city, its opinion made new law by extending the Just Compensation Clause of the Fifth Amendment to state action via the Due Process Clause of the Fourteenth Amendment. Writing for the Supreme Court, Justice John Marshall Harlan (the elder) asserted that "compensation for private property taken for public use is an essential element of due process of law as ordained by the 14th Amendment."

The decision in *Chicago B&Q Railroad* is reflective of the late nineteenth-century Court's preoccupation with property rights. As Justice Harlan noted in his opinion for the Court, "Due protection of the rights of property has been regarded as a vital principle of republican institutions." Harlan quoted Justice Joseph Story in asserting that "almost all other rights would become worthless if the government possessed an uncontrollable power over the private fortune of every citizen." Ironically, though, this precedent set by a conservative Supreme Court would be invoked later to incorporate most of the other Bill of Rights protections into the Fourteenth Amendment, thereby nationalizing the Bill of Rights. In retrospect the decision in *Chicago, B&Q Railroad v. City of Chicago* is an important landmark in the development of civil rights and liberties in the United States.

See also *Barron v. Baltimore;* Bill of Rights (American); Bill of Rights, Incorporation of; Fourteenth Amendment; Just Compensation Clause; Property Rights

John M. Scheb II and Otis H. Stephens, Jr.

CHICAGO SEVEN, THE

The Chicago Seven were seven antiwar activists who were tried on federal charges following the violence that took place on the streets of Chicago during the 1968 Democratic National Convention. In August 1968, thousands of young people convened in the streets and parks of Chicago to protest the Vietnam War and express their rage at the Democratic Party for not repudiating the war. While most of the protestors were well behaved, some taunted and provoked the police. At one point some protestors threw rocks and bottles. The police responded with massive force, launching tear gas into the crowds and beating protestors with batons. Nearly 700 protestors were arrested that week. More than 100 were treated in area hospitals, and hundreds more were treated by medical teams on the streets. Nearly 200 police officers were injured; about a fourth of them required hospitalization.

After the convention was over and the protesters left the city, a federal grand jury indicted eight of the protests' leaders, who were charged with conspiracy and incitement to riot under the Federal Anti-Riot Act of 1968. The defendants were some of the best-known leaders of the antiwar movement, including Rennie Davis, David Dellinger, Tom Hayden, Abbie Hoffman, and Jerry Rubin. Originally, there were eight defendants, but one of them, the Black Panther Party leader Bobby Seale, was severed from the other defendants and tried separately.

The trial of the Chicago Seven, which took place during the fall of 1969 and the winter of 1970, was marked by demonstrations outside the courthouse and a virtual circus inside the courtroom. The National Guard was mobilized to maintain order outside. During the trial, the defendants, most notably Jerry Rubin and Abbie Hoffman, mocked the judge incessantly and engaged in numerous antics that provoked the ire of the court. Eventually, all seven defendants were acquitted of the conspiracy charges, but five of them were convicted of crossing state lines to incite violence. All seven defendants, as well as their lawyers, William Kuntsler and Leonard Weinglass, were cited for contempt for courtroom misconduct. However, in *In re Dellinger* (1972), the U.S. Court of Appeals for the Seventh Circuit reversed the contempt convictions due to procedural irregularities. Several months later, in *United States v. Dellinger,* the same court reversed the defendants' substantive convictions as well. In this latter opinion the appellate court criticized the trial judge for his own antagonistic behavior during the trial. Given that the first trial had turned into a fiasco, the federal government chose not to proceed with a second trial.

See also Contempt, Power of; Inchoate Offenses; Kuntsler, William M.; Students for a Democratic Society

Bibliography

Alonso, Karen. 2002. *The Chicago Seven Political Protest Trial: A Headline Court Case.* Berkeley Heights, NJ: Enslow.

Schultz, John. 1993. *The Chicago Conspiracy Trial.* Cambridge, MA: Da Capo Press.

John M. Scheb II and Otis H. Stephens, Jr.

CHILD PORNOGRAPHY

The U.S. Supreme Court's first foray into the issue of child pornography came in *New York v. Ferber* (1982), in which the justices were required to determine the constitutionality of a New York statute prohibiting the production and distribution of a sexual performance by a child under the age of

16, even when the material was not legally obscene. Previously, in *Chaplinsky v. New Hampshire* (1942) the Court had recognized that obscenity was not protected speech under the First Amendment to the U.S. Constitution. For the next 30 years, in a series of cases including *Roth v. United States* (1957) and *Memoirs v. Massachusetts* (1966), the Court struggled to give legal definition to the meaning of obscenity. Eventually a majority of the justices agreed upon a three-part test for obscenity in *Miller v. California* (1973): "(a) whether the average person, applying contemporary community standards, would find that the work, taken as a whole, appeals to the prurient interest; (b) whether the work depicts or describes, in a patently offensive way, sexual conduct specifically defined by the applicable state law; and (c) whether the work, taken as a whole, lacks serious literary, artistic, political, or scientific value."

In *Ferber*, however, Justice Byron White's opinion for a unanimous Court held that, consistent with the First Amendment, pornographic depictions of children could be outlawed by authorities even if they were not, under the *Miller* standards, legally obscene. Although this created yet another category of speech not entitled to constitutional protection (thus joining obscenity, libel, fighting words, and advocacy of lawless action), the Court noted that the value of such speech was minimal, while the harm done was substantial. Unlike typical obscenity laws that put such materials off limits to protect the potential viewer from corrupting and immoral influences, child pornography laws are designed to protect minors not only from the immediate exploitation and abuse concomitant to the production but also from the continuing injury of having a permanent record of this exploitation and abuse. Consequently, whether the performance met the legal definition of obscenity or not was immaterial since, in either case, the child had been victimized by the production and distribution of the sexual performance. As a result, the Court held that child pornography laws limited to visual depictions of children need not conform to the legal definition of obscenity. However, this exception to the obscen-

ity standards does not apply to paintings, poems, short stories, novels, or other works depicting sexually explicit activity by minors when no child is, in fact, victimized by its production. Justices William Brennan, Thurgood Marshall, John Paul Stevens, and Sandra Day O'Connor concurred in the decision, but each expressed concern that the New York statute, in other contexts and other cases, might be overbroad and prohibit constitutionally protected speech, such as clinical photographs of children used for medical training or pictures in *National Geographic*.

That the rules applicable to obscenity are inapplicable in the context of child pornography is also apparent in the different fates of laws regulating private possession of such materials. In *Stanley v. Georgia* (1969) the Supreme Court held that a Georgia statute punishing the private possession of obscene matter violated the First Amendment. Justice Thurgood Marshall's opinion for a unanimous Court endorsed the view that "if the First Amendment means anything, it means that a State has no business telling a man, sitting alone in his own house, what books he may read or what films he may watch." However, in *Osborne v. Ohio* (1990) a six-to-three majority of the Court concluded that, apparently, a state does have that authority, at least in the context of child pornography. In *Osborne* a state law prohibiting the private possession of child pornography was upheld on the grounds that, unlike *Stanley*, the law at issue here did not rely on a "paternalistic interest" in regulating citizens' minds but on the interest in destroying the market for child pornography.

Twelve years after *Ferber*, the Supreme Court upheld as constitutional a federal version of New York's child pornography statute in *United States v. X-Citement Video* (1994). The Protection of Children against Sexual Exploitation Act of 1977, as this enactment is titled, prohibits the production or distribution of sexual performances by children under the age of 18. A seven-to-two majority, speaking through Chief Justice William Rehnquist, upheld the statute's classification of those under 18 as children (as opposed to 16 in *Ferber*) and mandated that a conviction could not be sustained absent a showing that the defendant had (1) knowledge of the sexually explicit nature of the material and (2) knowledge that at least one of the performers was underage.

Like the New York law at issue in *Ferber*, the federal statute prohibited the production and distribution of visual depictions of sexual performances by minors. However, in 1996 Congress passed the Child Pornography Prevention Act, amending the law to also punish any visual depiction that "appears to be of a minor engaging in sexually explicit conduct" or any material that "conveys the impression" that it depicts such activity. Both of these provisions were at issue when the Supreme Court decided *Ashcroft v. Free Speech Coalition* (2002).

The "appears to be" language of these amendments prohibited not only the use of adults who appeared to be minors but also punished those who might create computer-generated (i.e., virtual) child pornography. In passing this amendment Congress noted that such materials, even though they utilized no minors in their production, were virtually indistinguishable from child pornography and, therefore, could be prohibited consistent with the First Amendment. In Justice Anthony Kennedy's majority opinion, the Court found this "appears to be" provision unconstitutional. The Court observed that its initial decision in *Ferber* not to apply the *Miller* obscenity standards to child pornography was not based on the communication or message transmitted by the material but resulted from the fact that children were exploited and abused in its production. In the cases of adults posing as minors or computer-generated virtual child pornography, no children were used or exploited in their production; consequently, the exception carved out in *Ferber* to *Miller*'s test for obscenity simply was not applicable. Other arguments posited by the government (e.g., such materials are used by pedophiles to seduce minors, these materials encourage pedophiles to engage in illegal activity, virtual images promote child pornography trafficking) were ultimately unpersuasive to the majority.

The second 1996 amendment at issue in *Ashcroft* fared no better before the Court. That amendment prohibited sexually explicit materials that "conveyed the impression" that they depicted minors. For example, if one advertised the presence of sexually explicit conduct by minors in a film, the work was prohibited and punishable even if the illegal conduct were not actually present in the product. The Court found this provision of the statute overbroad in that it punished the possession of materials protected by the First Amendment merely because somewhere in the distribution chain someone had claimed them to be something they were not (e.g., child pornography).

In the area of child pornography, therefore, these precedents suggest that the Court defers to the legislature in protecting children from sexual exploitation and abuse by exempting child pornography from the usual legal standards applicable to obscenity cases. The work need only show visual depictions of minors engaged in sexual activity; it need not appeal to the prurient interest, be patently offensive, or lack serious literary, artistic, political, or scientific value. At the same time, however, the Court's First Amendment exception for child pornography does not extend to the production or distribution of nonobscene sexual performances in which minors are not used, even if those materials appear to be minors or are misleadingly advertised as such.

See also Brennan, William J., Jr.; Fighting Words Doctrine; First Amendment; Kennedy, Anthony; Marshall, Thurgood; *Miller v. California;* O'Connor, Sandra Day; Obscenity and Pornography; Overbreadth, Doctrine of; *Parens Patriae,* Doctrine of; Press, Freedom of the; Prior Restraint, Doctrine of; Rehnquist, William H.; Speech, Freedom of; Stevens, John Paul; White, Byron R.

Bibliography

Van Alstyne, William W. 2002. *The American First Amendment in the Twenty-first Century: Cases and Materials.* 3rd ed. New York: Foundation Press.

Volokh, Eugene. 2001. *The First Amendment: Problems, Cases, and Policy Arguments.* New York: Foundation Press.

Michael W. Bowers

CHILDREN'S INTERNET PROTECTION ACT OF 2000. *See United States v. American Library Association* (2003)

CHILD SHIELD STATUTES

The general legislative intent of child shield statutes is ostensibly to protect child victims and/or witnesses of traumatic crime from fear and intimidation while testifying in a traditional courtroom. Historically, children were considered incompetent to testify for a variety of reasons (i.e., the inability to distinguish reality from fiction or the lack of understanding of abstract concepts such as truth and oath). Due to this testimonial incompetence, it was virtually impossible to successfully convict defendants accused of offenses against children because the child was often the only direct witness. In the United States during the 1980s, the issues surrounding the testimony of children in criminal and civil courts came to the attention of the public via sensational cases such as the McMartin Preschool case and later the Little Rascals Daycare Center case in North Carolina. The defendants in the McMartin case were acquitted on all charges; however, their careers were damaged due to the seemingly over zealous prosecutors and the extraordinary testimony of the child victims. Unlike the defendants in the McMartin case, the Little Rascal Daycare case defendants were convicted.

To address these issues regarding children's lack of competency and provisions for allowances of their testimony, several state legislatures have enacted special provisions to facilitate their testimony as well as diminishing the accompanying stress of a criminal investigation. Some of these measures include the advent of child advocacy centers, where the child is not subjected to the overwhelming investigatory interviewing process. Others include limiting the child's involvement

in the criminal justice system where possible by limiting their appearance at pretrial hearings. Some states have enacted speedy trial provisions that take into account the stressful effects lengthy trials may present to young children. Several states have made it necessary to consider the best interest of the child before a delay in proceedings may be granted. These special accommodations for child victims and witnesses of crimes include, but not limited to:

- Out of court statements, usually in the form of videotaped testimony
- Closed-circuit camera testimony
- Competency-to-testify exceptions for child sexual abuse cases
- Altering the courtroom's physical layout to facilitate a child's testimony
- Testimonial aids in sexual abuse cases that make it easier for the child to communicate
- Permitting special forms of questioning child witnesses, such as leading questions and limiting the amount of time a child spends on the stand

In most states, the need for these special provisions must be judicially established, especially before closed-circuit testimony is allowed. The extent of proving the need for these special measures ranges from a strident showing of predictable traumatic effect on the child to a lesser showing of the preservation of the child's mental health. For example, the burden of proof in the state of Rhode Island shifts to the defendant in that the law presumes any child under the age of 13 is patently unable to testify without experiencing harm unless it can be shown otherwise.

These benevolent measures to protect the child witness have not been without controversy involving the interpretation of the Confrontational Clause of the Sixth Amendment and legal requirements of hearsay exceptions. The state of Illinois in the recent past experienced this particular conflict in the state constitution with an earlier attempt to enactment a child shield statute. Article I, Section 8 of the Illinois Constitution, before amended in 1994, guaranteed "[t]he accused shall have the right ... to meet the witnesses face to face," whereby the Illinois Supreme Court applied the plain meaning doctrine in that the face-to-face guarantee was meant literally. The face-to-face guarantee was removed from the Illinois constitution in a 1994 amendment to read "to be confronted with the witnesses against him or her."

Since 1990, courts have typically followed the U.S. Supreme Court's five-to-four ruling in *Maryland v. Craig* (1990), where the state of Maryland sought to invoke a procedure that allowed a judge to receive by one-way closed-circuit television the testimony of a child witness who was alleged to be a victim of child abuse. In *Craig*, defendant Sandra Craig was tried in a Maryland court on multiple charges of alleged sexual abuse of a young child. The child victim was removed from the courtroom and placed in a separate room with the prosecutor and defense counsel, while the defendant remained in the courtroom with the judge and jury. The trial court rejected Craig's assertion that she had not been afforded the "essence of the right of confrontation," including the right to cross-examine and have the jury observe the demeanor of the witness. On appeal, Maryland's State Court of Special Appeals affirmed the convictions. However, the Maryland Court of Appeals, while rejecting Craig's argument that the Confrontation Clause requires all court room confrontations be face-to-face, reversed and remanded for a new trial on the ground that the lower court failed to provide an adequate justification in allowing closed-circuit testimony in accordance with the strident requirement established in *Coy v. Iowa* (1988). The Supreme Court held that the use of the one-way closed-circuit television did not violate Craig's Sixth Amendment right of confrontation. Justice Sandra Day O'Connor delivered the opinion of the Court, stating, "We have never held ... that the Confrontation Clause guarantees criminal defendants the absolute right to a face-to-face meeting against them at trial." O'Connor recognized that the Sixth Amendment expresses an overall preference for face-to-face confrontation at trial but concluded that this preference must "occa-

sionally give way to considerations of public policy and the necessities of the case."

The importance of the *Craig* decision lies in the Court's assessment that the Maryland statutory "provisions for protection of child witnesses preserves all of the other elements of the confrontation right." The Court also concluded that "a state's interest in the physical and psychological well-being of child abuse victims may be sufficiently important to outweigh, at least in some cases, a defendant's right to face his or her accusers in court." Justice Antonin Scalia, joined by Justices William Brennan, Thurgood Marshall, and John Paul Stevens, dissented, asserting that the Sixth Amendment "provides, with unmistakable clarity, that "[i]n all criminal prosecutions, the accused shall enjoy the right ... to be confronted with the witnesses against him." Scalia reasoned that the purpose of this clarity was in effect to ensure that the right of confrontation was not subject to various public policy interests. Scalia was critical of O'Connor's reliance on the fact that "a majority of States has enacted statutes to protect child witnesses from the trauma of giving testimony in child abuse cases attests to the wide-spread belief in the importance of such a public policy." Scalia asserted in response, "Because the text of the Sixth Amendment is clear, and because the Constitution is meant to protect against, rather than conform to, current "widespread belief." I respectfully dissent." Justice Scalia, in his dissent, described a hypothetical situation where, in light of the majority opinion, an accused parent could not directly confront his or her child. Scalia speculated that society may favor such a procedure, but the Constitution did not.

Much progress has been made to create uniform laws to address the complicated legal and social issues surrounding the testimony of young children. The National Conference of Commissioners on Uniform State Laws approved and recommended the Uniform Child Witness Testimony by Alternative Methods Act for enactment in all states in 2002. The act contains 12 sections that include, among other things, definitions of alternative methods, provisions for applicability of the statute, guidelines for allowing testimony by alternative methods, right of party to examine child witnesses, standards for determining whether child witness may testify (clear and convincing in criminal matters and preponderance of the evidence in noncriminal matters) and uniformity of application and construction. Section 807(d) of the Uniform Rules of Evidence pertaining to child-witness testimony was eliminated to better accommodate exceptions to the hearsay rule and more individualized alternative means for taking the testimony of a child victim or witness.

A number of states have adopted many of the extensive and adaptive provisions of the Uniform Child Witness Testimony by Alternative Methods Act, not only in criminal matters, but in civil matters as well.

See also Accused, Rights of the; Brennan, William J., Jr.; Confrontation, Right of; Marshall, Thurgood; O'Connor, Sandra Day; Scalia, Antonin; Sex Offenders, Rights of; Sixth Amendment; Speedy Trial, Right to; Stevens, John Paul

Bibliography

McGough, Lucy. 1994. *Child Witnesses: Fragile Voices in the American Legal System.* New Haven, CT: Yale University Press.

National Conference of Commissioners on Uniform State Laws. 2002. *Uniform Child Witness Testimony by Alternative Methods Act.* Tucson, AZ: National Conference of Commissioners on Uniform State Laws.

U.S. Department of Justice. 1999. *Breaking the Cycle of Violence: Recommendations to Improve the Criminal Justice Response to Child Victims and Witness.* Washington, DC: U.S. Department of Justice.

Cassie Adams-Walls

CHILLING EFFECTS. *See* Overbreadth, Doctrine of

CHURCH COMMITTEE (SENATE SELECT COMMITTEE TO STUDY GOVERNMENTAL OPERATIONS WITH RESPECT TO INTELLIGENCE ACTIVITIES). *See* Foreign Intelligence Surveillance Act

CHURCH OF JESUS CHRIST OF LATTER-DAY SAINTS (LDS CHURCH)

The Church of Jesus Christ of Latter-day Saints, often called the Mormon religion, is a religious denomination of approximately 11 million members, about half of whom live outside the United States. Members are advised to refrain from consuming tobacco, alcohol, coffee, or tea and are expected to practice tithing, the giving of 10 percent of one's earnings to the church. Members celebrate the established Christian holidays of Christmas and Easter and also Pioneer Day, which celebrates the denomination's arrival in Utah. The religion was founded by Joseph Smith in upper New York in 1830 based on Smith's translation of golden plates supposedly delivered to him by the angel Moroni. The Book of Mormon, as the translation was called, established the new church's doctrine. Currently, the denomination is well established and is known for its strong emphasis on church and family. However, the Church of Jesus Christ of Latter-day Saints (LDS Church) is also associated in the minds of many with the practice of polygamy, which is not mentioned in the Book of Mormon, and which has been officially denounced by the church since 1890. It was the practice of plural marriage that first brought the Mormons to great public attention in the 1850s and created a question regarding the free exercise of religion as guaranteed under the First Amendment to the Constitution.

The Establishment of Polygamy as Religious Practice

It is not known exactly when the practice of polygamy began among the Mormons. In the years following the establishment of the LDS Church in 1830, its members, also known as Saints, settled first in Ohio, then in Missouri, and then in Illinois, where Joseph Smith, the founder, was killed by a lynch mob in 1844. While Smith is known to have taken multiple wives at some point, he never publicly advocated polygamy, and polygamy did not become a stated church doctrine until 1852, eight years after Smith died. The doctrine was said to be based on a revelation to Smith in 1843 that called for the restoration of polygamy as practiced in the Old Testament. Following Smith's death, church members migrated to Iowa and then in 1847 to the Great Salt Lake Valley, a territory claimed by Mexico. Moving to this area (and ignoring Mexican claims to the territory), the Mormons planned to establish their own theocratic state—the state of Deseret—where they could live without the interference they had encountered in Ohio, Missouri, Illinois, and Iowa. However, within a year, the Mexican government lost a war with the United States, and under the Treaty of Guadalupe Hidalgo (1848), the land occupied by the Mormons became U.S. territory once again. The LDS Church leaders' plans to remove themselves from U.S. control and to establish a theocratic state had been quickly thwarted. Nonetheless, in 1852, the LDS Church, now under the leadership of Brigham Young, was sufficiently bold to acknowledge the practice of taking multiple wives as an accepted religious practice. Thus, the private practice that had long been the subject of rumor was now made public as official church doctrine.

Several reasons were expressed for the sudden adoption of polygamy by revelation: it was a command from God to Joseph Smith; it brought the community closer; it increased the size of the community; and it was a return to a sacred and abandoned Hebrew tradition. The taking of multiple wives was a sacred act. Husbands, wives, and children were "sealed" for all eternity. Procreation was emphasized over sexual pleasure. Plural marriages, or celestial marriages, as they were also known, were viewed as a step toward divinity.

Mormons were not required to practice polygamy, but it was communicated that this was the *ideal* life, the one bringing members closest to God, and, importantly, it was the path to the highest levels of the LDS Church's hierarchy. Thus, even though the majority of Mormons may not have practiced polygamy, those who did practice it may have advanced, and those who did not practice it themselves ultimately accepted it as an LDS Church doctrine. Others may have left the church, perhaps to join the Reorganized Church of Jesus Christ of Latter-Day Saints, which did not practice polygamy.

Polygamy, Theocracy, and Utah's Road to Statehood

In 1852, when Smith's 1843 revelation was made public, there were no federal laws that prohibited polygamy. At this time, Utah was still a federal territory, not yet a state—and definitely not a Mexican territory. However, church leaders had designs on statehood—a goal that would turn out to be much delayed because of the LDS Church's unwillingness to renounce polygamy and because of the not unreasonable fear that church leaders were trying to establish a theocratic state in Utah.

Essentially, the Mormons lived in self-exile under a federally imposed government. LDS Church leaders served as territorial officials. Brigham Young was both the leader of the LDS Church and Utah's territorial governor—except for a period of four years when he was replaced during the disastrous U.S. military occupation of Utah. All petitions for statehood were denied, mainly due to concerns regarding polygamy but also out of fear that the citizens of Utah had more allegiance to the LDS Church than to the nation. It was not until after the LDS Church officially denounced polygamy that Utah was admitted as the forty-fifth state in 1896. Church leaders first denounced polygamy in an 1890 manifesto, which advised members not to enter into polygamous marriages. Leaders followed this manifesto with a stronger one in 1904, making the clearer, stronger statement that any who practiced polygamy would be excommunicated.

Anti-polygamy Legislation

Between 1862 and 1887, Congress passed several pieces of legislation aimed at outlawing polygamy—specifically directed at the religious practice of the Mormons. The Morrill Anti-bigamy Act (1862) made the practice of polygamy a felony. However, the law was ignored by Utah's Mormon-dominated courts. Later acts of legislation were intended to strengthen the Morrill Act. The Poland Act (1874) provided that polygamy cases would be tried in federal courts under federally appointed judges. In that same year, Brigham Young's assistant, George Reynolds, a practicing polygamist, agreed to take part in a test of the constitutionality of the Morrill Act.

Reynolds affirmed that he was a polygamist and claimed that because polygamy was an official tenet of his religion, the Free Exercise Clause of the First Amendment protected his right to this religious practice. The Supreme Court upheld the lower court rulings, establishing that polygamy was not protected by the First Amendment. In the decision, the justices affirmed the right of individuals to *believe* as they pleased but made a distinction between belief and actions or practices. Chief Justice Morrison Waite delivered the opinion of the Court in *Reynolds v. United States,* saying: "Laws are made for the government of actions, and while they cannot interfere with mere religious belief and opinions, they may [interfere with] with practices." Therefore, members of the LDS Church were free to believe in plural marriages, but the practice of plural marriage was prohibited. The Morrill Antibigamy Act was determined to be constitutional.

Subsequent legislative acts made it easier to prosecute polygamists. The Edmunds Act (1882) changed the violation from bigamy or polygamy to unlawful cohabitation, which was easier to prove since no proof of marriage was required. The Edmunds-Tucker Act (1887), possibly the most punitive of the laws, declared children of plural marriages to be illegitimate, disenfranchised many citizens, and froze many assets of the LDS Church. Faced with these sanctions, church leaders issued the Woodruff Manifesto in 1890, which recognized the law forbidding plural marriage, acknowledged the constitutionality of the law, and advised church members "to refrain from contracting any marriage forbidden by the laws of the land." Following the official change in the LDS Church's position, Utah became a state, and the prosecution of polygamy cases was no longer a national priority.

The Impact of Anti-polygamy Legislation

Polygamous marriages did not simply disappear in 1878. There was the difficult problem of determining the fates of so many wives and children.

Some practitioners went underground, moving to more remote areas. Others moved to Mexico. The laws of Mexico did not permit polygamy, but the Mexican government had no interest in prosecuting polygamists. Even after the Woodruff Manifesto in 1890, there was some concern as to whether the church had sufficiently denounced polygamy. Was the fact that the statements were expressed in a manifesto rather than a revelation significant? In 1904, the Smith Manifesto expressed the church's official position in much stronger terms, making it clear that those who entered into polygamous marriages would be excommunicated, the church's severest punishment. The Smith Manifesto had the desired effect for the most part. The practice of polygamy ended among mainstream Mormons. As those persons engaged in polygamous marriages prior to 1890 died, the practice died with them.

Polygamous marriages can be found in the United States today, but the LDS Church does not defend the practice. The LDS Church defines marriage very traditionally—as a covenant between one man and one woman—and is a strong critic of gay marriages. Some of today's polygamous marriages exist in isolation and are not connected with any established community of believers. Others of these marriages exist among members of various religious sects—a few, but certainly not all of them former Mormons—who call themselves Fundamentalists. Because most polygamists keep to themselves, few cases are prosecuted.

Will *Reynolds v. United States* Be Overturned?

The Supreme Court is generally supportive of a range of religious practices protected by the First Amendment. For example, in a series of decisions beginning with *Cantwell v. Connecticut* (1940), the Court established that the right to proselytize and solicit is protected by the Free Exercise Clause of the First Amendment to the Constitution. Decades later, the Court ruled in *Wisconsin v. Yoder* (1972) that the Amish practice of withdrawing children from formal education after the eighth grade was protected by the Free Exercise Clause. Interestingly, in his dissent to part of *Yoder,* Justice William O. Douglas wrote that the decision opened the way "to give organized religion a broader base than it has ever enjoyed; and it even promises that in time *Reynolds* will be overruled." In 1977, Robert G. Dyer, in an article in the *Utah Bar Journal,* noted that "[m]ore tolerant attitudes toward homosexuality, adultery, obscenity, prostitution, and unusual marriage styles [make] it difficult to attack polygamy as being violative of the peace and good order of society" (Dyer 1977, 45). However, the last time an appeals court decision upholding *Reynolds* was appealed to the Supreme Court, the Court declined to hear the case brought by Royston Potter. Thus, as of this writing, polygamy is not protected by the Constitution.

See also First Amendment; Free Exercise Clause; Douglas, William O.; Marriage, Rights Pertaining to; Religion, Freedom of; Waite, Morrison Remick

Bibliography

Dyer, Robert G. 1977. "The Evolution of Serial and Judicial Attitudes towards Polygamy." *Utah Bar Journal* 5 (Spring): 35–45.
Van Wagoner, Richard S. 1989. *Mormon Polygamy: A History.* Salt Lake City, UT: Signature Books.

Gay Henry Lyons

CICERO. *See* Natural Law and Natural Rights

CIR. *See* Center for Individual Rights

CITIZENSHIP

Citizenship is a legal concept denoting the fact that a person is a full member of a particular political community and possesses a full complement of rights and duties. Most of the protections of the United States Constitution are extended to "persons," rather than "citizens." But there are certain constitutional rights possessed exclusively by citizens, most notably the rights to vote, to hold public office, and to serve on a jury. In some states, citizenship is required as a condition of public employment.

In the Dred Scott decision of 1857, the Supreme Court held that persons of African descent were not and could never become citizens of the United States. That notorious holding was overturned by the ratification of the Fourteenth Amendment in 1868. It states: "All persons born or naturalized in the United States and subject to the jurisdiction thereof, are citizens of the United States and of the State wherein they reside."

In *Minor v. Happersett* (1874), the U.S. Supreme Court held that the right to vote is not an essential element of citizenship. In that case, the Court upheld Missouri's refusal to extend voting rights to women, which had been challenged under the Fourteenth Amendment. Of course, the Nineteenth Amendment (ratified 1920) extended suffrage to women. And the Fifteenth Amendment (ratified 1870) prohibited racial discrimination with respect to the right to vote. The effect of these amendments was to consign *Minor v. Happersett* to the constitutional dustbin. Today, it is assumed that voting and citizenship go hand in hand, although the right to vote is not enjoyed by minors and, in many states, by convicted felons, even though children and felons are still citizens.

While all persons within the jurisdiction of the United States have a duty to obey the laws and pay applicable taxes, only citizens bear the responsibility of serving in the armed forces when called to do so. And only citizens may serve on juries, which is generally regarded more as a duty than a privilege.

As noted above, the Fourteenth Amendment defines citizens as "persons born or naturalized in the United States." In Article I, Section 8, paragraph 4 of the Constitution, Congress is authorized to "establish a uniform Rule of Naturalization." Congress first exercised this power in enacting the Naturalization Act of 1795, which required an immigrant to reside in the United States continuously for a period of at least five years before becoming a citizen. In 1798, the Alien and Sedition Acts extended this period of residency to 14 years, but this measure was repealed in 1802. In 1882, Congress passed the Chinese Exclusion Act, which prohibited Chinese immigrants from becoming naturalized citizens. The Immigration Act of 1917 extended that restriction to virtually all

Asian immigrants. Ultimately, the Immigration and Nationality Act of 1952 removed all racial restrictions on naturalization.

Because citizenship by birth is conferred by the Constitution, it cannot be revoked through legislation. In *Trop v. Dulles* (1958), the Supreme Court held that Congress may not prescribe revocation of citizenship as punishment for a crime. Trop was convicted of desertion from the armed forces during the Second World War. A court-martial sentenced him to three years of hard labor and forfeiture of his military pay and ordered that he be dishonorably discharged from the army. In 1952 Trop applied for a passport but was denied on the ground that, under Section 401(g) of the Nationality Act of 1940, his citizenship had been revoked as the result of his conviction for wartime desertion. The U.S. Supreme Court reinstated Trop's citizenship and struck down the statute by which it had been revoked. Writing for the plurality, Chief Justice Earl Warren asserted that under the Eighth Amendment's Cruel and Unusual Punishments Clause, "statelessness is not to be imposed as punishment for crime." Concurring in the judgment, Justice William Brennan concluded that a law revoking citizenship is "beyond the power of Congress to enact."

The only way a native-born American citizen can lose citizenship is through voluntary renunciation. However, under federal law, naturalized citizens can have their citizenship revoked on the grounds that they illegally obtained a certificate of naturalization or misstated facts in their application for naturalization.

See also Brennan, William J., Jr.; Courts-Martial; Cruel and Unusual Punishments Clause; Eighth Amendment; Fifteenth Amendment; Fourteenth Amendment; Immigrants and Aliens, Rights of; Jury, Trial by; Military Conscription; Nineteenth Amendment; Vote, Right to; Warren, Earl

Bibliography

Wernick, Allan. 2002. *U.S. Immigration and Citizenship.* Rev. ed. Roseville, CA: Prima Publishing.

John M. Scheb II and Otis H. Stephens, Jr.

CIVIL DISOBEDIENCE

Civil disobedience is the nonviolent violation of the law to protest the presumed injustice of that law; a specific policy; or general social, political, or economic conditions. There is a venerable tradition of civil disobedience in the United States going back to the American Revolution. In modern times, civil disobedience has figured prominently in the civil rights movement, the antiwar movement, the antinuclear movement, and the environmental movement.

The nineteenth-century American writer Henry David Thoreau is best known for his advocacy of civil disobedience when the demands of conscience conflict with the dictates of law. In his famous essay "Civil Disobedience" (1849), Thoreau argued that the conscience of the individual is superior to the law of the state and that individuals have the right, indeed the duty, to violate the law when the law contravenes conscience. Thoreau's essay was born of personal experience. In 1847 Thoreau was jailed after refusing to pay his poll tax in order to protest the actions of his government in the Mexican-American War. Like most advocates of civil disobedience, Thoreau believed that it is the willingness to accept the consequences of the disobedience that justifies the violation of the law.

Like all philosophical positions, Thoreau's views on civil disobedience are not universally accepted. There are two principal criticisms. One is that citizens have an obligation to obey laws that are adopted by legitimate democratic procedures. Another objection is that individual conscience is an insufficient basis for disobedience—that an individual cannot be permitted to become a law unto oneself. Despite these objections, Thoreau's view of civil disobedience has been extremely influential in the United States and throughout the world.

Natural law theorists argue that without belief in some form of higher law, there is no way to justify a breach of the positive law. In their view, it is only the higher law or some higher standard of justice that allows one to evaluate the laws and policies, to object when a particular legal rule is established or a particular legal decision is rendered, and to argue for the need for legal change. In extreme circumstances, belief in a higher law may provide a justification for violating the positive law, as long as the violator is willing to accept the consequences of disobedience.

In 1963 Dr. Martin Luther King, Jr., was arrested in Birmingham, Alabama, after leading a civil rights demonstration in the city. The specific charge against him was parading without a permit. Dr. King had led the demonstration to protest segregation and had applied for a permit but had been denied. In his famous "Letter from the Birmingham Jail," King defended his disobedience of an unjust law. Echoing St. Thomas Aquinas, Dr. King wrote, "An unjust law is a human law that is not rooted in eternal and natural law." In a more modern vein, he also argued that an unjust law is one "that a majority inflicts on a minority that is not binding on itself." King was referring to the entire regime of laws that maintained racial segregation. King argued that "an individual who breaks a law that conscience tells him is unjust, and willingly accepts the penalty … is in reality expressing the very highest respect for the law." This expresses in a nutshell the justification for civil disobedience.

See also Civil Rights Movement; King, Martin Luther, Jr.; Natural Law and Natural Rights; Segregation, De Facto and De Jure; Thoreau, Henry David

Bibliography

King, Martin Luther, Jr. 1994. *Letter from the Birmingham Jail.* New York: Harper Collins.
Thoreau, Henry David. 2000. *Civil Disobedience.* Bedford, MA: Applewood Books.

John M. Scheb II

CIVIL LIBERTIES ACT OF 1988. *See* Civil Rights Act of 1988; Japanese Americans, Relocation of; Reparations for Slavery

CIVIL RIGHTS

By definition, a democratic society is one that is based on the legal and political equality of all citizens. Some would go further by insisting that a democratic society is one that seeks to maximize the social and economic equality of citizens as well. The term "civil rights" embraces the numerous and varied legal and political claims involving any of these aspects of equality, as well as the laws and policies adopted in response to such claims. Historically, the struggle for civil rights in the United States began with the movement to abolish slavery. In the early twentieth century, the focus shifted to the battle for women's suffrage. In the latter half of the twentieth century, the civil rights movement succeeded in advancing the cause of racial equality, most notably through the dismantling of segregation and the securing of voting rights for minority citizens. Beginning in the 1960s, the women's movement successfully challenged social and legal limitations on the status of women and the opportunities available to them. Over the last several decades, the United States has engaged in an ongoing national conversation about numerous forms of discrimination, the status of various minority groups in society, and the role that government should play in redressing inequalities and fostering opportunity.

See also Affirmative Action; Age Discrimination; *Alden v. Maine;* American Council of the Blind; Anthony, Susan B.; Anti-Defamation League; Baker Motley, Constance; Bilingual Education; Black Codes; *Bob Jones University v. United States; Boy Scouts of America v. Dale; Brown v. Board of Education;* Busing Controversy; Civil Rights Act of 1866; Civil Rights Act of 1870; Civil Rights Act of 1871; Civil Rights Act of 1875; Civil Rights Act of 1957; Civil Rights Act of 1964; Civil Rights Act of 1988; Civil Rights Cases, The; Civil Rights Restoration Act of 1991; Congress of Racial Equality; Congressional Women's Caucus; *Cooper v. Aaron;* Disabilities, Rights of Persons with; Discrimination by Private Actors; Diversity; Douglass, Frederick; Dred Scott Case; Du Bois, W.E.B.; *Edwards v. South Carolina;* Emancipation Proclamation; Employment Discrimination; Environmental Justice; Environmental Racism; Equal

Access to Justice Act; Equality; Equal Pay Act; Equal Protection Clause; Equal Protection Jurisprudence; Equal Rights Amendment; Evers, Medgar; Fair Housing Act of 1968; Federalism and Civil Rights and Liberties; Feminist Movement; Fourteenth Amendment; Freedom Rides; Freedom Summer; *Frontiero v. Richardson;* Gender-Based Discrimination; Grandfather Clause; Group Rights; *Heart of Atlanta Motel v. United States;* Housing, Discrimination in; Immigrants and Aliens, Rights of; Interracial Marriage; Jackson, Jesse; Japanese Americans, Relocation of; Jim Crow Laws; *Johnson v. Eisentrager; Katzenbach v. McClung;* King, Martin Luther, Jr.; *Korematsu v. United States;* Ku Klux Klan; Latino Americans, Civil Rights of; Lincoln, Abraham; Literacy Tests; Little Rock Crisis; *Loving v. Virginia;* Malcolm X; Marshall, Thurgood; *NAACP v. Alabama;* National Association for the Advancement of Colored People; National Organization for Women; Nation of Islam; Native Americans, Civil Rights of; *New York Times v. Sullivan;* Parks, Rosa; *Plessy v. Ferguson;* Poll Tax; Public Accommodation, Places of; Public Education, Right to; Racial Gerrymandering; Racial Profiling; Radical Republicans; Reconstruction; Reparations for Slavery; Restrictive Covenants; Rodney King Incident; *Romer v. Evans;* Roosevelt, Eleanor; Same-Sex Marriage and Civil Unions; Section 1983 Action; Segregation, De Facto and De Jure; Segregation in Public Education; Selective Prosecution; Seneca Falls Declaration; Sexual Harassment; Sexual Orientation, Discrimination Based on; Sharpton, Alfred Charles; Slavery; *South Carolina v. Katzenbach;* Southern Poverty Law Center; Stanton, Elizabeth Cady; Strict Scrutiny; Student Nonviolent Coordinating Committee; Thirteenth Amendment; Thomas, Clarence; Title IX, Education Amendments of 1972; Truth, Sojourner; Universal Declaration of Human Rights; Voting Rights Act of 1965; Warren Court; Washington, Booker T.; White Primary; Women's Suffrage; *Yick Wo v. Hopkins.*

John M. Scheb II and Otis H. Stephens, Jr.

CIVIL RIGHTS ACT OF 1866

The Civil Rights Act of 1866 was enacted by Congress after the Civil War largely in reaction to the Black Codes that Southern states had enacted to block the rights and liberties of the newly freed slaves. The Radical Republicans of the 39th Congress passed the Civil Rights Act of 1866, which declared African Americans to be citizens and granted them the equal protection of the laws in regard to contracts, lawsuits, trials, and property transactions. Although the Thirteenth Amendment had abolished slavery, it had not specifically conferred these rights. Thus, further legislation was needed to enforce the Thirteenth Amendment and to protect the rights of the former slaves and all African Americans.

The subheading of the act was titled An Act to Protect All Persons in the United States in Their Civil Rights, and Furnish the Means of Their Vindication. Specifically, Section 1 declared that all persons born in the United States and not subject to any foreign power, excluding Indians not taxed, were citizens of the United States without regard to previous condition of slavery or servitude. Section 2 stipulated that those who violated the equal protection of such persons were guilty of a misdemeanor and subject to fines and/or imprisonment. The act was also significant in that it expanded the jurisdiction of the federal courts, allowing these courts to punish violators of Section 1. Further, all federal law officers could initiate actions against violators. The federal courts were authorized to take appeals from state court rulings on such rights and to remove litigation from state courts. This authority was noteworthy in a time period when the authority of the states was greatly advocated.

President Andrew Johnson vetoed the act, arguing that it unconstitutionally conferred powers upon the federal government reserved to the states. In addition, Johnson claimed the legislation unwisely accorded citizenship to a people who were not prepared for it. Johnson's veto cost him the support of the many moderates deeply offended by both the Black Codes and the unrepentant Southern leaders experiencing a resurgence of control. The Radical Republicans in Congress were able to create enough support to override Johnson's veto by one vote. The Civil Rights Act was adopted by Congress on April 9, 1866.

To remove lingering doubts about the constitutionality of the Civil Rights Act of 1866, Congress quickly adopted another amendment to the Constitution. The Fourteenth Amendment, adopted by Congress in June of 1866 and ratified by the states two years later, prohibited states from denying equal protection of the laws to any persons within their jurisdictions and gave Congress power to enforce this prohibition through "appropriate legislation." During Reconstruction, Congress would use the authority provided by Section 5 of the Fourteenth Amendment to enact a series of important civil rights laws.

The Civil Rights Act of 1866 continues to be important in preventing racial discrimination in the sale and rental of housing. In *Jones v. Alfred H. Mayer* (1968), the Supreme Court held that provisions of the Civil Rights Act of 1866 codified at 42 U.S.C. §1982 prohibit private racial discrimination in the sale or rental of real or personal property. Writing for the Court, Justice Potter Stewart concluded that Congress intended to prohibit "all racial discrimination, private and public, in the sale ... of property," and that the Thirteenth Amendment empowered Congress "to determine what are the badges and the incidents of slavery, and ... to translate that determination into effective legislation."

The 1866 legislation has also been used to prohibit racial discrimination by private schools, which were unaffected by the Supreme Court's decision in *Brown v. Board of Education* (1954) striking down segregation in public schools. In *Runyon v. McCrary* (1976), the Supreme Court held that 42 U.S.C. §1981, which derives from the Civil Rights Act of 1866, forbids private schools from engaging in racially discriminatory admissions.

See also Black Codes; *Brown v. Board of Education;* Civil Rights Act of 1870; Civil Rights Act of 1871; Civil Rights Act of 1875; Federalism and Civil Rights and Liberties; Fourteenth Amendment; Fourteenth Amendment, Section 5 of the; Housing, Discrimination in; Lincoln, Abraham; Radical Republicans; Reconstruction; Slavery; Stewart, Potter; Thirteenth Amendment

Bibliography

Abernathy, Charles F. 2000. *Civil Rights and Constitutional Litigation: Cases and Materials.* 3rd ed. St. Paul, MN: West.

Foner, Eric. 1988. *Reconstruction: America's Unfinished Revolution.* New York: Harper Collins.

Jeffries, John C., Pamela S. Karlan, Peter W. Low, and George A. Rutherglen. 2000. *Civil Rights Actions: Enforcing the Constitution.* New York: Foundation Press.

McPherson, James. 1991. *Abraham Lincoln and the Second American Revolution.* New York: Oxford University Press.

Lynne Garcia

CIVIL RIGHTS ACT OF 1870

The Civil Rights Act of 1870, also known as the Enforcement Act, entitled all citizens to the right to vote at all elections without regard to race, color, or previous conditions of servitude (i.e., slavery). The act also included a section reaffirming the protections of the Civil Rights Act of 1866, which was included because Congress was concerned that the courts would claim the Fourteenth Amendment superseded the Civil Rights Act of 1866.

The 1870 act sought to strengthen the Fifteenth Amendment, which states, "The right of citizens of the United States to vote shall not be denied or abridged by the United States or by any State on account of race, color, or previous condition of servitude." The act outlined criminal penalties against anyone interfering with another citizen's right to vote. Any action that prohibited a citizen from taking actions to become registered to vote was made a misdemeanor. An action of conspiring to injure, oppress, threaten, or intimidate a citizen with the intent to violate this act was deemed a felony.

Because those who violated the act were subject to federal prosecution, there was a great deal of opposition from those who saw this as taking powers away from the state. Some claimed the act was a violation of the Fourteenth and Fifteenth amendments, which prohibit state action denying civil rights but do not extend to private action. Nevertheless, Congress then sought to strengthen the Enforcement Act with the passage of the Civil Rights Act of 1871 (better known as the Ku Klux Klan Act), which prohibits two or more persons from obstructing law enforcement by using violence, intimidation, or threats.

In two early decisions, the Supreme Court substantially weakened Congress's enforcement of the Civil Rights Act of 1870. In 1875 the Supreme Court ruled in *United States v. Cruikshank* (1875) that the act could not be used to indict whites who had murdered blacks who had assembled to defend officeholders. The Court said that individuals would have to rely on the state government to protect them during state elections. It further held that the Enforcement Act applied to discriminatory acts by states, not those committed by individuals. Similarly, in *United States v. Reese* (1875), the Court ruled against the indictments of two election inspectors in Kentucky who refused to count the vote of a black elector. The Court based its decision on the fact that the black elector was not prohibited from qualifying to vote (even though he was not actually allowed to cast a ballot). Moreover, the Court held that Congress did not have the power to punish those who refused to let him vote.

The Civil Rights Act of 1870 was later codified under Title XVIII of U.S. Code in sections 241 and 242 and in Title XLII in Section 1981. Under modern judicial interpretation, these provisions give the federal government broad enforcement powers in the civil rights field. For example, in *United States v. Price* (1966), the Supreme Court upheld a series of indictments under 18 U.S.C. § 241, saying:

[I]t is hardly conceivable that Congress intended § 241 to apply only to a narrow and relatively unimportant category of rights. We cannot doubt that the purpose and effect of § 241 was to reach assaults upon rights under the entire Constitution, including the Thirteenth, Fourteenth and Fifteenth Amendments, and not merely under part of it.

See also Civil Rights Act of 1866; Civil Rights Act of 1871; Civil Rights Act of 1875; Fifteenth Amendment; Fourteenth Amendment; Fourteenth Amendment, Section 5 of the; Ku Klux Klan; Radical Republicans; Reconstruction; Slavery; State Action Doctrine; Thirteenth Amendment

Bibliography

Howard, John R. 1999. *The Shifting Wind: The Supreme Court and Civil Rights from Reconstruction to Brown.* New York: State University of New York Press.

Katz, Ellen D. 2003. "Reinforcing Representation: Congressional Power to Enforce the Fourteenth and Fifteenth Amendments in the Rehnquist and Waite Courts." *Michigan Law Review* 101: 2341–408.

Glenn L. Starks

CIVIL RIGHTS ACT OF 1871

In the aftermath of the Civil War, Congress enacted five major pieces of civil rights legislation. Of these, none has had a greater impact than the Civil Rights Act of 1871, also known as the Ku Klux Klan Act.

The act grew out of a special one-paragraph message sent to the 42nd Congress on March 23, 1871, by President Ulysses S. Grant, urgently requesting the enactment of legislation:

A condition of affairs now exists in some States of the Union rendering life and property insecure.... That the power to correct these evils is beyond the control of State authorities I do not doubt; that the power the Executive of the United States, acting within the limits of existing law, is sufficient for present emergencies is not clear. Therefore, I urgently recommend such legislation as in the judgment of Congress shall effectually secure life, liberty, and property, and the enforcement of law in all parts of the United States.

The House of Representatives was quick to respond to the president's message. On the same day it was received, it was referred to a select committee chaired by Representative Samuel Shellabarger,

Republican of Ohio. Just five days later, on March 28, the committee brought forth a proposal that contained the essential provisions of the final version of the act.

Throughout the congressional debates, supporters of the act made repeated references to the depredations of the Ku Klux Klan. Numerous examples were cited of murders, whippings, intimidations, and other violence. Victims of these atrocities included not only blacks but also white Republicans. The crimes that were perpetrated were viewed not as isolated occurrences, but as part of an organized conspiracy political in its origins and aims. Moreover, the evidence adduced by supporters of the act demonstrated that these crimes were committed with at the least the tacit complicity of state and local officials, if not their outright support.

Three sections of the act are particularly noteworthy. In terms of contemporary civil rights litigation, the most important section was Section 1. It authorized a civil action for legal and equitable relief against any person who, under color of state law, deprived another of a right, privilege, or immunity secured by the Constitution of the United States. In the congressional debates, specific references to Section 1 were comparatively rare. The section has survived to the present and is the basis for what today are referred as Section 1983 actions, so called because Section 1 currently is codified in Title XLII of the United States Code as section 1983.

Section 2 of the Ku Klux Klan Act was far more extensively debated at the time of its enactment. As originally introduced, the section made it a felony for any "two or more persons" to conspire to commit certain enumerated crimes "in violation of the rights, privileges, and immunities of any person, to which he is entitled under the Constitution and laws of the United States." To the extent that Section 2 sought to regulate the conduct of one private person in relation to another, it occasioned debate over the fundamental question of the scope of the rights that may be secured under the Fourteenth Amendment of the Constitution, as well as the

power of Congress to enforce them. Eventually, Section 2 was amended in several respects, one of which authorized civil actions for the recovery of damages, and another of which limited the scope of conspiracies covered by the section to those motivated by a desire to deprive a person of the equal protection of the laws. Section 2 also has survived to the present and currently is codified in Section 1985 of Title XLII of the United States Code.

The third noteworthy section of the Ku Klux Klan Act is Section 6. Section 6 originated as an amendment to the act offered by Republican Senator John Sherman of Ohio. Through an intricate series of further amendments, Sherman's amendment evolved into a provision that imposed civil liability on persons who failed to assist in preventing violations of Section 2 of the act. That provision survives today as Section 1986 of Title XLII.

See also Civil Rights Act of 1866; Civil Rights Act of 1870; Civil Rights Act of 1875; Fourteenth Amendment; Ku Klux Klan; Reconstruction; Section 1983 Actions

Bibliography

Abernathy, Charles F. 2000. *Civil Rights and Constitutional Litigation: Cases and Materials.* 3rd ed. St. Paul, MN: West.

Cook, Joseph G., and John L. Sobieski, Jr. 1997. *Civil Rights Actions.* New York: Matthew Bender.

Jeffries, John C., Pamela S. Karlan, Peter W. Low, and George A. Rutherglen. 2000. *Civil Rights Actions: Enforcing the Constitution.* New York: Foundation Press.

Lewis, Harold S., Jr., and Elizabeth J. Norman. 2004. *Civil Rights Law and Practice.* 2nd ed. St. Paul, MN: West.

John L. Sobieski, Jr.

CIVIL RIGHTS ACT OF 1875

Enacted by the last biracial Congress of the nineteenth century, the Civil Rights Act of 1875 sought to guarantee equal access to and treatment in places of public accommodation, regardless of nativity, race, color, religion, or political persuasion. Affected places included trains, taverns, hotels, restaurants, and theaters. The act also sought to protect the rights of any individual serving on a jury. Individuals were authorized to bring federal suits against any persons who violated the rights guaranteed by this act.

Attempts to provide equal rights to former slaves following the Civil War created increased hostilities toward African Americans from former slave owners. This act sought to provide African Americans protection during the normal course of their daily lives by protecting their civil liberties in public places. Proposed by Charles Sumner and Benjamin F. Butler in 1870, the act entitled "all persons within the jurisdiction of the United States be entitled to the full an equal enjoyment of the accommodations, advantages, facilities, or privileges of inns, conveyances on land or water, theaters, and other places of public amusement; subject only to the conditions and limitations established by law, and applicable alike to citizens of every race and color, regardless of any previous condition of servitude." The act was criticized for its attempt to regulate what was seen as the noncriminal behavior of private citizens in determining whom they chose to serve in their businesses.

In 1883, the Supreme Court ruled that the act was unconstitutional on the grounds that Congress did not have the power to regulate the conduct of individuals. Only discriminatory state action was prohibited by the Fourteenth Amendment, and the Civil Rights Act of 1875 exceeded the power of Congress to enforce the amendment's provisions. In the Civil Rights Cases (1883) Justice Joseph P. Bradley wrote the majority opinion, asserting as follows that the Fourteenth Amendment:

does not invest Congress with power to legislate upon subjects which are within the domain of state legislation; but to provide modes of relief against state legislation, or state action, of the kind referred to. It does not authorize Congress to create a code of municipal law for the regulation of private rights; but to provide modes of redress against the operation of state laws, and the action of state officers, executive or judicial, when these are subversive of the fundamental rights specified in the amendment. Positive rights and privileges are undoubtedly secured by the Fourteenth Amendment; but they are secured by

way of prohibition against state laws and state proceedings affecting those rights and privileges, and by power given to Congress to legislate for the purpose of carrying such prohibition into effect; and such legislation must necessarily be predicated upon such supposed state laws or state proceedings, and be directed to the correction of their operation and effect.

This ruling brought strong criticism from civil rights advocates. For example, Frederick Douglass wrote, "The future historian will turn to the year 1883 to find the Supreme Court of the nation defeating the manifest purpose of the Constitution, nullifying the 14th Amendment, and placing itself on the side of prejudice, proscription, and persecution."

This act was the last congressional effort to protect the rights of African Americans for more than half a century, and many theorists date 1883 as the end of the Reconstruction period because of the Supreme Court's decision. Ultimately, the Civil Rights Act of 1964 prohibited racial discrimination by places of public accommodation by invoking Congress's broad powers to regulate interstate commerce.

See also Civil Rights Act of 1866; Civil Rights Act of 1870; Civil Rights Act of 1871; Civil Rights Act of 1964; Civil Rights Cases, The; Douglass, Frederick; Fourteenth Amendment; Fourteenth Amendment, Section 5 of the; Public Accommodation, Places of; Reconstruction; Slavery; State Action Doctrine

Bibliography

Green, Robert P. Jr., ed. 2000. *Equal Protection and the African American Constitutional Experience,* Westport, CT: Greenwood Press.

Howard, John R. 1999. *The Shifting Wind: The Supreme Court and Civil Rights from Reconstruction to Brown.* New York: State University of New York Press.

Glenn L. Starks

CIVIL RIGHTS ACT OF 1957

Proposed by President Dwight D. Eisenhower in early 1957, the Civil Rights Act of 1957 was the first in a series of landmark civil rights statutes enacted by the modern Congress. Not since Reconstruction had Congress undertaken significant legislation in this field. The measure faced considerable opposition from Southern members, especially in the Senate, where opponents filibustered for several weeks. On September 9, 1957, Congress enacted a watered-down version of Eisenhower's proposal.

The new law authorized U.S. attorneys to obtain injunctions from federal district courts to curtail interference with voting rights. It also established the Civil Rights Division of the Department of Justice to enforce existing federal laws in the civil rights field. In the early 1960s, under the leadership of Assistant Attorney General Burke Marshall, the Civil Rights Division played a crucial role in winning important legal victories in the civil rights arena. Finally, the Civil Rights Act of 1957 created the U.S. Civil Rights Commission to study problems of racial discrimination, especially with regard to voting rights, and make appropriate recommendations to Congress. The commission's landmark 1961 report provided the factual foundation for two important statutes: the Civil Rights Act of 1964 and the Voting Rights Act of 1965.

See also Civil Rights Act of 1964; Civil Rights Division, U.S. Department of Justice; Civil Rights Movement; Reconstruction; U.S. Civil Rights Commission U.S. Department of Justice; Voting Rights Act of 1965

John M. Scheb II and Otis H. Stephens, Jr.

CIVIL RIGHTS ACT OF 1960. *See* U.S. Civil Rights Commission

CIVIL RIGHTS ACT OF 1964

Called "the most far-reaching civil rights bill since the Emancipation Proclamation," the Civil Rights Act of 1964 takes up 27 pages in the *U.S. Statutes at Large* and addresses a number of important civil rights issues (Whalen and Whalen 1985, 101). Title I of the act limited the use of literacy tests, which had been used historically to disenfranchise minorities. Title IV allowed the Department of Justice to bring suit in federal court

to desegregate public schools that had not yet complied with the Supreme Court's mandate in *Brown v. Board of Education*. Title VI allowed funds to be withheld from any federally funded organization that practiced racial discrimination.

By far the most controversial provisions of the Civil Rights Act were Title II, which prohibited discrimination based on race, color, religion, or national origin in places of public accommodation, and Title VII, which prohibited employment discrimination based on race, color, religion, sex, or national origin by firms with 25 or more employees. Titles II and VII were based in part on the Equal Protection and Enforcement Clauses of the Fourteenth Amendment, and in part on Congress's power to regulate commerce among the states.

The Civil Rights Act was enacted only after its proponents were able to overcome numerous political obstacles. Democratic President John F. Kennedy had been hesitant to advance a civil rights agenda because he anticipated opposition from a coalition of Southern Democrats and conservative Republicans. Although the Democrats held the majority in both houses of Congress, 12 committee chairmen in each house were Southern Democrats who could be counted on to use their power to try to block passage of any significant civil rights legislation. Kennedy also feared that his support of civil rights legislation would invite retaliation against other parts of his legislative agenda. Finally, in 1963, he did send a civil rights bill to the House of Representatives. It received favorable treatment from the House Judiciary Committee but, following the president's assassination on November 22, 1963, the bill was held up in the House Rules Committee, chaired by Congressman Howard W. "Judge" Smith of Virginia, a long-time opponent of civil rights legislation.

The new president, Lyndon B. Johnson of Texas, was firmly committed to passage of the civil rights bill. He called it his first priority, and a memorial to President Kennedy. The mood of the nation, as well as of the House membership, was such that Judge Smith knew he was beaten. If he failed to convene his committee, he realized that the House would use a discharge petition to take the bill from him. After a public hearing, the Rules Committee granted the bill a special rule, which permitted it to go forward. When the final vote was taken, the bill passed the House by a margin of 290–130, with 152 Democrats and 138 Republicans supporting it.

In the Senate, Majority Leader Mike Mansfield bypassed the Judiciary Committee, chaired by a Southern Democrat, and placed the bill directly on the Senate calendar. He appointed Senator Hubert H. Humphrey of Minnesota, the Democratic whip, to be the bill's floor manager. Everyone knew that opponents of the bill would conduct a filibuster to try to prevent the bill from coming to a vote. It would be difficult to invoke cloture, the procedure for halting a filibuster, because of the large number of votes required for cloture. Although the number was later lowered to 60, in 1964 cloture required the vote of two-thirds of the senators present and voting. Senators Mansfield and Humphrey were doubtful that they could win a cloture vote unless they could win the support of the Republican leader, Senator Everett M. Dirksen of Illinois. Moderate Republicans already supported the bill, but Dirksen could bring more conservative Republican support with him.

Senator Dirksen ultimately joined the bill's supporters. He changed the bill in ways that made it somewhat more palatable to conservatives but still acceptable to liberals and moderates. On June 10, 1964, a filibuster led by Senator Richard Russell (D-GA) came to an end when 68 senators voted to impose cloture. On June 19, the bill itself passed the Senate by a vote of 73–27. On July 2, 1964, the House of Representatives accepted the changes made by the Senate, and President Johnson signed the bill into law that same day.

The constitutionality of Title II, which prohibited discrimination in public accommodations, was quickly challenged in the courts. In the Civil Rights Cases (1883), the Supreme Court had struck down similar legislation based on the Equal Protection and Enforcement clauses of the Fourteenth Amendment. According to the Court, the Fourteenth Amendment did not empower Congress to ban private discrimination but only to legislate against discriminatory state

action. For this reason, Congress tied the Civil Rights Act of 1964 to the Commerce Clause of Article I, Section 8, as well as the Fourteenth Amendment. In *Heart of Atlanta Motel v. United States* (1964), all nine members of the Supreme Court took note of the Commerce Clause justification and agreed that the legislation was constitutional. In the companion case of *Katzenbach v. McClung* (1964), the Court held that the Civil Rights Act could be applied to a small neighborhood restaurant with little or no out-of-state clientele because the business purchased products that had moved in interstate commerce. The Court noted that the cumulative effect of numerous small businesses would have a substantial impact on interstate commerce.

The Civil Rights Act of 1964 was followed by two other landmark enactments, the Voting Rights Act of 1965 and the Fair Housing Act of 1968. Not since Reconstruction had Congress enacted a series of significant civil rights bills. These three statutes, as amended over the years, along with the measures enacted after the Civil War, constitute the main corpus of contemporary federal civil rights law.

See also *Brown v. Board of Education;* Civil Rights Act of 1866; Civil Rights Act of 1870; Civil Rights Act of 1871; Civil Rights Act of 1875; Civil Rights Act of 1957; Civil Rights Cases, The; Civil Rights Division, U.S. Department of Justice; Civil Rights Movement; Discrimination by Private Actors; Emancipation Proclamation; Employment Discrimination; Equal Employment Opportunity Commission; Equal Protection Clause; Fair Housing Act; Federalism and Civil Rights and Liberties; Fourteenth Amendment; Fourteenth Amendment, Section 5 of the; *Heart of Atlanta Motel v. United States; Katzenbach v. McClung;* Literacy Tests; Public Accommodation, Places of; Reconstruction; State Action Doctrine; U.S. Civil Rights Commission; U.S. Department of Justice; Voting Rights Act of 1965

Bibliography

Cortner, Richard C. 2001. *Civil Rights and Public Accommodations: The Heart of Atlanta Motel and McClung Cases.* Lawrence: University Press of Kansas.

Loevy, Robert D., ed. 1997. *The Civil Rights Act of 1964: The Passage of the Law That Ended Racial Segregation.* Albany: State University of New York Press.

Whalen, Charles, and Barbara Whalen. 1985. *The Longest Debate: A Legislative History of the 1964 Civil Rights Act.* Cabin John, MD: Seven Locks Press.

Patricia A. Behlar

CIVIL RIGHTS ACT OF 1988

The Civil Rights Act of 1988 (also called the Civil Liberties Act of 1988), signed by President Ronald Reagan on August 10, provided a presidential apology and payment of $20,000 to each surviving Japanese citizen or permanent U.S. resident who was relocated, evacuated, or interned by the federal government during World War II. The $1.25 billion act also created an education fund administered by the Civil Liberties Public Education Fund to teach people about this period of history and to prevent the occurrence of any similar future events.

The bombing of Pearl Harbor on December 7, 1941, triggered the war between the United States and Japan and led to public hostility toward people of Japanese descent. On December 8 of that year the Federal Bureau of Investigation froze all assets of Japanese Americans and seized community leaders suspected of being sympathetic to Japan. On February 19, 1942, President Franklin Roosevelt signed Executive Order 9066, which authorized the exclusion and removal of any person from areas deemed as "military areas" for the use of federal troops, federal agencies, and state and local agencies. The right of any person to enter, remain in, or leave these areas was subject to whatever discretionary restrictions were imposed by the secretary of war or military commanders.

Japanese Americans and their children were removed from the western half of the Pacific coastal states and parts of Arizona, and taken to one of 16 assembly centers. These almost primitive centers were run by the army and the War Relocation Authority (a civilian agency). For example, one center was located in the desert, where temperatures during the day reached 115 degrees in the summer. At another, some

detainees were housed in latrines. On November 10, 1942, Japanese Americans were confined in 10 internment camps, which were ringed by barbed wire and armed guards in sentry towers. The first internment camp opened on March 21, 1942, and the last center closed on November 30, 1945. The largest center had a peak population of 18,789 detainees. By the end of 1946, 120,000 persons of Japanese descent had been interned, of whom 77,000 were American citizens.

The Civil Rights Act of 1988 was based on the recommendations of the Commission on Wartime Relocation and Internment of Civilians established by Congress in 1980. The commission was established as a result of a political movement mounted by Japanese Americans seeking reparations and an official apology by the U.S. government.

The act sought to remedy actions that the commission deemed to have been motivated by racial prejudice, wartime hysteria, and a failure of political leadership and carried out without adequate security reasons or proof of espionage or sabotage. Compensation was provided to remedy human suffering resulting from material and intangible losses suffered and losses in education and job training. During a public hearing held by the commission on July 14, 1981, 750 Japanese American witnesses testified about their wartime experiences.

The specific purposes of the act were the following: (1) to acknowledge the fundamental injustice of the evacuation, relocation, and internment of citizens and permanent resident aliens of Japanese ancestry during World War II; (2) to apologize on behalf of the people of the United States for the evacuation, internment, and relocation of such citizens and permanent resident aliens; (3) to provide for a public education fund to finance efforts to inform the public about the internment so as to prevent the recurrence of any similar event; (4) to make restitution to those individuals of Japanese ancestry who were interned; and (5) to make more credible and sincere any declaration of concern by the United States over violations of human rights committed by other nations.

On October 9, 1990, the first nine reparation payments were made at a Washington, D.C., ceremony. The first to receive a check was 101-year old Reverend Mamoru Eto of Los Angeles. The official presidential letter of apology was signed by President Bill Clinton on October 1, 1993.

See also Federal Bureau of Investigation; Japanese Americans, Relocation of; *Korematsu v. United States;* Roosevelt, Franklin D.; Wartime, Civil Rights and Liberties during

Bibliography

Hatamiya, Leslie T. 1993. *Righting a Wrong: Japanese Americans and the Passage of the Civil Liberties Act of 1988.* Stanford, CA: Stanford University Press.

Kurashige, Lon Yuki. 1996. "Righting a Wrong: Japanese Americans and the Passage of the Civil Liberties Act of 1988." *Journal of American Ethnic History* 15 (3): 63–65.

Glenn L. Starks

CIVIL RIGHTS AND LIBERTIES DURING WARTIME

In time of war, it is tempting for government to restrict individual rights and liberties for the greater good. Some of these restrictions may be necessary. Other restrictions, however, are counterproductive, offer no benefits for national security and eventually backfire on the government, at great cost to citizens and noncitizens. Erosions of civil liberties occur whenever the government exercises emergency power and argues that national interests must supersede individual rights.

The first experiment with this theory came from the Federalist Party during the quasi war against France from 1798 to 1800. President John Adams signed the repressive Alien and Sedition Acts of 1798, which deliberately tilted the nation toward England and against Jeffersonian supporters of France. The Sedition Act provided for fines and imprisonment for any person who wrote or spoke anything "false, scandalous and malicious" against the federal government, either House of Congress, or the president, with intent "to defame" those governmental bodies. The statute expired by its own terms on March 3, 1801, but by that time it had energized the Jeffersonian Republicans and helped

them gain control of Congress and the presidency in the 1800 elections. Once in office, Thomas Jefferson used his constitutional power to pardon all who had been prosecuted for sedition. So unpopular was the statute and its implementation that it dealt a mortal blow to the Federalist Party.

With the outbreak of the Civil War, President Abraham Lincoln used extraordinary powers to suspend the writ of habeas corpus. Unlike other presidents who claimed broad, unreviewable power in time of emergency, Lincoln conceded that the legality of his actions was uncertain. When Congress returned, he explained that his actions, "whether strictly legal or not, were ventured upon under what appeared to be a popular demand and a public necessity, trusting then, as now, that Congress would readily ratify them." Congress debated his request at length, with members supporting Lincoln despite the explicit assumption that his acts were illegal. Congress then passed legislation "approving, legalizing, and making valid all the acts, proclamations, and orders of the President, etc., as if they had been issued and done under the previous express authority and direction of the Congress of the United States."

During World War I, the federal government unleashed a campaign against opponents of military action against Germany. Before he asked Congress in 1917 to declare war on Germany, President Woodrow Wilson warned that the "gravest threats against our national peace and safety have been uttered within our own borders." These citizens, he said, "have poured the poison of disloyalty into the very arteries of our national life." With his urging, Congress passed the Espionage Act in June 1917, authorizing fines and imprisonment of anyone who "shall willfully cause or attempt to cause insubordination, disloyalty, mutiny, or refusal of duty, in the military or naval forces of the United States." The statute also categorized as "nonmailable" any "letter, writing, circular, postal card, … newspaper, pamphlet, book, or other publication" that advocated "treason, insurrection, or forcible resistance to any law of the United States."

Several thousand people were prosecuted under the Espionage Act, with their convictions regularly upheld by reviewing courts. The Supreme Court seemed to have no appreciation of the need for free speech during wartime. Challenging that attitude was Zechariah Chafee, Jr., whose article in the *Harvard Law Review* in 1919 argued strongly that free speech deserved special protection when the nation was at war. The war clauses of the Constitution, he said, "cannot be invoked to break down freedom of speech." Only through free debate could the government's war policy be "vigorously and constantly cross-examined" in order to ensure that war is not "diverted to improper ends, or conducted with an undue sacrifice of life and liberty, or prolonged after its just purposes are accomplished." Just as legal proceedings depended on cross-examination, so would it be "a disastrous mistake to limit criticism to those who favor the war."

Unlike the opposition to American involvement in World War I, Nazi aggression in Europe and the Japanese attack on Pearl Harbor generated broad support for U.S. intervention in World War II. In early 1942, President Franklin D. Roosevelt issued an executive order authorizing the military to "relocate" persons of Japanese descent living on the West Coast, which resulted in more than a 100,000 Japanese Americans being interned for the duration of the war. Upholding this massive deprivation of liberty in *Korematsu v. United States* (1944), the Supreme Court observed: "Citizenship has its responsibilities as well as its privileges, and in time of war the burden is always heavier."

Political conditions changed after the war when the United States confronted international communism. President Harry Truman issued an executive order to create loyalty review boards to supervise federal employees, and Congress passed legislation to prohibit aliens from entering the United States if they advocated communist doctrines. The Taft-Hartley Act of 1947 required union officers to file a non-Communist affidavit. This pattern ripened into the McCarthyist period of the 1950s, leading to congressional investigations into communist associations and the loss of jobs by many found guilty by association.

The Vietnam War triggered a number of civil liberties issues, including draft-card and flag burnings, and the wearing of black armbands to protest the war. The Supreme Court held in *United States* v. *O'Brien* (1968) that federal legislation prohibiting the destruction of a draft card did not unconstitutionally abridge free speech. Government, it said, has a legitimate interest in preserving draft cards. On the other hand, in the case of *Tinker v. Des Moines Independent Community School District* (1969), school children were permitted to wear black armbands to protest the war. Their conduct had been quiet and non-disruptive.

Flag burning also became a politically explosive issue. In *Texas v. Johnson* (1989), the Court held that a conviction for flag desecration (burning the flag during a protest) was contrary to the First Amendment because it was "expressive conduct" protected by the First Amendment. Congress responded by passing the Flag Protection Act of 1989, continuing the prohibition on flag burning but deleting from a 1968 statute the words "casts contempt." This change, the sponsors of the legislation argued, made the law "content neutral." The Supreme Court, in *United States* v. *Eichman* (1990), disagreed, holding that the government's interest in protecting the physical integrity of the flag could not justify its infringement on First Amendment rights. Efforts since that time to pass a constitutional amendment to protect the flag have been unsuccessful.

The terrorist attacks of 9/11 raised again the issue of civil liberties in wartime, but in a war that appears to have no likely termination date. The restoration of civil liberties that typically comes after the cessation of hostilities may not occur because no one knows when the war against terrorism will conclude.

In terms of the risk to civil liberties, the most significant action was passage of the USA PATRIOT Act on October 26, 2001, which strengthened the power of the administration to deter and punish terrorists. Yet the statute goes far beyond the threat of terrorism. It gives the government broad new powers to conduct any criminal investigation. Any increase in the power of the executive branch, especially over law enforcement, inevitably places at risk some constitutional rights and liberties. The risk is even greater when legislation moves through Congress at great speed without the regular care and deliberation of legislative hearings, markups, and floor debate. The House Judiciary Committee held one hearing on September 24, 2001, conducted a markup with amendments offered and agreed to, and issued a lengthy committee report. On the floor, however, that bill was put aside in favor of a substitute measure that few members had seen, with no opportunity for amendment. On the Senate side, there was no committee markup or vote in the Judiciary Committee, nor was there any opportunity to amend the measure when it reached the floor.

Senator Patrick Leahy (D-VT) laid down an early marker after the tragedy of 9/11. He cautioned against tipping the scales to the extent of endangering and jeopardizing civil liberties. "The worse thing that could happen is we damage our Constitution," he said. "If the Constitution is shredded, the terrorists win." Senator Russ Feingold (D-WI) issued a similar warning: "Preserving our freedom is the reason we are now engaging in this new war on terrorism. We will lose that war without a shot being fired if we sacrifice the liberties of the American people in the belief that by doing so we will stop the terrorists."

At such moments, citizens look to independent judges to check executive abuse, but, ironically, judicial safeguards are weakest in times of war and emergency. In the case of Yasser Esam Hamdi, held without charges as an enemy combatant, a Justice Department brief argued that courts "may not second-guess the military's enemy combatant determination." After a district judge had repeatedly rejected broad arguments advanced by the administration, the Fourth Circuit reversed each time, coming down squarely in favor of presidential power: "For the judicial branch to trespass

upon the exercise of the war-making powers would be an infringement of the right to self-determination and self-governance at a time when the care of the common defense is most critical."

When the government began to close deportation proceedings to the press and to the public, a district judge ordered the Justice Department to either give the suspect an open hearing or release him. The Sixth Circuit affirmed that ruling, noting that "Democracies die behind closed doors." The Third Circuit, however, declined to "lightly second-guess" the national security concerns of the Justice Department. Whatever the likelihood of judicial relief for litigants, safeguards for civil liberties will depend largely on the efforts of citizens, organizations, and the media to challenge practices and procedures of the executive branch. These outside forces, pressing their views upon Congress, are the true guardians of liberty.

See also Alien and Sedition Acts; Communist Party USA; Espionage Act of 1917; First Amendment; Habeas Corpus; Jefferson, Thomas; *Korematsu v. United States;* Liberty; Lincoln, Abraham; McCarthy, Joseph R.; Roosevelt, Franklin D.; *Schenck v. United States;* Speech, Freedom of; Symbolic Speech; Terrorism, War on; *Texas v. Johnson; Tinker v. Des Moines Independent Community School District;* USA PATRIOT Act; U.S. Department of Justice

Bibliography

Chafee, Zechariah, Jr. 1919. "Freedom of Speech in War Time." *Harvard Law Review* 32: 932–73.

May, Christopher N. 1989. *In the Name of War: Judicial Review and the War Powers since 1918.* Cambridge, MA: Harvard University Press.

Rabban, David M. 1997. *Free Speech in Its Forgotten Years.* Cambridge: Cambridge University Press.

Smith, James Norton. 1956. *Freedom's Fetters: The Alien and Sedition Laws and American Civil Liberties.* Ithaca, NY: Cornell University Press.

Smith, Jeffery A. 1999. *War and Press Freedom: The Problem of Prerogative Power.* New York: Oxford University Press.

Louis Fisher

CIVIL RIGHTS CASES, THE (1883)

The United States Supreme Court's decision in the Civil Rights Cases was arguably the most important civil rights decision of the late nineteenth century. While this decision is not as well known as *Plessy v. Ferguson* (1896), the decision in the Civil Rights Cases remains good law today, whereas the *Plessy* ruling was discarded long ago.

The Civil Rights Cases were actually five cases consolidated for decision in the Supreme Court. Specifically, they were denominated as follows: *Robinson and Wife v. Memphis and Charleston Railroad Company; United States v. Nichols; United States v. Ryan; United States v. Singleton;* and *United States v. Stanley.* All these cases arose under the Civil Rights Act of 1875, entitled An Act to Protect All Citizens in Their Civil and Legal Rights. With this legislation Congress attempted to eradicate racial discrimination in places of public accommodation, including hotels, taverns, restaurants, theaters, and "public conveyances."

The act was based primarily on the grant of legislative power contained in Section 5 of the Fourteenth Amendment, which grants Congress power to enforce the substantive provisions of the amendment "by appropriate legislation." In this context the relevant substantive provision was that clause of Section 1 that prohibits states from denying to persons within their jurisdictions the equal protection of the laws.

In the Civil Rights Cases the Supreme Court held that Section 5 of the Fourteenth Amendment limited congressional action to the prohibition of official state-sponsored discrimination, as distinct from discrimination practiced by privately owned places of public accommodation. Writing for the Court, Justice Joseph P. Bradley opined that Section 5 of the Fourteenth Amendment "does not authorize Congress to create a code of municipal law for the regulation of private rights; but to provide modes of redress against the operation of state laws, and the action of state officers, executive or judicial, when these are subversive of the fundamental rights specified in the amendment." This holding is the source of the state

action doctrine that is at the heart of the Supreme Court's Fourteenth Amendment jurisprudence. The doctrine requires that there be meaningful state action in order for there to be a possible violation of the Fourteenth Amendment. Discriminatory action that is solely private in character is beyond the ken of the Fourteenth Amendment.

In his solo dissent, Justice John Marshall Harlan (the elder) rejected the Court's narrow interpretation of the Fourteenth Amendment: "It was perfectly well known that the great danger to the equal enjoyment by citizens of their rights, as citizens, was to be apprehended, not altogether from unfriendly state legislation, but from the hostile action of corporations and individuals in the states. And it is to be presumed that it was intended, by [the Fourteenth Amendment] to clothe Congress with power and authority to meet that danger."

Not only did the Court's decision in the Civil Rights Cases preserve widespread practices of racial discrimination in restaurants, hotels, and the like, but it was also regarded as a green light for the passage of legislation mandating strict racial segregation.

Although the decision in the Civil Rights Cases has never been overturned, modern courts typically take a broad view of the concept of state action, thus allowing Congress wide authority under Section 5 of the Fourteenth Amendment. Moreover, Congress has used its broad powers to regulate interstate commerce to enact civil rights legislation applicable to virtually all places of public accommodation in this country.

See also Civil Rights Act of 1875; Civil Rights Act of 1964; Discrimination; Doctrine of State Action; Fourteenth Amendment; Fourteenth Amendment, Section 5 of the; Harlan, John Marshall; Public Accommodation, Places of; Segregation in Public Education

John M. Scheb II and Otis H. Stephens, Jr.

CIVIL RIGHTS DIVISION, U.S. DEPARTMENT OF JUSTICE

The Civil Rights Division is a branch of the United States Department of Justice. It was established by the

Civil Rights Act of 1957 and is charged with enforcing federal statutes and executive orders prohibiting discrimination on the basis of race, color, national origin, sex, age, disability, or religion in public accommodations and facilities, federally assisted programs, housing, education, employment, credit, and voting. The Civil Rights Division is under the supervision of an assistant attorney general, who is aided by deputy assistant attorneys general. These two individuals are responsible for the division's executive direction, presiding over enforcement duties and overseeing administrative management activities.

The Civil Rights Division has 11 sections, each responsible for ensuring enforcement and compliance in specific areas. For example, one section is responsible for coordinating federal agencies and preparing information under the Freedom of Information and Privacy Acts. The 11 sections are the Appellate Section, the Coordination and Review Section, the Criminal Section, the Disability Rights Section, the Educational Opportunities Section, the Employment Litigation Section, Housing and Civil Enforcement Section, the Office of Special Counsel for Immigration Related Unfair Employment Practices, the Special Litigation Section, the Voting Section, and the Administrative Management Section.

The Appellate Section deals with civil rights cases in the courts of appeals. This section also provides legal counsel to the Department of Justice regarding civil rights laws and appellate litigation. It also defends challenges to the constitutionality of antidiscrimination statutes and to federal procurement programs. The Coordination and Review Section works in a government-wide program to ensure that federal agencies enforce civil rights legislation correctly and effectively. This section is responsible for enforcing Executive Orders 12250, 13166, and 13160 and administrative complaint investigations. The Criminal Section prosecutes offenders in cases that involve violations of basic constitutional rights. These offenses include crimes based on race, ethnicity, or religion, and abuses of power by federal, state, and local law enforcement

officials. This section also prosecutes conspiracies to interfere with federally protected rights.

The Disability Rights Section was created to protect the rights of persons with disabilities by enforcing Titles I, II, and III of the Americans with Disabilities Act. Title I bans discrimination in the employment practices of state and local governments. Title II outlaws discrimination in the activities of state and local governments. Title III makes it illegal to discriminate against persons with disabilities in public areas like restaurants, retail stores, parks, and other places of public accommodation. This act also means that these facilities must reasonably accommodate the needs of persons with disabilities.

The Education Opportunities Section ensures that schools do not discriminate against students on the basis of race, national origin, religion, language, or disability. All students are supposed to have an equal opportunity to succeed in educational institutions. This section also ensures that sports programs in schools provide equal opportunities for women. The Employment Litigation Section is responsible for implementing the Equal Employment Opportunity Act and the Pregnancy Discrimination Act. It also protects against discrimination in employment policies and practices on the basis of race, sex, religion, national origin, and the like. The Housing and Civil Enforcement Section helps prevent discrimination in housing transactions. It also enforces the Equal Credit Opportunity Act, which prevents discrimination in lending.

The Office of Special Counsel for Immigration Related Unfair Employment Practices has three major functions. First, it protects U.S. citizens and legal immigrants from employment discrimination. Second, it prevents unlawful discrimination through outreach programs. Third, it provides advice and counseling on issues that affect the civil rights of U.S. citizens and immigrants. The Special Litigation Section was created in 2003, and it contains four major parts with which it enforces federal civil rights statutes. Part 1 deals with conditions of institutional confinement, part 2 deals with law enforcement, part 3 provides access to reproductive health facilities and places of religious worship, and part 4 protects a person's right to exercise his or her religion.

The Voting Section is responsible for implementing many acts, such as the Voting Rights Act of 1965 and the National Voter Registration Act of 1993. This section also helps the disadvantaged (the elderly, disabled, racial and language minorities) with voting. The Administrative Management Section provides management and technical services assistance to businesses. These services include budget formulation, litigation support, and mailing and filing for many operations.

See also Age Discrimination; Civil Rights Act of 1957; Disabilities, Rights of Persons with; Employment Discrimination; Freedom of Information Act; Gender-Based Discrimination; Housing, Discrimination in; Justice, U.S. Department of; Privacy, Informational; Public Accommodation, Places of; Voting Rights Act of 1965

Bibliography

Graham, Hugh Davis. 1998. "The Storm over Grove City College: Civil Rights Regulation, Higher Education, and the Reagan Administration." *History of Education Quarterly* 38 (4): 407–29.

Hutchings, Vincent L. 1998. "Issue Salience and Support for Civil Rights Legislation among Southern Democrats." *Legislative Studies Quarterly* 23: 521–44.

Shull, Steven A. 1999. *American Civil Rights Policy from Truman to Clinton.* Armonk, NY: M. E. Sharpe.

Maurice Mangum

CIVIL RIGHTS MOVEMENT

The civil rights movement was a massive collective social protest campaign led by African Americans aimed at ending segregation and other forms of racial discrimination and achieving the loftier goals of racial justice and equality. It is difficult to identify exactly when or where the Movement, as it was called by participants, began. In the early twentieth century, the NAACP was formed for the principal purpose of mounting a litigation campaign challenging the validity of state laws that severely restricted the voting rights of African Americans. Soon the NAACP broadened its goals by initiating legal assaults on racial segregation in such areas as residential housing and public education. By the middle of the twentieth century, this organization had achieved major victories in both of these areas. In *Shelley v. Kraemer* (1948), the NAACP successfully challenged the constitutionality of racially restrictive covenants by which white owners of real estate sought to maintain racial segregation in their neighborhoods. While not forbidding such covenants outright, the Supreme Court held that they were judicially unenforceable and therefore had no binding effect on the purchasers or sellers of residential property. *Brown v. Board of Education* (1954), in which the Supreme Court unanimously struck down racial segregation of public schools, was the NAACP's most celebrated victory and lifted the hopes of African Americans throughout the United States.

The *Shelley* and *Brown* decisions no doubt exercised long-range influence on the struggle for civil rights, but most observers agree that the catalyst of the movement can be traced to an afternoon in December 1955, when Rosa Parks, a leader of the Montgomery, Alabama, chapter of the NAACP, refused to give up her seat in the "whites only" section of a city bus. Ms. Parks's arrest for violating one of the infamous Jim Crow laws precipitated a year-long boycott of the city bus system led by a charismatic young minister by the name of Martin Luther King, Jr. Although segregation of Montgomery's bus system was ended by litigation (see *Browder v. Gayle,* 1956; affirmed per curiam in *Gayle v. Browder,* 1956), the boycott gave local black citizens a sense of empowerment and prompted other challenges to segregation across the South. It also provided the movement with a leader in the person of Dr. King. The Southern Christian Leadership Conference (SCLC), which would become Dr. King's principal organizational vehicle, likewise emerged out of the Montgomery bus boycott.

Black churches provided a ready-made organizational network for the civil rights movement. With coordination and direction provided by the SCLC, black churches throughout the South were soon pressed into service in the cause of civil rights. Other organizations, including the Student Nonviolent Coordinating Committee (SNCC) and the Congress on Racial Equality (CORE), played significant roles as well. In cities across the South, civil rights activists registered voters, conducted sit-ins at segregated facilities, led protest marches, held protest rallies, and organized boycotts. These grassroots actions, as well as the often violent responses of the police and reactionary mobs, galvanized the conscience of the nation.

The movement encountered its most violent resistance in Birmingham, Alabama. In the spring of 1963, the SCLC led a boycott of downtown merchants and a series of marches and demonstrations to protest the city's segregation laws. Birmingham's infamous police commissioner, Bull Connor, obtained a court order barring the demonstrations. When the civil rights marchers violated the order, numerous leaders, including Dr. King, were arrested. This was the occasion for Dr. King's famous "Letter from a Birmingham Jail," in which he so eloquently defended his course of nonviolent civil disobedience in protest of injustice. As the spring wore on, confrontations between demonstrators and police escalated. Despite growing pressure, Dr. King refused to call off the protests. The police continued to arrest protesters until the local jails were full. In early May, police used dogs and fire hoses against protestors, some of whom were school-age children. These brutal tactics created television images that shocked and outraged people around the world. Ultimately, the protests were called off when the city agreed to repeal its segregation laws.

The high point of the civil rights movement came in August 1963, when more than a quarter million people assembled in the National Mall in Washington, D.C. The highlight came when Dr. King, standing on the steps of the Lincoln Memorial, delivered his memorable "I have a dream" speech. But the optimism engendered by Dr. King's hopeful speech was shattered less than a month later when

terrorists bombed Birmingham's Sixteenth Street Baptist Church during Sunday school, killing four African American girls. And many despaired when President John F. Kennedy, a strong supporter of the movement's agenda, was assassinated on November 22, 1963.

Ironically, the tragic events of late 1963 helped prepare the political landscape for the adoption of landmark civil rights legislation. Of course, President Lyndon Johnson's decision to push the civil rights agenda through Congress was also crucial. The Civil Rights Act of 1964, while by no means eliminating the underlying problem of racism, went a long way toward abolishing the regime of racial segregation in America.

The political breakthrough that resulted in the passage of the Civil Rights Act of 1964 by no means meant the end of white resistance to the civil rights agenda. During the summer of 1964, Mississippi occupied center stage in the struggle for civil rights. When the NAACP, SNCC, and CORE began a campaign to register African Americans to vote, reactionary forces responded with violence. Civil rights workers were harassed, and some were even beaten by police and mobs. African American homes, businesses, and churches were bombed or burned. And three white civil rights workers, James Chaney, Andrew Goodman, and Michael Schwerner, were murdered by members of the Ku Klux Klan. Again, the nation was shocked, and support began to build for federal legislation to secure the right to vote in the South.

During the winter of 1965, another dramatic confrontation over civil rights took place in Selma, Alabama. Dr. King and the SCLC organized a march from Selma to Montgomery, the state capital. When marchers tried to cross the Edmund Pettis Bridge on March 7, they were beaten back by club-wielding police on horseback. Dubbed Bloody Sunday, this violent confrontation served as a catalyst for national political action. A week later, President Johnson introduced a voting rights bill into Congress. On national television, Johnson embraced the cause of civil rights, ending his speech by invoking the civil rights anthem, saying, "We shall overcome."

Johnson dispatched federal marshals and troops to keep the peace in Alabama, and Dr. King was able to complete the march on Montgomery. On August 6, 1965, Johnson signed the landmark Voting Rights Act of 1965, which would forever change the politics of the American South.

The last great legislative accomplishment of the civil rights movement, the Fair Housing Act of 1968, was achieved only after the greatest tragedy the movement had seen—the assassination of Dr. King in April of 1968. The Fair Housing Act became law on April 11, 1968, two days after Dr. King's funeral.

The year 1968 was perhaps the most turbulent year in American history since the Civil War. Outrage over Dr. King's assassination led to riots in cities across America. Just weeks after Dr. King's assassination in Memphis, Robert F. Kennedy was shot and killed in Los Angeles. Chicago became a virtual battleground as police clashed with demonstrators protesting the Vietnam War during the Democratic National Convention in August. Alabama governor George Wallace, an independent candidate for president, fanned the flames of white reaction. Meanwhile, voices in the movement became more militant and more radical. The most extreme elements, most notably the Black Panther party, went so far as to stage bank robberies and jailbreaks in an attempt to bring about revolution against the white-dominated society.

In retrospect, the civil rights movement of the late 1950s and 1960s was the most successful social movement in the nation's history. Although many in the movement were disappointed that more progress was not made toward the elimination of poverty, racism, and social injustice, the accomplishments of the movement are undeniable. Were it not for the movement, politicians—even liberal Democrats like Lyndon Johnson and Robert F. Kennedy—were unlikely to have manifested nearly as much concern for the rights of African Americans.

See also Abolitionist Movement; Baker Motley, Constance; Black Panther Party; Boycotts; *Brown v. Board of Education;* Busing Controversy; Civil Disobedience; Civil Rights Act of 1964; Congress on Racial Equality; *Edwards v. South Carolina;* Evers, Medgar; Fair Housing Act of 1968; Freedom Rides; Freedom Summer; Free Speech Movement; Housing, Discrimination in; Interest Groups; Jim Crow Laws; Kennedy, Robert F.; King, Martin Luther, Jr.; Ku Klux Klan; Little Rock Crisis; Marshall, Thurgood; Meredith, James; National Association for the Advancement of Colored People; Parks, Rosa; Restrictive Covenants; Segregation, De Facto and De Jure; Segregation in Public Education; *Shelley v. Kraemer;* Sit-Ins; Southern Christian Leadership Conference; Student Nonviolent Coordinating Committee; Voting Rights Act of 1965; Warren Court

Bibliography

Branch, Taylor. 1988. *Parting the Waters: America in the King Years.* New York: Simon & Schuster.

McWhorter, Diane. 2001. *Carry Me Home; Birmingham, Alabama—the Climactic Battle of the Civil Rights Revolution.* New York: Touchstone.

Vose, Clement E., 1959. *Caucasians Only: the Supreme Court, the NAACP, and the Restrictive Covenant Cases.* Berkeley and Los Angeles: University of California Press.

Williams, Juan. 1988. *Eyes on the Prize: America's Civil Rights Years, 1954–1965.* Reprint ed. New York: Penguin Books.

Otis H. Stephens, Jr., and John M. Scheb II

CIVIL RIGHTS RESTORATION ACT OF 1991

In the early 1990s, the House of Representatives found that existing protections and remedies under federal law were inadequate to deter unlawful discrimination in the workplace and compensate victims of discrimination. Congress found that the Supreme Court's decision in *Ward's Cove Packing v. Antonio* (1989) had weakened the scope and effectiveness of federal civil rights protections. Therefore, in November 1991, Congress passed the Civil Rights Restoration Act, which President George H. W. Bush signed into law on November 21, 1991.

The Civil Rights Restoration Act of 1991 was created with four purposes in mind. First, it was to provide appropriate remedies against discrimination and illegal harassment in the workplace. Second, the act codified the concepts of "business necessity" and "job related" outlined by the Supreme Court in *Griggs v. Duke Power* (1971) and in the other Supreme Court decisions before *Ward's Cove Packing v. Antonio*. Third, it bestowed statutory authority and discussed guidelines for adjudicating disparate-impact cases under Title VII of the Civil Rights Act of 1964. Lastly, the act sought to reverse the impact of previous decisions of the Supreme Court by expanding the scope of relevant civil rights provisions to provide protection to victims of discrimination.

Through its primary objective, the Civil Rights Restoration Act of 1991 granted employees more rights, including rights against discrimination and mistreatment, by circumventing approximately 12 Supreme Court decisions that narrowed civil rights protections. The Civil Rights Restoration Act made it easier for employees to sue their employers in job discrimination cases by clarifying and expanding earlier legislation. It also increased employer penalties for intentional and illegal discrimination against employees. That law expanded the remedies available to victims of employment discrimination under Title VII of the 1964 Civil Rights Act and the Americans with Disabilities Act of 1990.

Employees who are victims of employment discrimination found new financial incentives to redress discrimination imposed by businesses when Congress passed the Civil Rights Restoration Act of 1991. Businesses and corporations have more serious incentives to make sure there is no discrimination against any employees. Plaintiffs can sue for emotional stress and for just compensation that the company owes for its discriminatory behavior. This provision helps plaintiffs in a wide range of cases seek repayment of economic damages and attorneys' fees in addition to punitive damages and damages for emotional distress. Victims of employee

discrimination can obtain compensation from the employer on an economic basis as well as for pain that the employer caused.

Additionally, the Civil Rights Restoration Act of 1991 revitalized the Glass Ceiling Commission. The commission was established to provide different ways to remove the barriers frustrating the advancement of women and minorities. It also outlawed the adjustment of test scores based on a test taker's race, a practice known as race norming.

See also Civil Rights Act of 1964; Disabilities, Rights of Persons with; Employment Discrimination; Gender-Based Discrimination; Sexual Harassment

Bibliography

Graham, Hugh Davis. 1998. "The Storm over Grove City College: Civil Rights Regulation, Higher Education, and the Reagan Administration." *History of Education Quarterly* 38 (4): 407–29.

Shull, Steven A. 1999. *American Civil Rights Policy from Truman to Clinton.* Armonk, NY: M. E. Sharpe.

                                                Maurice Mangum

CIVIL SERVICE REFORM ACT OF 1978

The Civil Service Reform Act of 1978 is considered to be one of the most influential and comprehensive pieces of legislation relating to government personnel management. However, it was not a purely administrative instrument. The act represented a compromise among several political groups with different views on how to improve the performance of the federal bureaucracy (Ingraham 1984).

In addition to perceived internal inefficiency, there were economic conditions that produced pressures for a radical change in the federal personnel management system. According to Ingraham and Ban (1984), there were several internal issues the act was intended to address: (1) a general opinion that bureaucracy was inefficient, (2) career bureaucrats' perceptions of problems and rigidities in the personnel system, and (3) increased availability of management techniques from the private sector.

Similarly, according to Rosenbloom (1998), the Civil Service Reform Act of 1978 was an attempt to balance at least two conflicts within the personnel management system of the United States: first, the conflict between the merit system and political considerations of representation (affirmative action); and second, the conflict between appropriate legal rights for employees and stringent managerial guidelines needed to achieve agency goals. In general terms, the act tried to solve these problems by reforming and adding regulations relating to a variety of topics, such as protection for whistle-blowers, a new performance evaluation system, the creation of the Senior Executive Service, and a recommitment to affirmative action principles. The act also led to the creation of the Office of Personnel Management (OPM) and the new Federal Labor Relations Authority (FLRA).

The act delivered many of its promises but could not solve some of its internal conflicts. Ban and Ingraham state that the Civil Service Reform Act of 1978 contained several inconsistencies that influenced its implementation. The authors identify three important problems: (1) "The conflict between the desire for greater political responsiveness and the desire for greater managerial capability and independence, (2) The conflict between the concept of a management cadre with a sense of identity and esprit de corps and the concept of competition to increase productivity, and (3) The conflict between the goal of increasing managers' ability to fire problem employees and the goal of protecting whistle-blowers" (Ban and Ingraham 1984, 3)

As mentioned above, the implementation of the Civil Service Reform Act of 1978 had some positive results, one of the most important of which was the structural separation of managerial, legal, and political issues related to the federal personnel system (Rosenbloom 1998). Managerial functions were vested in the Office of Personnel Management. Some of OPM's responsibilities were training, retirement systems, and overseeing personnel management and policies in federal agencies. Political functions were assigned to the

Equal Employment Opportunity Commission (EEOC). This decision was based on the assumption that representation of minorities and women in the federal workforce was not a managerial, but a political, matter.

Finally, two public agencies shared important legal functions. The Merit System Protection Board (MSPB), created to deal with some of the legal functions, was able to impose sanctions on employees who violated personnel laws. MSPB was also assigned specific functions to protect whistle-blowers. The Federal Labor Relations Authority (FLRA) was created primarily to oversee collective bargaining in the federal agencies. The FLRA develops rules and procedures about fair labor relationships and can help resolve disputes between government and the unions.

It is important to clarify that the success of the act can be seen from different perspectives. Its comprehensiveness leads to multiple interpretations of its impact and ultimate success as a personnel policy.

See also Equal Employment Opportunity Commission; Merit Systems Protection Board; Public Employees, Constitutional Rights of

Bibliography

Ingraham, Patricia W. 1984. "The Civil Service Reform Act of 1978: Its Design and Legislative History." In *Legislating Bureaucratic Change: The Civil Service Reform Act of 1978,* ed. Patricia W. Ingraham and Carolyn Ban. Albany: State University of New York Press.

Ingraham, Patricia W., and Carolyn Ban. 1984. Introduction to *Legislating Bureaucratic Change: The Civil Service Reform Act of 1978,* ed. Patricia W. Ingraham and Carolyn Ban. Albany: State University of New York Press.

Rosenbloom, David H. 1998. *Public Administration: Understanding Management, Politics, and Law in the Public Sector.* New York: McGraw-Hill.

J. Ramon Gil-Garcia

CIVIL UNIONS. *See* Same-Sex Marriage and Civil Unions

CLARK, TOM C. (1899–1977)

President Harry Truman, who appointed Tom Clark to the Supreme Court, claimed, "[Clark] was no damn good as Attorney General, and on the Supreme Court … it doesn't seem possible, but he's been even worse" (Young 1998). That commonly recalled negative assessment of Clark is unfair to the justice, who, according to Supreme Court scholar Henry Abraham, was "a determined, if cautious, craftsman of the law who frequently became a swing man between the liberal and conservative blocs on the bench" (Abraham 1992). Although he was rated "average" in one poll seeking to assess Supreme Court justices, Clark still ranks higher than the other three Truman appointees to the Court, all of whom received "failure" ratings (Abraham 1992).

Clark was the son and grandson of lawyers. After service in World War I, he received a law degree from the University of Texas and joined his father's firm in Dallas, Texas. With the exception of a stint as civil district attorney in Dallas, he remained in private practice until 1937, when he began working for the Department of Justice. Among his major Justice Department positions were assistant attorney general in charge of the antitrust division, assistant attorney general in charge of the criminal division, and attorney general. In 1949, he was appointed to the Supreme Court, where he served until his retirement in 1967, when he left the Court to avoid ethical conflicts associated with the appointment of his son, Ramsey Clark, as attorney general. Clark, however, remained active and often served on the federal trial and appellate bench, serving on every federal circuit court. He had a strong interest in, and a vast influence over, judicial administration, especially in his capacity as the first director of the Federal Judicial Center, an educational and training center for the federal judiciary (Larrimer 1985; Young 1998).

Clark had an uncanny ability to make powerful friends who aided him in forwarding his career. Among his most influential allies were Texas senator Tom Connally, long-time Speaker of the House of Representatives Sam Rayburn, and presidents Harry Truman and Lyndon Johnson (Clark 1969).

Clark was involved in the removal and relocation of Japanese Americans during World War II, an action he later regretted. He pursued a strategy of filing amicus curiae briefs supporting racial equality claims as attorney general, as in *Shelley v. Kraemer* (1948), which challenged racially restrictive covenants in the sale of housing (Young 1998).

Although Clark was commonly labeled a conservative justice, he authored several major civil liberties opinions (Larrimer 1985). For example, Clark authored the eight-to-one decision in *Abington School District v. Schempp* (1963), a controversial decision that struck down the use of school prayers on First Amendment grounds. In *Mapp v. Ohio* (1961), Clark applied the exclusionary rule to the illegal seizure of evidence in state cases (Dorin 2001). *Heart of Atlanta Motel v. United States* (1964) and *Katzenbach v. McClung* (1964) addressed the constitutionality of the provisions of the 1964 Civil Rights Act dealing with desegregation of places of public accommodations. Clark wrote unanimous opinions upholding the act in both cases (Cortner 2001).

As the years have passed, history has tended to favorably reassess Clark. Henry Abraham wrote of Clark's record on the Court, "[It is] proof of man's inherent ability to grow remarkably in a position of high responsibility and authority" (Abraham 1992).

See also *Abington School District v. Schempp;* Civil Rights Act of 1964; Exclusionary Rule; First Amendment; Fourth Amendment; *Heart of Atlanta Motel v. United States;* Japanese Americans, Relocation of; *Katzenbach v. McClung; Mapp v. Ohio;* Restrictive Covenants; School Prayer Decisions; *Shelley v. Kraemer;* U.S. Department of Justice; Warren Court

Bibliography

Abraham, Henry J. 1992. *Justice and Presidents.* New York: Oxford University Press.

Clark, Tom C. 1969. "Oral History Interview I." By Joe B. Frantz. Internet Copy. 7 October. Lyndon B. Johnson Library, Austin, TX.

Cortner, Richard C. 2001. *Civil Rights and Public Accommodations.* Lawrence: University Press of Kansas.

Dorin, Dennis D. 2001. "Marshaling *Mapp:* Justice Tom Clark's Role in *Mapp v. Ohio*'s Extension of the Exclusionary Rule to State Searches and Seizures." *Case Western Reserve Law Review* 52 (4): 401–40.

Larrimer, Don. 1985. *Biobibliography of Justice Tom C. Clark.* Austin: University of Texas School of Law.

Young, Evan A. 1998. *Lone Star Justice: A Biography of Justice Tom C. Clark.* Dallas, TX: Hendrick-Long.

Anthony Champagne

CLEAR AND PRESENT DANGER DOCTRINE

The First Amendment to the United States Constitution protects freedom of speech from abridgment by the national government. By including this protection in the Bill of Rights, Congress and the states recognized freedom of expression as a fundamental right of citizens. In *Gitlow v. New York* (1925), *Fiske v. Kansas* (1927), and other decisions, the Supreme Court interpreted the Fourteenth Amendment to extend the protections of the First Amendment to encompass state action as well.

The right to freely express oneself has long been considered a "preferred freedom" by the courts and is robustly protected. There are restrictions, however, as no constitutional right is considered to be absolute. In 1919, Justice Oliver Wendell Holmes, Jr., made this point in observing that "the most stringent protection of free speech would not protect a man in falsely shouting fire in a theater, and causing a panic." Over the years courts have devised various tests in determining acceptable parameters for the right of expression. Historically, American courts followed the so-called bad tendency test developed under English common law in allowing government to restrict expression that might have a tendency to cause lawless action.

At the outbreak of World War I, the United States Congress passed the Espionage Act of 1917, which made it illegal to interfere with the process of recruiting and enlisting troops or to disclose information pertaining to national defense. Before it was repealed in 1921, approximately 900 persons were sentenced to prison under the act. In *Schenck v. United States* (1919), the U.S. Supreme Court upheld a conviction of a Socialist Party leader under the Espionage Act but in so doing adopted a new test for determining the scope of free speech protected by the First Amendment.

In what came to be known as the clear and present danger test, Justice Holmes's opinion for the Court in *Schenck* stated, "The question in every case is whether the words used are used in such circumstances and are of such a nature as to create a clear and present danger that they will bring about the substantive evils that Congress has a right to prevent." This represented a much higher level of judicial protection for First Amendment rights than was afforded by the traditional bad tendency test. Despite this heightened concern for freedom of speech, a unanimous Supreme Court concluded that Schenck's activities in opposing the military draft constituted a clear and present danger to the national security. It is important to keep in mind, however, that Schenck's prosecution occurred during World War I. As Justice Holmes observed in the *Schenck* opinion, "When a nation is at war many things that might be said in time of peace are such a hindrance to its effort that their utterance will not be endured so long as men fight, and that no court could regard them as protected by any constitutional right."

In subsequent First Amendment cases, Justice Holmes, along with his colleague Louis D. Brandeis, would continue to insist on the clear and present danger test as the proper standard for interpreting the scope of free speech. But in a series of decisions, a conservative Court would revert to the bad tendency test (see, e.g., *Abrams v. United States,* 1919).

It was not until the 1930s that the Supreme Court fully embraced the clear and present danger doctrine. In *Herndon v. Lowry* (1937), the Court first employed the clear and present danger doctrine to protect freedom of speech. In that case, the Court reversed a conviction for violation of a Georgia statute prohibiting "any attempt, by persuasion or otherwise" to incite insurrection. Following this decision, the Court began to apply the clear and present danger test not only to "seditious" speech but to other First Amendment issues as well.

The clear and present danger doctrine remains viable in First Amendment jurisprudence, albeit in a modified form. In its landmark decision in *Brandenburg v. Ohio* (1969), the Supreme Court said, in effect, that in order for a clear and present danger to exist, there must be "imminent lawless action." Although still not granting absolute protection to incendiary public speech, the imminent lawless action doctrine extends the protections of the First Amendment well beyond the point contemplated by Justice Holmes in *Schenck v. United States*.

In an opinion concurring in the Court's judgment in *Brandenburg*, Justice William O. Douglas called for a complete repudiation of the clear and present danger doctrine:

I see no place in the regime of the First Amendment for any "clear and present danger" test, whether strict and tight as some would make it, or free-wheeling.... The line between what is permissible and not subject to control and what may be made impermissible and subject to regulation is the line between ideas and overt acts.

Despite Justice Douglas's objection, the Supreme Court has not seriously reconsidered the clear and present danger doctrine, or the imminent lawless action reformulation, since 1969. Today, as Americans contemplate the ongoing threat of terrorism, there are those who would like to see the Court reconsider the doctrine, not to expand, but to restrict the protections of the First Amendment with respect to the advocacy of violence.

See also Alien and Sedition Acts; Bill of Rights (American); Bill of Rights, Incorporation of; Brandeis, Louis D.; *Brandenburg v. Ohio;* Clear and Probable Danger Doctrine; Common-Law Background of American Civil Rights and Liberties; Douglas, William O.; Espionage Act of 1917; First Amendment; First Amendment, Approaches to; Fundamental Rights; *Gitlow v. New York;* Holmes,

Oliver Wendell, Jr.; Preferred Freedoms Doctrine; *Schenck v. United States;* Smith Act; Speech, Freedom of; Terrorism, War on; Wartime, Civil Rights and Liberties during

Bibliography

Alonso, Karen. 1999. *Schenck v. United States: Restrictions on Free Speech.* Berkeley Heights, NJ: Enslow.

Bollinger, Lee. 1986. *The Tolerant Society: Freedom of Speech and Extremist Speech in America.* New York: Oxford University Press, 1986.

Haiman, Franklyn S. 1977. *Speech and Law in a Free Society.* Chicago: University of Chicago Press.

Kersch, Ken I. 2003. *Freedom of Speech: Rights and Liberties under the Law.* Santa Barbara, CA: ABC-CLIO.

Mendelson, Wallace. 1952. "Clear and Present Danger: From *Schenck* to *Dennis.*" *Columbia Law Review* 52:313–33.

Michael Haynes and John M. Scheb II

CLEAR AND PROBABLE DANGER DOCTRINE

Shortly after the end of World War II the United States was embroiled in the cold war, which pitted the ideals of democracy against those of communism. By the early 1950s the Soviet Union was expanding its influence throughout Eastern Europe; China, a previous American ally, was under communist control; and the United States had committed troops to defend southern Korea from being overrun by the communists to the north. At home there was fear bordering on paranoia that communists might attempt an overthrow of the U.S. government. Joseph McCarthy, a freshman senator from Wisconsin, was fueling the red scare by leading a national campaign to ferret out alleged communists whom he insisted had infiltrated the government. Against that backdrop, the Truman administration was feeling pressure to do something about the perceived internal communist threat.

On the morning of July 20, 1948, Eugene Dennis, the general secretary of the American Communist Party, was arrested along with 10 other members of the party for violation of the Alien Registration Act of 1940, better known as the Smith Act. Section 2 of the Smith Act made it illegal "to knowingly or willfully advocate, abet, advise, or teach the duty, necessity, desirability, or propriety of overthrowing or destroying any government in the United States by force or violence, or by the assassination of any officer of any such government." Dennis and the other codefendants were convicted in a highly publicized trial, which lasted for nine months. None of the defendants had publicly advocated the violent overthrow of the United States government but were convicted for their efforts in organizing the Communist Party within the United States, which the government deemed a threat to national security. The case was appealed to the United States Court of Appeals for the Second Circuit, where the decision was affirmed. In his opinion for the court, Chief Judge Learned Hand revised the clear and present danger test, articulating a more restrictive variation: the clear and probable danger test. Hand wrote, "In each case, we must ask whether the gravity of the evil, discounted by its improbability, justifies such invasion of free speech as is necessary to avoid the danger. Contexts too numerable to ponder exist and events are often too remote to foresee. Cases must be decided on an ad hoc, case-by-case basis, considering that the government's reasons for regulation are compelling." Under the new clear and probable danger standard it would no longer be necessary for the government to produce evidence that the speech in question would reasonably bring about the perceived danger. All that would be required was evidence that the speech could bring about an action that the government had a right to prevent. The case was appealed to the Supreme Court.

The *Dennis* case was argued before the Supreme Court on December 4, 1950, and on June 4, 1951, the Court rendered its decision. In a 6–2 vote the justices upheld the conviction of Dennis and the other codefendants under the Smith Act. Writing for a plurality, Chief Justice Fred Vinson stated, "It is the existence of the conspiracy which creates the danger. If the ingredients of the reaction are present, we cannot bind the Government

to wait until the catalyst is added." In the opinion, Vinson agreed with and accepted Judge Hand's revised clear and probable danger test. In effect the Court replaced the clear and present danger test with clear and probable danger, making it the new standard by which similar cases would be decided. In a concurring opinion Justices Felix Frankfurter and Robert Jackson agreed with the decision, Jackson saying he found "no constitutional right to 'gang up' on the Government." However, neither Frankfurter nor Jackson accepted the revised clear and probable danger as the new standard. Justices Hugo Black and William Douglas both dissented. Black disparaged the Court's decision as giving in to popular hysteria: "Public opinion being what it is few will protest the conviction of these communist petitioners. There is hope, however, that in calmer times, when present pressures, passions, and fears subside, this or some other Court will restore the First Amendment liberties to the high preferred place where they belong in a free society."

Senator McCarthy overplayed his authority and was censured by the Senate in December 1954. Public opinion started to change, and the force behind the red scare began to lose momentum. The Supreme Court was also changing as new members began to replace retiring justices. Just six years after the Court had accepted the more restrictive clear and probable danger standard, it reversed its decision. In *Yates v. United States* (1957) the Court reasoned that advocating and teaching communist ideology did not equal attempting to incite the immediate overthrow of the United States government. Speech that merely advocated such ideas was, therefore, protected by the First Amendment. In his majority opinion in *Yates,* Justice John M. Harlan (the younger) stated, "Throughout our decisions there has recurred a distinction between the statement of an idea which may prompt its hearers to take unlawful action, and advocacy that such action be taken." In *Yates,* the Court also drew a clear distinction between "active" and "nominal" membership in organizations such as the Communist Party. While not invalidating the Smith Act, the

Court made it much more difficult to bring charges under the act.

The Supreme Court slowly continued its move toward greater protection of First Amendment rights. In *Brandenburg v. Ohio* (1969) the Supreme Court established a new standard to apply when dealing with First Amendment issues. In a per curiam opinion, the Court noted that "later decisions have fashioned the principle that the constitutional guarantees of free speech and free press do not permit a State to forbid or proscribe advocacy of the use of force or of law violation except where such advocacy is directed to inciting or producing imminent lawless action and is likely to incite or produce such action." In *Brandenburg*, the Court had determined that just because ideas or speech were unpopular and even repugnant to reasonable persons, that in itself did not allow the government to prevent or punish those who espoused them. The government would now have to show that an action that it had a constitutional right to prevent was directly related to the idea or speech being advocated and that lawless action was imminent. The imminent lawless action test, also known as the *Brandenburg* test, is the standard applied today to First Amendment cases coming before the courts. The clear and probable danger standard had a short life, as the Supreme Court moved to restore and expand First Amendment rights, once again raising them to the level of preferred freedoms, as Justice Black had hoped in his *Dennis* dissent.

See also Black, Hugo L.; Clear and Present Danger Doctrine; Communist Party USA; Criminal Syndicalism; Douglas, William O.; Espionage Act of 1917; First Amendment, Approaches to; Frankfurter, Felix; Hand, Learned; Harlan, John Marshall, II; Holmes, Oliver Wendell, Jr.; Jackson, Robert H.; McCarthy, Joseph R.; Preferred Freedoms Doctrine; *Schenck v. United States;* Smith Act; Speech, Freedom of; Vinson, Fred M.

Bibliography

Antieau, Chester James. 1952. "*Dennis v. United States*: Precedent, Principle, or Perversion?" *Vanderbilt Law Review* 5:141.

Bollinger, Lee C., and Geoffrey R. Stone., eds. 2002. *Eternally Vigilant: Free Speech in the Modern Era.* Chicago: University of Chicago Press.

Gorfinkel, John A., and Julian W. Mack II. 1951. "*Dennis v. United States* and the Clear and Present Danger Rule." *California Law Review* 39:475.

Haiman, Franklyn S. 1977. *Speech and Law in a Free Society.* Chicago: University of Chicago Press.

Kersch, Ken I. 2003. *Freedom of Speech: Rights and Liberties under the Law.* Santa Barbara, CA: ABC-Clio.

Mendelson, Wallace. 1952. "Clear and Present Danger: From *Schenck* to *Dennis.*" *Columbia Law Review* 52:313–33.

Michael Haynes

CLEMENCY, EXECUTIVE

The United States Supreme Court enjoyed its first opportunity to comment on the definition of executive clemency in *United States v. Wilson* (1833). The case involved an act by President Andrew Jackson to pardon George Wilson after Wilson pleaded guilty to charges of "robbing the mail of the United States, and putting the driver in jeopardy." Invoking his executive prerogative, Jackson granted the pardon, and controversy ensued. A district attorney for the United States, frustrated by the president's intervention in the case, sought relief in the form of an additional punishment by the United States Supreme Court. The Supreme Court refused to comply. Claiming that executive clemency is "an act of grace, proceeding from the power entrusted with the execution of the laws, which exempts the individual, on whom it is bestowed, from the punishment the law inflicts for a crime he has committed," the justices noted that the judiciary is powerless to interfere with an executive's decision to grant clemency. According to the Court, "It is a constituent part of the judicial system, that the judge sees only with judicial eyes, and knows nothing respecting any particular case of which he is not informed judicially. A private deed, not communicated to him, whatever may be its character, whether a pardon or release, is totally unknown, and cannot be acted upon."

Broadly defined, executive clemency refers to the power of chief executives—governors and presidents—to change the specifics of a legal punishment, "to alter the outcome of a judicial decision by diminishing the impact of a defendant's punishment" (Breslin and Howley 2002, 235). Because clemency is always used to lessen the severity of a punishment, it is often synonymous with such terms as "mercy," "leniency," and "forgiveness." Throughout American history, clemency has been used in two ways: (1) as a grant of mercy and (2) as a political maneuver intended to appease particular individuals or groups. On the latter point, Alexander Hamilton wrote in *Federalist* no. 74 that the power of the executive to extend clemency provides a "golden opportunity" for rival political factions to win favors from opposition groups.

Typically, executives have three choices when exercising their clemency power: they can choose to grant pardons, which erase both the punishment and the guilt of the criminal; they can commute sentences, which reduces the length or severity of the punishment; or, in the case of capital sentences, they can grant reprieves, which act to temporarily postpone an execution. Indeed, the most visible use of executive clemency occurs in the arena of capital punishment.

Once a common practice in death penalty cases, the use of executive clemency has declined in recent years. Since the Supreme Court allowed the reinstatement of capital punishment in 1976 (see *Gregg v. Georgia*), less than 5 percent of death-row inmates have been granted clemency. Consequently, the steady decline in the number of clemency grants has caused abolitionists of capital punishment to seek reform of the entire clemency process. Yet some of the alarm emerging from abolitionist camps was muted in January 2003 when, in an unprecedented act of executive will, Governor George Ryan commuted the sentences of all 167 inmates on death row in Illinois. He cited concerns about his state's flawed criminal justice system as the primary reason for the blanket grant of clemency. He further insisted that until the criminal justice system could ensure that no

innocent person was being put to death, he would not tolerate any executions during his term in office. Over a firestorm of opposition from victims' families, religious leaders, public officials, and members of the legal community, Governor Ryan invoked his executive power and cleared Illinois of its death-row population.

See also Death Penalty and the Supreme Court; *Gregg v. Georgia*

Bibliography

Breslin, Beau, and John J. P. Howley. 2002. "Defending the Politics of Clemency." *Oregon Law Review* 81:231–54.

Beau Breslin

COHEN V. CALIFORNIA (1971)

At first glance, *Cohen v. California* (1971) seems too trivial to be considered by the United States Supreme Court. Yet it represents one of the greatest victories for freedom of speech in the history of American constitutional jurisprudence.

Paul Robert Cohen's jacket was emblazoned with the words "Fuck the Draft" to demonstrate his opposition to American involvement in Vietnam. When he wore his jacket to the Los Angeles County Courthouse, Cohen was arrested. He was convicted for violating a California law that prohibited the willful and malicious disturbing of the peace by offensive conduct, and he was sentenced to 30 days in jail. At the time, this was hardly a surprising result. In the 1960s, those with the temerity to violate the standards of polite society were condemned by an intolerant majority and frequently incarcerated for their rebelliousness. Cohen challenged the constitutionality of the California law, arguing that governmental efforts to ban offensive conduct violated the First Amendment. In an extraordinary decision, the Supreme Court agreed. The Court ruled that the First Amendment extends protection to a vast array of speech, from the sublime to the profane. When people choose to enter the public marketplace of ideas they expose themselves to some ideas that delight, others that challenge, and still others that infuriate. The precedent established by *Cohen v. California* is that it is a matter for the individual, not the government, to determine the value of speech.

Justice Harlan's majority opinion is an acknowledgment of the power of language. The Court recognized that words are frequently chosen for their emotional impact and that the First Amendment demands that speakers be allowed to express their positions in the most compelling manner possible. At the time, such a view was revolutionary. *Cohen v. California* stands for the proposition that if there are two ways to express a position, one genteel and the other noxious, a speaker should be free to choose the more controversial route. The adage of "go for the gut" became constitutional doctrine.

The Court indicated that words are not only powerful, but they are also intensely personal. They defy both easy classification as well as uniform characterization. Language that some may condemn as blasphemous and dangerous is embraced by others as wondrous and ingenious. As Justice Harlan wrote, "one man's vulgarity is another's lyric." Rather than allowing the government to take sides in this conflict over taste and propriety, the Court indicated that individuals should be able to decide for themselves which words to endorse and appreciate. If government is given the power to forbid the use of certain words as offensive, inevitably government would also be able to ban the ideas it finds unacceptable. Such a result would constitute a patent violation of the First Amendment.

Justice Harlan anticipated the outcry from this decision, writing, "To many, the immediate consequence of this freedom may often appear to be only verbal tumult, discord, and even offensive utterance." He offered an alternative interpretation. The Court's decision was a testament to our nation's commitment to freedom of expression and an acknowledgement of the people's ability to make decisions for themselves, free from government censorship.

There are two vastly contrasting views of *Cohen v. California*. One theory is that this case provided constitutional protection for offensive dissent that would have been otherwise crushed. Without *Cohen*, there would have been no *Texas v. Johnson* (1989), *RAV v. St. Paul* (1992), or *Reno v. ACLU* (1997). A second theory contends that *Cohen* created an "anything goes" mentality in America that has coarsened debate on issues of public import to the extent that profane howling has become an accepted, even routine, form of expressing ideas. It is beyond dispute that *Cohen v. California* changed the landscape of free speech in the United States.

See also Fighting Words Doctrine; First Amendment; Harlan, John Marshall, II; Profanity; *Reno v. American Civil Liberties Union;* Speech, Freedom of; Speech/Conduct Distinction; Symbolic Speech

Anthony Simones

COLLATERAL ATTACK. *See* Habeas Corpus; Postconviction Relief

COMMERCE CLAUSE. *See* Civil Rights Act of 1964; *Gonzales v. Raich; Heart of Atlanta Motel v. United States; Katzenbach v. McClung; United States v. Lopez;* RICO and Racketeering; Violence Against Women Act

COMMERCIAL SPEECH

Constitutional protections for commercial advertising have evolved consistently with the development of more general justifications of constitutional protection for free speech. During the mid-twentieth century, when expression rights were generally understood as a crucial element of the democratic process, courts tended to sustain legislation limiting business solicitations. Advertising enjoyed more protection beginning in the 1970s, as the First Amendment was understood as protecting a more general marketplace of ideas. Presently, truthful advertising enjoys almost as much judicial protection as political dissent.

Commercial advertising was heavily regulated throughout much of American history. State and local laws restricted what businesses could advertise, where they could advertise, and whether they could advertise. Many professionals, doctors and lawyers in particular, violated professional norms and were professionally sanctioned for soliciting business.

While some state courts struck down particular restrictions on advertising, others were sustained. Most were not even challenged in court.

Advertising did not immediately benefit when, during the 1930s and 1940s, federal courts began providing more protection for political dissent. That protection, Justice Harlan F. Stone's famous footnote 4 in *United States v. Carolene Products* (1938) declared, was aimed at "legislation which restricts those political processes that can ordinarily be expected to bring about repeal of undesirable legislation." Legislative bans on commercial solicitation were aimed at businesses, which every good New Dealer knew did not merit judicial protection.

Two judicial decisions during the 1940s reflected the nonconstitutional status of advertising. The first, *Valentine v. Chrestensen* (1942), bluntly declared that the Constitution placed no "restraint on government as respects purely commercial advertising." Government could regulate persons handing out handbills soliciting business, Justice Owen Roberts declared in a unanimous opinion, because "[w]hether, and to what extent, one may promote or pursue a gainful occupation in the streets ... are matters for legislative judgment." Seven years later, in *Railway Express Agency v. New York* (1949), the justices sustained a sharp limit on placing advertisements on commercial vehicles without discussing free speech issues at all. At late as 1973, the judicial majority in *Pittsburgh Press v. Pittsburgh Human Relations Commission* still opined that a publication that "did no more than propose a commercial transaction" was not constitutionally protected speech.

Commercial advertising evolved into "commercial speech" during the mid-1970s. The crucial decision was *Virginia Pharmacy Board v. Virginia Citizens Consumer Council* (1976). At issue was whether pharmacists had a constitutional right to advertise the prices of prescription drugs. Justice Harry Blackmun's majority opinion insisted that persons were not "disqualifie[d] ... for protection under the First Amendment" merely because their interest in speaking "is a purely economic one." "Society," he declared, "may have a strong interest

in the free flow of commercial information." For Blackmun and the *Virginia Pharmacy Board* majority, the First Amendment prohibited States from "suppress[ing] the dissemination of concededly truthful information about entirely lawful activity." Their concern was with paternalism, rather than the integrity of the political process. Blackmun observed that for most people, "the interest in the free flow of commercial information ... may be as keen, if not keener, by far, than ... interest[s] in the day's most urgent political debate." Justice William H. Rehnquist's dissent took the more traditional view, limiting the First Amendment to speech integral to the democratic process. The Constitution, in his view, protected "public decisionmaking as to political, social, and other public issues, rather than the decision of a particular individual as to whether to purchase one or another kind of shampoo."

The Supreme Court soon developed a four-part test for determining whether state regulations on advertising passed constitutional muster. Justice Lewis Powell in *Central Hudson Gas v. Public Service Commission* (1980) declared that the crucial First Amendment issues were (1) whether the advertisement "concern[ed] lawful activity" and was "not ... misleading," (2) "whether the asserted governmental interest is substantial," (3) "whether the regulation directly advances the governmental interest asserted," and (4) whether the regulation "is not more extensive than is necessary to serve that interest." Two differences exist between this test and the constitutional standard for regulating political speech. States may ban misleading advertising but prohibit only reckless or intentionally false political commentary. A substantial interest may justify prohibiting commercial speech, but a compelling interest is necessary to prohibit political dissent. Several justices, most notably Justice Clarence Thomas, would alter the *Central Hudson* test, permitting government to regulate truthful advertising only when a compelling interest is present.

Whether any alternation is actually necessary to protect business solicitors is doubtful. Most restrictions on commercial advertising fail the *Central Hudson* test. Supreme Court majorities almost always find that the advertisement before the court concerns lawful speech and that the state interest in regulating is substantial. The judicial majority also almost always concludes that the regulation either does not directly advance the asserted government interest or that the regulation is more extensive than necessary. *44 Liquormart v. Rhode Island* (1996) provides a good example of common judicial practice when businesses challenge bans on advertisements. The justices in that case agreed that promoting temperance was a substantial state interest. Nevertheless, a unanimous tribunal agreed that states could not constitutionally prevent liquor stores from widely publicizing their prices. Justices John Paul Stevens, Anthony Kennedy, David Souter, and Ruth Bader Ginsburg questioned whether the statutory ban was likely to be effective. In their view, there was "no evidence to suggest that [the] speech prohibition [would] significantly reduce market-wide consumption." Justices Sandra Day O'Connor, David Souter, and Stephen Breyer, along with Chief Justice Rehnquist, added that the ban was not necessary to serve the state interest. A sales tax, they pointed out, "would more directly accomplish" the state's goal of promoting temperance "without intruding on sellers' ability to provide truthful, nonmisleading information to customers." Given that sales taxes are always means for reducing consumption, this analysis suggests that justices applying the *Central Hudson* test will almost always strike down laws restricting truthful advertising. This has been the case for the past decade. The Supreme Court has declared unconstitutional bans on broadcasting advertisements for casinos (*Greater New Orleans Broadcasting Association v. United States,* 1999), bans on tobacco advertising (*Lorillard Tobacco v. Reilly,* 2001), and bans on advertising certain prescription drugs (*Thompson v. Western States Medical Center,* 2002).

The constitutional status of commercial advertising highlights several aspects of judicial policy making at the turn of the twenty-first century. Chief Justice Rehnquist aside, the other members of the Supreme Court have insisted that state and federal officials may rarely, if ever, prohibit businesses from truthfully advertising their wares. The more conservative justices are particularly prone to judicial activism when businesses attack bans on advertising. Justices Clarence Thomas and Antonin Scalia have consistently voted to strike down prohibitions enacted by elected officials. These votes are rarely justified by reference to the original meaning of constitutional provisions or legal practice at the time constitutional provisions were framed. Justice Thomas in *Lorillard* insisted that "all attempts to dissuade legal choices by citizens by keeping them ignorant are impermissible." This anti-paternal principle may have strong philosophical foundations, but no member of the Supreme Court has explained whether this value, as opposed to the values underlying democratic governance, is rooted in the First or Fourteenth amendments.

See also Blackmun, Harry A.; Breyer, Stephen G.; First Amendment; Fourteenth Amendment; Ginsburg, Ruth Bader; Judicial Activism; Kennedy, Anthony; New Deal; O'Connor, Sandra Day; Powell, Lewis F., Jr.; Rehnquist, William H.; Scalia, Antonin; Souter, David H.; Speech, Freedom of; Stevens, John Paul; Stone, Harlan Fiske; Thomas, Clarence; *United States v. Carolene Products*

Bibliography

Baker, C. Edwin. 1989. *Human Liberty and Freedom of Speech.* New York: Oxford University Press.

Collins, Ronald K. L., and David M. Skover. 1993. "Commerce and Communication." *Texas Law Review* 71 (4): 697–742.

Kozinski, Alex, and Stuart Banner. 1990. "Who's Afraid of Commercial Speech?" *Virginia Law Review* 76:627–53.

Mark A. Graber

COMMON-LAW BACKGROUND OF AMERICAN CIVIL RIGHTS AND LIBERTIES

The United States Constitution, as interpreted by the judicial branch, constitutes the primary source of civil rights and liberties in this country. This understanding of civil rights and liberties that underlies the Constitution derives from two principal sources: the English common law and the liberal tradition of political thought developed by John Locke and philosophers of the Enlightenment. From this the latter influence comes the concept of inalienable natural rights, which was incorporated into the Declaration of Independence in 1776 and later formed the basis for the adoption of the Bill of Rights. However, the concept of natural rights and their relation to the individual was not entirely new. This concept, along with ideas on the role and functions of the judiciary, was also a part of the common-law tradition.

In his *Commentaries on the Laws of England,* Sir William Blackstone defined the common law as "a positive law, fixed and established by custom, which custom is evidenced by judicial decisions." Based on the doctrine of stare decisis (following precedent), the common law developed over a long period of time and was continually evolving. In the thirteenth century, Henry de Bracton compiled early common-law decisions, thus providing the first attempt to state the common law in written form. In 1628, Sir Edward Coke's *Institutes* provided another important statement on key areas of common law. But Blackstone's *Commentaries* represented the first true codification of the English common law.

Beginning in the twelfth century, when Henry II unified the local systems of law by raising local customs to the national level, certain rights and liberties began to be protected as national customs. An initial statement referring to the fundamental rights and liberties protected in English common law is found in the Petition of Right of 1628, which was presented to King Charles I. This document described those rights that had been granted to all Englishmen but were being breached by the Crown. These rights included freedom from forced loans, arbitrary arrest, unlawful imprisonment as described in the Magna Carta, interference with property rights, protection of the right of habeas corpus, and the enforcement of due process of law for all citizens.

Following the Glorious Revolution, the most authoritative expression of the rights and liberties afforded to Englishmen is found in the English Bill of Rights of 1689. The basic tenets of the Bill of Rights relating to Parliament (representing the people) include freedom from royal interference with the law; freedom from arbitrary royal taxation; freedom to petition the king; freedom from a peacetime standing army, without agreement by Parliament; certain freedoms to bear arms for self-defense; freedom to elect members of Parliament without interference from the sovereign; freedom of speech in Parliament; freedom from cruel and unusual punishments, and excessive bail; and freedom from fines and forfeitures without trial.

It is from this background that the English colonists settling in America drew their sense of the law. Englishmen living in the American colonies believed themselves citizens of the English Crown and, as such, entitled to the rights granted to all Englishmen under the common law. The breach from this understanding of rights and liberties formed the basis of the Revolutionary War between the American colonies and England. The Declaration of Independence listed "certain unalienable rights; that among these are life, liberty and the pursuit of happiness," that had been abused, "evinc[ing] a design to reduce [the colonies] under absolute Despotism."

Following independence, numerous state constitutions referred to rights stemming from the English common law as characterized by its adherence to tradition, custom, and precedent. In *Federalist* no. 78, Alexander Hamilton acknowledged the influence of the common law on the judiciary and accepted the common-law understanding of the nature of law. In adopting the English common law, the United States "replaced the sway of the king with the sway of the people."

Adherence to the common-law protection of civil rights and liberty is expressed in the United States Constitution in the formation of the judiciary, the supremacy of the law and its interpretation by judicial holdings, adherence to *stare decisis,* the prohibition of the suspension of the writ of habeas corpus, the prohibition against ex post facto laws, the protection of property rights and the use of trial by jury. The United States Constitution and the subsequent adoption of the Bill of Rights codified English common law but limited the powers of the federal government and extended rights to freedom of speech and religion.

While the codification of common-law rights and liberties is found in the Constitution, there has been a continued evolution in the meaning and extent of these rights and liberties. This has been accomplished using the common-law vehicle of judicial review, which was expressly adopted by the United States Supreme Court in Chief Justice John Marshall's majority opinion in *Marbury v. Madison*. The common-law influence on American constitutional law is a process that is seen in the continuously evolving process of defining civil rights and liberties by the modern Court.

See also Accused, Rights of the; Arms, Right to Keep and Bear; Bill of Rights; Blackstone, William; Cruel and Unusual Punishments Clause; Declaration of Independence; Due Process, Procedural; Due Process Clauses; Bill of Rights (English); Excessive Bail, Prohibition of; Excessive Fines, Prohibition of; Ex Post Facto Laws; Habeas Corpus; Jury, Trial by; Liberalism; Locke, John; Magna Carta; Marshall, John; Natural Law and Natural Rights; Petition, Right of; Property Rights; U.S. Constitution

Bibliography

Blackstone, William. 1765–1769. *Commentaries on the Laws of England*. Oxford: Clarendon Press.

Hale, Matthew. 1971. *The History of the Common Law of England*. Chicago: University of Chicago Press.

Milsom, S.F.C. 2003. *A Natural History of the Common Law*. New York: Columbia University Press.

Stefanie A. Johnson

COMMUNIST PARTY USA

The Communist Party USA originated from a split in the Socialist Party of America (SPA) in 1919. Following the Russian Revolution, the Left Wing Section of the SPA sought to bring the party into the newly established Comintern (the Communist International). The moderate leadership of the SP resisted the move, expelling an array of state organizations and local and affiliated groups representing some two thirds of party members. In response, the left wing of the party split into two groups, those advocating a communist party separate from the SPA and those in favor of bringing the SPA into the Comintern. The former group founded the Communist Party of America in July 1919. The latter group, led by John Reed and Benjamin Gitlow, attempted to take their seats at the SPA convention on August 30, only to be expelled by the police at the request of the party leadership. The expelled delegates and the remaining leftists formed the Communist Labor Party on September 2, 1919. Under pressure from the Comintern, the two parties merged in 1920 to form a single U.S. Communist Party. The Socialist Party, which had had more than 108,000 members in 1918–1919, was left with just under 27,000 by 1920.

Until 1923 the party remained underground, having come under attack from state and federal governments. Under the Espionage Act of 1917 and Sedition Act of 1918, thousands of party members were arrested, and the foreign born deported. When the party finally resurfaced it did so as the Workers Party of America, only later adopting the name Communist Party USA (CPUSA). Through the 1920s the factional struggles in the Soviet Communist Party drove parallel factional conflicts in the CPUSA. Supporters of Trotsky, led by James P. Cannon, were expelled in 1928 and formed the Communist League of America, which in 1938 became the Socialist Workers Party. The following year, Stalin purged Nikolai Bukharin, until then head of the Comintern, leading Jay Lovestone and Benjamin Gitlow to break with the CPUSA and form the Communist Party (Opposition).

From the 1920s onward the party was active in campaigning for women's rights and on behalf of black workers and, during the Great Depression, organized the unemployed and the working poor and assisted farmers facing eviction. Initially the party worked within the American Federation of Labor (AFL), but with the onset of the Depression, party activists were instrumental in founding new "red" unions. These unions were, however, wound up in the wake of Roosevelt's election and the Comintern's development of the Popular Front strategy to combat Fascism. Party members also helped organize the Congress of Industrial Organizations (CIO), founded in 1935. Since that time the party has continued to work within the AFL-CIO.

During the war, as a result of the coalition with the Soviet Union, the party took a patriotic stance, supporting the war effort and opposing strike action. Indeed, in 1944 the party even ceased to exist and was replaced by a Communist Political Association in anticipation of a period of relatively good relations with the Soviet Union. The onset of the cold war and the renewal of state persecution shattered those hopes. Truman's loyalty oath of 1947, similar oaths developed by local governments, and the work of the House Un-American Activities Committee marked a period of intense government persecution of party members. Under the Alien Registration Act (1940, also called the Smith Act), which made it illegal to advocate or teach the desirability of overthrowing federal or state governments, party leaders were imprisoned, and thousands of ordinary members and sympathizers were blacklisted from public and private employment and expelled from the unions. Joseph McCarthy, Richard Nixon, and a number of other politicians achieved prominence by exposing or threatening to expose communists working in federal agencies. While the Supreme Court upheld the 1949 convictions of William Z. Foster and 11 other party leaders under the Smith Act (see *Dennis v. United States*, 1951) it eventually brought about an end to such convictions by requiring evidence of an actual conspiracy to overthrow the government, not the mere advocacy of such an idea (see *Yates v. United States*, 1957).

The persecution of communists substantially weakened the party's connection with wider society, membership plummeted, and front organizations were wound up. Khruschev's criticism of Stalin in a secret February 1956 speech and the Soviet invasion of Hungary later that year worsened the party's position yet further. Supporters of democratizing the party were expelled or forced out, a fate that was also to befall unreconstructed Stalinists in the early 1960s. Many former party members were instrumental in the development of the New Left and were active in the civil rights and peace movements of the 1960s. The Civil Rights Movement, however, shunned the party itself for fear of being labeled communist. Party membership grew in the 1970s, reaching 25,000, but the resumption of cold war hostilities under President Ronald Reagan in the 1980s presaged a further period of decline. The party had resumed running presidential candidates in 1968, after a lapse of some 28 years, but ceased to do so after 1984.

After rejecting Gorbachev's calls for reform of the Communist movement, the party's financial support from the Soviet Union was cut in 1989. The following year the party's newspaper, the *People's Daily World,* was forced to cut back to weekly publication as the *People's Weekly World.* The collapse of the Soviet Union two year later brought a further significant split in the party with a minority of reformers leaving in 1992 to form the Committees of Correspondence for Democracy and Socialism. Current membership is estimated at 2,500.

See also Civil Rights Movement; Criminal Syndicalism; Espionage Act of 1917; House Un-American Activities Committee; Legislative Investigations; McCarthy, Joseph R.; Smith Act

Bibliography

Buhle, Paul, and Dan Georgakas. 1992. *Encyclopedia of the American Left.* Urbana: University of Illinois Press.

Guenter, Lewy. 1997. *The Cause That Failed: Communism in American Political Life.* New York: Oxford University Press.

Klehr, Harvey, and John Earl Haynes. 1992. *The American Communist Movement: Storming Heaven Itself.* New York: Twayne.

Ian Down

COMMUNITY CONTROL

Within the field of criminal law, community control refers to a broad range of alternative sanctions to imprisonment or probation. Community control options are intermediate sanctions on a continuum between incarceration and probation and are also known as community corrections programs. Offenders typically participate in community control programs outside a prison or jail setting. A prison sentence may be shortened when some jail time is replaced with a community control component. Corrections statutes in a majority of states have been modified to include provisions for community control programs.

These programs are operated at the discretion of local courts and units of local government, such as cities and counties. Programs vary widely across jurisdictions and include combinations of penalties and services for offenders. Program content is determined by local needs, and preferences and programs vary from community to community. Common program concepts include intensive supervised probation, day reporting, work release, house arrest, and electronic monitoring.

In an intensive supervised probation program, offenders live at home and participate in work or school, mental health treatment, and/or drug treatment and perform community service. Program participants meet regularly with probation officers, sometimes as often as daily. In day reporting programs, offenders report daily to a central location and file a daily activity plan with supervising staff. Work release programs release offenders from a community residential setting such as a halfway house in order to work. House arrest confines an offender to home for all or most of every day. Offenders on house arrest are typically monitored through an electronic transmitter worn on the wrist or ankle. Electronic monitoring has become more sophisticated with the introduction of global positioning technology in combination with mapping systems.

The overarching goal of community control programs is rehabilitation. That goal is achieved by controlling behavior within the community in which the offender resides. To that end, employment checks, curfews, and drug and alcohol testing are commonly required across all types of community control programs. Offenders perform community service activities, pay fines, and provide restitution to compensate their victims. Drug treatment and mental health services are also commonly incorporated. Increasingly, employment and education, including basic literacy needs, are recognized as critical elements for long-term behavioral change.

Community control programs are operated by government agencies such as probation departments. In addition to operating entire community control programs, private service providers also furnish specific services to public agencies.

Principles of community control have been articulated in many states in conjunction with community corrections statutes. As an example, the Wisconsin Department of Corrections has replaced felony probation with a program called Community Confinement and Control. The Wisconsin community control program incorporates structured, rigorous supervision and surveillance to establish a community-intensive probation system. Mandatory program components include frequent contact with a probation officer, drug testing, electronic monitoring, and either work or community service. Similar principles have been articulated at the federal level with respect to the juvenile justice system.

Public sentiment appears to support community control programs rather than prison or jail for nonviolent offenders. This public support includes an increasing preference for drug treatment in lieu of incarceration for nonviolent drug offenders.

Community control programs have been adopted in many locations as a policy response to overcrowded prisons and jails. In recent decades, state departments of corrections and local communities have experienced increased pressure on prisons and jails as a result of three strikes laws for habitual offenders, mandatory sentencing practices, and severe increases in the penalties for drug offenses. Supporters argue that community control programs represent a wise use of public funds because they promote the rehabilitation of offenders within their home communities.

The federal government has also determined that there are benefits to community control options. The Federal Bureau of Prisons undertakes community corrections programs for federal prisoners through contracts with state and local governments and private service providers. The federal sentencing guidelines and similar state schemes recognize community confinement, home detention, and intermittent confinement as formal sentencing options.

The halfway house nature of many community control programs has given rise to challenges by offenders that the programs do not sufficiently restrict personal liberty. Time spent in a federal halfway house under sentence has long been considered to constitute incarceration, despite the nonsecure aspects of some types of programs. Time spent in community-based programs, however, while one is on bail or bond is not creditable against the length of an individual's sentence (see *Moreland v. United States,* 1992; *Reno v. Koray,* 1995).

See also Bail, Right to; Eighth Amendment; House Arrest; Prisoners' Rights; Probation and Parole; Sentencing, Eighth Amendment and; Sentencing Guidelines

Bibliography

Cullen, Francis T., Bonnie S. Fisher, and Brandon K. Applegate. 2000. "Public Opinion about Punishment and Corrections." In *Crime and Justice, A Review of Research,* ed. Michael Tonry. Chicago: University of Chicago Press.

Latessa, Edward J., and Harry E. Allen. 1999. *Corrections in the Community.* 2nd ed. Cincinnati, OH: Anderson Publishing.

Petersilia, Joan. 2002. "Community Corrections." In *Crime: Public Policies for Crime Control,* ed. James Q. Wilson and Joan Petersilia. Oakland, CA: ICS Press.
                                                          Kathleen Hale

COMPULSORY PROCESS

The term "compulsory process" refers to a legal mechanism called a subpoena by which courts, legislatures, and government agencies can compel witnesses to appear, give sworn testimony, and, in some instances, bring with them documents or other articles than can be entered into evidence. An interested party in a legal proceeding requests a subpoena from an administrative official, usually a court clerk, who issues a subpoena commanding a witness to appear at a specified time and place. When a witness is required to produce books, documents, or other articles, the subpoena is called a subpoena duces tecum. Court clerks generally issue subpoenas to a named person but often are allowed to issue a subpoena in blank, which the party requesting it is required to fill in before the subpoena is served. A subpoena is usually served by a sheriff or process server. Disobedience of a subpoena is punishable by contempt of court or other branch of government authorized to compel attendance of witnesses.

The Sixth Amendment to the United States Constitution guarantees a defendant in a criminal trial the right "to have compulsory process for obtaining witnesses in his favor." This right to subpoena witnesses extends to state prosecutions through the Due Process Clause of the Fourteenth Amendment; however, state constitutions contain similar provisions. The Compulsory Process Clause affords an accused the right to compel witnesses to appear in court. Courts hold the right does not apply to prison discipline hearings. Although courts are liberal in allowing defendants to subpoena witnesses, a defendant cannot subpoena numerous witnesses to offer cumulative testimony and can be required to show that a witness's testimony can be material to his or her defense. Statutes and court rules ordinarily require a defendant to advance witness fees when seeking a subpoena; however, Rule 17 of the Federal Rules of Criminal Procedure provides for issuance of a subpoena if the defendant does not have the ability to pay witness fees and expenses. A similar provision is common in the states. Statutes and court rules allow prosecutors to subpoena witnesses for investigations and trials.

By the late 1960s the U.S. Supreme Court began interpreting the language "to have compulsory process for obtaining witnesses in his favor" in a broader context than simply requiring witnesses to show up for trial. When the state of Texas charged Jackie Washington with a 1964 murder, he sought to present testimony by Charles Fuller, an accomplice who had already been convicted of the murder. The judge denied his request, citing a state law that prohibited principals, accomplices, or accessories in the same crime to testify as witnesses for each other. Washington was convicted, and the Texas Court of Criminal Appeals affirmed. In *Washington v. Texas* (1967), the U.S. Supreme Court reversed Washington's conviction, holding that the Texas law denied Washington's right to have compulsory process for obtaining witnesses in his favor. Chief Justice Earl Warren wrote,

[Washington] was denied his right to have compulsory process for obtaining witnesses in his favor because the State arbitrarily denied him the right to put on the stand a witness who was physically and mentally capable of testifying to events that he had personally observed, and whose testimony would have been relevant and material to the defense. The Framers of the Constitution did not intend to commit the futile act of giving to a defendant the right to secure the attendance of witnesses whose testimony he had no right to use.

Vickie Rock was charged with manslaughter for the 1983 shooting of her husband in Arkansas. After undergoing hypnosis to refresh her memory about the shooting, she remembered that her gun was defective and had misfired. Her recollection was corroborated by an expert. The trial court denied her request to offer her hypnotically refreshed testimony, and she was convicted. The Arkansas Supreme Court affirmed, noting, "The dangers of admitting this kind of testimony outweigh whatever probative value it may have." Writing for a five-to-four majority, the U.S. Supreme Court reversed her conviction in *Rock v. Arkansas* (1987). Justice Harry Blackmun explained that the Due Process Clause of the Fourteenth Amendment, the Compulsory Process Clause, and the Fifth Amendment right against compelled testimony afforded her the right to testify in her own defense.

In 1988, in *Taylor v. Illinois,* the Supreme Court rejected the state's contention that the Compulsory Process Clause merely enables an accused to compel attendance of witnesses in his or her favor. "The Compulsory Process Clause," the Court wrote, "is not merely a guarantee that the accused shall have the power to subpoena witnesses, but confers on the accused the fundamental right to present witnesses in his own defense." Nevertheless, the Court cautioned that a defendant does not have the absolute right to present witnesses; rather that right is governed by the legitimate demands of the adversarial system.

A person subpoenaed can challenge the issuance of the subpoena by filing a motion in court to quash or modify it on grounds that the evidence sought is otherwise available, the subpoena is for harassment, or the evidence sought is privileged. For example, a person subpoenaed might argue the evidence sought would violate spousal or clergy-penitent privilege or compel the witness to waive the Fifth Amendment privilege against self-incrimination. Neither a corporation nor the custodian of corporate records can resist a subpoena on the grounds of self-incrimination.

Subpoenas are commonly employed in civil and administrative proceedings as well as criminal cases. Federal and state statutes and court rules define the mechanics of subpoenaing witnesses and documents and make provision for payment of certain expenses witnesses incur.

See also Accused, Rights of the; Adversary System of Justice; Blackmun, Harry A.; Contempt, Power of; Due Process Clauses; Fifth Amendment; Fourteenth Amendment; Self-Incrimination Clause; Warren, Earl

Bibliography

Scheb, John M., and John M. Scheb II. 2006. *Criminal Procedure.* Belmont, CA: Thomson/Wadsworth.

Hon. John M. Scheb

COMPULSORY STERILIZATION

In the early twentieth century, states enacted laws allowing for the sterilization of persons suffering from mental retardation, mental illness, and other disabilities. These laws reflected the goal of the eugenics movement, namely, to improve society by manipulating the gene pool.

In *Buck v. Bell* (1927), the United States Supreme Court upheld a Virginia statute adopted to promote the "health of the patient and the welfare of society" through the sterilization of "mental defectives." Carrie Buck, an 18-year-old woman, was committed to the Virginia State Colony for Epileptics and Feeble Minded, where her mother was also confined. Before being committed, Carrie had been raped by a guest at the home where she had been in foster care. Officials at the Virginia institution concluded that Carrie and her mother shared hereditary traits of "feeble-mindedness and sexual promiscuity" and sought to have Carrie sterilized. After conducting an evidentiary hearing required by the statute, the Circuit Court of Amherst County ordered the director to proceed with the sterilization. The Virginia Supreme Court affirmed, as did the United States Supreme Court, dividing eight-to-one.

Writing for the U.S. Supreme Court, Justice Oliver Wendell Holmes, Jr., concluded that the principle that allows states to compel vaccinations to stave off epidemics (see *Jacobson v. Massachusetts,* 1905) is "broad enough to cover cutting the Fallopian tubes." Expressing support for the eugenics movement, Holmes wrote, "It is better for all the world, if instead of waiting to execute degenerate offspring for crime, or to let them starve for their imbecility, society can prevent those who are manifestly unfit from continuing their kind." Somewhat gratuitously, Holmes added, "Three generations of imbeciles are enough." Justice Pierce Butler was the sole dissenter in *Buck v. Bell,* but he did not produce an opinion to explain his dissenting vote.

After the Supreme Court's decision, Carrie Buck was sterilized by tubal ligation. She was eventually released from the institution and went to work as a housekeeper. Carrie Buck died in 1983 at the age of 77. Her daughter, who was also sterilized even though she was performing well in elementary school, died at age eight.

The Supreme Court's decision in *Buck v. Bell* prompted other states to enact laws modeled after the Virginia statute and during the next 15 years thousands of mentally retarded men and women across the United States were sterilized pursuant to these laws. However, the Court's decision in *Skinner v. Oklahoma* (1942) reversed this trend. In *Skinner,* the Court struck down a state law allowing for the sterilization of habitual criminals. Although the decision was based on the Equal Protection Clause of the Fourteenth Amendment, *Skinner* in effect recognized a constitutional right of procreation. Speaking for the Court, Justice William O. Douglas characterized the right to procreate as "one of the basic civil rights of man." He also stressed the need for strict judicial scrutiny of all sterilization laws:

The power to sterilize, if exercised, may have subtle, far-reaching and devastating effects. In evil or reckless hands it can cause races or types which are inimical to the dominant group to wither and disappear. There is no redemption for the individual whom the law touches. Any experiment which the State conducts is to his irreparable injury. He is forever deprived of a basic liberty. We mention these matters not to reexamine the scope of the police power of the States. We advert to them merely in emphasis of our view that strict scrutiny of the classification which a State makes in a sterilization law is essential, lest unwittingly, or otherwise, invidious discriminations are made against groups or types of individuals in violation of the constitutional guaranty of just and equal laws.

The *Skinner* decision effectively ended the practice of sterilizing prison inmates. Sterilization of the mentally retarded continued, though at a greatly reduced pace, until well into the 1960s. By then the eugenics movement had fallen into disrepute, in large part due to its association with racism and, in particular, to the atrocities perpetrated by the Nazis in the name of improving society. In recent years, a number of state governors have issued apologies for their state's actions in furtherance of this discredited movement.

See also Douglas, William O.; Due Process, Substantive; Equal Protection Clause; Fourteenth Amendment; Fundamental Rights; Holmes, Oliver Wendell, Jr.; Liberty; Privacy, Constitutional Right of; Reproductive Freedom; Strict Scrutiny

Bibliography

Lombardo, Paul A. 2003. "Taking Eugenics Seriously: Three Generations of ??? Are Enough." *Florida State University Law Review* 30:191–218.

Selden, Steven. 1999. *Inheriting Shame: The Story of Eugenics and Racism in America.* New York: Teachers College Press.

John M. Scheb II and Otis H. Stephens, Jr.

CONCERNED WOMEN FOR AMERICA (CWA)

Concerned Women for America (CWA) was founded in 1979 by Beverly LaHaye. LaHaye is the wife of Tim LaHaye, coauthor of the bestselling *Left Behind* book series and a founding member of Jerry Falwell's now defunct Moral Majority. Beverly La Haye founded the group because she was disturbed by increasing attention to what she viewed as the "anti-God, anti-family" feminist "agenda." CWA now has chapters in most states and national headquarters in Washington, D.C. Over the years it has formed affiliated entities, including the Culture and Family Institute, which works on a variety of issues including opposition to legal rights for homosexuals; the Concerned Women for America Legal Defense Foundation; and the Beverly LaHaye Institute, a think tank. CWA claimed 500,000 members in 2004. The organization is involved in everything from the grassroots organization of letter-writing campaign to providing legal representation.

Concerned Women for America has a six-part mission. First, the organization supports a traditional definition of family, which manifests itself in opposition to homosexuality and gay rights (including gay marriage). CWA has also consistently opposed the equal rights amendment. Second, CWA believes in the sanctity of human life and thus opposes abortion and cloning. Third, the organization has been involved in various aspects of education, supporting abstinence-only sex education and Christian-based education. For example, CWA attorneys represented a group of Tennessee families who sued to protect their children, who were enrolled in public schools, from textbook material they found objectionable (*Mozert v. Hawkins County Public Schools,* 1987). Fourth, CWA is opposed to obscenity and has supported legislation known as cable choice, which would allow cable subscribers to opt out of receiving channels to which they object. The group has also been outspoken about the dangers of child pornography. Fifth, CWA has supported greater freedom of religious expression. In *Witters v. Washington Department of Services for the Blind* (1986), CWA successfully sued on behalf of a blind student who had been denied education benefits based on the fact that he was a ministerial student. Sixth, CWA is opposed to the United States' involvement in the United Nations due to their objection to UN policies concerning gender equity and population control.

In addition to these six categories of action, the CWA has also at various times been involved in opposition to hate crimes legislation, support of right-to-work legislation, opposition to women in combat, and support for the impeachment of President Clinton. The CWA and its highly visible founder have supported a number of controversial presidential appointments, including the Supreme Court nominations of Robert Bork, Antonin Scalia (in which case LaHaye testified before the Senate Judiciary Committee), Anthony Kennedy (in which LaHaye also testified), David Souter, and Clarence Thomas, and the appointment of John Ashcroft to the position of attorney general.

See also Abortion, Right to; Ashcroft, John; Bork, Robert H.; Equal Rights Amendment; Freedom of Access to Clinic Entrances Act; Hate Crimes; Kennedy, Anthony; Obscenity and Pornography; Pro-life Movement; Religious Right; Same-Sex Marriage and Civil Unions; Scalia, Antonin; Souter, David H.; Thomas, Clarence

Bibliography

Beverly LaHaye Institute. www.beverlylahayeinstitute.org (accessed 10 May 2004).

Concerned Women for America. www.cwfa.org (accessed 10 May 2004).

Culture and Family Institute. www.cultureandfamily.org (accessed 10 May 2004).

Kara E. Stooksbury

CONFESSIONS. *See* Interrogation and Confessions Confrontation Clause; Confrontation, Right of

CONFRONTATION, RIGHT OF

The Sixth Amendment to the United States Constitution gives the accused in all criminal prosecutions "the right ... to be confronted with the witnesses against him." Despite the brevity of the Confrontation Clause, as this part of the Sixth Amendment is called, and notwithstanding the simplicity of its eight words, the Confrontation Clause has been interpreted in varied and inconsistent ways.

There is little controversy that the Confrontation Clause provides a trial right for the criminally accused. By its very terms, it has no application except in criminal prosecutions. It is uniformly regarded as inapplicable to any proceeding except a criminal trial. Equally well established is that the only beneficiary of the right to confrontation is the accused, not the prosecution.

That the right of confrontation is a rule that enhances reliability is also reasonably well accepted. It is premised on the belief that evidence is more reliable if it is offered by a witness who testifies under oath, in the presence of the fact finder, and who is subject to confrontation, consisting of leading questions posed by the lawyer for the accused, referred to as cross-examination. Under such circumstances, the solemnity of the proceeding and the administration of the oath impresses upon the witness the significance of the occasion. The fact finder not only hears the witness's testimony but observes the witness's demeanor during the testimony and during the cross-examination by the lawyer for the accused. In *Mattox v. United States* (1895), the Supreme Court described the Confrontation Clause as providing the accused "an opportunity, not only of testing the recollection and sifting the conscience of the witness, but of compelling him to stand face to face with the jury in order that they may look at him, and judge by his demeanor upon the stand and the manner in which he gives his testimony whether he is worthy of belief."

While there is some dispute as to the origins of the right of confrontation, it is not disputed that its roots predate the American Constitution. Many scholars, and ultimately the United States Supreme Court, have traced the right to early Roman times. Notwithstanding its ancient beginnings, the Supreme Court has held that the "founding generation's immediate source of the concept [of confrontation]" was the English common law. The common-law tradition required witnesses in criminal trials to give "live testimony in court subject to adversarial testing." Underlying the tradition was the belief that reliability would be enhanced by in-court testimony, subject to cross-examination.

While the right of confrontation is a rule of constitutional proportion, the hearsay rule is an evidence rule with similar purposes. The hearsay rule prohibits the introduction of certain out-of-court statements that are not offered under oath in the presence of the fact finder by a witness subject to cross-examination. The exclusion of hearsay is based upon the belief that such evidence is not reliable, or at least not as reliable as it would be if offered by a live witness under oath. Because the two rules serve similar purposes, they became linked, and by the early 1980s, the United States Supreme Court had virtually equated the two, admitting out-of-court statements in criminal trials despite confrontation objections if the statements satisfied a "firmly rooted" hearsay exception. If the out-of-court statement did not satisfy a firmly rooted hearsay exception, it could still be admitted if the statement itself contained sufficient "particularized guarantees of trustworthiness" (*Ohio v. Roberts,* 1980). In these situations, a judge would have to determine, based on countless factors, whether the statement was sufficiently reliable to be admitted.

In 2004, the Supreme Court acknowledged that the test it had established in *Ohio v. Roberts* had not only proved unpredictable and subjective but was also inconsistent with the original intent behind the Confrontation Clause. Roberts was an "open-ended balancing test," which replaced a "categorical constitutional guarantee" and thereby "did violence to [the framers'] constitutional design." In a now landmark decision, *Crawford v. Washington* (2004), a divided Supreme Court overruled the *Roberts* test and established a new test for determining whether the Confrontation Clause was violated. In *Crawford*, the court held that the Confrontation Clause prohibits the introduction of "testimonial statements" made by one not testifying at trial unless that person, referred to as a declarant, is unavailable and the accused had a prior opportunity to cross-examine the declarant.

This test derived from two conclusions reached by the Court. First, the Court found that the "primary evil at which the [Confrontation Clause] was directed was ... particularly [the] use of *ex parte* examinations as evidence against the accused." The Court focused on the amendment's use of the phrase "witnesses against the accused" to conclude that only certain kinds of statements were implicated by the Confrontation Clause. Because a witness is one who "bears testimony," and testimony is "a solemn declaration or affirmation made for the purpose of establishing or proving some fact," the Confrontation Clause applies only to "testimonial statements." While the Court declined to fully define the phrase "testimonial statements," it suggested that included within the phrase were "extrajudicial statements ... contained in formalized testimonial materials, such as affidavits, depositions, prior testimony, or confessions" and other similar statements that one would expect to be used by the prosecution at trial. Unless a statement is "testimonial," the Confrontation Clause is not implicated.

The second finding that affected the Court's new formulation was the conclusion "that the Framers would not have allowed the admission of testimonial statements of a witness who did not appear at trial unless he was unavailable to testify and the defendant had a prior opportunity for cross-examination." Because the English common law allowed the introduction of those statements without confrontation, the Court reasoned that the Sixth Amendment must do likewise. Thus, the prosecution may not introduce a testimonial statement made by one not testifying (a declarant), unless the declarant is unavailable at the time of trial

(presumably as determined by traditional evidence rules), and the defendant has had a prior opportunity to cross-examine the declarant. For example, if a witness testified at trial against a defendant who was convicted, but who later won a retrial on appeal, that witness's testimony would be admissible in a subsequent trial if the witness died or was unable to be located for the subsequent trial.

If the statement offered by the prosecution is not testimonial, the Confrontation Clause does not affect its admissibility. State evidence rules, such as hearsay rules, may disallow its introduction, but the constitutional right to confrontation does not. An examples of a nontestimonial statement is an offhand, overheard remark.

The Supreme Court decision in *Crawford v. Washington* has had and will continue to have a dramatic effect on criminal trials. Courts struggle to apply the test, trying to decide when a statement is testimonial, when a declarant is unavailable, and, on occasion, when a defendant had prior opportunity to cross-examine. Like the *Roberts* test, the *Crawford* formulation is not without its complications and ambiguities; it too will undoubtedly be subject to much refinement and interpretation over the years to come.

See also Accused, Rights of the; Adversary System of Justice; Common-Law Background of American Civil Rights and Liberties; Counsel, Right to; Impeachment of Witnesses; Sixth Amendment

Bibliography

Chase, Carol A. 2003. "The Five Faces of the Confrontation Clause." *Houston Law Review* 40:1003.

Counseller, W. Jeremy, and Shannon Rickett. 2005. "The Confrontation Clause after *Crawford v. Washington:* Smaller Mouth, Bigger Teeth." *Baylor Law Review* 57:1.

Hermann, Frank R., and Brownlow M. Speer. 1994. "Facing the Accuser: Ancient and Medieval Precursors of the Confrontation Clause." *Virginia Journal of International Law* 34 (1): 481–552.

Jonakait, Randolph N. 1995. "The Origins of the Confrontation Clause: An Alternative History." *Rutgers Law Review* 27:77–168.

White, Penny J. 2003. "Rescuing the Confrontation Clause." *South Carolina Law Review* 54 (3): 537–625.

Penny White

CONGRESSIONAL WOMEN'S CAUCUS

A congressional caucus is comprised of members of Congress who share similar views on an issue or set of issues. These groups then attempt to influence the national policy agenda by drawing attention to those issues to enact legislation on those topics. The Congresswomen's Caucus was created in 1977 to address women's issues when there were only 18 women in the House of Representatives. The name of the organization was changed in 1981 to the Congressional Caucus for Women's Issues (CCWI) to reflect male membership. In 1995, the House changed the rules regarding such organizations so that they were stripped of funding, staff, and formal status. As a result, the caucus reorganized itself and no longer allows male members.

Several scholars have found that an organized caucus for women's issues and interests is a central factor in bringing about legislation favorable to women (Ford 2002, 144). Ironically, a handful of influential early congresswomen were opposed to the idea of a women's caucus because they believed it would draw attention to divisions within the country rather than women's issues (Gertzog 2004, 8). Others expressed concern that election opponents might use membership in such an organization against incumbents. Therefore, the creation of the original caucus came about only after many of the older veteran congresswomen had left the House of Representatives. Fifteen congresswomen, led by Margaret Heckler (R-Mass.) and Elizabeth Holtzman (D-N.Y.), initially joined the Congresswomen's Caucus in 1977. According to Gertzog, the most significant strategic decision made by the caucus was to make its membership bipartisan. The reasoning behind the decision was that unless women from both parties were members, the group would be "dismissed as narrowly partisan and self-serving" (Gertzog 2004, 9). Bipartisanship is also evident in the structure of the organization, which is led by co-chairs, one from each political party.

The caucus had two early legislative successes: (1) a bill preventing employer discrimination against pregnant women, which was enacted into law, and (2) drawing attention to gender disparities in federal employment and social security benefits (Ford 2002, 145). In 1978 the caucus was instrumental in securing an extension on the ratification deadline for the proposed equal rights amendment, a feat few members of Congress thought possible. This was a significant victory, as it brought much-needed credibility to the organization.

Since its inception, the influence of the caucus has fluctuated. The zenith of the group's influence was during the 103rd Congress when it supported 66 bills benefiting women's interests that were passed into law, including the Violence Against Women Act, the Gender Equity in Education Act, and the Freedom of Access to Clinic Entrances Act. These legislative successes came on the heels of the "year of the woman," a phrase used to refer to 1992, when a large number of female candidates won office in the congressional elections. As more women were elected to Congress, more legislation advancing women's interests was enacted.

The organization's influence has waned since 1995 due to a number of factors, including the aforementioned House rule changes, fewer financial resources, less sympathetic House leaders, and the war on terrorism (Gertzog 2004, 177). Interestingly, as more women have been elected to Congress, the influence of the caucus has weakened because the female officeholders are now more diverse, and women's issues have become more publicized since the late 1970s (Gertzog 2004).

See also Equal Rights Amendment; Freedom of Access to Clinic Entrances Act; Gender-Based Discrimination; Violence Against Women Act

Bibliography

Bingham, Clara. 1997. *Women on the Hill: Challenging the Culture of Congress.* New York: Times Books.

Ford, Lynne E. 2002. *Women and Politics: The Pursuit of Equality.* Boston: Houghton Mifflin.

Gertzog, Irwin N. 2004. *Women and Power on Capitol Hill: Reconstructing the Congressional Women's Caucus.* Boulder, CO: Lynne Rienner.

                                    Kara E. Stooksbury

CONGRESS OF RACIAL EQUALITY (CORE)

The Congress of Racial Equality (CORE) was founded in 1942 (although it was originally named the Committee of Racial Equality) by a group of students in Chicago who had been significantly influenced by Mahatma Gandhi and Henry David Thoreau and their beliefs on nonviolent protest. The interracial group of students believed that those same tactics could be employed in an effort to gain civil rights for African Americans. CORE pioneered the use of sit-ins, jail ins, and Freedom Rides.

In 1947, an interracial group of 16 men (8 white, 8 African American) traveled on a Journey of Reconciliation in an attempt to test a Supreme Court ruling invalidating segregation in interstate travel. In *Morgan v. Virginia* (1946), the Supreme Court invalidated state laws that segregated interstate passengers. Most Southern railroad and bus companies, however, did not comply with the ruling (Klarman 2004). Many civil rights leaders, including Thurgood Marshall, were opposed to such direct action due to the potential for severe consequences. The members were arrested several times during this journey and gained national attention after their arrest in North Carolina for violating segregated bus policies. Two of the African American men were sentenced to 30 days on a chain gang. Overall, the CORE members found that most people had never heard of the *Morgan* ruling, that they were the only African Americans protesting the segregation of bus transportation, and that bus drivers rejected their attempts to violate the policy. Their activities were limited to the upper South, as fear of violence and retribution prevented such actions in the Deep South (Klarman 2004, 266).

During the 1950s, the organization became involved in organizing sit-ins and was instrumental in ending segregation at lunch counters as well as other public places. The organization was also a motivating force behind the Freedom Rides during May 1961; the rides were modeled after the 1947 Journey of Reconciliation. The purpose behind Freedom Rides was for members of the organization to test Southern compliance with court rulings concerning desegregation in interstate transportation. In the towns of Anniston and Birmingham, Alabama, the interracial teams from CORE were attacked by angry segregationists. The actions of the group did not sit well with Attorney General Robert Kennedy, who expressed a desire for a cooling-off period; nevertheless, Kennedy ordered the Federal Bureau of Investigation (FBI) to investigate the attacks and made it clear that the group members would be protected. Kennedy was forced to send 600 deputy marshals to Montgomery, Alabama, after a mob firebombed a bus that Freedom Riders were on when local police reluctantly intervened (Franklin 1980, 467). Other organizations committed to civil rights, such as the Student Nonviolent Coordinating Committee (SNCC), began using Freedom Rides to draw attention to segregation in public transportation.

CORE was involved in the March on Washington in 1963, which culminated in Martin Luther King, Jr.'s "I have a dream" speech. That same year, members of CORE joined forces with SNCC and the NAACP to promote the Freedom Summer campaign, in which members of the organizations conducted voter registration drives in Mississippi and in freedom schools, which taught others African American history and the principles of the civil rights movement. Members of the groups were assaulted by angry whites, and three men were murdered by the Ku Klux Klan in 1964. The nationwide attention to the murders and the cause of voting rights were part of the social climate supportive of the Voting Rights Act of 1965, which effectively curtailed racial discrimination in voting.

CORE had historically suffered from organizational problems, and as some members began to advocate more militant tactics, the organization was fractured. Today, the organization is still active in promoting equal opportunity for African

Americans. Its Web site is located at www.core-online.org.

See also *Brown v. Board of Education;* Civil Disobedience; Civil Rights Act of 1964; Civil Rights Movement; Freedom Rides; Freedom Summer; Jim Crow Laws; Kennedy, Robert F.; King, Martin Luther, Jr.; Ku Klux Klan; Marshall, Thurgood; National Association for the Advancement of Colored People; Sit-Ins; Student Nonviolent Coordinating Committee; Thoreau, Henry David; U.S. Department of Justice; Vote, Right to; Voting Rights Act of 1965

Bibliography

Franklin, John Hope. 1980. *From Slavery to Freedom: A History of Negro Americans.* 5th ed. New York: Alfred A. Knopf.

Klarman, Michael J. 2004. *From Jim Crow to Civil Rights: The Supreme Court and the Struggle for Racial Equality.* New York: Oxford University Press.

Kara E. Stooksbury

CONSCIENCE, FREEDOM OF

Historically, the term "freedom of conscience" was employed most often to denote the right of the individual to adopt or reject religious ideas and affiliations. In his celebrated *Memorial and Remonstrance* (1785), James Madison wrote: "The Religion then of every man must be left to the conviction and conscience of every man; and it is the right of every man to exercise it as these may dictate." Without question, freedom of conscience in this sense is protected by the Free Exercise Clause of the First Amendment. It is also protected by the same amendment's prohibition against the official establishment of religion. As one scholar has noted, "In the time between the proposal of the Constitution and of the Bill of Rights, the predominant, not to say exclusive, argument against established churches was that they had the potential to violate liberty of conscience" (Feldman 2002, 398).

In the modern era, freedom of conscience has come to be viewed more broadly as the right of the individual to accept or reject any creed, religious or otherwise. In this broad sense, freedom of conscience

is supported by the Free Speech Clause as well as the religion clauses of the First Amendment. In *Wallace v. Jaffree* (1985), the U.S. Supreme Court identified freedom of conscience as "the central liberty that unifies the various Clauses in the First Amendment." Perhaps the best statement of this broad view of freedom of conscience as it relates to the First Amendment is found in Justice Robert H. Jackson's opinion for the Supreme Court in *West Virginia Board of Education v. Barnette* (1943): "If there is any fixed star in our constitutional constellation, it is that no official, high or petty, can prescribe what shall be orthodox in politics, nationalism, religion, or other matters of opinion or force citizens to confess by word or act their faith therein."

See also Conscientious Objection to Military Service; Establishment Clause; First Amendment; Free Exercise Clause; Jackson, Robert H.; Madison, James; "Memorial and Remonstrance"; Religion, Freedom of; Separation of Church and State; Speech, Freedom of

Bibliography

Feldman, Noah. 2002. "Intellectual Origins of the Establishment Clause." *New York University Law Review* 77:346.

John M. Scheb II and Otis H. Stephens, Jr.

CONSCIENTIOUS OBJECTION TO MILITARY SERVICE

Conscientious objection to military service is rooted in a belief that certain moral, ethical, and religious principles forbid individuals from participating in organized killing or the carrying of arms. Therefore, conscientious objection is the act of refusing to serve in the armed forces because of conscience. Conscientious objection is applicable to all categories and aspects of war. Therefore, it may be expressed through a variety of actions, including refusal to register for the draft and/or refusal to serve in the armed forces. The roots of conscientious objection in the United States can be traced to specific Christian sects that settled in colonial America. Three of the more notable groups were the Quakers, the Brethren, and the Mennonites. The failure of these sects to participate in ongoing conflicts resulted in their persecution by the government and other religious factions. Colonial governments adopted a variety of ways to deal with conscientious objectors. Some governments exempted members of these sects from military service. Others forced conscientious objectors to find substitutes to fight in their place. Still others imposed fines, confiscated property, or imprisoned those who refused to serve in the military.

The emergence of peace groups in the nineteenth century elevated the issue of conscientious objection into the national arena with the outbreak of the Mexican-American War. Henry David Thoreau, whose refusal to pay war taxes resulted in his brief imprisonment, galvanized conscientious objection in the United States. The Civil War was accompanied by conscription legislation that required all males between 20 and 45 years old to serve in the military if called to duty. This legislation contained no provisions to exempt individuals for reasons of conscience.

The outbreak of World War I was accompanied by a more developed approach to dealing with issues of conscientious objection. Only members of churches recognized as having a historical record of conscientious objection were allowed to participate in noncombatant or alternative forms of military service. Members of other religious groups or those who attempted to object for political reasons were forced to enlist. If these individuals remained noncompliant, they were subject to imprisonment. While efforts were undertaken by peace groups to protect conscientious objectors under the First Amendment, the majority of the American population viewed conscientious objectors as unpatriotic dissidents.

Although protected from compulsory service through the Selective Training and Service Act of 1940, conscientious objectors during World War II were often obliged to work on projects seen as serving the national interest. Conscientious objectors found themselves working on conservation projects and construction projects or as staff in medical facilities. Some conscientious objectors took part in government-sponsored experiments.

Public support for conscientious objection, including objection based on political grounds, grew throughout the Vietnam War. A powerful antiwar movement lent its support to those filing for conscientious objection status as well as to those denied such status. It is estimated that there were 50,000 conscientious objectors in the United States by the end of the Vietnam War. High rates of noncompliance with the draft, growing numbers of conscientious objectors, and United States military failures were contributing factors to the government's decision to withdraw from Vietnam in 1975.

Modern conscientious objection encompasses several categories: conscientious objectors, noncombatant conscientious objectors, conscientious objectors to paying for war, selective objectors, nuclear pacifists, and noncooperators with the draft. A conscientious objector is an individual whose opposition to war in all forms is based on deeply held religious, moral, or ethical beliefs. This category of objectors is excused from military service, and in the event of war, is allowed to perform alternative service in a civilian capacity. The second category is noncombatant conscientious objectors. While their beliefs prevent participation as combatants, noncombatant conscientious objectors do not oppose participation in the armed services as noncombatants. Conscientious objectors to paying for war refuse to pay the military portion of their taxes because of their beliefs and are often subjected to legal consequences for their failure to pay. Selective objectors are persons whose religious, ethical, and moral beliefs only allow for participation in "just" wars. Nuclear pacifists refuse to participate in nuclear wars because of conscience. And finally, noncooperators with the draft are individuals whose religious, moral, and ethical beliefs prevent participation and cooperation with draft requirements.

While federal law allows for conscientious objector and noncombatant conscientious objector status, it does not acknowledge conscientious objectors to paying for war, selective objectors, Nuclear pacifists, or noncooperators with the draft.

In fact, the category of noncooperators with the draft is deemed illegal and carries federal penalties.

See also First Amendment; Quakers; Thoreau, Henry David

Bibliography

Cooney, Robert, and Helen Michalowski, eds. 1987. *Power of the People: Active Nonviolence in the United States*. Philadelphia: New Society.

Wittner, Lawrence S. 1984. *Rebels against the War: The American Peace Movement, 1933–1983*. Philadelphia: Temple University Press.

Denise DeGarmo

CONSCRIPTION. *See* Military Conscription

CONSENT OF THE GOVERNED. *See* Declaration of Independence

CONSENT SEARCHES

It is established law that persons may waive their constitutional rights, including their Fourth Amendment protection against unreasonable searches and seizures. When police do not have probable cause to justify a search, they frequently ask persons they have detained to consent to a search of their person, belongings, or automobile. More often than not, people grant consent to search, even when they have something to hide. Thus consent searches often result in fruitful seizures of contraband or other evidence of crime.

To be valid, consent must be truly voluntary. If a person actually assists the police in conducting a search, or consents after having been advised that consent is not required, courts have little difficulty in finding that consent was voluntary. Yet consent has to involve more than mere acquiescence to the authority of the police. Thus, in *Bumper v. North Carolina* (1968), the Supreme Court held that a claim of police authority based on a nonexistent warrant was so coercive as to invalidate the defendant's consent.

In *Schneckloth v. Bustamonte* (1973), the Supreme Court held that "when the subject of a search is not in custody and the State attempts to justify a search on the basis of his consent, the Fourth and Fourteenth Amendments require that it demonstrate that the consent was in fact voluntarily given, and not the result of duress or coercion, express or implied." Yet the Court ruled that law enforcement officers have no constitutional duty to inform suspects of their right to refuse to consent to a search, writing, "It would be thoroughly impractical to impose on the normal consent search the detailed requirements of an effective warning." In dissent, Justice Brennan wrote, "It wholly escapes me how our citizens can meaningfully be said to have waived something as precious as a constitutional guarantee without ever being aware of its existence."

More recently, in *Ohio v. Robinette* (1996), the Court ruled that police are not required to inform lawfully stopped motorists that they are free to go before asking them to consent to an automobile search. Justice Ruth Bader Ginsburg's concurring opinion in *Robinette* succinctly summarizes the facts in the case and suggests the importance of consent searches in the war on drugs:

Robert Robinette's traffic stop for a speeding violation on an interstate highway in Ohio served as prelude to a search of his automobile for illegal drugs. Robinette's experience was not uncommon in Ohio. As the Ohio Supreme Court related, the sheriff's deputy who detained Robinette for speeding and then asked Robinette for permission to search his vehicle "was on drug interdiction patrol at the time." ... The deputy testified ... that he routinely requested permission to search automobiles he stopped for traffic violations.... According to the deputy's testimony in another prosecution, he requested consent to search in 786 traffic stops in 1992, the year of Robinette's arrest.

A perennial problem in the area of consent searches is that of third-party consent. The problem is especially acute in situations where several persons share a single dwelling. In *United States v. Matlock* (1974), the Supreme Court said that third-party consent is valid only when there is mutual use of the property by persons generally having joint access or control. Thus, any of the co-occupants has the right to consent to a search. The others have assumed the risk that any member of the group might permit the common area to be searched. *Matlock* stands for the principle that the validity of third-party consent is tested by the degree of dominion and control exercised by the third party over the searched premises and that a joint occupant may provide valid consent only if the other party is not present. For the most part, state courts have followed the *Matlock* approach.

In *Illinois v. Rodriguez* (1990), the Supreme Court shifted the focus from the dominion and control of the third party to the police officer's subjective belief that the third party has the authority to grant consent to a search of the premises. Writing for the Court, Justice Antonin Scalia opined that a warrantless entry of a residence is valid when based on the consent of a third party whom the police reasonably believe to possess common authority over the premises, even if the third party does not in fact have such authority. In dissent, Justice Thurgood Marshall insisted that "the weighty constitutional interest in preventing unauthorized intrusions into the home overrides any law enforcement interest in relying on the reasonable but potentially mistaken belief that a third party has authority to consent to such a search or seizure."

There are a number of well-established situations in which third-party consent is not valid. Tenancy arrangements are a good example. As the Supreme Court held in *Chapman v. United States* (1961), a landlord does not have the implied authority to consent to the search of a tenant's premises. Similarly, in *Stoner v. California* (1964), the Court ruled that a hotel manager or clerk does not have the right to consent to the search of a guest's room during the time the guest has a legal right to occupy the room.

Some current problems in the area of third-party consent involve parental consent to searches of premises occupied by their adult children, and spousal consent to searches of the other spouse's property, such as an automobile. Most courts have taken the view that either spouse may consent to search all property belonging to the couple (see,

e.g., *United States v. Duran,* 1992). It remains an open question whether one spouse may consent to property owned solely by the other spouse.

See also Brennan, William J., Jr.; Fourth Amendment; Marshall, Thurgood; Scalia, Antonin; War on Drugs

Bibliography

Scheb, John M., and John M. Scheb II. 2006. *Criminal Procedure.* Belmont, CA: Thomson/Wadsworth.

Stephens, Otis H., Jr., and Richard A. Glenn. 2006. *Unreasonable Searches and Seizures: Rights and Liberties under the Law.* Santa Barbara, CA: ABC-Clio.

John M. Scheb II and Otis H. Stephens, Jr.

CONSERVATISM

The meaning of the term "conservatism" varies across countries and over time. As such, it is difficult to formulate a single definition with a single set of prescribed outcomes. In its broadest sense, conservatism embraces order, stability, and tradition; takes a dim view of human nature, distrusts innovation; and is skeptical as to the possibility of social progress. Inasmuch as these attitudes describe a certain personality orientation, as distinct from a well-conceived philosophy or ideology, conservatism has always been and will likely always be well represented in human societies.

Periods of conservatism in the population have always followed periods of swift political changes. Political philosophy, even at its beginnings, has contained strains of what we would consider conservatism. However, most early conservatives did not create an integrated political theory beyond advocacy of slow evolutionary changes in traditional institutions. It was not until the late eighteenth century that it became a coherent theory of politics, when, in 1790, Edmund Burke wrote what would become the Vulgate for conservatives.

The French Revolution of 1789 served as Burke's catalyst. In his *Reflections on the Revolution in France,* Burke predicted that the French Revolution would eventually degenerate into anarchy and horror because the revolutionary government had created a complete break with the past—a rupture so complete that no connection existed between what was and what was to come. This lack of historical continuity in the government eliminated the usual constraints on tyranny. As a result, the French people, according to Burke, would find themselves without any civil checks on their behavior. Thus, either the new government would have to become tyrannical to force the French to follow the new rules, or it would completely fail. In other words, power is protected by tradition; without tradition, it is raw, naked, and extremely dangerous. Both the people and the state suffer because of it—the former because they are exposed to tyranny; the latter, because they must expend so much energy in control. To understand this, it is necessary to examine the underpinnings of Burke's traditional conservatism.

Like the other contractarians, those political philosophers who considered the social contract, Burke reflected on humans in the state of nature. Where Hobbes felt that humanity was a battle between passions and reason, with reason ultimately checking passion in the willing formation of the state, Burke denied the triumph of reason. Where Hobbes, Locke, and Rousseau all held that men were created equal in nature, Burke did not. For Burke, two fundamental points characterize human nature: inability of reason to consistently trump human passions, and natural inequality of humans. These two points, in conjunction with the presupposition that stability is a good, lead to the three basic arguments of Burke's traditional conservatism. First, traditional institutions are of paramount importance. Traditional institutions include the family, the church, and the government in its guise as lawgiver. These institutions have the duty of passing on traditional moral teachings.

Second, because of the human tendency toward irrational behavior, we need guidance from traditional authorities in order for society to enjoy stability. Because he lacked faith in the individual, Burke elevated the collective rationality of people above the rights of the individual much in the same manner as did Rousseau. Burke's collective rationality compares easily with Rousseau's sovereign.

However, while Rousseau held that private property was the prime source of corruption, Burke held that private property was one of the more important traditions. In his *Reflections on the Revolution in France,* Burke stated, "The power of perpetuating our property in our families is one of the most valuable and interesting circumstances belonging to it, and that which tends most to the perpetuation of society itself."

Third, compliance with traditional morality is more important than individual liberty; that is, people should not have the liberty to contravene moral principles. This also conflicts with Rousseau's liberalism. For Rousseau, society's restrictions on personal liberty were the chains that fettered man's natural goodness. For Burke, these restrictions provided man a framework within which he knew ethical behavior and responsible liberty.

For conservatives, stability is of utmost importance; the stability of the state and the stability of the society are inseparable. This requires neither a stagnant society nor a regressive one; change is allowed. However, because of the premium placed on stability, conservative logic results in two major tenets: first, reforms must contribute to the well-being of the community; second, present generations have a responsibility to both past and future generations. These two principles illustrate why Burke supported the American Revolution. While a member of Parliament, Burke pled the cause of the colonists, even calling for the repeal of the Stamp Act, not because Britain had no right to tax the colonists, but because it was unfair to them. After the Treaty of Paris, the Americans refused to break completely with their history. The government they created drew heavily from English institutions. Furthermore, the framers created the new constitution with the expressed purpose of restricting the power of the government to help society.

The very structure of the American government is conservative. Madison built upon Montesquieu's separation of powers with his own system of checks and balances. This helped ensure that no single branch of government would be able to seize power at the expense of society. To further circumscribe the powers of the government and to check populist demagogues, the Federalists allowed only the House of Representatives to be popularly elected, and thus subject to the passions of the governed. The other three bodies were chosen by the Electoral College, the state legislatures, and the president. Furthermore, the Constitution became the new holy scripture. The law is supreme, and the Constitution is even more so. Each of these guarantees that the government changes slowly. Moreover, basing the American legal system on English common law and stare decisis makes even clearer this dedication to tradition, to legal conservatism.

Today, there are two distinctive strains of American conservatism. In the economic sphere, modern American conservatives champion the free enterprise system and abhor governmental intervention into the economy. They champion free trade and low taxes and oppose regulation and redistribution of wealth. Indeed, with respect to economics, modern American conservatives have adopted the philosophy of classical liberalism.

In the sphere of social policy, contemporary American conservatives echo the traditionalism of Edmund Burke and the classical conservatives. They still tend to adhere to the three basic arguments of Burke's conservatism; that is, they still emphasize American heritage over American progress, and they still emphasize traditional over progressive institutions. It is fair to say that, by and large, conservatives have been far less likely than liberals to support expansion of civil rights and liberties. Whether the issue has been expansion of the suffrage, abolition of racial segregation, or recognition of sexual and reproductive freedom, conservatives have always been less willing to support civil rights and liberties claims. The only exception to this trend has been the tendency for conservatives to support claims of religious freedom, especially in the Judeo-Christian context, as well as those rights associated with the free enterprise system.

The faith-based initiatives championed by President George W. Bush demonstrate the continuing power of Edmund Burke in modern American politics, as does the ongoing debate over gay marriage. Under the mantle of compassionate conservatism, the Bush administration sought to strengthen the traditional institutions of the family and religion in order to reinforce traditional values and thereby promote stability and social cohesion.

Is this surge in conservatism a new event? Not at all. Writing in 1962, Clinton Rossiter identified the cyclical nature of this phenomenon. After each period of intense political change, be it the American Revolution, Reconstruction, the New Deal, the Civil Rights Movement, or globalization, American society has reacted by becoming more conservative, less willing to change again. Thus do the conservative strains echo through the ages: evolution, not revolution.

See also Civil Rights Movement; Common-Law Background of American Civil Rights and Liberties; Declaration of Independence; Economic Freedom; Gay Rights Movement; Hobbes, Thomas; Liberalism; Locke, John; Madison, James; New Deal; Reconstruction; Religion, Freedom of; Reproductive Freedom; Rousseau, Jean-Jacques; Same-Sex Marriage and Civil Unions; Segregation, De Facto and De Jure; Women's Suffrage

Bibliography

Ball, Terence. 2003. "The Federalist Papers." In *Political Thinkers: From Socrates to the Present*, ed. David Boucher and Paul Kelly. New York: Oxford University Press.

Boucher, David. 2003. "Burke." In *Political Thinkers: From Socrates to the Present*, ed. David Boucher and Paul Kelly. New York: Oxford University Press.

———. 2003. "Rousseau." In *Political Thinkers: From Socrates to the Present*, ed. David Boucher and Paul Kelly. New York: Oxford University Press.

Burke, Edmund. [1790] 2001. *Reflections on the Revolution in France*. Ed. J.C.D. Clark. Stanford, CA: Stanford University Press.

Rossiter, Clinton. 1962. *Conservatism in America: The Thankless Persuasion*. New York: Vintage Books.

———. 1963. *The Political Thought of the American Revolution*. New York: Harcourt, Brace & World.

Ole J. Forsberg

CONSPIRACY

In common law the agreement between two or more persons to commit a crime has always been regarded as an offense separate and apart from the substantive crime that was the objective of the conspirators. Separate and distinct punishment for the agreement was supported by the belief that the combination of persons to achieve a criminal objective made the accomplishment of that objective far more likely. Today states and Congress have defined conspiracy by statute. Generally, the law of conspiracy seeks to punish an illegal agreement or compact to commit a crime, even in those instances where no criminal conduct ultimately occurs.

In most states, and under the general federal conspiracy statute (18 U.S.C. §371) conspiracy requires an agreement between two or more individuals to commit a crime together with the occurrence of at least one overt act in furtherance of the conspiracy. In those instances, a criminal agreement, standing alone, does not become an actionable conspiracy until one of the members of the compact does some act in furtherance of the criminal objective. Once an overt act is performed, the crime of conspiracy is complete, even if the criminal objective is never attained.

However, the Model Penal Code, a series of criminal statutes used to guide states in codifying various crimes, does not require an overt act, while almost all states do. Further, some states that did not always do so now require overt acts. Certain federal crimes do not require proof of both an agreement and an overt act. For example, in *Whitfield v. United States* (2005), the U.S. Supreme Court held that under the federal money laundering statute, the government need not prove that a defendant committed an overt act. An examination of the specific statute in each jurisdiction is necessary to understand the elements of the crime of conspiracy that pertain in that particular jurisdiction.

The agreement to commit a crime is the *actus reus* of conspiracy. Some states permit conviction under a unilateral conspiracy statute, in which only one party actually intends to conspire. Under the unilateral theory, one may be convicted of conspir-

ing with a police informant or undercover officer. In bilateral jurisdictions, such as Connecticut, conviction requires proof that two or more persons entered into the criminal agreement (see §53a-48, Conn. Gen. Stat.). A bilateral construction of conspiracy statutes finds support in decisions by the federal courts, which hold that one cannot conspire with an informant as a matter of law.

In like manner, the mens rea or intent element of the crime differs among the various jurisdictions. Under one theory the conspirator need only posses the intent to conspire; while in other jurisdictions, one must possess both the intent to conspire as well as the intent to commit the underlying crime. In those jurisdictions the absence of either intent is sufficient to acquit, even if proof of the agreement is substantial.

Proof of an agreement can be inferred from the conduct of the conspirators. There need not be a formal compact or contract, since criminal conspiracies are formed in secret. Thus the conduct of two persons acting in concert to achieve a common criminal goal can give rise to an inference that a conspiracy exists.

Wharton's Rule, a principle not embraced in all jurisdictions, prohibits conviction for conspiracy where the substantive crime (e.g., incest) requires the participation of two persons. In contrast, federal gambling and RICO offenses, which require the participation of at least two persons, commonly punish the conspiracy in addition to the substantive offense.

In *Pinkerton v. United States* (1946), the Supreme Court announced what has become known as the *Pinkerton* Rule. Generally a member of a conspiracy is liable for all offenses committed in furtherance of the conspiracy that are the reasonably foreseeable result of the unlawful agreement of the conspirators. Conspirators are deemed to be agents of one another and are bound by the acts of their co-conspirators within the framework of the conspiracy. The rationale is that one who joins a criminal confederation assumes responsibility for all crimes committed in furtherance of the main objective of the confederation This is particularly relevant in determining other relevant conduct pursuant to the federal sentencing guidelines. For example, a court can apply penalty enhancements for one conspirator when another employs a firearm in the course of the conspiracy, even though the defendant being sentenced was unaware of the existence of the gun or that any member of the conspiracy used it.

The offense of conspiracy has become a potent weapon for prosecutors, particularly due to the wide-ranging scope of evidence allowed in such prosecutions. Generally out-of-court statements of another individual are inadmissible hearsay. However, where hearsay statements are made during the course of, and in furtherance of a conspiracy, the extrajudicial statements of co-conspirators are admissible in the absence of the speaker for cross-examination. Generally, prosecutors must demonstrate prima facie proof of the conspiracy and a co-conspirator's participation before such statements are allowed. However, many courts permit the use of the proffered statements to establish this prima facie showing. This rule applies to statements of unindicted or uncharged co-conspirators as well. As a consequence, great latitude is given in the presentation of evidence, leading to convictions where prosecutors could not otherwise meet the burden of proof.

Many states prohibit charging multiple conspiracies where the various crimes are part of an overall criminal confederation among the same conspirators. Thus there is but one conspiracy with multiple objectives, rather than a series of separate conspiracies.

Renunciation is a defense in many jurisdictions; that is, a conspirator may withdraw from the conspiracy and avoid prosecution, but the extent of the efforts at withdrawal required varies. In some instances, merely withdrawing from the conspiracy is sufficient, while in others the actor must take affirmative steps to thwart the conspiracy, such as alerting the police.

Punishment for conspiracy is generally the same as for the underlying substantive crime. As the U.S. Supreme Court held in *Blockburger v. United States* (1932), a court may impose consecutive sentences for conspiracy and the completed underlying crime,

and doing so does not constitute a double jeopardy violation.

See also Accused, Rights of the; Common-Law Background of American Civil Rights and Liberties; Double Jeopardy, Prohibition of; Fifth Amendment; Inchoate Offenses; Racketeering and RICO Laws; Sentencing Guidelines

Richard T. Meehan, Jr.

CONSTITUTION. *See* United States Constitution

CONSTITUTIONAL DEMOCRACY

When the framers of the United States Constitution met in Philadelphia in the summer of 1787, the right to vote was, for the most part, limited to propertied white men. In fact, all 55 of the delegates to the Constitutional Convention were drawn from this segment of the population. Women were regarded as second-class citizens, and most persons of African descent, as slaves, held no legal rights whatsoever.

The political system established by the Constitution could hardly be called a democracy, inasmuch as democracy requires universal suffrage, representation of all segments of society in their government, and equal rights under the law for all citizens. But the framers did not set out to create a democracy, a term they equated with mob rule. Rather, their project was the creation of a constitutional republic in which individual rights, and above all property rights, would be protected from the tyranny of the majority.

The Civil War, industrial and commercial expansion, and waves of immigration in the late nineteenth century, together with two world wars and the Great Depression in the twentieth century, produced fundamental changes to American society and ultimately in the legal and political systems. Consequently, American government at all levels has become much more democratic, that is, more open to meaningful participation by groups that once were excluded. This fundamental change in the character of the political system testifies to the remarkable adaptability of the Constitution itself.

The Bill of Rights and the Fourteenth Amendment

By protecting the rights of all citizens against the power of the national government, the Bill of Rights took a major stride in the march toward constitutional democracy. Certainly, the First Amendment, which protects the right of all citizens to express their views and organize for the purpose of influencing policy, has proved to be essential to American democracy. Without question, the Fourteenth Amendment, which provided broad protection for the civil rights of all Americans, must be regarded as a giant step forward in the evolution of American democracy. The Fourteenth Amendment guarantees, among other things, equal protection of the laws. This provision rests on the premise that individuals should be equal before the state, which is *the* fundamental principle of democracy.

Enfranchising African Americans

In *Scott v. Sandford* (1857)—better known as the Dred Scott case—the Supreme Court ruled that persons of African descent were not, and could not become, citizens of the United States. Indeed, they had no constitutional rights. This decision, which is now considered morally outrageous, was overturned by the ratification of the Fourteenth Amendment in 1868. The Fourteenth Amendment conferred citizenship on "all persons born or naturalized in the United States." It did not, however, specifically guarantee African Americans the right to vote. Congress corrected this oversight by adopting the Fifteenth Amendment (1870), which provides that "the right of citizens of the United States to vote shall not be denied or abridged by the United States or by any State on account of race, color, or previous condition of servitude."

Of course, the Constitution is not a self-executing document. Nearly a century passed before the promise of the Fifteenth Amendment was fulfilled. A number of states resisted the extension of the franchise to African Americans, and some adopted measures that frustrated black citizens' efforts to register and vote. Eventually, however, these impediments were swept away by Supreme Court

decisions and acts of Congress, such as the landmark Voting Rights Act of 1965. These decisions and enactments involved both assertions of power by the national government vis-à-vis the states and changes in constitutional interpretation. As a result of the enforcement of the Fifteenth Amendment, African Americans can register and vote without encountering legal and structural obstacles.

Direct Popular Election of the Senate

The U.S. Constitution initially provided that members of the U.S. Senate would be elected by the state legislatures. The Seventeenth Amendment, ratified in 1913, required that the Senate be chosen directly by the people. The House of Representatives had proposed the amendment on several occasions, but the Senate had resisted. Finally, in 1912, after public opinion became aroused, the Senate relented. It took only one year for the states to ratify the measure, which had attracted widespread popular support. In reality, though, the Seventeenth Amendment merely formalized what had been occurring informally in half the states, where the legislatures routinely followed the will of the people expressed at the ballot box.

Women's Rights

The Nineteenth Amendment (1920), which guaranteed women the right to vote, was the culmination of a movement that began in the 1840s. But the Nineteenth Amendment applied only to voting. It said nothing about the numerous state and federal laws that discriminated against females in matters of property, marriage and divorce, employment, and the professions. In 1923, an amendment was introduced in Congress to provide wider constitutional protection for women's rights. Not until 1972, however, did Congress submit the equal rights amendment to the states. After a protracted and, in some states, bitter struggle, the amendment failed to win ratification. But its failure did not leave women's rights without protection under the federal Constitution. The Equal Protection Clause of the Fourteenth Amendment has been interpreted to provide a substantial degree of protection against official government-sponsored sex discrimination. Moreover, Congress has used its enforcement powers under the Fourteenth Amendment to enact statutes that further protect women against discrimination.

Lowering the Voting Age

The Twenty-sixth Amendment (1971) effectively lowered the voting age to 18 in both state and federal elections. Congress had already decided in 1970 to lower the voting age in federal elections; the amendment came in response to *Oregon v. Mitchell* (1970), in which the Supreme Court held that a constitutional amendment was necessary to force the states to lower their voting ages. Considerable impetus for lowering the voting age came from young men ages 18 to 21, who were eligible to be drafted into military service and sent to die in the jungles of Vietnam but were unable to vote for or against the politicians who formulated policies like the draft and the conduct of the Vietnam War. The amendment was ratified quickly and with little opposition. Even state legislatures that supported maintaining the voting age at 21 were reluctant to deal with the costly administrative problems that would follow if the federal and state voting ages were different.

Eliminating Economic Restrictions on Voting

When the Constitution was framed, the states were given almost total discretion in determining eligibility to vote. They were limited only in that those who were deemed to be eligible to vote for members of the state house—technically, "the most numerous branch of the state legislature"—would be eligible to vote in elections to the U.S. House of Representatives. In all states, voting was restricted to propertied white men, although specific property requirements varied somewhat. By the time Andrew Jackson was elected president in 1832, all states except New Jersey and North Carolina had abolished property requirements for voting.

One of the ways in which states limited the vote was through the poll tax. Throughout the nineteenth century, many states, especially in the South, charged a tax for the privilege of voting. Of course, the idea was to limit the participation of the poor, both black and white. In 1964, the Twenty-fourth Amendment was ratified to eliminate the poll tax, which had already fallen into disfavor. However, the new amendment applied only to federal elections, and some states continued the practice. Two years later, in *Harper v. Virginia State Board of Elections* (1966), the Supreme Court ruled that state poll taxes violated the Fourteenth Amendment's Equal Protection Clause, thus dealing a death blow to poll taxes.

Reapportionment: One Person, One Vote

Prior to the 1960s, many congressional districts, state legislative districts, school board districts, county commission districts, and city council districts were grossly unequal in terms of population, a condition known as malapportionment. When districts are unequal, the influence of each voter in the more populous districts is diminished, and the influence of voters in the less populated districts is enhanced. Arguably, the right to vote is devalued if one person's vote counts for less than the votes of other citizens.

In its landmark decision in *Baker v. Carr* (1962), the Supreme Court overturned a precedent that had prevented the lower courts from intervening in matters of apportionment. Then, in *Reynolds v. Sims* (1964), the high court held that state legislative districts had to be reapportioned according to the principle of one person, one vote. Districts then had to be redrawn to be made equal in population. Other Supreme Court decisions extended this requirement to U.S. House districts and to districts for local governing bodies.

Considered fairly revolutionary in the 1960s, reapportionment is now an accepted part of American political life. Every 10 years, after the federal government completes its census, state legislatures reapportion themselves and the congressional districts in their respective states. Failure to do so inevitably means that they will be sued and ordered to undertake reapportionment by a federal court. Although reapportionment can be contentious, both legally and politically, unquestionably the reapportionment revolution has rendered the political system more democratic.

Through constitutional amendments, changing judicial interpretations of existing constitutional language, the enactment of landmark statutes, and, ultimately, profound changes in political culture, the constitutional republic designed by the framers has become a constitutional democracy.

See also At-Large Elections; *Baker v. Carr;* Bill of Rights (American); Dred Scott Case; Equality; Equal Protection Clause; Fifteenth Amendment; First Amendment; Fourteenth Amendment; Fourteenth Amendment, Section 5 of the; Free and Fair Elections; Gender-Based Discrimination; Grandfather Clause; Literacy Tests; Living Constitution; Nineteenth Amendment; Petition, Right of; Poll Tax; Pluralism; Racial Gerrymandering; Reapportionment; Representative Democracy; *Reynolds v. Sims*; Slavery; Speech, Freedom of; Twenty-fourth Amendment; Tyranny of the Majority; United States Constitution; Universal Suffrage; Vote, Right to; Voting Age; Voting Rights Act of 1965; White Primary; Women's Suffrage

Bibliography

Amar, Akhil Reed. 2000. *The Bill of Rights: Creation and Reconstruction.* New Haven, CT: Yale University Press.

Ford, Lynne E. 2002. *Women and Politics: The Pursuit of Equality.* Boston: Houghton Mifflin.

Grofman, Bernard, and Chandler Davidson, eds. 1994. *The Quiet Revolution in the South: The Impact of the Voting Rights Act, 1965–1990.* Princeton, NJ: Princeton University Press.

Keyssar, Alexander. 2000. *The Right to Vote: The Contested History of Democracy in the United States.* New York: Basic Books.

Schwartz, Bernard. 1977. *The Great Rights of Mankind: A History of the American Bill of Rights.* New York: Oxford University Press.

Stephenson, Donald Grier, Jr. 2004. *The Right to Vote: Rights and Liberties under the Law.* Santa Barbara, CA: ABC-Clio.

John M. Scheb II

CONSTITUTIONAL TORTS. *See Bivens v. Six Unknown Named Federal Narcotics Agents*; Civil Rights Act of 1871; Section 1983 Actions

CONSUMER DISCRIMINATION

Discrimination on the basis of race, ethnicity, and gender occurs in a variety of retail settings and transactions. Consumer discrimination is a broad term encompassing a number of discriminatory behaviors that take place in stores, restaurants, gas stations, banks, and other businesses. Anecdotal and empirical evidence exists to support claims that retailers and lenders may discriminate against customers on the basis of race, ethnicity, gender, and perceived religious affiliation (Ayres 1991; Ayres 1995; Pan 1997; *60 Minutes* 2001; *20/20* 1998). The informal use of testers and some empirical studies have revealed discrimination on the basis of race and gender exists in automobile purchase prices, automobile financing, accepting payment in the form of checks and gift certificates, heightened surveillance by store and security personnel in retail settings, and refusal of entry and denial of or substandard service in restaurants, stores, and taxicabs (Ayres 1991; Ayres 1995; Broman, Mavaddat, and Hsu 2000; Feagin 1991).

Victims of consumer discrimination historically have relied on a variety of nonlegal and legal means to respond to the problem of consumer discrimination. Individuals, for example, have engaged in sit-ins and boycotts as extralegal methods of combating racial discrimination at lunch counters and public transportation (Chafe 1980, 99). In fact, images of these protests are synonymous with the Civil Rights Movement of the 1960s. Although boycotts of offending businesses continue today, contemporary complainants who seek redress for consumer discrimination-related harms most commonly rely on a combination of federal and state statutes and state common law to attempt to obtain legal relief for consumer discrimination. While no single federal statute is directly aimed at providing relief for consumers who experience differential treatment on the basis of race or ethnicity in retail settings, federal statutes prohibit discrimination in contracting, in the purchase of personal property, and in places of public accommodation.

Section 1981 of the Civil Rights Act of 1866, as amended in 1991, provides that "[a]ll persons within the jurisdiction of the United States shall have the same right in every State and Territory to make and enforce contracts ... as enjoyed by white citizens." The amended act further provides that "for the purposes of this section, the term 'make and enforce contracts' includes the making, performance, modification, and termination of contracts, and the enjoyment of all benefits, privileges, terms and conditions of the contractual relationship." In order to articulate a viable claim under Section 1981, plaintiffs generally must allege that they are members of a racial minority, that the defendants intentionally discriminated against them on the basis of race, and that the discrimination was directed toward one or more of the activities protected by the statute. Courts vary substantially in determining what activities are protected by the statute and in defining "making and enforcing contracts." Plaintiffs can prove intentional discrimination through direct, indirect, or circumstantial evidence. Absent direct evidence of intentional discrimination, courts allow plaintiffs to establish discrimination by relying on the burden-shifting framework of *McDonnell Douglas v. Green* (1973). Under the *McDonnell Douglas* framework, consumer discrimination plaintiffs can meet their burden by showing that (1) they are a member of a protected class; (2) they attempted to make, enforce, or secure the performance of a contract; and (3) they were denied the opportunity to make, enforce, or secure the performance of a contract for goods or services that remained available to similarly situated persons outside the protected class. Once plaintiffs meet that burden, the defendant must then "articulate some legitimate, nondiscriminatory reason for the plaintiff's rejection." If the defendant can do so, the burden shifts back to the plaintiff to establish that the defendant's response is a pretext for discrimination.

In addition to establishing discrimination on the basis of race or ethnicity, courts require plaintiffs to establish that they were prevented from completing an activity protected by the act. Most jurisdictions have determined that activities protected under Section 1981 are fairly limited to being denied admittance or service, or being prohibited from completing a retail transaction that was in process. Courts have interpreted "completing a retail transaction" fairly narrowly, and plaintiffs generally have been required to establish more than a general interest in the merchandise or an intent to shop. Courts have been largely unsympathetic to claims that shoppers have a right to browse unmolested and not be subject to heightened surveillance on the basis of race.

Section 1982 of the Civil Rights Act of 1866 is similarly aimed at discouraging discrimination based on race in business dealings. Section 1982 prohibits discrimination in the purchase of personal property: "All citizens of the United States shall have the same right, in every State and Territory, as is enjoyed by white citizens thereof to inherit, purchase, lease, sell, hold, and convey real and personal property." Courts construe Section 1982 in a manner similar to Section 1981 (*Tillman v. Wheaton-Haven Recreation Association*, 1973). Under Section 1981, as under Section 1982, successful plaintiffs must establish that their rights enumerated in the statute were violated on account of race and that the discrimination was intentional.

Section 2000a of the Civil Rights Act of 1964 broadens the prohibited bases of discrimination beyond those provided in sections 1981 and 1982. Section 2000(a) provides: "All persons shall be entitled to the full and equal enjoyment of the goods, services, facilities, privileges, advantages, and accommodations of any place of public accommodation ... without discrimination or segregation on the ground of race, color, religion, or national origin." Although the prohibited bases of discrimination are broadened under Section 2000(a), "place of public accommodation" is narrowly defined. It includes hotels, motels, restaurants, gas stations, theaters, concert halls, and sports arenas but does not include all businesses and excludes retail establishments. Customers who assert that they were denied entrance or service or received substandard service in restaurants, hotels, motels, or other places of public accommodation on the basis of race have articulated an actionable claim under Section 2000(a) of the Civil Rights Act of 1964.

A number of states have civil rights or human rights statutes that mirror the language of the Civil Rights Acts. Other state statutes are drafted more broadly than the federal statutes and include retail stores within their definitions of "places of public accommodation." For example, the New Jersey state statute defines "public accommodations" to include all retail stores. Similarly, California prohibits discrimination in all business establishments. A number of states have expanded the prohibited bases of discrimination beyond those included in the federal statutes. For example, Michigan prohibits discrimination in places of public accommodation on grounds that include height, weight, familial status, or marital status. New Jersey statutes prohibit discrimination based on, among other things, "affectional" or sexual orientation. In addition to relying on federal and state statutes for legal relief, plaintiffs may find relief under various state common claims that may include claims for false imprisonment, defamation, intentional infliction of emotional distress, and assault. State law may also provide immunity from liability for retailers who reasonably believed there was probable because to suspect the accused was stealing merchandise.

See also Civil Rights Act of 1964; Civil Rights Act of 1866; Civil Rights Movement; Civil Rights Restoration Act; Discrimination; Discrimination by Private Actors; Gender-Based Discrimination; Public Accommodation, Places of; Sexual Orientation, Discrimination Based on

Bibliography

Ayres, Ian. 1991. "Fair Driving: Gender and Race Discrimination in Retail Car Negotiations." *Harvard Law Review* 104 (4): 817–72.

———. 1995. "Further Evidence of Discrimination in New Car Negotiations and Estimates of Its Cause." *Michigan Law Review* 94 (1):109–47.

Broman, Clifford L., Roya Mavaddat, and Shu-yao Hsu. 2000. "The Experience and Consequences of Perceived Racial Discrimination: A Study of African Americans." *Journal of Black Psychology* 26 (2): 165–80.

Chafe, William H. 1980. *Civilities and Civil Rights: Greensboro, North Carolina, and the Black Struggle for Freedom.* New York: Oxford University Press.

Feagin, Joe R. 1991. "The Continuing Significance of Race: Antiblack Discrimination in Public Places." *American Sociological Review* 56:101–16.

Pan, Philip P. 1997. "More Black Suing over Retail Bias." *Washington Post,* 8 October.

Singer, Joseph William. 1996. "No Right to Exclude: Public Accommodations and Private Property." *Northwestern University Law Review* 90 (4): 1283–497.

60 Minutes. 2001. "Widespread Allegations of Racial Profiling at Dillard's." CBS television broadcast, 25 March.

Sullivan, Barry. 1989. "Historical Reconstruction, Reconstruction History, and the Proper Scope of Section 1981." *Yale Law Journal* 98:541.

20/20. 1998. "Under Suspicion; Security Guards Unfairly Target Black Shoppers." ABC television broadcast, 8 June.

Deseriee A. Kennedy

CONTEMPT, POWER OF

Contempt is conduct that disrupts the proceedings or impedes the functioning of a court or legislative body. Judicial officers have inherent authority to impose penalties for persons found to be in contempt of court. Nevertheless, Congress has specifically recognized this power of federal courts (see 18 U.S.C. § 401). In *Anderson v. Dunn* (1821), the U.S. Supreme Court recognized Congress's power to punish for contempt.

Although state courts possess an inherent common-law power to punish for contempt, state constitutions and statutes frequently provide for courts and legislative bodies to exercise the power. The power to impose contempt is essential to uphold the dignity of courts, but because it carries a potential for abuse, in *Cooke v. United States* (1925), the U.S. Supreme Court cautioned that it is a power to be used sparingly.

Contempt may be criminal or civil, direct or indirect, and the processes for imposing contempt depend on the character of contempt. Federal and state statutes and rules of court procedure outline these procedures.

Criminal and Civil Contempt

Courts impose criminal contempt to punish a person for offensive conduct directed against the court or its processes. Criminal contempt may occur in criminal or civil proceedings and may be either direct or indirect.

Direct criminal contempt consists of speaking contemptuous words, for example, openly insulting the court or committing contemptuous acts such as disorderly conduct in the immediate presence of the court. Courts may summarily punish such contemptuous actions but before finding a person in contempt must first inform the contemnor (person accused of contempt) that the court is considering imposing contempt, explain why, and afford the contemnor an opportunity to show cause why he or she should not be adjudged guilty of contempt. Contempt before a legislative body usually involves refusal of a witness who has been subpoenaed to testify or produce documents. Legislative contempt charges are usually referred to a court for resolution.

Indirect criminal contempt consists of a person uttering contemptuous words or committing contemptuous acts outside the presence of the court. In some instances it may involve intentional violation of an injunction or restraining order. The alleged contemptuous acts are usually brought to the attention of the court by an affidavit from a witness to such words or conduct. The court must issue an order alleging grounds for contempt and directing the contemnor to show cause why he or she should not be held in contempt. The contemnor must be afforded an opportunity for a hearing before a court to determine the issue of contempt.

Civil contempt consists of willful disobedience of a court order. Civil contempt is coercive, sometimes remedial, and is usually initiated by a party to a civil proceeding. Common instances involve willful failure to pay court-ordered alimony or child support. The contemnor must be given notice of the alleged contemptuous actions and provided a hearing on the issue. As in any civil case, the initiating party must establish the grounds.

Judgment and Sentence for Contempt

In both criminal and civil contempt proceedings the court's judgment finding a contemnor in contempt must recite factual findings, and before imposing a sentence the court must allow the contemnor to present any mitigating circumstances.

In *Bloom v. Illinois* (1968), the U.S. Supreme Court held that criminal contempt must be treated like other crimes insofar as the right to a jury trial is concerned. Thus, before a person can be sentenced for criminal contempt in excess of six months he or she must be afforded the right to a jury trial.

In civil contempt a sentence may be confinement for a fixed period, a fine, or both and must include a provision allowing the respondent to purge the contempt. The idea is usually expressed by the saying "The contemnor must be given a key to the jail cell."

See also Accused, Rights of the; Common-Law Background of American Civil Rights and Liberties; Due Process, Procedural; Jury, Trial by

Bibliography

Gray, Lawrence N. 1999. "Criminal and Civil Contempt: Some Sense of a Hodgepodge." *Journal of the Suffolk Academy of Law* 13:1.

Hanger, Teresa S. 1987. "The Modern Status of the Rules Permitting a Judge to Punish Direct Contempt Summarily." *William and Mary Law Review* 28:553.

Zimmerman, Deborah J. 2003. "Civil Contemnors, Due Process, and the Right to a Jury Trial." *Wyoming Law Review* 3:205–31.

Hon. John M. Scheb

CONTINUANCE, MOTION FOR

A motion for a continuance is one of a variety of pretrial motions available to parties in a civil or criminal case. The term "continuance" is legal jargon for postponement; hence, a motion for a continuance is an attempt by counsel for a party to delay a scheduled trial or hearing. Motions for continuance are very common in complex cases in which considerable time is needed to prepare for a trial or a contested hearing. Such motions are also used to extend the time available for negotiations that may avert a trial or hearing altogether. Other grounds that may be asserted in support of the motion for continuance include an illness or emergency that prevents a litigant, lawyer, or witness from appearing in court as scheduled; the unavailability of a significant witness or piece of documentary evidence; or the lack of adequate time to depose an opposing party's witnesses. The trial judge has broad discretion whether to grant or deny a motion for continuance. Appellate courts have consistently held that trial judges do not abuse their discretion in denying a motion for continuance unless the moving party can show that specific prejudice has resulted from the denial.

Although continuances are most commonly sought in matters pending before a trial court, parties can also seek continuances of proceedings before administrative and regulatory agencies, usually for same reasons as outlined above. In addition, counsel may file a motion for continuance in an appellate court in an effort to postpone oral arguments before the court because of scheduling conflicts or personal emergencies of counsel. As where a continuance is sought in trial court, the grant or denial of a continuance by a governmental agency or appellate court is discretionary with the agency or court.

See also Accused, Rights of the; Adversary System of Justice; Counsel, Ineffective Assistance of; Critical Pretrial Stages; Plea Bargaining

John M. Scheb II and Otis H. Stephens, Jr.

CONTRACT, LIBERTY OF. *See* Due Process, Substantive; Economic Freedom; *Lochner v. New York*

CONTRACTS CLAUSE

When the delegates to the Constitutional Convention met in Philadelphia in the summer of 1787, the memory of Shays' Rebellion was still fresh in their minds. Neither the state of Massachusetts nor the national government under the Articles of Confederation was able to deal effectively with this revolt of debtor farmers in western Massachusetts during the summer of 1786. The rebellion was finally squelched

by a "band of mercenaries hired by wealthy citizens who feared a popular uprising" (Stephens and Scheb 2003, 3). Shays' Rebellion underscored the general economic unrest throughout the 13 states at the time of the drafting of the U.S. Constitution.

One of the most important objectives of the framers was the protection of property rights. A central tenet of these rights was the freedom to enter into contracts unhampered by governmental regulation. Such regulation at that time was most likely to come from state laws passed by elected legislatures likely to be sympathetic to the concerns of debtors who would obviously benefit from the suspension or termination of contract obligations. It is not surprising, therefore, that one of the specific limitations that the framers placed on the states was the prohibition of "any … Law impairing the Obligation of Contracts" (Article I, Section 10, clause 1).

During the 1800s, and especially prior to the death of Chief Justice John Marshall in 1835, the Contracts Clause proved to be a major restriction on state legislation. For example, in *Fletcher v. Peck* (1810) the Supreme Court ruled that a Georgia law rescinding the state's sale of some 25.5 million acres of public land, stretching to the Mississippi River and comprising much of what is now Alabama and Mississippi, was unconstitutional either on the basis of "general principles which are common to our free institutions" or because it violated the Contracts Clause. By linking contractual obligations with "general principles … common to our free institutions," Chief Justice Marshall's opinion for the Court reflected the view that the Contracts Clause was grounded in a philosophy of natural rights. As Marshall saw it, the original sales contract had created "absolute rights," and these rights had become "vested" in the subsequent purchasers; that is, those "innocent third parties" who had acquired it from the original investors. It made no difference to Marshall and his colleagues that private speculators had obtained the land in the first place by bribing members of the Georgia legislature.

While *Fletcher v. Peck* greatly broadened the scope of the Contracts Clause, the Court's decision nine years later in *Dartmouth College v. Woodward* (1819) had far greater influence on economic development in nineteenth-century America. Here the Court held that the corporate charter establishing Dartmouth College in 1769 was a contract that could not be changed by the state of New Hampshire without violating the U.S. Constitution. It made no difference that the American Revolution had intervened between the date of the original charter and the attempt by the state to convert this private educational institution into a public college in 1816. As Chief Justice Marshall explained in his opinion for the Court, the state of New Hampshire had simply succeeded to the rights and obligations of the British Crown specified in the original charter. In attempting to modify the governing structure of the college, the state had violated the Contracts Clause. No specific language in the charter required this limitation on New Hampshire's power to amend it half a century after it was granted, when all the original parties to the contract were dead. Marshall concluded, nevertheless, that the challenged legislation violated the spirit if not the letter of the Contracts Clause. Any ambiguity in the charter, Marshall declared, should be construed in favor of "the adventurers," the founders of the college and their successors, and against the state.

The broad principle that Marshall enunciated in the *Dartmouth College* case was soon extended by lower courts beyond charitable educational institutions to include profit-seeking corporations. The *Dartmouth College* decision came at a time when business was rapidly expanding in such fields as insurance, canal building, and road construction. Companies were tangibly assisted throughout the country by an interpretation of the Contracts Clause that gave their corporate charters firm constitutional protection.

While early interpretation of the Contracts Clause contributed to the expansion of business and industry, the demand for more effective state regulation of private enterprise also increased as a countervailing force in American society. By the early 1830s, even before the end of the Marshall Court era, the state police power was gaining

judicial recognition as a valid rationale for protecting the public health, safety, and general welfare. Responding to the forces of economic and political change accompanying the rise of Jacksonian democracy, the Supreme Court began to narrow the property rights protections afforded by the early interpretation of the Contracts Clause. In *Charles River Bridge Company v. Warren Bridge* (1837), the new Chief Justice, Roger B. Taney, upheld a Massachusetts law of 1828 that authorized the Warren Bridge Company to build a bridge across the Charles River a short distance from the previously chartered, privately owned Charles River Bridge Company, which had for a number of years enjoyed a private monopoly in exacting tolls from the traveling public. Within a short time the Warren Bridge was to become free to the public as part of the Massachusetts highway system. Relying on a 1785 charter authorizing it to build a bridge and charge tolls for a period of 70 years, the Charles River Bridge Company challenged the 1828 law as a violation of its rights under the Contracts Clause, claiming that its charter implied "that the legislature would not authorize another bridge, and especially a free one," alongside the original one. Interpreting the language of the 1785 charter literally, Chief Justice Taney rejected this argument. The charter had not literally granted exclusive rights to the Charles River Bridge Company. Taney reasoned that "while the rights of private property are sacredly guarded, we must not forget that the community also have rights, and that the happiness and well-being of every citizen depends on their faithful preservation."

The long-range decline of the Contracts Clause as a bulwark of vested rights began with the *Charles River Bridge* case of 1837. In *Stone v. Mississippi* (1880) the Court held that Mississippi could prohibit the sale of lottery tickets by a company previously chartered to conduct the lottery business in that state. By the late 1880s the Due Process Clause of the Fourteenth Amendment had supplanted the Contracts Clause as a significant restriction on state regulation of business.

The demise of the Contracts Clause as a limitation on state power was vividly illustrated by the 1934 Supreme Court decision in *Home Building and Loan Association v. Blaisdell.* Here the Court upheld, by a five-to-four vote, a Depression-era state law authorizing a maximum two-year postponement of mortgage foreclosures. Writing for the majority, Chief Justice Charles Evans Hughes concluded that "the reservation of the reasonable exercise of the protective power of the state is read into all contracts." The state's abridgement of the literal terms of thousands of real estate contracts was thus upheld as a matter of public policy.

While the Contracts Clause is no longer a significant restriction on the states, it is still invoked on rare occasions as a constitutional limitation. For example, the Supreme Court held in 1977 that a New Jersey statute violated the Contracts Clause because it impaired the state's obligation to holders of bonds issued by the Port Authority of New York and New Jersey. Neither that decision nor any other rendered by the Court in recent years, however, has resurrected the Contracts Clause as a meaningful restraint on state authority.

See also Articles of Confederation; Due Process, Substantive; Due Process Clauses; Economic Freedom; Fourteenth Amendment; Natural Law and Natural Rights; Marshall, John; Property Rights; Taney, Roger B.

Bibliography

Horowitz, Morton. 1977. *The Transformation of American Law, 1780–1860.* Cambridge, MA: Harvard University Press.

Stephens, Otis H., Jr., and John M. Scheb II. 2003. *American Constitutional Law.* 3rd ed. Belmont, CA: Wadsworth.

Wright, Benjamin F. 1938. *The Contract Clause.* Cambridge, MA: Harvard University Press.

  Otis H. Stephens, Jr., and John M Scheb II

COOPER V. AARON (1958)

This celebrated case stemmed from the efforts of state and local officials to block court-ordered desegregation of a public school. After the Supreme Court's decision in *Brown v. Board of Education* (1954), the federal district court ordered the desegregation of Central High School in Little Rock, Arkansas, effective at the beginning of the 1957–1958 school year. But Governor Orval Faubus called out the National Guard to prevent nine African American students from entering the school. The guard remained on the scene for three weeks

The governor's action prompted the Little Rock School Board to petition the federal district court for instructions. After conducting hearings, the court issued an order "enjoining the Governor and the officers of the Guard from preventing the attendance of Negro children at Central High School, and from otherwise obstructing or interfering with the orders of the court in connection with the plan." Governor Faubus removed the National Guard, but this only exacerbated tensions and increased the likelihood of mob violence. When the African American students attempted to enter the school on September 23, 1957, they were confronted by a large, angry mob. Fearing for the students' safety, local law enforcement officers whisked them from the scene. Two days later President Dwight D. Eisenhower, who had reservations about court-ordered desegregation, sent federal troops to Little Rock to restore public order and provide protection to the black students. The Little Rock Nine, as they were called, were able to complete the school year.

Citing the difficulties created by the continuing opposition of state and local officials, the school board returned to court with a petition to delay implementation of desegregation for two and a half years. The Supreme Court refused to allow the delay. Attaching great importance to the case, the justices heard oral arguments in a special session on September 11, 1958, and rendered their decision two and a half weeks later on September 29. In an unusual step, the Court produced an opinion coauthored by all nine justices. The opinion issued a stern rebuke to Governor Faubus, reminding him of his duty to uphold the Constitution. The Court insisted that "law and order are not here to be preserved by depriving the Negro children of their constitutional rights." The Court acknowledged that "public education is primarily the concern of the States" but pointed out "that such responsibilities, like all other state activity, must be exercised consistently with federal constitutional requirements."

Cooper v. Aaron is important in that the Court, despite changes in its membership, unanimously reaffirmed its commitment to the desegregation of public schools. One might question, however, whether the Court would have been able to take the constitutional high ground had President Eisenhower decided not to send federal troops to Little Rock. In using military force to implement a Supreme Court decision about which he had doubts, Eisenhower was recognizing the authority of the Court to speak with finality on matters of constitutional interpretation. However, the ultimate decision to enforce the Court's authority belonged to the president. Accordingly, *Cooper v. Aaron* is as much a testament to judicial dependency on the executive as an assertion of judicial authority. The lesson is that courts of law alone are ill equipped to protect civil rights and liberties in times of crisis.

See also *Brown v. Board of Education;* Little Rock Crisis; Segregation in Public Education; Warren Court

Bibliography

Patterson, James T. 2002. *Brown v. Board of Education: A Civil Rights Milestone and Its Troubled Legacy.* New York: Oxford University Press.

John M. Scheb II and Otis H. Stephens, Jr.

CORE. *See* Congress of Racial Equality

CORPORAL PUNISHMENT

In colonial America, persons convicted of misdemeanors were generally subjected to corporal punishments such as flogging. In keeping with the English common law and centuries of practice, the misdemeanant would be taken into the public square, bound to the whipping post, and administered as many lashes as were prescribed by law for the offense. The underlying idea was that the public spectacle of painful and humiliating punishment would deter others from engaging in criminal acts.

The American Bill of Rights, ratified in 1791, prohibited the imposition of "cruel and unusual punishments." The framers of the Bill of Rights sought to prevent the use of torture, which had been common in Europe as late as the eighteenth century. However, they did not intend to abolish all forms of corporal punishment. And even if they had so intended, it would have had no effect on the punishments meted out by the state courts, because prior to *Robinson v. California* (1962), the Cruel and Unusual Punishments Clause was deemed to apply only to sentences imposed by the federal courts.

In *Weems v. United States* (1910), the U.S Supreme Court invalidated a sentence of 12 years in irons at hard and painful labor imposed on a man convicted of falsifying public records. In its opinion the Court noted that state courts had up to that time generally sustained corporal punishments in various cases brought under the provisions of state constitutions. However, the Court also noted that the Cruel and Unusual Punishments Clause "is not fastened to the obsolete, but may acquire meaning as public opinion becomes enlightened by a humane justice." This view is very similar to that expressed by Chief Justice Earl Warren in *Trop v. Dulles* (1958): "The Amendment must draw its meaning from the evolving standards of decency that mark the progress of a maturing society."

By the twentieth century, incarceration and monetary fines had replaced corporal punishment as legislatively prescribed and judicially imposed penalties for those convicted of misdemeanors. Still, corporal punishment remained in use in some of the jails and prisons of this country as a mechanism of insuring discipline among inmates. Without question, in many instances the use of corporal punishment in jails and prisons was unnecessary to the maintenance of order and discipline and amounted to wanton violence against inmates. In some cases, this violence took place without the knowledge of supervisory officials. In other cases, it resulted from their consent, explicit or otherwise. Of course, prior to the 1960s, there was little judicial review of and even less public concern for what went on inside the walls of America's prisons and jails. That would change as prisoners acquired and began to exercise the right of access to the courts.

In *Jackson v. Bishop* (1968), the U.S. Court of Appeals for the Eighth Circuit held that the practice of beating inmates with leather straps violated the Cruel and Unusual Punishments Clause. The inmates confined to penal farms within the Arkansas prison system were routinely beaten when they failed to meet performance standards in picking crops. Writing for the court, Judge (later Supreme Court Justice) Harry Blackmun concluded that "the use of the strap in the penitentiaries of Arkansas is punishment which, in this last third of the twentieth century, runs afoul of the Eighth Amendment" and "that the strap's use, irrespective of any precautionary conditions which may be imposed, offends contemporary concepts of decency and human dignity and precepts of civilization which we profess to possess."

Although prison and jail officials no longer prescribe corporal punishment for misconduct in the prison, sometimes guards must use force to maintain discipline and order in the prison or jail, and the courts have recognized their right to do so. However, sometimes guards administer force wantonly and without justification, and sometimes prison officials turn a blind eye to such practices. In *Whitney v. Albers* (1986), the Supreme Court made it clear that the Eighth Amendment prohibits the "unnecessary and wanton infliction of pain" on inmates. Guards who engage in such conduct, and other officials who condone it, are subject to being found liable for damages under 42 U.S.C. § 1983.

Corporal Punishments Administered by Schools and Parents

Historically, public schools routinely administered corporal punishment, usually in the form of paddling, to students who misbehaved. This tradition is reflected in the words of a popular early twentieth-century song: "School days, school days, dear old golden rule days. Reading and writing and 'rithmetic, taught to the tune of a hick'ry stick." The justification for this practice, aside from the need to maintain order and discipline in the schools, was that teachers and principals were acting in loco parentis, that is, in the place of the parents. And, until recently, there were no legal prohibitions against parents subjecting their children to corporal punishments. Of course, corporal punishments that were excessive or lacking in justification could result in criminal charges or civil suits for battery.

In *Ingraham v. Wright* (1977), the U.S. Supreme Court rejected a challenge to the constitutionality of paddling public school students. The Court held that the Cruel and Unusual Punishments Clause was intended only to protect persons convicted of crimes and is inapplicable to corporal punishment administered by public schools. The Court noted that remedies already existed under common law for instances of excessive or unjustified punishments. In the wake of the *Ingraham* decision, some state courts opted to limit school punishment under applicable provisions of their respective state constitutions. In other states, legislatures enacted statutes prohibiting or restricting corporal punishments in schools. And in other cases, restrictions on corporal punishment were enacted at the local level by school boards or other governing bodies. Today, in school districts where paddling is still permitted, parents have the right to exempt their children from such punishments and, if they do not, must be notified when such punishments have been administered.

Recent concern over child abuse has led to a national rethinking of corporal punishment, whether it is imposed by parents or others acting in their stead. And with changing public attitudes, some parents have found themselves the object of official attention after they spanked their children in public. In some instances parents have even been arrested for child abuse after spanking their children in the presence of strangers. Still, polls show that most Americans continue to support the right of parents to administer corporal punishment to their children.

See also Accused, Rights of the; Bill of Rights (American); Bill of Rights, Incorporation of; Blackmun, Harry A.; Common-Law Background of American Civil Rights and Liberties; Criminal Confinement, Conditions of; Cruel and Unusual Punishments Clause; Eighth Amendment; Living Constitution; Parental Rights; Prisoners' Rights; Warren, Earl

Bibliography

Dayton, John. 1994. "Corporal Punishment in Public Schools: The Legal and Political Battle Continues." *Education Law Reporter* 89:729–40.

Scott, George Ryley. 1996. *The History of Corporal Punishment.* n.p.: Merchant Book Company.

Straus, Murray A. 1994. *Beating the Devil out of Them: Corporal Punishment in American Families.* Lexington, MA: Lexington Books.

John M. Scheb II and Otis H. Stephens, Jr.

COUNSEL, INEFFECTIVE ASSISTANCE OF

The Sixth Amendment to the United States Constitution sets forth the essential elements of a fair trial—that it be speedy and public, that witnesses be available and subject to confrontation, and that the accused have the "[a]ssistance" of counsel. Even before the United States Supreme Court interpreted the Sixth Amendment to require states to provide attorneys to those who could not afford their own (see *Gideon v. Wainwright,* 1963), the Court recognized that the assistance of counsel means more than the mere presence of an attorney (see *Powell v. Alabama,* 1932). Counsel, whether retained by the accused or appointed by the state, must provide effective assistance to the accused.

To understand what is meant by effective assistance of counsel, one must understand the essence of the adversarial American criminal justice system. In *Herring v. New York* (1975), the Supreme Court said that the main premise of the adversary system of justice is that "partisan advocacy on both sides of a case will best promote the ultimate objective that the guilty be convicted and the innocent go free."

Thus, effective counsel puts the adversary system to its test, assuring that the system produces just and fair results.

While the Sixth Amendment's assistance of counsel provision has been interpreted to require "effective" assistance, it has not been interpreted to require specific standards of conduct. Lawyers owe basic duties to their clients, including the duty of loyalty, the duty of advocacy, the duty to consult with and keep the client informed, and the duty to use their skill and knowledge to test the evidence offered against the client and ensure the reliability of the trial. Since the purpose of having counsel for the accused is to ensure that the accused receives a fair trial that produces just results, counsel's duty is simply to render "reasonably effective assistance considering all the circumstances."

The Sixth Amendment's right to effective assistance of counsel does not envision the development of a checklist of lawyer's duties. Rather, in evaluating effectiveness, courts must presume that counsel acted reasonably, fulfilling the role envisioned by the adversary system. Courts must also give deference to counsel's decision, recognizing the "countless ways to provide effective assistance of counsel." A court reviewing counsel's performance must evaluate the performance based on the circumstances existing at the time of counsel's performance and not with the unfair benefit of hindsight.

As a result, it is not every error by counsel that renders counsel ineffective. Instead, counsel is ineffective only when "counsel's conduct so undermine[s] the proper functioning of the adversarial process that the trial cannot be relied on as having produced a just result." This is the standard developed by the United States Supreme Court in the landmark case of *Strickland v. Washington* (1984).

The ineffective assistance of counsel standard has two separate parts. The first focuses on counsel's conduct; the second focuses on the result of the trial. For counsel's conduct to fall below the standard for ineffectiveness, counsel must have made serious professional errors resulting in "deficient performance." Second, counsel's deficient performance must have "prejudiced" the client such that the client was deprived of a "trial whose result is reliable." The practical result of the two-prong *Strickland* standard is that an accused who claims to have received ineffective assistance of counsel at trial must prove that counsel engaged in specific acts or omissions that were deficient, and that without those deficiencies a "reasonable probability" exists that "the factfinder would have had a reasonable doubt [as to] guilt."

Because the role of counsel at a sentencing hearing in a capital case is similar to that of counsel at trial, the ineffective assistance of counsel standard applies there as well. When the accused is challenging counsel's performance at a capital sentencing, the accused must establish that "there is a reasonable probability that, absent the errors, the sentencer ... would have concluded that the balance of aggravating and mitigating circumstances did not warrant death."

In three situations, ineffective assistance of counsel is presumed, removing the need for the accused to prove deficient performance and prejudice. These situations are when counsel is "totally absent" or "prevented from assisting" at an important stage of the trial or sentencing, when counsel "entirely fails to subject the prosecution's case to meaningful adversarial testing," and when counsel is asked to assist the accused "under circumstances where competent counsel very likely could not." The three situations are intentionally construed very narrowly.

Most ineffective assistance of counsel claims are raised after an accused has been convicted and has lost on appeal. In collateral proceedings known as postconviction or habeas proceedings, which may be raised in both state and federal courts, the convicted defendant petitions the court for a new trial or capital sentencing, claiming that the earlier trial or sentencing was tainted by ineffective assistance of counsel. On occasion, the defendant will challenge a guilty plea, claiming that counsel was ineffective in advising the defendant to plead guilty. In the collateral proceeding, the defendant bears the burden of satisfying the two prongs of *Strickland*. If the defendant fails to satisfy either requirement, the petition is denied, and

the conviction and sentence stand. If the defendant is successful, the court will order a new trial or sentencing, or, in the event of a set-aside guilty plea, a trial.

See also Accused, Rights of the; Adversary System of Justice; Bill of Rights, Incorporation of; Confrontation, Right of; Counsel, Right to; *Gideon v. Wainwright;* Pleas in Criminal Cases; Public Trial, Right to; Sixth Amendment; Speedy Trial, Right to

Bibliography

Coyne, Randall, and Lyn Entzeroth. 2001. *Capital Punishment and the Judicial Process.* Durham, NC: Carolina Academic Press.

Dripps, Donald A. 1997. "Ineffective Assistance of Counsel: The Case for an *Ex Ante* Parity Standard." *Journal of Criminal Law & Criminology* 88:242–308.

Duncan, Meredith J. 2002. "The (So-Called) Liability of Criminal Defense Attorneys: A System in Need of Reform." *Brigham Young University Law Review* 2002:1–52.

Kirchmeier, Jeffrey L. 1996. "Drink, Drugs, and Drowsiness: The Constitutional Right to Effective Assistance of Counsel and the *Strickland* Prejudice Requirement." *Nebraska Law Review* 75:425 –75.

Penny White

COUNSEL, RIGHT TO

The Sixth Amendment to the United States Constitution provides, "In all criminal prosecutions, the accused shall enjoy the right ... to have the Assistance of Counsel for his defense." State constitutions contain similar provisions. The right to counsel may be the single most important right possessed by persons accused of serious crimes. As the Supreme Court observed in *Gideon v. Wainwright* (1963), "the right of one charged with crime to counsel may not be deemed fundamental and essential in some countries, but it is in ours."

Historically, the right to counsel meant the right to hire an attorney if one could afford to do so. Under the early English common law, persons accused of treason or felonies did not have the right to be represented by counsel, but the common law did recognize a right to counsel in misdemeanor cases. In 1695 Parliament enacted a law recognizing a right to counsel in cases of treason. By the late eighteenth century, the common law recognized a limited right to counsel in felony cases, and in 1836 Parliament passed legislation recognizing the right to counsel for all criminal defendants. Under the common law and the aforementioned acts of Parliament, the right to counsel meant the right to hire a barrister (a lawyer admitted to trial practice) at a person's own expense. It was not until 1903 that Parliament passed the Poor Prisoner's Defense Act, authorizing courts to appoint counsel to represent indigent defendants at public expense.

In the United States, the right to counsel has likewise evolved through both judicial decisions and legislation. The Sixth Amendment has been consistently interpreted to allow defendants to employ counsel in all federal prosecutions, including treason, felony, and misdemeanor cases. Similar provisions in the 50 state constitutions have been interpreted to allow defendants to retain counsel in state criminal prosecutions. Irrespective of state constitutional protection, the accused is protected by the federal Constitution. In *Gideon v. Wainwright* (1963) the Supreme Court held that the Sixth Amendment right to counsel applies to prosecutions in the state courts by way of the Due Process Clause of the Fourteenth Amendment. Today, criminal defendants have the right to retain attorneys to represent them in all types of criminal prosecutions, whether in state court, federal court, or before military tribunals.

The Supreme Court has recognized that indigent defendants have the right to court-appointed counsel in serious criminal cases. The first preliminary statement of this doctrine came in *Powell v. Alabama* (1932), in which the Court ruled that in state death penalty cases, indigents unable to defend themselves because of handicaps such as illiteracy must be given court-appointed counsel.

Although the rule of law in *Powell* covered few defendants, Justice Sutherland, speaking for the Court, made a now classic statement about the critical nature of counsel in many criminal cases:

The right to be heard would be, in many cases, of little avail if it did not comprehend the right to be heard by counsel. Even the intelligent and educated layman has small and sometimes no skill in the science of law.... He lacks both the skill and knowledge adequately to prepare his defense, even though he had a perfect one. He requires the guiding hand of counsel at every step in the proceedings against him. Without it, though he be not guilty, he faces the danger of conviction because he does not know how to establish his innocence.

In 1963, the Supreme Court ruled in *Gideon v. Wainwright* that in all state felony cases, indigent defendants are entitled to court-appointed counsel. Writing for the majority, Justice Black supported his contention that the right to counsel is a fundamental right by noting that the government always hires lawyers for its prosecutorial positions and that when people of means are charged with crime, they tend to hire the best lawyers they can afford. Moreover, Black observed, "From the very beginning, our state and national constitutions and laws have laid great emphasis on procedural safeguards designed to assure fair trials before impartial tribunals in which every defendant stands equal before the law."

In *Argersinger v. Hamlin* (1972), the Supreme Court held that in state cases, defendants cannot be sentenced to jail unless the assistance of court-appointed counsel is made available, regardless of the length of time for which the defendant may be incarcerated. The ruling meant that judges who wished to preserve the option of a jail sentence would have to appoint counsel to indigent defendants prior to trial. This ruling also served to make court-appointed counsel available in misdemeanor cases where the defendant was not entitled to a jury trial. Insofar as the great majority of misdemeanor defendants in state court are not sentenced to jail, however, only a relatively small minority are entitled to appointed counsel under *Argersinger*. This narrow right in state court contrasts sharply with federal cases; in *Johnson v. Zerbst* (1938) the Supreme Court recognized that, in the absence of valid waiver, indigent defendants in federal criminal cases are entitled to appointed counsel.

The right to appointed counsel is not limited to the trial itself, and various Supreme Court cases have extended it to such critical pretrial stages as in-custody interrogation (*Miranda v. Arizona,* 1966), postindictment lineups (*United States v. Wade,* 1967), and the preliminary hearing (*Coleman v. Alabama,* 1970). Indigent defendants are also entitled to appointed counsel when they exercise the right to appeal (*Douglas v. California,* 1963).

The Supreme Court has never indicated how to determine which defendants are able to afford counsel, and different courts use different criteria: whether the defendant has excess of assets over liabilities, whether income falls within or close to federal poverty standards, if one has been released on bail, and the like. Some of the criteria are poor indicators of indigence. For example, many people must borrow money to secure their release on bail, only to have the mere fact of release equated with ability to hire their own counsel.

Although the Supreme Court expanded the right to court-appointed counsel, it never specified the mechanisms by which assistance would be granted. States and counties use three different systems to furnish counsel to indigents, who comprise perhaps 80 to 90 percent of all defendants in criminal court. The commonly used mechanism is the public defender system, under which public defender offices are established to provide representation to indigent defendants on a routine basis. A second system is that of assigned counsel, where indigents are assigned to private attorneys who continue their private practice of law. Finally, a minority of jurisdictions adopt the contract system, under which they invite attorneys or law firms to submit a lump-sum bid for undertaking all or some of the cases over a specified period of time.

The system used to defend indigents often varies considerably from county to county within a state. Large metropolitan areas are most likely to employ public defenders, while less populated areas tend toward assigned counsel. The same county often makes use of two or more systems. For example, the public defender may refer cases in which he or she has a conflict of interest to assigned counsel, or

the contract system may take surplus cases from the public defender.

There are numerous problems with court-appointed counsel. Public defenders are often understaffed and carry huge caseloads. Because the pay is not competitive with private practice, assigned attorneys are commonly younger, relatively inexperienced lawyers or older, less successful ones. The contract system often hires whichever lawyer or firm submits the lowest bid, without regard to reputation or quality of service.

As the law and order movement has gathered momentum during recent decades, many jurisdictions have shifted some of the funding responsibility to indigent defendants, and the courts have generally upheld these provisions. It is now very common for courts to charge defendants for court-appointed counsel—albeit well under market price for private attorneys.

Bibliography

Fellman, David. 1979. *The Defendant's Rights Today.* Madison: University of Wisconsin Press.

George Kiser

COUNTERCULTURE

The term "counterculture" was coined in the 1960s to refer to a social movement among disaffected youth. The movement began with the beatniks of the 1950s, celebrated in Jack Kerouac's iconoclastic novel *On the Road.* It evolved into the hippies of the 1960s and the freaks of the 1970s. The counterculture rejected, or attempted to reject, mainstream social, political, and economic values. The counterculture's protest went beyond the realm of the political. It challenged conventional notions about success and the realization of the American dream. While the New Left advocated radical social change through political means, the counterculture rejected politics altogether. Rather, the counterculture advocated "dropping out" of mainstream society and "doing one's own thing." For the beatniks, hippies, and freaks, dropping out meant rejecting traditional values, institutions, and lifestyles. It meant growing one's hair, wearing unusual clothing, and experimenting with illegal drugs, most notably marijuana and hallucinogens.

In the late 1960s some adherents of the counterculture attempted to "get back to the land" by establishing communal farms dedicated to producing organic vegetables, but most such efforts were soon abandoned. Some, following the example of Jack Kerouac, became vagabonds. Others dabbled in Eastern religions or took up transcendental meditation. Nearly all reveled in rock music—especially the acid rock of Jimi Hendrix, Jefferson Airplane, the Doors, and the Grateful Dead.

Some commentators viewed the counterculture as the beginning of a new phase of American social development—the achievement of a higher consciousness (see, e.g., Roszak 1969). In retrospect, those interpretations seem naive, even comical. Eventually, most of those who had dropped out drifted back into more or less conventional lifestyles, although the illegal drug use often continued. By the mid-1970s, there was little talk of a counterculture. It had not disappeared per se, but it had been absorbed into the larger societal culture. As that occurred, "recreational" use of illicit drugs became more widespread, leading the government to declare the war on drugs that continues to the present time.

The principal significance of the counterculture for civil rights and liberties lies in the expansion of personal freedom that has taken place in the United States since the 1960s. Today, there is greater appreciation for social diversity and less social pressure to conform to rigid notions of social and economic roles. Ultimately, the scope of civil rights and liberties in the United States or any country is determined not by legal or political actions or agencies, but by the people themselves through the evolution of culture.

See also Drugs, Private Use of; Drugs, War on; Liberalism

Bibliography

Anderson, Terry H. 1996. *The Movement and the Sixties.* New York: Oxford University Press.

Gitlin, Todd. 1993. *The Sixties: Years of Hope, Days of Rage.* New York: Bantam.

Roszak, Theodore, 1969. *The Making of a Counter-Culture: Reflections on the Technocratic Society and Its Youthful Opposition.* Garden City, NY: Anchor Books.

John M. Scheb II and Otis H. Stephens, Jr.

COURTS-MARTIAL

A court-martial is a tribunal that has jurisdiction over persons belonging to the military or otherwise subject to military or naval laws. Judges in courts-martial are members of the military and may preside individually or as part of a panel of judges. There is no jury in a court-martial. Courts-martial, however, do not have any jurisdiction over civilians, except in cases of espionage.

Courts-martial arise out of military law. Military law is similar to civilian law, but it is applicable to all members of the military and contains provisions that are not relevant to civilian legal codes. In particular, military law has provisions regarding the military police and the chain of command. For example, it is considered a crime to be late for your job in the military (Article LXXXVI of the Uniform Code of Military Justice [UCMJ]). The UCMJ, which governs the armed forces, sets out its own system of laws and regulations, and it also provides its own set of penalties, including a death penalty. The UCMJ was first enacted by Congress in 1951. Prior to the code's enactment, the military was governed by another body of codes, which had proved to be insufficient during World War II. Notably, the UCMJ expanded the role that lawyers and legal professionals play in courts-martial.

The Constitution provides sufficient authority for the use of courts-martial and military law. Articles I and II give the Congress and the president, respectively, powers over the military, and the Fifth Amendment states that "[n]o person shall be held to answer for a capital, or otherwise infamous crime, unless on a presentment or indictment of a grand jury, except in cases arising in the land or naval forces, or in the militia, when in actual service in time of war or public danger."

Any commanding officer can order that a subordinate be subject to a court-martial hearing. There are three levels of courts-martial. The summary court-martial is heard by a single judge and can only impose penalties of up to one month in prison. In a special court-martial there is a panel of three judges, and these panels can impose penalties of up to six months' imprisonment. Finally, the general court-martial is heard by five judges and can impose penalties up to and including death. The UCMJ allows any person subject to a court-martial to request that the panel of judges include at least one enlisted member of the military; otherwise, judges must hold officers' ranks. Any conviction by a court-martial is considered a felony.

Aside from courts-martial, there are many other measures a commanding officer can take to reprimand a subordinate. The officer may order counseling, give reprimands, assign extra training, take administrative measures (including demotion and discharge), and use Article 15 procedures. Article 15 procedures are akin to courts-martial, except that the commanding officer serves as the judge, and an accused person can refuse an Article 15 procedure. The courts-martial themselves are the most significant forms of military justice.

See also Accused, Rights of the; Death Penalty and the Supreme Court; Due Process, Procedural; Fifth Amendment; Grand Jury; Military Tribunals; Uniform Code of Military Justice

Bibliography

Lurie, Jonathan. 2001. *Pursuing Military Justice: The History of the United States Court of Appeals for the Armed Forces, 1951–1980.* 2nd ed. Princeton, NJ: Princeton University Press.

Rant, James, James J. W. Rant, Jeffrey Blackett, and Jeff Blackett, eds. 2003. *Courts Martial, Discipline, and the Criminal Process in the Armed Forces.* 2nd ed. New York: Blackstone.

Tom Clark

CRIME VICTIMS, RIGHTS OF

Just as definitions of crime have changed over time, so have the protections afforded to crime victims. In earlier epochs, victims of criminal acts were avenged by family or tribal members, not through some formal mechanism or legal system. "Prior to the establishment of centralized political authority associated with the rise of the nation-state, wrongs were typically private matters between victim and offender in the context of their kinship groups" (Reisner and Nelligan 2002, 239). However, in a civil society, the means to restore what was lost must be institutionalized to redress these grievances publicly and peacefully to prevent blood feuds, thereby justifying the categorization of crime based on level of harm inflicted.

Fewer aspects of the American criminal justice system have changed more noticeably than the recent recognition of the rights of crime victims. Previously in the United States, it was generally considered inflammatory and prejudicial for the victims of crime to participate in the judicial process, as it might infringe upon the criminal defendant's constitutional right to a fair trial. Furthermore, because crime was perceived as a wrong against society and the state, victims were given a further subordinated role (Elias 1986). So while it was appropriate for victims to file police reports or participate in trials as witnesses for the prosecution, their participation in the criminal justice process was typically minimized.

However, in recent decades, largely due to an increased social consciousness of the plight of rape victims, changes were instituted that paved the way for the victim's rights movement and the greater participation of victims in the legal process. This coincides with a growing acceptance of the idea that, beyond serving the goals of retribution, deterrence of crime, and the incapacitation or rehabilitation of offenders, the criminal justice system should promote restorative justice. "Of special concern to restorative justice are the needs of crime victims that are not being adequately met by the criminal justice system" (Zehr 2002, 14). According to the restorative justice perspective, the legal system should focusing on redressing harm to individuals and communities through a process of confrontation, mediation, restitution, and reconciliation, all of which require that victims play a significant role in the criminal justice process (Zehr 2002, 22–25).

Because most criminal cases are resolved through negotiated guilty pleas, victims' rights advocates often call for crime victims to become involved in the plea negotiations process. Prosecutors and defense counsel typically resist such efforts and often see victims as interlopers whose participation will make it more difficult to reach agreements. Of course, nothing is more discouraging to the victims of violent crimes than to read in the newspaper that those who victimized them have been released on probation pursuant to a deal with the prosecutor's office. This is why many jurisdictions now require that crime victims be informed of the progress of the cases against those who harmed them so that they will at least be able to come to court to observe the resolution of the process. Indeed, many prosecutors offices now have victim advocates or victims' rights specialists whose job is to keep victims informed.

The needs of victims are addressed through greater participation in the criminal justice process, offender accountability, restitution, and other means of compensation. To institutionalize these changes, some states have adopted Victims' Rights Amendments (VRAs) to their state constitutions as well as other statutes to include victim impact testimony in death penalty cases, restitution, and victim compensation funds.

One way to reduce the financial harm of victims is through restitution, where courts order the offender to repay victims for their losses. The means and goals of restitution are varied and may include direct compensation to the victim, community service, working for the victim, and "sometimes unusual paybacks devised between victim and offender" (Umbreit 2003, 29). One important point is that financial compensation is often not the main issue, but rather the acknowledgement of the defendant's responsibility that accompanies the payment of restitution or reparations. Another example of restitution involves victim compensation funds, where in some states court-imposed costs are accompanied by a small fee, which is placed in a victim compensation fund. These funds are tapped in cases when the defendant is unable to pay restitution or is be incarcerated and not in a position to provide any compensation. Unfortunately, in most jurisdictions it is difficult to qualify for the money, and funds are unavailable for many types of victims.

Another controversial component of victims' rights concerns the effect of their testimony during the sentencing phase of capital cases. Victim impact statements describe the tragedy and suffering of the victim and his or her family (Territo, Halsted, and Bromley 2004, 405). Sentencing judges take these statements into account when considering the physical, financial, and emotional impact of crimes upon victims and others (Territo, Halsted, and Bromley 2004, 156). One perceived problem of victim impact statements is their allegedly prejudicial effect on capital cases, where a judge or jury might be moved to execute a defendant based upon the emotional impact of these statements. Nevertheless, in *Payne v. Tennessee* (1991), the U.S. Supreme Court ruled that the Eighth Amendment does not prohibit the consideration of victim impact statements that relate the emotional impact of murder upon the family or other loved ones.

This ruling cemented the additional participation of victims (or others on their behalf) within the criminal justice process. The enhanced focus on victims' rights and restorative justice is an important change in American criminal justice.

See also Accused, Rights of the; Plea Bargaining; Restitution; Retribution; Victim Impact Evidence in Death Penalty Cases

Bibliography

Elias, Robert. 1986. *The Politics of Victimization: Victims, Victimology, and Human Rights*. New York: Oxford University Press.

Reisner, Ronald L., and Peter J. Nelligan. 2002. "A Comparative Analysis of Victim Impact Testimony in Capital Cases in New Jersey and Texas." In *Visions for Change: Crime and Justice in the Twenty-First Century*, ed. Rosalyn Muraskin and Albert R. Roberts. 3rd ed. Upper Saddle River, NJ: Prentice Hall.

Territo, Leonard, James B. Halsted, and Max L. Brom-
ley. 2004. *Crime and Justice in America: A Human
Perspective.* 6th ed. Upper Saddle River, NJ: Pearson
Hall.

Umbreit, Mark S., Betty Vos, Robert B. Coates, and
Katherine A. Brown. 2003. *Facing Violence: The Path
of Restorative Justice and Dialogue.* Monsey, NY:
Criminal Justice Press.

Zehr, Howard. 2002. *The Little Book of Restorative
Justice.* Intercourse, PA: Good Books.

Keith Clement

CRIMINAL CONFINEMENT, CONDITIONS OF

In recent decades the federal courts have made
it clear that the Eighth Amendment prohibition
of "cruel and unusual punishments" applies to
conditions of confinement in the nation's prisons
and jails. This was not always the case. Prior to the
1960s the courts adopted a hands-off approach
when dealing with questions of prisoners' rights.
The reasons for this attitude ranged from the notion that prisoners were essentially slaves of the
states to the argument that the separation of powers doctrine required the judiciary to stay out of
the affairs of the executive branch, which manages
the prisons. Other reasons given were the lack of
judicial expertise in prison affairs, the potential for
a flood of litigation, and the need to conserve state
fiscal resources. Beginning in the 1960s, the federal
courts rejected these arguments and moved into the
area of prisoners' rights.

Originally the Eighth Amendment was only
intended to prevent the use of barbarous types of
punishment, such as those suffered by the English
under the reigns of the Stuart kings. In 1910 the
United States Supreme Court slightly widened
this interpretation in *Weems v. United States* when
it stated that for "a principle to be vital, [it] must
be capable of wider application than the mischief
which gave it birth." After being convicted of falsifying a document, Weems had been sentenced to 12
years and one day in prison, where he was forced to
wear chains and perform hard labor. In overturning his sentence, the Supreme Court held that the
Cruel and Unusual Punishments Clause "is not
fastened to the obsolete but may acquire meaning as
public opinion becomes enlightened by a humane
justice." The Court went on to declare that "it is a
precept of justice that punishment for crime should
be graduated and proportioned to offense."

In *Trop v. Dulles* (1958), Chief Justice Earl Warren stated that the Eighth Amendment's Cruel and
Unusual Punishments Clause "must draw its meaning from the evolving standards of decency that
mark the progress of a maturing society." Although
this comment was dictum, it reflected Warren's
belief that the Constitution was a living document
that should not be bound solely by the conditions
existent when it was written. This decision set the
stage for increased judicial receptivity to claims
brought by prisoners.

In *Monroe v. Pape* (1961) the Supreme Court
held that government officials could be held liable
under 42 U.S.C. § 1983 for depriving an individual, under color of state authority, of rights guaranteed by the Fourteenth Amendment. Additionally
Monroe allowed individuals' claims to be brought in
the federal courts. Section 1983 became the normal
means by which free people and prisoners could
challenge civil rights violations, including those
related to conditions of confinement and Eighth
Amendment rights.

One of the most notorious cases involving prison conditions was that of the Arkansas prison
system, which was scrutinized in a series of federal
lawsuits beginning in 1969. The worst conditions
existed at prison farms run largely by senior prisoners entrusted with the job of controlling their fellow
inmates. Without proper supervision by prison officials, the so-called trusties smuggled in weapons,
liquor, and drugs and sold them to other inmates.
They hoarded food purchased for the inmates and
forced them to pay for their meals. The trusties
employed fear, intimidation, violence, and even torture to maintain their grip over the other prisoners.
Prisoners were held in "punitive isolation" (solitary
confinement) for indeterminate periods of time.
Medical care was almost totally inadequate at these

prison farms, and the prisoners endured appalling sanitary conditions.

In a series of decisions handed down during the 1970s, a federal district judge issued detailed orders aimed at remedying the conditions in the Arkansas prison system. In *Hutto v. Finney* (1978), the Supreme Court upheld these orders, affirming the conclusion that conditions of confinement were subject to judicial review under the Eighth Amendment. The Court also recognized that trial judges should have broad discretion in fashioning orders to remedy unconstitutional prison conditions, although this discretion would be limited in 1996 when Congress passed the Prison Litigation Reform Act. Furthermore, in *Rhodes v. Chapman* (1981) the Court stated that prison conditions, alone or in combination, may be violative if inmates are deprived of the minimal civilized measure of life's necessities.

In 1992, the American Civil Liberties Union reported that 24 out of 53 jurisdictions (50 states plus the District of Columbia, Puerto Rico, and the Virgin Islands) in the United States were operating their prisons under court orders or consent decrees. Eleven states had their entire prison systems under court control, according to the report. Courts were looking into challenges relating to conditions such as sanitation, fire safety, medical care, mental health care, diet, exercise, and protection of inmates from assaults. In recent years, courts have examined the conditions existing in many city and county jails, which are often worse than conditions of large-scale state and federal prisons.

The Court began a partial retreat in the area of prisoners' rights when it held in *Wilson v. Seiter* (1991) that prisoners challenging their conditions of confinement would have to prove that officials had a culpable state of mind. The minimum threshold standard of culpability was held to be deliberate indifference by the officials, a standard that previously had been applied in a case where a prisoner challenged the quality of medical care he received (*Estelle v. Gamble,* 1976).

The Prison Litigation Reform Act of 1996 restricted a prisoner's ability to file lawsuits and further narrowed judicial remedies. Legislative history reveals that the intention of the bill was to limit frivolous prisoner litigation and to end micromanagement by the courts of the prisons. The U.S. Department of Justice (1996), however, has found that there have been many meritorious prisoner suits that demonstrated sadistic beatings by guards, failure to provide security against rapes and assaults by inmates, prison overcrowding, sewage overflows in cells, and mixing the insane in with other inmates.

The number of prisoners' conditions of confinement suits in federal courts has dropped since the bill required that inmates exhaust the facility's grievance process prior to filing in the federal courts and pay their own court costs. While inmates continue to bring suits, the barriers are higher today then they were when the Court first began accepting these cases. Today inmates seek relief in the state courts more often than in the federal judiciary.

See also Corporal Punishment; Cruel and Unusual Punishments Clause; Eighth Amendment; Prisoners' Rights; Warren, Earl

Bibliography

Palmer, John W., and Stephen E. Palmer. 2003. *Constitutional Rights of Prisoners.* 7th ed. Cincinnati, OH: Anderson Publishing.

Sanabria, Jason D., and Farmer V. Brennan. 1995. "Do Prisoners Have Any Rights Left under the Eighth Amendment?" *Whittier Law Review* 16:1113.

Wilson, Jennifer. 2002. "The Prison Litigation Reform Act's Physical Injury Requirement Bars Meritorious Lawsuits: Was It Meant To?" *UCLA Law Review* 49:1655.

Caryl Segal

CRIMINAL SYNDICALISM

"Criminal syndicalism" is an antiquated term, a relic of the first Red scare of the early twentieth century. After the Communist Party seized power in Russia in 1917, there was an upsurge in radical political activity in the United States and Europe. In the United States, political authorities sought to suppress radical activity through a variety of legal and extralegal means. One measure was the enactment of the criminal syndicalism laws by state legislatures across America. Between 1917 and 1920, 20 states adopted laws proscribing criminal syndicalism. California's version of the law, enacted in 1919, defined criminal syndicalism as "any doctrine or precept advocating, teaching or aiding and abetting the commission of crime, sabotage, or unlawful acts of force and violence or unlawful methods of terrorism as a means of accomplishing a change in industrial ownership or control or effecting any political change." The statute made it a felony, punishable by imprisonment, for any person to organize or knowingly become a member of "any organization, society, group or assemblage of persons organized or assembled to advocate, teach or aid and abet criminal syndicalism."

In *Whitney v. California* (1927), the U.S. Supreme Court upheld California's criminal syndicalism statute against a challenge based on, among other things, the First Amendment freedoms of speech and assembly. Writing for the Court, Justice Edward T. Sanford noted that

the offense denounced by the Act is the combining with others in an association for the accomplishment of the desired ends through the advocacy and use of criminal and unlawful methods. It partakes of the nature of a criminal conspiracy. That such united and joint action involves even greater danger to the public peace and security than the isolated utterances and acts of individuals is clear.

Forty-two years later, a very different Supreme Court reflecting a very different time in American history struck down the criminal syndicalism laws as violations of the First Amendment. In *Brandenburg v. Ohio* (1969), the Supreme Court ruled that a state cannot prohibit "mere advocacy," regardless of its content, nor can it prohibit "assembly with others merely to advocate the described type of action" unless there is "imminent lawless action." The Court concluded its opinion in *Brandenburg*

by explicitly overruling *Whitney v. California,* noting that it had been "thoroughly discredited by later decisions." This decision sounded the death knell for criminal syndicalism laws throughout the United States.

See also *Brandenburg v. Ohio;* Clear and Present Danger Doctrine; Clear and Probable Danger Doctrine; Communist Party USA; First Amendment; Smith Act; Speech, Freedom of

Bibliography

Dowell, Eldridge Foster. 1939. *A History of Criminal Syndicalism Legislation in the United States.* Baltimore: Johns Hopkins University Press.
Stephens, Otis H., and John M. Scheb II. 1998. *American Civil Liberties.* Belmont, CA: Wadsworth.

John M. Scheb II and Otis H. Stephens, Jr.

CRITICAL PRETRIAL STAGES

The term "critical pretrial stages" refers to steps in the criminal process prior to trial that the courts have identified as being crucial to the fair administration of justice. As the Supreme Court pointed out in *United States v. Wade* (1967), "today's law enforcement machinery involves critical confrontations of the accused by the prosecution at pretrial proceedings where the results might well settle the accused's fate and reduce the trial itself to a mere formality." It should also be pointed out that the overwhelming majority of criminal cases do not result in trials but rather are resolved through plea bargaining. It is therefore extremely important that defendants be represented by counsel during the pretrial process.

In *Gideon v. Wainwright* (1963), the Supreme Court held that indigent persons accused of felonies are entitled to representation at public expense. But the *Gideon* decision left open the question as to when the right to appointed counsel comes into play. Writing for the Supreme Court in *United States v. Wade* (1967), Justice William Brennan observed that "the accused is guaranteed that he need not stand alone against the State at any stage of the prosecution, formal or informal, in court or out, where counsel's absence might derogate from the accused's right to a fair trial." Brennan noted that "[t]he presence of counsel at such critical confrontations, as at the trial itself, operates to assure that the accused's interests will be protected consistently with our adversary theory of criminal prosecution." In *Wade* the Court reversed a conviction where an indigent defendant was required to participate in a lineup without giving notice to his appointed lawyer. Noting that the lineup "was a critical stage of the prosecution," Justice Brennan concluded that the failure to notify Wade's appointed attorney prior to the procedure was a denial of the right to counsel.

In other cases, the Supreme Court has identified preliminary hearings (see *White v. Maryland,* 1963), postindictment interrogations (see *Massiah v. United States,* 1964), and arraignments (see *Hamilton v. Alabama,* 1961) as critical pretrial stages. The government's failure to provide indigent defendants with counsel at these crucial events will result in a reversal of a defendant's conviction on the ground that the right of counsel has been abridged. However, because the Supreme Court has held that the right to counsel means the "effective assistance of competent counsel" (see *McMann v. Richardson,* 1970), it is necessary that public defenders and other appointed counsel do more than merely appear with the accused at the critical pretrial stages. As Justice Sandra Day O'Connor noted in her opinion for the Supreme Court in *Strickland v. Washington* (1984), counsel must "consult with the defendant on important decisions and ... keep the defendant informed of important developments in the course of the prosecution."

See also Arraignment; Brennan, William J., Jr.; Counsel, Ineffective Assistance of; Counsel, Right to; *Gideon v. Wainwright;* Initial Appearance in Criminal Cases; Interrogation and Confessions; Lineups and Identification Procedures; O'Connor, Sandra Day; Plea Bargaining; Preliminary Hearing; Probable Cause; Self-Representation

John M. Scheb II and Otis H. Stephens, Jr.

CRUEL AND UNUSUAL PUNISHMENTS CLAUSE

The Eighth Amendment to the United States Constitution provides that "[e]xcessive bail shall not be required, nor excessive fines imposed, nor cruel and unusual punishments inflicted." Its provisions were copied nearly verbatim from the English Bill of Rights, which had been enacted a century earlier, and its roots can be traced back to the Magna Carta (1215). The framers intended for the prohibition against cruel and unusual punishments to prevent the federal government from torturing, quartering, disemboweling, or otherwise inflicting barbarous sanctions upon criminal defendants.

The Supreme Court arguably expanded the scope of the Cruel and Unusual Punishments Clause in *Weems v. United States* (1910), when it struck down a sentence as disproportionate to the crime committed. Weems, convicted of making a false entry into a public financial ledger, was sentenced to 15 years of hard labor in chains. The Court found that such harsh punishment, which was more severe than that authorized for some forms of homicide, inciting rebellion, robbery, and other crimes, violated the Eighth Amendment.

The ambiguity of the phrase "cruel and unusual punishments" raises a fundamental question about how it should be interpreted. Does it prohibit only those sanctions considered cruel and unusual at the time it was enacted or does its meaning change over time?

The Supreme Court confronted this issue in *Trop v. Dulles* (1958). After being convicted of desertion during World War II, Trop was dishonorably discharged from the army and stripped of his United States citizenship. In a plurality opinion, Chief Justice Earl Warren applied contemporary values, not historical arguments, to conclude that denationalization of Trop violated the Eighth Amendment. He noted that the contours of the Cruel and Unusual Punishments Clause are not fixed; instead, the "[a]mendment must draw its meaning from the evolving standards of decency that mark the progress of a maturing society."

Originally, the Eighth Amendment only applied to the federal government. In *Robinson v. California* (1962), however, the Court extended the application of the Cruel and Unusual Punishments Clause to states via the Fourteenth Amendment, striking down a state statute that criminalized the mere status of being a narcotic addict.

A number of important Supreme Court cases interpreting the Cruel and Unusual Punishments Clause have involved the death penalty. In *Furman v. Georgia* (1972), a sharply divided Court concluded that the death penalty as it was being applied constituted cruel and unusual punishment in violation of the Eighth Amendment. The Court held that capital punishment could not be imposed without specific legal guidelines as to both the crimes and conditions meriting a death sentence.

Furman resulted in a four-year moratorium on executions in the United States. In *Gregg v. Georgia* (1976), however, a plurality of the Court held that capital punishment for the crime of murder did not constitute a per se violation of the Cruel and Unusual Punishments Clause where the discretion of a judge or jury to impose death was properly constrained and where it was limited to cases where one or more statutory aggravating factors were present.

Other significant Supreme Court decisions involving Eighth Amendment challenges to capital punishment include *Coker v. Georgia* (1977), which prohibits the imposition of death for rape; *Ford v. Wainwright* (1986), which bars the execution of a prisoner who is insane; *Stanford v. Kentucky* (1989), which permits the death penalty for criminal defendants who were minors at the time they committed their crimes; and *Atkins v. Virginia* (2002), which invalidates the execution of the mentally retarded. *Atkins* is particularly significant because it reversed the earlier decision of the Court in *Penry v. Lynaugh* (1989) due to a significant shift in societal values during the intervening 13 years, as more states had enacted specific prohibitions against the practice.

The conflict observed within the Supreme Court over capital cases is mirrored to a large degree in proportionality challenges to noncapital sentences.

In *Rummel v. Estelle* (1980), a five-to-four Court affirmed a Texas three strikes statute, which imposed a mandatory life sentence with the possibility of parole upon the conviction of a third felony. Rummel, who had previously been convicted of the fraudulent use of a credit card and passing a forged check for a combined total of slightly more than $100, was subsequently found guilty of theft in the amount of $120.75. He challenged his sentence of life in prison as grossly disproportionate to the seriousness of his offenses in violation of the Cruel and Unusual Punishments Clause.

The majority distinguished its prior decision in *Weems* on the basis that it had involved a challenge not just to the length of the sentence, but also to the other particularly harsh conditions that were imposed after conviction. In the end, the Court said it was unwilling to substitute its judgment for that of the Texas legislature in determining under what circumstances a sentence of life in prison is justified for a three-time felon both to deter future recidivism and to separate from the rest of society those individuals who repeatedly violate its norms.

Just three years later, however, the Supreme Court seemingly contradicted itself in *Solem v. Helm* (1983). Helm was sentenced to life in prison without the possibility of parole after being convicted of his seventh nonviolent felony. This time a bare majority concluded that the sentence constituted cruel and unusual punishment contrary to the Eighth Amendment. The Court said that its decision was guided by three objective factors: (1) the seriousness of the offense and the severity of the punishment, (2) the sentences imposed upon other defendants in the same state, and (3) sentences for the same crime in other states. It distinguished its earlier decision on the ground that Rummel had been eligible for release after just 12 years, while Helm had no opportunity whatsoever for parole.

The Court appeared to shift course yet again in *Harmelin v. Michigan* (1991), when a five-to-four majority held that a mandatory sentence of life in prison without the possibility of parole for a single conviction of possessing more than 650 grams of cocaine did not violate the Cruel and Unusual Punishment Clause. It rejected Harmelin's claim that the individualized sentencing and consideration of mitigating factors required by the Eighth Amendment in death penalty cases should be extended to the noncapital context. Noting that severe mandatory punishments indeed may be cruel under some circumstances, it nevertheless insisted that they were not unusual because they have been imposed throughout the history of the United States.

The Cruel and Unusual Punishments Clause has been at the center of some of the Supreme Court's most important and controversial decisions. As both legislative sanctions for criminal conduct and contemporary societal values toward punishment continue to evolve, sometimes in opposite directions, the Eighth Amendment promises to remain one of the most dynamic areas of constitutional jurisprudence well into the future.

See also Accused, Rights of the; Bill of Rights, Incorporation of; Corporal Punishment; Criminal Confinement, Conditions of; Death Penalty, Crimes Punishable by the; Death Penalty and Mental Competence; Death Penalty and Racial Discrimination; Death Penalty and the Supreme Court; Death Penalty for Juveniles; Death-Qualified Jury; Due Process, Procedural; *Furman v. Georgia; Gregg v. Georgia;* Habitual Offender Laws; Magna Carta; Prisoners' Rights; *Robinson v. California;* Three Strikes Laws

Bibliography

Melusky, Joseph A., and Keith A. Pesto. 2003. *Cruel and Unusual Punishment: Rights and Liberties under the Law.* Santa Barbara, CA: ABC-Clio.

Tubb, Kristin O'Donnell. 2005. *Freedom from Cruel and Unusual Punishment.* San Diego, CA: Greenhaven Press.

Danton Asher Berube

CRUZAN, NANCY. *See* Right to Die

CURFEWS

A curfew is a regulation, usually established in the criminal law, that requires that people be off the streets by a certain time of night. Although most curfews involve restrictions on juveniles, the law recognizes that governments can also impose curfews to cope with emergencies. State laws usually grant local governments the authority to impose limited curfews during emergencies where floods, fires, riots, looting, and other situations threaten the safety and welfare of a community. Curfews restrict a person's right of movement, but the Supreme Court has stated that the constitutional right to travel may be legitimately curtailed when a community has been ravaged by flood, fire, or disease, and its safety and welfare are threatened (see *Zemel v. Rusk,* 1965). Courts generally uphold the exercise of emergency powers by local governing bodies or their authorized representatives to declare a curfew where life and property are threatened as long as the curfew regulations are reasonable. To be reasonable, curfew regulations must not be directed at any one class of persons, must not unduly restrict the right of expression, and must allow necessary exemptions.

In April 1992, widespread rioting, looting, and arson occurred in Los Angeles County following the jury verdict acquitting police officers in the Rodney King beating. Long Beach, California, imposed curfew regulations that prohibited anyone from being on the public streets and in public places between 7:00 p.m. and 6:00 a.m. as long as the emergency existed. The regulations were not directed at any particular class or group, regulated conduct and not the content of speech, exempted law enforcement and firefighters, and permitted arrest of only those who refused, after notice, to obey the curfew. A California appellate court upheld curfew regulations (see *In re Juan C.,* 1994).

In an attempt to combat juvenile crime and protect children by keeping them off the streets at night, most large cities and many counties have enacted curfew ordinances. While restrictions vary considerably, most curfew laws define juveniles as unmarried persons under age 18 and prohibit them from being on public streets or in other public places from midnight to 6:00 a.m., unless accompanied by a parent or guardian or another adult approved by the juvenile's parent or guardian. Many curfew ordinances provide that parents and guardians violate the ordinance if they knowingly allow their child to commit a violation. Curfew laws often provide exceptions concerning work, school and civic events, travel, and emergencies.

Considerable litigation has ensued concerning the validity of curfews for juveniles. Those who seek to sustain them argue that a juvenile curfew is a valid exercise of the government's police power and its power as *parens patriae*. They liken the curfew regulations to requirements that minors are required to attend school and are prohibited from purchasing alcoholic beverages and are subject to restrictions on operation of motor vehicles. Challengers contend that curfew regulations are vague and violate First Amendment rights of association, abridge Fourth Amendment rights to be free from unreasonable detention, deny juveniles the equal protection of the law, and interfere with parental rights.

In *City of Wadsworth v. Owens* (1987), the Ohio Supreme Court struck down a city ordinance that prohibited anyone under age 18 from being on the streets, sidewalks, or other public places during certain nighttime hours, unless accompanied by a parent or some other responsible adult having the parent's permission. The court found the ordinance was unconstitutionally overbroad, pointing out that it contained no exceptions, thereby restricting a minor's church, school, and work activities. Courts in New Jersey, Hawaii, and Washington State have also found curfew ordinances unconstitutional. On the other hand, in *Panora v. Simmons* (1989), the Iowa Supreme Court upheld an ordinance making it unlawful for any minor to be or remain upon any street or in any public place between 10:00 p.m. and 5:00 a.m. The ordinance provided exceptions for a minor accompanied by a parent or other adult custodian and for a minor traveling between home and places of employment, and to church, civic, or school functions.

More recent curfew ordinances that have been upheld have included an expanded number of exceptions. For example, in May 1997, Pinellas Park, Florida, adopted a curfew ordinance along the lines described above. In addition to permitting a juvenile to be accompanied by a parent or adult when authorized by a custodial parent, the ordinance includes numerous exceptions, such as instances when a juvenile is exercising First Amendment rights to attend religious, political, and governmental meetings or events sponsored by civic and governmental groups, during or when a juvenile is going to and from lawful employment and school-sponsored or theme-park events, when a juvenile is on the sidewalk at home or at a neighbor's home with the neighbor's permission, or when a juvenile is involved in interstate travel. The trial court, applying a strict scrutiny test, invalidated the ordinance on the basis that it violates a juvenile's parents' fundamental right to raise their children without governmental intrusion. In *State v. T. M.* (2000), a Florida appellate court applied a heightened scrutiny test and reversed the trial court, noting that the ordinance includes adequate exceptions to limit the scope of the curfew. A few months later, in *J. P. v. State,* the same appellate court upheld the juvenile curfew ordinance of Tampa, Florida, pointing out that the ordinance substantially relates to important governmental interests, provides adequate exceptions that limit the scope of the curfew, and focuses enforcement on the prevention of juvenile crime and victimization. Courts in Texas; Virginia; and Washington, D.C., have also upheld curfew ordinances.

Those who oppose curfews recognize the authority of parents to impose the restrictions, but they claim the government should not intrude into the parental sphere. They also point to studies showing no correlation between arrests for curfew violations (which are quite common) and the incidence of juvenile crime. The American Civil Liberties Union has been very active in attacking curfew laws in the courts. In a September 1999 press release, ACLU of New Jersey legal director Lenora Lapidus observed that "police already have the ability to arrest juvenile criminals; the curfew adds nothing more than the discretion to arrest the innocent as well." In her view, "[t]he proper response to juvenile crime is to arrest the criminals, not to place thousands of law-abiding young people under house arrest."

Despite the controversial nature of juvenile curfews, law enforcement officials and local governing bodies overwhelmingly support these measures. They are likely to remain on the scene as long as juvenile crime continues to plague our nation's cities, although to be upheld, the ordinances must recognize reasonable exceptions.

See also American Civil Liberties Union; Association, Freedom of; Equal Protection Clause; First Amendment; Fourth Amendment; House Arrest; Juvenile Justice; *Parens Patriae,* Doctrine of; Parental Rights; Police Power; Rodney King Incident; Vagueness Doctrine

John M. Scheb II and Otis H. Stephens, Jr.

CURTILAGE. *See* Open Fields Doctrine

CWA. *See* Concerned Women for America

D

DARROW, CLARENCE. *See* Evolution/Creationism Controversy

DARWIN, CHARLES. *See* Evolution/Creationism Controversy

DEATH PENALTY, CRIMES PUNISHABLE BY THE

American legal tradition has always countenanced capital punishment. Murder and treason were enduring colonial capital offenses, just as they are today. The 1641 Massachusetts "Body of Liberties," for example, listed treason and four types of biblically referenced murder (willfully, in passion, by guile, as the result of false witness) among its 12 capital offenses. But petty property crimes (Virginia had many relating to tobacco), crimes against morality and religion (as in New England), and even the striking of one's parent (New York, 1665) were also, at least nominally, death penalty offenses. Subsequently, when the Constitution gave both individual states and the federal government the authority to write laws, the very first Congress made rape and murder capital offenses.

Murder, in all its permutations, is the constant core offense in capital crime statutes. Treason, rape, arson, and kidnapping are historically, after murder, the most frequently cited crimes worthy of the death penalty. Still others, such as colonial bestiality, pre-Civil War slave crimes, horse theft,

drug kingpin statutes, train wrecking and airline hijacking, reflect a *guerre de jour* fear that is often regional or particular to a given time.

A number of the reform efforts have shaped modern death penalty cases. Pennsylvania, intending to limit mandatory death penalty for murder, introduced "degrees of murder" in 1794. Tennessee introduced "discretionary use" of the death penalty for all capital crimes in 1838. The United States Supreme Court's ruling in *Furman v. Georgia* (1972), which held the death penalty unconstitutional as then applied, resulted in the rewriting of all death penalty laws, using the previously crafted Model Penal Code as a guide. Capital punishment cases became bifurcated into guilt and penalty phases. Where previously only a plea of guilty could also accommodate a plea for mercy, now mercy or death was a tailored judgment rendered after a finding of guilt, in a separate proceeding that considered mitigating and aggravating circumstances. *Coker v. Georgia* (1977) found death a disproportionate and therefore unconstitutional penalty for the rape of an adult woman. Finally, many individual state reforms now set age limits for executions and prohibit execution of the mentally retarded.

Thirty-eight states currently mandate the death penalty for crimes of murder (generally called first-degree or capital murder) with at least one (from as many as 18) aggravating circumstances. Few states still have non-homicide capital crimes. Since *Furman*, approximately 60 offenses have been designated as federal death penalty crimes. Most involve murder with qualifying circumstances, but espionage, treason, attempted or planned murder of particular targets, and major drug trafficking are also included. Federal judicial guidelines regarding "cruel and unusual punishments" are also applicable to the states through the Fourteenth Amendment's Due Process Clause.

Jurisdictions without capital crimes are also part of the American legal tradition. The Quaker colony of West Jersey was founded without a death penalty. Territorial Michigan was the first to abolish the death penalty in 1846 for all crimes except treason. Rhode Island (1852–1882) and Wisconsin (since 1853) were the first states to decapitalize all crimes without exception. 24 states have, sometime in their history (some more than once), abolished the death penalty. Currently, 12 states, since the date cited, have no death penalty: Alaska (1957), Hawaii (1957), Iowa (1965), Maine (1887), Massachusetts (1984), Michigan (1846), Minnesota (1911), North Dakota (1915), Rhode Island (1852), Vermont (1965), West Virginia (1965), and Wisconsin (1853).

See also Bill of Rights (American); Bill of Rights, Incorporation of; Cruel and Unusual Punishments Clause; Death Penalty and Racial Discrimination; Death Penalty for Juvenile Offenders; Eighth Amendment; *Furman v. Georgia; Gregg v. Georgia;* Sentencing, Eighth Amendment and

Bibliography

Bedau, Hugo Adam, ed. 1997. *The Death Penalty in America.* New York: Oxford University Press.

Bowers, William J. 1984. *Legal Homicide.* Boston: Northeastern University Press.

Kevin Collins

DEATH PENALTY AND MENTAL INCOMPETENCE

Since the reinstatement of the death penalty in *Gregg v. Georgia* (1976) the issue of the execution

of mentally disabled defendants has created controversy and debate. In 1986, the United States Supreme Court addressed the issue in review of a habeas corpus petition challenging Florida's procedure for reviewing the competency of mentally disabled condemned defendants. In *Ford v. Wainwright* (1986), the Supreme Court prohibited the execution of mentally incompetent offenders and mandated adversarial competency proceedings prior to such attempted executions.

The Court was asked to examine a Florida statutory scheme to determine if it violated Fourteenth Amendment due process standards. Under that statutory scheme, a panel of three psychiatrists conducted a 30-minute group interview with the condemned prisoner. In this instance the panel determined that the defendant, Alvin Ford, understood the death penalty; however, four other psychiatrists found him to be psychotic and concluded that he did not understand why he was being executed. Under Florida's scheme the governor was empowered to make an unreviewable decision based solely upon the conclusions of the three-member panel despite the findings of the dissenting group.

A five-member majority of the U.S. Supreme Court held that the Eighth Amendment's Cruel and Unusual Punishment Clause prohibited the execution of an insane person. The Court did not define insanity, but the plurality decision ruled that a person must be aware of the impending execution and the prisoner must understand why he or she is going to be executed. The plurality and Justices Lewis Powell and Sandra Day O'Connor agreed that Florida's competency procedure violated due process standards and that Ford had not been afforded a full and fair hearing.

Mental health professionals urged a comprehensive psychological assessment in the process, rather than the single interview conducted only by psychiatrists. The Court determined that the condemned should be permitted to present evidence from mental health experts as well.

The debate did not end there, however, and in 1989 the Court again addressed the issue of whether the execution of the mentally retarded violated the

Eighth Amendment proscription against cruel and unusual punishments. In *Penry v. Lynaugh* the Court declined to find an Eighth Amendment violation, determining instead that mental retardation would be considered as a mitigating factor. Penry, who had the mental age of a seven-year-old, was convicted of rape and murder in Texas and sentenced to death. He challenged the trial court's refusal to instruct the jury that it could consider his mental retardation as a mitigating factor.

Penry's attorneys urged the Texas Supreme Court to adopt a per se rule that the execution of the retarded constituted cruel and unusual punishment. That Court declined, and the case proceeded into the federal court on habeas corpus review, eventually reaching the U.S. Supreme Court. Justice O'Connor, writing for a majority, rejected the claim that the Eighth Amendment's proscription of cruel and unusual punishment prohibits the execution of the retarded. Instead, the Court ruled that the jury should have been allowed to consider the defendant's mental retardation as a mitigating factor in weighing the punishment to be imposed. The Court determined that such instructions were essential to a jury expressing its sentence as a "reasoned moral response." The Court declined to establish a per se rule, rather, ruling that cases should be reviewed on an individual basis to weigh personal responsibility based on individual cognitive, volitional, and moral capacity to act with the degree of culpability required in capital cases. Mental age alone is too vague a factor upon which to establish a per se rule.

In 2002, the Supreme Court revisited the issue in the case of *Atkins v. Virginia* and ruled that the application of the death penalty to defendants with mental retardation is per se cruel and unusual, overturning its decision in *Penry v. Lynaugh*. Drawing on earlier language that the basic concept underlying the Eighth Amendment is the dignity of man, Justice John Paul Stevens concluded that a review of legislation in 19 states, and the federal government, established a consistency of the direction of change and as powerful evidence that society views mentally retarded defendants as "categorically less culpable than the average offender."

The majority discussed three policy considerations that weigh against executing the mentally retarded: relative culpability, the relationship between mental retardation and the purposes served by the death penalty, and the strength of the procedural protections that may not be afforded mentally retarded defendants. Because of problems with "reasoning, judgment, and control of their impulses," there is "serious question" whether either justification advanced for the death penalty—"retribution and deterrence of capital crimes by prospective offenders"—applies to retarded offenders.

The Court also acknowledged that the mentally retarded face risks not associated with the average offender: (1) These defendants may be more apt to give false confessions; (2) They may have lesser ability to effectively argue mitigation; (3) They may be less able to give meaningful assistance to their counsel; (4) They often make poor witnesses; and (5) Their demeanor may create an impression of lack of remorse.

According to the National Coalition to Abolish the Death Penalty, despite ranking among those states with statutory proscriptions against the execution of incompetent offenders, Texas has since 2002 executed two prisoners who arguably fell short of the *Ford v. Wainwright* competency standard. On May 19, 2004, the NCADP issued a press release urging Congress and the Texas state legislature to study this issue, relating this trend to the type of conduct revealed as socially abhorrent in the treatment of prisoners in Abu Ghraib prison in Baghdad.

See also Bifurcated Trial; Counsel, Right to; Cruel and Unusual Punishments Clause; Death Penalty and the Supreme Court; Due Process, Procedural; Due Process Clauses; Eighth Amendment; Fourteenth Amendment; *Furman v. Georgia; Gregg v. Georgia;* Habeas Corpus; Insanity Defense; Interrogation and Confessions; O'Connor, Sandra Day; Powell, Lewis F., Jr.; Stevens, John Paul

Richard T. Meehan, Jr.

DEATH PENALTY AND RACIAL DISCRIMINATION

One of the more common criticisms leveled at the criminal justice system today is that criminal penalties are often assessed against defendants in a racially discriminatory manner. While this is a concern in any type of case, the practice becomes especially problematic in cases where capital punishment is an option. Americans have consistently supported the use of capital punishment over the past several decades, but they have also become increasingly concerned about the nature of the system that sentences criminal defendants to death.

A number of studies have shown that the death penalty has historically been applied to blacks and other racial minorities at a level disproportionate to their numbers in the overall U.S. population. This trend has been especially apparent in the South. While such numbers do not necessarily prove that the death penalty has been applied in a racially discriminatory manner, they do give many scholars and civil libertarians cause for concern. Indeed, the U.S. Supreme Court recognized the race factor in *Furman v. Georgia* (1972), where a slim majority struck down Georgia's death penalty.

States retooled their death penalty statutes in the wake of *Furman,* and the Court upheld these new laws in the 1976 case of *Gregg v. Georgia.* In an effort to reduce what the *Furman* court described as the "arbitrary and capricious" nature of capital sentencing, states built new protections into their sentencing schemes. Common elements included a separate sentencing hearing, the consideration of aggravating and mitigating factors, and an automatic review in all capital cases. Such protections were designed to provide more concrete guidelines for juries in capital cases and reduce the likelihood that improper factors such as race, gender, or social class would be considered in the sentencing decision.

Numerous scholars have attempted to isolate the effect that race has on capital sentencing. Most studies that have examined race and capital punishment since *Gregg* have had trouble isolating race as a single causal variable that determines a sentencing outcome. These studies have, however, suggested that the racial dyad, the racial characteristics of the offender and the victim, is a significant predictor of whether a defendant will receive the death penalty. Black offenders who killed white victims were, by far, the most likely to receive the death penalty, while white offenders who killed black victims were the least likely to be sentenced to death.

Only once has the United States Supreme Court directly addressed the issue of racial discrimination and capital punishment. In the 1987 case of *McCleskey v. Kemp,* the Court heard the case of Warren McCleskey, a black man convicted and sentenced to death for murdering a white police officer in Atlanta, Georgia. In the course of his defense, McCleskey's counsel offered a detailed statistical study authored by Professor David Baldus concluding that blacks in Georgia were significantly more likely to receive the death penalty than whites. McCleskey argued that such evidence supported the conclusion that Georgia's capital sentencing procedure violated the Equal Protection Clause of the Fourteenth Amendment and was therefore unconstitutional.

By a narrow five-to-four decision, the Court ruled against McCleskey and held that even if statistical studies showed that the death penalty was applied in a manner that appeared to be racially discriminatory, this did not sufficiently show that McCleskey was discriminated against on the basis of race in his particular case. The Court was clearly leery of opening the door for the use of statistical studies to bolster legal arguments regarding criminal sentencing. Dissenting justices countered that studies, which showed a significant possibility of racial discrimination in the sentencing process were sufficient to sustain McCleskey's contention that Georgia's capital sentencing scheme violated the Eequal Protection Clause.

In recent years the Supreme Court has shown a willingness to revisit several important holdings in the area of capital punishment. Juries, not judges, must weigh aggravating and mitigating factors at sentencing. Juveniles and the mentally retarded may not be executed. Such a trend perhaps demonstrates an increased sensitivity of the Court to the issue of capital punishment and means that it may be more receptive to hearing claims related to race and capital sentencing.

Racial bias can enter capital cases at many junctures of the criminal justice system. The case of *Miller-El v. Cockrell* (2003) illustrates this point. When a Dallas County prosecutor used peremptory challenges to dismiss 10 of 11 eligible blacks in the jury pool at his capital murder trial, Miller-El sought to introduce evidence that the Texas prosecutor had engaged in racially discriminatory behavior that violated his equal protection rights. The Supreme Court overturned a lower court decision and ordered the trial court to consider Miller-El's evidence.

The public and government officials may likewise be reconsidering the application of death penalty statutes. Recently, Illinois governor George Ryan commuted the sentences of Illinois' entire death-row contingent because he had determined that the sentencing system in Illinois was fraught with error.

While it is often difficult to say whether or not race plays a role in individual capital sentencing decisions, the aggregate statistics showing blacks and other racial minorities disproportionately receiving death sentences have led many to question whether there are larger, if more subtle, racial biases in the criminal justice system.

See also Bifurcated Trial; Death Penalty, Crimes Punishable by the; Death Penalty and Mental Incompetence; Death Penalty and the Supreme Court; Death Penalty for Juvenile Offenders; Death-Qualified Jury; Equal Protection Clause; Fourteenth Amendment; *Furman v. Georgia; Gregg v. Georgia*

Bibliography

Baldus, David, et al. 1990. *Equal Justice and the Death Penalty: Legal and Empirical Analysis.* Boston: Northeastern University Press.

Keil, Thomas, and Gennaro Vito. 1990. "Race and the Death Penalty in Kentucky Murder Trials: An Analysis of Post-*Gregg* Outcomes." *Justice Quarterly* 7:189–207.

Neubauer, David. 2002. *America's Courts and the Criminal Justice System.* 7th ed. Belmont, CA: Thompson.

Russell, Gregory. 1994. *The Death Penalty and Racial Bias: Overturning Supreme Court Assumptions.* Westport, CT: Greenwood Press.

Darren A. Wheeler

DEATH PENALTY AND THE SUPREME COURT

Since this nation's founding there have been efforts to eliminate capital punishment. Until the mid-twentieth century, death penalty abolitionists focused primarily on state laws and state legislatures, because the states prosecute the great majority of criminal cases. In challenging the death penalty, abolitionists usually relied on moral arguments to either repeal or narrow the scope of capital punishment laws. These efforts were intermittently successful. For instance, during the first two decades of the 1900s, several state legislatures repealed the death penalty. Most of those states, however, reinstituted capital punishment within the next few years. The abolitionist movement has also prompted changes in the method of execution. Most prisoners were hanged until the late 1800s, when the electric chair was developed as a more humane means of execution. In the early twentieth century, a number of states adopted the gas chamber. Today, lethal injection is the predominant means of execution.

For most of its history, the Supreme Court presumed that capital punishment was constitutionally permissible. Both the Fifth and Fourteenth Amendments declare that life can be taken so long as the prisoner is provided due process of law. It was not until after the Cruel and Unusual Punishments Clause of the Eighth Amendment was applied to the states in *Robinson v. California* (1962) that state prisoners could challenge their punishment under the Eighth Amendment.

By the mid-1960s, the Supreme Court slowly began to examine procedural issues related to the death penalty. Though several cases presented direct challenges to the constitutionality of the death penalty, the Court generally avoided ruling directly on that issue. In *McGautha v. California* (1971), the Court finally addressed the constitutionality of the death penalty. It held that the Due Process Clause of the Fourteenth Amendment was not violated by a single proceeding in a capital case in which both guilt and punishment were decided. According to the Court, "To identify before the fact those characteristics of criminal homicides and their perpetrators which call of the death penalty and to express these characteristics in language which can be fairly understood and applied by the sentencing authority appear to be tasks which are beyond present human ability." The majority did note that in capital cases the concerns raised by the defendants might be better addressed by bifurcated trial proceedings and detailed standards. The Court, however, was unwilling to interpret the Due Process Clause as mandating such procedures and standards.

The next year, in June 1972, in four cases often collectively referred to as *Furman v. Georgia* (1972), the Court, by a five-to-four vote, concluded that the death penalty violated the Eighth Amendment. Each justice wrote separately and emphasized different aspects of the cases.

The state legislatures and Congress responded to *Furman* by rewriting their capital punishment laws. Four years later, in *Gregg v. Georgia* (1976), the Court ruled that the death penalty did not invariably violate the Constitution. The Court read *Furman* as declaring unconstitutional any death penalty scheme under which there was a substantial risk of arbitrary and capricious sentencing. Thus, it was unnecessary to overrule that decision. According to the *Gregg* Court, the statutes before it ensured that the decision to impose a death sentence was "suitably directed and limited so as to minimize the risk of wholly arbitrary and capricious action." *Gregg* and four companion cases established the structure of the modern death penalty. Since then, the Court has been heavily involved in fine-tuning the constitutional parameters of capital punishment.

Gregg and its companion cases relied on conscientious judicial review of capital cases as the means of ensuring a rationally functioning system of capital punishment. Some states provide for an automatic appeal of a conviction and death sentence to the

state's highest court, while others have capital cases travel the same route as other criminal appeals. An important part of that appellate review is comparative proportionality review. Under comparative proportionality review, the reviewing appellate court considers whether the death sentence has been imposed in cases and on defendants similar to the one under review. The goal of comparative review is to ensure that on a statewide basis the death penalty is not being imposed in an arbitrary manner. In *Pulley v. Harris* (1983), Court held that such review was not constitutionally required. Since *Pulley,* some states have legislatively repealed their comparative review requirements and most other states, through their courts, have relaxed their comparative review requirements.

Federal habeas corpus law has been an important, but often overlooked, part of the Supreme Court's involvement in the death penalty. Frequently, a capital defendant's case is before the Supreme Court on a writ of habeas corpus. To file the writ, the defendant must allege that he is being held in custody in violation of federal law. Thus, the federal habeas statutes have provided the jurisdictional basis for the Court to decide most constitutional issues that have come before it. From 1963 to about 1976 the availability of the writ was interpreted expansively, making it relatively easier for state court capital defendants to litigate their federal claims in federal court. The availability of the writ was limited, when Congress enacted the Antiterrorism and Effective Death Penalty Act of 1996 (AEDPA), which made it more difficult for prisoners to file successive habeas corpus petitions in federal courts.

On several occasions the Supreme Court has been asked to declare that the execution of a class of defendants would be cruel and unusual punishment and therefore in violation of the Eighth Amendment. To answer this question, the Court applies the standard announced in *Trop v. Dulles* (1958), namely, whether the "evolving standards of decency that mark the progress of a maturing society" have developed to prohibit the execution of that class of defendants. In an effort to ensure that its decisions do not represent merely the predilections of its members, the Court turns to objective societal factors. The Court considers capital punishment statutes, jury verdicts in capital cases, whether that class of defendants historically has been subject to the death penalty, and judicial precedents. Sometimes the Court discusses whether the penological objectives of the death penalty—deterrence and retribution—would be achieved by the execution. The Court has also considered international law and developments in other countries. The evolving standards of decency test and the factors on which it relies provide an air of authenticity to some of the Court's more dramatic legal declarations, particularly rulings that force the states to change their methods of prosecution and their criteria for determining the persons they can realistically prosecute for capital crimes.

Perhaps the ultimate violation of a person's civil or political right is the execution of an innocent person. This concern has always hovered over the capital punishment process. The Supreme Court has twice directly addressed the issue. In *Herrera v. Collins* (1993), the Court was faced with a capital habeas petitioner who submitted affidavits that tended to show that his now-dead brother was the actual perpetrator of the crime. The Court ruled that a claim of newly discovered evidence of factual innocence, standing alone, was an insufficient reason to grant federal habeas relief. To qualify for relief, in addition to the innocence claim, a habeas petitioner must also be able to establish a federal constitutional violation in the state proceeding. The Court suggested alternatively that a defendant would be entitled to a hearing on a free-standing innocence claim if he made a truly persuasive showing of innocence and if there were no mechanism by which he could present the claim in the state. The Supreme Court was apparently fearful that capital defendants could, years after their convictions, too easily manufacture evidence casting doubt on their guilt. Two years later the Court decided *Schulp v. Delo* (1995), which involved claims of factual innocence and independent constitutional violations that occurred during trial. The Court

held that when a constitutional violation is alleged along with a factual innocence claim, a defendant only has to show that it is more likely than not that no reasonable juror would have found him guilty but for the constitutional error. The AEDPA modified this standard so that a habeas petitioner now has to show by clear and convincing evidence that he would not have been found guilty of the capital crime. In the October 2005 term, the Court had a chance to address the matter in *House v. Bell*. Bell involves DNA-based evidence that was tested years after conviction, suggesting that the prisoner did not commit the crime. *Bell* is important because since 1972 more than 110 death-row prisoners have been exonerated or acquitted in retrials, though not all exonerations have been based on DNA evidence.

Despite the complexity and extensive amount of death penalty law, most of what the U.S. Supreme Court does in capital cases, short of declaring certain practices unconstitutional, has relatively little impact. When the Court affirms a capital sentence, it allows the government—state or federal—to execute a defendant, if it so chooses. When the Court issues a ruling favorable to capital defendants, it prevents that execution from occurring, at least until the error is corrected. At most, the Court's ruling creates a ripple of issues that lower courts, prosecutors, and defense attorneys will have to consider in future capital cases.

The debate over the death penalty has continued for centuries. The Supreme Court is likely to remain influential in the legal regulation and discussion of the death penalty in this country. More than a generation of litigation on the issue strongly suggests that ending the legal regulation of the death penalty may be most effectively done by legislation. For a legislature to repeal or resist efforts to reinstate capital punishment, there has to be popular support for abolition, and that support has to withstand the occasional calls for reinstatement of the death penalty. Importantly, abolitionists have to provide meaningful alternatives to the death penalty; these alternatives have to ensure both that defendants who commit the most horrible crimes are punished and that society's interests are not undermined in doing so.

See also Bifurcated Trial; Bill of Rights, Incorporation of; Burger Court; Clemency, Executive; Counsel, Ineffective Assistance of; Cruel and Unusual Punishments Clause; Death Penalty, Crimes Punishable by the; Death Penalty and Mental Incompetence; Death Penalty and Racial Discrimination; Death Penalty for Juvenile Offenders; Death-Qualified Jury; Due Process Clauses; Execution, Methods of; Fifth Amendment; Fourteenth Amendment; *Furman v. Georgia; Gregg v. Georgia;* Habeas Corpus; Habeas Corpus, Federal; International Law; Rehnquist Court; *Robinson v. California;* Sentencing, Eighth Amendment and; Victim Impact Evidence in Death Penalty Cases; Warren Court

Bibliography

Acker, James R., Robert M. Bohm, and Charles S. Lanier, eds. 1998. *America's Experiment with Capital Punishment: Reflections on the Past, Present, and Future of the Ultimate Penal Sanction.* Durham, NC: Carolina Academic Press.

Bedau, Hugo Adam, ed. 1997. *The Death Penalty in America: Current Controversies.* New York: Oxford University Press.

Mandery, Evan J., ed. 2005. *Capital Punishment: A Balanced Examination.* Sudbury, MA: Jones and Bartlett.

Megivern, James J. 1997. *The Death Penalty: An Historical and Theological Survey.* Mahaw, NJ: Paulist Press.

Dwight Aarons

DEATH PENALTY FOR JUVENILES

If the death penalty ranks among the more volatile issues in constitutional jurisprudence, then the question of the death penalty for juveniles towers as one of the most controversial matters in the modern era. Twelve years after the United States Supreme Court upheld the death penalty in *Gregg v. Georgia,* the Court was called on to determine if there are murderers who are simply too young to be executed and whether the killing of these juvenile offenders constitutes a violation of the Eighth Amendment's prohibition against cruel and unusual punishment. In *Thompson v. Oklahoma,* a case involving a brutal murder committed by a 15-year-old, the Supreme

Court responded in the affirmative. The execution of juveniles who were younger than 16 at the time of their offense would violate the stricture against cruel and unusual punishment. Writing for the majority, Justice John Paul Stevens stated that the Eighth Amendment must be interpreted according to "the evolving standards of decency that mark the progress of a maturing society." To identify these standards of decency, Justice Stevens looked to the actions of state legislatures and the verdicts of juries across the nation indicating the line should be 16 years of age.

However, Justice Stevens was not willing to defer to other actors in defining what was constitutional, citing the fact that "it is for us ultimately to judge whether the Eighth Amendment permits imposition of the death penalty" in a case like Thompson's. In making this determination, Stevens argued that it is the Court's responsibility to inquire whether the sentence of death is proportionate to the moral culpability of a 15-year-old killer. For the Court in *Thompson,* the answer was a resounding no. Justice Stevens wrote that "less culpability should attach to a crime committed by a juvenile than to a comparable crime committed by an adult. The basis for this conclusion is too obvious to require extended explanation. Inexperience, less education, and less intelligence make the teenager less able to evaluate the consequences of his or her conduct while at the same time he or she is more apt to be motivated by mere emotion or peer pressure than is an adult." The Court had been asked to establish a bold precedent that would forbid the execution of any person who was under the age of 18 at the point at which he or she killed. Stevens refused, writing, "Our task today, however, is to decide the case before us; we do so by concluding that the Eighth and Fourteenth Amendments prohibit the execution of a person who was under sixteen years of age at the time of his or her offense." Those younger than 16 could not be executed. Those who were older than 18 could be. The fate of 16 and 17 year olds remained unresolved.

This question would be addressed in the following year. In *Stanford v. Kentucky,* the Supreme

Court ruled that the execution of those who were 16 or 17 years of age at the time of their offenses did not violate the Eighth Amendment. Writing for the majority, Justice Antonin Scalia took the "evolving standards of decency" principle cited in *Thompson* and used it to achieve a very different result. For Justice Scalia, these standards were to be identified, not announced, by the Court. He examined the decisions of the people's elected representatives and concluded that no national consensus existed against the execution of those younger than 18 years of age. Thus, the Eighth Amendment was not violated. Justice Scalia seemed to view this matter as an issue of judicial power, writing, "When this Court cast loose from the historical moorings consisting of the original application of the Eighth Amendment, it did not embark rudderless upon a wide-open sea. Rather, it limited the Amendment's extension to those practices contrary to the 'evolving standards of decency that mark the progress of a maturing society.' It has never been thought that this was a shorthand reference to the preferences of a majority of this Court." If the people wanted to execute those under 18, it was not for the Court to stand in their way.

The seeds of the reversal of *Stanford* were planted, not in a case involving the specific issue of age, but instead in a line of cases involving mental retardation. On the same day the Supreme Court decided *Stanford v. Kentucky*, it handed down its decision in *Penry v. Lynaugh*, ruling that the Eighth Amendment was not violated by the execution of the mentally retarded. Not surprisingly the *Penry* case came down to the by-now oft-repeated questions of the standards of decency and national consensus. Writing for the majority, Justice Sandra Day O'Connor concluded that "at present, there is insufficient evidence of a national consensus against executing mentally retarded people convicted of capital offenses for us to conclude that it is categorically prohibited by the Eighth Amendment."

13 years later the Court would reverse its decision in *Penry*. In *Atkins v. Virginia* the Supreme Court ruled that a consensus had developed in opposition to executing the mentally retarded.

However, Justice Stevens did not rest the Court's decision exclusively on agreement among state legislators. As he did in *Thompson*, Stevens evaluated the proportionality of the death sentence and the moral culpability of those to be executed. Stevens argued that because of the impairments of the mentally retarded:

By definition they have diminished capacities to understand and process information, to communicate, to abstract from mistakes and learn from experience, to engage in logical reasoning, to control impulses, and to understand the reactions of others. There is no evidence that they are more likely to engage in criminal conduct than others, but there is abundant evidence that they often act on impulse rather than pursuant to a premeditated plan, and that in group settings they are followers rather than leaders. Their deficiencies do not warrant an exemption from criminal sanctions, but they do diminish their personal culpability.

For Stevens the minimized personal culpability of these defendants made execution an unacceptable option.

Much of what the Supreme Court stated in *Atkins* to justify its reversal of *Penry* set the stage for a reexamination of its decision in *Stanford v. Kentucky*. This reexamination would be forced by an extraordinary decision of the Missouri Supreme Court. In *Simmons v. Roper* the Missouri Supreme Court overturned the death sentence of Christopher Simmons, who committed a horrific murder at the age of 17. While the precedent established by the United States Supreme Court in *Stanford v. Kentucky* would seem to preclude such a decision, the Missouri Supreme Court read the *Atkins* decision as rendering *Stanford* invalid as a precedent. Judge Laura Denvir Stith wrote, "[T]his Court finds that the Supreme Court would today hold such executions are prohibited by the Eighth and Fourteenth Amendments. It therefore sets aside Mr. Simmons'[s] death sentence and resentences him to life imprisonment without eligibility for probation, parole, or release."

Many expected the United States Supreme Court to rebuke the Missouri Court with an admonition that if precedents established by the United States

Supreme Court are to be overturned, the United States Supreme Court, not a state supreme court, would do the overturning. Instead the United States Supreme Court upheld the Missouri Supreme Court's decision in *Roper v. Simmons.* Writing for the majority, Justice Kennedy followed the path established by the Missouri Supreme Court, conceding that "[j]ust as the *Atkins* Court reconsidered the issue decided in *Penry,* we now reconsider the issue decided in *Stanford."* Justice Kennedy would use *Atkins* as a veritable template for his analysis, looking first to the question of consensus and then engaging in an analysis of proportionality. On the first issue, Kennedy identified a shift in the national consensus since the *Stanford* decision, writing, "As in *Atkins,* the objective indicia of consensus in this case—the rejection of the juvenile death penalty in the majority of States; the infrequency of its use even where it remains on the books; and the consistency in the trend toward abolition of the practice—provide sufficient evidence that today our society views juveniles, in the words *Atkins* used respecting the mentally retarded, as 'categorically less culpable than the average criminal.'"

Justice Kennedy also adopted the *Atkins* approach: determining whether execution was proportional to the moral culpability of those under 18. Kennedy's conclusions mirrored those of the Missouri Supreme Court, noting "a lack of maturity and an underdeveloped sense of responsibility," a greater susceptibility "to negative influences and outside pressures," and the reality that "the character of a juvenile is not as well formed as that of an adult." These factors led Kennedy to conclude that those under 18 years of age possess a lower level of moral culpability. Kennedy wrote, "Once the diminished culpability of juveniles is recognized, it is evident that the penological justifications for the death penalty apply to them with lesser force than to adults."

The final point noted by the majority focused on the dubious company in which the United States placed itself by executing juveniles. Kennedy listed an ignoble array of nations, including Iran, Pakistan, Saudi Arabia, Yemen, Nigeria, and China, which had previously employed the death penalty for juveniles but renounced the practice throughout the 1990s. Kennedy then identified "the stark reality that the United States is the only country in the world that continues to give official sanction to the juvenile death penalty." With its decision in *Roper v. Simmons* that the Eighth Amendment is violated by the execution of those who were younger than 18 at the time of their crime, the Supreme Court removed the United States from this list as well.

See also *Atkins v. Virginia,* Bill of Rights (American); Cruel and Unusual Punishments Clause; Death Penalty and the Supreme Court; Eighth Amendment; Fourteenth Amendment; *Furman v. Georgia; Gregg v. Georgia;* Juvenile Justice; Kennedy, Anthony; Living Constitution; O'Connor, Sandra Day; Stevens, John Paul

Bibliography

Streib, Victor. 1987. *Death Penalty for Juveniles.* Bloomington: Indiana University Press.

Anthony Simones

DEATH-QUALIFIED JURIES

The right to a trial by jury is an essential component of the American justice system. In various state and federal constitutional provisions, the right is preserved, both in civil and criminal trials, with some variations. The Sixth Amendment establishes the right in "all criminal prosecutions" to a "speedy and public trial, by an impartial jury of the state and district wherein the crime shall have been committed." Its provisions are incorporated within the Due Process Clause of the Fourteenth Amendment so as to make the right to a neutral jury a right in state as well as federal courts.

A neutral jury is comprised of impartial jurors. An impartial juror is a juror who is free from bias or favor toward or against any party in the trial. Thus, in a criminal case impartiality includes freedom from jury bias in favor of or against the prosecution or the accused. An impartial juror begins a trial with an "impartial frame of mind" and decides the trial based on the evidence admitted and the law that is to be applied. Therefore, to be an impartial juror, a juror must be able to follow the law as given to the jury in the court's jury instructions.

In capital cases, juries are called upon not only to determine the guilt or innocence of the accused, but also to set the sentence. A juror in a capital case must be able to follow both the law that applies to determining guilt or innocence and the law that applies to sentencing. Otherwise, the juror is not impartial and does not satisfy the constitutional guarantee.

At the beginning of a capital trial, it is unknown whether the accused will ultimately face the death penalty. If, for example, the jury does not find the accused to be guilty of a capital offense in the guilt phase of the proceeding, no sentencing hearing will follow. But if the defendant is found guilty of a crime that carries the death sentence, the same jury will have to decide whether the defendant should be sentenced to death or to a lesser sentence, such as life imprisonment or life imprisonment without the possibility of parole. Therefore, at the beginning of the trial, potential jurors must be questioned not only about their willingness to follow the law pertaining to culpability, but also about the law pertaining to sentencing.

The process by which a juror's willingness to follow the law pertaining to the imposition of a death sentence is known as death qualification. Specifically, jurors are questioned regarding their beliefs about capital punishment. If the juror's answers reveal that the juror is impartial, that is, able to follow the jurisdiction's law on capital punishment, then the juror is death qualified. If the juror is not able to follow the law on capital punishment, the juror is excused from participation, just as a juror who is unable to follow the law on culpability would be excused.

The United States Supreme Court, in a series of cases, has established standards for selecting death-qualified juries. In an early case, *Witherspoon v. Illinois* (1968), the Court set aside a death sentence imposed by a jury from which all jurors who voiced religious or conscientious objections to the death penalty had been excused. The Court reasoned that a "[s]tate may not entrust the determination of whether [one] should live or die to a tribunal organized to return a verdict of death." Ultimately, however, the Court became dissatisfied with the effect that semantics had on its application and replaced the *Witherspoon* standard with a more pliable one. The present standard for determining whether a juror is death qualified, articulated by the Court in *Wainwright v. Witt* (1985), is "whether the juror's views would prevent or substantially impair the performance of [the juror's] duties as a juror in accordance with [the juror's] instructions and … oath."

Under the *Witt* standard, it is not a juror's belief or conviction against capital punishment that disqualifies the juror from sitting on a capital jury. It is the juror's unwillingness or inability to follow the law *despite* personal opinion. As the Supreme Court explained in *Witt*:

It is entirely possible that a person who has a "fixed opinion against" or who does not "believe in" capital punishment might nevertheless be perfectly able as a juror to abide by existing law—to follow conscientiously the instructions of a trial judge and to consider fairly the imposition of the death sentence in a particular case.

A juror whose personal viewpoint renders him or her unable to impose a death sentence in any case, no matter what the law requires, is not death qualified and may be excused for cause. Similarly, as the Supreme Court held in *Morgan v. Illinois* (1992), a juror who will automatically vote for the death penalty in every case in which it is an available sentence is excused from the jury by a process known as excusing for cause.

During the jury selection process, jurors are questioned concerning their attitudes about the death penalty. If they express a willingness to follow the law and abide by the juror oath, despite their personal opinions, they are death qualified. Conversely, if they cannot follow the law or if they are unable to impose a death sentence in any circumstance, they are excused from service by a process known as challenging for cause. Many jurors may not be able to predict precisely how their personal opinions might affect their ability to follow the law.

In situations of ambiguity, the trial judge will decide whether the juror will be unable to "faithfully and impartially apply the law." The trial judge's decision whether to remove the juror for cause or allow the juror to remain on the jury will be given deference by appellate courts reviewing the issue.

The process of death qualification, by which jurors who cannot impose a death sentence are also excluded as jurors from the guilt phase, arguably produces conviction-prone juries. In addition, it has the effect of producing a nonrepresentative jury, one that is without individuals who oppose capital punishment. In *Lockhart v. McCree* (1986), the Supreme Court was faced with mounting social science evidence that death-qualified juries were more likely to convict than juries that included those unable to impose a capital sentence. Despite the accepted validity of the studies, the Court held that the use of death-qualified juries during the guilt phase of capital trials does not violate the Constitution.

See also Accused, Rights of the; Bifurcated Trial; Bill of Rights, Incorporation of; Challenges for Cause; Death Penalty and the Supreme Court; Due Process Clauses; Fourteenth Amendment; Jury, Trial by; Peremptory Challenges to Prospective Jurors; Sixth Amendment

Bibliography

Bowers, William J., Maria Sandys, and Benjamin D. Steiner. 1998. "Symposium: Foreclosed Impartiality in Capital Sentencing: Jurors' Predispositions, Guilt-Trial Experience and Premature Decision Making." *Cornell Law Review* 83:1476.

Coyne, Randall, and Lyn Entzeroth. 2001. *Capital Punishment and the Judicial Process.* Durham, NC: Carolina Academic Press.

Rozelle, Susan D. 2002 "The Utility of *Witt:* Understanding the Language of Death Qualification." *Baylor Law Review* 54:677–99.

Penny White

DEBS, EUGENE VICTOR (1855–1926)

Born and raised in Terre Haute, Indiana, Debs was a prominent labor union leader, political activist, and founder and five-time presidential candidate for the Socialist Party of America (1900, 1904, 1908, 1912, and 1920). Of his five presidential campaigns, the most notable was the last, which was conducted from an Atlanta prison and brought his largest vote tally.

At the age of 20, Debs joined the Brotherhood of Locomotive Firemen, becoming Grand Secretary within five years. He came to national prominence as a founder and leader of the American Railway Union (ARU), established in 1893. The ARU was the first industrial union in the United States. In contrast to the brotherhoods, the ARU sought to organize all workers on the railroad, not just those within specific crafts. The ARU scored notable successes, in particular managing to extract signed contracts for its members from two of the strongest corporations in the country, and in a very short time achieved a membership larger than all the brotherhoods combined.

In 1894, Debs led the ARU in a boycott of the Pullman Company. In July of that year, he was arrested for violating an injunction not to aid the boycott by word or deed and was subsequently imprisoned until 1895. Debs's imprisonment effectively broke the strike and brought about the demise of the ARU, as the railroad companies subsequently monitored, blacklisted, and fired any workers associated with the ARU.

The experience of the strike, his imprisonment, and the realization that the government was not an impartial arbiter between capital and labor—the federal government, the courts, and the military had all been marshaled to break the boycott—propelled Debs toward socialism. In 1897, he helped establish the Social Democracy of America (SDA) and in 1900 undertook his first run for the presidency. The following year, the SDA merged with splinter groups from Daniel De Leon's Socialist Labor Party to form the Socialist Party of America (SPA).

In 1905, along with De Leon, Debs helped establish the Industrial Workers of the World (IWW, aka, the "Wobblies"), an industrial union designed to compete with the AFL and shift unionism in the United States from a craft to a mass industrial basis. However, the IWW became a very different type of entity from that envisaged by Debs. While expert at organizing and conducting strikes, the IWW lacked a facility for basic day-to-day union activity, and in 1908 Debs allowed his membership to lapse.

In the 1912 election, the proportion of the popular vote won by Debs rose to its highest level at 6 percent. Nevertheless, in 1916 at the age of 61, ill health and his wife's wishes led Debs to reject the idea of another run. In 1919, he was again imprisoned, this time under the Sedition Act (1918), for speaking out against the war. He was persuaded to run one last time in the 1920 presidential election from his jail cell in Atlanta. Despite tight restrictions placed on his ability to communicate from prison, and a split in the party when the Communists left in 1919 (reducing membership in the SPA by some three-quarters), he polled a larger absolute number of votes (915,302) than at any previous election. Debs was finally released from prison in late 1921. Yet prison had taken its toll; his health had deteriorated dramatically, and despite continuing to work he spent most of the remaining five years of his life recuperating from the experience.

See also Communist Party USA

Bibliography

Ginger, Ray. 1949. *The Bending Cross: A Biography of Eugene Victor Debs.* New Brunswick, NJ: Rutgers University Press.

Morgan, Howard Wayne. 1962. *Eugene V. Debs: Socialist for President.* Syracuse, NY: University Press.

Salvatore, Nick. 1982. *Eugene V. Debs: Citizen and Socialist.* Urbana: University of Illinois Press.

Shannon, David A. 1955. *The Socialist Party of America: A History.* New York: Macmillan.

Ian Down

DECLARATION OF INDEPENDENCE (1776)

The Declaration of Independence is the most important and influential document to the founding of the United States of America. Its primary purpose was to convince the world that the American colonies had a moral and legal right to separate from Great Britain, a struggle that had been waging

on battlefields for about a year before the delegates to the Second Continental Congress voted on independence. Thomas Jefferson authored the first draft of the Declaration in less than one month's time in June 1776 and by his own admission turned "to neither book [n]or pamphlet while writing it" (Becker 1960, 25). However, the final draft of "The Unanimous Declaration of the Thirteen United States of America," on which the delegates voted on the pleasantly cool morning of July 4, 1776, was the product of several of America's greatest minds and ardent patriots.

Jefferson's draft was revised first by his colleagues John Adams and Benjamin Franklin, who along with Robert R. Livingston and Roger Sherman served on a regionally balanced Committee of Five (chaired by Jefferson) that Congress appointed to draft a resolution for a motion offered for debate by Richard Henry Lee on June 7, 1776, "that these colonies are and ought to be, free and independent states" (McCullough 2001, 118; Gaustad 1996, 46). After the committee's review, Jefferson's draft was then edited by the entire Second Continental Congress, which acted as a committee of the whole. Delegates made several notable improvements as well as changes that resulted in the removal of more than one-quarter of Jefferson's original text. For Jefferson, Adams, and others, perhaps the most painful deletion made by Congress was Jefferson's poignant and passionate references to the king's "execrable commerce" in slavery (Becker 1960, 212–13).

Nonetheless, the final draft of the Declaration of Independence, a mere 1,342 words, brilliantly articulates a general theory of democratic government that identifies the rights of individuals; the origin of those rights; and the responsibility that government has, with the consent of the governed, to secure and protect those rights. It also clarified for both domestic and international audiences the circumstances that made the American Revolution unavoidable, necessary, and justifiable.

There are five distinct parts to the Declaration of Independence: an introduction, a preamble, a main body that consists of two sections, and a conclusion. The introduction states the purpose of the document: to declare the causes that made it necessary for the American colonies to leave the British Empire. Uppermost in Jefferson's mind when he penned the introduction was the concept of the law. The king, after all, had already declared the colonists to be traitors and had committed the bulk of the British land and naval forces to quell the rebellion (McCullough 2005). In fact, by the summer of 1776, King George had dispatched a fleet of more than 120 ships and 32,000 troops, which included Scot brigades and Hessian mercenaries, an army that was larger than the entire population of either New York or Philadelphia and the largest yet gathered on the American continent. Estimates place the number of men in General Washington's force at no more than 10,000 (McCullough 2005, 135, 148, 162). What made the courage and fortitude of those who voted for independence in July 1776 so remarkable was that the war, underway since 1775 when the British advanced on Lexington and Concord, was in real danger of being completely lost by the Americans.

The many loyalists in the colonies also considered the rebellion to be a lawless act. Jefferson wanted the world to know that the colonists were not lawless rebels but were rather exercising their right to be free—a right to which they were entitled and that is derived from "the laws of Nature and Nature's God" (Amos 1989, 35).

While often misunderstood by many contemporary readers, Jefferson and his colleagues, especially those trained in the law, were quite familiar with the phrase "law of Nature and of Nature's God." Although the phrase did not originate with Sir William Blackstone, his *Commentaries on the Laws of England,* required reading at almost all colonial universities, served as the major source for the founders' legal terminology and defined these terms (Amos 1989, 42). Following mainstream theological tradition that had been in place for centuries, Blackstone defined the concepts "law of nature" and the "law of God" as being two sides of the same coin:

the revealed or divine law ... are to be found only in the holy scriptures.... These precepts ... are found upon comparison to be really part of the original law of nature.... As then the moral precepts of this law are indeed of the same original with those of the law of nature ... the revealed law ... is the law of nature expressly declared to be so by God himself; ...Upon these two foundations, the law of nature and the law of revelation, depend all human laws. (Amos 1989, 44)

What Jefferson was saying to the world in the introduction to the Declaration of Independence was that the document would explain why it was necessary and even unavoidable in the course of human events for the American people to separate from Great Britain and to assume "a separate and equal station" to which they were entitled by God.

The declaration's second section, the preamble, draws on the same immutable natural laws to declare that certain truths were recognized to be "self-evident," at least by most eighteenth-century Englishmen. These truths required "no Aristotelian syllogism, no Platonic presupposition, and no authority whatsoever except Reason to establish their validity" because they "came, like creation itself, fresh from the hand of God" (Gaustad 1996, 47–48). Why the focus on certain self-evident truths? The framers realized that if kings ruled by divine right (*Lex Rex*), as was commonly claimed at the time, there could be no right of rebellion, no matter how long the list of grievances or how oppressive a king's acts. Something more would be required to prove to the world that in declaring independence, the colonies were not really rebelling against rightful authority (Becker 1960, 7). Historian Carl Becker has explained that what the founders needed was a "theory of government that provided a place for rebellion, that made it respectable, and even meritorious under certain circumstances" (Becker 1960, 7–8).

Therefore, the preamble, so labeled because it precedes the list of grievances against the king, articulates a general political philosophy upon which the case of the colonies would rest. This philosophy affirms the right of a people to establish and to overturn its own government whenever the people are convinced that the government, whatever its form, has become destructive of the ends for which all government is instituted among men and women (Becker 1960, 8–9). Accordingly, the preamble states:

> We hold these truths to be self-evident, that all men are created equal, that they are endowed by their Creator with certain unalienable Rights, that among these are Life, Liberty and the pursuit of Happiness.—That to secure these rights, Governments are instituted among Men, deriving their just powers from the consent of the governed,—That whenever any Form of Government becomes destructive of these ends, it is the Right of the People to alter or to abolish it, and to institute new Government, laying its foundation on such principles and organizing its powers in such form, as to them shall seem most likely to effect their Safety and Happiness.

Even though it was not at all clear that a majority of "the People" in the colonies favored independence from the king, the framers found it politically expedient to suggest that the colonies were united in their desire to institute a new government. Having affirmed the right of revolution under certain conditions, the preamble states that these conditions do indeed exist, that the people have suffered under them long enough, and that "when a long train of abuses and usurpations, pursuing invariably the same Object evinces a design to reduce them under absolute Despotism, it is their right, it is their duty, to throw off such Government, and to provide new Guards for their future security."

Alone in his upstairs parlor at Seventh and Market streets in the warm June days and nights of Philadelphia in June 1776, Jefferson worked on drafts of the declaration without benefit of any his library resources at Monticello (McCullough 2001, 120). While he later admitted that he had no need of his books since his objective was not to be original but only to "place before mankind the common sense of the subject," Jefferson (and the other framers) nonetheless used ideas about limiting the power of kings and princes that stemmed from sources including John Locke, David Hume, Jean-Jacques Rousseau, the English poet Daniel Defoe, and even Cicero ("The people's good is the highest law")

(McCullough 2001, 120–21). By his own account, Jefferson drew from his own recent work on the new Virginia Constitution and no doubt also was familiar with the declaration of rights authored by his fellow Virginian George Mason, which appeared in the *Pennsylvania Evening Post* on June 12 and declared that "all men are born equally free and independent and have certain natural rights … among which are the enjoyment of life and liberty." (McCullough 2001, 121). Both of these documents were informed by the language of England's Declaration of Rights of 1689 (Maier 1997, 55). Some scholars suggest that America's Declaration of Independence must be numbered among the few elegant works in history intended both to be read and to be read aloud (Fliegelman 1993).

Jefferson also was familiar with a pamphlet written by Pennsylvania delegate James Wilson and published in Philadelphia in 1774, which claimed: "All men are, by nature equal and free: no one has a right to authority over another without his consent: all lawful government is founded on the consent of those who are subject to it" (McCullough 2001, 121). In addition, Thomas Paine's popular and widely read *Common Sense* also made a persuasive and passionate case against monarchy and for independence of the colonies.

Jefferson and the framers were especially familiar with ideas about limiting the power of kings and princes as argued by John Locke in his first and second *Treatises on Government.* In his *Second Treatise* for example, Locke refuted a divine right monarchy because no "law of nature" or "positive law of God" existed to make one man inherently superior to another (Amos 1989, 57). Locke used the term "law of nature" to refer to God's general revelation of moral law in nature, and the term "positive law of God" to describe how God had revealed eternal moral law in the Bible (Amos 1989, 57). Locke found no law in creation or in scripture that prefers one man over another and that therefore divine right monarchy has no support in either general or special revelation (Amos 1989, 57). Such ideas were central to demonstrate the moral rectitude of the revolution.

Having formulated a philosophy of government that embraced certain self-evident and unalienable rights, popular sovereignty, and conditions that justify revolution, the declaration then presents in the first part of the main body of the text, in a manner similar to a legal indictment, evidence of the "long train of abuses and usurpations" of the colonists' rights by Great Britain's monarch, King George III. Among these grievances are taxation without representation, the dissolution of elected houses of representatives, the quartering of large numbers of troops among the colonists in peacetime, deprivation of the benefits of trial by jury, obstruction of justice, and the hiring of large armies of foreign mercenaries to complete "the works of death, desolation and tyranny, already begun with circumstances of Cruelty and perfidy scarcely paralleled in the most barbarous ages." It was this section of Jefferson's original draft that delegates to the Second Continental Congress edited most extensively, toning down some of Jefferson's most passionate language and striking completely other charges against the king such as his "cruel war against human nature itself, violating the most sacred rights of life and liberty," which was part of Jefferson's long passage on the slave trade (Gaustad 1996, 48; Maier 1997, 146).

These grievances and the seeds for revolution can be traced to a series of acts instituted during the previous 12-year period by the king and Parliament, even though the latter actually had no legal jurisdiction at all over the American colonies. Passage of the Sugar Act of 1764 was only the first in a series of measures designed to raise revenue for the Crown and to protect British trade that were considered onerous by the colonists. That same year, Parliament passed the Currency Act, which prohibited any assembly in America from issuing any paper bills or bills of credit. The Quartering Act of 1775 dictated that if no room for British soldiers could be found in normal barracks then they were to be housed and fed by American colonists. The infamous Stamp Act of 1765 produced an immediate uproar, especially in Massachusetts, where Boston mobs stoned the residence of the province secretary (McCullough 2001,

59). This act required that nearly everything written on paper, other than private correspondence, was to carry revenue stamps, some of which cost as much as 10 pounds (McCullough 2001, 59). This first British attempt to tax Americans directly to meet the expense of the French and Indian War was the catalyst for the Stamp Act Congress. This body was the first collective effort, by 27 delegates from nine colonies, to compile a list of grievances that eventually led to repeal of the act by Parliament in 1766.

The Townsend Act of 1767 and the Tea Act of 1773 placed further duties on imported goods and provided that colonists could be taxed for tea merely if it were unloaded and set on the docks (Amos 1989, 30). These acts provoked another wave of colonial resistance that led to the Boston Tea Party in which "Indians" boarded three British ships and tossed tea in Boston harbor to avoid having to pay the tax. In retaliation, Parliament passed a series of laws in 1774 that collectively came to be known as the Intolerable Acts among Americans. These included the Boston Port Act, which closed Boston harbor until the tea tax was paid; the Administration of Justice Act, which allowed the Crown-appointed governor to suspend the court system; and the Massachusetts Government Act, which revised the colony's charter and gave the British Government more extensive and direct control over all internal affairs. In response to the Intolerable Acts, representatives from 12 of the 13 colonies gathered in Philadelphia in 1774 in the First Continental Congress to attempt to present a united front to persuade the British people that they were "dead earnest about their rights" and united in their determination to defend them (Becker 1960, 115).

That all appeals to their "British brethren" for a redress of these grievances had been in vain is the focus of the second part of the main body of the declaration. This section begins with the passage:

In every stage of these Oppressions We have Petitioned for Redress in the most humble terms: Our repeated Petitions have been answered only by repeated injury. A Prince whose character is thus marked by every act which may define a Tyrant, is unfit to be the ruler of a free people.

Having stated the conditions that made independence necessary, and having shown that those conditions existed in the American colonies despite all appeals to their "British brethren," who have been "deaf to the voice of justice," the declaration concludes:

That these United Colonies are, and of Right ought to be Free and Independent States; that they are Absolved from all Allegiance to the British Crown, and that all political connection between them and the State of Great Britain, is and ought to be totally dissolved; and that as Free and Independent States, they have full Power to levy War, conclude Peace, contract Alliances, establish Commerce, and to do all other Acts and Things which Independent States may of right do.

The framers of the Declaration of Independence were clear that their list of grievances alone did not justify rebellion. These grievances were presented as evidence to persuade the world that they were part of the king's deliberate "design to reduce [a people] under absolute Despotism." The case presented to the world was that the circumstances that prevailed in the colonies were not caused by anything the colonists had done or left undone; rather, they were "solely on account of the deliberate and malevolent purpose of their king to establish over them an absolute tyranny" (Becker 1960, 16). The implicit choice as framed by Jefferson was clear: either to abandon the unalienable rights with which they had been endowed by the creator or to submit to the slavery of despotic rule.

Jefferson was asking a candid world to "deny that the colonies were rightly absolved from allegiance to so malevolent a will" (Becker 1960, 14). There was no ambiguity about the correct course of action among the 56 delegates who affixed their signatures to the declaration, most of whom signed the document by August 2, 1776. They pledged their lives, fortunes, and sacred honor and appealed to "the Supreme Judge of the world for the rectitude" of their intentions in supporting America's Declaration of Independence.

See also Articles of Confederation; Bill of Rights (English); Blackstone, William; Common-Law Background of American Civil Rights and Liberties; Jefferson, Thomas; Liberalism; Locke, John; Natural Law and Natural Rights; Rousseau, Jean-Jacques; United States Constitution

Bibliography

Amos, Gary T. 1989. *Defending the Declaration*. Charlottesville, VA: Providence Foundation.

Becker, Carl. 1960. *The Declaration of Independence: A Study in the History of Political Ideas*. New York: Alfred A. Knopf.

Fliegelman, Jay. 1993. *Declaring Independence: Jefferson, Natural Language, and the Culture of Performance*. Stanford, CA: Stanford University Press.

Gaustad, Edwin S. 1996. *Sworn on the Altar of God*. Grand Rapids, MI: William B. Eerdmans.

Maier, Pauline. 1997. *American Scripture*. New York: Alfred A. Knopf.

McCullough, David. 2001. *John Adams*. New York: Simon & Schuster.

———. 2005. *1776*. New York: Simon & Schuster.

David H. Folz

DEFAMATION

Defamation is a tort that consists of publishing communications that cause a person to be held in ridicule or disgrace or that injure another's reputation or business interests. The requirement of publishing is fulfilled when defamatory statements are intentionally or negligently communicated to a third party.

Civil actions for injury to one's reputation emerged as the English common law developed in the thirteenth and fourteenth centuries. With the use of the printing press in the sixteenth century, common-law courts identified the tort of defamation and began to distinguish between oral and written defamatory statements. Today defamation laws vary according to state and federal jurisdictions, but in general they have common features.

Oral defamation is called slander. Certain slanderous statements, for example, charging someone with a crime, publishing a statement that a female is unchaste or that someone has a sexually transmitted disease, or making statements disparaging a person's business or professional conduct, are considered slander per se. In such instances a plaintiff, even without proof of economic losses, can recover damages called special damages. Slander that does not qualify as slander per se requires a plaintiff to prove that special damages resulted from a defamatory statement; however, some modern court decisions have found that even loss of friendship can have a monetary value that qualifies as proof of special damages.

Defamation of a permanent nature, that is, defamation that is expressed in writing, pictures, signs, or even electronic broadcasts, are classified as libel. Libel per se consists of statements that literally injure a person's reputation or hold a person up to ridicule or adversely affect a person's business or profession. Where the defamatory character of a statement is not apparent on its face but is established by proof from innuendo or other extrinsic circumstances, it is called libel *per quod* and historically has been actionable only when the plaintiff proves special damages. The trend of modern judicial decisions is to hold that once a plaintiff proves a libelous statement, damages are presumed.

Truth is a defense to a suit for slander and libel. Some states, however, add that the truth of a published statement must be accompanied by good motives of one who publishes it. The defense of privilege applies to statements by witnesses, lawyers, and judges in judicial proceedings and statements by legislators on the floor of the legislature. Courts also generally recognize a person has a right to publish a "fair comment" about matters of public interest.

News media jealously guard their rights of under the First Amendment to the U.S. Constitution. However, in *Chaplinsky v. New Hampshire* (1942) the U.S. Supreme Court said that libelous publications are outside the protection of the First Amendment. Because "names make news," libel suits by "public persons" pose a significant threat to the news media, especially because courts generally hold the media responsible for publication of a libelous story received from others. Many states have enacted statutes that require advance notice to a newspaper or other media before filing a suit for defamation. This allows a prospective defendant to make a retraction. A retraction does not excuse a defamatory publication, but it can mitigate any damages awarded.

Once nationwide circulation of newspapers and national audiences for radio and television broadcast became a reality in the twentieth century, the media became increasingly concerned about their liability under laws in various jurisdictions for publishing news accounts involving people in public life. When sued for publishing articles about public officials and people often identified as public figures, they began asserting constitutional defenses.

The issue of First Amendment protection came into sharp focus during the civil rights struggle of the 1960s. A public official in Montgomery, Alabama, sued the *New York Times* for publishing an advertisement chastising public officials for police responses to civil rights demonstrations. After a state supreme court affirmed a $500,000 verdict for a plaintiff against the newspaper, the U.S. Supreme Court granted review. In *New York Times v. Sullivan* (1964), the Court found that the Alabama courts failed to provide the constitutional safeguards for freedom of speech and of the press required by the First and Fourteenth amendments when a libel action is brought by a public official against critics of his official conduct. The Court's decision effectively precludes public officials from recovering damages for defamatory falsehoods related to their official conduct unless they can prove "that the statement was made with … knowledge that it was false or with reckless disregard whether it was false or not."

In *Curtis Publishing v. Butts* (1967), the Supreme Court expanded the principle to apply to all "public figures" that sue for libel. The theory underlying this holding is that public figures have sufficient access to the mass media to defend themselves against false accusations and thus do not require the assistance of libel suits. In a later decision, *Time v. Firestone* (1976), the Court held that a wealthy Palm Beach socialite could not be considered a public figure simply because she was involved in a highly publicized divorce case. This public figure doctrine has made it difficult, but certainly not impossible, for celebrities to prevail in the libel suits they frequently file against the tabloid press. Many jurisdictions have recently adopted statutes that permit private individuals to bring suits against the media for unwarranted invasions of their privacy.

Finally, some states have laws proscribing criminal libel, for example maliciously imputing unchastity to a female or falsely alleging insolvency of financial institutions. The strictures of the First Amendment pose roadblocks to enforcement of such laws. Indeed, statutes criminalizing libel that remain on the books seldom result in criminal prosecutions.

See also Common-Law Background of American Civil Rights and Liberties; First Amendment; Fourteenth Amendment; *Hustler Magazine v. Falwell; New York Times v. Sullivan;* Press, Freedom of the; Privacy, Invasion of

Bibliography

Lewis, Anthony. 1992. *Make No Law: The Sullivan Case and the First Amendment.* New York: Random House.

Smolla, Rodney A. 1988. *Jerry Falwell v. Larry Flynt: The First Amendment on Trial.* New York: St. Martin's Press.

_____. 2001. *Law of Defamation.* 2nd ed. St. Paul, MN: West.

Tiersma, Peter Meijes. 1987. "The Language of Defamation." *Texas Law Review* 66 (2): 303–50.

Walker, Erik. 1993. "Defamation Law: Public Figures— Who Are They?" *Baylor Law Review* 45:955–.

Hon. John M. Scheb and John M. Scheb II

DEFENSE OF MARRIAGE ACT. *See* Same-Sex Marriage and Civil Unions

DEFINITE AND DETERMINATE SENTENCING

Sentencing statutes are an important part of criminal law and are generally categorized in three broad groups: determinate, indeterminate, and guideline. Determinate sentencing can take a variety of forms and is sometimes referred to as definite sentencing. There are, though, differences between definite and determinate sentences and even alternate types within the latter.

Strictly speaking, definite sentences refer to those criminal penalties that impose a specific period of imprisonment with no reduction by parole (Inciardi 2002). Determinate sentences consist of those where a term of imprisonment is fixed for a specific period but is also subject to possible reduction by parole (Cole and Smith 2004). Although both definite and determinate definitions of sentencing focus on a period of incarceration, it is possible that a definite penalty could be specified for an offense that required a particular punishment (e.g., fixed fine) but no imprisonment. In the United States, however, the terms "definite" and "determinate" are generally used in conjunction with penalties that require incarceration, with corresponding terms referred to as fixed.

For most of the twentieth century, indeterminate and indefinite sentences were the norm, resting on the rehabilitative ethic and providing early prison release by parole authorities. Since the 1970s, many state legislatures have enacted definite and determinate sentencing provisions. The federal government, however, adopted a guidelines system in 1984.

Changes in state and federal sentencing laws over the past 30 years stemmed from several concerns. The rehabilitative ethic underlying indefinite and indeterminate sentencing provisions was challenged by a philosophical shift to retribution and deterrence. Indefinite and indeterminate sentencing provisions were also criticized for their uncertainty for both offenders and the justice system, disparate and discriminatory effects, and the poor quality of both judicial and administrative (e.g., parole board) decision making. In 1975, Maine became the first state in the country to shift to a definite sentencing system where flat or fixed terms of imprisonment were specified, and parole abolished.

After Maine, several states adopted definite and determinate sentencing provisions. The latter typically includes three basic forms: determinate discretionary sentencing, presumptive sentencing, and mandatory sentencing (Branham 2002). Determinate discretionary statutes set out sentencing minimums and maximums for each category or type of offense and direct judges to set a specific term within those limits. Arizona, Colorado, and Illinois' sentencing provisions are examples. Presumptive sentencing statutes consist of legislatively directed penalties for each offense. When imprisonment is required, the legislature identifies the modal or presumptive term and indicates reductions ranges for mitigating factors and additions for aggravating circumstances. California was one of the first of a small group of states to adopt presumptive sentencing systems and in the process joined Maine in the abolition of parole. The third type of determinate sentences consists of mandatory terms. Typically, these are defined in terms of a minimum that a judge must apply for conviction of a specific offense but can also include those cases where a definite term is fixed and absolute for the conviction offense. Georgia's sentencing provision for armed robbery (mandatory five-year minimum) is an example of the former, while Michigan's firearms provision (two-year term for carrying or possessing a firearm when committing or attempting a felony) illustrates the latter. It is important to recognize that sentencing statutes in states with indefinite or indeterminate sentencing structures can also feature mandatory penalties for specific crimes. The aforementioned mandatory minimums and life terms for some habitual offenses (e.g., three strikes laws) are examples. In California, the three strikes provision applies to the third conviction for any felony, while in Georgia state statutes require life imprisonment for the second conviction of one of a small number of serious criminal offenses.

Definite and determinate sentencing has come under considerable criticism. Some argue that legislatures set unnecessarily harsh terms or that they are not even capable of staying focused to determine sentencing options and terms. Others call attention to the shift of discretion from judges to prosecutors in cases where the charged offense is often the critical determinant of sentence severity.

Still others complain that these changes in sentencing laws have resulted in costly and unnecessary incarceration and that they have not helped to reduce unjustifiable or discriminatory application of punishment. At a more philosophical level, critics charge that the underlying demise of the rehabilitative ethic has resulted in prison facilities that do little to assist in personal reformation and even intensify the likelihood of recidivism. On the other hand, advocates argue that more definite or determinate sentences have contributed to the decline in crime, reflect more honest correctional policy, and have introduced greater predictability and equity in sentencing. Like the problem of crime itself, it is not likely that debate over sentencing laws and policies will decline.

See also Accused, Rights of the; Indefinite and Indeterminate Sentencing; Plea Bargaining; Presentence Investigation Reports; Sentencing, Eighth Amendment and; Sentencing, Proportionality in; Sentencing Guidelines; Sentencing Hearing; Sixth Amendment

Bibliography

Branham, Lynn S. 2002. *The Law of Sentencing, Corrections, and Prisoners' Rights.* St. Paul, MN: West.

Cole, George F., and Christopher E. Smith. 2004. *The American System of Criminal Justice.* Belmont, CA: Wadsworth/Thomson.

Inciardi, James A. 2002. *Criminal Justice.* New York: Oxford University Press.

Susette M. Talarico

DEMOCRACY. *See* Constitutional Democracy; Representative Democracy

DEPARTMENT OF JUSTICE. *See* U.S. Department of Justice

DEPARTMENT OF LABOR. *See* Employment Discrimination

DESEGREGATION. *See Brown v. Board of Education;* Busing Controversy; Civil Rights Act of 1964; Civil Rights Movement; *Cooper v. Aaron;*

Jim Crow Laws; Little Rock Crisis; Marshall, Thurgood; Meredith, James; National Association for the Advancement of Colored People; *Plessy v. Ferguson;* Segregation, De Facto and De Jure; Segregation in Public Education

DEWEY, JOHN (1859–1952)

A philosopher, educator, and social reformer in the liberal tradition, John Dewey wrote extensively on the connection between a proper educational system and the development of democracy. A strong advocate of public education, Dewey saw education as a fundamental part of maintaining and expanding a free and democratic society. At the beginning of the twentieth century he sought to change the method of educating students so as to produce citizens who could reason and make decisions on their own. He wanted to change the then-current approach where students memorized and recited information back to their teachers. This method, according to Dewey, did not help students learn how to reason or make decisions about their own futures.

Experimentation in education also advanced the cause of liberal democracy, according to Dewey. Different methods of teaching for different students would eliminate the type of absolutist thought that Dewey believed undermined democratic principles. Experimentation in education would also lead to the same in politics. Dewey believed in constant change and reorganization in society and democracy. Adhering to traditional values would only slow progress. Only teaching students how to think and analyze would allow them to move with the inevitable and positive changes in a democracy. Hence Dewey tied together the change in the methods of teaching with the demands of change created by a democratic society.

Dewey complained that those with the most education under the old system also tended to be the least willing to support change within the system. He attributed this on the tendency of schools to teach memorization and repetition. He saw this as indoctrination rather than learning. For Dewey, the properly educated student would know how to engage in social action to actively pursue change in society. Dewey's students would follow what was known as the Progressive movement. Progressives believed the state, using government programs, could improve the lives of its citizens.

At the same time, Dewey did not agree with the argument that freeing people from the constraints of government would allow a democracy to flourish. Dewey believed that liberty could best be practiced by those with an adequate education that allowed them to logically consider their actions and act responsibly. A free population without the proper educational basis would create a less than democratic system.

For Dewey a democratic system was also one that included many different groups and viewpoints, all able to participate within that system. The more people involved in making policy, the more democratic the system. This could be achieved only through systematic education that favored experience and teaching how to solve problems over rote memorization.

See also Constitutional Democracy; Liberalism; Liberty; Public Education, Right to; Representative Democracy

Bibliography

Boisvert, Raymond D. 1998. *John Dewey: Rethinking Our Time.* Albany: State University of New York Press.

Hickman, Larry, and Thomas Alexander, eds. 1998. *The Essential Dewey.* Vol. 1. Bloomington: University of Indiana Press.

Martin, Jay. 2002. *The Education of John Dewey: A Biography.* New York: Columbia University Press.

Savage, Daniel. 2002. *John Dewey's Liberalism: Individual, Community and Self Development* Carbondale: Southern Illinois University Press.

Douglas Clouatre

DHS. *See* Homeland Security, Department of

DIALLO, AMADOU. *See* Force, Use of by Law Enforcement

DISABILITIES, RIGHTS OF PERSONS WITH

Historically, government has taken a paternalist approach in dealing with people with disabilities. Disabled individuals were not viewed as constituents, but as people who needed protection or institutionalization. It was not until the civil rights consciousness of the 1960s that people with disabilities began articulating a different vision for governmental involvement and began mobilizing into a politically active force. Previously, advocates for the disabled had been social workers who emphasized medical cures and rehabilitation. The new movement argued that many of the limitations placed on those deemed disabled did not come from actual physical limitations but from societal constraints. These constraints include antiquated stereotypes of helplessness, and inaccessible and inadaptable physical environments, as well as the cultural stigma of incompetence. Motivated by the slogan, "nothing about us, without us," these groups fought for access to mainstream society and accommodations by society to allow their inclusion. People with disabilities argued that they had faced years of persecution, stereotypes, and paternalism, as had other oppressed groups that had been successful in legislating and litigating formal equality. Consequently, they initially attempted to follow the approach used by women and racial minorities, seeking to amend the Civil Rights Act of 1964 to include people with disabilities. This attempt, however, failed, and the disabilities movement became increasingly radicalized by the glacial pace of governmental and societal recognition of their existence.

Over the past 50 years, virtually every president has designated a commission designed to demonstrate concern for the disabled community; generally, the reports generated by these commissions articulate a need for greater societal inclusion, especially in employment. Legislation, however, rarely resulted from these efforts. With mounting frustration, competing elements of the disability movement became sophisticated in the use of traditional political tools such as civil disobedience and staging direct-action media events. These competing groups and multiple strategies resulted in the serial passage of disability legislation ranging from provision of access to some buildings (Architectural Barriers Act of 1968) to aspects of mass transportation (Urban Mass Transportation Assistance Act of 1970) and to educational opportunities for children previously excluded from public education (Education of All Handicapped Children Act of 1975). None of the legislation, however, addressed what many disability activists perceived to be the primary barrier to their societal involvement—the attitudes and assumptions of the able bodied. Two revolutionary pieces of congressional legislation dramatically changed the response of the government to people with disabilities: the Rehabilitation Act of 1973 and the Americans with Disabilities Act of 1990.

The Rehabilitation Act of 1973 required the federal government, for the first time, to address the issue of societal discrimination against people with disabilities. The act, as amended in 1974, defined the disabled as "any individual who (1) has a physical or mental impairment which substantially limits one or more of such person's major life activities, (2) has a record of such an impairment, or (3) is regarded as having such an impairment." This definition, adopted by Congress in the 1990 Americans with Disabilities Act, moves beyond the definition of formal equality assumed by the Civil Rights Act of 1964 and extends discrimination protection not only to people with disabilities but to people who were previously disabled or might be assumed to be disabled. This definition recognized that the stereotypes regarding disabilities were frequently as handicapping as the disability itself.

Section 504, a simple sentence at the end of the statute, was the most important element of the Rehabilitation Act. "No otherwise qualified handicapped individual in the United States, as defined in Section 7(6), shall, solely by reason of his handicap, be excluded from participation in, be denied the benefits of, or be subjected to discrimination under any program or activity receiving federal financial assistance." While the rules under the 1973 act required all new buildings constructed with federal dollars be made accessible, many organizations (including public schools and universities) only complied when they were legally compelled to do so. The result was extensive federal litigation in order to clarify the statutory requirements. Of specific concern was the statutory expectation that buildings and workplaces need to make "reasonable accommodation" for accessibility without causing an "undue hardship" on the organization or entity. This accommodation could mean the removal of physical barriers, the purchase of specific technology or equipment, the alteration of a job description, or the reevaluation of employer expectations. In *Southeastern Community College v. Davis* (1979) the United States Supreme Court determined that to avoid an undue hardship on the complying organization, any mandated accommodation could not create an "undue financial or administrative" burden.

The Americans with Disabilities Act (ADA) expanded Section 504 by applying these guidelines and protections to private employers, institutions, and businesses. Like the 1973 act, the ADA not only requires that disabled individuals be treated no worse than similarly situated able-bodied individuals but that in certain circumstances they be provided accommodations or treated differently to acquire an equal effect. Critics of the ADA feared that the costs of these accommodations in the workplace would potentially harm the economy, driving small businesses out of profitable competition. Others warned that the resulting litigation would create a cottage industry of lawyers and unworthy litigants who would exploit the ADA for their own personal gain. Supporters of the ADA responded that the average cost for workplace accommodations ranges from $50 to $100. They observed that while much litigation has resulted from the ADA, studies conducted demonstrate the employers/defendants win these cases 80 to 90 percent of the time and that settlements for victorious plaintiffs are typically quite small. In fact, many scholars and advocates have noted that the potential of the ADA to radically transform the workplace for people with disabilities has not been met.

The Supreme Court has heard several cases related to the ADA, and according to most scholars it has significantly restricted its coverage. In three cases decided in 1999 (*Sutton v. United Airlines, Murphy v. United Parcel Services,* and *Albertson's v. Kirkingburg*), the Court significantly narrowed who is covered under the ADA. While the goal of the ADA is to force employers to evaluate employment and workplace norms to see if they unnecessarily discriminate against the disabled by limiting who can file lawsuits under the ADA, the utility of the ADA to change the workplace has been significantly conscribed. The Court has found consistently that people whose disabilities are mitigated through medication or technology (e.g., use of corrective lenses) do not have an impairment of substantial life activity and are therefore not covered by the act. For example, the myopic pilot cannot use the ADA to force the airline to demonstrate that the barrier against pilots who require corrective lenses is necessary in order the meet the requirements of the position. Activists argue that the point of the ADA was not to guarantee that all workers can be accommodated in the workplace, but to allow workers to demonstrate that their needs can be met without an undue burden on the employer. Simultaneously, several lower federal court decisions have found that citizens who can demonstrate that they are so seriously disabled that they have protection under the ADA may require such substantial accommodation that they create an "undue hardship" on the employer. This combination of judicial interpretations may result in the ADA having a more limited impact on the workplace for people with disabilities than intended by its framers.

In *University of Alabama v. Garrett* (2001), the Supreme Court found Section 1 of the ADA unconstitutional because it provided a disabled individual the opportunity to sue for state discrimination in federal court. Because disability is not a suspect classification under the Fourteenth Amendment, states are permitted to enact legislation and take other actions that disadvantage disabled people. According to the *Garrett* ruling, such action would not violate equal protection principles as long as the state can articulate a rational justification for its action. While there is much more statutory protection for people with disabilities in the twenty-first century, the judicial limitations on these protections may prevent the full participation of these citizens in the workplace and in their communities.

See also Civil Rights Act of 1964; Disability Rights Organizations; Equal Protection Clause

Bibliography

Krieger, Linda Hamilton, ed. 2003. *Backlash Against the ADA: Reinterpreting Disability Rights.* Ann Arbor: University of Michigan Press.

O'Brien, Ruth. 2001. *Crippled Justice: The History of the Modern Disability Policy in the Workplace.* Chicago: University of Chicago Press.

Switzer, Jacqueline Vaughn. 2003. *Disabled Rights: An American Disability Policy and the Fight for Equality.* Washington, DC: Georgetown University Press.

Tucker, Bonnie P. 1989. "The Americans with Disabilities Act: An Overview." *University of Illinois Law Review* 4:923–39.

Michelle D. Deardorff

DISABILITY RIGHTS ORGANIZATIONS

Organizations at the local, state, and national levels of American government have been working for many years to advance the rights and opportunities of people with disabilities. The National Association of the Deaf (NAD) was formed in 1880, and the National Federation of the Blind (NFB), building on the work of many state and local organizations, was established in 1940. The American Council of the Blind (ABC) was formed in 1961, following a protracted conflict within the National Federation of the Blind. The National Council of Independent Living dates from the early 1980s and is distinguished from ACB, NFB, and NAD as a cross-disability rather than a single-disability organization. All four groups share common concerns in such vital areas as employment, education, transportation, communication, and access to public accommodations.

The modern disability rights movement at the national level came of age with Congress's passage of the Rehabilitation Act of 1973. The movement achieved a high level of visibility during the political struggle that led to President George H. W. Bush's signing of the Americans with Disabilities Act in July 1990. Singly and in combination, the various disability organizations have contributed significantly to the ongoing education of the public regarding the capabilities of people with disabilities and the challenges that must be met in achieving social equality.

The National Association of the Deaf (NAD)

The National Association of the Deaf (on the Web at www.nad.org) was founded in 1880 in Cincinnati, Ohio. The mission of NAD is "to promote, protect, and preserve the rights and quality of life of deaf and hard of hearing individuals in the United States." NAD, the oldest and largest membership organization of deaf and hard-of-hearing people in this country, seeks to "safeguard the accessibility and civil rights of 28 million deaf and hard of hearing Americans in education, employment, health care, and telecommunications." The NAD is a dynamic organization of 51 state affiliates, a number of other organizational affiliates, and individual members. The NAD advocates, primarily on the federal level, for the deaf and hard-of-hearing community on legislative and public policy issues. The group deals with the implementation and enforcement of various civil rights laws that affect deaf people, including the Americans with Disabilities Act, the Individuals with Disabilities Education Act, and the Fair Housing Act. The NAD is involved in various other endeavors relating to captioned media, certification of sign language interpreters, certification of American Sign Language professionals, deafness-related publications, legal assistance, and youth development. Through its activities, the NAD has improved the quality of life of deaf and hard-of-hearing people in numerous ways.

The National Federation of the Blind (NFB)

Founded in 1940, the National Federation of the Blind (on the Web at www.nfb.org) has more than 700 local affiliate organizations located in all 50 states, Washington D.C., and Puerto Rico and claims a national membership of over 50,000 members. The NFB has a twofold purpose: (1) to help blind persons achieve self-confidence and self-respect and (2) to act as a vehicle for collective self-expression by the blind. It provides public education about blindness, information and referral services for the blind, scholarships, adaptive equipment and appliances for the visually impaired, and advocacy services.

The NFB has also developed two telephone systems for use by visually impaired individuals. One system, NFB-Newsline, offers the complete text of leading national and local newspapers through the use of a touch-tone phone. The other system, Jobline, offers national employment listings and job openings through a telephone menu system. Additionally, the Federation publishes two magazines: the *Braille Monitor* and *Future Reflections*. The *Braille Monitor*, a monthly publication, "provides a positive philosophy about blindness" and discusses various events, activities, and issues relevant to the blind community. *Future Reflections*, a magazine for the parents and teachers of blind children, is published quarterly and addresses the issues that a blind child will confront from birth to college and how to deal with these issues.

The American Council of the Blind (ACB)

Founded in 1961, the American Council of the Blind (on the Web at www.acb.org) is one of the nation's leading advocacy groups representing the interests of blind and visually impaired people. ACB has 51 state affiliates with approximately 500 local chapters, as well as 20 other special interest affiliates, including the American Association of Visually Impaired Attorneys, the National Association of Blind Teachers, Blind Information Technology Specialists (BITS), and Guide Dog Users, Inc. Although a large majority of the Council's membership consists of blind and visually impaired people, it has a number of fully sighted members as well.

The Council's main purpose is "to improve the well-being of all blind and visually impaired people

by: serving as a representative national organization of blind people; [and] elevating the social, economic and cultural levels of blind people." In implementing this broad objective, ACB seeks to improve elementary and secondary educational services available to blind and visually impaired students. It also awards merit scholarships to qualified individuals at all levels of postsecondary education. In addition, the Council works to improve rehabilitation facilities and programs while cooperating with "public and private institutions and organizations" providing other services to the blind and visually impaired. Consistent with its positive philosophy, ACB encourages all blind people to "develop their abilities" and to achieve independence as fully contributing members of society. ACB challenges negative stereotypes of blindness by conducting programs designed to "promote greater understanding of blindness and the capabilities of blind people."

ACB has been an active advocate for the visually impaired community on a number of important issues, including (1) educational opportunities; (2) improvement of rehabilitation services; (3) employment discrimination; (4) equal access to public accommodations, including an effort to require the U.S. Treasury Department to adapt currency so that it can be identified by blind and visually impaired people; (5) early implementation of the Help America Vote Act and independent access to the secret ballot in national, state, and local elections; (6) pedestrian safety; (7) advancement of descriptive video, in which verbal description details visual action occurring on-screen that is otherwise inaccessible to blind people (i.e., body language, scene changes, etc.); and (8) availability and affordability of adaptive technology such as computer software that provides direct access to printed material.

The Council has been a major driving force in the production and use of reading materials in formats such as Braille, recordings, and large print. As part of this effort, the ACB publishes its own free monthly national magazine, the *Braille Forum*. The magazine, which has a readership of over 26,000 people, is produced in Braille, large-print format, cassette, and computer-readable disc. It addresses topics of national interest including employment, legislation, and sports and leisure activities.

The Council's advocacy role extends to the provision of legal assistance to blind and visually impaired persons who have encountered discrimination in employment, education, housing, transportation, access to public accommodations, and related areas. In this forum, ACB has supported and participated directly in litigation aimed at protecting and extending the rights of blind and visually impaired people.

For a number of years, ACB has produced and distributed various television and radio public service announcements containing information about the organization's activities and emphasizing the capabilities and accomplishments of blind and visually impaired people. Recognizing the growing impact of the Internet on communications, the Council began webcasting *ACB Radio* in the year 2000. This popular program provides timely information and commentary on issues of interest to blind and visually impaired people throughout the world. It also offers descriptions of new products and services, as well as entertainment programs. *ACB Radio* is available to Internet users free of charge.

The American Council of the Blind maintains a national office, in Washington, D.C., headed by an executive director and staffed by blind and sighted employees. The Council is strongly committed to principles of democratic governance. Policies are initially formulated and recommended or approved by an elected 16-member board of directors. The president and other officers may serve a maximum of three consecutive two-year terms, and the non-officer directors are limited to two consecutive terms of four years. Ultimate authority rests with the National Convention, which meets annually. Individual members and affiliates are entitled to full voting rights at the National Convention.

The National Council on Independent Living (NCIL)

The National Council on Independent Living (online at www.ncil.org) is the "oldest cross disability, grassroots organization run by and for people with disabilities." The Council represents more than 700 various organizations that advocate for the civil rights of disabled people throughout the United States, including centers for independent living and statewide independent-living councils.

The NCIL was established in 1982 in response to the 1978 amendments to the Rehabilitation Act of 1973, which added statutory language and funding for the formation of centers for independent living. Executive directors of local centers for independent living agreed that a national organization was needed to advocate for the development and expansion of a nationwide network of centers for independent living. The Council's main philosophy is "that individuals with disabilities have the right to live with dignity and with appropriate support in their own homes, fully participate in their communities, and to control and make decisions about their lives."

Other Important Organizations

Other important groups in the disability rights arena include the National Coalition for Disability Rights (online at www.adawatch.org), the Bazelon Center for Mental Health Law (www.bazelon.org), the Disability Rights Education and Defense Fund (www.dredf.org), and the National Alliance for the Mentally Ill (www.nami.org).

See also Interest Groups; Disabilities, Rights of Persons with

Bibliography

Fleischer, Doris Zames, and Frieda Zames. 2000. *The Disability Rights Movement*. Philadelphia: Temple University Press.

Megivern, James, and Marjorie. 2003. *People of Vision: A History of the American Council of the Blind*. Bloomington, IN: Authorhouse Publishing.

Switzer, Jacqueline Vaughn. 2003. *Disabled Rights: An American Disability Policy and the Fight for Equality*. Washington, DC: Georgetown University Press.

Otis H. Stephens, Jr.

DISCRETE AND INSULAR MINORITIES. *See* Equal Protection Jurisprudence; Fundamental Rights; Strict Scrutiny; *United States v. Carolene Products*

DISCRIMINATION

To discriminate is to separate or draw a distinction. In the legal context, discrimination refers to differential treatment of people based on their membership in some group or category. Discrimination can be public or private. Public discrimination is that based on law, public policy, or the actions of government officials. Private discrimination is that which occurs outside the governmental context. The object of civil rights law is to delineate between permissible and impermissible forms of discrimination.

The Equal Protection Clause of the Fourteenth Amendment prohibits states from denying to persons within their jurisdiction the equal protection of the laws. Although it is well known that the amendment was adopted primarily to protect the rights of the newly freed former slaves, it makes no mention of race. The Equal Protection Clause is the legal basis upon which various forms of state-sponsored discrimination can be attacked. In *Bolling v. Sharpe* (1954), the Supreme Court held that the Due Process Clause of the Fifth Amendment imposes on the federal government a similar prohibition against discrimination. Federal laws, state laws, and local ordinances prohibit various forms of public and private discrimination.

At the outset it is important to recognize that most forms of discrimination are perfectly legal. For example, federal and state laws prohibit persons from dispensing medicinal drugs unless they are licensed pharmacists. The law requires a driver's license to operate an automobile on a public street and prohibits children under a certain age (usually 16) from obtaining a license. People cannot perform surgery in hospitals unless they are licensed to do so. All of these restrictions involve discrimination, yet few (other than the most hard-core libertarians) would challenge the propriety of such restrictions.

Most instances of official discrimination are valid because they are rationally related to a legitimate governmental objective. As the Supreme Court observed in *New Orleans v. Dukes* (1976), courts in most instances "presume the constitutionality of the statutory discriminations and require only that the classification challenged be rationally related to a legitimate state interest." In *Barrett v. Indiana* (1913), the Supreme Court observed, "The equal protection of the laws requires laws of like application to all similarly situated; but in selecting some classes and leaving out others the legislature, while it keeps within this principle, is, and may be, allowed wide discretion."

More recently, in *Ferguson v. Skrupa* (1963), the Supreme Court noted that laws "create many classifications which do not deny equal protection; it is only 'invidious discrimination' which offends the Constitution." In *Loving v. Virginia* (1967), Chief Justice Earl Warren pointed out that "the Equal Protection Clause requires the consideration of whether the classifications drawn by any statute constitute an arbitrary and invidious discrimination." The word "invidious" refers generally to that which arouses resentment, animosity, or ill will. Invidious discrimination is that which is oppressive or tends to elevate the status of one group over that of another.

The courts have held that some forms of discrimination are inherently suspect. Because one's race bears no relationship to one's ability or performance, discrimination based on race has come to be viewed as nothing more than the manifestation of racism. In *Korematsu v. United States* (1944), the Supreme Court said that "all legal restrictions which curtail the civil rights of a single racial group are immediately suspect." The courts have used this suspect classification doctrine to strictly scrutinize laws, policies, and programs discriminating on the basis of race. With the notable exception of affirmative action programs, which are characterized by their defenders as benign forms of discrimination, virtually all instances of official race discrimination have been declared invalid. Likewise, courts strictly scrutinize governmental actions that discriminate on the basis of religion, alienage, or ethnicity. Strict judicial scrutiny means that the challenged discrimination is presumed to be invalid; the government carries the burden of persuasion to demonstrate otherwise. To carry that burden, the government must show that its policy is necessary to the achievement of a compelling interest and that it is "narrowly tailored" to further that interest.

Official discrimination based on sex is not currently considered to be inherently suspect but is subject to heightened scrutiny, which means that the government must show that a challenged policy bears a substantial relationship to an important governmental interest.

In *Kirchberg v. Feenstra* (1981), the Supreme Court said that "the burden remains on the party seeking to uphold a statute that expressly discriminates on the basis of sex to advance an 'exceedingly persuasive justification' for the challenged classification." Using this standard, courts have invalidated numerous instances of gender-based discrimination.

Other forms of official discrimination that have been successfully attacked in the courts include discrimination based on age, wealth, disability, and, most recently, sexual orientation. In many instances these challenges have been based not on the Equal Protection Clause of the Fourteenth Amendment or the implicit equal protection component of the Fifth Amendment, but on similar protections found in state constitutions and in federal and state statutes. Every state constitution has some provision analogous to the Equal Protection Clause of the Fourteenth Amendment. Moreover, Congress, the 50 state legislatures, and numerous local governing bodies have enacted laws prohibiting various forms of discrimination in both public and private contexts. One who is the victim of private discrimination in employment, housing, banking, or the enjoyment of places of public accommodation may well have remedies based on federal, state, or local antidiscrimination laws.

See also Affirmative Action; Age Discrimination; Disabilities, Rights of Persons with; Employment Discrimination; Equality; Equal Protection Clause; Equal Protection Jurisprudence; Equal Rights Amendment; Fifth Amendment; Fourteenth Amendment; Gender-Based Discrimination; Housing, Discrimination in; Immigrants and Aliens, Rights of; Private Actors, Discrimination by; Sexual Orientation, Discrimination Based on

Bibliography

Baer, Judith. 1983. *Equality Under the Constitution: Reclaiming the Fourteenth Amendment.* Ithaca, NY: Cornell University Press.

Davis, Abraham L., and Barbara Luck Graham. 1995. *The Supreme Court, Race, and Civil Rights: From Marshall to Rehnquist.* Thousand Oaks, CA: Sage.

Farley, John E. 2004. *Majority-Minority Relations.* 5th ed. Upper Saddle River, NJ: Prentice Hall.

Graham, Hugh Davis. 1990. *The Civil Rights Era: Origins and Development of a National Policy.* New York: Oxford University Press.

Rossum, Ralph. 1980, *Reverse Discrimination: The Constitutional Debate.* New York: Dekker.

John M. Scheb II and Otis H. Stephens, Jr.

DISCRIMINATION BY PRIVATE ACTORS

In a series of decisions beginning with *Brown v. Board of Education* (1954) and culminating in *Loving v. Virginia* (1967), the Supreme Court repudiated the separate but equal doctrine and invalidated the regime of Jim Crow laws that mandated racial segregation. Yet these decisions did not address the widespread practice of racial discrimination by private actors including businesses, civic groups, and social clubs as well as individuals. Because, as the Supreme Court held in The Civil Rights Cases (1883), private discrimination lies beyond the prohibitions of the Fourteenth Amendment, such discrimination must be addressed by legislation.

Congress first attempted to prohibit racial discrimination by privately owned businesses when it enacted the Civil Rights Act of 1875, but the Supreme Court held in The Civil Rights Cases that the act exceeded congressional enforcement powers under the Fourteenth Amendment. Ultimately, in passing Title II of the Civil Rights Act of 1964, Congress was able to prohibit racial discrimination on the part of restaurants, hotels and other public accommodations by invoking its broad power to regulate interstate commerce (see *Heart of Atlanta Motel v. United States,* 1964; *Katzenbach v. McClung,* 1964). Title VII of the 1964 Civil Rights Act prohibited racial discrimination in private-sector employment, again relying on Congress's power in the field of interstate commerce. And in 1972, Congress amended Title VII to prohibit gender-based employment discrimination as well.

Congress also relied on the Commerce Clause to enact the Fair Housing Act of 1968, which prohibited racial discrimination in the rental or sale of homes where the transaction is handled by a licensed agent. In *Jones v. Alfred Mayer* (1968), the Supreme Court interpreted the Civil Rights Act of 1866 broadly to prohibit racial discrimination in real estate transactions not covered by the Fair Housing Act. And in *Runyon v. McCrary* (1976), the Court interpreted the 1866 statute broadly to prohibit racial discrimination by private schools. As the Supreme Court recognized in *Runyon*, "It is now well established that Section 1 of the Civil Rights Act of 1866 ... prohibits racial discrimination in the making and enforcement of private contracts."

Historically, the state governments were anything but leaders in the struggle for civil rights. Yet today, all states have their own civil rights laws that parallel and, in many instances, go beyond the scope of federal law. Many cities and counties have also enacted ordinances along these lines. In some instances these laws have been applied to organizations such as civic groups and social clubs that are not covered by the federal civil rights statutes. By and large these measures have met with judicial approval, especially when the affected organizations have an economic or commercial character. For example, in *Roberts v. United States Jaycees* (1984) the Supreme Court upheld a Minnesota law that had been interpreted to require a civic organization to accept women as full members. Writing for the Court, Justice William Brennan recognized the Jaycees' right to freedom of association under the First Amendment but held that this right was trumped by the state's "compelling interest" in eradicating sex discrimination. Three years later, in *Board of Directors of Rotary International v. Rotary Club of Duarte* (1987), the Court allowed the state of California to require Rotary clubs within the state to accept women. And in *New York Club Association v. City of New York* (1988), the Court upheld a New York City ordinance that required certain all-male social clubs to admit women.

It should be understood that there remain numerous private clubs in this country that continue to discriminate among members on the basis of race, gender, and religion. Because the federal civil rights laws do not apply to such organizations (unless they qualify as public accommodations or their discriminatory policies are sanctioned by state action), it is up to state and local authorities to enact, and then enforce, laws that do apply in this context. In many states and communities, public opinion does not support governmental intrusion into a sphere of activity that historically has been considered private. Moreover, noncommercial groups can challenge governmental actions of this kind by invoking the First Amendment freedom of association.

In recent years, a number of cities and states have enacted laws prohibiting discrimination based on sexual orientation in employment, housing and the use of public accommodations. While these laws have generally been upheld by the courts, the U.S. Supreme Court has not been willing to allow state and local governments to interpret these laws to require private organizations to abolish their policies of excluding people based on sexual orientation. In *Hurley v. Irish-American Gay, Lesbian and Bisexual Group of Boston* (1995), the Court held that the state of Massachusetts could not prohibit the organizers of the annual St. Patrick's Day parade from excluding gay-rights groups. And in *Boy Scouts of America v. Dale* (2000), the Court refused to permit the state of New Jersey to force the Boy Scouts to accept gay scout leaders. In the Court's view, this requirement would be a "severe intrusion on the Boy Scouts' right to freedom of expressive association" guaranteed by the First Amendment. In dissent, Justice John Paul Stevens quoted Justice Louis D. Brandeis, who once wrote that "we must be ever on our guard, lest we erect our prejudices into legal principles."

See also Association, Freedom of; *Boy Scouts of America v. Dale;* Brandeis, Louis D.; Brennan, William J., Jr.; *Brown v. Board of Education;* Civil Rights Act of 1866; Civil Rights Act of 1875; Civil Rights Act of 1964; Civil Rights Cases;

Employment Discrimination; Equal Protection Clause; Fair Housing Act of 1968; First Amendment; Fourteenth Amendment; Gay Rights Movement; *Heart of Atlanta Motel v. United States;* Housing, Discrimination in; *Loving v. Virginia;* Public Accommodations, Places of; Segregation, De Facto and De Jure; Sexual Orientation, Discrimination Based on; State Action Doctrine; Stevens, John Paul

Bibliography

Abernathy, Charles F. 2000. *Civil Rights and Constitutional Litigation: Cases and Materials.* 3rd ed. St. Paul, MN: West.

Cortner, Richard C. 2001. *Civil Rights and Public Accommodations.* Lawrence: University Press of Kansas.

Jeffries, John C., Pamela S. Karlan, Peter W. Low, and George A. Rutherglen. 2000. *Civil Rights Actions: Enforcing the Constitution.* New York: Foundation Press.

John M. Scheb II and Otis H. Stephens, Jr.

DISCOVERY. *See* Pretrial Discovery

DISPARATE IMPACT. *See* Civil Rights Act of 1964; Civil Rights Restoration Act of 1991; Employment Discrimination

DIVERSITY

Diversity is not just a code word for consideration of race and gender issues. Diversity is the principle that all people and groups, without regard to differences, should be respected, valued, and appreciated to maximize the potential for a greater common good. Diversity in public institutions continues to be a hot-button issue in American society.

Many Americans recognize that diversity is an important issue in public organizations, especially colleges and universities. Americans also generally agree that colleges and universities should have racially diverse campuses; however, Americans do not agree on the best method of achieving diversity. The changing demographic characteristics of the workforce present both challenges and opportunities to individuals and the organizations that they represent (Chemers, Oskamp, and Costanzo 1995).

Diversity is important in many different organizations, including places of business, institutes of higher learning, and divisions of government. A diverse membership gives an organization access to a broader spectrum of strengths, ideas, and views. Diversity is often defined to encompass a variety of factors; differences in race, ethnicity, religion, ability, and other traits are characteristics of a diverse group. Individuals and groups who value diversity strive to include all kinds of people in their activities and organizations.

Affirmative action is a widely used method for promoting diversity. Proponents of affirmative action contend that it is necessary to reduce the lingering effects of past discrimination and that it fosters diversity in a wide range of fields without unduly prejudicing hiring decisions. They also point out that African Americans and Hispanics are still underrepresented in student enrollment when compared to their proportion of the total U.S. population. Hispanics comprise 12.5 percent and African Americans comprise 12.3 percent of the total population. But when it comes to total enrollment at U.S. colleges and universities, Hispanics comprise only 4.4 percent, and African Americans comprise 7.6 percent (Jost 2005). Proponents of affirmative action also argue that members of minority groups are not the only beneficiaries under affirmative action programs. They maintain that society as a whole stands to benefit from the increases in equality and diversity achieved through affirmative action.

Opponents of affirmative action believe that it is no longer needed to assist African Americans, Hispanics, and other minority groups. Critics of affirmative action as a means of encouraging diversity allege that the policy allows less qualified minority individuals to obtain positions simply to fulfill quotas, thereby enforcing a system of reverse discrimination for nonminorities. It is important to recognize that the achievement of diversity has been cited by the courts as a compelling interest to offset claims of reverse discrimination.

Diversity benefits organizations, companies, and the economy as a whole. A diverse workforce is better able to serve a diverse world and its inhabitants. Flourishing businesses help keep our economy stable. A diverse population brings about creative and groundbreaking ideas in organizations and businesses. Diversity serves to educate the young and the privileged about the challenges faced by people outside their peer group. It is vital, however, that programs promoting the goals of diversity be explained and implemented in a way that is tolerable to minority and majority groups alike. Programs like affirmative action can encourage the development of a more morally defensible society.

The leadership within any organization must be committed to the concept of diversity before it will become an ingrained value. The primary means of increasing diversity's role in organizational culture are (1) through the selection process, especially for managerial personnel; (2) through changes in the management systems; and (3) through ongoing education and communication activities (Cox 1994). Diversity values must be incorporated, learned, and applied in everyday life so that all groups of individuals are prized, appreciated, and able to reach new heights of success.

See also Affirmative Action; Employment Discrimination; Equality; Gender-Based Discrimination; Pluralism

Bibliography

Cox, Taylor, 1994. *Cultural Diversity in Organizations.* San Francisco: Berrett-Koehler.

Chemers, Martin, Stuart Oskamp, and Mark Costanzo. 1995. *Diversity in Organizations: New Perspectives for Changing Workplace.* Thousand Oaks, CA: Sage.

Jost, Kenneth. 2005. *Issues in Race, Ethnicity and Gender.* Washington DC: CQ Press.

F. Erik Brooks and Ashley Scruggs

DNA EVIDENCE. *See* Postconviction Relief

DOCTOR-ASSISTED SUICIDE

In doctor-assisted suicide (also known as physician-assisted suicide), a physician provides a patient with a lethal dose of drugs, and the patient takes the drug to end his or her own life. The distinction between doctor-assisted suicide and euthanasia is that in assisted suicide the doctor only provides the means of death; the patient causes his or her own death (Brock 1992). "Euthanasia," however, is the Greek term meaning good or easy death (Glick 1992). In contemporary terms, euthanasia is the act of painlessly putting to death a person who is suffering from an incurable, painful disease or condition (Quill 1993).

The practice of an assisted death is not a modern phenomenon. In ancient Greece, the government gave hemlock, a poison, to those who requested it. The Greeks felt that a death caused by disease or suffering was dishonorable; a good death, or euthanasia, was one that occurred when the person was in good health and was therefore honorable (Leone 1997). Most of the Greek philosophers endorsed assisted suicide to escape the pains of disease and public humiliation. This stoic attitude prevailed until the rise of Christianity in the third century (Emmanuel 1998).

In the sixteenth century, Renaissance philosophers rediscovered the Greek and Roman concept of euthanasia. Writings by Sir Thomas Moore (*Utopia*, 1516), Francis Bacon (*New Atlantis*, 1629) and David Hume ("Of Suicide," 1757) advocated euthanasia and assisted suicide in intellectual terms, and had very little impact on medicine and public opinion (Schere and Simon 1999).

In the United States, modern interest in euthanasia and assisted suicide began in 1870, when a nonphysician, Samuel Williams, addressed the Birmingham Speculate Club on the topic of euthanasia. He advocated the use of chloroform "in all cases of hopeless and painful illness," not just to relieve pain, but to bring about "a quick and painless death" (Leone 1997). The idea of euthanasia and assisted suicide began gaining ground in the twentieth century because of new medical technologies to prolong life and the development of new drugs, such as morphine, that could relieve pain and could also painlessly induce death (Leone 1997).

Williams's comments sparked debate and opposition to euthanasia among the medical community. As a result, more than half of the 17 states in the nation prohibited assisted suicide (Leone 1997). Other states, such as Ohio (1906), Nebraska (1937), and New York (1939) attempted to pass legislation legalizing assisted suicide but failed.

When the Nazis took power in Germany in 1933, they used the ideas of Alfred Hoche and Karl Binding to purge Germany of "undesirables" and "the impaired." Hoche and Binding asserted that "death assistance" by a physician was consistent with medical ethics in instances of brain damage, mental retardation, and psychiatric illness, where termination of a life was not homicide, but a "useful act" (Worsnop 1997). This program, which the Nazis called euthanasia, culminated in the mass extermination of millions. As a result, the idea of medical assistance in the termination of life became an untouchable social policy in the United States and Europe until the 1970s (Worsnop 1997).

In that decade assisted suicide reemerged as a widely debated public issue. Interest focused on "death with dignity," a phrase that describes the right of a terminally ill person to refuse life-sustaining medical treatment (Worsnop 1997). Many states attempted to pass bills allowing terminally ill patients to refuse heroic treatment, none of which were successful. However, by 1990, most states successfully passed legislation expanding patient autonomy, including the medical right to refuse treatment, advance directives, the durable power of attorney, and the do-not-resuscitate order (Glick 1992).

After passage of these laws, the assisted suicide movement focused on the rights of competent terminally ill patients who wished to end their lives before they became dependent on life support-systems. Euthanasia groups in the United States addressed the rights of individuals who are not terminally ill but desire to hasten their deaths to escape lifelong pain that accompanies their illnesses (i.e., AIDS, Alzheimer's, certain cancers, and Lou Gehrig's disease) (Desimone 1996). By the 1990s, the advancement and legalization of the rights of competent patients to refuse treatment were widely accepted. As a result, right-to-die groups argued that if one has the right to refuse life-sustaining treatment, knowing that the refusal will result in death, why should one not have a similar right to request physician assistance to hasten death (Hamel and DuBose 1996).

In the 1990s, Jack Kevorkian, a Michigan pathologist, heightened the debate of assisted suicide. Kevorkian, who is now in prison in the state of Michigan, claims to have assisted more than 100 people to end their lives with the use of his suicide machine, a machine that allowed patients to commit suicide with the self-administration of a lethal infusion of intravenous drugs (Worsnop 1995).

In 1994, the right-to-die movement achieved the legislation it had pursued for a century. The Oregon Death with Dignity Act, a citizen initiative legalizing physician-assisted suicide, was passed by Oregon voters. The 1994 Death with Dignity Act was enjoined and later reinstated after a failed legislative repeal campaign. In 1997, after unsuccessful initiative attempts in Washington, California, and Michigan, Oregon became the first state to legalize physician-assisted suicide.

In 1994, a federal judge declared unconstitutional Washington State's law criminalizing assisted suicide. The U.S. Court of Appeals for the Ninth Circuit agreed, concluding that the law was unconstitutional as applied to "terminally ill competent adults who wish to hasten their deaths with medication prescribed by their physicians." In *Washington v. Glucksberg* (1997), the Supreme Court reversed the Ninth Circuit's decision. Writing for a unanimous Court, Chief Justice William H. Rehnquist observed that nearly every state makes it a crime to assist in a suicide, and that the statutes banning assisted suicide are long-standing expressions of the states' commitment to the protection and preservation of all human life. Rehnquist rejected any parallel between a person's right to terminate medical treatment and the right to have assistance in committing suicide. Rehnquist recognized that a serious debate was taking place throughout the nation on doctor-assisted suicide—a debate that the Court's decision permitted to continue.

See also Due Process, Substantive; Fourteenth Amendment; Liberty; Medical Treatment, Right to Refuse; Privacy, Constitutional Right of; Pro-life Movement; Pro-life Position; Rehnquist, William H.; Right to Die

Bibliography

Brock, Dan. 1992. "Voluntary Active Euthanasia." *Hastings Center Report* 22 (2): 10–21.

Desimone, Cathleen. 1996. *Death on Demand: Physician-Assisted Suicide in the United States.* New York: William S. Hein.

Emmanuel, Linda, ed. 1998. *Regulating How We Die: The Ethical, Medical and Legal Issues.* Cambridge, MA: Harvard University Press.

Glick, Henry. 1992. *The Right to Die.* New York: Columbia University Press.

Hamel, Ronald, and Edwin DuBose. 1996. *Must We Suffer Our Way to Death?* Dallas, TX: Southern Methodist University Press.

Leone, Bruno. 1997. *Assisted Suicide.* CA: Greenhaven Press.

Quill, Timothy. 1993. *Death and Dignity: Making Choices and Taking Charge.* New York: W. W. Norton.

Schere, Jennifer, and Rita Simon. 1999. *Euthanasia and the Right to Die: A Comparative View.* Lanham, MD: Rowman & Littlefield.

Worsnop, Richard. 1995. "Assisted Suicide Controversy." *CQ Researcher* 5:393–416.

_____. 1997. "Caring for the Dying." *CQ Researcher* 7:769–92.

Dina M. Krois

DOGS, USE OF BY POLICE

The use of dogs to detect crimes or suspects goes back to ancient times (Taslitz 1990). In *Hodge v. State* (1893) the Alabama Supreme Court noted that "it is common knowledge that dogs may be trained to follow the tracks of a human being with considerable certainty and accuracy." During Prohibition there was some use of dogs in tracking down moonshiners (Taslitz 1990, 26). The use of dogs in detecting drugs and explosives is a modern practice; in fact, the United States Customs Service did not begin using drug dogs until about 1970 (Taslitz 1990, 26n53).

Today, although police dogs are commonplace in law enforcement, questions as to limits on the use of dogs remain. In particular, there are concerns regarding the use of dogs as potentially lethal force against persons and the use of dogs in conducting searches and seizures.

Use of Force

The early use of dogs as force dates back to ancient times, when the Greeks and Romans used them in combat. The modern use of dogs to control persons invokes memories of their use against civil rights marchers in 1963 Birmingham, Alabama. Today concerns remain about police dogs and their use as force. In general, cases of dogs used as force are subject to the standards articulated by the United States Supreme Court in *Graham v. O'Connor* and *Tennessee v. Garner.* There appears to be little divide with regard to the standards set forth in *Graham* and their application in dog cases; however, the same cannot be said about *Garner.* The courts are divided as to when the use of a dog constitutes deadly force. The Sixth Circuit faced the issue in a Tennessee case where, during the search of a darkened building, a police dog bit a suspected burglar on the neck, causing his death. In *Robinette v. Barnes* (1988), the court, in discussing the standard of review for cases involving dogs as force, stated that with regard to deadly force, "the use of a properly trained police dog to apprehend a felony suspect does not carry with it a substantial risk of causing death or serious bodily harm," and furthermore that when the use of a dog causes a death, it is an "extreme aberration from the outcome intended or expected." The Court indicated that in order for there to be a use of deadly force reviewable under *Garner,* there must be intent on the part of the officer involved to inflict "death or serious bodily harm," or possibly the use of an untrained dog.

More recently, in *Marquez v. City of Albuquerque* (2005), the Tenth Circuit stated, "While we have not addressed whether use of a police dog is properly considered deadly force, every circuit to consider the question has held that it is not…. And for the purposes of this case, we assume that use of a police dog is not deadly force ipso facto." However, in *Chew v. Gates* (1994), the Ninth Circuit left open the question as to whether the use of a dog could be considered deadly force by noting that deadly or not, the question is whether the force used was excessive. Judge Norris, concurring in part and dissenting in part, stated:

Whether a particular instrument of force qualifies as an instrument of deadly force is a question of fact. Indeed, whether particular *dogs* as trained and deployed qualify as deadly weapons has been uniformly treated as a question of fact for the jury.... [T]he question whether or not the LAPD dogs, as trained to bite and hold suspects, constitute instruments of deadly force is an issue of fact that cannot be decided at summary judgment.

Thus, the use of a dog against a person may constitute an excessive use of force reviewable under the standards of *Graham* and may possibly be considered deadly force subject to the standards of *Garner*.

Use of Dogs in Searches

In *United States v. Place* (1983), the Supreme Court considered the use of dogs in drug searches. The Court found that:

a "canine sniff" by a well-trained narcotics detection dog... discloses only the presence or absence of narcotics, a contraband item. Thus, despite the fact that the sniff tells the authorities something about the contents of the luggage, the information obtained is limited.... In these respects, the canine sniff is *sui generis*. We are aware of no other investigative procedure that is so limited both in the manner in which the information is obtained and in the content of the information revealed by the procedure. Therefore, we conclude that the particular course of investigation that the agents intended to pursue here—exposure of respondent's luggage, which was located in a public place, to a trained canine—did not constitute a "search" within the meaning of the Fourth Amendment.

Recently the Court reaffirmed its finding in *Place*. In *Illinois v. Caballes* (2005), the Court held that "the use of a well-trained narcotics-detection dog ... during a lawful traffic stop, generally does not implicate legitimate privacy interests." Noting that the dog was used only to sniff the exterior of a car that was lawfully stopped for a traffic violation,

the Court found that the "intrusion on respondent's privacy expectations does not rise to the level of a constitutionally cognizable infringement."

While the line of federal cases from *Place* and *Caballes* has reinforced the use of dogs to detect drugs, state courts, interpreting state constitutions, have been willing to limit the use of dogs for this purpose. For example, in *State v. Ortiz* (1999), the Supreme Court of Nebraska, in a case involving the use of a dog to sniff outside a door to an apartment to establish the basis for a search warrant, wrote:

We agree with the courts which conclude an individual's Fourth Amendment privacy interests may extend in a limited manner beyond the four walls of the home, depending on the facts, including some expectation of privacy to be free from police canine sniffs for illegal drugs in the hallway outside an apartment or at the threshold of a residence, and that a canine sniff under these circumstances must be based on no less than reasonable, articulable suspicion ... under the facts of this case, we conclude that, given the legitimate expectation of some measure of privacy in the hallway, the canine sniff for illegal drugs which lacked reasonable suspicion violated the Fourth Amendment and Neb. Const. art. I, § 7.

Similarly, in *State v. Tackitt* (2003), the Montana Supreme Court interpreted its state constitution as providing its citizens broader privacy protections than the Federal Constitution. Regarding the use of a drug dog to sniff a vehicle, the court stated, "Montana's citizens have a reasonable expectation of privacy in areas of their vehicles that are out of plain view," and thus "when a person stores something in a concealed area of a vehicle and seeks to preserve their privacy, that privacy has constitutional protections." Consequently, the court held that "the balance between governmental interests and individual interests in this case can best be struck by requiring particularized suspicion as a prerequisite for the use of a drug-detecting canine."

Finally, in a Maryland case police received an anonymous tip regarding the possession of drugs by occupants of an apartment complex. Officers went to the complex with a drug dog. They entered through a public doorway and remained in the common areas and hallways of the building. They then proceeded to use the dog to sniff the exterior doors of various apartments in order to confirm their information. Using the information of the drug dog's alert to a particular residence, the officer obtained a search warrant and returned to the residence. In *Fitzgerald v. State* (2004), the Maryland Court of Appeals, in affirming the denial of the suppression of evidence, concluded "that binding and persuasive authority compel our holding that a dog sniff of the exterior of a residence is not a search under the Fourth Amendment." These cases are evidence of a continuing divide that exists among various jurisdictions with regards to the use of drug dogs in detecting contraband.

Given the ongoing war on drugs and the current threat of terrorism, police will continue to use dogs in their searches for drugs, explosives, and suspects; consequently, there will continue to be litigation in both the federal and state courts.

See also Accused, Rights of the; Arrest, Constitutional Limits on; Automobile Stops and Searches; Drugs, War on; Fourth Amendment; Privacy, Reasonable Expectations of; Stop and Frisk; Terrorism, War on

Bibliography

Audero, Maria A. 1999. "From Man's Best Friend to Deadly Force? *Vera Cruz v. City of Escondido*." *Southwestern University Law Review* 29:139–66.

Hall, Hope Walker. 1994. "Sniffing out the Fourth Amendment: *United States v. Place*—Dog Sniffs—Ten Years Later." *Maine Law Review* 46:151.

Hunter, Dave. 2002. "Common Scents: Establishing a Presumption of Reliability for Detector Dog Teams Used in Airports in Light of the Current Terrorist Threat." *Dayton Law Review* 28:89–109.

Paul, Nina, and Will Trachman. 2005. "Fidos and Fi-Don'ts: Why the Supreme Court Should Have Found a Search in *Illinois v. Caballes*." *California Criminal Law Review* 9:1.

Sloman, Lisa K. 2004. "Throw a Dog a Suspect: When Using Police Dogs Becomes an Unreasonable Use of Force under the Fourth Amendment." *Golden Gate University Law Review* 34:191–215.

Taslitz, Andrew E. 1990. "Does the Cold Nose Know? The Unscientific Myth of the Dog Scent Lineup." *Hastings Law Journal* 42 (1): 17–134.

Weintraub, Mark. 2001. "A Pack of Wild Dogs? *Chew v. Gates* and Police Canine Excessive Force." *Loyola of Los Angeles Law Review* 34 (2): 937–78.

Fermin De La Torre

DOJ. *See* U.S. Department of Justice

DOMESTIC PARTNERSHIPS. *See* Same-Sex Marriage and Civil Unions

DOUBLE JEOPARDY, PROHIBITION OF

The Fifth Amendment of the U.S. Constitution provides that no person shall "be subject for the same offence to be twice put in jeopardy of life or limb." Rooted in English common law, this language originally referred only to capital punishment. The Double Jeopardy Clause, however, has since been applied to all types of punishments resulting from retrials for the same offense. In *Benton v. Maryland* (1969), the Supreme Court ruled that the Double Jeopardy Clause also applies to state courts via the Due Process Clause of the Fourteenth Amendment.

The concept of double jeopardy is derived from the common-law concept of res judicata, which is Latin for "a thing decided." This doctrine bars the retrial of cases between the same parties on the same issue when a prior court has handed down a final judgment. Judges presented with the case a second time would dismiss it and uphold the original judgment. The double jeopardy language in the Constitution is attributed to William Blackstone, who wrote in his *Commentaries on the Laws of England* of the "universal maxim of the common law of England, that no man is to be brought into jeopardy of his life more than once for the same offence. And hence it is allowed as a consequence, that when a man is once fairly found not guilty upon any indictment or other prosecution, before any court having competent jurisdiction of the offence, he may plead such acquittal in bar of any subsequent accusation for the same crime." The Supreme Court noted in *Benton v. Maryland* (1969) that a bar against double jeopardy was "carried out into the jurisprudence of this country through the medium of Blackstone."

The reason for disallowing double jeopardy was best articulated in *Green v. United States* (1957):

The underlying idea, one that is deeply ingrained in at least the Anglo-American system of jurisprudence, is that the State with all its resources and power should not be allowed to make repeated attempts to convict an individual for an alleged offense, thereby subjecting him to embarrassment, expense and ordeal and compelling him to live in a continuing state of anxiety and insecurity, as well as enhancing the possibility that even though innocent he may be found guilty.

Three distinct protections are offered by the Double Jeopardy Clause: (1) protection from being prosecuted for the same crime after a defendant has been acquitted of that crime, (2) protection from being retried for the same crime after a defendant has been convicted of that crime, and (3) protection from multiple punishments for the same crime.

The Supreme Court has ruled that in certain situations the double jeopardy defense cannot be invoked. A second trial can be held when the first was ruled a mistrial, since no final judgment was rendered. A second trial may also be held when the first trial has been ruled a fraud or sham. A defendant may be tried for separate offenses stemming from a single act. Separate punishments may be rendered in multiple criminal prosecutions if each punishment is based upon additional facts or elements arising from the same act. A defendant may be retried in a separate jurisdiction or by a separate governmental body. An appeal is also not a violation of double jeopardy because it does not invalidate the judgment reached at the trial level. Plaintiffs may also appeal a case when a judge sets aside a jury verdict with a judgment not withstanding the verdict for the defendant (i.e., the jury's verdict is reversed because the judge rules it was not based on facts). Lastly, double jeopardy does not apply if the second charge is a civil charge and the first was a criminal charge, or when a convicted person is tried for parole violations.

See also Accused, Rights of the; Appeal, Right of; Bill of Rights, Incorporation of; Blackstone, William; Common-Law Background of American Civil Rights and Liberties; Death Penalty and the Supreme Court; Fifth Amendment; Fourteenth Amendment

Bibliography

Amar, Akhil Reed. 1997. "Double Jeopardy Law Made Simple." *Yale Law Journal* 106 (6):1807–48.

Blackstone, William. 1769–1769. *Commentaries on the Laws of England.* Oxford: Clarendon Press.

Thomas, George C., III. 1998. *Double Jeopardy: The History, the Law.* New York: New York University Press.

Wiet, Elizabeth J. 1996. "Double Jeopardy and the United States Sentencing Guidelines." *Journal of Criminal Law and Criminology* 86 (4): 1539–70.

Glenn L. Starks

DOUGLAS, WILLIAM O. (1898–1980)

William Orrville Douglas, the longest-serving justice in Supreme Court history, was born in rural Maine, Minnesota, but is generally associated with Yakima, Washington, and the Pacific Northwest. His family moved there after the death of his father. The family was poor, and as a child Douglas may have been afflicted with polio, although this claim has been challenged by biographer Bruce Murphy. To compensate for his affliction, Douglas became an outdoorsman and an avid hiker. His background instilled in Douglas a sense of individualism, a desire to protect the downtrodden, and a mistrust of governmental power. These principles would guide his judicial philosophy. Douglas graduated from Whitman College and Columbia Law School. He was at the center of the fledgling legal realism movement at Columbia and Yale law schools, where he taught. This movement challenged the conventional explanations for judicial decision making. Legal realists maintained that decisions reflected the attitudes and backgrounds of the judges as well as the social, political, and economic context of the times. They downplayed formalist adherence to legal principles and precedent.

Douglas was appointed to the Securities and Exchange Commission in 1936 and named its chairman in 1937. He was nominated to the Supreme Court by his friend President Franklin D. Roosevelt in 1939 to take the seat formerly held by Louis

Brandeis. Roosevelt, fresh from a protracted battle with the Supreme Court over the constitutionality of New Deal legislation, felt Douglas's populist views on regulation would protect his economic recovery program. In 1944, Roosevelt initially considered asking Douglas to leave the Court to run as his vice presidential candidate but ultimately opted for Harry Truman of Missouri. Truman, who succeeded to the presidency following Roosevelt's death in April 1945, considered Douglas for the vice presidential nomination in 1948. Douglas was more interested, however, in seeking the presidential nomination himself and briefly considered, but later rejected, the idea of leaving the Court to enter the 1948 campaign.

Controversy surrounded Douglas as a consequence of his stands on many issues, his off-the-bench-writings, and his personal life (Douglas was married four times and divorced three times). Impeachment of Douglas was discussed in 1951 after the justice publicly advocated recognition of Communist China. Congressman Gerald Ford led a more serious attempt to impeach Douglas in 1970. While questions about a conflict of interest were the stated reasons for beginning impeachment proceedings, it is clear that Justice Douglas's liberal views and his lifestyle were the underlying motivation.

Douglas's judicial behavior characterized him as a moderate in his early years on the Court. Some claim that this was because he harbored political ambitions and wanted to appear palatable to the public. The evidence suggests, however, that Douglas's early behavior and that of his frequent ally on the Court, Hugo Black, was a function of the times (the early forties), the novelty of the issues before the Court, and his lack of prior judicial experience. By the early fifties, Douglas was espousing the liberal views that are typically associated with his name. As the Warren Court matured and ideological allies were appointed, Douglas's views were increasingly read into constitutional doctrine. He supported the incorporation doctrine, applying the Bill of Rights to the states through the Fourteenth Amendment; absolutism in First Amendment matters; greater protection of criminal defendants; and a broad view of state action

to permit the government to attack discrimination. Douglas was a supporter of civil liberties and civil rights, upholding these values in approximately 90 percent of the cases decided during his tenure.

Douglas was the very epitome of the judicial activist. He was a result-oriented jurist whose judgment was often not controlled by precedent or strict adherence to constitutional text. He supported open-ended theories of the law. His opinion in *Griswold v. Connecticut* (1965) was perhaps the best example of this activism as Douglas helped create the right to privacy out of "the shadows and penumbras" cast by the First, Third, Fourth, and Fifth amendments as well as the long-dormant Ninth Amendment. The privacy doctrine would become the constitutional foundation for the effective legalization of abortion in *Roe v. Wade* (1973).

Douglas was criticized for his result-oriented jurisprudence. Critics claimed that his work was hastily constructed and his ideas underdeveloped, but defenders admired the passionate manner in which he decided the question in each case. He felt it was important to consider the social, political, and economic consequences of cases. While most members of the Court complained about the workload justices faced, this did not seem to bother Douglas, who wrote many opinions as well as numerous articles and some 30 books.

His opinions were characterized by a commitment to individual rights and a distrust of government power. He believed that the Constitution and the Bill of Rights were designed to take government off the backs of the citizens. Douglas did not write majority opinions in many of the landmark decisions that were issued during his lengthy tenure. He did, however, author many concurring and dissenting opinions, a sign of his fierce independence and a reflection of the fact that his position was often more liberal than the center of the Court.

Many adjectives have been used to describe the justice who served 36 years and seven months. He was considered brilliant, eccentric, independent, iconoclastic, and controversial. Douglas was a legal pragmatist who did not have a broad theory of constitutional jurisprudence.

An ailing Douglas left the Court in November 1975, allowing his old nemesis, then president Gerald Ford, to nominate his successor, John Paul Stevens. Douglas died January 19, 1980.

See also Accused, Rights of the; Bill of Rights (American); Bill of Rights, Incorporation of; Black, Hugo L.; Brandeis, Louis B.; Civil Rights; First Amendment; First Amendment, Approaches to; Fourteenth Amendment; Fourth Amendment; *Griswold v. Connecticut;* Judicial Activism; Ninth Amendment; Preferred Freedoms Doctrine; Privacy, Constitutional Right of; Reproductive Freedom; *Roe v. Wade;* Roosevelt, Franklin D.; Stevens, John Paul; Third Amendment

Bibliography

Ball, Howard. 1992. *Of Power and Right: Hugo Black, William O. Douglas, and America's Constitutional Revolution.* New York: Oxford University Press.

Douglas, William O. 1981. *The Court Years, 1939–1975: The Autobiography of William O. Douglas.* New York: Vintage Books.

Murphy, Bruce. 2003. *Wild Bill: The Legend and Life of William O. Douglas.* New York: Random House.

Simon, James F. 1980. *Independent Journey: The Life of William O. Douglas.* New York: Harper & Row.

Richard L. Pacelle, Jr.

DOUGLASS, FREDERICK (1818–1895)

While no one person can claim sole credit for moving the public mind toward acceptance of the ideas underlying the Thirteenth, Fourteenth, Fifteenth, and Nineteenth amendments to the U.S. Constitution, Frederick Douglass probably accomplished more toward that goal than did any other American. Frederick Douglass began his career as a public spokesman agitating for social justice on March 12, 1839, and he ended it on the day he died, shortly after having lectured at a women's rights rally on February 20, 1895.

Born into slavery on the eastern shore of Maryland as Frederick Augustus Bailey, he escaped from slavery on September 3, 1838. Once in the North, he changed his name to Frederick Douglass in order to evade capture by the bounty hunters who

pursued escaped slaves. He settled in Massachusetts and soon thereafter spoke out publicly at a church meeting. His first lecture topics that evening were on the evil nature of the slavery system, the need to abolish it, and the wrongfulness of African colonization as a policy for dealing with free blacks. The Garrisonian abolitionists in the area quickly noticed his oratorical talents and hired him as a full-time lecturer. In 1845, he published *Narrative of the Life of Frederick Douglass, An American Slave*—the first of three popular versions of his autobiography. Douglass quickly rose to prominence as an abolitionist, lecturer, author, journalist, and, after Lincoln freed the slaves, spokesperson for the Republican Party. He served as a consultant to Abraham Lincoln; a marshal of the District of Columbia; and, in the 1890s, U.S. minister to Haiti. His career in public office was short lived, and in the last two decades of his life, he returned to his work as an advocate for social justice in the dual role of journalist and orator.

From the start of his public career, Douglass campaigned for full citizenship rights for black Americans—first by seeking constitutional guarantees and then by seeking enforcement of those laws from a reluctant police force. His speeches and writings concerning the struggles of American blacks touched on more than just the evils of chattel slavery and the rightfulness of immediate abolition. Douglass also spoke out about the character of the antebellum U.S. Constitution with respect to slavery, the rightfulness of blacks serving in the Union army, the appropriate voting behavior for conscientious persons favoring abolition, the importance of black leadership within the black community, the dire need for vocational training for free blacks, and the indispensability of strength of character for a people attempting to overcome past subjugation. But Douglass did not limit his advocacy to the needs of his own people. Over the course of his half-century career, he appealed to the public at large on behalf of Irish freedom from Britain, women's rights—including voting—and temperance.

But by far, Douglass's most consistent and persistent theme was the justice owed by America to its black slaves and citizens. That obligation was, first, to end chattel slavery; second, to accord full, equal protection of the laws securing the privileges and immunities of U.S. citizenship to all Americans irrespective of skin color; and, third, to accord the vote to black Americans as a necessary part of the rights of citizenship. Douglass saw these goals attained at the level of constitutional reform, but he also witnessed the post-1876 failure to enforce the Fourteenth and Fifteenth amendments. He did not live long enough to see that enforcement restored (in the Civil Rights Movement of the 1960s and 1970s), nor did he see the fulfillment of the women's suffrage movement in 1920. Nonetheless, he devoted a lifetime to using his gifts for what he called "moral suasion" to move the U.S. public to constitutionalize principles of equality. His leadership in moving the country to embrace full civil equality for all its adults, irrespective of race or gender, left a legacy that endures to the present.

See also Abolitionist Movement; Civil Rights Movement; Equal Protection Clause; Fifteenth Amendment; Fourteenth Amendment; Lincoln, Abraham; Nineteenth Amendment; Slavery; Thirteenth Amendment; Women's Suffrage

Bibliography
Douglass, Frederick. 1941. *Life and Time of Frederick Douglass.* New York: Pathway Press.
                                    Leslie Friedman Goldstein

DRAFT CARDS, BURNING OF

The United States Supreme Court confronted the constitutionality of draft card burning in *United States v. O'Brien* (1968). In this case the Court had to decide whether burning a draft card was protected as symbolic speech under the First Amendment.

On the morning of March 31, 1966, David O'Brien and three others burned their selective service registration certificates (draft cards) on the steps of a south Boston courthouse to protest the Vietnam War. This action took place in front of a sizable crowd. The men were convicted under a 1965 amendment to the Universal Military Training and Service Act, which prohibited "forging, altering, knowingly destroying, knowingly mutilating, or in any manner changing a draft card." O'Brien argued that the statute violated the First Amendment's guarantee of free speech because it limited his ability to convey his antiwar views.

The Court, however, disagreed in a 7–1 ruling (Justice Thurgood Marshall did not participate). In the majority opinion, Chief Justice Earl Warren pointed out that "when 'speech' and 'nonspeech' elements are combined in the same course of conduct, a sufficiently important governmental interest in regulating the nonspeech element can justify incidental limitations" on free speech. In other words, in order for a statute limiting speech to withstand a constitutional challenge, the government must have a valid and important interest, and the government's interest must be unrelated to the suppression of free speech.

In this instance, the Constitution gave Congress the power to raise and support armies and to make all laws necessary to that end. Warren characterized this power as "broad and sweeping." Part of that power included the ability to create a registration system for military service, which included the issuance of draft cards. Draft cards served a number of important governmental interests including providing proof of draft registration, facilitating communication between individuals and local draft boards, and providing a reminder that the registrant must notify his local board of changes in address or status. According to the Court, the issuance of draft cards was the only way to achieve these interests. Thus, draft card destruction would significantly interfere with the administration of the Selective Service System, and it was on this basis, not the content of his speech, that O'Brien was convicted.

Justice William O. Douglas dissented from the majority opinion. He agreed with the Chief Justice that the congressional power to raise and maintain armies and navies was sweeping during a time of declared war; however, the extent of this power during an armed conflict without a declaration of war needed to be examined.

Since *O'Brien,* the Court has dealt with a number of issues concerning symbolic speech. The Court has invalidated statutes prohibiting flag burning and even those prohibiting cross burning. A general principle of these cases is that symbolic speech is protected by the First Amendment, but like other forms of speech, there are circumstances under which it may be regulated by the government.

See also Douglas, William O.; First Amendment; Flag Burning; Hate Speech; Military Conscription; Speech, Freedom of; Symbolic Speech; Warren, Earl

Kara E. Stooksbury

DRAFT, MILITARY. *See* Military Conscription

DRED SCOTT CASE (1857)

In *Scott v. Sandford* (1857), better known as the Dred Scott Case, the Supreme Court ruled that neither Congress nor the territorial legislatures had the power to ban slavery from the territories of the United States. In striking down the Missouri Compromise of 1820, the Court declared unconstitutional an act of Congress, something it had not done since *Marbury v. Madison* (1803). Speaking through Chief Justice Roger Taney, the Court further held that persons of African descent, whether free or slave, were not citizens of the United States and could therefore "claim none of the rights and privileges which that instrument provides for and secures to citizens of the United States."

The refusal by both the Democratic and Republican parties to support the Dred Scott decision led 11 Southern states to secede from the Union, a reaction that precipitated the Civil War. Ultimately, the issue of slavery was decided on the battlefield. The Thirteenth, Fourteenth and Fifteenth amendments, ratified following the Civil War, nullified the Dred Scott decision by abolishing slavery and granting to the emancipated slaves and their descendants civil and political rights.

Dred Scott was born a slave in Virginia around 1800. His owner, Peter Blow, moved to St. Louis in 1830 and sold him to a doctor in the U.S. Army,

John Emerson. In 1834 Emerson took Scott with him when he was transferred to Illinois, a state that had entered the union as a free state under the terms of the Northwest Ordinance of 1787. In 1836 Scott accompanied Dr. Emerson to Fort Snelling, located in the portion of the Louisiana Territory from which Congress had banned slavery in the Missouri Compromise of 1820. Emerson and Scott returned to Missouri in 1838. In 1846, following Emerson's death, Scott sued in state court to prove that he, his wife, and their two daughters were legally entitled to their freedom because they had resided in a free state and a free territory. In 1850 a jury of 12 white men found him to be free, but the Supreme Court of Missouri, hearing the case on appeal, held in 1852 that Scott was still a slave. The judges pointed to the intemperance of the Northern abolitionists in their attacks on the South as the basis for their decision.

Because Article III of the U.S. Constitution grants the federal courts jurisdiction over suits between citizens of different states, in 1854 Dred Scott sued for his freedom in the United States Circuit Court in St. Louis. Scott, as a citizen of Missouri, sued his owner, John F. A. Sandford, a citizen of New York. Sandford, Emerson's brother-in-law, had inherited Scott. Sandford argued that blacks could never be citizens of the United States and therefore could never sue in federal court. Federal judge Robert Wells, agreeing with the Missouri Supreme Court, decided that Scott was still a slave even though he had lived in the free state of Illinois and the free territory of Louisiana. Scott then appealed to the U.S. Supreme Court. The Court heard arguments in the case in the spring of 1856, but instead of issuing a decision, Chief Justice Taney asked for reargument of the issues in December. Taney announced the Court's decision in March 1857. For the first time in the Supreme Court's history, each of the nine justices wrote an opinion in the same case, making it difficult to ascertain what the majority's position was on the important questions before it.

The Dred Scott case followed a long history of controversy over the status of slavery in the West.

African slavery was an important feature of British imperial policy toward its North American colonies. When 13 of the colonies declared their independence from the British crown in 1776, seven of the new states within a few years abolished slavery. The principle was established that states could choose for themselves whether to recognize the right of whites to own Negro slaves. In 1787, however, the Congress under the Articles of Confederation passed the Northwest Ordinance, prohibiting slavery in the territory north of the Ohio River. This territory soon became the states of Ohio, Michigan, Indiana, Illinois, and Wisconsin. The Constitution, which replaced the Articles of Confederation the following year, authorized Congress to stop the importation of slaves from Africa, a step Congress took in 1808, the earliest date allowed. In 1803 the United States greatly expanded its territory by purchasing from France an immense tract of land watered by the Mississippi and Missouri rivers. The Louisiana Purchase offered Congress the opportunity to extend the principle of the Northwest Ordinance. The proslavery faction, however, had grown measurably since 1787, and in the Missouri Compromise of 1820 Congress admitted Missouri as a slave state even though it was north and west of the Ohio River. The Compromise, however, banned slavery in the territory west and north of Missouri's southern border. Congress found the middle ground again in 1850, when it admitted California as a free state, even though much of it lay south of Missouri, but allowed slavery in the other territory acquired in the war with Mexico in 1846–1847. The Wilmot Proviso, a bill that would have banned slavery from the acquired territory, passed the House but failed in the Senate.

The Democratic Party abandoned the Missouri Compromise altogether in a bill introduced by Stephen Douglas, a senator from Illinois who needed Southern support for his bid for the presidency. The Kansas-Nebraska Act of 1854 lifted the ban on slavery in the territory west of Missouri and left it to the legislature of each territory whether to petition Congress for admission as a free or slave state, a principle Douglas termed "popular sovereignty."

The Republican Party was formed two months later to bring about the repeal of this legislation. Popular sovereignty soon degenerated into civil war in the Kansas Territory. This ensuing Border War in what came to be known as Bleeding Kansas brought slaveholders into violent conflict with opponents of slavery.

It was in this highly charged political atmosphere that Chief Justice Taney in 1857, speaking for seven of the nine justices in the case *Scott v. Sandford,* delivered three blows to the efforts to contain or abolish slavery. Taney ruled that the question of whether residency in a free state emancipated a slave was to be left to the courts of the state where the slave brought suit for his or her freedom. He thus supported the Missouri Supreme Court's rejection of the long-standing rule in England and the United States of "once free, always free."

Taney further held that Congress had no power to exclude slavery from the territories because slave owners had a right under the Due Process Clause of the Fifth Amendment of the Constitution to carry their property into federal territory, land held by the United States in trust for all Americans, Southerners and Northerners. He read the Constitution as "distinctly and expressly" affirming the right of property in slaves, even though the document nowhere uses the terms "slave" or "slavery." The Missouri Compromise, therefore, was in Taney's view an abuse of Congress's legislative power.

Finally, Taney proclaimed that because whites had founded the United States for the benefit of whites, persons of African descent, whether free or slave, could never become citizens of the United States. He argued that the drafters of the Constitution had viewed them as "beings of an inferior order, and altogether unfit to associate with the white race, either in social or political relations, and so far inferior that they had no rights which the white man was bound to respect." Taney acknowledged that some Northern states allowed free blacks to vote and hold office. The U.S. Constitution, however, he said, did not regard them as citizens of the state where they lived for the purposes of Article III, because blacks were excluded as a race from the

American political community at the time of its founding in 1776.

Because the Court found that Scott was not a citizen of Missouri, Taney could have dismissed the suit for lack of jurisdiction. He chose not to take this course, however, and thus inserted the judiciary into the most salient political dispute of his day. The Taney Court, however, failed miserably in its effort to settle the slavery issue. Antislavery settlers in Kansas Territory ignored the decision and continued to drive out slave-owning migrants from Missouri and other slave states. Despite the Supreme Court's and President James Buchanan's support of slave-holding interests, Kansas entered the union as a free state in 1861.

In a series of debates with Stephen Douglas during the 1858 senatorial contest in Illinois, Republican candidate Abraham Lincoln alleged a conspiracy among the Democrats Taney, Douglas, Buchanan, and Franklin Pierce. Pierce was president from 1853 until March 4, 1857, when Buchanan took the oath of office. The purpose of the conspiracy, said Lincoln, was to allow slavery to spread first into the territories and then into the Northern states. Douglas had authored the Kansas-Nebraska bill, and Pierce signed it into law. More suspiciously, Dred Scott's appeal of the U.S. Circuit Court's decision arrived at the Supreme Court in the spring of 1856, but Taney insisted on reargument, which he scheduled after the presidential election in November, and did not announce the Court's decision until March 6 of the following year, two days after Buchanan's inauguration. Buchanan apparently knew what the Court's decision was going to be because of allusions he made to it in his inaugural address. There is also evidence that Buchanan successfully pressured one of the associate justices of the Supreme Court, Robert Grier, a fellow Pennsylvania Democrat, to vote with the Southern justices so that at least one member of the majority would be from outside the South. The Republican Party called for resistance to Taney's reading of the Constitution as soon as he announced it.

Despite the accommodations of Douglas, Pierce, and Buchanan, the Democratic Party could not sustain consensus on the future of slavery. In the second 1858 debate between Lincoln and Douglas at Freeport, Illinois, Lincoln asked Douglas whether he supported the Dred Scott decision, according to which slave owners had a constitutional right to take their human property into the federal territories. Douglas replied that he believed in popular sovereignty, the right of the people of a territory to decide for themselves whether to permit slavery. Douglas's answer made clear that popular sovereignty was contradictory to the Court's opinion in the Dred Scott case. This so-called Freeport Doctrine split the Democratic Party into Northern and Southern wings. In the 1860 presidential election, both factions of the Democratic Party nominated candidates. Douglas, the nominee of the Northern wing of the party, won only 12 electoral votes, while John C. Breckinridge, the choice of the Southern splinter, carried 72. The division of the Democratic vote allowed the Republican nominee, Lincoln, to win with 180 electoral votes, even though he received fewer popular votes than the Democrats Douglas and Breckinridge combined. (John Bell, a fourth-party candidate, won 39 electoral votes.)

The Dred Scott decision was one of the most significant events that precipitated the Civil War. Through its holding, the Court suffered a self-inflicted wound. The Court lost much of the public's respect, and its legitimacy as a coequal branch of government was challenged. Republicans, who controlled both Congress and the presidency during the Civil War (1861–1865) and Reconstruction (1865–1877), further weakened the Court by altering the number of justices three times between 1863 and 1869. In the years following the Dred Scott decision, the Supreme Court reached its lowest ebb since the early years of the Republic.

The Dred Scott Case, however, furnished the Court with a powerful weapon that it would later employ against Congress and the state legislatures. Taney's use of the Fifth Amendment's language— "nor shall any person be deprived of life, liberty or property without due process of law"—to strike down an act of Congress was the first application of the doctrine of substantive due process. Between 1895 and 1936, conservative justices employed the doctrine to declare unconstitutional efforts by Congress to regulate economic activity, such as manufacturing, oil production, mining, and agriculture. In the 1960s and 1970s, a more liberal Supreme Court would employ substantive due process to protect privacy, personal autonomy, and other unenumerated rights.

See also Abolitionist Movement; Declaration of Independence; Due Process, Substantive; Equality; Lincoln, Abraham; Lincoln-Douglas Debates; Privacy, Constitutional Right of; Slavery; Taney, Roger B.

Bibliography

Fehrenbacher, Don E. 2001. *The Dred Scott Case: Its Significance in American Law and Politics.* New York: Oxford University Press.

Finkelman, Paul. 1997. *Dred Scott v. Sandford: A Brief History with Documents.* New York: Palgrave.

Kutler, Stanley I. 1967. *The Dred Scott Decision: Law or Politics?* Boston: Houghton-Mifflin.

Latham, Frank Brown. 1968. *The Dred Scott Decision, March 6, 1857: Slavery and the Supreme Court's Self-Inflicted Wound.* New York: F. Watts.

Wilson, Charles Morrow. 1973. *The Dred Scott Decision.* Philadelphia: Auerbach.

Kenneth Holland

DRUG COURIER PROFILES

In prosecuting the war on drugs, law enforcement has employed many controversial tactics. One of these methods is drug courier profiling, in which a set of behavioral characteristics believed to typify drug smugglers is employed to identify, monitor and sometimes detain suspected drug couriers. First developed by the Drug Enforcement Administration (DEA) in the mid-1970s, drug courier profiling has generated considerable controversy among criminal justice scholars and professionals. Sean P. Trende (2000) has argued that the drug courier profile:

is not, as its name would imply, a single, coherent list of characteristics commonly found among drug dealers. Rather, it consists of a virtual laundry list of sometimes contradictory factors that agents have deemed useful in apprehending suspects. Examples of factors used by agents include, among other things, being the first off the plane, being the last off the plane, using a one-way ticket, using a round-trip ticket, traveling alone, traveling with a companion, acting too nervous, and acting too calm. To say that profiling is an inexact science is, thus, something of an understatement. (Trende 2000, 335–36)

Drug courier profiling has also generated considerable litigation, albeit with mixed results. The Supreme Court first dealt with drug courier profiles in *Reid v. Georgia* (1980). The case stemmed from an incident in the Atlanta airport in which a federal drug enforcement agent seized cocaine from Reid's shoulder bag. In its brief per curiam opinion, the Supreme Court enumerated the elements of the drug courier profile that Reid's behavior matched and that caused the agent to become suspicious:

(1) the petitioner had arrived from Fort Lauderdale, which the agent testified is a principal place of origin of cocaine sold elsewhere in the country, (2) the petitioner arrived in the early morning, when law enforcement activity is diminished, (3) he and his companion appeared to the agent to be trying to conceal the fact that they were traveling together, and (4) they apparently had no luggage other than their shoulder bags.

The Court held that the agent "could not, as a matter of law, have reasonably suspected the petitioner of criminal activity on the basis of these observed circumstances." In the Court's view, these facts, even if they are typical of drug couriers, were not sufficient to produce the "reasonable suspicion" required for an investigatory detention.

In *United States v. Montoya de Hernandez* (1985), the Court upheld a protracted detention of a young woman whose behavior aroused suspicion because it appeared to customs officials to be typical of drug smugglers. Although no formal profile was used, officials took note of the fact that the suspect had arrived from Bogotá, Colombia, a known source city for drugs, and had made frequent trips between Colombia and the United States. Officials were also suspicious of the fact that she was carrying $5,000 in cash, had no hotel reservation, and could not recall how she had purchased her airline ticket. The woman was detained and strip-searched. Justice William H. Rehnquist's opinion for the Supreme Court describes what happened next:

During the search the female inspector felt respondent's abdomen area and noticed a firm fullness, as if respondent were wearing a girdle. The search revealed no contraband, but the inspector noticed that respondent was wearing two pairs of elastic underpants with a paper towel lining the crotch area.

Sixteen hours after her flight had landed, the suspect had still not used the restroom. At that point customs officials obtained a court order allowing them to transport the suspect to a hospital for a rectal examination. In his opinion for the Supreme Court, Justice Rehnquist noted that:

a physician conducted a rectal examination and removed from respondent's rectum a balloon containing a foreign substance. Respondent was then placed formally under arrest. By 4:10 A.M. respondent had passed 6 similar balloons; over the next four days she passed 88 balloons containing a total of 528 grams of 80% pure cocaine hydrochloride.

Dividing seven-to-two, the Supreme Court upheld the detention, holding that customs officials had reasonable suspicion that Montoya de Hernandez was a drug courier. Justice Rehnquist's opinion did not discuss the issue of profiling per se but noted that "trained customs inspectors had encountered many alimentary canal smugglers and certainly had more than an 'inchoate and unparticularized suspicion or hunch' … that respondent was smuggling narcotics in her alimentary canal."

Dissenting in the case, Justice Brennan characterized the detention as a "disgusting and saddening episode" and suggested that the suspect had been detained solely "because she fit the profile of an 'alimentary canal smuggler.'" Brennan opined that "[t]he nature and duration of the detention here may well have been tolerable for spoiled meat or diseased animals, but not for human beings held on simple suspicion of criminal activity."

In *United States v. Sokolow* (1989), the Supreme Court upheld a similar investigatory detention in which a drug courier profile was employed. Upon arriving at Honolulu International Airport, Andrew Sokolow was detained by agents of the Drug Enforcement Administration because his behavior

matched elements of the DEA's drug courier profile. Specifically, the DEA cited the facts that Sokolow paid for his ticket in cash; traveled under an alias; flew round-trip to Miami; considered to be a source city for drugs; stayed in Miami for only 48 hours; checked no luggage; and appeared nervous during his flight back to Honolulu. A search of Sokolow's carry-on luggage recovered more than 1,000 grams of cocaine. Citing *Reid v. Reid,* the U.S. Court of Appeals for the Ninth Circuit held that agents did not have reasonable suspicion to detain Sokolow and thus invalidated the subsequent search and seizure. The Supreme Court reversed, splitting seven-to-two. Chief Justice Rehnquist, writing for the majority, commented on the suspicious elements of Sokolow's behavior that led the DEA to detain him: "Any one of these factors is not by itself proof of any illegal conduct and is quite consistent with innocent travel. But we think taken together they amount to reasonable suspicion."

Rehnquist also commented on an assertion by Sokolow's counsel that the DEA's reliance on a drug courier profile invalidated the detention:

We do not agree with respondent that our analysis is somehow changed by the agents' belief that his behavior was consistent with one of the DEA's "drug courier profiles." A court sitting to determine the existence of reasonable suspicion must require the agent to articulate the factors leading to that conclusion, but the fact that these factors may be set forth in a "profile" does not somehow detract from their evidentiary significance as seen by a trained agent.

In dissent, Justice Thurgood Marshall objected to the use of the drug courier profile, arguing that it poses "a far greater risk than does ordinary, case-by-case police work of subjecting innocent individuals to unwarranted police harassment and detention." Citing cases where lower courts reviewed detentions based on different profiles with contradictory characteristics, Marshall insisted that the risk of unwarranted detention "is enhanced by the profile's 'chameleon-like way of adapting to any particular set of observations.'"

The most controversial aspect of drug courier profiling has been the tendency of some agencies to include race or ethnicity as an element of the profile and the fact that some courts have approved detentions where race was employed as an element of forming reasonable suspicion (D'Ambrosio 1987). There is consensus that race can never be the sole basis of suspicion, but courts are divided as to whether race and/or ethnicity can be included, along with various other factors, in profiling drug couriers.

See also Brennan, William J., Jr.; Drugs, War on; Fourth Amendment; Probable Cause; Racial Profiling; Rehnquist, William H.; Stop and Frisk; Warrantless Searches

Bibliography

Becton, Charles L. 1987. "The Drug Courier Profile." *North Carolina Law Review* 65:417–.

D'Ambrosio, Joseph P. 1987. "The Drug Courier Profile and Airport Stops: Reasonable Intrusions or Suspicionless Seizures?" *Nova Law Review* 12:273.

Scheb, John M., and John M. Scheb II. 2006. *Criminal Procedure.* Belmont, CA: Thomson/Wadsworth.

Trende, Sean P. 2000. "Why Modest Proposals Offer the Best Solution for Combating Racial Profiling." *Duke Law Journal* 50 (1): 331–80.

John M. Scheb II and Otis H. Stephens, Jr.

DRUG COURTS

Researchers have long questioned the efficacy of legal sanctions in addressing problems of substance abuse and addiction. In recent years, judges and other public officials have come to recognize that traditional court processes do not deter substance abusers, nor do they deal with the underlying medical, social, and economic problems of substance abuse and addiction. The drug court is an effort to modify the judicial process to address these types of issues. Rather than sending nonviolent drug offenders to jail, the drug court emphasizes community-based rehabilitation. Working in collaboration with prosecutors, defense counsel, and other criminal justice professionals, judges monitor offenders' progress through regular status hearings. Judges prescribe rewards and restrictions in an attempt to modify behavior. Of course, the threat of removing someone from the program and applying the traditional punitive sanction always hangs, like the proverbial sword of Damocles, over the head of the participant in the drug court program.

Drug courts began to operate in the late 1980s and during the 1990s proliferated throughout most urban jurisdictions. The Violent Crime Control and Law Enforcement Act of 1994 authorized federal grants for drug court programs that include court-supervised drug treatment. By 2005, there were more than 1,200 drug courts that were fully operational in the United States and nearly 600 more in the planning stages (Office of Justice Programs 2005).

The methodology of processing defendants who might be eligible for participation in a drug court program varies from standard postarrest processes. After an individual who has not committed a violent crime is arrested for possession of a controlled substance, a background check is made. If the arrestee meets the drug court eligibility requirements and the prosecuting attorney agrees, the defendant may opt to be diverted to a drug court program. Prosecution is deferred as long as the participant progresses. Once in the program, the participant must obtain a sponsor, attend certain meetings and counseling sessions, give frequent urine samples, and attend required court status hearings. The participant signs a contract to complete the program within a specified period, usually 12 months. The treatment phases consist of detoxification, counseling sessions, and often assistance in job training or employment. In some programs a participant who agrees is given acupuncture treatments to aid in detoxification and to make the participant more receptive to counseling sessions.

The status hearings before the drug court are central to the program. They are held in open court with all participants present. The judge may begin with a short orientation emphasizing the need for sobriety and gainful employment. The judge then reviews each participant's progress file and commends those whose urine samples are clean and who are in complete compliance with their contract. Participants applaud those with outstanding records of performance. The judge encourages those who have minor deviations in their performance and admonishes those who have relapsed. Often the court prescribes additional counseling, treatment, community service, or a short stay in jail for those who have seriously relapsed in their efforts.

Most programs countenance some relapse; however, positive urine tests, additional arrests, and/or failure to attend status hearings or treatment sessions may cause a participant to be terminated and prosecution resumed. Successful completion of a drug court program usually results in the charges against the participant being dropped or the plea of guilty being stricken from the record.

Though still a new and innovative institution, drug courts appear to hold considerable promise to deter repetitive criminal behavior of drug abusers. They also hold a promise to relieve courts and other agencies of the burden of repetitive arrests and overloaded trial and sentencing dockets of criminal cases, where drugs play an important role. Moreover, the proliferation of drug courts has made judges and other criminal justice professionals more receptive to new approaches to dealing with other social problems (e.g., domestic violence) that drive criminal court caseloads.

See also Accused, Rights of the; Drug Testing; Drugs, War on; Plea Bargaining; Pleas in Criminal Cases; Restitution

Bibliography

Gebelein, Richard S. 2000. "The Rebirth of Rehabilitation: Promise and Perils of Drug Courts." *Sentencing and Corrections: Issues for the 21st Century* 6. Washington, DC: National Institute of Justice.

Nolan, James L. 2003. *Reinventing Justice: The American Drug Court Movement.* Princeton, NJ: Princeton University Press.

Office of Justice Programs. 2005. *Drug Court Activity Update: January 1, 2005.* Washington, DC: U.S. Department of Justice.

John M. Scheb II

DRUG ENFORCEMENT ADMINISTRATION (DEA). *See* Drugs, War on

DRUG-FREE WORKPLACE ACT. *See* Drugs, War on; Drug Testing

DRUGS, PRIVATE USE OF

Libertarians argue that governments lack authority to impose criminal penalties on conduct that does not harm others. Following this argument, they have claimed that private recreational drug use is one such victimless crime, and that criminalizing the personal use of certain drugs is costly, ineffective, and wasteful. When prosecuted for minor drug crimes, criminal defendants have sometimes invoked their federal or state constitutional rights to privacy by way of defense. All federal courts and most state courts have been unreceptive to such claims, but one state high court has recognized that its state constitution protects the right of an adult to use small amounts of marijuana in the privacy of his or her home.

Unlike the United States Constitution, the Alaska State Constitution contains a provision explicitly recognizing a right of privacy. In *Ravin v. State* (1975), the Alaska Supreme Court determined that this state constitutional right to privacy was violated when an Alaska resident was prosecuted for possessing marijuana in his home. Ravin argued that there was no legitimate state interest in prohibiting the possession of marijuana by adults for personal use. He also argued that principles of equal protection were violated by classifying marijuana as a dangerous drug when alcohol and tobacco were not so classified. The Alaska court rejected his equal protection argument, holding that state legislators were not required to criminalize possession of all dangerous substances equally. The court agreed with Ravin, however, that the home is a place deserving of special protection and overturned his conviction on the grounds that his state constitutional right to privacy was violated. The court did not determine that there was a constitutional right to the private use of drugs in general, but rather that a person's home was entitled to special protection.

Despite efforts to overturn the *Ravin* decision legislatively, the Alaska Supreme Court has continued to uphold the right of an adult to possess for personal use less than four ounces of marijuana in his or her home. The decision has not been extended to cover other recreational drugs, nor has it been held to cover the sale of drugs or the cultivation of large amounts of marijuana. In addition, some Alaska state law enforcement officials have referred marijuana possession cases for prosecution by the federal government because a state constitutional right is not a defense to a federal criminal prosecution.

Efforts to enforce a similar right to the private use of recreational drugs in other states have uniformly failed. In states where there is no explicit state constitutional right to privacy, all state high courts considering the issue have distinguished *Ravin* as being based on an explicit state constitutional right. Even in cases where a state constitution has an explicit privacy right, no other high court has chosen to follow Alaska's lead. For example, the Hawaii Constitution also contains an express right to privacy, but the Hawaiian Supreme Court has ruled that this privacy right does not prevent criminal prosecution for marijuana possession. The *Ravin* case may be viewed as a product of the unique environment of Alaska, "the home of people who prize their individuality," in the words of the Alaska Supreme Court.

See also Castle Doctrine; Drugs, War on; Federalism and Civil Rights and Liberties; Libertarianism; Liberty; Police Power; Privacy, Constitutional Right of

Bibliography

Boire, Richard Glen. 1996. *Marijuana Law.* 2nd ed. Oakland, CA: Ronin.

Williams, John C. 2004. "Constitutionality of State Legislation Imposing Criminal Penalties for Personal Possession or Use of Marijuana." *American Law Reports 3d* 96:225–.

Margaret Stock

DRUGS, WAR ON

The "war on drugs" was officially declared by President Richard M. Nixon in 1971. While the war was carried forward and even sharpened in later administrations, it is traceable to the influence of consummate bureaucrat and former prohibitionist Harry Anslinger. Director of the Federal Bureau of Narcotics (FBN) from 1931 to 1961 and one of the architects of the 1937 Marijuana Tax Act, Anslinger produced 1930s U.S. government propaganda like that depicted in the movie *Reefer Madness* and the book *Marihuana: Assassin of Youth.*

At the outset, it must be clear that the phrase "War on Drugs" is misleading, as there has never been a U.S. war on all drugs, or even only the most dangerous drugs. Though heroin, cocaine, LSD, and marijuana have long been targeted, highly addictive and often far more dangerous drugs like alcohol, nicotine, and various pharmaceuticals have not.

President Nixon declared the War on Drugs at a pivotal moment in U.S. history. Recreational marijuana use had increased during the 1960s, and *Leary v. United States* (1969) declared the 1937 act unconstitutional. That same year, however, New York enacted the first of the Rockefeller Drug Laws, state laws mandating minimum sentences for drug offenses. Seizing the moment, Congress produced and Nixon signed the 1971 Controlled Substances Act (CSA), which criminalized possession of even small amounts of all the substances targeted in the War on Drugs and provided for forfeiture of property connected to federal drug crimes. Soon thereafter, Nixon created the Drug Enforcement Agency (DEA), the successor to the FBN.

In spite of these advances in the War on Drugs, the 1970s also saw some setbacks for the war. The Shafer Commission, appointed by Nixon, reported that marijuana's dangers had been greatly exaggerated and recommended eliminating state and federal penalties for its possession and use. Many states thus decriminalized possession of small amounts of marijuana, and in 1977 President Jimmy Carter advocated eliminating all federal penalties for such possession, declaring that "penalties against possession of drug should not be more damaging to an individual than the use of the drug itself." In light of evidence of marijuana's value in treating diseases like glaucoma, the FDA established the Compassionate Investigative New Drug (IND) program. In *Ravin v. State* (1975), finally, the Alaska Supreme Court declared a state constitutional right to private possession and use of small amounts of marijuana by adults.

The 1980s however, saw the ascent of a Republican president and Congress. In 1982, thus, Ronald Reagan redeclared the War on Drugs, and this new war took many forms. Congress used civil forfeiture more aggressively in the Comprehensive Crime Control Act of 1984, for example, and it imposed Rockefeller-type mandatory minimum sentences for federal drug crimes in 1986. As for the administration, Nancy Reagan launched her Just Say No campaign in 1984, the Office of National Drug Control Policy was created in 1988, and the Campaign Against Marijuana Production (CAMP) targeted the cannabis industry of northern California. For its part, the Supreme Court upheld a federal policy requiring drug testing for those seeking positions as customs inspectors in *Treasury Employees Union v. Von Raab* (1989), and in response to a flood of applications from AIDS patients, the first Bush administration terminated the Compassionate IND program in 1992.

Having attacked the first Bush administration's hard line on drugs in his campaign, Bill Clinton was elected president in 1992. The 1990s thus seemed poised, like the 1970s, to deal the War on Drugs some setbacks. Yet studies published soon after Clinton's election suggested that cannabis use by teenagers had been increasing. Republicans, moreover, regained control of Congress in 1994, thus controlling key committees and forcing Clinton to moderate his drug policy rhetoric. In 1991, however, San Francisco enacted Proposition P, which legalized the medicinal use of cannabis in the city, and officially made pursuit of cannabis offenders a low priority for police. In 1996, California and Arizona became the first states to enact a new wave of medical cannabis laws, which addressed the problems with some of the earlier attempts

to protect medicinal cannabis use by state law. In California, this took the form of Proposition 215, codified in state law as the Compassionate Use Act (CUA), which is designed to:

> ensure that seriously ill Californians have the right to obtain and use marijuana for medical purposes where that medical use is deemed appropriate and has been recommended by a physician who has determined that the person's health would benefit from the use of marijuana in the treatment of cancer, anorexia, AIDS, chronic pain, spasticity, glaucoma, arthritis, migraine, or any other illness for which marijuana provides relief.

The CUA has led to several federal lawsuits illuminating both the reinvigoration of the War on Drugs under the second Bush administration and continuing opposition to the war. In *United States v. Oakland Cannabis Buyers Cooperative* (2001), the Supreme Court held that in spite of state laws like the CUA, there is no implied medical necessity exception to enforcement of the CSA. In *Conant v. Walters* (2002), conversely, the U.S. Court of Appeals for the Ninth Circuit held that the First Amendment prohibits the U.S. government from revoking a physician's medical license for recommending the use of medicinal cannabis. Most recently, the Supreme Court held in *Gonzales v. Raich* (2005) that the DEA is empowered under the CSA to raid the homes and confiscate and destroy the cannabis of sick patients, even those using it under a doctor's recommendation in states with laws like the CUA. Writing for a 6–3 majority, Justice Stevens expressed concern for sick patients but said that Congress is where reformers should apply for changes in the CSA. Nonetheless, law enforcement authorities, physicians, and patients in the 12 states that have now legalized medicinal cannabis announced that *Raich* would be irrelevant to the operation of cannabis law in their states.

The War on Drugs thus drags on, even while the trend in several states as well as other Western democracies is toward the policy of harm reduction articulated by President Carter. The principle that "penalties against possession of drug should not be more damaging to an individual than the use of the drug itself" seems indisputably rational, yet the

United States government spent $19 billion on the War on Drugs in 2002. Congress, moreover, has not only refused for decades to reschedule marijuana as a Schedule II drug under the CSA but consistently declines even to defund the DEA's operations where they conflict with state laws protecting medicinal cannabis. While *Raich* is a victory for the War on Drugs, if the states and other Western democracies continue to lead the way toward more rational drug policy, Congress will eventually have to follow.

See also Drug Courier Profiles; Drug Courts; Drug Testing; Drugs, Private Use of; *Gonzales v. Raich;* Privacy, Constitutional Right of; Prohibition

Bibliography

Bock, Alan. 2000. *Waiting to Inhale: The Politics of Medical Marijuana.* Santa Ana, CA: Seven Locks Press.

MacCoun, Robert J., and Peter Reuter. 2001. *Drug War Heresies: Learning from Other Vices, Times and Places.* Cambridge: Cambridge University Press.

Miron, Jeffrey. 2004. *Drug War Crimes: The Consequences of Prohibition.* Oakland, CA: Independent Institute.

Sloman, Larry. 1998. *Reefer Madness: A History of Marijuana in the United States.* New York: St. Martin's Press.

Torgoff, Martin. 2004. *Can't Find My Way Home: America in the Great Stoned Age, 1945–2000.* New York: Simon & Schuster.

Martin Carcieri

DRUG TESTING

Drug testing of public employees became common in the late 1980s as part of the federal government's War on Drugs. In the 1990s many private employers followed the government's example and began testing their employees for drugs. Numerous public schools have instituted drug testing of students as a condition of participation in athletics or other extracurricular activities. Collegiate athletes in both public and private institutions are routinely subjected to drug testing.

Many favor the use of drug testing as a way to combat the increasing drug problem both in the workplace and in schools. Others oppose the use of drug testing and view it as a violation of the Fourth Amendment's implied right to privacy. The potential for invasion of privacy arises in a number of contexts: testing of bodily fluids (particularly urine) and the potential breach of confidentiality through release of drug testing results to employers, school administrators, and law enforcement officials. Some maintain that in addition to search and seizure problems, drug testing also violates due process standards of the Fifth and Fourteenth amendments applicable to federal and state governments respectively.

In *Committee for GI Rights v. Callaway* (1975), the U.S. Court of Appeals for the D.C. Circuit upheld random drug testing of military personnel based on the "administrative search exception" to the Fourth Amendment. The Court reasoned that the state's strong public interest to ensure military readiness outweighs the privacy interests of soldiers, who already serve under considerably diminished Fourth Amendment rights. Thus, the administrative search exception balances the state's interest against the constitutional interest of the individual and allows for a relaxing of the Fourth Amendment when the state's interest is viewed to be overwhelming and/or predominant.

In 1986, President Ronald Reagan issued Executive Order 12564, requiring federal agencies to implement urine-testing programs. The purpose was to create a drug-free federal work environment and launch the War on Drugs policy initiative. The order specifically authorizes testing of individuals who meet certain criteria: (1) when there is a reasonable suspicion that any employee uses illegal drugs; (2) in postaccident examinations; (3) as part of or as a follow-up to counseling or rehabilitation for illegal drug use through an Employee Assistance Program; and (4) preemployment screening for evidence of drug use.

In *Shoemaker v. Handel* (1986), the United States Court of Appeals for the Third Circuit approved mass urinalysis procedures in the public workplace for the first time. Citing the administrative search exception, the court stipulated, "warrantless searches or seizures by voluntary participants in a highly state regulated industry ... are reasonable." Again citing the administrative search exception, the Eighth Circuit Court of Appeals in *McDonell v. Hunter* (1987) found that urine testing of federal prison guards is constitutional. And in *Rushton v. Nebraska Public Power District* (1988), the Eighth Circuit upheld testing of nuclear power plant employees.

In *National Treasury Employees Union v. Von Raab,* the U.S. Supreme Court relied on the administrative search exception in upholding a policy that required all employees who were seeking promotions to certain sensitive positions to submit to urinalysis even in the absence of probable cause or individualized suspicion of drug use. In the Court's view, drug tests for employees seeking sensitive positions were seen as reasonable per se. In this context, the government's interest in maintaining a drug-free workplace outweighed individual concerns about the potential violation of Fourth Amendment rights. Those individuals seeking employment in sensitive positions must assume that inquiries will be made into their drug use, and therefore they have a diminished expectation of privacy.

In 1988 Congress passed the Drug-Free Workplace Act, extending drug testing to companies that have been awarded federal contracts. Not long after the implementation of drug testing by the public sector, private-sector employers joined the War on Drugs and implemented various kinds of drug testing. Private-sector drug testing can take many forms, including preemployment, causal testing, post-rehabilitation, timed testing, random selective, and safety-sensitive testing. In 1998, Congress again passed another Drug-Free Workplace Act, which provided federal funds to small businesses that utilize drug testing of their employees.

States, cities, and counties have established their own drug testing programs for public employees in various occupations and, by and large, these programs have survived judicial review. In 1998, the U.S. Court of Appeals for the Sixth Circuit upheld a mandatory drug testing requirement for public school teachers in Knox County, Tennessee. In *Knox County Education Association v. Knox County Board of Education* (1998), the court held that drug testing of teachers is justified by the "unique role" that teachers play in school children's lives. The court observed that teachers "must expect that with this extraordinary responsibility, they will be subject to scrutiny to which other civil servants or professionals might not be subjected, including drug testing."

Public- and private-sector employees are no longer the only individuals subject to drug testing. In *Vernonia School District v. Acton,* the Supreme Court, relying on a "special needs" exception to the Fourth Amendment, upheld a school district policy forcing students to consent to drug testing in order to participate in interscholastic sports, regardless of suspicion. The Court held that students are under the supervision of the state and are thus subject to more extensive searches than might otherwise be permissible. Moreover as student athletes, they also have a lesser expectation of privacy largely because of the communal nature of the locker room. With respect to urine collection, the Court maintained that the conditions of collection are similar to those one encounters in a public restroom. Taking into account "the decreased expectation of privacy, the relative unobtrusiveness of the search, and the severity of the need met by the search," Justice Scalia, the author of the Court's opinion, concluded that Vernonia's drug testing policy was "reasonable and hence constitutional."

In *Board of Education of Independent School District No. 92 of Pottawatomie County v. Earls* (2002), the Supreme Court expanded the special needs exception by extending it to mandatory drug testing of all students engaged in extracurricular activities. Writing for the Court, Justice Clarence Thomas characterized the drug testing policy as a "reasonably effective means of addressing the School District's legitimate concerns in preventing, deterring, and detecting drug use." In dissent, Justice Ruth Ginsburg argued that "schools' tutelary obligations to their students require them to 'teach by example' by avoiding symbolic measures that diminish constitutional protections."

See also Administrative Searches; Drugs, War on; Fourth Amendment; Ginsburg, Ruth Bader;

Privacy, Invasion of; Privacy, Reasonable Expectations of; Thomas, Clarence

Bibliography

Persico, Deborah A. 1999. *Vernonia School District v. Acton: Drug Testing in Schools.* Berkeley Heights, NJ: Enslow.

Potter, Beverly A. 1998. *Drug Testing at Work: A Guide for Employers.* Berkeley, CA: Ronin.

Kimberly Gill

DU BOIS, W.E.B. (1868–1963)

William Edward Burghardt Du Bois was born on February 26, 1868, in Great Barrington, Massachusetts. He graduated from Fisk University in Nashville, Tennessee, a school he attended only because he lacked the funds to attend Harvard University. Du Bois was shocked by the racial divisions in the South and "believed that the aspirations of his people were being destroyed by racial prejudice, and he began to concentrate on a race-centered program designed to improve Negro living conditions" (Rudwick 1960, 20). Du Bois earned a bachelor of arts in 1888 and then entered Harvard University as a junior, where he studied history and philosophy. He earned a bachelor's degree from Harvard in 1890, followed by a master's degree in 1891. After study in Berlin, Germany, Du Bois completed his doctorate at Harvard in 1895, becoming the first African American to receive a PhD from that institution. Du Bois taught sociology at several universities and spent a great deal of time studying the social conditions of African Americans. He became an early civil rights activist as a result of his academic study of racism.

Du Bois's fundamental views of civil rights stood in stark contrast to those of the most powerful African American leader at the time, Booker T. Washington. Washington had argued that blacks would have to prove to whites that they were qualified for civil rights through vocational training and a willingness to live in a segregated society. He believed that economic success would lead to political rights. Du Bois and others criticized Washington's approach, and the conflict between the two men grew to be personal. In setting forth his own ideas about the status of blacks in American society, Du Bois noted a triple paradox in Washington's program (Davis 1996). Du Bois asserted that (1) political participation was fundamental to the protection of African American rights; (2) a willingness to embrace segregation would deprive African Americans of their dignity; and (3) vocational education was insufficient for the progress of African Americans (Davis 1996, 273). In his now classic work, *The Souls of Black Folk,* Du Bois devoted an entire chapter entitled "Of Booker T. Washington and Others" to a critique of Washington's views. Du Bois also articulated in that work a concept called "the Talented Tenth," which would be composed of intelligent, educated, and accomplished blacks who would "pull the black masses forward" (Davis 1996, 274).

Washington retaliated and attempted to bring the two groups together so that he could control both. In 1906, as a result of what he perceived to be Washington's underhanded tactics, Du Bois, along with 28 other men, designed the structure of the Niagara Movement, which reflected Du Bois's ideas. This group would ultimately become part of a larger reform group: the National Association of the Advancement of Colored People (NAACP). While Du Bois was not entirely pleased with the group, as whites held many of the leadership positions, he became editor of the group's magazine, *The Crisis,* and used it as a vehicle for disseminating his ideas and criticisms of society.

Shortly after World War I, Du Bois became heavily involved with the pan-African movement, which advocated the global unification of Africans in the struggle for freedom. In the face of the economic struggles of the Great Depression, Du Bois argued for a separate black economy, a position that alienated him from the NAACP. Du Bois left the organization and returned to his teaching post at Atlanta University in 1934. Without the *Crisis* as an outlet, however, Du Bois was no longer considered an effective leader of the early Civil Rights Movement. He became increasingly critical of the U.S. government and enamored with Communist ideologies.

When, as chairman of the Peace Information Center in 1950, he spoke out about ending nuclear weapons, his views were considered pro-Communist. As a result, in 1951, a federal grand jury indicted Du Bois on charges that he failed to register as an agent of a foreign principal. He was ultimately acquitted, as the Peace Information Center was determined not to be a foreign principal. In 1961, he formally joined the Communist Party and had his membership announced in the *New York Times*. That same year, he accepted the invitation of Ghana president Kwame Nkrumah to direct the *Encyclopedia Africana*. When he was refused a new U.S. passport because of his communist affiliation, he and his wife renounced their U.S. citizenship and became citizens of Ghana. Du Bois died in Ghana on August 27, 1963, at the age of 95. His death, ironically, was on the same day as the March on Washington, when Martin Luther King, Jr., delivered his "I Have a Dream" speech.

According to Rudwick, "shortly after his departure from the United States, Du Bois's reputation soared, and he was transformed into a prophet" (Franklin and Meier 1982, 82). His early views on political participation for African Americans and the abolition of the "color line" dividing the country resonated with a new generation of Americans who were involved in the Civil Rights Movement of the 1960s.

See also Civil Rights Movement; Communist Party USA; Discrimination; King, Martin Luther, Jr.; National Association for the Advancement of Colored People; Washington, Booker T.

Bibliography

Davis, Sue. 1996. *American Political Thought: Four Hundred Years of Ideas and Ideologies*. Englewood Cliffs, NJ: Prentice Hall.

Franklin, John Hope, and August Meier, eds. 1982. *Black Leaders of the Twentieth Century*. Urbana: University of Illinois Press.

Moore, Jack B. 1981. *W.E.B. Du Bois*. Boston: Twayne.

Rudwick, Elliott M. 1960. *W.E.B. Du Bois: A Study in Minority Group Leadership*. Philadelphia: University of Pennsylvania Press.

Kara E. Stooksbury

DUE PROCESS, PROCEDURAL

The Due Process Clauses of the Fifth and Fourteenth Amendments provide that no citizen shall be "deprived of life, liberty or property without due process of law." The Fifth Amendment ensures this right with respect to the federal government, the Fourteenth with respect to the state governments. The U.S. Supreme Court has interpreted the Due Process Clause to include two elements: substantive due process and procedural due process. The former involves the extent to which the government may enact legislation that infringes on a fundamental right not otherwise specified in the U.S. Constitution, such as the right to travel or the right to marry. The latter focuses on the procedural mechanisms that must be followed before the government may deprive an individual of life, liberty, or property.

According to the prevailing interpretation of procedural due process, unless life, liberty, or property is at risk through governmental action, whether civil or criminal in nature, no legal process—involving notification of the potential deprivation and some form of hearing—is due. Situations in which an individual is subject to the deprivation of life are not difficult to identify. If the government seeks the death penalty, it must follow certain procedures, including a fair trial, before that penalty may be imposed. On the other hand, the meaning of "liberty" or "property" or "due process" is not self-evident. Thus, the Court has focused much of its jurisprudence in this area on the definition of those terms.

Liberty Interests

In the criminal context, "liberty" has at least one obvious meaning: imprisonment involves the loss of liberty, and thus legal process is required before it may be imposed as punishment. In addition, the Court has held that, where an individual has received a sentence of probation, allegations that the terms of probation were violated also involve the potential loss of liberty, thus triggering the application of the Due Process Clause (*Morrissey v. Brewer*, 1972). Where a state creates a system of "good time credits" that enables prisoners to seek early release from their sentence, revocation of such credits similarly carries a potential loss of liberty in the future (*Wolf v. McDonnell*, 1974), creating a protected liberty interest in those credits. More recently, however, the Court has held that changes in a prisoner's confinement not involving the length of imprisonment, such as the imposition of disciplinary segregation, do not give rise to a liberty interest unless such changes involve an "atypical and significant hardship on the inmate in relation to ordinary incidents of prison life" (*Sandin v. Conner*, 1995). In *Conner*, the Court held that no process in the form of notice or hearing was required prior to the imposition of the disciplinary measure.

The Court has held that deprivation of liberty outside the criminal context may also trigger application of the Due Process Clause. Of particular importance is the liberty interest that is affected when the government engages in some action that adversely affects a person's reputation. For example, where a state government required that liquor stores post the names of "public drunkards," the Court held that individuals on the list were deprived of a liberty interest in their reputations. As a result, the state must provide a hearing to contest such a designation prior to its publication (*Wisconsin v. Constantineau*, 400 U.S. 433, 1971). Of course, where a state posts the names of criminals who have already been convicted at trial, such as in the case of certain sexual offender notification Web sites, process has already been provided through the criminal justice system. No further hearing is required (*Connecticut Department of Public Safety v. Doe*, 2003). Moreover, the Court has limited this form of liberty interest in reputation by requiring that imposition of a reputational stigma alone is not sufficient to trigger application of the Due Process Clause, which could be remedied by a state law defamation suit rather than a constitutional challenge. Instead, the Court has required that the stigma be accompanied by some other form of deprivation (referred to as stigma plus) before a liberty interest may be recognized. Thus, where an employee is fired and the employer simultaneously issues a statement that the employee is incompetent, it may

give rise to a liberty interest since the individual is deprived of both reputation and employment at the same time (cf. *Siegert v. Gilley*, 1991).

Property Interests

The Due Process Clause clearly applies to traditional forms of tangible and intangible property. Thus, where the government seeks to deprive an individual of real property, money, or other similar valuables, it may not do so without first providing notification and a hearing to allow the affected individuals to contest the deprivation. The 1960s and 1970s witnessed a substantial expansion of the definition of property, however. In the landmark case of *Goldberg v. Kelly* (1970), the Supreme Court held that continued payment of welfare benefits—traditionally viewed as a privilege rather than a property right—did constitute a property interest protected by the Due Process Clause. As a consequence, when the government seeks to terminate the stream of welfare or other benefits to an individual, it must first provide notice and some form of a hearing before the termination may take effect. Another important expansion of the term involved its application to public employment. In a series of cases decided in the early 1970s, the Court held that where an individual has more than a unilateral expectation of continued employment, it gives rise to a property interest in the position. Thus, where some restrictions exist on managerial discretion to fire or demote an employee—which may arise from an employment contract or through state law—such action may not be taken without procedural protections for the employee (*Board of Regents v. Roth*, 1972; *Perry v. Sinderman*, 1972).

What Process Is Due?

Once it is determined that its action is likely to implicate a protected interest in life, liberty, or property, the government must provide "due process" prior to the deprivation. In general, due process involves (1) notification to the affected individual of the proposed governmental action and (2) some form of hearing to enable the individual to challenge the deprivation. Notification must take place at a meaningful time in advance of the proposed deprivation to enable the affected individual to respond. As for the form the hearing must take, not all deprivations require a full trial-type hearing prior to their execution. In *Mathews v. Eldridge* (1976) the Supreme Court held that three factors must be considered in constructing an appropriate hearing mechanism to protect the individual's rights: (1) the private interest that will be affected by the official action, (2) the rise of erroneous deprivation under any existing procedures and the reduction in that risk by the procedures proposed by the affected individual, and (3) the government's interest in using any existing procedures, as compared to any enhanced procedural protections. This standard allows for a sliding scale of procedural rights depending on the individual's interest, the cost to the government, and the likelihood that the government will make an erroneous deprivation without additional procedures. An example makes this standard easier to understand. Assume a student has been disciplined with a suspension for smoking in school but was provided with no opportunity to defend the charges and avoid the suspension. Public education constitutes a property right. In such a case, a full trial would be too costly to the school district. Instead, oral or written notification of the charges and an explanation of evidence from the authorities, with an opportunity for the student to present his or her side of the story, may be sufficient (*Goss v. Lopez,* 1975). On the other hand, where the individual's interest is more profound—such as in the case of the termination of welfare benefits that enable the beneficiary to subsist—a more extensive and involved hearing, involving witnesses, cross-examination, and so forth, is required (*Goldberg v. Kelly,* 1970).

See also Accused, Rights of the; Bill of Rights, Incorporation of; Due Process, Substantive; Due Process Clauses; Due Process Rights of Government Beneficiaries; Fifth Amendment; Fourteenth Amendment; Liberty; New Property; Privilege/Right Distinction; Property Rights

Bibliography

Farina, Cynthia R. 1991. "Conceiving Due Process." *Yale Journal of Law and Feminism* 3:189.

Mashaw, Jerry. 1985. *Due Process in the Administrative State.* New Haven, CT: Yale University Press.

Monaghan, Henry Paul. 1977. "Of 'Liberty' and 'Property.'" *Cornell Law Review* 62:405–44.

Reich, Charles A. 1964. "The New Property." *Yale Law Journal* 73 (5): 733–87.

Stefanie A. Lindquist

DUE PROCESS, SUBSTANTIVE

The Fifth Amendment to the United States Constitution, ratified in 1791 as part of the Bill of Rights, provides that no person shall be "deprived of life, liberty, or property, without due process of law." Although this provision applies solely to actions of the federal government, the Fourteenth Amendment, ratified in 1868, imposes the same injunction on the states by stating "nor shall any State deprive any person of life, liberty, or property, without due process of law." These clauses restate an idea that is at the very core of the Anglo-American legal tradition—that the law protects against the arbitrary exercise of governmental power. Magna Carta (1215) stated the principle as follows: "No Freeman shall be taken, or imprisoned, or be disseised of his Freehold, or Liberties, or free Customs, or be outlawed, or exiled, or any otherwise destroyed; nor will we pass upon him, nor condemn him, but by lawful Judgment of his Peers, or by the Law of the Land."

To one untutored in the complex jurisprudence of due process, the protection afforded by the Fifth and Fourteenth amendments would appear to be primarily, if not exclusively, of a procedural nature. The term "due process" suggests a set of legal procedures to be followed when government seeks to take life, liberty, or property. Thus the government is permitted to take someone's life, as in the execution of a death sentence imposed for the commission of a capital crime, as long as due process of law has been observed. It can deprive a person of liberty, usually because that person has been accused or convicted of a crime, again assuming that the procedural dictates of due process have been followed. Government may even take someone's land through eminent domain as long as the landowner is given fair notice and a meaningful opportunity to challenge the taking in court. Procedural due process always requires fair notice and in most instances affords the right to some sort of hearing, but as the Supreme Court noted in *Morrissey v. Brewer* (1972), "[D]ue process is flexible and calls for such procedural protections as the particular situation demands."

In addition to providing procedural protections against arbitrary and capricious government action, due process has been held to impose substantive limits on government policies as well. Under the doctrine of substantive due process, government is barred from enforcing policies that are arbitrary, capricious, irrational, unfair, unreasonable, or unjust in their infringements on life, liberty, or property, even if such policies are not prohibited by explicit constitutional constraints. In their joint opinion in *Planned Parenthood v. Casey* (1992), Justices Sandra Day O'Connor, Anthony Kennedy, and David Souter noted: "Although a literal reading of the [Due Process] Clause might suggest that it governs only the procedures by which a State may deprive persons of liberty, for at least 105 years... the Clause has been understood to contain a substantive component as well, one 'barring certain government actions regardless of the fairness of the procedures used to implement them.'"

There are two levels of judicial review associated with substantive due process. The more lenient approach, and the one more frequently applied by the courts, requires that any governmental restriction of personal liberty be rationally related to a legitimate governmental interest. The stricter standard of review applies only to those liberties deemed to be "fundamental." To meet this standard, government must show that the infringement of liberty is necessary to achieve a compelling governmental interest. This standard of review is essentially the same as the strict scrutiny of suspect classifications developed in modern equal protection jurisprudence. Indeed, the two are so closely intertwined that many

commentators refer to them jointly as the new due process/equal protection.

Origins of the Doctrine

The jurisprudential origins of substantive due process are somewhat murky, but there are obvious precursors in the English common law. In *Dr. Bonham's Case* (1609), Sir Edward Coke asserted that "when an Act of Parliament is against common right and reason," the "common law will controul it, and adjudge such Act to be void." While foreshadowing the emergence of judicial review in *Marbury v. Madison* (1803), Coke's dictum also reflects the spirit, if not the vocabulary, of substantive due process.

Substantive due process made its first appearance in American law in *Wynehamer v. New York* (13 N.Y. 378, 1856), where the New York Court of Appeals held that a state criminal law prohibiting the sale of liquor restricted the liberty of a Buffalo tavern owner who had been prosecuted for violating its provisions. The court ruled that the police power of the state could not be used to deprive the defendant of a liberty protected by the state constitution, namely, the liberty to earn his livelihood.

The following year, in the infamous Dred Scott decision, the United States Supreme Court employed substantive due process for the first time. In *Scott v. Sandford* (1857), the Court invalidated the Missouri Compromise of 1820, under which Missouri was admitted to the Union as a slave state, but slavery was prohibited in the remainder of the Louisiana Purchase north of Missouri's southern border. Writing for the Supreme Court, Chief Justice Roger B. Taney opined that "[a]n Act of Congress which deprives a citizen of the United States of his liberty or property, merely because he came himself or brought his property into a particular Territory of the United States, and who had committed no offense against the laws, could hardly be dignified with the name of due process of law." Of course, the "property" Taney referred to was the human being held in slavery. Robert Bork has suggested that Chief Justice Taney's substantive interpretation of the Due Process Clause of the Fifth Amendment was "an obvious sham" (Bork 31) contrived to mask his personal support for the institution of slavery. Despite the infamy of the Dred Scott decision and its nullification by the Thirteenth and Fourteenth amendments to the Constitution, the Supreme Court in the late nineteenth century resurrected the doctrine of substantive due process in a very different context.

Economic Due Process

In the Slaughterhouse Cases (1873), a narrowly divided Supreme Court upheld Louisiana's grant of a monopoly in the slaughtering business in and around New Orleans. Although officially designated as "An Act to Protect the Health of the City of New Orleans," the law was not in any meaningful sense a health measure. Its only apparent effect was to deprive more than 1,000 persons of their right to engage in the slaughtering trade. A number of these persons filed suit, maintaining that the state had conferred "odious and exclusive privileges upon a small number of persons at the expense of the great body of the community of New Orleans." Arguing that the law should have been invalidated under the Fourteenth Amendment, Justice Joseph L. Bradley's dissenting opinion asserted that "a law which prohibits a large class of citizens from adopting a lawful employment previously adopted, does deprive them of liberty as well as property, without due process of law."

More than a decade later the Court signaled that it was moving in the direction suggested by Bradley's dissent in the Slaughterhouse Cases. Writing for the Court in *Mugler v. Kansas* (1887), Justice John Marshall Harlan (the elder) warned that not all exercises of the state police power would be automatically approved: "The Courts are not bound by mere forms, nor are they to be misled by mere pretenses. They are at liberty—indeed, are under a solemn duty—to look at the substance of things." But it was not until the late 1890s that the doctrine came into full flower.

In *Chicago, Burlington and Quincy Railroad v. Chicago* (1897), the Court held that the Due Process Clause of the Fourteenth Amendment incorporates the Fifth Amendment protection against governmental takings of private property without "just compensation." Writing for the Court, Justice Harlan asserted: "In determining what is due process of law, regard must be had to substance, not to form." Invoking "natural equity" and "universal law," Harlan concluded that "[t]he mere form of the proceeding instituted against the owner, even if he be admitted to defend, cannot convert the process used into due process of law, if the necessary result be to deprive him of his property without compensation." Thus was born the doctrine of incorporation, a doctrine by which the Supreme Court in the twentieth century would render most of the provisions of the Bill of Rights enforceable against the states. Although one can criticize the Court's reasoning in the *Chicago B&Q* case, the principle incorporated into the Due Process Clause of the Fourteenth Amendment was one recognized in the text of the Constitution, albeit in the Fifth Amendment. Subsequent decisions would make clear that substantive due process would not be limited to the incorporation of substantive rights found in the Bill of Rights.

In another landmark decision rendered in 1897, the Court would make clear that substantive due process was not only a means of extending Bill of Rights provisions to the states. In *Allgeyer v. Louisiana*, the Supreme Court invalidated Louisiana's effort to regulate out-of-state insurance companies transacting business in the state. Writing for the Court, Justice Rufus Peckham found this regulation to be an infringement of the liberty protected from state interference by the Fourteenth Amendment:

The "liberty" mentioned in that amendment means, not only the right of the citizen to be free from the mere physical restraint of his person, as by incarceration, but the term is deemed to embrace the right of the citizen to be free in the enjoyment of all his faculties; to be free to use them in all lawful ways; to live and work where he will; to earn his livelihood by any lawful calling; to pursue any livelihood or avocation; and for that purpose to enter into all contracts which may be proper, necessary, and essential to his carrying out to a successful conclusion the purposes above mentioned.

Lochner v. New York (1905) is generally regarded as the quintessential economic due process decision. In *Lochner,* the Supreme Court struck down a state law specifying a maximum 60-hour workweek for bakery employees. The Court held that the law unreasonably interfered with the "general right to make a contract in relation to [one's] business," which the Court insisted was "part of the liberty of the individual protected by the 14th Amendment of the Federal Constitution." The Court acknowledged the police powers of the state but refused to view the law as a valid public health measure. Rather, Justice Peckham's opinion for the sharply divided Court characterized the statute as an unjustified infringement on "the right to labor, and with the right of free contract on the part of the individual, either as employer or employee." In one of the most famous dissenting opinions ever issued, Justice Oliver Wendell Holmes, Jr., attacked the majority for reading its conservative policy preferences into the Constitution and accused the Court of deciding the case not on legal principle but rather "upon an economic theory which a large part of the country does not entertain."

In the early decades of the twentieth century, substantive due process was by and large confined to the protection of economic liberties from government regulation. For example, in *Adair v. United* States (1908), the Supreme Court relied on the Due Process Clause of the Fifth Amendment in striking down a federal law outlawing yellow dog contracts (employment contracts in which workers agree not to join labor unions). Seven years later, in *Coppage v. Kansas* (1915), the Court voided a similar state provision as a violation of the "liberty of contract" protected by the Fourteenth Amendment. In these cases, the Court seemed unconcerned with the blatant inequality in the bargaining positions of individual nonunion employees and their corporate employers. Indeed, in the Court's view, it was unreasonable for the legislature to interfere with the "natural order" of inequalities, no matter how great the resulting disparities between employer and employee.

In *Adkins v. Children's Hospital* (1923), a divided Supreme Court struck down a congressional measure authorizing the setting of minimum wages for women and minors employed in the District of Columbia. As in *Lochner,* the government's perceived interference with liberty of contract was held to violate due process—in this instance, the Fifth Amendment's restriction on federal authority. In dissent, Chief Justice William Howard Taft accused the majority of overstepping its authority, reminding his brethren that "it is not the function of this Court to hold congressional acts invalid simply because they are passed to carry out economic views which the Court believes to be unwise or unsound." In a separate dissenting opinion, Justice Holmes asserted that the power of Congress to enact minimum-wage legislation was "absolutely free from doubt." Holmes sharply criticized the Court's development of what he called the "dogma" of liberty of contract. The word "contract," he pointed out, is not mentioned in the Due Process Clause. Holmes viewed contract merely as "an example of doing what you want to do, embodied in the word liberty. But pretty much all law," he added, "consists in forbidding men to do some things that they want to do, and contract is no more exempt from law than other acts."

The Decline of Economic Due Process

In *Morehead v. New York ex rel. Tipaldo* (1936), the Supreme Court reaffirmed its controversial *Adkins* ruling by striking down a New York minimum-wage law for women. In seeking Supreme Court review of a New York Court of Appeals decision invalidating this statute, attorneys failed to ask specifically for reconsideration of the *Adkins* precedent. Rather, they sought to distinguish the New York minimum-wage law from the congressional act invalidated in *Adkins.* Writing for a five-member majority, Justice Pierce Butler seized on this omission and considered only the question of whether the two cases were distinguishable. He found that they were not and thus struck down the New York law. In separate dissenting opinions, Chief Justice Charles Evans Hughes and Justice Harlan Fiske

Stone maintained that the two laws were, in fact, distinguishable. More significantly, however, they criticized the Court for its refusal to reconsider the validity of *Adkins,* especially in light of the country's experience during the Great Depression.

Ten months later, the Supreme Court, again by a five to four vote (Justice Owen Roberts having changed sides), dramatically overruled the *Adkins* and *Tipaldo* decisions in *West Coast Hotel Company v. Parrish* (1937). Although the votes of the justices had occurred in conference several weeks before President Franklin Roosevelt unveiled his controversial Court-packing plan on February 5, 1937, most political observers and the public in general regarded the *Parrish* decision, announced on March 29, as a clear indication that the Court had caved in to pressure from a popular presidential administration. Justice Roberts later claimed he had voted with the majority in *Tipaldo* simply because he believed that the only question presented in that case was whether the New York minimum-wage law could be distinguished from the provision struck down in *Adkins.* Whatever the true motivations of Justice Roberts, his change of position in this and several other major constitutional decisions in the spring of 1937 figured prominently in the constitutional revolution that to this day marks the single most important jurisprudential shift in Supreme Court history.

In *West Coast Hotel,* the Court considered the constitutionality of a Washington State minimum-wage law enacted in 1913. Chief Justice Hughes delivered the majority opinion. He noted that in upholding the minimum wage, the Washington Supreme Court had "refused to regard the decision in the *Adkins* case as determinative." Such a ruling, Hughes declared, "demands on our part a reexamination" of the *Adkins* case. This reexamination began with the dismantling of the liberty of contract doctrine on which *Adkins* was based. Hughes pointed out that this freedom is not absolute. Moreover, "the liberty safeguarded is liberty in a social organization which requires the protection of law against the evils which menace the health, safety, morals, and welfare of the people." Thus, constitutional

liberty is "necessarily subject to the restraints of due process, and regulation which is reasonable in relation to its subject and is adopted in the interests of the community as due process." Hughes enumerated a wide array of state laws in the field of employer-employee relations previously upheld by the Supreme Court. Then, after quoting approvingly from the dissenting opinions of Chief Justice Taft and Justice Holmes in *Adkins,* he branded that decision "a departure from the true application of the principles governing the regulation by the state of the relation of employer and employed."

West Coast Hotel Company v. Parrish marked the end of an era in American constitutional law. Although the fact might not have been fully recognized at the time, substantive due process as a limitation on governmental power in the field of economic regulation was dead. Justice Sutherland, the author of the *Adkins* majority opinion, sounded a defensive, subdued note in a dissenting opinion. For him, the Constitution had a fixed meaning that did not change "with the ebb and flow of economic events." He attempted, with little success, to distinguish between the "judicial function" of constitutional interpretation and "the power of amendment under the guise of interpretation." "To miss the point of difference between the two," he said, "is to miss all that the phrase 'supreme law of the land' stands for and to convert what was intended as inescapable and enduring mandates into mere moral reflections." That was precisely what the critics of the *Lochner-Adkins-Tipaldo* approach charged that the Court had been doing. But Sutherland insisted that "if the Constitution, intelligently and reasonably construed in the light of these principles, stands in the way of desirable legislation, the blame must rest upon that instrument, and not upon the Court for enforcing it according to its terms."

Personnel changes, beginning only a few months after announcement of the *Parrish* decision, soon resulted in the replacement of all four dissenting justices in that case. The newly constituted so-called Roosevelt Court continued the trend begun in *Parrish* and in other 1937 decisions upholding far-reaching economic and social legislation. In

United States v. Darby (1941), the Court sustained sweeping federal regulatory power in the areas of employer-employee relations by sustaining the Fair Labor Standards Act. The constitutional revolution begun by the *Parrish* case in 1937 thus applied directly not only to due process interpretation but also to other key provisions of the Constitution, including the Commerce Clause, the taxing and spending power, and the Tenth Amendment.

Since 1936, no significant state or federal regulation of business or labor-management relations has been struck down on due process grounds. The 1963 decision in *Ferguson v. Skrupa* is representative of the modern approach in this area. Here, the Supreme Court, in an opinion by Justice Hugo Black, upheld the validity of a Kansas statute conferring a virtual monopoly on the legal profession to engage in the business of "debt adjusting." Black noted that the doctrine prevailing in the *Lochner-Coppage-Adkins* line of cases authorizing courts to invalidate laws because of a belief that the legislature acted unwisely "has long since been discarded." The Court, he continued, had "returned to the original constitutional proposition that courts do not substitute their social and economic beliefs for the judgment of legislative bodies, who are elected to pass laws." Once again, we see how the "original" meaning of the Constitution can mean diametrically opposing things to various Supreme Court justices. In any event, for Justice Black, objections to the law on grounds of social utility should be addressed by the legislature, not the courts. "Whether the legislature takes for its textbook Adam Smith, Herbert Spencer, Lord Keynes, or some other," Black concluded, "is no concern of ours." He also found no violation of the Equal Protection Clause of the Fourteenth Amendment in the legislative decision to provide lawyers a monopoly in the field of debt adjusting.

For the most part, the Supreme Court during the last four decades has followed the approach taken in the *Skrupa* case. Substantive due process has virtually disappeared as a barrier to economic policy making by Congress and state legislatures. However, as a constitutional doctrine, substantive due process is anything but dead. It lives on in recent Court decisions recognizing various noneconomic rights under the Fifth and Fourteenth amendments.

Recognition of Noneconomic Rights

Just two months before the Court handed down its controversial decision in *Lochner v. New York*, it refused to find in the Due Process Clause a prohibition against compulsory vaccination laws. However, Justice Harlan's majority opinion in *Jacobson v. Massachusetts* (1905) recognized that "there is, of course, a sphere within which the individual may assert the supremacy of his own will and rightfully dispute the authority of any human government, especially of any free government existing under a written constitution, to interfere with the exercise of that will." For Justice Harlan and most of his brethren, the state's interest in promoting the public health through compulsory vaccination was superior to the individual "exercise of will." Nevertheless, in *Jacobson*, the Court suggested that the Fourteenth Amendment might protect certain noneconomic aspects of individual autonomy.

The expansion of substantive due process to include noneconomic rights took a quantum leap in *Meyer v. Nebraska* (1923), in which the Supreme Court recognized that citizens have the right to teach and study foreign languages in private schools, state statutes to the contrary notwithstanding. Writing for the Court, Justice James C. McReynolds averred that the liberty protected by the Fourteenth Amendment "denotes not merely freedom from bodily restraint but also the right of the individual to contract, to engage in any of the common occupations of life, to acquire useful knowledge, to marry, establish a home and bring up children, to worship God according to the dictates of his own conscience, and generally to enjoy those privileges long recognized at common law as essential to the orderly pursuit of happiness by free men."

Two years later, in *Pierce v. Society of Sisters* (1925), the Court struck down an Oregon law that required parents to send their children to public schools. Relying on *Meyer v. Nebraska*, the Court held that the statute "unreasonably interferes with the liberty of parents and guardians to direct the upbringing and education of children under their control." Justice McReynolds again spoke for the Court, stressing that "rights guaranteed by the Constitution may not be abridged by legislation which has no reasonable relation to some purpose within the competency of the state."

In the wake of the constitutional revolution of 1937, the Supreme Court turned its attention to the protection of noneconomic civil rights and liberties. In this endeavor the Court relied heavily on the Due Process Clauses of the Fifth and Fourteenth Amendments. For example, in *Bolling v. Sharpe* (1954), the Court struck down the De Jure racial segregation of the public schools in the District of Columbia. Because the Fourteenth Amendment has never been held to apply to the District, the Court relied on substantive due process under the Fifth Amendment. Chief Justice Earl Warren's opinion for the Court brushed aside the inconvenient fact that the Fifth Amendment contains no explicit guarantee of equal protection, noting that in some instances "discrimination may be so unjustifiable as to be violative of due process." Finding that segregation of public schools "is not reasonably related to any proper governmental objective," Warren concluded that segregation of students by race "constitutes an arbitrary deprivation of their liberty in violation of the Due Process Clause."

In *Kent v. Dulles* (1958), the Supreme Court held that the right to travel abroad "is a part of the 'liberty' of which the citizen cannot be deprived without due process of law under the Fifth Amendment." Six years later, in *Aptheker v. Secretary of State* (1964) the Court struck down a provision of the Subversive Activities Control Act of 1950 that deprived members of Communist organizations of the freedom to hold passports. And in *Shapiro v. Thompson* (1969), the Court invoked the right to travel freely across state lines in striking down state laws that precluded newly arriving state residents from obtaining welfare benefits. Because the Court's opinion intertwined substantive due process with an equal protection analysis, *Shapiro v. Thompson*

is often viewed as the archetypal example of the new due process/equal protection.

Marriage and Reproductive Freedom

In *Skinner v. Oklahoma* (1942), the Supreme Court struck down a state law providing for the compulsory sterilization of criminals. Although the decision was based explicitly on the Equal Protection Clause of the Fourteenth Amendment, rather than on substantive due process, the Court characterized the right to procreate as "one of the basic civil rights of man, fundamental to our very existence and survival." Thus, *Skinner* in effect recognized a right of procreation as one of the freedoms implicit in the term "liberty."

The Court's decisions in *Meyer v. Nebraska, Pierce v. Society of Sisters,* and *Skinner v. Oklahoma* paved the way for the landmark 1965 decision in *Griswold v.* Connecticut, which recognized an independent constitutional right of privacy. In *Griswold,* the Court invalidated as applied to married couples a Connecticut law making it a crime to use birth control devices. Justice William O. Douglas's majority opinion attempted to locate the right of marital privacy in various "emanations" from the Bill of Rights. Justices John M. Harlan (the younger) and Byron White, who also voted to strike down the Connecticut law, were not altogether persuaded by Justice Douglas's analysis. In their separate opinions concurring in the judgment, Harlan and White resorted to the time-honored substantive due process approach. Justice Arthur Goldberg invoked the Ninth Amendment's protection of rights "reserved to the People" to buttress the Court's recognition of marital privacy as a constitutional liberty. In Goldberg's view, "the Ninth Amendment simply lends strong support to the view that the 'liberty' protected by the Fifth and Fourteenth Amendments from infringement by the Federal Government or the States is not restricted to rights specifically mentioned in the first eight amendments." In a strongly worded dissent, Justice Hugo Black objected to what he perceived as overstepping the judicial role: "I do not believe that we are granted power by the Due Process Clause or any other constitutional provision or provisions to measure constitutionality by our belief that legislation is arbitrary, capricious or unreasonable, or accomplishes no justifiable purpose, or is offensive to our own notions of 'civilized standards of conduct.'"

Although it is widely recognized as the jurisprudential origin of the constitutional right of privacy, the *Griswold* decision was limited to the marital context. Two years after Griswold, the Court strengthened the constitutional protection of marital freedom by striking down a Virginia law that forbade interracial marriage. In *Loving v. Virginia* (1967), the Court held that such laws violate the Equal Protection Clause of the Fourteenth Amendment, but it also grounded its decision in substantive due process. Noting that free choice in marriage "has long been recognized as one of the vital personal rights essential to the orderly pursuit of happiness by free men," Chief Justice Warren concluded that "[t]o deny this fundamental freedom on so unsupportable a basis … is surely to deprive all the State's citizens of liberty without due process of law."

Because the *Griswold* holding was limited to married couples, the question remained as to whether anti-contraception laws could be enforced against single adults. In *Eisenstadt v. Baird* (1972), the Court answered that question in the negative. Justice William Brennan, writing for the Court, asserted that the right of privacy is "the right of the individual, married or single, to be free from unwarranted governmental intrusion into matters so fundamentally affecting a person as the decision whether to bear or beget a child." Thus the stage was set for the most dramatic and consequential application of substantive due process since *Dred Scott*: the Supreme Court's 1973 decision in *Roe v. Wade*.

Justice Blackmun's opinion for the Court in *Roe* did not elaborate on the interpretive foundations of the right to privacy. But it made clear that the decision to strike down the Texas abortion statute was based on a species of substantive due process: "This right of privacy, whether it be founded in the Fourteenth Amendment's concept of personal liberty and restrictions upon state action, *as we feel it is,* or, as the District Court determined, in the Ninth Amendment's reservation of rights to the people, is broad enough to encompass a woman's decision whether or not to terminate her pregnancy" (emphasis added). Nineteen years later, in *Planned Parenthood v. Casey* (1992), the controlling opinion made clear that "[c]onstitutional protection of the woman's decision to terminate her pregnancy derives from the Due Process Clause of the Fourteenth Amendment."

While not rejecting the substantive due process approach altogether, Justice William H. Rehnquist's dissent in *Roe v. Wade* objected to the recognition of the right to abortion as an aspect of Fourteenth Amendment liberty: "The fact that a majority of the States reflecting, after all, the majority sentiment in those States, have had restrictions on abortions for at least a century is a strong indication, it seems to me, that the asserted right to an abortion is not 'so rooted in the traditions and conscience of our people as to be ranked as fundamental.'" Dissenting in the *Casey* decision 19 years later, Rehnquist would elaborate on this theme. Reviewing the history of criminal prohibitions of abortion, Rehnquist concluded: "On this record, it can scarcely be said that any deeply rooted tradition of relatively unrestricted abortion in our history supported the classification of the right to abortion as 'fundamental' under the Due Process Clause of the Fourteenth Amendment."

Refusal of Medical Treatment and the Right to Die

In the 1970s, state courts around the country began to recognize that terminal patients have a right to refuse medical treatments that artificially prolong life. This so-called right to die is rooted in the common-law doctrine of informed consent as well as the modern constitutional right to privacy. Some state courts have engaged quite explicitly in a substantive due process analysis of such claims. In *Cruzan v. Missouri Health Department* (1990), the U.S. Supreme Court recognized under the Fourteenth Amendment a "constitutionally protected liberty interest in refusing unwanted medical treatment." However, the Supreme Court upheld a state policy under which courts are required to find clear and convincing evidence of a noncommunicative patient's wish to forego life-extending treatments before ordering that such measures be halted. Similarly, in *Washington v. Glucksberg* (1997), the Supreme Court upheld a state ban on doctor-assisted suicide. However, the Court's analysis of the issue was strikingly different. Writing for the Court in *Glucksberg*, Chief Justice Rehnquist refused to recognize a "right to suicide" under the Due Process Clause of the Fourteenth Amendment. Warning of the dangers of an unfettered substantive due process, Rehnquist stressed the "consistent and almost universal tradition that has long rejected the asserted right, and continues explicitly to reject it today, even for terminally ill, mentally competent adults." The effect of the *Glucksberg* ruling was to allow states to make their own policies in this area without federal judicial supervision, but no doubt state courts will continue to wrestle with these issues.

Gay Rights

Some commentators viewed the *Glucksberg* decision as an indication that the Supreme Court was curtailing the further development of the constitutional right of privacy. Six years later, however, in *Lawrence v. Texas* (2003), the Court employed substantive due process in striking down a Texas law criminalizing private, consensual homosexual conduct by adults. In so doing, the Court overturned its 1986 decision in *Bowers v. Hardwick*, where the Court had flatly refused to recognize "a fundamental right to homosexuals to engage in acts of consensual sodomy." Writing for the Court in *Lawrence*, Justice Anthony Kennedy summarized the decision as follows:

> Liberty presumes an autonomy of self that includes freedom of thought, belief, expression, and certain intimate conduct…. When sexuality finds overt expression in intimate conduct with another person, the conduct can be but one element in a personal bond that is more enduring. The liberty protected by the Constitution allows homosexual persons the right to make this choice.

In a strident dissent, Justice Antonin Scalia argued that for the state of Texas to criminalize homosexual conduct is "well within the range of traditional democratic action, and its hand should not be stayed through the invention of a brand-new 'constitutional right' by a Court that is impatient of democratic change." In a statement reminiscent of Justice Holmes's dissent in *Lochner v. New York*, Scalia asserted that the Court's decision was less a product of legal reasoning than of "a law-profession culture that has largely signed on to the so-called homosexual agenda."

Substantive Due Process and the Judicial Role

Substantive due process has been controversial ever since its inception in American constitutional law. This is partially because it is based on a less than obvious—some might say counterintuitive—interpretation of the Fifth and Fourteenth amendments. Moreover, it has served as a vehicle for judicial forays into some of the most contentious issues of public policy, including slavery, the minimum wage, segregation, birth control, abortion, euthanasia, and, most recently, gay rights. Critics of substantive due process argue that it provides judges a license to "substitute their social and economic beliefs for the judgment of legislative bodies," as Justice Hugo L. Black argued in his opinion for the Supreme Court in *Ferguson v. Skrupa* (1963). These critics would agree with Chief Justice Charles Evans Hughes, who observed in *Sproles v. Binford* (1932) that "debatable questions as to reasonableness are not for the courts but for the Legislature." They would also concur with Justice Harlan Fiske Stone, whose dissenting opinion in *United States v. Butler* (1936) insisted that it is not "the business of courts to sit in judgment on the wisdom of legislative action" and that "courts are not the only agency of government that must be assumed to have capacity to govern." Critics contend that judges employing substantive due process set themselves over and above the legislative branch, acting more like Platonic guardians than jurists.

Defenders of substantive due process argue that merely procedural protections of life, liberty, and property are inadequate. Justice John Marshall Harlan (the younger), dissenting in *Poe v. Ullman* (1961), observed that "were due process merely a procedural safeguard it would fail to reach those situations where the deprivation of life, liberty or property was accomplished by legislation which by operating in the future could, given even the fairest possible procedure in application to individuals, nevertheless destroy the enjoyment of all three." In *Washington v. Glucksberg* (1997), the Supreme Court noted that "by barring certain government actions regardless of the fairness of the procedures used to implement them," substantive due process "serves to prevent governmental power from being 'used for purposes of oppression.'"

Justice Lewis Powell, writing for the plurality in *Moore v. City of East Cleveland* (1985), recognized that substantive due process "has at times been a treacherous field for this Court." Powell noted the "risks when the judicial branch gives enhanced protection to certain substantive liberties without the guidance of the more specific provisions of the Bill of Rights." Quoting Justice Harlan's concurrence in *Griswold v. Connecticut* (1965), Powell insisted that "appropriate limits on substantive due process come not from drawing arbitrary lines but rather from careful 'respect for the teachings of history [and] solid recognition of the basic values that underlie our society.'" Of course, judges and justices can and do disagree as to the "teachings of history" and the application of "basic values."

Although strong arguments continue to be made against its validity, substantive due process is now firmly rooted in the American constitutional tradition and is not likely to be repudiated by the courts. Political controversy is not likely to focus on substantive due process per se but will ebb and flow depending on the "basic values" the Court chooses to emphasize in defining the scope of liberty.

See also Bill of Rights (American); Bill of Rights, Incorporation of; Black, Hugo L.; Bork, Robert H.; *Chicago, Burlington and Quincy Railroad v. Chicago;* Douglas, William O.; Dred Scott Case; Due Process, Procedural; Due Process Clauses; Fundamental Rights; Gay Rights Movement; *Griswold v. Connecticut;* Harlan, John Marshall; Harlan, John Marshall, II; Holmes, Oliver Wendell, Jr.; *Lawrence v. Texas;* Liberty; *Lochner v. New York; Loving v. Virginia; Meyer v. Nebraska; Pierce v. Society of Sisters;* Powell, Lewis F., Jr.; Privacy, Constitutional Right of; Rational Basis Test; Right to Die; *Roe v. Wade;* Scalia, Antonin; Strict Scrutiny; Taney, Roger B.; Travel, Right to;

Bibliography

Berger, Raoul. 1977. *Government by Judiciary: The Transformation of the Fourteenth Amendment.* Cambridge, MA: Harvard University Press.

Bork, Robert H. 1990. *The Tempting of America: The Political Seduction of the Law.* New York: Free Press.

Haynes, Charles Grove. 1930. *The Revival of Natural Law Concepts.* Cambridge, MA: Harvard University Press.

Keynes, Edward. 1996. *Liberty, Property and Privacy: Toward a Jurisprudence of Substantive Due Process.* University Park: Pennsylvania State University Press.

Orth, John V. 2003. *Due Process of Law: A Brief History.* Lawrence: University Press of Kansas.

John M. Scheb II and Otis H. Stephens, Jr.

DUE PROCESS CLAUSES

There are two Due Process Clauses in the United States Constitution. The first is found in the Fifth Amendment, which is part of the Bill of Rights. That amendment provides: "No person shall be ... deprived of life, liberty, or property, without due process of law." The second instance, found in Section 1 of the Fourteenth Amendment, provides that "nor shall any State deprive any person of life, liberty, or property, without due process of law." The first of these clauses applies specifically to the federal government. The second, like the other provisions of Section 1 of the Fourteenth Amendment, applies specifically to the states.

Due process is the broadest and most basic protection afforded by the Constitution. In its most general sense, due process of law requires government to exercise power within legal parameters and show due regard for the rights and interests of the individuals under its authority. In other words, due process protects citizens against the arbitrary and capricious exercise of governmental power.

Courts have recognized two aspects of due process. Procedural due process requires government to provide fair notice and a fair hearing to persons whose "life, liberty, or property" interests are adversely affected by governmental action. Substantive due process prohibits government from enforcing policies that unreasonably restrict liberty or property rights, even if such policies do not run counter to other specific constitutional prohibitions.

Procedural due process has enormous implications for public administration and, in particular, the administration of the criminal justice system. All government agencies, including educational institutions, law enforcement agencies, social welfare programs, and regulatory agencies, must provide procedural due process to their employees as well as to other persons subject to their authority. In the criminal context, procedural due process encompasses the various procedures established by courts to ensure that a person accused of a crime has a reasonable opportunity to contest the charges brought by the government.

Substantive due process was important historically in protecting property rights and economic liberty. In the modern era, courts have relied on substantive due process to protect rights of personal privacy and autonomy.

The Due Process Clause of the Fourteenth Amendment is particularly important in the development of civil rights and liberties in the United States, as the Supreme Court has used this clause to apply the provisions of the Bill of Rights to the actions of state and local governments. Under the doctrine of incorporation, most of the provisions of the Bill of Rights now apply with equal force to state and local governments because they are held to be incorporated within the substantive or procedural protections of the Due Process Clause of the Fourteenth Amendment.

See also Accused, Rights of the; Bill of Rights, Incorporation of; Due Process, Procedural; Due Process, Substantive; Fifth Amendment; Fourteenth Amendment; Hearing, Elements of a; Liberty; New Property; Property Rights

Bibliography

Orth, John V. 2003. *Due Process of Law: A Brief History.* Lawrence: University Press of Kansas.

John M. Scheb II and Otis H. Stephens, Jr.

DUE PROCESS OF LAW. *See* Accused, Rights of the; Bill of Rights, Incorporation of; Due Process, Procedural; Due Process, Substantive; Due Process Clauses; Hearing, Elements of a; Magna Carta

DUE PROCESS RIGHTS OF GOVERNMENT BENEFICIARIES

The Due Process Clauses of the Fifth and Fourteenth Amendment guarantee that no citizen shall be deprived of life, liberty, or property by either the federal or state government without first receiving due process of law. The meaning of this clause is not self-evident. As the U.S. Supreme Court noted in *Hannah v. Larche* (1960), due process is "an elusive concept. Its exact boundaries are undefinable, and its content varies according to specific factual contexts."

One question that has required resolution by the U.S. Supreme Court, for example, involves whether the word "property" applies to the future stream of government entitlements, such as welfare or social security. If the word "property" includes such future benefits, then the Due Process Clause requires that the government provide the affected individual with legal process should it choose to terminate those benefits. For example, the government may determine that a welfare recipient's eligibility for benefits has, for some reason, expired. In that case, the question arises whether the Due Process Clause requires the government to provide the recipient with notification of the proposed termination and the opportunity to challenge the termination at a hearing.

Defining the New Property

The word "property" in the Due Process Clause clearly applies to more traditional forms of tangible and intangible property, such as real property, money, personal property, or stocks. Government financial benefits distributed via beneficiary programs such as welfare become such traditional property once they are transferred to the beneficiary, since at that point the beneficiary owns them in the traditional sense. Thus, where the government seeks to recoup such benefits, the Due Process Clause would apply. On the other hand, government entitlement programs also create an expectation that the beneficiary will receive a stream of benefits *in the future* if he or she qualifies under the relevant statutory requirements.

Until the 1960s, the expectation of future government benefits did not constitute a property right entitled to protection under the Due Process Clause. Rather, government benefits were considered "privileges" or "gratuities" donated to the beneficiary by the government. In a series of decisions in the 1960s culminating in the landmark decision of *Goldberg v. Kelly* (1970), however, the U.S. Supreme Court made clear that government "benefits are a matter of statutory entitlement for persons qualified to receive them." As such, they deserve protection under the Due Process Clause, which cannot be avoided "by an argument that public assistance benefits are 'a 'privilege' and not a 'right.'" Since the Court has held that public assistance benefits constitute a property interest under the Due Process Clause, they may not be revoked without some form of legal process.

What Process Is Due?

In *Goldberg*, the plaintiffs, who received aid under the federally assisted program of Aid to Families with Dependent Children, originally brought suit because the state government failed to provide any legal procedures prior to termination of such aid. Once the plaintiffs filed suit, however, the state altered its regulations to provide for seven days' notice of the proposed termination of benefits, as well to provide the beneficiary with the opportunity to participate in a written correspondence with welfare officials concerning the propriety of the termination. The plaintiffs then claimed that these procedures were themselves inadequate.

Once the Court made clear that the termination of welfare benefits constituted a deprivation of property under the Due Process Clause, it turned to what process was constitutionally required. Like the term "property," the words "due process" have no inherent meaning. As a result, the Court was forced to determine how much notice and what type of hearing the government must provide upon the termination of welfare benefits. In answering these questions, the Court noted the importance of balancing the individual's interest in the benefits (in the case of welfare, benefits that often enable recipients to eat and obtain shelter), against the cost to the government in providing additional procedures. In the context of welfare benefits, the Court held that the government must provide meaningful notice and a pre-termination hearing at which the beneficiary has the opportunity to cross-examine witnesses and be represented by legal counsel. In addition, the hearing must be presided over by an impartial decision maker who is required to state the basis for his or her decision for or against the beneficiary.

Some years after *Goldberg*, the Supreme Court clarified these rules by providing a more specific balancing test to determine the form a hearing must take to satisfy due process. In *Mathews v. Eldridge* (1976) the Court considered the type of hearing required when the government terminates social security disability benefits. In resolving that matter, the Court set forth three elements that courts must consider in determining hearing rights under the Due Process Clause: (1) the private interests affected by the government's action, (2) the risk that the existing procedures will result in error and the probable value of the proposed procedures in reducing such error, and (3) the government's cost in providing additional procedures. Because social security beneficiaries do not necessarily rely on their benefits for subsistence, the Court held in *Mathews* that a *post*-termination hearing before an administrative law judge was sufficient to satisfy the Due Process Clause. This conclusion substantially differed from *Goldberg,* in which the Court held that, in the case of welfare benefits, a hearing must be held *prior* to termination of those benefits.

The Due Process Clause thus requires hearing rights in cases involving the termination of government benefits, but the extent of those hearing rights (i.e., when the hearing is held—before or after termination—whether it requires confrontation and cross-examination of witnesses, whether counsel must be permitted, etc.) depends upon the particular context. To avoid litigation and to protect their clients, however, most government agencies err on the side of extensive procedural protections for their beneficiaries, as set forth in agency regulations.

See also Bill of Rights, Incorporation of; Due Process, Procedural; Due Process Clauses; Fifth Amendment; Fourteenth Amendment; Liberty; New Property; Privilege/Right Distinction; Property Rights

Bibliography

Mashaw, Jerry. 1985. *Due Process in the Administrative State.* New Haven, CT: Yale University Press.

Reich, Charles A. 1964. "The New Property." *Yale Law Journal* 73 (5): 733–87.

Shapiro, Sidney A., and Richard E. Levy. 2005. "Government Benefits and the Rule of Law: Toward a Standards-Based Theory of Due Process." *Administrative Law Review* 57:107–53.

Stefanie A. Lindquist

DUI FIELD TESTS AND BREATH TESTS

When police stop a motorist and have reasonable suspicion that the driver is under the influence of alcohol, they will often administer a battery of field sobriety tests. Most law enforcement agencies utilize three standardized field sobriety tests. In 1977, the National Highway Transportation Safety Administration (NHTSA) began to study various roadside sobriety tests. The purpose of this research was to develop the most reliable and accurate of these tests and to then standardize the tests (Burns and Moskowitz 1977). After evaluating a number of field tests, the study concluded that a group of three tests including Horizontal Gaze Nystagmus (HGN), one-leg stand, and walk and turn would be the most reliable to determine if a driver was impaired.

The process of standardization involved a set procedure for administering each of the tests and evaluating those tests by set criteria or clues. The researchers then set forth test conditions such as a designated straight line and a reasonably dry, hard, level, nonslippery surface for the walk-and-turn test. One of the most important points the researchers made was that validation of these tests applies only when the tests are administered in the prescribed standardized manner, the standard clues are used to assess the suspect's performance, and the standard criteria are employed to interpret that performance. If any one of the standard field sobriety test elements is changed, the validity is compromised (NHTSA 2004).

In *State v. Homan* (2000), the Ohio Supreme Court held that any variation in the use of NHTSA standardized field sobriety tests makes the result completely unreliable as it relates to probable cause, a much lower standard than proof beyond the reasonable doubt needed for conviction. The *Homan* court stated: "It is well established that in field sobriety testing even minor deviations from the standardized procedures can severely bias the results." This is due, the court reasoned, to "the small margins of error that characterize field sobriety tests, making strict compliance critical." The court found that "when field sobriety testing is conducted in a manner that departs from established methods and procedures, the results are inherently unreliable." It concluded that "for the results of a field sobriety test to serve as evidence of probable cause to arrest, the police must have administered the test in strict compliance with standard testing procedures."

On the other hand, courts in Florida (*State v. Meador,* 1996), Wisconsin (*City of West Bend v. Wilkens,* 2005), and a federal district court in Maryland (*United States v. Horn,* 2002), have approached the admissibility of field sobriety tests on a different basis. In *City of West Bend v. Wilkens,* the Wisconsin Court of Appeals stated:

Other than the bare assertion that the recommended standardized tests are both scientifically reliable and valid, the record contains no indication that they are based on science. Any scientific explanation for why the standardized procedures yield any particular result is completely absent. Standardization may lead to reliability in the sense that where examiners look for the same "clues" to shape their observations of the subject, their observations are likely to be more similar. Similarity does not equate to more correct observations, however. "The mere fact that the NHTSA studies attempted to quantify the reliability of the field sobriety tests in predicting unlawful [blood alcohol content] does not convert all of the observations of a person's performance into scientific evidence."

If the police believe the motorist has failed the field sobriety tests, this generally leads to the driver's arrest, especially when there are other signs of impairment such as the odor of alcohol, unsteadiness, slurred speech, and bloodshot or watery eyes. The driver is generally taken to jail, where he or she is requested to submit to a chemical test of his breath, blood, or urine. In most cases, the test will be a breath test. Refusal to take the requested chemical test generally results in suspension of driving privileges. There are a number of breath tests used throughout the United States, including the Intoxilyzer, models 5000 and 8000; the Drager Alcotest; and BAC Data Master.

Currently there is heated debate and controversy over the science underlying chemical breath testing. There are three basic assumptions utilized in chemical breath testing. The first is that the driver is in the post-absorptive phase when tested. This assumption can be easily disputed by defense attorneys and expert witnesses. Most breath tests occur within an hour and a half after driving. The absorption phase can last as long as two hours or more, depending on what the driver has eaten and the time and amount of alcohol consumption. Numerous studies have shown that breath tests are least accurate during the absorptive phase. The disparity between breath alcohol concentrations and blood alcohol concentrations during the absorption phase are of great concern to the defense bar, since many state statutes do not distinguish between an unlawful breath alcohol concentration or an unlawful blood alcohol concentration.

The second assumption used in breath testing since its inception in the 1950s is that the exchange of alcohol from blood to breath occurs in the deep lung alveoli. More recent studies show that the exchange of ethanol occurs across the conducting airways of the lungs, not the alveoli. Hlastala (2002) has concluded that breath test machines currently favor people with large lung capacity since they may stop breathing into the machine sooner, thus causing the machine to sample non-alviolar air that is lower in alcohol concentration. He states:

A consequence of continuing to use the old model is that subjects with larger lung volume may have a lower BrAC than a subject with a small lung volume because these subjects do not need to exhale as great a fraction of their vital capacity as subjects with smaller lung volume to fulfill the minimum volume exhalation required before stopping exhalation…. A person with smaller lung volume must breathe farther into the exhaled breath, resulting in a greater BrAC-to-BAC ratio. (Hlastala 2002, 406)

The third assumption used in current breath test machines is that the true blood-to-breath partition ratio for alcohol is 2100/1. It is agreed that a single partition ratio will not apply to all people. NHTSA has adopted the 2100/1 partition ratio as a population mean. All breath test instruments are calibrated at the 2100/1 partition ratio. However, studies on large study groups have shown that the mean alcohol partition ratio between blood and breath is closer to 2300/1 (Dubowski 1985).

The Gaussian distribution for these newer partition ratios in the post-absorptive phase is 1797/1 to 2763/1 for 95 percent of the population and 1555/1 to 3005/1 for 99.7 percent of the population. An examination of these new findings shows that the current partition ratio of 2100/1 accounts for less than 80 percent of the population. This means that approximately 20 percent of persons tested in this study at 2100/1 would have a false high reading. The 1555/1 partition ratio would have to be used to achieve 99.7-percent confidence.

It is important to understand, however, that a conviction for driving while intoxicated (DWI) or driving while under the influence (DUI) does not require chemical testing; and it is not uncommon for defendants to be convicted of these offenses solely on the basis of driving patterns, field observations, and field sobriety tests.

See also Automobile Stops and Searches; Implied Consent Statutes; Probable Cause

Bibliography

Burns, Marcelline, and Herbert Moskowitz. 1977. *Psycho Physical Tests PT 4 DWI.* Washington, DC: U.S. Department of Transportation, National Highway Transportation Safety Administration.

Dubowski, Kurt M. 1985. "Absorption, Distribution and Elimination of Alcohol: Highway Safety Aspects." *Journal of Studies on Alcohol.* Suppl. 10:98–108.

Hlastala, Michael P. 2002. "Invited Editorial on 'The Alcohol Breath Test.'" *Journal of Applied Physiology* 93 (2): 405–6.

National Highway Traffic Safety Administration. 2004. *DWI Detection and Standardized Field Sobriety Testing, Student Manual, VIII-19.* Washington, DC: U.S. Department of Transportation, National Highway Transportation Safety Administration.

James R. Dirmann

DUNCAN V. LOUISIANA (1968)

Gary Duncan was accused in a Louisiana court of misdemeanor battery. He requested a trial by jury but was denied because Louisiana law at the time granted jury trials only in capital cases and felony cases where imprisonment at hard labor could be imposed. Duncan was convicted, sentenced to 60 days in jail, and ordered to pay a $150 fine. After the Louisiana Supreme Court denied review, Duncan obtained a writ of certiorari from the United States Supreme Court.

At issue before the High Court was whether the right of trial by jury guaranteed by the Sixth Amendment is applicable to state courts by way of the Fourteenth Amendment. In a line of cases beginning with *Chicago, Burlington and Quincy Railroad v. Chicago* (1897), the Court had held that various provisions of the Bill of Rights were applicable to the states because they were incorporated into the Due Process Clause of the Fourteenth Amendment. In *Palko v. Connecticut* (1937), the Court had

held that particular provisions of the Bill of Rights would be made applicable to the states if they were essential "to a scheme of ordered liberty" and necessary to maintain "a fair and enlightened system of justice."

After reviewing the line of incorporation cases, Justice Byron White's majority opinion held that "in the American States, as in the federal judicial system, a general grant of jury trial for serious offenses is a fundamental right, essential for preventing miscarriages of justice and for assuring that fair trials are provided for all defendants." However, White stopped short of holding that jury trials are required in cases of petty offenses, noting that such cases "were tried without juries both in England and in the Colonies and have always been held to be exempt from the otherwise comprehensive language of the Sixth Amendment's jury trial provisions." White concluded that criminal violations "carrying possible penalties up to six months do not require a jury trial if they otherwise qualify as petty offenses." Because Louisiana law allowed Duncan to be sentenced to up to two years in prison, the Court held that he was entitled to a jury trial.

Justice Hugo Black, a long-time advocate of the idea that all the provisions of the Bill of Rights should be applied to the states via the Fourteenth Amendment, expressed his satisfaction with what the Court had done under the mantle of selective incorporation, In a concurring opinion joined by Justice William O. Douglas, Black wrote, "I believe as strongly as ever that the Fourteenth Amendment was intended to make the Bill of Rights applicable to the States. I have been willing to support the selective incorporation doctrine, however, as an alternative, although perhaps less historically supportable than complete incorporation…. [T]he selective incorporation process has the virtue of having already worked to make most of the Bill of Rights protections applicable to the States."

In a dissenting opinion joined by Justice Potter Stewart, Justice John Marshall Harlan (the younger) objected to what he perceived as an unwarranted departure from the idea that the states have "primary responsibility for operating the machinery of criminal justice within their borders, and adapting it to their particular circumstances." Harlan insisted that the Fourteenth Amendment "does not impose on the State the rules that may be in force in the federal courts except where such rules are also found to be essential to basic fairness." Evidently, in Justice Harlan's view, the right to trial by jury in a nonpetty criminal case was not in that category. For him, maintaining state judicial autonomy under traditional notions of federalism was of a higher value.

See also Bill of Rights (American); Bill of Rights, Incorporation of; Black, Hugo L.; *Chicago, Burlington and Quincy Railroad v. Chicago;* Douglas, William O.; Due Process Clause; Fourteenth Amendment; Harlan, John Marshall, II; Jury, Trial by; *Palko v. Connecticut;* Sixth Amendment; Stewart, Potter; White, Byron R.

John M. Scheb II and Otis H. Stephens, Jr.

DWORKIN, ANDREA (1946–2005)

Andrea Dworkin was born in Camden, New Jersey, on September 26, 1946. Her father, a sometime teacher and postal worker, encouraged his daughter to read extensively and to think for herself. Dworkin attended Bennington College, then a women's college, where she studied music and was politically active. Her studies were interrupted in 1965 when she was arrested while protesting at the United Nations and was taken to New York's Women's House of Detention. She later testified before a grand jury that while at the jail she had been denied phone calls, kept in squalid conditions, and subjected to a brutal physical examination that caused hemorrhaging. Although the grand jury dismissed Dworkin's claims, her testimony was widely credited with leading to the eventual closing of the prison. Following the grand jury's decision, Dworkin escaped for a year to Greece before returning to Bennington. However, she soon parted ways with the college, which she later described as a "brothel" in which young women were groomed to be the mistresses of artists and intellectuals (rather than to be artists and intellectuals themselves) (Dworkin

2002, 4, 60). Dworkin felt the grand jury decision enforcement was a paternalistic and hypocritical moral code.

Dworkin emigrated to Amsterdam; her memoirs from this period describe being battered by an anarchist she married there. After leaving him and returning to New York she published *Woman Hating* (1976), a sharp critique of what she saw as a violent sexual culture. For a time she held various jobs and continued to be active in the antiwar movement, though she was disgusted by the sexism of the political left. Eventually Dworkin cultivated a career as a lecturer in some demand.

Dworkin claimed to have been sexually assaulted three times before she was 19 (Dworkin 1992), and her memoirs recount experiences with a pedophilic high school teacher. During her youth she worked at times as a prostitute. Her writings are full of rage, pain, sweeping condemnations of gender roles, and, in most cases, a refusal to soften or qualify her claims. Dworkin wrote that "violence ... is the prime component of male identity" (Dworkin 1981, 51)—and not just identity but also pleasure: "male pleasure is inextricably tied to victimizing, hurting, exploiting" (Dworkin 1981, 69).

Around 1980 Dworkin began to focus primarily on pornography. A 1981 book, *Pornography: Men Possessing Women,* describes a link between the submissive and often victimized roles women play in pornography and their continued subjugation in society at large. Driven by violent urges, she wrote, "[m]en act out pornography ... [and w]omen's lives become pornography" (Dworkin 1992). In 1983 Dworkin and Catherine MacKinnon, an attorney and University of Minnesota law professor, drafted legislation that would define pornography as a form of discrimination against women and that would allow any woman residing in the area covered by the law to sue pornographers in civil court. Although a handful of cities considered passing the draft legislation as an ordinance, only two city councils—those of Minneapolis and Indianapolis—did so. Minneapolis mayor Don Fraser vetoed that city's ordinance early in 1984, citing First Amendment concerns.

However, on May 1, 1984, Mayor William Hudnut of Indianapolis signed that city's version of the civil rights ordinance into law. The Indianapolis ordinance would have allowed any woman to file in the city's Office of Equal Opportunity a complaint against a purveyor of pornography. A hearing, followed in some cases by a trial, could result in a cease-and-desist order being issued against the pornographer or seller. Within the hour of Mayor Hudnut's signing the ordinance, a coalition of bookstores, trade associations, and a cable television station submitted a challenge to it in federal court. An injunction preventing the city from allowing suits under the law was issued a few days later, and the case went to trial. A federal district court and the Seventh Circuit Court of Appeals agreed that the Indianapolis ordinance impermissibly burdened free speech; the U.S. Supreme Court affirmed this decision without comment (See *American Booksellers v. Hudnut,* 1984; *American Booksellers v. Hudnut,* 1985; *American Booksellers v. Hudnut,* 1986).

In 1986, Dworkin testified before Attorney General Edwin Meese's Commission on Pornography, and the commission gave consideration to the MacKinnon-Dworkin civil rights approach to punishing pornography. The commission's final report endorsed a somewhat narrowed version of this approach but declined to recommend that lawmakers create opportunities for any and all women in the governed area to sue purveyors of pornography (part 3, chapter 5, June 1986).

In 1998, Dworkin married John Stoltenberg, although both identified themselves as gay. In 2000 she published an account of a traumatic experience; she believed that she had been drugged and raped in a French hotel the year before. A new round of controversial and largely bitter media attention brought Dworkin again to the public mind. On April 9, 2005, she passed away, and as of April 20, 2006, the cause of her death is not generally known. She died as she had lived: a controversial figure vilified by both conservatives for her rejection of traditional gender definitions and for liberals for being supposedly antisex and anti-free speech in her views on pornography. Besides Dworkin's

writings mentioned above, works left behind by the author include *Our Blood: Prophecies and Discourses on Sexual Politics* (1976) and *Heartbreak: The Political Memoir of a Militant Feminist* (2002).

See also *American Booksellers v. Hudnut;* Feminist Movement; First Amendment; Gay Rights Movement; Gender-Based Discrimination; Obscenity and Pornography; Speech, Freedom of

Bibliography

Dworkin, Andrea. 1976. *Our Blood: Prophecies and Discourses on Sexual Politics.* New York: Harper & Row.
_____. 1976. *Woman Hating: A Radical Look at Sexuality.* New York: E. P. Dutton.
_____. 1981. *Pornography: Men Possessing Women.* New York: G. P. Putnam's Sons.
_____. 2002. *Heartbreak: The Political Memoir of a Militant Feminist.* New York: Basic Books.

Rachel Pearsall

DWORKIN, RONALD (1931–)

Ronald Dworkin is one of the most influential and prolific theorists in Anglo-American legal philosophy. While serving in academic appointments both in the United States and in Britain, he has contributed to the conversations regarding the nature of judicial decision making and constitutional interpretation in both countries. Generally considered a liberal, he advocates an approach to law that defies easy categorization. He is clearly not a positivist, given his rejection of the mechanical approach to constitutional interpretation, but then neither is he a postmodernist. Although he fully concedes the inescapably political nature of interpreting the law, Dworkin rejects the decisionist contentions most often associated with postmodernism. In other words, the law is not simply the expression of judicial opinion. It is not arbitrary and it does not gain legitimacy based upon majority belief. According to Dworkin, argument, coherence, and reason giving are central aspects of the law, and from those sources the law derives its authority.

Dworkin's unique approach features the values of integrity, principle, and equality. Integrity is the idea that "judicial decision [must] be a matter of principle, not compromise or strategy or political accommodation" (Dworkin 1996, 83). What Dworkin is arguing is that even though judges are necessarily in a position of having to make hermeneutical judgments, their decisions must not be arbitrary. They display integrity insofar as they do not simply declare legal decisions by fiat. Judges are bound by the power of effective argument and must be prepared to situate their decisions within the historical context of the relevant legal area. Precedent, then, becomes a constraining factor in judicial decision making. Furthermore, judges must be prepared to apply the thematic findings of a single decision across the board to other decisions. This is what Dworkin means by principle.

Dworkin's view of principle, drawing on his asserted need for a law with integrity, stands in contrast to the view of principle held by positivists. Positivists of all stripes stress the importance of seeing the law as somehow already existing prior to judicial decision making. To judge with integrity, according to positivists, is to apply the general principle of the law to the particular case pending before the court. This mechanical view is designed to reduce the arbitrariness of law by explicitly identifying the data by which judges render their verdict. Dworkin shares the concerns of positivists that the law should not be wanton or arbitrary. Citizens must be able to identify the patterns in judicial decisions. Otherwise, power would be left unchecked and citizens would be at the mercy of an unrestrained bench. The problem that Dworkin identifies is that such a view of principle does not really comport with the actual practice of constitutional adjudication.

Judges are not simply collecting information whereby they might turn to the relevant statute and render a quick decision. They are, rather, in a position that Dworkin describes as Herculean. The law is a forum for argument and counterargument, structured debate, and evidence giving. The court is, then, a place of persuasion based upon reasoned discourse. It is the judge's job to declare a winner. This elevates the position of the judge inasmuch as the judge is the one who must determine the actual content of the law in any given case. Distancing himself from postmodernists, however, Dworkin does not concede that this makes the law ultimately arbitrary. The requirement that the decision be justified by coherent and compelling arguments marks the boundaries of his power. To judge with integrity means that the judge must identify the principles involved in a given case, and this can only be done through effective argumentation.

Dworkin fully recognizes that his view of the Herculean judge presiding over rational debate and carefully weighing the arguments presented before him does not offer the relatively pristine view of judicial decision making championed by positivists. Dworkin therefore relies heavily on political theory and philosophy to defend his position. This willingness to reach beyond the domain of legal theory is demonstrative of one of Dworkin's most identifying characteristics—his rejection of the idea that a rigid taxonomy can be applied to academic disciplines. The law, according to Dworkin, does not exist in a vacuum. To champion argument and reason giving as the means by which legal legitimacy might be gained is to effectively take a side in the debates now animating the fields of political theory and social philosophy regarding the nature of democratic society. It is to reject the postmodern assumption that arguments are always ephemeral expressions of the powerful. Dworkin is an Enlightenment modernist in that he believes in the fundamental soundness of reason as a means of adjudicating the difficult claims raised by citizens of the same polity. Because he is aware of the philosophical ramifications of his legal theories, Dworkin routinely peppers his essays with references to philosophy, linguistic theory, and social criticism. This makes him a truly eclectic legal theorist.

See also Interpretivism; Liberalism

Bibliography

Dworkin, Ronald. 1978. *Taking Rights Seriously.* Cambridge, MA: Harvard University Press.

_____. 1996. *Freedom's Law: The Moral Reading of the American Constitution.* Cambridge, MA: Harvard University Press.

Guest, Stephen. 1991. *Ronald Dworkin.* Stanford, CA: Stanford University Press.

John Wilson Wells

ECONOMIC DUE PROCESS. *See* Due Process, Substantive

ECONOMIC FREEDOM

Just as the terms "freedom" and "liberty" can be defined in different ways, "economic freedom" is conceived differently in the capitalist and socialist traditions. In socialist thought, economic freedom is associated with the empowerment of the exploited worker through the equalization of material conditions. In sharp contrast, the prevailing understanding of economic freedom in the American tradition is the absence of governmental interference with private property, private enterprise, and the private acquisition of wealth.

In the American tradition, economic freedom means the right to acquire real and personal property without limitation as to how much one can own. It means the right to use and develop one's resources to satisfy one's needs and wants. The right to choose one's own occupation, enter into contracts, form business associations, and buy and sell goods and services, as well as one's labor, in the marketplace is reserved to the individual. It also encompasses the right to conduct one's own business as one sees fit, from the hiring and firing of employees to determining the conditions and wages under which they will labor. In other words, ideal economic freedom is associated with a pure market economy—one in which the government's role is limited to the enforcement of contracts, providing a medium of exchange (money), and setting standards of weights and measures.

In many ways, this definition of economic freedom describes the prevailing economic policy in the United States until the late 19th century, although it should be noted that America has never had a purely laissez-faire economy. Obviously, today law and public policy increasingly play a larger role in the lives of Americans, thus limiting economic freedom in many ways. A few of the more prominent examples include antitrust laws, environmental regulations, consumer protection laws, labor laws, civil rights laws, licensure requirements, subsidies, the minimum wage, building codes, and zoning ordinances. These polices exist because political decisions were made (by and large) through democratic procedures to limit economic freedom in order to promote various collective interests. Yet economic freedom becomes a political issue as the number of government employees increases dramatically, and government, through the power of taxation, becomes a de facto partner in economic pursuits.

For the most part, courts have allowed government to impose these constraints as long as lawful procedures were employed in their adoption. In the modern era the courts have broadly interpreted Congress's power to regulate interstate commerce. Moreover, today courts tend to defer to legislative (as well as bureaucratic) decisions that impinge on property rights, thus marginalizing economic freedom.

The federal constitution affects economic freedom to a limited extent by forbidding laws that impair contracts and by empowering Congress to provide for patent and copyright protection. Both federal and state constitutions protect economic freedom in a number of other important ways, such as the right guaranteed by the Fifth Amendment to just compensation when private property is taken through eminent domain, and the broader right, found in both the Fifth and Fourteenth amendments, to due process of law (i.e., adequate notice and a fair hearing) when government deprives a person of property interests. This was not always the case. During the late nineteenth and early twentieth centuries, the U.S. Supreme Court tended to view economic freedom as an essential component of the liberty protected by the Due Process Clauses of the Fifth and Fourteenth amendments. Even though laws affecting private property and private enterprise were adopted through proper procedures, the Court often found these laws to be unconstitutional as unreasonable or arbitrary deprivations of liberty.

The classic example is *Lochner v. New York* (1905), where the Court struck down a state law limiting the hours employees could work in bakeries. The Court said that the law violated both the employer and the employee's "liberty of contract," a right not specifically enumerated in the Constitution but embraced within the substantive prohibitions of the Due Process Clause of the Fourteenth Amendment. In a widely quoted dissenting opinion, Justice Oliver Wendell Holmes, Jr., attacked the majority for grafting Social Darwinism onto the Constitution, observing, "The Fourteenth Amendment does not enact Mr. Herbert Spencer's *Social Statics.*"

In a series of controversial decisions between the late 1880s and the late 1930s, the Supreme Court invoked substantive due process and various other constitutional provisions and doctrines to strike down numerous state and federal laws regulating economic activity. This period of intense judicial activism came to an abrupt end with the constitutional revolution of 1937, a sea change in constitutional interpretation engendered by a confrontation between the Court and President Franklin D. Roosevelt over the constitutionality of the series of New Deal statutes enacted by Congress beginning in 1933 designed to manage and regulate the national economy.

The Supreme Court's decision in *Ferguson v. Skrupa* (1963) is representative of the modern approach to judicial review of economic regulation. Here the Court upheld a state law conferring a virtual monopoly on lawyers to engage in the business of debt adjusting. Writing for a unanimous bench, Justice Hugo L. Black noted that the doctrine prevailing in *Lochner* and other cases of that era "has long since been discarded." The Court, Black wrote, had "returned to the original constitutional proposition that courts do not substitute their social and economic beliefs for the judgment of legislative bodies, who are elected to pass laws." In Black's view, "[w]hether the legislature takes for its textbook Adam Smith, Herbert Spencer, Lord Keynes, or some other is no concern of ours."

The English economist John Maynard Keynes (1883–1946), who advocated active government intervention in the market, was probably the most influential economist of the twentieth century. Keynes actively supported such programs as the New Deal. In contrast, the American economist Milton Friedman (1912–) is among the strongest advocates of economic freedom. Friedman, who served as an economic advisor during President Ronald Reagan's administration, supports government programs to foster education and to reduce poverty. But Friedman's emphasis is on economic freedom and individual responsibility. He advocates that government's role in the management of the economy should be severely restricted.

For the most part, the Supreme Court during the last four decades has followed the approach taken in the *Skrupa* case and has allowed the government to intervene into the economy to an extent never imagined by the founders. Despite the numerous restrictions on economic freedom, the United States still maintains a strong legal, political, and cultural commitment to the idea of economic liberty, and individuals and corporations in the United States are subject to less burdensome regulations than those in most of the world's other democracies.

See also Bill of Rights, Incorporation of; Black, Hugo L.; Conservatism; Constitutional Democracy; Due Process, Procedural; Due Process, Substantive; Due Process Clauses; Fifth Amendment; Fourteenth Amendment; Holmes, Oliver Wendell, Jr.; Judicial Activism; Judicial Restraint; Just Compensation Clause; Liberalism; Libertarianism; Liberty; *Lochner v. New York;* New Deal; Property Rights; Public Use Clause; Representative Democracy; Right to Work Laws; Roosevelt, Franklin D.; Slaughterhouse Cases, The; Zoning

Bibliography

Ackerman, Bruce. 1977. *Private Property and the Constitution.* New Haven, CT: Yale University Press.

Conant, Michael. 1974. *The Constitution and Capitalism.* St. Paul, MN: West.

Dorn, James A., and Henry G. Manne, eds. 1987. *Economic Liberties and the Judiciary.* Fairfax, VA: George Mason University Press.

Friedman, Milton. 1962. *Capitalism and Freedom.* Chicago: University of Chicago Press.

Mendelson, Wallace. 1960. *Capitalism, Democracy, and the Supreme Court.* New York: Appleton-Century-Crofts.

Seigan, Bernard H. 1981. *Economic Liberties and the Constitution.* Chicago: University of Chicago Press.

John M. Scheb II and Hon. John M. Scheb

ECONOMIC INDIVIDUALISM. *See* Individualism

ECONOMIC RIGHTS. *See* Affirmative Action; Consumer Discrimination; Due Process Clauses; Economic Freedom; Employment Discrimination; Equal Protection Clause; Equal Protection Jurisprudence; Liberalism; Liberty; Property Rights

EDUCATION OF ALL HANDICAPPED CHILDREN ACT OF 1975. *See* Disabilities, Rights of Persons with; Disability Rights Organizations

EDWARDS V. SOUTH CAROLINA (1963)

In *Edwards v. South Carolina* (1963), the Court reversed the convictions of 187 African American college students who had participated in a peaceful civil rights demonstration on the grounds of the state capitol in Columbia, South Carolina. The students met at a local church, marched to the state capitol, and congregated on the grounds. They made speeches and sang songs. They did not obstruct pedestrian or vehicular traffic. Although the protest was loud and boisterous, there was no violence, no call to violence, nor any indication that violence was imminent. A crowd gathered to watch the demonstration, but as the Supreme Court noted in its opinion, "nobody among the crowd actually caused or threatened any trouble." Nevertheless, the police ordered the students to disperse. The students refused and continued their protest, singing patriotic and religious songs. They were then arrested and charged with breach of the peace. The students were convicted and received sentences ranging from a $10 fine or 5 days in jail to a $100 fine or 30 days in jail. In reversing the convictions, the Supreme Court held that South Carolina had infringed the students' "constitutionally protected rights of free speech, free assembly, and freedom to petition for redress of their grievances." In his opinion for the majority, Justice Potter Stewart observed that "the Fourteenth Amendment does not permit a state to make criminal the peaceful expression of unpopular views."

See also Assembly, Freedom of; Civil Rights Movement; First Amendment; Fourteenth Amendment; Speech, Freedom of; Stewart, Potter; Petition, Right of; Segregation, De Facto and De Jure

John M. Scheb II and Otis H. Stephens, Jr.

EEOC. *See* Equal Employment Opportunity Commission

EIGHTEENTH AMENDMENT. *See* Prohibition

EIGHTH AMENDMENT (1791)

The Eighth Amendment to the United States Constitution, adopted by Congress in 1789 and ratified by the states in 1791 along with the other amendments that constitute the Bill of Rights, explicitly protects persons accused of crimes from being subjected to excessive bail to secure pretrial release. The amendment also protects persons convicted of criminal offenses from being subjected to excessive fines or cruel and unusual punishments. Accordingly, the Eighth Amendment plays an important role in shaping the criminal law and the policies and practices of the criminal justice system.

See also Bail, Right to; Bill of Rights (American); Bill of Rights, Incorporation of; Cruel and Unusual Punishments Clause; Excessive Bail, Prohibition of; Excessive Fines, Prohibition of

John M. Scheb II and Otis H. Stephens, Jr.

ELECTRONIC MEDIA. *See FCC v. Pacifica Foundation;* Federal Communications Commission; Internet, Access to; Internet, Free Speech on; Press, Freedom of the; *Reno v. American Civil Liberties Union*

ELECTRONIC MONITORING. *See* House Arrest

ELECTRONIC SURVEILLANCE

Historically, the Fourth Amendment's prohibition of unreasonable searches and seizures was limited to physical entries into "places." Thus, in *Olmstead v. United States* (1928), the Supreme Court held that wiretapping without a physical entry into the home was beyond the scope of the Fourth Amendment. Writing for the majority in *Olmstead,* Chief Justice William Howard Taft observed that "one who installs in his house a telephone instrument with connecting wires intends to project his voice to those quite outside" and concluded that "that the wires beyond his house, and messages passing over them, are not within the protection of the Fourth Amendment." For Chief Justice Taft, it was irrelevant that federal agents had violated state law by intercepting Mr. Olmstead's conversations: "Whether the state of Washington may prosecute and punish federal officers violating this law, and

those whose messages were intercepted may sue them civilly, is not before us." Dissenting, Justice Oliver Wendell Holmes, Jr., called wiretapping a "dirty business" and argued that federal courts should not countenance lawbreaking by federal agents. In his oft-quoted dissent, Justice Louis D. Brandeis argued that "every unjustifiable intrusion by the government upon the privacy of the individual, whatever the means employed, must be deemed a violation of the Fourth Amendment."

The *Olmstead* decision left the regulation of wiretapping and electronic eavesdropping to the state legislatures and state courts. Most states had statutes prohibiting unauthorized interception of telephone conversations, but these prohibitions were rarely applied to the police. In 1959, Samuel Dash published *The Eavesdroppers,* which showed the extent to which law enforcement agencies at all levels of government were employing wiretapping, often in disregard of state law. Dash's landmark study played an important role in changing judicial and legislative attitudes toward electronic surveillance.

Justice Brandeis's *Olmstead* dissent was vindicated in 1967 when the United States Supreme Court held in *Katz v. United States* that the "Fourth Amendment protects people, not places." In *Katz* the Court ruled that electronic eavesdropping by law agencies without prior judicial authorization was a violation of the Fourth Amendment. Reflecting on *Katz* several years later, the Supreme Court observed in *United States v. United States District Court* (1972) that while "physical entry of the home is the chief evil against which the wording of the Fourth Amendment is directed, its broader spirit now shields private speech from unreasonable surveillance."

In *Berger v. New York* (1967), the Supreme Court struck down a state statute that authorized courts to issue wiretap orders in cases where there was "reasonable ground to believe that evidence of a crime may be thus obtained." Justice Tom Clark's opinion for the Court compared this permissive statute to the infamous general warrants of colonial times. In holding that electronic eavesdropping can be permitted only on the basis of probable cause, Justice Clark insisted that "officers be required to comply with the basic command of the Fourth Amendment before the innermost secrets of one's home or office are invaded."

The upshot of the Court's seminal decisions in *Katz* and *Berger* is that the use of wiretaps, hidden microphones, concealed cameras, and other devices that permit law enforcement agencies to intercept the content of what would otherwise be private communications implicates the Fourth Amendment. Therefore, in order to employ such means of surveillance, agents must obtain prior judicial authorization, which in turn must be based on probable cause.

It is important to understand, however, that for the police to use technology to augment their natural senses does not necessarily trigger Fourth Amendment protections. The question is whether the police use methods that infringe on a person's reasonable expectations of privacy. For example, in *Smith v. Maryland* (1979), the Supreme Court determined that the police's employment of a pen register (a device that records the phone numbers that are dialed from a particular phone number) is not a search within the meaning of the Fourth Amendment. Writing for the Court, Justice Harry Blackmun observed that merely by using the phone, the defendant "voluntarily conveyed numerical information to the telephone company and 'exposed' that information to its equipment in the ordinary course of business." Blackmun concluded that in so doing, the defendant "assumed the risk that the company would reveal to police the numbers he dialed." Similarly, in *Dow Chemical Company v. United States* (1986), the Court held that high-altitude photography of a chemical plant was not a search within the meaning of the Fourth Amendment. The Court concluded that that means of surveillance was incapable of revealing intimate activities that would give rise to constitutional concerns.

In the 1980s, police looking for marijuana being grown indoors under artificial light began to use infrared imaging devices, which can provide a strong indication if marijuana is being grown inside a closed structure. In *Kyllo v. United States* (2001), the U.S. Supreme Court held that when "the Government uses a device that is not in general public use, to explore details of the home that would previously have been unknowable without physical intrusion, the surveillance is a 'search' and is presumptively unreasonable without a warrant."

Federal Legislation Affecting Electronic Eavesdropping

In the wake of *Katz v. United States,* Congress enacted legislation governing the interception of electronic communications, both by law enforcement agencies and by private parties. Title III of the Omnibus Crime Control and Safe Streets Act of 1968, known generally as the Wiretap Act, prohibits interception of electronic communications without a court order unless one party to the conversation consents. Interception is defined as "aural or other acquisition of the contents of any wire, electronic or oral communication through the use of any electronic, mechanical, or other device." In 1986 Congress expanded the meaning of "wire communications" to include conversations heard through switching stations, thus making the statute applicable to cellular telephones.

Title III permits issuance of wiretap orders by federal and state courts on sworn application authorized by the United States Attorney General, a specially designated assistant, or a state official at a similar level. To permit the use of electronic surveillance by its own agents, a state must adopt legislation along the lines of the federal act, and most states have done so.

Before a court may issue a wiretap order, it must find probable cause that the subject of the wiretap has committed or is committing one of a series of enumerated crimes for which wiretapping is authorized and conventional modes of investigation will not suffice. Court orders permit surveillance for a 30-day period. At the period's expiration, the recordings made of intercepted communications must be delivered to the judge who issued the order. They are then sealed under the judge's direction.

The Electronic Communications Privacy Act of 1986 established federal standards for access to email and other electronic communications and to "transactional records," including subscriber identifying information, call logs, phone bills, and the like. The new law established a high standard for access to the contents of electronic communications but allowed agencies to easily gain access to transactional records. One part of the act governs the use of pen registers and trap-and-trace devices. It requires judges to issue orders to allow the use of such devices when properly requested by prosecutors. There is no standard of proof that prosecutors have to meet to obtain such orders. The courts have generally taken the position that users of telephones have no reasonable expectations of privacy with regard to numbers associated with incoming or outgoing phone calls. Congress has chosen not to provide significant statutory protection in this area, much to the chagrin of civil libertarians.

Shortly after the terrorist attacks of September 11, 2001, Congress enacted the USA PATRIOT Act to facilitate government counterterrorism efforts. Title II of this controversial act, entitled Enhanced Surveillance Procedures, includes a number of provisions expanding the federal government's authority to engage in electronic eavesdropping. Among other things, Title II facilitates use of pen registers and trap-and-trace surveillance. To secure a pen register or trap-and-trace order, agents have only to certify that the information they are seeking is relevant to an "ongoing investigation" of terrorism or various other federal crimes.

Under Title II, agents are authorized to obtain court orders allowing the use of technology that records e-mail addresses and URLs of Web sites being accessed from particular computers. Federal courts may issue "roving" surveillance orders in connection with foreign intelligence matters, enabling investigators to intercept e-mail and cell phone communications where suspects frequently change their account numbers. The act also permits federal agents to seize voice mail messages pursuant to a search warrant instead of issuing a wiretap order.

The USA PATRIOT Act also permits federal agents to use easily obtained administrative subpoenas to require Internet providers to turn over subscriber records and other information without notice to subscribers. In *Doe v. Ashcroft* (2004), a federal judge in the Southern District of New York declared this provision of the PATRIOT Act invalid under the First and Fourth amendments. At the time of this writing, the case was pending in the U.S. Court of Appeals for the Second Circuit. Despite strenuous objections by civil libertarians, and a flurry of lawsuits attacking various provisions of the act, Congress in 2006 reauthorized the PATRIOT Act, albeit with some modifications.

Changes in technology always create new problems for the law. The rapid diffusion of personal computers and the Internet has created an exciting new medium of communication for many millions of law-abiding citizens. It has also provided new opportunities for terrorists, child molesters, and con artists. Law enforcement agencies insist that they need broad powers to monitor Internet communication, but civil liberties advocates worry about the threat to privacy inherent in online surveillance. Courts have only just begun to sort out the Fourth Amendment issues in this area.

See also Blackmun, Harry A.; Brandeis, Louis D.; Clark, Tom C.; Foreign Intelligence Surveillance Act; Fourth Amendment; Holmes, Oliver Wendell, Jr.; Internet, Free Speech on; *Katz v. United States;* Privacy, Reasonable Expectations of; Search Warrants; Taft, William Howard; USA PATRIOT Act

Bibliography

Dash, Samuel. 1959. *The Eavesdroppers: The Unknown Story of Wiretapping Today—Its Victims, Its Practitioners, the Techniques, and What the Law Says about It.* New Brunswick, NJ: Rutgers University Press.

Freiwald, Susan. 2004. "Online Surveillance: Remembering the Lessons of the Wiretap Act." *Alabama Law Review* 56 (9): 9–84.

John M. Scheb II

ELEVENTH AMENDMENT (1798)

The Eleventh Amendment to the U.S. Constitution was proposed by Congress on March 4,

1794, and ratified by the states on January 8, 1798. The amendment explicitly prohibits suits in federal courts against states brought by citizens of another state and thus implicitly establishes a state sovereign immunity doctrine with respect to federal jurisdiction. This amendment is widely viewed as the movement toward states' rights in the early development of the American governmental system.

The doctrine of sovereign immunity evolved from the conceptualization of sovereignty embodied in the English common-law tradition. However, in the United States, there is a dual sovereignty resulting from citizenship under both federal and state governments and this "mixed" government as James Madison termed it, is a constitutional hybrid between a confederation of sovereign states and a unitary government with subnational administrative functionalities. If both the national government and states were sovereign, then each was cloaked with sovereign immunity, at least with respect to suits brought by their own citizens in their own courts. But what of lawsuits brought in federal courts against state governments by citizens of other states? Would the doctrine of sovereign immunity insulate states from such claims?

This was precisely the question before the U.S. Supreme Court in its first major constitutional law case, *Chisholm v. Georgia* (1793). In a suit brought in federal court by residents of South Carolina, the Court rejected Georgia's claim of sovereign immunity, thus strongly endorsing the authority of the federal judiciary in relation to the states. This decision drew an intense reaction from states' rights advocates and resulted in the ratification in 1798 of the Eleventh Amendment.

The principal reason for the creation of federal courts was to allow for the effective judicial resolution of interstate legal disputes. The Eleventh Amendment, while reducing the ability of the federal courts to perform this function, did not apply to federal lawsuits between rival state governments. That being the case, state governments sometimes acted as surrogate plaintiffs for their own citizens to bring disputes into federal court. In *New Hampshire v. Louisiana* (1883), the Supreme Court invalidated this practice. And in *Hans v. Louisiana* (1890), the Court held that the Eleventh Amendment barred citizens from suing their *own* state governments in federal court.

In the early twentieth century, the heyday of dual federalism, the Court continued to strengthen state sovereign immunity under the Eleventh Amendment. In 1921, in *Ex parte New York*, the Court held that the Eleventh Amendment applied to admiralty suits, and in *Monaco v. Mississippi* (1934), it held that foreign sovereigns are barred from bringing federal actions against states.

The nationalist jurisprudence that dominated the Supreme Court from the New Deal era through the 1980s produced an erosion of the doctrine of sovereign immunity generally but particularly for state governments. For example, in *Fitzpatrick v. Bitzer* (1976), the Court recognized the power of Congress to abrogate the states' sovereign immunity in order to vindicate individual rights protected by the Fourteenth Amendment. Similarly, in *Pennsylvania v. Union Gas Company* (1989) the Court held that Congress had similar authority under the Commerce Clause of Article I, Section 8. These decisions meant that Congress could authorize certain types of federal lawsuits against states, notwithstanding the provisions of the Eleventh Amendment.

The dominance of nationalism reflected in these and other Supreme Court decisions led some scholars to question whether national power had eclipsed dual sovereignty to such an extent that federalism itself was dead (Corwin 1950; Derthick 1996). However, as part of a larger agenda to restore balance to the federal system, the Rehnquist Court revived the Eleventh Amendment. In *Seminole Tribe of Florida v. Florida* (1996), the Court overturned *Pennsylvania v. Union Gas Company*, holding that nothing in Article I, Section 8, of the Constitution gives Congress the power to abrogate state sovereign immunity. Writing for a sharply divided Court, Chief Justice William H. Rehnquist asserted: "Even when the Constitution vests in Congress complete law-making authority over a particular area [in this case, interstate commerce], the Eleventh Amendment prevents congressional authorization of suits by private parties against unconsenting states."

In *Fitzpatrick v. Bitzer* (1976) the Supreme Court had recognized the power of Congress under Section 5 of the Fourteenth Amendment to allow citizens to sue unconsenting state governments in federal court in matters involving civil rights and liberties. But in *Alden v. Maine* (1999), the Rehnquist Court, again dividing five-to-four, held that congressional authority under the Commerce Clause "does not include the power to subject unconsenting States to private suits for damages in state courts." Justice Anthony Kennedy, speaking for the Court, insisted that "our federalism requires that Congress treat the States in a manner consistent with their status as residuary sovereigns and joint participants in the governance of the Nation."

The Rehnquist Court took seriously the limitations placed by the Eleventh Amendment on the jurisdiction of the federal courts. Whether the Roberts Court will do so, as conservatives hope and liberals fear, remains to be seen.

See also Common-Law Background of American Civil Rights and Liberties; Conservatism; Fourteenth Amendment; Fourteenth Amendment, Section 5 of the; Kennedy, Anthony; Liberalism; Madison, James; New Deal; Rehnquist, William H.; Rehnquist Court; Sovereign Immunity; States' Rights, Doctrine of; Tenth Amendment

Bibliography

Corwin, Edward S. 1950. "The Passing of Dual Federalism." *Virginia Law Review* 36:1.

Derthick, Martha. 1996. "Whither Federalism?" *Future of the Public Sector* 2. Washington DC: Urban Institute.

McDonald, Forrest. 2000. *States Rights and the Union*. Lawrence: University Press of Kansas.

Orth, John V. 1986. *The Judicial Power of the United States: The Eleventh Amendment in American History*. New York: Oxford University Press.

Michael W. Hail

ELLSBERG, DANIEL. *See* Pentagon Papers Case

ELY, JOHN HART. *See* Interpretivism

EMANCIPATION PROCLAMATION (1863)

President Abraham Lincoln formally signed the Emancipation Proclamation in the White House on January 1, 1863. In his first inaugural address, Lincoln had tried to pacify Southern voters by stating that he would not eliminate slavery. The onset of a protracted and bloody Civil War, however, changed America and altered Lincoln's position during the time between the first inaugural address in March 1861 and the Emancipation Proclamation in January 1863. With the country embroiled in the Civil War, Lincoln no longer viewed slavery as an economic necessity. He became convinced that freeing the slaves had become necessary for the preservation of the Union. Lincoln had always been personally opposed to the institution of slavery, but he waited until there was institutional support as well before issuing his famous proclamation to end this unfortunate chapter in American history.

A Preliminary Emancipation Proclamation was drafted in July 1862 and read on September 22, 1862, after the Battle of Antietam. While the preliminary proclamation did not abolish slavery as an institution (this would be accomplished later with passage of the Thirteenth Amendment), it did promise this outcome with the advent of a Union victory. In his early draft, Lincoln promised that all slaves in states then opposing the North would be free effective January 1, 1863, or 100 days after the issuance of the preliminary proclamation. He then followed up as promised with the official Emancipation Proclamation, noting in a letter written shortly after the signing of the proclamation: "If slavery is not wrong, nothing is wrong" (Nelson 73). In drafting the proclamation, he also freed persons in the military, "recommended" that they be allowed to work for fair wages, and promised that they would be eligible for full military service. He cautioned against violence and claimed this to "be an act of justice."

Although Lincoln privately doubted whether Article II of the Constitution gave him the authority to free the slaves, he did not betray these misgivings to the public. Indeed, he claimed authority to issue the Proclamation by virtue of his status as commander in chief of the armed forces and further claimed that it was "warranted by the Constitution, upon military necessity" (Mitgang 330). Interestingly, Lincoln waited until Congress had already abolished slavery in the District of Columbia and in the territories before he freed slaves in those states still in rebellion with the Emancipation Proclamation.

In the Emancipation Proclamation, Abraham Lincoln furthered the cause of equality for this great nation. However, it is important to note that political motivations influenced his decision to promise freedom. Indeed, earlier he had claimed that if he could have "saved the Union without freeing any slaves," he would have done so (Mitgang 300). Many Northerners supported the Emancipation Proclamation not because it would advance civil rights but because they wanted to punish the South. Lincoln himself delayed issuing the proclamation until he had secured the support of Great Britain and until he was sure that he would not lose the support of the border states (DiClerico 360). Moreover, in correspondence with A. G. Hodges, Lincoln noted that he stopped short of allowing one of his generals to free slaves at an earlier point during the war. He also opposed the arming of blacks and military emancipation in the early years of the war as unnecessary (Cohen and Nice 17). Clearly, political expediency dictated Lincoln's decision making and the timing of the Emancipation Proclamation. Nevertheless, to quote Ralph Waldo Emerson, the Emancipation Proclamation resulted in "the silent joy which has greeted it in all generous hearts and the new hope it has breathed into the world" (Mitgang 328).

See also Abolitionist Movement; Lincoln, Abraham; Slavery; Thirteenth Amendment

Bibliography

Cohen, Jeffrey, and David Nice. 2003. *The Presidency: Classic and Contemporary Readings.* Boston: McGraw-Hill.

DiClerico, Robert E. 2000. *The American President.* 5th ed. Upper Saddle River, NJ: Prentice Hall.

Mitgang, Herbert. 1956. *Lincoln as They Saw Him.* New York: Rinehart.

Nelson, Michael. 2000. *The Presidency and the Political System.* 8th ed. Washington, DC: CQ Press.

Lori Maxwell

EMERGENCY SEARCHES

The Fourth Amendment to the United States Constitution guarantees protection against "unreasonable searches and seizures" and expresses a strong preference for law enforcement to obtain a warrant before conducting a search or seizure. As interpreted by the U.S. Supreme Court, the Fourth Amendment binds all courts; however, state constitutions include similar proscriptions, which state courts sometimes interpret even more strictly. Consequently, searches conducted without prior approval by a judge or magistrate are per se unreasonable, subject only to specifically established exceptions based on exigent circumstances.

Federal and state courts recognize that one of the most compelling exceptions that gives rise to exigent circumstances is the occurrence of an emergency, which permits police and public safety officers to enter private premises and conduct a warrantless search if they have probable cause to believe that an emergency mandates immediate action. The emergency exception to the warrant requirement reflects a commonsense understanding that exigent circumstances often require public safety officials, such as the police, firefighters, or paramedics, to enter a dwelling or a vehicle without a warrant for the purpose of protecting life or preventing serious injury. As the Supreme Court observed in *Michigan v. Tyler* (1978), "it would defy reason to suppose that firemen must secure a warrant or consent before entering a burning structure to put out the blaze."

In *United States v. Al-Azzawy* (1985), the U.S. Court of Appeals for the Ninth Circuit upheld a warrantless search where a suspect was believed to be in possession of explosives and was in such an agitated state as to create a risk of endangering the lives of others. Federal and state courts have approved warrantless emergency searches involving various scenarios, including entry into a home to investigate a report of a dead body, to render aid to drug overdose or poisoning victims and to search for the drug or poison container, or to render aid to a child victim of sexual assault. Other scenarios that have met judicial approval include police responding to screams in the night coming from a home, the need to rescue a woman and her child from a crack house, search of an apartment where an explosion has occurred, and a fire marshal's search to determine the cause of a fire and assure it was completely extinguished.

The issue of whether a warrantless emergency search was justified usually arises when during the search, police discover and seize evidence of a crime. When the prosecution seeks to introduce such evidence, the defendant generally moves the court to suppress it on the grounds there was no emergency that mandated a warrantless search, or that the police exceeded the bounds of the scope of an emergency search. Before a court admits such evidence against a defendant, the prosecution must demonstrate to the court that the search that produced fruits of a crime was justified. The prosecution seeks to do this by establishing that the police acted on information that someone was in distress, and they were not motivated to search simply to find evidence of a crime. There is a limit, however, to the scope of a search conducted pursuant to the emergency exception. For example, in *Flippo v. West Virginia* (1999), the U.S. Supreme Court reviewed a case where the police responded to a 911 call alerting them that a man and his wife had been attacked in a cabin at a state park. When the police arrived on the scene, they found the woman dead. They opened a briefcase and seized photos that tended to incriminate the woman's husband. The Court rejected the prosecution's contention that a crime scene exception justified the seizure of the photos from the briefcase.

As the New Jersey Supreme Court observed in *State v. Frankel* (2004), a police officer entering a home looking for a person injured or in danger may not expand the scope of a warrantless emergency by peering into drawers, cupboards, or wastepaper baskets; however, where an officer who is lawfully on the premises seizes evidence in plain view, that evidence will be admissible.

See also Exclusionary Rule; Fourth Amendment; Plain View Doctrine; Search Warrants; Warrantless Searches

Hon. John M. Scheb

EMINENT DOMAIN. *See Kelo v. City of New London*

EMPLOYMENT DISCRIMINATION

Over the last 40 years, Congress has enacted a number of civil rights statutes attacking various forms of discrimination in employment. These include the Equal Pay Act of 1963, Title VII of the Civil Rights Act of 1964, the Age Discrimination in Employment Act of 1967, the Equal Employment Opportunity Act of 1972, Title IX of the Education Amendments of 1972, Title I of the Americans with Disabilities Act of 1990, and the Family and Medical Leave Act of 1993. Collectively, these statutes require fair treatment of employees regardless of their race, national origin, gender, age, or disability. By virtue of the Equal Employment Act of 1972 and subsequent federal legislation, these protections apply to teachers and government workers as well as employees in the private sector. State and local governments have enacted their own laws addressing employment discrimination, some of which even protect workers against discrimination on the basis of sexual orientation. Thus, as the result of enactments at all levels of government, virtually all workers in the United States now have some degree of legal protection against employment discrimination.

The purpose of the Equal Pay Act of 1963 was to prohibit gender-based payment discrimination by employers engaged in interstate commerce. The act requires that men and women be given equal pay for equal work in the same establishment. The jobs do not have to be completely identical, but they must be substantially equal. It is the job content not the job title that determines if a job is equal (Cayer 1996). The factors of equality are defined by the Equal Employment Opportunity Commission, an independent federal agency created in 1964.

When considering job content, evaluators weigh the skill, effort, responsibility, and working conditions that are required by the work. Skill refers to the experience, ability, education, and training required to perform a job. For the purpose of assessing skill equality in employment, the evaluator must consider the skill required for the job, not the actual skill of the employees. Effort is measured by factors such as the physical and mental exertion considered necessary to perform the job. Responsibility is the degree of accountability required in performing a job. Working conditions encompass the physical surroundings and occupational hazards inherent in a job. Pay can be different for the same job only when the pay difference is based on factors other than sex, such as seniority, merit, or quality of job performance. When an employer is attempting to remedy inequities in pay, employees' pay cannot be lowered; rather, lower-paid employees must be brought up to the higher pay level.

In enacting Title VII of the Civil Rights Act of 1964, Congress prohibited employment discrimination on the basis of race, color, religion, sex, or national origin by employers with 25 or more employees. Title VII bars employers not only from intentional discrimination against members of protected classes, but also from using "facially neutral" employment practices that have a "disparate impact" on those groups. Once the plaintiff has made out a prima facie case of disparate impact, the burden shifts to the employer to prove that the challenged practices result from "business necessity." Actionable issues under Title VII include not only discrimination in hiring practices and promotions but the controversial questions of affirmative action and sexual harassment as well.

The Age Discrimination in Employment Act of 1967 (ADEA) was designed to protect workers age 40 and over from an onslaught of younger workers entering the American workforce. The statute states that employers should not discriminate in hiring, setting wages, or promoting workers on the basis of age without a bona fide reason. In adopting the Older Workers Protection Act of 1990, Congress amended the ADEA to protect older workers from discrimination with regard to pensions and other fringe benefits.

Enacted to strengthen Title VII of the Civil Rights Act of 1964, the Equal Employment Act of 1972 lowered from 25 to 15 the number of employees required to make an employer subject to Title VII and, as noted above, extended the protections of Title VII to government workers and teachers. It also gave the EEOC the power to sue companies and unions on behalf of workers claiming employment discrimination.

In 1971, only 18 percent of American women, as compared to 26 percent of men, had completed four or more years of higher education. Title IX of the Education Amendments of 1972 was enacted to close this gap by providing that "[n]o person in the United States shall, on the basis of sex, be excluded from participation in, be denied the benefits of, or be subjected to discrimination under any education program or activity receiving Federal financial assistance." As a result of the aggressive enforcement of Title IX by the U.S. Department of Education, women now constitute the majority of students in America's colleges and universities. By greatly enhancing educational opportunities for women, Title IX has worked indirectly to open access to fields of employment once dominated by males, most notably professions such as law and medicine. For example, while in 1972, women accounted for less than 10 percent of the recipients of law degrees awarded in this country, today nearly half of all law degrees are being earned by women.

With the passage of the Americans with Disabilities Act of 1990 (ADA), Congress sought a more comprehensive set of tools for dealing with disability discrimination. The Americans with

Disabilities Act seeks to eliminate discrimination in hiring, training, promotions, and other terms of employment. Title I of the ADA prohibits discrimination against a qualified employee with a disability because of the disability. It requires that employers must provide "reasonable accommodation" to disabled applicants and employees, although courts have held that the ADA does not require accommodations that would create an "undue hardship" on employers. Like the other federal prohibitions against employment discrimination, Title I is enforced by the EEOC.

The Family and Medical Leave Act of 1993 seeks to ensure equality by allowing employees to take 12 months of unpaid leave in order to care for a newborn child, an adopted infant, or a seriously ill family member while maintaining job security and medical benefits.

The U.S. Department of Labor has taken further steps to ensure equality in the workplace by developing the Equal Pay Initiative, which focuses on three crucial elements of employment discrimination within the department's authority. These elements include eliminating pay discrimination and occupational segregation, and promoting equity. The Department of Labor seeks to strengthen civil rights enforcement, increase the public's education and awareness, and build strategic partnerships to help the department bring about equal pay and equal employment opportunity in America's workplaces. The Department of Labor is responsible for enforcing laws regarding pay discrimination. In doing so, the agency monitors companies that hold government contracts and make sure that these companies have equity in employment and pay. Through the Equal Pay Initiative, companies with federal contracts can take advantage of community outreach and technical assistance to advance their efforts to find and hire diverse employees.

Despite significant progress as a result of legislative action, most women still earn less than their male counterparts. This wage gap is even wider for women of color. The wage gaps mean more than just standard pay; they mean a difference in pension earning and retirement savings. It is also significant because earnings are major factors in regard to a person's social status and health-care options. It is also a major factor in the choice of quality K–12 education options, and the neighborhood in which one resides. Clearly, more progress is needed to realize the goal of equal employment opportunity.

See also Affirmative Action; Age Discrimination; Civil Rights Act of 1964; Civil Rights Restoration Act of 1991; Disabilities, Rights of Person with; Diversity; Equal Employment Opportunity Commission; Equality; Equal Pay Act; Gender-Based Discrimination; Title IX, Education Amendments of 1972

Bibliography

Cayer, Joseph N. 1996. *Public Personnel Administration in the United States.* New York: St. Martin's Press.

Klingner, Donald, and Nalbandian, John. 1993. *Public Personnel Management: Context and Strategies.* Englewood Cliffs, NJ: Prentice Hall.

Office of Civil Rights. 1999. *Impact of the Civil Rights Laws.* Washington DC: United States Department of Education.

Porette, Maureen, and Brian Gunn. 1993. "The Family and Medical Leave Act of 1993: The Time Has Finally Come for Governmental Recognition of True Family Values." *St. John's Journal of Legal Commentary* 8:587.

F. Erik Brooks and Ashley Scruggs

EMPLOYMENT DIVISION, DEPARTMENT OF HUMAN RESOURCES OF OREGON V. SMITH (1990)

In *Reynolds v. United States* (1879) the U.S. Supreme Court upheld a federal anti-polygamy statute as applied to a member of the Mormon faith, rejecting the appellant's claim that his polygamous behavior was shielded by the Free Exercise of Religion Clause of the First Amendment. In *Reynolds,* the Court drew a sharp distinction between religious belief on one hand and conduct on the other, holding that while government could not in any way restrict religious belief, it could restrict religiously motivated conduct that the people's elected representatives had determined was inimical to the public welfare.

In the wake of the Reynolds decision, the belief/ action dichotomy became well established in Free Exercise Clause jurisprudence. Although government could not regulate religious belief, it could restrict harmful religious practices. However, in *Sherbert v. Verner* (1963) Justice William Brennan's majority opinion made it more difficult for government to regulate religious action. In a seven-to-two decision the Court held that a state could not deny unemployment compensation to a Seventh-Day Adventist who was fired because she refused to work on Saturday, her day of worship. Brennan made it clear that when a law limits free exercise, the government has a burden of showing that it is preserving a significant compelling governmental interest in the least restrictive manner possible. Between 1963 and 1990, the Supreme Court applied this standard consistently, with, however, a few exceptions, the most notable of which upheld governmental actions that intruded upon the unique religious beliefs and rites of Native Americans (*Bowen v. Roy,* 1986; *Lyng v. Northwest Indian Cemetery Protective Association,* 1988). These cases and others in which the Rehnquist Court upheld government actions over free exercise claims set the stage for the *Smith* decision in 1990.

Alfred Smith and Galen Black, two members of the Native American Church, were fired from their jobs as drug and alcohol rehabilitation counselors at a private clinic for ingesting peyote at a religious ceremony. Oregon law treated peyote as a controlled substance that was illegal to possess and use without a doctor's prescription. Smith and Black applied for unemployment compensation and were declared ineligible because of their violation of state law. Relying on the *Sherbert* decision and similar cases, they appealed this action in state court. Although the state court of appeals ruled against them, the Oregon Supreme Court, relying on *Sherbert,* reversed the trial court's decision. The case first reached the U.S. Supreme Court in 1988 and was remanded for a determination of whether sacramental peyote use was proscribed by the state's controlled substance law. On remand, the state supreme court held that sacramental peyote use violated, and was not excepted from, the state-law prohibition but concluded that that prohibition was invalid under the Free Exercise Clause. The state then appealed to the U.S. Supreme Court.

By a six-to-three vote the Court overturned the Oregon Supreme Court's ruling, with Justice Antonin Scalia writing the majority opinion. Scalia selectively reviewed case law from *Reynolds v. United States* (1879) through the 1980s and drew a stark contrast between *Sherbert* and other unemployment compensation cases (e.g., *Thomas v. Review Board,* 1981; *Hobbie v. Unemployment Appeals Commission of Florida,* 1987) by noting that the claimants in those cases had not broken any laws. He noted that the Court "had never invalidated any governmental action" on the basis of the *Sherbert* compelling governmental interest standard *except* the denial of unemployment compensation. This statement by Scalia ignored or at least obscured the fact that in *Wisconsin v. Yoder* (1972), Chief Justice Warren Burger specifically applied *Sherbert* in the ruling favoring Amish objections to the Wisconsin compulsory school attendance law. In 1983, Burger again cited the *Sherbert* rule in *Bob Jones University v. United States.* Even though the Court ruled that the government could withdraw the school's tax exemption status because of its racially discriminating policies, Burger noted that this sectarian school could still practice its religion. Scalia distinguished these cases and others like them by asserting that they involved other constitutional protections such as freedom of speech along with free exercise rights.

Scalia continued by arguing that the compelling interest test, taken at face value in the context of free exercise, could lead to "anarchy" and "open the prospect of constitutionally required religious exemptions from civic obligations of almost every kind." He offered several examples of activities that could possibly require religious exemptions, including "compulsory military service [and] payment of taxes" along with "health and safety regulations" concerning manslaughter, child neglect, animal cruelty, and environmental protection. He surmised that free exercise does not require these exemptions.

But the government has recognized the legitimacy of conscientious objector status to military service and tax exemption for churches. To have equated these policies with the acts of manslaughter and child neglect and ignore the fact that government can easily overcome religious objections to the restriction of these acts is a shortcoming of his argument.

Scalia also insisted that if the Court were to continue using the *Sherbert* standard in free exercise cases, the application of the compelling governmental interest test in cases of race and speech would produce inconsistent interpretation of what makes for a "constitutional norm." Equality of treatment on the basis of race and unrestricted free speech are norms, but a religious right to ignore generally applicable laws is "a constitutional anomaly," he insisted. Did Scalia mean that free speech is to be more highly valued than free exercise of religion? Justice Sandra Day O'Connor thought so.

While O'Connor concurred in the judgment of the Court, she wrote a scathing critique of Justice Scalia's rationale. The three dissenters, Brennan, Thurgood Marshall, and Harry Blackmun, joined this part of O'Connor's opinion. O'Connor bluntly stated that Scalia's rationale "dramatically departs from well-settled First Amendment jurisprudence" and noted that this case can be easily distinguished from the *Sherbert* line of unemployment compensation cases due to the fact that Smith and Black violated the law. O'Connor warned that as a result of the majority rationale, government can restrict "without justification" actions required by a person's religious beliefs so long as it is done under a law of general applicability. Laws that limit religious conduct "manifestly" prohibit free exercise rights, and to do that the state should be required to carry a burden of proof. She ridiculed Scalia's "parade of horribles" and ironically emphasized that it is such a list of varying acts that compels the Court to honor the *Sherbert* precedent and trust the courts to "strike sensible balances" between free exercise rights and competing governmental interests and duties. Scalia's rationale would not allow courts to make such distinctions as they would almost always be required to side with the government.

In her concluding remarks O'Connor pointed to the most probable result of the Court's reasoning. Scalia had suggested that an "unavoidable consequence" when religious minorities clash with the government is that government will prevail as a part of the normal political process. She reminded the Court of the impact that "harsh majoritarian rule" has had on such minorities like the Amish and Jehovah's Witnesses at various times in American history. Her only point of agreement with the majority was to uphold Oregon's law on peyote, but she did so only after applying *Sherbert* and concluding that there was a compelling interest on the part of the state to prohibit it. The dissenters agreed with O'Connor on every point of her opinion except the last one.

As Frederick Gedricks noted in 1992, the Court completed a "full circle" of free exercise review by returning to the *Reynolds* rationale and rejecting *Sherbert*. It could be argued that Scalia's rationale goes even beyond the *Reynolds* decision. At least when the *Reynolds* Court upheld a law prohibiting polygamy over Mormon religious objections, it described the possible societal harms that could result from an opposite conclusion. In short, there was some burden of proof required of the government. Scalia's reasoning suggests that government need only claim a need of general applicability to negate free exercise rights.

See also *Bob Jones University v. United States;* Blackmun, Harry A.; Brennan, William J. Jr.; Burger, Warren E.; First Amendment; Marshall, Thurgood; O'Connor, Sandra Day; Rehnquist Court; Religion, Freedom of; *Reynolds v. United States;* Scalia, Antonin; *Wisconsin v. Yoder*

Bibliography

Barsh, Russell Lawrence. 1986. "The Illusion of Religious Freedom for Indigenous Americans." *Oregon Law Review* 65:363–412.

Collins, Richard B. 2003. "Sacred Sites and Religious Freedom on Government Land." *Journal of Constitutional Law* 5(2): 241–70.

Joe Bill Sloan

ENDANGERED SPECIES ACT. *See* Animal Rights

ENGLISH COMMON LAW. *See* Common-Law Background of American Civil Rights and Liberties

ENTRAPMENT DEFENSE

Entrapment was defined by the Supreme Court in *Sorrells v. United* States (1932) as "the conception and planning of an offense by an officer, and his procurement of its commission by one who would not have perpetrated it except for the trickery, persuasion, or fraud of the officer." Two opposing versions of the entrapment defense have been formulated and defended by various members of the Court; both, it should be emphasized, limit the defense to cases where causing or threatening bodily harm is not an element of the offense charged.

The first may be referred to as the federal approach, since it has been adopted by a majority of the Court in each of its major entrapment decisions and is generally followed by the lower federal courts. The federal defense focuses on the conduct and propensities of the particular defendant in each individual case. If defendants are not predisposed to commit crimes of the nature charged, they may avail themselves of the defense. However, if they are ready and willing to commit such an offense at any favorable opportunity, then the entrapment defense will fail, regardless of the nature or extent of the government's inducement or participation. Because of its focus on the defendant's predisposition, this approach is frequently referred to as the subjective test.

The other version of the entrapment defense may be labeled the hypothetical-person approach. Expressed by justices in both concurring and dissenting opinions, this approach concentrates on the quality of police or government conduct rather than on the predisposition of the accused. It subscribes to the view that governmental conduct that falls below certain minimum standards will not be tolerated, thus relieving from criminal responsibility a defendant who commits a crime as a result of such conduct. This approach will not condone conduct by law enforcement officials that presents too great a risk that hypothetical law-abiding persons will be induced to commit a crime that they would not otherwise have committed. Thus, the individual who commits the criminal offense, although technically guilty, will be relieved of criminal responsibility, and further prosecution will be barred. Proponents of this approach hope to deter unlawful governmental activity in the instigation of crime and to preserve the purity of the criminal justice system. Like all questions involving the legality of law enforcement methods, the hypothetical-person defense submits the issue in question (here, entrapment) to the judge; by contrast, the jury decides the issue under the federal defense. Because of its exclusive concentration on the conduct of the police and its disregard of the defendant's predisposition, this approach is often referred to as the objective test.

In *Jacobson v. United States* (1992), the Supreme Court's latest consideration of the entrapment defense, all the justices employed the federal approach but split over whether or not the defendant was predisposed to purchase child pornography when he was induced to do so by an undercover police sting operation. Five justices concluded that the police had implanted in the defendant the disposition to purchase illegal child pornography; four insisted that he was already predisposed to make such a purchase (he had purchased child pornography before Congress had made it illegal to do so) and that all the government did was induce him to act on that predisposition.

Bibliography

Dilloff, Anthony M. 2004. "Unraveling Unlawful Entrapment." *Journal of Criminal Law and Criminology* 94 (4): 827–70.

Ralph A. Rossum

ENVIRONMENTAL JUSTICE

The Environmental Protection Agency (EPA) defines environmental justice as "Fair treatment and equal protection under federal environmental laws to ensure that all people, regardless of race, culture, or income level, live in clean, safe, and sustainable communities."

The movement for environmental justice is distinct from, but related to, the movement against environmental racism. Environmental justice is a broader concept incorporating two central issues: inequity in the distribution of environmental risk and recognition of the diversity of participants and experiences in the environmental justice movement. Inequity in the distribution of risk includes factors such as class, effects on future generations, and fairness among geographical areas in siting. Integration of distributional equity and recognition manifests in demands for more public participation in the development, implementation, and oversight of environmental policy.

Environmental racism denotes the disproportionate exposure to environmental hazards borne by communities of color and is central to the debate over whether there is a pattern of racial discrimination in the siting of hazardous-waste facilities. A significant body of research concludes that low-income persons and people of color carry a heavier toxic load than the rest of society. Environmental justice focuses on improvement in the overall quality of life for those affected populations. It is manifest in continuous struggles among many groups for access to valuable resources—ecological, material, social, political, psychological, and symbolic. Symbolic resources are words, phrases, images, and group affiliations associated with social movements. These can evoke powerful social responses.

The environmental justice movement represents a fusion of the grassroots environmental movement's economic analysis of environmental problems with the Civil Rights Movement's racial critique of political and economic institutions. Environmental justice activists mobilize collective resistance by claiming that minority and low-income groups are disproportionately exposed to environmental risks because of racism and classism. Their grievances concern the inequity of exposure to sources of contamination and a desire for environmental, economic, and social justice.

More recently, the environmental justice movement has expanded its environmental focus to include where people live, work, play, and go to school, and the physical world. The environmental justice movement addresses the inequities that result from human settlement, industrial facility siting, and industrial development; educates and assists groups by organizing and mobilizing them to take charge of their lives, their communities, and their surroundings; addresses power imbalances and the lack of political enfranchisement; and urges the redirection of resources to create healthy, livable, and sustainable communities.

The environmental justice movement formed from the confluence of three important groups that brought to public attention the inequitable imposition on poor and minority communities of hazardous waste facilities: the antitoxics grassroots movement, the Civil Rights Movement, and scientific researchers. The antitoxics movement emerged in the wake of the 1978 Love Canal (and Times Beach) revelations of toxic contamination in residential communities, and the 1979 Three Mile Island nuclear accident. The movement is primarily composed of working-class individuals without prior movement experience who organize when faced with environmental contamination in their communities. They seek avoidance of environmental threat, remediation of environmental damages, and compensation for the adverse health effects of contamination. They use direct-action tactics to pressure government agencies to enforce existing environmental regulations. They sometimes resort to litigation, using expert testimony from behavioral and natural scientists, to force regulatory compliance.

The Civil Rights Movement had become a fixture in American politics with a focus on bringing social justice to poor communities and improving the economic conditions of minorities and people of color. In the 1980s the national movement for environmental justice took root in several mainstream civil rights organizations, sparked by two incidents of community protest against hazardous waste landfills. In 1979, residents of Houston's Northwood Manor suburban neighborhood filed the first lawsuit charging environmental discrimination. Citing Houston's long history of locating its solid-waste facilities in African American communities, Houston residents fought Browning-Ferris Industries' location of a municipal solid-waste landfill in their community. The citizens lost the 1979 lawsuit, *Bean v. Southwestern Waste Management,* but it was the first case to use civil rights law to challenge the siting of a waste facility.

In 1982, when North Carolina state officials decided to locate a new hazardous landfill for polychlorinated biphenyl (PCBs) in Warren County, the people of the county organized to oppose the proposed landfill. Warren County was the poorest county in one of the poorest states in the nation, with a 65-percent African American population. Residents formed a grassroots organization to protest the siting of the PCB landfill and requested assistance from the United Church of Christ's Commission for Racial Justice (CRJ), a civil rights organization formed in 1963. Warren County residents, CRJ members, and representatives of the Southern Christian Leadership Conference and the National Association for the Advancement of Colored People engaged in civil disobedience to protest racial discrimination in the choice of a black community for the landfill site. Even though the PCB landfill was constructed, the incident brought national attention to a new aspect of the civil rights movement and jump-started the movement for environmental justice.

In 1983, chairman of the Congressional Black Caucus Walter Fauntroy asked the General Accounting Office (GAO) to investigation hazardous-waste landfill sites in the Environmental Protection Agency's (EPA) Region IV. The findings showed a strong relationship between location of the landfills and the race and socioeconomic status of surrounding communities. In three of the four communities containing the hazardous-waste sites, blacks made up the majority of the population. In all four communities, at least 25 percent of the population had incomes below the poverty level, and most of this poor population was black. Sociologist Robert Bullard published his study of Houston's municipal waste disposal sites, which revealed that six of eight city incinerators, all five city landfills, and three of

four privately owned landfills were located in black neighborhoods.

In 1987 the United Church of Christ Commission for Racial Justice published its study "Toxic Wastes and Race in the United States: A National Report on the Racial and Socio-Economic Characteristics of Communities with Hazardous Waste Sites," which concluded that the poor and members of racial minority groups were being treated inequitably in the siting of such facilities. At the press conference marking the release of the study, CRJ executive director Ben Chavis, Jr., coined the term "environmental racism" to describe the findings on racial disparity in locating hazardous waste sites.

This report was followed in October 1991 by the First National People of Color Environmental Leadership Summit in Washington, D.C., which produced a set of "Principles of Environmental Justice." The summit's leaders called upon people of color to secure their economic and social liberation and demand the right to participate as equal partners in environmental decision making.

In 1994 President Clinton's Executive Order 12898, Federal Actions to Address Environmental Justice and Low-Income Populations, reinforced Title VI of the Civil Rights Act of 1964 and created the Office of Environmental Justice and the National Environmental Justice Advisory Council (NEJAC) to advise EPA on how to attain environmental justice.

Siting of hazardous waste and radioactive waste facilities has numerous dimensions—scientific, economic, political, sociological, psychological, and legal. Prior to the environmental legislation of the 1970s, decisions of siting private disposal facilities were made by private companies and based on key factors such as low land and development costs. Even after environmental regulations took effect, they played only a secondary role in location decisions, with more traditional factors retaining primacy. Inconsistency among state laws adds to the problem of inconsistent siting criteria, although most of these laws provide for enhanced public participation and for technical siting criteria. A great irony is that the principal environmental impact of stringent siting rules, ineffective siting strategies, and an illusory search for the nonexistent perfect site has been to continue the life of old, substandard, and poorly sited hazardous- and radioactive-waste facilities.

See also Civil Rights Act of 1964; Civil Rights Movement; Environmental Racism; Interest Groups; National Association for the Advancement of Colored People; Southern Christian Leadership Conference

Bibliography

Bullard, Robert. 1994. *Unequal Protection: Environmental Justice and Communities of Color.* San Francisco: Sierra Club.

Cable, Sherry, and Michael Benson. 1993. "Acting Locally: Environmental Injustice and the Emergence of Grassroots Environmental Organizations." *Social Problems* 40 (4): 464–77.

Cable, Sherry, Donald W. Hastings, and Tamara L. Mix. 2002. "Different Voices, Different Venues: Environmental Racism Claims by Activists, Researchers, and Lawyers." *Human Ecology Review* 9 (1): 26–42.

Cole, Luke W., and Sheila R. Foster. 2001. *From the Ground Up: Environmental Racism and the Rise of the Environmental Justice Movement.* New York: New York University Press.

Gerrard, Michael B. 1994. *Whose Backyard, Whose Risk: Fear and Fairness in Toxic and Nuclear Waste Siting.* Cambridge, MA: MIT Press.

Pellow, David Naguinb. 2002. *Garbage Wars: The Struggle for Environmental Justice in Chicago.* Cambridge, MA: MIT Press.

Schlosberg, David. 1999. *Environmental Justice and the New Pluralism.* New York: Oxford University Press.

Switzer, Jacqueline Vaughn. 2001. *Environmental Politics: Domestic and Global Dimensions.* 3rd ed. Boston: Bedford/St. Martin's Press.

Nancy Brannon

ENVIRONMENTAL RACISM

One important offshoot of American environmentalism in the 1970s was increased attention to the phenomenon of environmental racism. Civil rights leaders and grassroots organizations as well as community groups across the United States claimed decision makers at the local, state, and federal levels consistently placed or urged the placement of hazardous-waste sites, toxic landfills, and other polluting operations in low-income communities populated largely by people of color. Consequently, these communities and minorities were disproportionately affected by environmental hazards.

Were these accusations true? Were low-income communities and people of color more likely than other segments of society to experience increased exposure to environmental risks? In order to evaluate these claims, a variety of studies were undertaken by members of the economic, political, and environmental communities. Once the data was collected and analyzed, it became evident that minorities and low-income communities were indeed exposed to greater environmental risks in their neighborhoods than society at large. Even worse, the evidence suggested that environmental agencies claiming to protect the people and the environment had failed to recognize that their policies were perpetuating the cycle of environmental racism. The failure of government agencies to acknowledge their role in this matter led to the birth of the environmental justice movement.

Environmental justice consists of two important components. The first component addresses the fair treatment of all people in regard to environmental law, policies, and practices. Fair treatment within this context ensures that no one specific ethnic, racial, or socioeconomic group bears the brunt of negative environmental effects resulting from economic operations or government policies and programs at the local, state, and federal levels.

The second component of environmental justice focuses on the broader incorporation of those with a vested interest in the policy outcome (regardless of racial origin and income status) into the development, implementation, and enforcement mechanisms of environmental policies and practices. The incorporation of interested parties ensures that the outcome of the decision-making process is acceptable to the majority rather than to the minority of stakeholders. Environmental justice then seeks to equally enforce policies and practices across racial, ethnic, and socioeconomic lines.

The environmental justice framework employs several strategies to prevent, reduce, and/or eliminate environmental racism. The preferred strategy is to eliminate the threat of environmental injustice before damage or harm can occur. This is accomplished by employing ethical analyses to determine whether the underlying assumptions embedded in the decision-making or policy process create disparities in environmental outcomes among groups. If faulty assumptions are found to exist, then the basis of the decision or policy can be reevaluated. In this way, communities can more closely examine the political, social, and economic assumptions upon which environmental racism is built and reinforced. Additionally, the environmental justice framework compels the polluter to provide evidence that people of color or low-income groups are not unduly discriminated against when it comes to decisions regarding environmental hazards or harm.

As environmental justice has become an important consideration in domestic environmental matters, it has also taken on increasing importance in the international environmental realm. The inequitable distribution of environmental risks found in the domestic sphere is being replicated at the international level. Globalization has led to growing exportation of polluting industries from the Northern to the Southern hemisphere. It has also fostered the growing influence abroad of multinational corporations, along with their environmentally destructive behavior. The absence of environmental laws and lax enforcement mechanisms, combined with existing tensions between economic development and environmental degradation in the developing world, have only reinforced the pattern of unequal distribution of risk between the developing and developed world. Hence, developing countries and impoverished populations around the world are disproportionately bearing the negative environmental consequences of globalization. Because the developing world has fewer resources available to deal effectively with negative environmental outcomes, these impoverished countries are especially vulnerable to environmental change. Policy choices being made at the international level threaten to embed patterns of global environmental racism into international relations.

Environmental justice must be understood in the domestic as well as global contexts. That being the case, environmental justice is the right of all members of the global community to environmental protection irrespective of race, culture, and income. Environmental protection within this context not only includes the equal allocation of environmental costs and risks, but it also promotes strategies that target resources where environmental problems are the greatest. It requires the participation of stakeholders around the globe to enhance the effectiveness of environmental protection both domestically and internationally.

See also Civil Rights Movement; Environmental Justice

Bibliography

Bullard, Robert D. 1999. "Dismantling Environmental Racism in the USA." *Local Environment* 4 (1): 5–19.
Moore, Donald S., Jake Kosek, and Anand Pandian, eds. 2003. *Race, Nature and the Politics of Difference.* Durham, NC: Duke University Press.
Williams, Christopher, ed. 1998. *Environmental Victims.* London: Earthscan Press.

Denise DeGarmo

EPPERSON V. ARKANSAS (1968)

Sensationally labeled the second monkey trial by the press, *Epperson v. Arkansas* was the 1968 case in which the U.S. Supreme Court decided that a state may not prohibit the teaching of the theory of evolution in the public schools. The decision struck down as unconstitutional a 1928 Arkansas statute that made it a misdemeanor, and a cause for dismissal, for a teacher at a state-supported school or university "to teach the theory or doctrine that mankind ascended or descended from a lower order of animals" or "to adopt or use in any such institution a textbook that teaches" the proposition. *Epperson* invalidated the Arkansas law on the grounds that the legislation violated the First Amendment's Establishment of Religion Clause. By the force and tenor of its reasoning, the ruling also repudiated the result of the notorious 1925 Scopes case, or the so-called first monkey trial, in which high school biology teacher John T. Scopes was convicted of transgressing Tennessee's antievolution statute, a measure upon which the Arkansas law was modeled.

Epperson v. Arkansas was brought by Susan Epperson, a tenth-grade biology teacher at Central High School in Little Rock, Arkansas. The educator sought to obtain a judicial order allowing her to use a new textbook adopted by the school administration that contained a chapter on evolution. Writing for a six-member Court majority, Justice Abe Fortas determined that the state statute banning the textbook had been enacted to prevent "teachers from discussing the theory of evolution because it is contrary to the belief of some that the Book of Genesis must be the exclusive source of doctrine as to the origin of man." The Arkansas law violated the Constitution's bedrock principle of state neutrality on religious questions, Fortas reasoned, and could not be allowed to stand. "Government in our democracy, state and national, must be neutral in matters of religious theory, doctrine, and practice," Fortas declared. "It may not be hostile to any religion or to the advocacy of no-religion; and it may not aid, foster, or promote one religion or religious theory against another or even against the militant opposite. The First Amendment mandates governmental neutrality between religion and religion, and between religion and nonreligion."

A native Tennessean who had been deeply dismayed by the outcome of the Scopes trial, Fortas took particular pleasure in voiding Arkansas' antievolution law. He joked to a friend that while he wrote the *Epperson* opinion, he would occasionally glance at a portrait of himself, stored in a corner of his office, and wonder whether it indicated mankind had "ascended from or descended from apes" (Kalman 1990, 275). John Scopes, in

his sixties when the *Epperson* ruling came down, applauded the ruling, saying, "It is what I have been working for all along" (Associated Press 1968, 24).

In the years since it was decided, *Epperson* has been used as a precedent in other evolution-related disputes. The decision has been cited in cases such as *Edwards v. Aguillard* (1987) to strike down so-called balanced treatment acts mandating that "creation science" be taught alongside any teaching of evolution.

See also Establishment Clause; Evolution/Creationism Controversy; First Amendment; Fortas, Abe; Religion, Freedom of; Separation of Church and State

Bibliography

Associated Press. 1968. "Ruling Pleases Scopes." *New York Times*, 13 November.

Kalman, Laura. 1990. *Abe Fortas: A Biography*. New Haven, CT: Yale University Press.

Alain L. Sanders

EQUAL ACCESS TO JUSTICE ACT

The Equal Access to Justice Act, codified at 28 U.S.C. § 2412, allows a prevailing party involved in a civil lawsuit against the United States to recover its costs as well as attorneys' fees spent in the lawsuit. Not all who are involved in lawsuits against the United States are automatically entitled to recoupment of their fees and expenses, nor does the statute provide for unlimited payoffs. Rather, the statute has numerous requirements with which the parties must comply before any type of recovery can be had.

To be eligible for such an award, a request must be made in a timely manner. Under Section 2412(d)(1)(B), an application must be filed no later than 30 days from the entry of the final judgment in the case. According to Section 2412(d)(2)(G), that means a judgment that is "final and not appealable."

Next, the party must show that he is the prevailing party in the lawsuit. Although there are times when that determination can be very easily made, such as when judgment is rendered in favor of the party after trial, at other times the issues can become more complex. For instance, in *Yarborough v. Cuomo* (2000), the U.S. Court of Appeals for the Eighth Circuit noted that a prevailing party was one who obtained "actual relief on the merits of his claim," while in *United States v. Marolf* (2002), the Ninth Circuit concluded that fees could be awarded without regard to "whether the [government's action] could have succeeded on the merits."

If a party can show that he or she did indeed prevail against the government, then the issue becomes, under Section 2412 (d)(1)(A), whether "the position of the United States was substantially justified or that special circumstances make an award unjust." So, if the government's position had a reasonable basis in law and fact, it will be deemed substantially justified under the statute. If the court makes such a determination, recovery against the United States will not be permitted. However, if the position of the government was not substantially justified, then the court must determine the reasonable fee award.

According to Section 2412 (d)(2)(A) of the statute, the amount of the fees awarded depends "upon prevailing market rates for the kind and quality of the services furnished," although ordinarily fees should not exceed $125 per hour unless there is a special factor involved. The reasonable expenses of expert witnesses can be recouped as well as the costs of studies, analyses, certain reports, and projects as long as they are found by the court to have been a necessary part of preparing the case for litigation.

Finally, under Section 2412 (d)(2)(B), an individual party must establish that his or her net worth did not exceed two million dollars at the time that the civil action was filed. If the party is a business, it must establish that its net worth did not exceed seven million dollars, nor did it have more than 500 employees at the time of the filing of the civil action.

Hon. Virginia M. Hernandez Covington

EQUAL EMPLOYMENT OPPORTUNITY COMMISSION (EEOC)

The Equal Employment Opportunity Commission (EEOC) was established by Title VII of the Civil Rights Act of 1964 on July 2, 1965. The EEOC is charged with enforcing the same provisions of the Act. Title VII prohibits employment discrimination on the basis of race, color, national origin, sex, age, disability, and religion in practices including testing, hiring, layoffs, firing, training, apprenticeship, wages, privileges, promotion, disciplinary action, and other terms, conditions, or benefits of employment. Title VII provides protection from discrimination for employees of state and local governments, public and private employment agencies, public and private educational institutions, labor unions with 15 or more members, and joint-labor management committees. If a person believes that he or she is being mistreated due to employment practices and a lack of equal opportunities within the workplace, he or she may file a grievance against his or her employer through the EEOC. This law gives employees who would normally not have an outlet to voice their frustration an opportunity to be heard and ensure that their rights are observed. Employees or applicants of the federal government, government-owned institutions, and Indian tribes are exempt from this law's protection.

The EEOC is composed of five members appointed by the president and confirmed by the Senate. The members serve staggered five-year terms, and there can be no more than three members from one political party on the commission. The president appoints one member as the chairperson of the commission. This person takes responsibility for the commission's administrative operations. He or she is also responsible for appointing other officers, agents, hearing examiners, and attorneys to represent the commission, and employees to assist the commission. The commission operates through about 50 field offices, each of which processes grievances and complaints.

Because its mission is to enforce Title VII of the Civil Rights Act of 1964, the EEOC has the authority to prevent discrimination in the workplace and ensure equal employment opportunity.

Persons protected under Title VII may lodge their complaints by contacting the appropriate EEOC district office where they will be given a Charge of Discrimination form. Charges must be made under oath and are not made public. Once the form is completed, the fair employment agencies at the state and local levels have priority jurisdiction over the complaint. If the agency does not take action on the complaint within 60 days, then the EEOC takes responsibility for investigating the complaint. When the EEOC obtains the complaint, the commission investigates the claim and determines whether the practices carried out by the employer are discriminatory. If the EEOC does not find probable cause, the commission will dismiss the charge and notify both the plaintiff and the employer. If the EEOC finds probable cause, then the commission begins the conciliation process in which it attempts to persuade the employers to remove that discrimination voluntarily. If this fails, then the EEOC may sue in a federal district court. Nonetheless, the main goal is to promote and effectuate voluntary equal opportunity action programs by employers, unions, and community organizations.

At the end of each fiscal year, the EEOC reports to Congress and the president all the complaints made and actions taken. The commission also reports all causes and methods of eliminating discrimination and any recommendations for new legislation. This is no small matter, for the EEOC has helped to create numerous pieces of legislation in its effort to further protect Americans against employment-based discrimination. With the assistance and guidance of the EEOC, Congress has passed a number of important pieces of legislation, including: the Equal Opportunity Employment Act in 1972, which granted the EEOC more power to enforce equality in the workplace; the Rehabilitation Act of 1973; the Pregnancy Discrimination Act of 1978; the Civil Service Reform Act; the Immigration Reform Act of 1986; the Americans with Disabilities Act of 1990; the Omnibus Budget Reconciliation Act of 1986; the Civil Rights Restoration Act of 1991; and the EEOC Education, Technical Assistance and Training Revolving Fund

Act of 1992, which combats age discrimination in the workplace.

See also Affirmative Action; Civil Rights Act of 1964; Civil Rights Restoration Act of 1991; Employment Discrimination

Bibliography

United States Equal Employment Opportunity Commission. 1987. *Laws Enforced by the U.S. Equal Employment Opportunity Commission.* Washington, DC: U.S. Government Printing Office.

———. 2000. *Ensuring the Promise of Opportunity for 35 Years.* Washington, DC: U.S. Government Printing Office.

United States Office of Public Affairs. 1976. *EEOC at a Glance.* Washington, DC: U.S. Government Printing Office.

Maurice Mangum

EQUALITY

When the framers of the Declaration of Independence (1776) asserted the "self-evident" truth "that all men are created equal," they obviously were not making an empirical statement about the distribution of talent, ability, or virtue among human beings. Rather, they were stating one of the core values of liberal democracy—that all persons are equal before the state and equal before the law. Political philosophers from Aristotle to John Rawls have debated the meaning and obligations of equality. This debate will no doubt continue as long as constitutional democracy continues to evolve.

Political Equality

In the American philosophical and legal traditions, political equality does not mean that political influence must be equally shared. Were that the case, the American system of government (and all others aspiring to its constitutional ideals) would have to be considered dismal failures. Rather, it means that there is universal suffrage—that all citizens (at least adults) have the right to vote and otherwise participate in the political process. It also means, as the Supreme Court recognized in *Reynolds v. Sims* (1964) and many decisions since then, that political equality is impaired by systems of representation that weight individual votes unequally. Thus in *Reynolds* and succeeding decisions, the Court has demanded reapportionment of state legislatures and other representative bodies according to the principle of one person, one vote, requiring that districts must be drawn so as to make their populations of voters as equal as is practicable.

Legal Equality

Inscribed above the entrance to the Supreme Court building in Washington, D.C., is the phrase "Equal Justice Under Law." The same value is enshrined in the Fourteenth Amendment which provides that "no state shall... deny to any person within its jurisdiction the equal protection of the laws." A considerable proportion of constitutional litigation over the last century has been devoted to determining the meaning of this sweeping commitment to the "equal protection of the laws." In *Plessy v. Ferguson* (1896), the Supreme Court held that de jure racial segregation was not ipso facto a denial of legal equality. Speaking for the Court, Justice Henry Billings Brown opined that "[t]he object of the [Fourteenth A]mendment was undoubtedly to enforce the absolute equality of the two races before the law, but, in the nature of things, it could not have been intended to abolish distinctions based upon color, or to enforce social, as distinguished from political, equality, or a commingling of the two races upon terms unsatisfactory to either." This notion that segregation was not tantamount to legal inequality was ultimately rejected by the Supreme Court in a series of decisions beginning with *Brown v. Board of Education* (1954) and culminating in *Loving v. Virginia* (1967), in which the Court made clear that racial segregation was a denial of equal protection of the law. Since then the courts (as well as Congress and the state legislatures) have proceeded to tackle other forms of legal inequality, including discrimination based on gender, alienage, age, disability, and, most recently, sexual orientation.

Economic Equality

Socialists argue that there can be no real legal and political equality without social and economic equality, which they propose to achieve through redistribution of property. In the capitalist tradition, in which the United States is firmly embedded, for government to act in this way violates property rights and economic freedoms that are viewed as implicitly guaranteed by the Constitution. In the capitalist tradition, equality means equality of opportunity, not equality of result. Courts have played a limited but significant role in addressing some public manifestations of economic inequality. While the U.S. Supreme Court has been unwilling to extend the equal protection guarantee of the Fourteenth Amendment in an effort to remove disparities in public school spending at the local level (*San Antonio Independent School District v. Rodriguez*, 1973), many state courts have addressed this problem through state constitutional interpretation. These courts have in some instances required state legislatures to provide equal financing of education to all public schools within their jurisdictions, irrespective of the differences in property values among school districts.

Social Equality

Social equality, a condition in which all members of society enjoy equal status, is by far the least attainable. Human beings in groups inevitably form hierarchies of power and status. While there is no caste system in this country, there are inequalities in status that result from deeply imbedded cultural tendencies, including racism, sexism, religious prejudice, nativism, homophobia. Although the law cannot directly attack these attitudes, in that people have a First Amendment right to feel and believe as they will, the law can address the discrimination that results from these cultural tendencies. Although perfect social equality will never be achieved, the law can reduce the extent to which social inequality is based on characteristics such as race, gender, religion, alienage, and sexual preference.

See also Affirmative Action; Age Discrimination; Aristotle; At-Large Elections; *Baker v. Carr;* Bilingual Education; Black Codes; *Brown v. Board of Education;* Busing Controversy; Catholicism and Anti-Catholicism; Civil Rights; Civil Rights Act of 1866; Civil Rights Act of 1870; Civil Rights Act of 1871; Civil Rights Act of 1875; Civil Rights Act of 1957; Civil Rights Act of 1964; Civil Rights Act of 1988; Civil Rights Movement; Civil Rights Restoration Act of 1991; Constitutional Democracy; Consumer Discrimination; Declaration of Independence; Disabilities, Rights of Persons with; Discrimination; Discrimination by Private Actors; Diversity; Economic Freedom; Emancipation Proclamation; Employment Discrimination; Environmental Justice; Environmental Racism; Equal Access to Justice Act; Equal Pay Act; Equal Protection Clause; Equal Protection Jurisprudence; Equal Rights Amendment; Fair Housing Act of 1968; Federalism and Civil Rights and Liberties; First Amendment; Fourteenth Amendment; Free and Fair Elections; Gay Rights Movement; Gender-Based Discrimination; *Gideon v. Wainwright;* Grandfather Clause; Group Rights; Housing, Discrimination in; Immigrants and Aliens, Rights of; Interracial Marriage; Japanese-Americans, Relocation of; Jim Crow Laws; Latino Americans, Civil Rights of; Liberalism; Liberty; Literacy Tests; *Loving v. Virginia; Native Americans, Civil Rights of; Plessy v. Ferguson;* Pluralism; Poll Tax; Property Rights; Public Accommodation, Places of; Public Education, Right to; Racial Gerrymandering; Racial Profiling; Rawls, John; Reapportionment; Reparations for Slavery; Representative Democracy; Restrictive Covenants; *Reynolds v. Sims;* Same-Sex Marriage and Civil Unions; Section 1983 Action; Segregation, De Facto and De Jure; Segregation in Public Education; Selective Prosecution; Seneca Falls Declaration; Sexual Harassment; Sexual Orientation, Discrimination Based on; Slavery; Speech, Freedom of; Title IX, Education Amendments of 1972; Universal Suffrage; Violence Against Women Act; Vote, Right to; Voting Age; Voting Rights Act of 1965; White Primary; Women's Suffrage

Bibliography

Barcalow, Emmett. 2003. *Justice, Equality and Rights.* Belmont, CA: Wadsworth.

Johnston, David, ed. 2000. *Equality.* Indianapolis, IN: Hackett.

Pojman, Louis P., and Robert Westmoreland, eds. 1997. *Equality: Selected Readings.* Oxford: Oxford University Press.

Otis H. Stephens, Jr., and John M. Scheb II

EQUAL PAY ACT (1963)

Equal pay legislation first was introduced in Congress in 1945, and thereafter some form of equal pay proposal was introduced in each Congress for the next 17 years. Not until 1961, however, was enactment of equal pay legislation into law a realistic possibility. In that year, President Kennedy created a Commission on the Status of Women. At its very first meeting, the commission endorsed the principle of equal pay for comparable work, the same principle that had been incorporated into the very first equal pay bill introduced into Congress in 1945.

Both the House and the Senate took up consideration of equal pay legislation in 1962. After extensive hearings, the House Committee on Education and Labor recommended adoption of legislation requiring equal pay for comparable work. On the House floor, however, the legislation was amended to require equal pay for equal work, rather than equal pay for comparable work. The Senate also passed equal pay legislation in 1962, but the Senate action came so late in the session that the differences between and House and Senate bills could not be reconciled before the 87th Congress adjourned.

After the convening of the 88th Congress, the Kennedy administration again proposed enactment of equal pay legislation. After further hearings, the House and Senate approved similar equal pay bills. For the first time, however, equal pay protection was tied to the minimum-wage provisions of the Fair Labor Standards Act. President Kennedy signed the Equal Pay Act into law on June 19, 1963.

Two conditions prompted enactment of the Equal Pay Act. One was the dramatic increase of women in the workforce. Between 1940 and 1960, the number of women in the workforce nearly doubled from 12.8 million to 23 million, increasing the percentage of women from one-fourth to approximately one-third of the total workforce. Of those joining the workforce a higher proportion were married women from low-income families. The second condition contributing to enactment of the Equal Pay Act was the compelling evidence that women were not paid wages equal to those of men who performed equal work. In 1960, the median annual income of women working full time was only 60.7 percent of the earnings of men. The Senate Committee on Labor and Public Welfare reported that "it is overwhelmingly apparent that ... women are not rewarded in the same manner as are ... men" (S. Rep. No. 176, 88th Cong., 1st Sess. 2, 1963).

As a general rule, coverage under the Equal Pay Act is tied to the minimum-wage provisions of the Fair Labor Standards Act. Thus, an employer required to pay minimum wage under the Fair Labor Standards Act also is required to pay equal wages for equal work regardless of sex. The act also applies to labor organizations that "cause or attempt to cause" an employer to discriminate in violation of the equal pay requirement.

The Equal Pay Act prohibits covered employers from discriminating on the basis of sex by paying unequal wages for equal work. Although wage discrimination against women was the principal reason for enactment of the Equal Pay Act, because the act prohibits discrimination "on the basis of sex," men are as protected by the act as are women.

There are four elements of an Equal Pay Act claim: (1) that within the *same establishment,* (2) an employer discriminates *on the basis of sex,* (3) by paying *unequal wages,* for (4) *equal work.* One of the most frequently litigated issues arising under the Equal Pay Act involves the question of equal work. The act does not require that the jobs be identical to warrant application of the equal pay requirement. What the act does require is that the jobs involve "equal skill, effort, and responsibility" and that they be performed "under similar working conditions."

Different pay for concededly equal work does not violate the act, however, if the pay differential can be justified under one of the four exceptions listed in the act. The first three exceptions are quite specific: they apply to pay differentials based on seniority, merit, or productivity. The fourth exception is open ended: it permits a pay differential "based on any other factor," as long as that factor is one "other than sex."

An employee underpaid in violation of the act may institute a civil action to recover the wages that should have been paid, plus an additional equal amount as liquidated damages. Reasonable attorneys' fees and costs also are recoverable. Employees may not recover compensatory or punitive damages or obtain injunctive relief.

Litigation to enforce the act also may be instituted by the Equal Employment Opportunity Commission. Under one section of the act, the EEOC may recover the same remedies available to an employee, except for attorneys' fees and costs. Under a separate section of the act, the EEOC may seek injunctive relief not only to restrain future violations of the act but also to restrain the withholding of wages found to be due for past violations of the Equal Pay Act. In actions for injunctive relief, however, the EEOC may not recover liquidated damages, nor may it recover attorneys' fees or costs.

See also Civil Rights Act of 1964; Employment Discrimination; Equal Employment Opportunity Commission; Feminist Movement; Gender-Based Discrimination

Bibliography

Cook, Joseph G., and John L. Sobieski, Jr. 1997. *Civil Rights Actions.* New York: Matthew Bender.

John L. Sobieski, Jr.

EQUAL PROTECTION CLAUSE

One of the ethical pillars of constitutional democracy is the norm of equality under the law.

The United States Constitution expresses this norm in the Equal Protection Clause of the Fourteenth Amendment (1868), which provides that no state shall "deny to any person within its jurisdiction the equal protection of the laws." Like other provisions of the Civil War amendments, the Equal Protection Clause was motivated by a desire to protect the civil rights of the newly freed slaves. In the Slaughterhouse Cases (1873), the Supreme Court observed that the purpose of the Fourteenth Amendment was "the protection of the newly-made freeman and citizen from the oppressions of those who had formerly exercised unlimited dominion over him." On the basis of this narrow understanding of the Fourteenth Amendment, the Supreme Court held in *Plessy v. Ferguson* (1896) that state-mandated racial segregation was not a violation of the Equal Protection Clause. That view of the Equal Protection Clause was repudiated by the Supreme Court in *Brown v. Board of Education* (1954), where the Court invalidated compulsory racial segregation in public schools, and in a series of subsequent decisions in which the Court struck down other types of Jim Crow laws.

In the wake of *Brown*, the Equal Protection Clause figured prominently in the civil rights struggles of African Americans and other racial and ethnic minorities. However, the text of the clause makes no mention of race. Rather, it refers to any person within the jurisdiction of a state. Accordingly, the Equal Protection Clause has developed, largely through judicial interpretation, into a broad prohibition against unreasonable governmental discrimination directed at any identifiable group. In the modern era, the Equal Protection Clause has been invoked to challenge discrimination not only against racial, ethnic, and religious minorities, but against women, the poor, out-of-wedlock children, immigrants and aliens, persons with physical and mental disabilities, and, most recently, gay men and lesbians.

Because the Bill of Rights contains no explicit equal protection provision, does it follow that the national government is under no constitutional obligation to provide equal protection of the laws? The Supreme Court has answered this question emphatically in the negative, finding an "equal protection component" implicit in the Due Process Clause of the Fifth Amendment. In *Bolling v. Sharpe* (1954), the Court concluded that the values underlying the equal protection guarantee are embraced within the broad definition of due process of law. Of course, had the Court ruled otherwise, there would have been no constitutional basis to challenge discriminatory policies and actions initiated by the federal government.

Without question, the scope of the Equal Protection Clause has been expanded far beyond the intentions of its Reconstruction-era framers and has become a means of challenging the constitutionality of a broad range of state laws, actions, and policies. It must be understood, however, that the constitutional requirement of equal protection does not automatically invalidate every instance of differential treatment by government. As the Supreme Court recognized in *Reed v. Reed* (1971), "the Fourteenth Amendment does not deny to States the power to treat different classes of persons in different ways." Chief Justice Warren E. Burger's opinion for the Court in *Reed* noted that any official classification of persons "must be reasonable, not arbitrary, and must rest upon some ground of difference having a fair and substantial relation to the object of the legislation, so that all persons similarly circumstanced shall be treated alike."

The fact that similarly situated groups are unequally affected by public policy is not enough to constitute a denial of equal protection of the laws. In *Washington v. Davis* (1976), the Supreme Court noted that its decisions "have not embraced the proposition that a law or other official act, without regard to whether it reflects a racially discriminatory purpose, is unconstitutional solely because it has a racially disproportionate impact." Thus the key to prevailing in an equal protection claim is proving discriminatory intent on the part of decision makers.

The jurisprudence of the Equal Protection Clause has become extremely complex, involving various levels of judicial scrutiny of different sorts of discrimination claims. Moreover, under what is often termed the new due process/equal protection, equal protection jurisprudence blends into substantive due process with regard to the protection of fundamental rights. Thus, contemporary courts will strictly scrutinize public policies that discriminate among groups with regard to the exercise of fundamental rights, even when those rights are not specifically enumerated in the Constitution. For example, a state law that restricts minors' access to abortion will be strictly scrutinized by the courts, whereas other forms of age discrimination are subjected to less stringent judicial review.

The Equal Protection Clause has provided the basis on which courts have invalidated numerous discriminatory laws and policies. The Clause has also been interpreted to require fundamental fairness in the political process (see, for example, *Reynolds v. Sims,* 1964). The most dramatic and controversial application of the Equal Protection Clause in this area was the Supreme Court's decision in *Bush v. Gore* (2000), where the Court effectively determined the outcome of the 2000 presidential election. Clearly, the Equal Protection Clause is among the most important constitutional provisions with respect to civil rights, but its highly abstract character provides a wide range for judicial policy making in this area.

See also Affirmative Action; Age Discrimination; *Brown v. Board of Education;* Civil Rights Movement; Constitutional Democracy; Disabilities, Rights of Persons with; Discrimination; Diversity; Due Process, Substantive; Equality; Equal Protection Jurisprudence; Fourteenth Amendment; Fundamental Rights; Gay Rights Movement; Gender-Based Discrimination; Group Rights; Immigrants and Aliens, Rights of; Interracial Marriage; Jim Crow Laws; *Plessy v. Ferguson;* Rational Basis Test; Reconstruction; Segregation, De Facto and De Jure; Sexual Orientation, Discrimination Based on; State Action Doctrine; Strict Scrutiny

Bibliography

Baer, Judith. 1983. *Equality under the Constitution: Reclaiming the Fourteenth Amendment.* Ithaca, NY: Cornell University Press.

Berger, Raoul. 1977. *Government by Judiciary: The Transformation of the Fourteenth Amendment.* Cambridge, MA: Harvard University Press.

Brest, Paul. 1976. "In Defense of the Antidiscrimination Principle." *Harvard Law Review* 90:1–54.

Fiss, Owen M. 1976. "Groups and the Equal Protection Clause." *Philosophy and Public Affairs* 5:107–77.

Perry, Michael J. 1979. "Modern Equal Protection: A Conceptualization and Appraisal." *Columbia Law Review* 79:1023–83.

Schwartz, Bernard, ed. 1970. *The Fourteenth Amendment.* New York: New York University Press.

John M. Scheb II and Otis H. Stephens, Jr.

EQUAL PROTECTION JURISPRUDENCE

According to the Equal Protection Clause of the Fourteenth Amendment, "No state shall … deny to any person within its jurisdiction the equal protection of the laws." The clause does not mean that government is prohibited from making classifications when it adopts laws, because laws by their nature establish classifications of people and actions. The task for the courts has been to determine the constitutionality of state and federal policies challenged as violations of equal protection. Over time, the Supreme Court has adopted three levels of scrutiny for deciding equal protection cases: (1) minimal, (2) strict, and (3) intermediate or heightened. The level of scrutiny utilized in a given case determines how closely the Court examines the challenged policy, particularly the degree of deference accorded to the government.

With minimal scrutiny, which involves the rational basis test, the justices ask whether the government has a legitimate interest or objective in making the classification and whether the means chosen are rationally related to the objective and are not arbitrary or capricious. Here the burden of proof is on the individual(s) challenging the policy. Under strict scrutiny, or the compelling interest test, the burden is on the government to demonstrate that it has a compelling interest in making the classification and that the means chosen are narrowly tailored to achieve that interest. When intermediate/heightened scrutiny or the important government objective test is used, the reviewing court must determine whether the government has an important objective and whether the means employed in the classification are substantially related to achieving that objective. Again, the burden of proof is on the government. Minimal scrutiny ordinarily applies to basic economic classifications and to classifications based on age and mental retardation. Strict scrutiny is used to examine suspect classifications and alleged deprivations of fundamental rights. Intermediate scrutiny is applied to gender-based classifications and to those based on illegitimacy. Classifications involving alienage have been reviewed under all three levels, depending upon the specific issue, and claims alleging discrimination on the basis of indigence are subject to minimal scrutiny unless they involve deprivation of a fundamental right.

Minimal Scrutiny/The Rational Basis Test

Minimal scrutiny is the traditional level used by the Court to decide equal protection cases. A good summary of minimal scrutiny is found in the majority opinion in *Lindsley v. Natural Carbonic Gas Company* (1911):

A classification having some reasonable basis does not offend against the [Equal Protection] clause merely because it is not made with mathematical nicety, or because in practice it results in some inequality.... One who assails the classification in such a law must carry the burden of showing that it does not rest upon any reasonable basis, but is essentially arbitrary.

With this analysis, the Court usually defers to the judgments of policy makers, and the policy or classification challenged is normally upheld. For example, when individuals challenged Texas's property tax system of school financing as a violation of equal protection because of disparities in funding among school districts, by a vote of five-to-four the Court upheld the system as a rational method of promoting local control of public education (*San Antonio Independent School District v. Rodriguez,* 1973).

The facts of the case showed the disparities to be quite extensive. After taking into account the revenue from property taxes and additional state and federal funding, funding per student in the poorest district in the state was $333, while the per-student amount in the wealthiest district was $594. Because of a state ceiling on the property tax, residents of poorer districts could not tax themselves at rates high enough to increase funding and reduce the disparities. Although Justice Lewis Powell's majority opinion conceded that the school financing system was in need of reform, he said that this was the job of the state legislature, not the federal courts.

Occasionally, a policy reviewed under minimal scrutiny is found invalid. For example, in *Romer v. Evans* (1996), the Court struck down a Colorado amendment that precluded local governments or the state from making policies that prohibit discrimination on the basis of sexual orientation. A six-member majority led by Justice Anthony Kennedy held that the law was not "directed to any identifiable legitimate purpose or discrete objective," that it was "a status-based enactment divorced from any factual context from which [they] could discern a relationship to legitimate state interests," and that it was "a classification of persons undertaken for its own sake." Kennedy rejected the state's argument that it was respecting other citizens' freedom of association and conserving its resources to fight other types of discrimination. In a sharp dissent, Justice Antonin Scalia argued that the Colorado amendment was a rational attempt by the state to preserve "traditional sexual mores against the efforts of a politically powerful minority."

Other types of classifications determined by the Court to require minimal scrutiny are those related to age and mental retardation. In *Massachusetts Board of Retirement v. Murgia* (1976), the Court upheld a state law that required uniformed police officers to retire at the age of 50. In a per curiam opinion, the justices ruled that age classifications would be examined using the rational basis test and concluded that "old age does not define a 'discrete and insular' group ... in need of 'extraordinary protection from the majoritarian political process.'"

The justices held that the mandatory retirement policy passed minimal scrutiny because having physically fit police officers was reasonably related to the state's legitimate interest in promoting public safety. Fifteen years later, in rejecting a claim that the Missouri Constitution's mandatory retirement provision for state judges violated equal protection, the Court reiterated the principle that age classifications would be subject only to minimal scrutiny (*Gregory v. Ashcroft,* 1991). Justice Sandra Day O'Connor's majority opinion held that the state's legitimate interest in maintaining a judiciary capable of performing demanding tasks was reasonably furthered by the requirement that state judges retire at age 70. She pointed to the effects of aging on physical and mental capacity and the insufficiency of removing judges from office through voluntary retirement, impeachment, or the regular election process. Two dissenters saw the mandatory retirement provision as a violation of the federal Age Discrimination and Employment Act and did not consider the equal protection aspect of the case.

The Court refused to adopt anything higher than minimal scrutiny for reviewing policies regarding mental retardation in *Cleburne v. Cleburne Living Center* (1985). The majority held, nonetheless, that the city ordinance requiring a special use permit for the operation of a group home for the mentally retarded was invalid as applied. Justice Byron White's majority opinion first noted that special permits were not required for operating other multiple-use dwellings and, most importantly, the state had no rational basis for believing that the home for mentally retarded individuals would pose any particular threat. Three justices concurred in the outcome, but they maintained that a higher level of scrutiny should apply to cases alleging discrimination against the mentally retarded. In 1993, in upholding a Kentucky law that established different standards for committing mentally retarded and mentally ill individuals, the high court affirmed its earlier principle that the rational basis test was the appropriate standard of review (*Heller v. Doe*). The majority was persuaded by the government's reasoning that differences in the diagnosis of and treatment for the mentally ill and mentally retarded prompted different standards for commitment.

Justice Hugo Black's opinion in a 1956 case involving poor criminal defendants led to speculation that the Court was poised to include classifications based on wealth/indigence in the suspect category, which would trigger the use of strict scrutiny. Black wrote, "In criminal trials a State can no more discriminate on account of poverty than on account of religion, race, or color" (*Griffin v. Illinois*). Despite this language, the Court reviews wealth/indigence classifications under minimal scrutiny. For example, a Maryland law that limited AFDC benefits to a specific amount, regardless of family size or needs, was upheld by a six-to-three vote as reasonably furthering the state's interest in "encouraging employment and in avoiding discrimination between welfare families and the families of the working poor" (*Dandridge v. Williams,* 1970).

Perhaps the Court's clearest statement about whether classifications based on indigence/wealth belong in the suspect category was provided in the *Rodriguez* case introduced above. Rejecting arguments that the state's property tax system for financing public education unconstitutionally discriminated against the poor, Justice Lewis Powell maintained that there was no evidence that the system "discriminate[d] against any definable category of 'poor' people" (*San Antonio Independent School District v. Rodriguez,* 1973). Justice Thurgood Marshall, joined by Justice William O. Douglas, dissented, contending that the children in poor school districts were members of a "suspect class" deserving of special protection. The Court also applied minimal scrutiny in rulings that upheld the state's right to limit appointed counsel for indigent defendants to first appeals (*Ross v. Moffitt,* 1974) and a federal law prohibiting the use of federal funds to pay for abortions for Medicaid recipients (*Harris v. McRae,* 1980).

Strict Scrutiny

In 1944, the Court introduced a more stringent level of scrutiny for resolving equal protection disputes. The Court had offered a hint that it might do so in a footnote in Justice Harlan F. Stone's majority opinion in a routine case six years earlier. In *United States v. Carolene Products* (1938), Stone noted in what came to be known as Footnote Four that prejudice against "discrete and insular minorities" may require a "more searching judicial inquiry." The justices officially established such an inquiry in *Korematsu v. United States* (1944). At issue in *Korematsu* was the constitutionality of the federal government's World War II exclusion order sending Japanese Americans to relocation camps after the bombing of Pearl Harbor. At the outset of the opinion, Justice Black wrote that some classifications, specifically those regarding race, are automatically suspect and require a closer examination:

[All] legal restrictions which curtail the civil rights of a single racial group are immediately suspect. That is not to say that all such restrictions are unconstitutional. It is to say that courts must subject them to the most rigid scrutiny.

Classifications analyzed under strict rather than minimal scrutiny are more likely to be declared unconstitutional. This was not the case in *Korematsu,* however, as strict scrutiny was applied in a way that upheld the government's exclusion orders. According to Black, Japanese Americans were not being sent to these centers because of racial hostility but because the nation was "at war with the Japanese Empire, because the properly constituted military authorities … decided that the military urgency of the situation demanded that all citizens of Japanese ancestry be segregated from the West Coast temporarily."

Korematsu notwithstanding, the Court has utilized strict scrutiny to invalidate racial classifications. For example, in *Loving v. Virginia* (1967), the Court unanimously struck down Virginia's anti-miscegenation statute. The state argued that it had a compelling interest in preventing sociological and psychological problems that burden spouses in interracial marriages. Chief Justice Earl Warren's majority opinion did not accept this reasoning, concluding that Virginia's clear intent was to maintain white supremacy.

The Court's initial use of strict scrutiny in equal protection cases involving racial classifications was directed at laws that discriminated against racial minorities. By the late 1980s, however, the Court held that strict scrutiny also applies to policies designed to remedy or redress such discrimination. This controversy began in 1978 in *University of California Regents v. Bakke* (1978), a case concerning affirmative action in higher education. In *Bakke,* while striking down a University of California–Davis Medical School admissions policy that set aside 16 of 100 seats for minority applicants, the Court also held that race can be considered as a factor in the admissions process. The vote on each of these issues was five-to-four, with Justice Powell providing the deciding vote and announcing the Court's decision. Four of the justices argued for using intermediate scrutiny in reviewing remedial race-based classifications, while the other four maintained that equal protection analysis was not necessary to decide the case because the set-aside policy violated the Civil Rights Act of 1964. In what became the controlling opinion, Justice Powell applied strict scrutiny, concluding that "[r]acial and ethnic distinctions of any sort are inherently suspect and thus call for the most exacting judicial examination." Powell also concluded that promoting diversity in the student body is a compelling interest justifying the use of race as one element in a range of factors to be considered in admissions decisions.

In several affirmative action cases decided after *Bakke,* the justices could not agree on the appropriate level of judicial scrutiny, but in a 1989 case concerning government contracting, a majority ruled for the first time that the affirmative action plans of state and local governments would be examined under strict scrutiny. Justice O'Connor's majority opinion held that "the standard of review under the Equal Protection Clause is not dependent on the race of those burdened or benefited by a particular classification." One year later, the Court held that intermediate scrutiny was the standard for determining the constitutionality of federal affirmative action programs (*Metro Broadcasting v. FCC,* 1990), but in 1995, the Court reversed itself.

In *Adarand Constructors v. Pena,* the majority held that *all* government affirmative action programs, whether federal, state, or local, must be reviewed using strict scrutiny. Justice O'Connor reiterated the earlier conclusion that strict scrutiny applies equally to classifications that discriminate against racial minorities and remedial classifications seeking to redress such discrimination. Justice John Paul Stevens disagreed:

There is no moral or constitutional equivalence between a policy that is designed to perpetuate a caste system and one that seeks to eradicate racial subordination. Invidious discrimination is an engine of oppression, subjugating a disfavored group to enhance or maintain the power of the majority. Remedial race-based preferences reflect the opposite impulse: a desire to foster equality in society.

Despite the clarity in *Adarand* regarding the use of strict scrutiny for examining government contracting programs, an important question remained about the level of scrutiny to be applied to the affirmative action policies of public educational institutions. In addition, the U.S. Court of Appeals for the Fifth Circuit concluded in *Hopwood v. Texas* (1996) that the decisions in *Adarand* and other cases had effectively overturned the *Bakke* decision. An appeal to the Supreme Court was rejected without comment. Two landmark cases in 2003 finally answered this question. In companion cases involving the University of Michigan's undergraduate and law school admissions programs (*Gratz v. Bollinger* and *Grutter v. Bollinger,* respectively), the Court, led by Justice O'Connor, affirmed Justice Powell's *Bakke* reasoning. The majority ruled that strict scrutiny was the correct standard for reviewing race-based affirmative action in university admissions. Moreover, the Court held that student body diversity is a compelling interest that can justify the use of race in university admissions as long as the policy is narrowly tailored to achieve that interest. Consequently, the law school's program met the narrow tailoring test (*Grutter v. Bollinger*), while the undergraduate program did not (*Gratz v. Bollinger*). Unlike the undergraduate program, which involved a selection index or point system that

awarded points for a number of factors, including race, the law school's program sought a "critical mass" of minority students based on individualized consideration of applications, with no bonus points for race/ethnicity. The dissenters in *Grutter* agreed that the use of strict scrutiny was appropriate, but they concluded that the law school policy did not meet the narrow tailoring test.

In addition to classifications involving race, the Court has extended the use of strict scrutiny to some policies that discriminate against aliens. The Court ruled in *Graham v. Richardson* (1971) that alienage, like race is a suspect classification requiring the government to demonstrate a compelling interest being achieved by narrowly tailored means. In this case, the Court unanimously invalidated an Arizona law that denied welfare benefits to noncitizens, rejecting the state's argument that discrimination against aliens was justified by its "special public interest" in providing for its citizens. Subsequently however, the Court ruled that not all laws discriminating against aliens require the highest level of review; thus, the justices used minimal scrutiny to uphold a New York law that prohibited aliens from becoming state troopers (*Foley v. Connellie,* 1978). The Court upheld the law on the grounds that positions involving discretionary government power in which the potential for abuse can have "serious impact on individuals" could be limited to citizens; law enforcement officers were included in that category.

Strict scrutiny or the compelling interest test also applies to cases involving claims of violations of fundamental rights. The Court has identified four categories of implicit constitutional rights: marriage and procreation, access to justice, voting rights, and interstate travel. Marriage and procreation were declared to be fundamental rights deserving of rigorous scrutiny in *Skinner v. Oklahoma* (1942). A unanimous Court declared Oklahoma's law authorizing the compulsory sterilization of habitual criminals convicted of certain crimes a violation of the Equal Protection Clause. Justice Douglas's majority opinion emphasized that "[m]arriage and procreation are fundamental to the very existence and survival of the race" and that "strict scrutiny of the classification which a State makes in a sterilization law is essential, lest unwittingly or otherwise invidious discriminations are made against groups or types of individuals."

Access to justice was declared to be a fundamental right with the decision in *Griffin v. Illinois* (1956). The justices ruled that indigent defendants must be provided a free transcript of their trial when necessary for preparing an appeal. In an important case regarding reapportionment of state legislatures, the Court held that the right to vote is fundamental to a free and democratic society (*Reynolds v. Sims,* 1964). As such, infringements on that right must be carefully examined. In 1969, the Court invalidated durational residency requirements for eligibility for welfare benefits on the grounds that such requirements violated the freedom to travel among the states (*Shapiro v. Thompson*). The state offered several objectives for the policy: assistance in planning the welfare budget; providing an objective test of residency; minimizing the possibility of fraud; and encouraging new residents to enter the labor force. Applying strict scrutiny, the Court found none of these interests to be compelling.

The Court refused to include education in the fundamental rights category despite being encouraged to do so in the *Rodriguez* case. In his majority opinion, Justice Powell declared that education "is not one of the rights afforded explicit protection under our Federal Constitution," nor is it implicitly protected. After criticizing the majority for retreating from its "historic commitment to equality of educational opportunity," Justice Marshall insisted that the Court's two-tiered approach to equal protection (minimal scrutiny or strict scrutiny) was too rigid. He suggested a "sliding scale" approach:

The task in every case should be to determine the extent to which constitutionally guaranteed rights are dependent on interests not mentioned in the Constitution. As the nexus between the specific constitutional guarantee and the nonconstitutional interest draws closer, the nonconstitutional interest becomes more fundamental and the degree of judicial scrutiny applied when the interest is infringed on a discriminatory basis must be adjusted accordingly.

The Court did not adopt Marshall's approach, but, as explained in the next section, a majority eventually did agree that the traditional two-tiered approach was inadequate.

Intermediate/Heightened Scrutiny

While the Court adopted strict scrutiny for determining whether classifications based on race and alienage violate equal protection, the justices rejected its use for gender-based classifications. In 1971, by a 7–0 vote, the Court for the first time declared a gender classification to violate the Equal Protection Clause (*Reed v. Reed*), but minimal scrutiny was used to decide the case. The case concerned an Idaho law that stipulated that in appointing administrators of estates, courts were to prefer males over equally qualified females. The state maintained that the purpose of the law was reduce the probate courts' workloads by reducing the number of competitive hearings in estate matters. Using the rational basis test, Chief Justice Warren E. Burger found this argument unsatisfactory, concluding that the policy was precisely the "kind of arbitrary legislative choice forbidden by the Equal Protection Clause."

Three years later, in *Frontiero v. Richardson* (1973), while a majority struck down the policy being challenged, only a plurality of justices agreed that gender is a suspect classification requiring the highest level of review. The case concerned a federal policy that permitted married male members of the Air Force to receive housing benefits without proving the dependency of their wives but that required similarly situated females to prove that their husbands depended on them for more than one-half of their support. The plurality argued that gender, like race, met the criteria for suspect classification: (1) Women were subject to a long history of purposeful discrimination; (2) Sex is an immutable characteristic of birth; and 3) Women lacked the ability to bring about change through the political arena. In his opinion concurring only in the judgment, Justice Powell argued that the *Reed* precedent was sufficient for deciding the case and that it was unnecessary to include gender as a suspect classification because passage of the Equal Rights Amendment, which was in the ratification process at the time, would resolve the issue. The ERA fell three states short of the three-quarters necessary for ratification by the seven-year deadline specified in the amendment. And although Congress extended the deadline for an additional three years, the ERA lacked sufficient support and was eventually defeated.

While refusing to place gender in the suspect category, the Court also determined that minimal scrutiny was insufficient for examining gender-based classifications. Consequently, in 1976, the justices introduced a midlevel standard: intermediate or heightened scrutiny (*Craig v. Boren*). The intermediate scrutiny standard was initially proposed to the Court by Ruth Bader Ginsburg, then director of the ACLU's Women's Rights Project, in her brief in a 1975 case, *Weinberger v. Weisenfeld*. Earlier in *Frontiero*, she had tried to persuade the Court to adopt strict scrutiny, but after failing in that attempt, she subsequently advised the attorney representing the individuals in *Craig* to push for adoption of intermediate scrutiny and to downplay strict scrutiny.

The issue in *Craig* was an Oklahoma law that permitted 18-year-old females to purchase beer containing 3.2 percent alcohol but prohibited males from doing so until age 21. After announcing that the important government objective test/intermediate scrutiny was the appropriate standard of review, Justice William Brennan accepted the promotion of traffic safety as an important government objective but held that the gender classification was not substantially related to it. He said that statistics regarding drinking and driving among teenagers, including arrests and traffic accidents, were insufficient and that the goal of traffic safety was undermined by the classification because the law prohibited only the sale, not the consumption, of 3.2 beer to males. Consequently, an underage male could drink and drive after his female companion purchased the beverage for him. In separate dissents, Chief Justice Burger and Justice William H. Rehnquist maintained that the rational basis test/minimal scrutiny should have

been used to decide the case, and they would have upheld the classification.

Since its adoption in 1976, intermediate scrutiny has been used both to invalidate and to uphold gender-based classifications. The Court has used this standard to strike down laws that made husbands but not wives liable for alimony payments (*Orr v. Orr*, 1979), gave husbands the right to dispose of property jointly owned with their wives without obtaining the wives' consent (*Kirchberg v. Feenstra*, 1981), and excluded men from enrolling in a state-supported professional nursing school (*Mississippi University for Women v. Hogan*, 1982). By contrast, intermediate scrutiny was used to sustain a provision of the Social Security Act that permitted women to exclude more low-earning years from the calculation of their retirement benefits than men were allowed to do (*Califano v. Webster*, 1977), uphold statutory rape laws that punished males for having sex with females under a specified age but excluded females from punishment (*Michael M. v. Sonoma County*, 1981), and affirm a federal policy excluding females from registering for the draft (*Rostker v. Goldberg*, 1981).

Following Justice Ginsburg's appointment to the high court in 1993, some Court observers speculated that she might try to persuade her colleagues to revisit the issue of extending strict scrutiny to gender-based classifications. Her brief concurrence in a case involving sexual harassment under Title VII of the Civil Rights Act fueled such speculation. In a footnote to that opinion Ginsburg wrote that "under the Court's equal protection jurisprudence, which requires 'an exceedingly persuasive justification' for gender-based classifications, it remains an open question whether 'classifications based upon gender are inherently suspect'" (*Harris v. Forklift Systems*, 1993).

Three years later, Ginsburg wrote the majority opinion in *United States v. Virginia* (1996), a landmark case concerning the exclusion of women from Virginia Military Institute (VMI). The Court's ruling contained two findings: (1) the male-only admission policy violated the Equal Protection Clause, and (2) the creation of a parallel program for women at Mary Baldwin College, a private liberal arts school for women, did not remedy the violation. Ginsburg held that the admission policy was not substantially related to the achievement of an important government objective and thereby failed the important government objective test. "A purpose genuinely to advance an array of educational options … is not served by VMI's historic and constant plan—a plan to 'affor[d] a unique educational benefit only to males.' However 'liberally' this plan serves the Commonwealth's sons, it makes no provision whatever for her daughters." In applying intermediate/heightened scrutiny, Ginsburg used the phrases "skeptical scrutiny" and "exceedingly persuasive justification," and Justice Antonin Scalia took issue with her analysis in his lone dissent. Scalia said that the majority opinion incorrectly applied intermediate scrutiny and redefined it in a way that "makes it indistinguishable from strict scrutiny." In an opinion concurring only in the judgment, Chief Justice Rehnquist also was troubled by the phrase "exceedingly persuasive justification" and suggested that the majority was introducing confusion to the important government objective test.

As stated earlier, intermediate scrutiny also is used in reviewing some policies that discriminate against aliens. In *Plyler v. Doe* (1982), a sharply divided Court invalidated a Texas law that withheld from school districts funds for educating the children of illegal aliens and that authorized school districts to deny a free public education to those children. The state claimed three main interests for the statute: preventing an influx of illegal immigrants, improving the overall quality of education, and ensuring that those the state educates make a productive use of their education within the state. The majority found none of these objectives to be substantial. The dissenters, however, argued for the use of minimal scrutiny and concluded that in allocating its resources, the state has a reasonable interest in making distinctions between "persons who are lawfully within the state and those who are unlawfully there."

Heightened scrutiny also has been applied to classifications based on illegitimacy. Initially, however, it

was not clear what standard would be used in cases concerning discrimination against illegitimate children. For example, when the Court struck down a law permitting only legitimate children to recover damages for the wrongful death of their mother, it was unclear whether the majority used minimal or strict scrutiny (*Levy v. Louisiana*, 1968). After conceding that the state has broad power in making classifications, Justice Douglas said that "it may not draw a line which constitutes an invidious discrimination against a particular class." This seems to entail the use of strict scrutiny. In the next sentence, however, Douglas continued, "Though the test has been variously stated, the end result is whether the line drawn is a rational one." In a 1971 case, minimal scrutiny was used to uphold a state law restricting the inheritance rights of illegitimate children (*Labine v. Vincent*). Two cases in 1976 and 1977 suggested that while illegitimacy classifications would not be reviewed under strict scrutiny, minimal scrutiny was not sufficient (*Matthews v. Lucas* and *Trimble v. Gordon*, respectively). "Despite the conclusion that classifications based on illegitimacy fall in a 'realm of less than strictest scrutiny,' *Lucas* … establishes that the scrutiny 'is not a toothless one'" (*Trimble*). Over a decade later, the Court reaffirmed this principle in *Clark v. Jeter* (1988). In this case, the Court invalidated a Pennsylvania statute of limitations for undertaking paternity actions. Under the law, actions to establish paternity of an illegitimate child ordinarily must be commenced within six years of the child's birth. Although the state had an important objective in preventing fraudulent claims, the Court said the law was not substantially related to this objective because Pennsylvania had permitted claims in some circumstances to be litigated more than six years after the birth of an illegitimate child.

Conclusion

Since 1976, the high court has utilized this three-tiered approach to examine policies challenged under the Equal Protection Clause. It remains to be seen whether Justice Ginsburg's use of the terms "skeptical scrutiny" and "exceedingly persuasive justification" in *United States v. Virginia* portends a shift from intermediate to strict scrutiny for reviewing gender discrimination claims. Also, despite the fact that the justices were able to use minimal scrutiny to invalidate Colorado's law that discriminated against same-sex partners, some civil rights activists continue to hope that the Court will eventually adopt a higher level of scrutiny for such claims. At this point, however, the Court appears committed to its current approach and has generally been unwilling to extend its highest level of scrutiny to classifications beyond those involving race or fundamental rights.

See also Abortion, Right to; Affirmative Action; Age Discrimination; American Civil Liberties Union; Black, Hugo L.; *Brown v. Board of Education;* Burger, Warren E.; Busing Controversy; Civil Rights Movement; Disabilities, Rights of Persons with; Discrimination; Diversity; Douglas, William O.; Equality; Equal Protection Clause; Equal Rights Amendment; Fourteenth Amendment; *Frontiero v. Richardson;* Fundamental Rights; Gay Rights Movement; Gender-Based Discrimination; Ginsburg, Ruth Bader; Group Rights; Immigrants and Aliens, Rights of; Interracial Marriage; Jim Crow Laws; Kennedy, Anthony; *Korematsu v. United States;* Little Rock Crisis; *Loving v. Virginia;* Marshall, Thurgood; O'Connor, Sandra Day; *Plessy v. Ferguson;* Powell, Lewis F., Jr.; Public Education, Right to; Rational Basis Test; Rehnquist, William H.; *Reynolds v. Sims; Romer v. Evans;* Same-Sex Marriage and Civil Unions; Scalia, Antonin; Segregation, De Facto and De Jure; Sexual Orientation, Discrimination Based on; Stevens, John Paul; Stone, Harlan Fiske; Strict Scrutiny; *United States v. Carolene Products; United States v. Virginia;* Warren, Earl; White, Byron R.

Bibliography

Baer, Judith. 1983. *Equality under the Constitution: Reclaiming the Fourteenth Amendment.* Ithaca, NY: Cornell University Press.

Goldstein, Leslie F. 1988. *The Constitutional Rights of Women: Cases in Law and Social Change.* 2nd ed. Madison: University of Wisconsin Press.

Hensley, Thomas R., Christopher E. Smith, and Joyce A. Baugh. 1997. *The Changing Supreme Court: Constitutional Rights and Liberties.* St. Paul, MN: West/Wadsworth.

Schwartz, Bernard, ed. 1970. *The Fourteenth Amendment.* New York: New York University Press.

Joyce Baugh

EQUAL RIGHTS AMENDMENT (ERA)

On the heels of a victorious suffrage movement, women in the United States turned their attention to a new cause: an equal rights amendment to the Constitution. Women who had been involved in the battle for suffrage were aware that a voting rights amendment alone would not guarantee equal rights under the law. Alice Paul proposed an equal rights amendment at the 1923 National Woman's Party Convention; it was subsequently introduced in Congress by Representative Daniel Anthony, nephew of Susan B. Anthony, later that year. The proposed amendment read: "Men and women shall have equal rights throughout the United States and every place subject to its jurisdiction." Not all the women's groups involved in the quest for suffrage were in favor of such an amendment. In fact, it deeply divided many of the groups that had worked together for voting rights. Some feared that the amendment would nullify several state minimum-wage provisions applicable to female workers. Ultimately, this fear proved to be unfounded, since the amendment was not even taken seriously until after World War II. In 1950 and again in 1953, an equal rights amendment was passed by the United States Senate; however, both times it was amended to include language that would negate any meaningful impact of the provisions (Hillyard 1996). While an equal rights amendment had been introduced in every session of Congress since 1923, it was not until the late 1960s that a new wave of feminism sparked widespread interest in passing the amendment.

This wave of feminism arose out of changes in attitudes toward women's rights. Women were inspired by the Civil Rights Movement to reevaluate their status in life. They were also influenced by Betty Friedan's book *The Feminine Mystique,* which documented the emptiness experienced by American women who had remained at home to raise children. These societal and cultural changes helped lead to the formation of the National Organization for Women (NOW), which played a major role in lobbying for the Equal Rights Amendment (ERA). The key provisions of the proposed amendment declared that "Equality of rights under the law shall not be denied or abridged by the United States or by any State on account of sex."

The House of Representatives passed the ERA by a margin of 354–24 on October 12, 1971. On March 22, 1972, the Senate approved the amendment by a vote of 84–8 and established a March 22, 1979, deadline for ratification. Within hours of the Senate vote, Hawaii ratified the amendment, and in the following three months 19 other states followed suit. By 1977, 35 states had approved the amendment (Hillyard 1996). The momentum for ratification was thwarted by an anti-ERA organization, STOP ERA, headed by conservative activist Phyllis Schafly. STOP was an acronym for Stop Taking Our Privileges. The organization's primary argument was that passage of the ERA would deny women the privileges they enjoyed under state and federal law. Schafly suggested that the ERA would be detrimental to women by forcing them into combat, allowing for government-funded abortions, requiring both private schools (including military academies) and sports to become coeducational, legalizing gay marriage and the adoption of children by homosexuals, and eliminating the segregation of public restrooms on the basis of sex (McGlen et al. 2002).

While the Schafly organization was instrumental in mobilizing opposition at the grassroots level, ERA proponents focused on a national strategy touting the amendment's benefits. The most important argument for passage of the ERA was equal pay for equal work. Although the amendment likely would have done little to eliminate the wage gap, it was an important issue for supporters (Mansbridge 1986). Supporters also argued that it would allow for medically necessary abortions if states provided medically necessary health-care services for men.

And because many proponents were advocates of full equality, they argued that women could be drafted and serve in combat roles alongside their male counterparts (Mansbridge 1986). Even though this argument did little to engender additional support, it was important because it emphasized that women were not seeking special treatment but rather equal treatment under the law.

On October 6, 1978, both houses of Congress voted to extend the time period for ratification until June 30, 1982. Despite this extension, the amendment failed to achieve the approval of the 38 states needed for ratification. This defeat did not mean, however, that women's rights were not protected under the law. In *Reed v. Reed* (1971) the United States Supreme Court held that the Fourteenth Amendment's Equal Protection Clause prohibited sex discrimination. In 1973 however, a majority of the Court declined to apply the same standard of review used for racial discrimination cases in sex discrimination suits partly because the ERA was pending (see *Frontiero v. Richardson,* 1973). Since *Craig v. Boren* (1976), the Court has applied intermediate scrutiny to instances of sex discrimination, which requires that classifications based on gender must serve important government objectives and must be substantially related to the achievement of those objectives. While this is a lower standard than the strict scrutiny standard used in racial discrimination suits, the Court has invalidated a number of discriminatory practices based on intermediate scrutiny.

The failure of the ERA at the federal level did not preclude states from amending their respective constitutions to guarantee equality on the basis of sex. While Wyoming and Utah had these guarantees as part of their state constitutions when they were adopted in the late 1800s, 15 states were sufficiently inspired by the federal debate to amend their own constitutions to include "little" ERAs (Hillyard 1996).

Although the ERA was not ratified, it was significant in that it drew attention to discriminatory laws. The specific impact of the ERA on women's rights is unknown. However, the Court's interpretation of the

Equal Protection Clause has eliminated many vestiges of the male-dominated society early feminists were fighting against. Although much has changed regarding legal equality for women, ERA supporters have reintroduced the amendment in every session of Congress since its failure.

See also Anthony, Susan B.; Civil Rights Movement; Discrimination; Equality; Equal Protection Clause; Equal Protection Jurisprudence; Feminist Movement; Fourteenth Amendment; *Frontiero v. Richardson;* Gender-Based Discrimination; Women's Suffrage

Bibliography

Hillyard, Carrie. 1996. "The History of Suffrage and Equal Rights Provisions in State Constitutions." *BYU Journal of Public Law* 10 (1): 117–38.

Mansbridge, Jane J. 1986. *Why We Lost the ERA*. Chicago: University of Chicago Press.

McGlen, Nancy, Karen O'Connor, Laura van Assendelft, and Wendy Gunther-Canada. 2002. *Women, Politics, and American Society*. 3rd ed. New York: Pearson.

Kara E. Stooksbury

EQUITY

The term "equity" comes from the Latin *aequitas,* which means justice or equality. The idea of equity as a supplement to law can be traced to the Roman law and ultimately to Aristotle. The idea is that when existing legal rules and procedures are insufficient to remedy injustice, a court should rely on general principles of fairness in granting relief.

From early English law down through the century following the Norman Conquest in 1066, law was handed down by oral tradition and administered in "people's courts." These were bodies of local men lacking in any legal training. Relief afforded was often informal. In its formative period, the English common law developed with trained judges who were appointed by the king and traveled about the country with the objective of providing law common to the country. By the thirteenth century this common law developed the writ system and by the fourteenth century had become highly technical

and rigid. The common law focused on remedies for recovery of land and left money damages as the only remedy in personal actions. Moreover, technical rules of procedure and proof required litigants to secure the services of barristers. As a consequence litigation was expensive and did not afford specific remedies.

Aggrieved parties who were unable to secure a remedy at common law would appeal to the king directly for justice. The king often delegated such matters to his chancellor, who was also a cleric and a member of the king's court and was often referred to as the "keeper of the King's conscience." Eventually this practice of referring disputes to the chancellor evolved into a secular tribunal called the Court of Chancery, which developed its own system of jurisprudence called equity.

The Court of Chancery did not follow the writ system, nor did it utilize juries—chancellors made their own factual determinations and fashioned equitable remedies. The Court of Chancery did not follow the common law or the doctrine of stare decisis (precedent); instead chancellors eventually came to rely on maxims derived from previous equitable decisions, for example, "He who seeks equity must do equity; He who comes into equity must do so with clean hands."

Perhaps the chief distinction between the common law and equity was that common-law courts were limited to awarding damages to plaintiffs who prevailed in most civil actions, while the Court of Chancery could issue an injunction to prevent or terminate injurious conduct and order specific performance in cases of breach of contract. This became especially important as commerce, and later the Industrial Revolution, began to develop.

Eventually, common law and equity would be merged, both in England and the United States, at least in the sense that law and equity jurisdiction would be vested in the same courts. Notably, Article III, Section 2, of the U.S. Constitution extends the judicial power "to all Cases, in Law and Equity, arising under this Constitution, the Laws of the United States, and Treaties made, or which shall be made, under their Authority."

Many of the procedures followed and remedies afforded by American courts today originated in equity. Modern examples include injunctive relief against trespass and nuisance; protection of patents, copyrights, trademarks, and trade secrets; and enforcement of easements and deed restrictions.

See also Aristotle; Common-Law Background of American Civil Rights and Liberties; Equality; Precedent, Doctrine of

Bibliography

Scheb, John M., and John M. Scheb II. 2002. *An Introduction to the American Legal System.* Albany, NY: Delmar.

Hon. John M. Scheb and John M. Scheb II

ERA. *See* Equal Rights Amendment

ESPIONAGE ACT OF 1917

As America's intervention into World War I loomed, many in the United States were concerned about the internal threat of subversion by radical forces from within. Organizations such as the Socialist Party were gaining support within industrial labor unions, and some of the more radical labor leaders openly opposed entering the war. They claimed the capitalist elites were starting the war, but the working class would be asked to fight and die. On April 6, 1917, the United States Congress declared war against Germany, and six weeks later on May 18, the Congress passed the Selective Service Act in order to raise an army to fight the war. Many within the radical labor organizations declared the Selective Service Act unconstitutional and encouraged young men to violate the law. The Supreme Court quickly upheld the constitutionality of the act.

Against this backdrop, on June 15, 1917, the United States Congress passed the Espionage Act of 1917. The act provided the government with broad authority to restrict civil liberties during time of war. Its aim was to prevent all forms of sabotage and the communicating of military secrets to the enemy. Another provision of the act empowered the

postmaster general to remove from the mail all letters, circulars, newspapers, books, pamphlets, and other materials that violated the act. The Justice Department suggested to Congress that the act be strengthened to prohibit even informal expressions of disloyalty. On May 16, 1918, the Congress amended the act by adding what is referred to as the Sedition Act. Under this amendment it became a crime to criticize the sale of war bonds, to question the constitutionality of the draft, or even to express that the war was contrary to the teachings of Christ. Following the lead of Congress, many states passed similar laws, and by 1925 approximately two-thirds of the states had their own criminal syndicalism statutes on the books.

The act was immediately challenged in the courts; however, none of the cases reached the Supreme Court until after World War I was over. In virtually every case the argument was that the Espionage Act violated the First Amendment right of freedom of expression. In every case the Supreme Court rejected the claim and upheld the law. The armistice ending World War I was signed on November 11, 1918, and the first Espionage Act case was argued before the Supreme Court in January 1919. The Court's first decision in an Espionage Act case was *Schenck v. United States* (1919), where it rejected in a nine-to-zero vote the claim that enforcement of the Espionage Act had violated Charles Schenck's First Amendment rights. Schenck, the general secretary of the American Socialist Party, was charged under the act for conspiring to obstruct recruiting for the draft and for causing insubordination within the armed forces. Schenck had distributed leaflets opposing both the war and the draft. Copies of the leaflets had been sent through the mail to young men who had recently been drafted.

The *Schenck* case was the first time Justice Oliver Wendell Holmes defined the clear and present danger test, which established the level of governmental limitation of free speech that the courts would accept when considering First Amendment rights. This standard would later replace the bad tendency test that American courts had carried over from the English common law.

The Espionage Act was vigorously enforced, and during the period between 1917 and 1921 over 2,000 people were prosecuted under the federal statute, from which the government obtained 1,050 convictions. Many other prosecutions occurred under the various state laws. The Sedition Act, the amendments to the act, was repealed in 1921. The Espionage Act itself remains on the books to this day and can be enforced in time of war.

See also Clear and Present Danger Doctrine; Common-Law Background of American Civil Rights and Liberties; Communist Party USA; Criminal Syndicalism; First Amendment; Holmes, Oliver Wendell, Jr.; Speech, Freedom of; U.S. Department of Justice; Wartime, Civil Rights and Liberties during

Bibliography

Bollinger, Lee C., and Geoffrey R. Stone, ed. 2002. *Eternally Vigilant: Free Speech in the Modern Era.* Chicago: University of Chicago Press.

Haiman, Franklyn S. 1977. *Speech and Law in a Free Society.* Chicago: University of Chicago Press.

Schweber, Howard. 2003. *Speech, Conduct, and the First Amendment.* New York: Peter Lang.

Tedford, Thomas L. 1985. *Freedom of Speech in the United States.* New York: Random House.

Michael Haynes

ESTABLISHMENT CLAUSE

The Establishment Clause of the First Amendment states that "Congress shall make no law respecting an establishment of religion." Although this language seems clear and concise, the United States Supreme Court has experienced great difficulty in interpreting this important constitutional command as it applies to such controversial topics as prayer in public schools, government assistance to religious schools, and religious displays on public property.

Since its first major Establishment Clause decision in *Everson v. Board of Education* in 1947, the justices of the Supreme Court have utilized three conflicting interpretations of the Establishment Clause. These are the accommodation approach, the neutrality approach, and the strict separation approach. None of these approaches has been embraced consistently by a majority of the justices, however, and this failure to agree on guiding principles to interpret the Establishment Clause has resulted in confusion and conflict in the Court's opinions. Before tracing the historical development of the Court's Establishment Clause jurisprudence, it is necessary to discuss briefly these three competing approaches of accommodation, neutrality, and strict separation.

The strict separation approach calls for a "high and impregnable wall of separation" between church and state. Strict separationists frequently cite the writings of Madison and Jefferson for support, and they express grave concern over the many dangers, such as civil strife, that can result from church-state involvement.

In sharp contrast, accommodationists argue that the Establishment Clause permits substantial involvement between church and state. Accommodationists claim that their approach is most consistent with the views of those who authored the First Amendment as well as with the original understanding of the clause. In addition, accommodationists emphasize the lack of danger in church-state interactions, and they argue that the United States has always recognized the importance and centrality of religion for both private and public matters.

The neutrality approach occupies a middle position between strict separation and accommodation. Neutralists tend to view both alternative approaches as too extreme, and they argue that the Establishment Clause simply requires the government to be neutral regarding religion, neither promoting nor inhibiting religion.

The Supreme Court did not decide a major Establishment Clause case until *Everson v. Board of Education* in 1947, and all three approaches to interpreting the Establishment Clause were given recognition. *Everson* involved a claimed violation of the Establishment Clause because a school district was reimbursing parents for the costs of sending their children to parochial school on public buses. The justices of the Vinson Court (1946–1953) made two important decisions in this case. First, they nationalized or incorporated the Establishment Clause, thus making it applicable to state and local governments. Second, they found no constitutional violation with the bus system under challenge.

Justice Hugo Black wrote the five-to-four majority opinion, in which he referenced all three major approaches. He asserted strongly the strict separation view: "The First Amendment has erected a wall between church and state. That wall must be kept high and impregnable. We could not approve the slightest breach." The dissenters argued that despite this strict separationist language, the Court majority reached an accommodationist result by ruling constitutional this busing system, which provided state support for religious schools. The neutrality approach was also emphasized in *Everson* with Black arguing that the Establishment Clause only requires "the states to be neutral in its relations with groups of religious believers and non-believers; it does not require the state to be their adversary."

The ambiguous interpretation of the Establishment Clause by the Vinson Court can also be seen in the closely related Vinson Court cases of *McCollum v. Board of Education (*1948) and *Zorach v. Clauson* (1952). Both cases involved "released time" programs in which public school children were released from their regular activities to receive religious training. Black authored the majority opinion in the eight-to-one decision in *McCollum,* an Illinois case, using strong separationist language and using again the "high and impregnable wall" metaphor. But four years later in *Zorach,* Justice William O. Douglas, for a six-person majority, ruled that a released time program in New York City did not violate the Establishment Clause. Douglas argued that the New York program was constitutional because the children were given religious instruction away from the schools rather than being given within the schools in the Illinois program. In reaching this decision, Douglas and five other justices used

strong accommodationist language: "[W]e are a religious people whose institutions presuppose a Supreme Being. When the State encourages religious instruction or cooperates with religious authorities … it follows the best of our traditions. For it then respects the religious nature of our people and accommodates the public service to their spiritual needs."

The Warren Court (1953–1968) was thus faced with an ambiguous jurisprudential legacy regarding the Establishment Clause in which all three completing interpretations had been recognized and supported. The Warren Court heard relatively few Establishment Clause cases (six), and, not surprisingly, they utilized all three approaches.

In their first major school prayer case—*Engel v. Vitale* (1962)—Justice Black, writing for the majority in this six-to-one decision, utilized strong strict separation language in finding unconstitutional an optional nondenominational prayer in the state of New York. Although public outcry to *Engel* was intense, the Warren Court continued its opposition to state-sponsored religious activities in the public schools. But in ruling eight-to-one against Pennsylvania's law requiring daily Bible readings in the public schools, in *Abington School District v. Schempp* (1963) the Court avoided the harsh, strict separationist language of *Engel* and instead employed softer, neutralist language while still finding the program unconstitutional.

Very importantly in *Schempp,* Justice Clark for the majority set forth two requirements for analyzing the Establishment Clause. First, any government activity involving religion must have a "secular legislative purpose." Second, the government must show that the activity has a "primary effect that neither advances nor inhibits religion."

The Warren Court also handed down a decision in *Board of Education v. Allen* (1968) that accommodated a New York City program that loaned secular textbooks free of charge to all students, public and parochial alike. Ruling six-to-three that the program did not violate the Establishment Clause, the Court used the two-pronged test from *Schempp* in finding that the purpose of the program was secular and that the primary effect was neither to advance nor to inhibit religion.

Thus, despite hearing few Establishment Clause cases, the Warren Court moved away from strict separation to neutrality as the proper approach. Furthermore, a two-part test had emerged to analyze Establishment Clause cases.

Unlike the Warren Court, the Burger Court gave a great deal of attention to Establishment Clause cases, ruling in 26 decisions compared to only six for the Warren Court. During the 1970s the Burger Court expanded the two-part *Schempp* test into a three-part *Lemon* test that supported the neutrality approach to the Establishment Clause. The *Lemon* test was not popular with the accommodationists on the Burger Court, however, and in the early 1980s the accommodationists gained control of the Court. By the end of the Burger Court era in the mid-1980s, however, the neutralists managed to regain control over interpretations of the Establishment Clause.

The first major Establishment Clause case for the Burger Court was *Lemon v. Kurtzman* (1971). An eight-to-zero Court ruled unconstitutional a Pennsylvania law that provided a variety of forms of financial aid to parochial schools, including teachers' salaries. In his majority opinion for the Court, Chief Justice Burger added a third prong to the two-part *Schempp* test, thereby creating the three-prong *Lemon* test. In order to be declared constitutional under the Establishment Clause, a government activity being challenged must. (1) have a secular purpose, (2) have a primary effect that neither advances nor inhibits religion, and (3) avoid excessive government entanglement with religion.

During the 1970s the Burger Court used the *Lemon* test and the neutrality approach to strike down a variety of government programs, especially parochial aid. *Meek v. Pittenger* (1975) and *Wolman v. Walter* (1977) provide good examples. *Meek* involved Pennsylvania parochial aid programs that provided textbooks, instructional materials, and auxiliary services and speech therapy to parochial students. A six-person majority found the programs to be unconstitutional under the second and third prongs

of the *Lemon* test. The Burger Court similarly ruled unconstitutional various Ohio parochial aid programs in *Wolman v. Walter* in 1977.

Chief Justice Burger, who supported the accommodationist approach, became increasingly opposed to the Court's direction in Establishment Clause cases, and he was able, with the addition of Sandra Day O'Connor to the Court, to rework Establishment Clause jurisprudence in a series of decisions in the eighties. In *Mueller v. Allen* (1983) the Court approved of tax breaks to the parents of parochial students; in *Marsh v. Chambers* (1983) the justices found no constitutional violation in the practice of prayer by a minister to begin Nebraska's legislative sessions; and in the 1984 case of *Lynch v. Donnelly*, the Burger Court ruled in favor of a local government that sponsored a Christmas display that included a nativity scene. From a doctrinal perspective, the most important results of these three cases involved the strong assertion of the accommodation approach to the Establishment Clause and the minimizing or outright rejection of the *Lemon* test.

Quite surprisingly, however, in three major 1985 cases the Burger Court returned to the neutrality approach and the *Lemon* test. The lead case was *Wallace v. Jaffree* (1985), in which a six-to-three Court ruled unconstitutional an Alabama law that allowed silent prayer at the beginning of each school day. Justice Stevens wrote the majority opinion. He gave no attention to the recent accommodationist decisions of *Mueller, Marsh,* and *Lynch.* Instead, he simply asserted "the established principle that government must pursue a course of complete neutrality toward religion." He also stated that Establishment Clause cases must begin with the three-part *Lemon* test. In this case, Stevens concluded, the Alabama law failed the first prong because the law did not have a secular purpose.

Two additional 1985 Establishment Clause cases were *Grand Rapids v. Ball* and *Aguilar v. Felton.* The cases involved the constitutionality of parochial programs in Michigan and New York. In the Grand Rapids, Michigan, case, the challenged program involved remedial programs of a secular nature taught by public school teachers in parochial classrooms. The *Aguilar* case was similar, involving a New York City program in which public school teachers were paid to teach remedial programs to disadvantaged children in parochial schools. A major difference between the programs was that the teachers were not monitored for religious activities in Michigan, but they were monitored in New York.

Justice Brennan wrote the majority opinion—joined by Justices Marshall, Blackmun, Stevens, and Powell—emphasizing the neutrality approach and the *Lemon* test. Regarding neutrality, Brennan argued that the Establishment Clause requires "the government to maintain a course of neutrality among religions and between religion and nonreligion. "As to the *Lemon* test, Brennan asserted: "We have particularly relied on *Lemon* in every case involving the sensitive relationship between government and religion in the education of our children."

Brennan used the *Lemon* test to find both programs unconstitutional. In the Michigan case, the program violated the Establishment Clause because the teachers were *not* monitored, thus creating the possibility that the effect of the program could be to advance religion, violating the second prong of the *Lemon* test. The New York program was unconstitutional because the teachers *were* monitored, violating the third prong of the *Lemon* test prohibiting excessive entanglement of church and state. This decision had the effect of making it necessary to hold these classes in mobile units that had no religious symbols in them, and this issue would be reconsidered by the Rehnquist Court.

The Rehnquist Court thus inherited a highly ambiguous jurisprudence from past Supreme Court eras. Unfortunately, interpretation of the Establishment Clause has become even more confused and confusing during the Rehnquist Court era. Neutrality has been the dominant approach to the Establishment Clause during this period, but the liberal justices tend to interpret neutrality from a separationist perspective, while the more conservative justices view neutrality from an accom-

modationist perspective. The *Lemon* test has been used in a seemingly random fashion; few members of the Court seem happy with it, but no alternative test has emerged.

The Rehnquist Court's initial major Establishment Clause case suggested that neutrality and the *Lemon* test would guide Establishment Clause analysis. *Edwards v. Aguillard* (1987) involved Louisiana's Creationism Act, which forbade the teaching of evolution in the public schools unless "creation science," teachings based upon the biblical story of creation, was also taught. The Court ruled this unconstitutional by a seven-to-two majority, using both neutrality and the *Lemon* test, finding that the law violated the first prong of *Lemon* because it had a religious purpose.

Changes in the Court's membership in the next few years created the possibility of a dramatic shift away from neutrality and *Lemon*. One change involved Kennedy's 1988 replacement of Powell. Even more significantly, the Court's two leading liberals, Brennan and Marshall, retired in 1990 and 1991 and were replaced by Souter and Thomas, respectively. The Court's new alignment thus had as many as seven justices who might reject *Lemon* and the neutrality approach, including Rehnquist, Scalia, Thomas, O'Connor, Kennedy, White, and Souter.

The first major case to confront the new group of justices was *Lee v. Weisman* in 1992. This case challenged the common practice of prayer at public school graduation exercises. The Bush administration thought the moment was ripe to change the guiding principles for analyzing the Establishment Clause, filing an amicus brief that asked the Court to overturn *Lemon* and rule the practice constitutional. Surprisingly, however, a five-person majority of Kennedy, O'Connor, Stevens, Blackmun, and Souter ruled the practice unconstitutional. Kennedy wrote the majority opinion, in which he rejected the call to overturn *Lemon*, which he said could be considered in a future case. Instead, Kennedy argued that the concept of coercion was the key to this case, just as it was in the key school prayer precedents of *Engel* and *Schempp*. The future of *Lemon* and the neutrality approach were thus left in limbo by the *Lee* decision, and subsequent Establishment Clause cases did little to resolve this uncertain status of Establishment Clause jurisprudence.

In the Court's next major Establishment Clause case, *Agostini v. Felton* (1997), the Court ruled five-to-four to overturn the Burger Court's 1985 decision in *Aguilar v. Felton*. This new decision approved the practice of allowing public school teachers to teach in parochial schools without monitoring under Title I of the 1965 Elementary and Secondary Act, which provided remedial education for disadvantaged students. O'Connor's majority opinion, joined by Rehnquist, Scalia, Thomas and Kennedy, did not break new doctrinal grounds, however, because she adhered closely to the neutrality principle and the *Lemon* test.

The Rehnquist Court modified additional Burger Court decisions in the 2000 case of *Mitchell v. Helms*. This case involved a federal parochial aid program that provided both public and private schools with a variety of secular educational equipment and materials, including computer hardware and software. In reaching its decision in *Mitchell*, the Rehnquist Court modified the Burger Court precedents of *Meek v. Pittinger* (1975) and *Wolman v. Walter* (1977). Thomas wrote a plurality opinion that was joined by Rehnquist, Scalia, and Kennedy and set forth highly accommodationist principles for interpreting the Establishment Clause, arguing that a parochial aid program is constitutional as long as it is offered on a neutral basis and is secular in nature. O'Connor and Breyer agreed that the program was constitutional, but they disagreed with Thomas's statement of Establishment Clause principles. Writing a strong dissent, Souter was joined by Ginsburg and Stevens in rejecting Thomas's plurality opinion, arguing that "the plurality would break with the law" and that "there is no mistaking the abandonment of doctrine that would occur if the plurality were to become a majority."

An additional 2000 Establishment Clause case (*Santa Fe v. Doe*) produced a triumph for the liberal justices, with a six-to-three majority finding that public prayers before Friday night high school football games violate the Establishment Clause. Justice Stevens wrote the majority opinion, joined by Souter, Ginsburg, Breyer, Kennedy, and O'Connor. Citing the Court's long line of decisions opposing state-sponsored religious activities in the public schools, Stevens used both the coercion test and the first prong of the *Lemon* test in finding the practice to be unconstitutional.

The *Lemon* test was utilized again in the 2003 case of *Zelman v. Simmons-Harris*, but in this case it was the conservative justices who employed the test. The case involved the constitutionality of Cleveland's voucher program, which provided tuition payments for children attending parochial schools. The Court found the program to be constitutional in a five-to-four majority opinion written by Chief Justice Rehnquist and joined by Scalia, Thomas, Kennedy, and O'Connor. Rehnquist utilized the first two prongs of the *Lemon* test, arguing that the program had a secular purpose and that the primary effect of the program was neutral, neither advancing nor inhibiting religion. In a concurrence, O'Connor argued quite correctly that the Court's approach was similar to the test set forth by the Warren Court in the 1963 *Schempp* case. Souter wrote a stinging dissent joined by Stevens, Ginsburg, and Breyer. The liberals accused the conservative majority of reaching "doctrinal bankruptcy" and ignoring the clear meaning of the principle of neutrality.

The Rehnquist Court's most recent Establishment Clause cases involved the display of the Ten Commandments on public property. *Van Orden v. Perry* (2005) involved a challenge to the placement of a six-foot-high monolith containing the Ten Commandments on the grounds of the Texas state capitol. In *McCreary County v. ACLU* (2005), the posting of the Ten Commandments in public courthouses was challenged as a violation of the Establishment Clause. The Rehnquist Court found the display of the Ten Commandments on the state capitol grounds to be constitutional but ruled unconstitutional the posting of the Ten Commandments in courthouses. The Court not only reached opposite conclusions in these cases but also set forth in the controlling opinions diametrically opposed ideas regarding the proper interpretation of the Establishment Clause, thus muddying the waters even more.

In the *McCreary County* case, Souter's majority opinion, joined by Stevens, O'Connor, Breyer, and Ginsburg, utilized the *Lemon* test and the neutrality approach to find unconstitutional the display of the Ten Commandments in public courthouses. Souter's opinion argued that the county's activities violated the first prong of the *Lemon* test because the purpose of the display was religious in nature. Souter also stressed that neutrality is the key principle in Establishment Clause analysis: "The importance of neutrality as an interpretive guide is no less true now than it was when the Court broached the principle in *Everson* (1947)." Scalia authored a dissenting opinion that was joined in its entirety by Rehnquist and Thomas and in part by Kennedy. Scalia made three major arguments. First, he rejected the neutrality argument of the majority, arguing that the United States has a long and continuous history of government accommodation of religion. Kennedy did not join this part of Scalia's dissent, but he did join the rest of Scalia's opinion. Scalia's second argument was that the majority used *Lemon* in a manner that both modified the test and increased the Court's hostility toward religion. Scalia's third major argument was that even under the *Lemon* test, the posting of the Ten Commandments in courthouses was constitutional because the displays have a valid secular purpose.

Scalia and his fellow accommodationists prevailed, however, in *Van Orden,* where a five-to-four majority found the six-foot monolith containing the Ten Commandments on the grounds of the state capitol to be constitutional. Rehnquist wrote the controlling opinion, but it was joined by only Scalia, Thomas, and Kennedy. Breyer concurred with the judgment, but he did not join any of Rehnquist's plurality opinion.

The conservative accommodationists agreed that *Lemon* was not an appropriate test for this type of case, but they were badly fragmented regarding the proper test to utilize. Rehnquist's plurality opinion argued that the Court should rely on "the monument's nature and the Nation's history" in deciding this case. Scalia in a concurring opinion indicated he could support Rehnquist's opinion, but he called for a more strongly accommodationist approach to interpreting the Establishment Clause: "I would prefer to reach the same result by adopting an Establishment Clause jurisprudence that is in accordance with our Nation's past and present practices, and that can be consistently applied—the central relevant feature of which is that there is nothing unconstitutional in a State's favoring religion generally, honoring God through public prayer and acknowledgement, or in a nonproselytizing manner, venerating the Ten Commandments." Thomas also wrote a concurring opinion, calling for a coercion approach to Establishment Clause analysis; and Breyer, who did not join any of Rehnquist's opinion, argued that a case like this requires an "exercise of legal judgment."

The dissenting group of Stevens, Ginsburg, Souter, and O'Connor produced three separate opinions, with the common theme being that the proper general approach to Establishment Clause cases is neutrality. In Stevens's words, "This nation's resolute commitment to neutrality with respect to religion is flatly inconsistent with the plurality's wholehearted validation of an official state endorsement of the message that there is one and only one, God."

To conclude, the Supreme Court's Establishment Clause jurisprudence has long been and remains today a confusing and controversial area of constitutional analysis. Justice Thomas correctly observed in 1995 that "our Establishment Clause jurisprudence is in hopeless disarray" (*Rosenberger v. Rector and Visitors of the University of Virginia,* 1995). A decade later, Thomas had not seen much improvement and declared that "a more fundamental rethinking of our Establishment Clause jurisprudence is in order" (*Van Orden v. Perry,* 2005).

The Court has long been in disagreement regarding both a general approach to analyze the Establishment Clause and a specific test. In regard to general approaches, the strict separation view has largely vanished from opinions, but strong disagreements exist among the justices concerning the appropriateness of the competing neutrality and accommodationist approaches. In regard to a specific test, the three-part *Lemon* test has been the most widely cited, but its status is far from clear. In some cases, it has been used with all three prongs; in other cases, only the first two prongs have been employed; in one of the Court's most recent cases involving the Ten Commandments, only the first prong was utilized, and in yet other cases the *Lemon* test has not been used at all. Furthermore, no alternative test has commanded the support of a Court majority.

The Supreme Court thus seems to be confronting an intractable problem in analyzing the Establishment Clause. This problem had its origin in *Everson* in 1947, when the Court recognized three competing approaches to the Establishment Clause: strict separation, neutrality, and accommodation. Subsequently, the Warren, Burger, and Rehnquist Courts have struggled unsuccessfully to find a majority consensus on the basic principles for analyzing Establishment Clause cases. Unfortunately, little reason exists to expect anything different in the future. Establishment Clause cases are certain to remain an important part of the Court's agenda, but resolution of these cases is most likely to be ad hoc and contentious, with no agreement on guiding principles.

See also *Abington School District v. Schempp;* Bill of Rights, Incorporation of; Black, Hugo L.; Blackmun, Harry A.; Brennan, William J., Jr.; Breyer, Stephen G.; Burger, Warren E.; Burger Court; Clark, Tom C.; Douglas, William O.; *Epperson v. Arkansas; Everson v. Board of Education;* Evolution/Creationism Controversy; First Amendment; Free Exercise Clause; Ginsburg, Ruth Bader; Jefferson, Thomas; Kennedy, Anthony; *Lemon v. Kurtzman;* Madison, James; Marshall, Thurgood; Moment of Silence Laws; O'Connor, Sandra Day; Powell, Lewis F., Jr.; Rehnquist, William H.; Rehnquist Court; Religion, Freedom of; Religion, Official Endorsements of; Religious Schools, Government Aid to; Scalia, Antonin; School Prayer Decisions; Separation of Church and State; Souter, David H.; Stevens, John Paul; Stewart, Potter; Tax Exemptions for Religious Organizations; Ten Commandments, Public Display of the; Thomas, Clarence; Vinson, Fred M.; Warren, Earl; Warren Court; White, Byron R.

Bibliography

Alley, Robert. 1988. *The Supreme Court on Church and State.* New York: Oxford University Press.

Hensley, Thomas R., Chris E. Smith, and Joyce A. Baugh. 1997. *The Changing Supreme Court: Constitutional Rights and Liberties.* St. Paul, MN: West/Wadsworth.

Levy, Leonard. 1986. *The Establishment Clause: Religion and the First Amendment.* New York: Macmillan.

Thomas R. Hensley

EUTHANASIA. *See* Die, Right to; Doctor-Assisted Suicide; Medical Treatment, Right to Refuse

EVANESCENT EVIDENCE. *See* Warrantless Searches

EVERS, MEDGAR (1925–1963)

Medgar Wiley Evers was born on July 2, 1925, near Decatur, Mississippi, to James and Jessie Evers. He attended school in Mississippi until he joined the United States Army in 1943 to fight in World War II. After his service in the Army, he attended Alcorn Agricultural and Mechanical College (now Alcorn State University), where he majored in business administration. While at Alcorn, Evers was involved in several extracurricular activities, including the debate team, college choir, football team, track team, student government, and the school newspaper and annual, of which he was editor. Because of his accomplishments at Alcorn, he was listed in *Who's Who in American Colleges.*

At Alcorn, he met Myrlie Beasley, and they later married in 1951. In 1952, Evers received his bachelor of arts degree, and he and his wife moved to Mound Bayou, near Jackson, Mississippi. While working as an insurance agent, Evers established local chapters of the NAACP throughout Mississippi to promote equal rights for African Americans. He sought to accomplish this through voter registration campaigns and boycotts of racially discriminating businesses.

In 1954, Evers left his insurance job in order to fight for the enforcement of the U.S. Supreme Court's *Brown v. Board of Education* decision, which ruled school segregation unconstitutional. Despite the ruling, the University of Mississippi law school denied admission to Evers. Because of his attempt to integrate the state's oldest public university, he attracted the attention of the NAACP's national office. Later that year, he was appointed Mississippi's first field secretary for the NAACP.

The murder of Emmett Till in 1955 had profound effects on Mississippi civil rights activists. Evers urged the NAACP national leadership to become involved in the case. Evers and two NAACP field workers, Ruby Hurley and Amzie Moore, clandestinely searched for witnesses willing to come forward. Some local leaders courageously stepped forward after the Till murder. A physician and civil rights leader, Dr. T.R.M. Howard, offered his own personal bodyguards to protect witnesses in the case, as well as family members of Emmett Till. After they testified, Howard, Evers, and other NAACP officials helped the witnesses leave Jackson.

Evers gained national prominence when he boycotted all racially discriminatory Jackson merchants. As a result, he received federal assistance to support James Meredith in his admission to the University of Mississippi in 1962. Meredith's admittance was a major step in securing civil rights in the state. However, a race riot on campus ensued and left two people dead. This and other controversial activities created negative feelings toward Evers and his work.

On June 12, 1963, Medgar Evers was killed by an assassin's bullet as he stepped out of his vehicle. His funeral was held in Jackson, Mississippi, and his internment was at Arlington National Cemetery. Many leaders of all races from around the nation attended these events.

The shotgun used in the assassination was found in nearby bushes and still held the perpetrator's fingerprints. The accused killer, a white supremacist member of the Ku Klux Klan named

Byron De La Beckwith, stood trial twice in the 1960s. However, both trials, consisting of all-white juries, ended in deadlock despite the overwhelming evidence against Beckwith. In 1989, allegations of jury tampering emerged after a Mississippi newspaper found evidence that a state agency had helped Beckwith's lawyers screen potential jurors in both trials. Ultimately, no evidence of jury tampering was found, but new witnesses were. As a result, the assistant district attorney and Evers's widow put together a new case. On February 5, 1994, 31 years after the murder, he was retried before a multiracial jury, which found him guilty of the crime. The 74-year-old Beckwith was sentenced to life imprisonment. He died after serving six years of that sentence.

In *For Us, the Living*, a memoir of her slain husband, Myrlie Evers wrote: "There will, I believe, be a day when Medgar Evers will be remembered, in Mississippi as elsewhere, as a true friend of his state. Surely the day must come when his assassin and people like him will be remembered as the state's real enemies" (Evers 1996, 6).

See also *Brown v. Board of Education;* Civil Rights Movement; Ku Klux Klan; Meredith, James; National Association for the Advancement of Colored People

Bibliography

Evers, Myrlie. 1996. *For Us, the Living.* Oxford: University Press of Mississippi.

Nossiter, Adam. 1994. *Of Long Memory: Mississippi and the Murder of Medgar Evers.* Cambridge, MA: Perseus Books.

Ann M. Bennett

EVERSON V. BOARD OF EDUCATION (1947)

Although it is the first clause in the First Amendment to the Constitution, the Establishment Clause was not the focus of a serious examination by the Supreme Court until *Everson v. Board of Education* (1947). As such, *Everson* stands to the Establishment Clause much as *Marbury v. Madison* (1803) stands to judicial power—the initial determinative gloss on its constitutional meaning. Although the decision of the Court was delivered with a five-to-four split among the justices, the vote on the central interpretational issue in the case—the meaning of the Establishment Clause—was unanimous. "In the words of Jefferson, the clause against establishment of religion by law was intended to erect 'a wall of separation between Church and State.'" The divided vote of the justices, however, demonstrates that there is a difference between meaning and application.

Everson grew out of a political conflict rooted in an increasingly pluralist religious environment, the increased importance of public financing of schools, and the battles that ensued over who could receive tax revenue (Sorauf, 1976). It involved an ACLU-sponsored challenge to a New Jersey statute permitting state reimbursement of transportation costs to the parents of all eligible students, including those who attended sectarian (here, predominantly Catholic) schools. Due to the issues involved in the case, a number of Protestant groups filed amicus briefs on behalf of Everson, challenging the statute, and various state attorneys general and Catholic organizations filed amicus briefs on behalf of New Jersey.

The doctrinal difficulty of Justice Hugo Black's majority opinion lies in its tying separationist logic ("No tax in any amount, large or small, can be levied to support any religious activities or institutions, whatever they may be called, or whatever form they may adopt to teach or practice religion.") with an accommodationist result and wrapping it with the "wall" metaphor. Justice Robert Jackson expressed this tension best in his dissent: "[T]he undertones of the opinion, advocating complete and uncompromising separation of Church from State, seem utterly discordant with its conclusion yielding support to their commingling in educational matters." From his perspective, the majority got the test right but botched its application.

Everson ensconced a daunting ambiguity into the Court's Establishment Clause jurisprudence

and set the stage for the twisted doctrinal confusion that characterizes this area of law to this day. Separationists seize on its "no tax" language to support a stark separation of church and state, and accommodationists focus on its "child benefit" result—a state cannot directly aid religions, but it can assist children (and parents) who make choices that advance religion—to justify governmental assistance to religious activities and institutions.

Although the ambiguity of *Everson*'s "wall" has created seemingly inconsistent decisions since its erection, its existence was not seriously questioned until the mid-1980s. In his dissent in *Wallace v. Jaffree* (1985), Justice Rehnquist argued that the *Everson* Court got it all wrong: the Establishment Clause erects no wall of separation between church and state. This brought academic debates into the Court and opened the issue of the wall's long-term viability.

See also American Civil Liberties Union; Black, Hugo L.; Establishment Clause; First Amendment; Jackson, Robert H.; Jefferson, Thomas; Rehnquist, William H.; Religion, Freedom of; School Choice Programs; Separation of Church and State; Tax Exemptions for Religious Organizations

Bibliography

Sorauf, Frank J. 1976. *The Wall of Separation: The Constitutional Politics of Church and State.* Princeton, NJ: Princeton University Press.

Joseph F. Kobylka

EVOLUTION/CREATIONISM CONTROVERSY

In 1859, Charles Darwin published *On the Origin of Species,* a book offering an account of the complexity and apparent design of the world's diverse life forms that relied on a purely natural mechanism that did not require an appeal to a divine agent. Darwin argued for two points that are central to his case. First, all life forms—whether human beings, butterflies, or amoebas—share a common ancestor; that is, they are the result of a single-cell organism that came to be at some point in the distant past. This is called common descent. Second, Darwin offered the theory of natural selection to account for the a wide range of life forms that arose from this one cell. According to this theory, all life forms, in their struggle for survival, gradually, through small incremental changes, develop new characteristics that are in turn passed on to their progeny. Consequently, over eons, different species—with different body plans, characteristics, and a wide range of complexities—develop as a result of the sorts of attributes that are needed for their survival in their particular regions of the globe and for the sorts of challenges they face in striving for survival. In the early to mid-twentieth century, Darwin's views were merged with the growing knowledge of genetics. This is called the neo-Darwinian synthesis.

Although Darwin's theory did not concern the origin of the first one-celled organism or even the origin of the universe as a whole, today the term "evolution" is typically understood in this wider sense as an entirely materialist account of the universe as a whole and the particular entities in it, including the earth and all its biological organisms. In fact, the commitment to evolution on the part of some scientists bears little relation to the plausibility of Darwinism or neo-Darwinism. Some scientists—such as the paleontologist Stephen Jay Gould—have challenged Darwin's gradualism, largely as a result of the fossil record. For example, the Cambrian explosion shows a geologically abrupt appearance (530 million years ago) of a diversity of fully formed, highly complex species with apparently no antecedents. But this is inconsistent with Darwin's prediction that the fossil record would reveal gradual development from simple to more complex species. Gould offered what he called punctuated equilibrium as an alternative evolutionary account to Darwinian gradualism.

The Scopes Trial

Because Darwinism appeared to conflict with the dominant reading of the Bible in late nineteenth- and early twentieth-century America, some states passed laws that prohibited the teaching of evolution in public school classes. One of those states, Tennessee, featured the first real legal battle over such a law, the Scopes trial. The trial took place in 1925 in the small town of Dayton. The case involved John Scopes, a local teacher who used a textbook that included sections explaining and defending Darwinism. Scopes's arrest was orchestrated with his consent by a group of prominent Dayton officials and businessmen who wanted to increase the visibility of their small town. Drawing the attention of a worldwide audience, the Scopes trial featured the legendary civil liberties attorney Clarence Darrow, who represented Scopes, and the three-time Democratic presidential candidate William Jennings Bryan, who was part of the prosecution's legal team. Although Scopes was convicted, it is widely believed that the Scopes trial was a cultural victory for Darwinism.

Creationism/Evolution and the Federal Courts

It was not until 1968 that the U.S. Supreme Court dealt with an antievolution statute. In *Epperson v. Arkansas* (1968), the Court struck down an Arkansas law that was similar to the statute upheld in Scopes. The Court held that the statute "must be stricken because of its conflict with the constitutional prohibition of state laws respecting an establishment of religion or prohibiting the free exercise thereof." The Court concluded that the statute proscribed evolution solely because it is inconsistent with the creation story in the book of Genesis. Thus, the statute had no secular purpose. In the face of *Epperson*, opponents of evolution developed a balanced treatment approach, a strategy that resulted in the crafting of statutes that require a balanced treatment in public schools between evolution and "creation science," a unique religious doctrine transparently derived from a literal reading of the first chapters of the book of Genesis, though portrayed by its proponents as a scientific alternative to evolution.

Balanced-treatment acts in Arkansas and Louisiana were struck down as unconstitutional by a federal district court in *McLean v. Arkansas* (1982) and by the U.S. Supreme Court in *Edwards v.*

Aguillard (1987). Although the statutes were not identical, they were similar, and the reasoning that the courts applied to each was similar as well. The courts held that the real purpose of the acts was to advance a particular religious viewpoint, creation science, and thus held that the acts violated the Establishment Clause. Four issues dominated the analysis in both cases: (1) the statute's historical continuity with *Scopes* as well as the creation/evolution battles throughout the twentieth century; (2) how closely the curricular content required by the statute parallels the creation story in Genesis, and/or whether the curricular content prohibited or regulated by the statute is treated as such because it is inconsistent with the creation story in Genesis; (3) the motives of those who supported the statute in either the legislature or the public sphere; and (4) whether the statute was a legitimate means to achieve appropriate state ends.

The Challenge of Intelligent Design Theory

The Court held in *Edwards* that it is permissible for legislatures to require and/or allow public schools to teach scientific critiques of predominant scientific theories as well as to expose students to a diversity of scientific perspectives on human origins as long as it is done "with the clear secular intent of enhancing the effectiveness of science instruction." For this reason, some have argued that noncreationist alternatives to evolution (broadly defined), such as intelligent design (ID) theory, may pass the *Edwards* test and could be taught in public schools without violating the Establishment Clause. In the case of ID, its proponents offer arguments that do not directly involve the book of Genesis and its tenets as explicit or implicit propositions. Unlike their creationist predecessors, many proponents of ID are well-credentialed scholars who hold or have held academic appointments at respected institutions and who have published peer-reviewed monographs and anthologies with academic presses and have contributed to professional journals.

See also Academic Freedom; *Epperson v. Arkansas;* Establishment Clause; Religion, Freedom of

Bibliography

Beckwith, Francis J. 2003. *Law, Darwinism and Public Education: The Establishment Clause and the Challenge of Intelligent Design.* Lanham, MD: Rowman & Littlefield.

Greenawalt, Kent. 2003. "Establishing Religious Ideas: Evolution, Creationism, and Intelligent Design." *Notre Dame Journal of Law, Ethics and Public Policy* 17 (2): 321–97.

Larson, Edward J. 1997. *Summer of the Gods: The Scopes Trial and America's Continuing Debate over Science and Religion.* New York: Basic Books.

Strickberger, Monroe W. 2000. *Evolution.* 3rd ed. Sudbury, MA: Jones & Bartlett.

Francis J. Beckwith

EXCESSIVE BAIL, PROHIBITION OF

Bail refers to the pretrial release of a person arrested on criminal charges, usually with the requirement that the accused post a bond to ensure that he or she will appear in court when required to do so. The Eighth Amendment to the United States Constitution states that "excessive bail shall not be required." Bail becomes excessive when a court sets it higher than reasonably necessary to ensure a defendant's appearance at trial.

In *Stack v. Boyle* (1951), the U.S. Supreme Court made it clear that the purpose of bail is to ensure the appearance of the accused in court, not to inflict punishment. Writing for the Court, Chief Justice Fred Vinson observed, "Bail set at a figure higher than an amount reasonably calculated to fulfill this purpose is 'excessive' under the Eighth Amendment."

Stack v. Boyle was a federal criminal case that came to the Supreme Court via the writ of habeas corpus. The case involved 12 defendants accused of conspiring to violate the Smith Act, which made it an offense to advocate the overthrow of the U.S. government by force. Chief Justice Vinson noted that "bail was fixed for each petitioner in the widely varying amounts of $2,500, $7,500, $75,000 and $100,000" and also pointed out that, if convicted, the defendants faced a maximum fine of $10,000. Vinson observed that "bail for each petitioner has been fixed in a sum much higher than that usually imposed for offenses with like penalties and yet there has been no factual showing to justify such action in this case." The Court instructed the federal district court to reconsider the defendants' bail in light of its opinion.

The Supreme Court has never held that the Excessive Bail Clause of the Eighth Amendment is enforceable against the states via the Fourteenth Amendment, thus leaving the matter of excessive bail in state criminal cases to the state constitutions, legislatures, and courts. But all states have adopted some form of prohibition against excessive bail in criminal cases. For example, the Texas Code of Criminal Procedure states that "the power to require bail is not to be so used as to make it an instrument of oppression." Similarly, the Illinois Code of Criminal Procedure provides that "the amount of bail shall be: (1) Sufficient to assure compliance with the conditions set forth in the bail bond; (2) Not oppressive; and (3) Considerate of the financial ability of the accused."

As the Supreme Court has observed, the purpose of bail is to ensure the accused's presence in court. In considering the probability of the accused appearing, courts look to the gravity of the offense and weight of the evidence supporting the charge and potential danger to the victims, as well as the accused's family ties, employment history, and reputation in the community. An accused may challenge the denial of the right to or excessiveness of the amount or conditions of bail. This usually takes the form of a petition for a writ of habeas corpus.

See also Bail, Right to; Bill of Rights (American); Bill of Rights, Incorporation of; Eighth Amendment; Fourteenth Amendment; Habeas Corpus; Smith Act; Vinson, Fred M.

John M. Scheb II and Otis H. Stephens, Jr.

EXCESSIVE FINES, PROHIBITION OF

The Eighth Amendment to the United States Constitution provides that "excessive bail shall not be required, nor excessive fines imposed, nor cruel and unusual punishments inflicted." This language

was borrowed from the English Bill of Rights of 1689. As the U.S. Supreme Court observed in *Ingraham v. Wright* (1977), "Bail, fines, and punishment traditionally have been associated with the criminal process, and by subjecting the three to parallel limitations the text of the Amendment suggests an intention to limit the power of those entrusted with the criminal-law function of government."

Monetary fines are the most common punishments meted out in criminal cases. Most misdemeanors carry monetary fines, especially for first offenses. Some felonies, especially serious economic crimes defined by federal law, carry heavy monetary fines as penalties. The Supreme Court has yet to say what constitutes an excessive fine in a criminal case. Furthermore, the Court has never ruled that the Excessive Fines Clause is incorporated within the Due Process Clause of the Fourteenth Amendment; thus it has not been made applicable to the state courts. State constitutions, however, have provisions that parallel the Eighth Amendment. For example, Article I, Section 13, of the Texas Constitution provides, "Excessive bail shall not be required, nor excessive fines imposed, nor cruel or unusual punishment inflicted."

Fines in criminal cases are set by federal and state statutes, that is, laws of general applicability enacted by Congress and the state legislatures, respectively. Appellate courts are unlikely to second-guess the level of the fines imposed, restricting their function to addressing fines that exceed a statutory maximum or instances where a trial court has failed to impose a mandatory fine. Indeed, it is rare to find a judicial decision where an appellate court has invalidated a particular fine on the ground that it is excessive.

In the latter part of the twentieth century the U.S. Supreme Court has addressed whether the Excessive Fines Clause applies to monetary awards in civil cases as well as statutes authorizing asset forfeiture in connection with a variety of criminal offenses. In 1989, in *Browning-Ferris Industries v. Kelco Disposal*, the Supreme Court made it clear that the Excessive Fines Clause does not apply to monetary awards in civil cases. Writing for the

Court, Justice Harry Blackmun noted that "nothing in English history suggests that the Excessive Fines Clause of the 1689 Bill of Rights, the direct ancestor of our Eighth Amendment, was intended to apply to damages awarded in disputes between private parties." Rather, Blackmun concluded, "the Excessive Fines Clause was intended to limit only those fines directly imposed by, and payable to, the government." Because punitive damages are, by definition, a form of punishment inflicted on a tortfeasor who has committed gross negligence or engaged in outrageous conduct, the Court's decision in *Browning-Ferris* dashed the hopes of tort reform advocates that the Court would view punitive damages as a civil fine subject to the Excessive Fines Clause.

In the 1970s, Congress began enacting numerous statutes authorizing civil asset forfeiture in connection with a variety of criminal offenses. This resulted in numerous challenges, and the issue eventually ended in the Supreme Court in 1990, when it reviewed a case involving Richard Lyle Austin, who was indicted on four counts of violating South Dakota's drug laws. Austin ultimately pleaded guilty to one count of possessing cocaine with intent to distribute, and a state court sentenced him to seven years' imprisonment. Subsequently, the United States filed an action in federal district court seeking forfeiture of Austin's mobile home and auto body shop. The government's action proceeded under the Comprehensive Drug Abuse Prevention and Control Act of 1970, Title XXI, sections 881(a)(4) and (a)(7) of the U.S. Code, which provides for the forfeiture of property used to facilitate the commission of drug crimes. The federal government argued that Austin's assets facilitated his offense, obtained an order from the federal court forfeiting Austin's home and business, and ordered forfeiture. The Supreme Court granted review, and in *Austin v. United States* (1993), the Court held that the Excessive Fines Clause can be used to challenge forfeitures of property by persons convicted of crimes, even though the legal actions resulting in the forfeitures are technically civil and not criminal cases. Again writing for the Court, Justice Blackmun said the key question is not whether a particular

legal procedure is formally denominated as civil or criminal, but whether it amounts to punishment. But noting that Congress intended the forfeiture laws to "deter and to punish," Blackmun concluded that "forfeiture under these provisions constitutes 'payment to a sovereign as punishment for some offense, ... and, as such, is subject to the limitations of the Eighth Amendment's Excessive Fines Clause."

In 1998, the Supreme Court continued down the path it blazed in *Austin*, and in *United States v. Bajakajian*, in a five-to-four decision, the Court invalidated a civil forfeiture under 18 U.S.C. § 982(a)(1), which provides that "a person convicted of willfully not reporting the transport of more than $10,000 shall forfeit to the government any property ... involved in such offense." In 1994, Hosep Bajakajian attempted to leave the United States without reporting to the authorities that he was transporting $357,144 in U.S. currency. The United States sought forfeiture of all the money. Bajakajian argued that such a forfeiture would violate the Excessive Fines Clause of the Eighth Amendment. By a five-to-four vote the Supreme Court agreed and held the forfeiture would be unconstitutional.

After explaining that a civil forfeiture is a fine, Justice Clarence Thomas's majority opinion observed that "[Bajakajian's] failure to report his currency affected only one party: the government, and in a relatively minor way.... Had his crime gone undetected, the government would have been deprived only of the information that $357,144 had left the country." Thomas then proceeded to discuss the standard for determining its "excessiveness," observing:

The touchstone of the constitutional inquiry under the Excessive Fines Clause is the principle of proportionality: The amount of the forfeiture must bear some relationship to the gravity of the offense that it is designed to punish.... Until today, however, we have not articulated a standard for determining whether a punitive forfeiture is constitutionally excessive. We now hold that a punitive forfeiture violates the Excessive Fines Clause if it is grossly disproportional to the gravity of a defendant's offense.

Justice Kennedy, writing on behalf of the four dissenting justices, argued that the sanctions involved were remedial and not subject to the Excessive Fines Clause.

Based on the reasoning of the Court in *Austin* and *Bajakajian,* one could argue that large fines imposed by federal regulatory agencies, at least in some contexts, might be subject to challenge under the Excessive Fines Clause, but the Supreme Court has not yet addressed this question. Lower courts that have addressed the question of the excessiveness of administrative fines have generally taken the position that any administrative fine that does not exceed the limits prescribed by the statute authorizing it does not violate the Eighth Amendment. For example, in *Newell Recycling v. EPA* (2000), the Fifth Circuit said, "No matter how excessive (in lay terms) an administrative fine may appear, if the fine does not exceed the limits prescribed by the statute authorizing it, the fine does not violate the Eighth Amendment." Other courts have applied the grossly disproportional standard discussed in *Bajakajian* but have continued to grant great deference to legislative sanctions imposed for administrative violations and have held penalties not excessive (see, for example, the Ninth Circuit's decision in *Balice v. U.S. Department of Agriculture,* 2000).

See also Bill of Rights (English); Bill of Rights, Incorporation of; Blackmun, Harry A.; Cruel and Unusual Punishments Clause; Drugs, War on; Due Process Clauses; Eighth Amendment; Excessive Bail, Prohibition of; Fourteenth Amendment; Sentencing, Eighth Amendment and; Sentencing, Proportionality in; Thomas, Clarence

Bibliography

Jochner, Michele M. 1999. "The U.S. Supreme Court Expands Excessive Fines Clause Protection in *Austin* and *Bajakajian*." *Illinois Bar Journal* 87:78.

Lee, Youngjae. 2005. "The Constitutional Right Against Excessive Punishment." *Virginia Law Review* 91:677–745.

Hon. John M. Scheb and John M. Scheb II

EXCLUSIONARY RULE. *See* Fourth Amendment Exclusionary Rule

EXCULPATORY EVIDENCE, DISCLOSURE OF

American courts have long recognized a prosecutor's duty to disclose to the defense information that tends to vindicate the accused. This duty to disclose exculpatory evidence is based on constitutional requirements of due process of law and, more specifically, the value of fundamental fairness it has been held to encompass. In *Brady v. Maryland* (1963), the seminal case in this area, the Warren Court held that "the suppression by the prosecution of evidence favorable to the accused upon request violates due process where the evidence is material either to guilt or punishment, irrespective of the good faith or bad faith of the prosecution." The Court's opinion in *Brady* stressed the idea that "[s]ociety wins not only when the guilty are convicted but when criminal trials are fair; our system of the administration of justice suffers when any accused is treated unfairly."

In general, it is incumbent on the defense to request the disclosure of exculpatory evidence. Indeed, the failure of a defense lawyer to do so may give rise to a claim of ineffective assistance of counsel. Of course, unless the defense is aware of the existence of the evidence, such a request is impossible. In *United States v. Agurs* (1976), the Supreme Court held that a prosecutor's failure to inform the defense of the existence of exculpatory evidence is not the basis for the reversal of a conviction, unless the admission of such evidence would have created a reasonable doubt that would not otherwise exist as to the defendant's guilt. Justice John Paul Stevens, writing for the Supreme Court, observed that the prosecutor's failure to disclose evidence:

must be evaluated in the context of the entire record. If there is no reasonable doubt about guilt whether or not the additional evidence is considered, there is no justification for a new trial. On the other hand, if the verdict is already of questionable validity, additional evidence of relatively minor importance might be sufficient to create a reasonable doubt.

In *United States v. Bagley* (1985), the prosecutor failed to disclose evidence that tended to impeach the credibility of government witnesses. The Supreme Court reversed the conviction, holding that "impeachment evidence" falls within the *Brady* rule. Writing for the Court, Justice Harry Blackmun observed, "Such evidence is 'evidence favorable to an accused' … so that, if disclosed and used effectively, it may make the difference between conviction and acquittal." However, in *Bagley* the Supreme Court adopted a somewhat different view of the scope of the prosecutor's duty in this area, saying that "the prosecutor is not required to deliver his entire file to defense counsel, but only to disclose evidence favorable to the accused that, if suppressed, would deprive the defendant of a fair trial."

Under *Bagley,* nondisclosed evidence is "material" and therefore subject to the *Brady* rule "only if there is a reasonable probability that, had the evidence been disclosed to the defense, the result of the proceeding would have been different." One commentator has pointed out that the Court in *Bagley* "placed a heavy post-trial burden upon the defense by requiring the defense, on appeal, to demonstrate that it has suffered such prejudice from the prosecution's withholding of exculpatory evidence and that the withheld evidence is reasonably likely to have changed the trial's outcome" (Joseph 2004, 36). This commentator concludes, "Numerous cases of *Brady* violations nationwide suggest that *Bagley* has set too high a standard for the determination of materiality" (Joseph 2004, 38).

See also Accused, Rights of the; Adversary System of Justice; Blackmun, Harry A.; Counsel, Ineffective Assistance of; Due Process, Procedural; Due Process Clauses; Stevens, John Paul; Warren Court

Bibliography

Joseph, Jannice E. 2004 "The New Russian Roulette: *Brady* Revisited." *Capital Defense Journal* 17:33–60.

Nofer, Paul G. 1986. "Specific Requests and the Prosecutorial Duty to Disclose Evidence: The Impact of *United States v. Bagley.*" *Duke Law Journal* 1986 (5): 892–914.

Scheb, John M., and John M. Scheb II. 2006. *Criminal Procedure.* Belmont, CA: Thomson/Wadsworth.

John M. Scheb II and Otis H. Stephens, Jr.

EXECUTION, METHODS OF

From colonial times to today, American methods of execution for capital crimes have undergone many changes, most in the pursuit of a more humane and efficient death penalty. The physical suffering of colonial cruelty has been replaced by the painless chemistry of lethal injection. Executions, once great public spectacles, are now private and somber events. Sophisticated legal safeguards are now embedded in the same judicial processes that were once quick to carry out a death sentence. The agency of the hangman has given way to the clinical, impersonal, hidden, and self-disguised functions of group and machine.

Executions in colonial America were primarily, although not exclusively, realized by the European methods of hanging or firing squad. Sometimes, selective measures of great brutality were also employed to produce terror as a means of intensifying the moral teaching or coercive warning known to be inherent in the execution itself. These added punishments were most often directed at slaves, Native Americans, pirates, mutineers, and traitors. Examples of these punishments included burning at the stake (sometimes alive, sometimes after hanging), a rare punishment inflicted not for witchcraft but for crimes of petit treason (slaves who plotted revolt or murdered their owners, as in New Jersey, 1753, or white women who murdered their husbands, as Pennsylvanian Catherine Bevan did in 1731); public display of the corpse, in whole (called gibbeting when the body is encased in an iron cage or hung by chains, as was the fate of a Boston pirate in 1724) or in part (such as a spiked Native American's head, which was displayed in Rhode Island in 1639, or the quartered corpse of a Virginia slave, each quarter of which was displayed at a different location, in 1755); dismemberment (sometimes carried out while the condemned was still alive); for treason (as in New York in 1691 or North Carolina in 1771);

and dissection (in colonial law, called *anatomie*), a judge's added discretionary penalty for murderers (first exercised on a Boston Native American in 1735, and still legal in Massachusetts as late as 1904).

There have been three American innovations in capital punishment: the electric chair (1890), the gas chamber (1924), and lethal injection (1982). Each method was intended as an improvement on its predecessor. Together with hanging and the firing squad, these five methods have accounted for an estimated 20,000 sanctioned executions between 1608 and the present and still constitute the legal means of capital punishment in America today.

Of 52 separate legal jurisdictions (one for each state, the federal government, and the military), 40 were death penalty jurisdictions in 2003. 12 states are without a death penalty, while one state that has the death penalty, Illinois, has suspended executions (in 2000, pending administrative review) and pardoned or commuted all death sentences (in 2003). Presently, 21 death penalty jurisdictions authorize an exclusive method of execution (electrocution in Nebraska, lethal injection in 19 states and the military). The remaining 19 jurisdictions provide for multiple means of execution.

Hanging

Ideally, the correct result of drop force in a hanging (a function primarily of body weight and length of rope) should produce an immediate broken neck and severed spinal cord, causing shock and unconscious strangulation. When the drop is too short, death is by slow, painful, conscious asphyxiation; when too long, it is by decapitation.

Hanging was the primary method of execution in the United States until the 1890s and has accounted for two-thirds of the executions in America since 1608. Presently, two states still maintain hanging along with lethal injection—New Hampshire (as a fallback option) and Washington (convict's choice). Delaware abolished hanging in July 2003. The first American execution by hanging was *Mayflower* passenger John Billington in colonial Massachusetts in

1630; the last to date was William Bailey, for murder, in Delaware in 1996.

The Firing Squad

Death by firing squad is achieved by blood loss when the heart and lungs are ruptured. Modern protocol employs five rifles, one with a blank round. The condemned is seated, hooded, bound, and placed with a target on his heart.

Execution by shooting, a military tradition, first became a civil statute in territorial Utah around the 1850s. There are three states that presently provide for execution by firing squad while maintaining lethal injection—Idaho, Oklahoma (as a fallback options), and Utah (convict's choice). The first American execution by shooting (also the first execution in America) was Captain George Kendall, for mutiny and espionage in colonial Virginia around 1608; the last to date was John Taylor for murder in Utah in 1996.

The Electric Chair

Electrocution causes death by ventricular fibrillation (uncontrolled heart muscle contractions that prevent blood flow). The electric volts (between 500 and 2,000 for 30 seconds, repeated as necessary until death), however, can also produce burning flesh, tissue swelling, and cooked organs.

Invented by engineer Harold P. Brown and adopted by the New York state legislature in 1888 as a more humane option than hanging, 10 states presently sanction electrocution (9 with a lethal injection option). Nebraska requires it. Between 1890 and 1951, 25 states had executed felons by electrocution. The first was William Kemmler, for murder, in New York in 1890; the last to date was Robert Williams, also for murder, in Nebraska in 1997.

The Gas Chamber

Sodium or potassium cyanide crystals released into sulfuric acid produce hydrogen cyanide gas. When breathed within a sealed environment, the gas causes death by hypoxia (deprivation of oxygen to the brain) within 6 to 18 minutes. Some assert the method is excruciatingly painful, while others disagree.

Invented by Major D. A. Turner as a humane alternative to electrocution, five states presently maintain the gas chamber along with lethal injection. Between 1924 and 1960, 11 states executed felons by lethal gas. The first was Gee Jon, for murder, in Nevada in 1924; the last to date was Walter LeGrand (a German national) for murder in Arizona in 1999.

Lethal Injection

A combination of two or three drugs, sequentially delivered intravenously, produces death by respiratory and cardiac arrest while the condemned is unconscious. In 1988 Frederick A. Leuchter invented a computerized controlled, blind-agency, fully automated three-syringe delivery system a process now known as the Missouri Protocol (this system came with an instruction manual). The first injection (sodium thiopental) sedates, the second (pavulon or pancuronium bromide) paralyzes the complete muscle system, and the third (potassium chloride) stops the heart. Death occurs within nine minutes.

Asserted to be humane and pain free, lethal injection is the overwhelming choice of method of execution in America and is now authorized by 37 states, the military service, and the federal government. The first execution by lethal injection was of Charles Brooks for murder in Texas in 1982. The first Missouri Protocol execution was of George Mercer for murder in Missouri in 1989.

Throughout United States history, there have been multiple methods of execution employed to carry out death sentences. This evolution has occurred due to concerns regarding the efficiency and humanity of inflicting the ultimate punishment.

See also Cruel and Unusual Punishments Clause; Death Penalty, Crimes Punishable by the; Eighth Amendment; *Furman v. Georgia; Gregg v. Georgia*

Bibliography

Banner, Stuart. 2002. *The Death Penalty, an American History.* Cambridge, MA: Harvard University Press.

Bowers, William J., 1984. *Legal Homicide.* Boston: Northeastern University Press.

Palmer, Louis J., Jr. 2001. *Encyclopedia of Capital Punishment in the United States.* Jefferson, NC: McFarland.

Kevin Collins

EXECUTIVE CLEMENCY. *See* Clemency, Executive

EXIGENT CIRCUMSTANCES. *See* Warrantless Searches

EX POST FACTO LAWS

Article I, Section 9, clause 3 of the United States Constitution specifies that Congress may not pass ex post facto laws, and clause 1 of Section 10 also prohibits states from passing such laws. The latter provision has induced many states to include the same provision in their constitutions. In general terms, ex post facto laws have a retroactive application. They seek to impose penalties on individuals for actions that were not subject to punishment when committed. In *The Federalist Papers,* no. 84, Alexander Hamilton wrote that "the creation of crimes after commission of the fact, in other words, the subjecting of men to punishment for things which, when they were done, were breaches of no law" was an instrument of tyranny.

For two reasons a very early case is the most important one on the subject of ex post facto laws. In *Calder v. Bull* (1798) the Supreme Court echoed and elaborated upon Hamilton's point: "there are certain vital principles in our free Republican government, which will determine and over-rule an apparent and flagrant abuse of legislative power.... An act of the Legislature (for I cannot call it a law) contrary to the great principles of social compact, cannot be considered a rightful exercise of legislative authority." In *Calder v. Bull* the Court also specified four categories of ex post facto laws and, in the process, began one of the lines of cases on that subject by implying that only criminal laws can be ex post facto. The four categories are:

1. Every law that makes criminal an action done before the passing of the law and that was innocent when done and punishes such action

2. Every law that aggravates a crime or makes it greater than it was when committed

3. Every law that changes the punishment and inflicts a greater punishment than the law annexed to the crime when committed

4. Every law that alters the legal rules of evidence and receives less, or different, testimony than that required by the law at the time of the commission of the offence in order to convict the offender

Contrary to *Calder v. Bull,* another early case began a line of decisions holding that civil laws could be ex post facto. In *Fletcher v. Peck* (1810), Justice John Marshall acknowledged that some ex post facto laws "may inflict penalties on the person," that is, be criminal, but also wrote that others "may inflict pecuniary penalties," which would include those that are civil. *Fletcher v. Peck* involved title to a parcel of land, and Marshall thought that the legislation "had the effect" of an ex post facto law. While his reasoning was a bit wobbly, later cases more clearly held that civil laws could be ex post facto. The best examples are two cases that were decided on the same day and held that laws retroactively denying individuals the right to practice a profession are ex post facto: *Cummings v. Missouri* (1867) and *Ex Parte Garland* (1867).

Although courts have occasionally held that certain civil laws are ex post facto and thus invalid, they have consistently refused to treat one class of civil laws in that fashion. That class is laws that require deportation for persons who have been found to have engaged in specified kinds of activity. The reasoning has always been the same: deportation is not punishment, so laws that impose it for past actions do not fit in any of the categories of ex post facto laws. That reasoning is, to be charitable, surprising in light of the severe role of banishment in many societies and the moving accounts of exile in literature (e.g. in *The Divine Comedy)* and in biographies and autobiographies (e.g. Vladimir Nabokov's). Another recurrent element of those deportation cases is that the activity was political. Reading the cases, one ought to become suspicious of political bodies that retroactively punish political behavior.

Like the peculiar assertion that deportation is not punishment, certain rules of statutory interpretation have limited the number of times that courts have invalidated laws on the ground that they are ex post facto. Two rules of statutory interpretation that have had that effect are that statutes should be interpreted so as to render them constitutional and that statutes are not to be given a retroactive effect unless they are explicitly made retroactive. The former applies to all laws, but the latter applies specifically to laws that are alleged to be ex post facto. In any event, there are a number of cases in which courts, by interpreting statutes less than convincingly, have upheld them against charges that they are ex post facto.

To this point it appears that the ex post facto clauses in the United States Constitution have been less effective means to invalidate questionable laws than they might have been. However, they also have had an invisible effect, one that does not appear in the case law. They are deterrents. The most important features of these prohibitions, the statements of the characteristics of criminal laws that make them ex post facto, are clear and definite. Thus, legislatures realize that there are boundaries beyond which they cannot go. It can thus be said of the ex post facto clauses that "they also serve who only stand and wait" (Milton 1919).

See also Accused, Rights of the; *Federalist Papers*; Marshall, John

Bibliography

Milton, John. 1919. "On His Blindness." In *The Oxford Book of English Verse: 1250–1900,* ed. Arthur Quiller-Couch. Oxford: Clarendon Press.

Jack Stark

EXPRESSIVE CONDUCT. *See* Symbolic Speech

EXTRADITION, INTERNATIONAL

Extradition refers to the delivery of a person who is suspected or has been convicted of a crime by a country or other jurisdiction where the person has taken refuge to the country or jurisdiction that asserts legal authority over said person. The purpose of extradition is to prevent criminals who flee a jurisdiction to escape from punishment for a criminal offense they have been accused or convicted of.

Historically, extradition dates back as far as the ancient days of the Egyptian, Greek, and Roman empires and often would concern political refugees. The modern system of extradition evolved in Europe from the eighteenth century onward. With the rise of national states and the centrality of the concept of sovereignty, more than 100 extradition treaties were signed during the eighteenth and the early part of the nineteenth centuries. The development of bilateral treaties between nations has become the norm to regulate extradition. By present-day standards, extradition between countries is not considered an obligation in the absence of a formal treaty. A multitude of bilateral extradition treaties exists, but there is no country that has such treaties with all other countries in the world.

Extradition treaties typically spell out the conditions under which an extradition can take place. An extradition treaty provides that the crime involved is serious, and that there exists sufficient evidence for the prosecution against the wanted individual, or that the person to be extradited has been convicted under conditions of due process of law. Furthermore, extradition treaties rely on a principle of double criminality, which specifies that the offense for which extradition is requested is regulated by law in both countries. Other common provisions include that the conditions of the treaty are reciprocal between the two parties, that the extradited person can expect or already had a fair trial in the requesting country, and that the punishment will be proportionate to the crime. Most countries, including the United States, will not surrender a fugitive wanted for a political crime. The rise in terrorism, however, has brought about some limitations to the political offense exception.

In some respects, the provisions of extradition treaties vary considerably depending on the countries involved. Many countries, including most European states, Mexico, and Canada, do not allow an extradition to countries that have capital punishment unless assurances are made that the death penalty will not be imposed on the extradited person. In some countries, such as Germany and France, extradition of a citizen of that country is always prohibited, although those countries will allow prosecution of their own citizens when they have committed serious crimes abroad. The political structure of countries, such as the federal structure of the United States, can bring about an additional difficulty in extradition proceedings, inasmuch as the governments of foreign nations have official relations only with federal governments, not with the governments of a country's constituent states. It is not always clear whether an extradition agreement with the federal government is also binding to the states when a matter of state jurisdiction is involved. Also, extradition among states in a federal country is separately regulated. In the United States, interstate extradition (or rendition) is regulated by Article IV, Section 2, of the U.S. Constitution, which specifies that interstate extradition applies irrespective of the nature of the crime.

Extradition has gained attention in recent years because international criminality has become an increasing problem, while at the same time human rights have also been more universally recognized. Therefore, there is presently a sharper need in extradition cases to find a proper balance between the recognition of states' claims to sovereignty, on one hand, and respect for individuals' civil and human rights, on the other. The existing system of extradition already incorporates safeguards for individuals' rights, such as the political offense exception, the rule of double criminality, and the principle of specialty, which specifies that the extradited individual will only stand trial for the offense specified in the extradition. But not all civil and human rights concerns are as easily dealt with in extradition. Conflicts in specific cases have revolved around the use of the death penalty, torture in criminal proceedings; harsh interrogation methods; questionable trial and incarceration conditions; and cruel, inhumane, or degrading treatment and punishment.

In order to more effectively protect human rights, extradition could benefit from a conditional agreement whereby the state that receives an extradition request is allowed to monitor the judicial process of the extradited individual. This would also include monitoring the extradited person in prison. Because of sovereignty concerns, however, such a monitoring system would be politically unacceptable to many countries, making extradition ironically more difficult.

An important problem with the present system of multiple bilateral extradition treaties is that there is no overarching international law or treaty guiding their application. Yet inasmuch as human rights have begun to be recognized across nations, there has been a relative loss in nations' sovereignty and a streamlining of extradition provisions. In specific cases, also, nations have agreed to multilateral extradition treaties on particular offenses. Furthermore, when nations explicitly agree upon a shared system of criminal law provisions as members of a supranational political entity, the need for extradition is eliminated altogether. With the increasing development of multilateral treaties and the formation of supranational entities, the current system of extradition is changing and might lead to an increase in extradition agreements between supranational entities rather than between national states.

See also Accused, Rights of the; Death Penalty and the Supreme Court; Extradition, Interstate; Human Rights Watch; International Law; Terrorism, War on

Bibliography

Dugard, John, and Christine Van den Wyngaert. 1998. "Reconciling Extradition with Human Rights." *American Journal of International Law* 92(2): 187–212.

Epps, Valerie. 2003. "The Development of the Conceptual Framework Supporting International Extradition." *Loyola of Los Angeles International and Comparative Law Review* 25: 369–87.

Gilbert, Geoff. 1991. *Aspects of Extradition Law.* Boston: Martinus Nijhoff.

Pyle, Christopher H. 2001. *Extradition, Politics, and Human Rights.* Philadelphia: Temple University Press.

Rose, Thomas. 2002. "A Delicate Balance: Extradition, Sovereignty, and Individual Rights in the United States and Canada." *Yale Journal of International Law* 27: 193–215.

Mathieu Deflem and Kyle Irwin

EXTRADITION, INTERSTATE

Extradition is the legal process by which one jurisdiction surrenders to another jurisdiction an individual accused or convicted of an offense in the latter jurisdiction. The objective is to prevent escape of persons who stand accused or convicted of crimes and to secure their return to the jurisdiction from which they fled. Extradition can be interstate or international in character. Although the process is similar, different legal considerations are involved.

Article IV, Section 2, of the Constitution, known generally as the Rendition Clause, governs interstate extradition within the United States. The clause provides: "A Person charged in any State with Treason, Felony or any other crime, who shall flee from Justice, and be found in another state, shall on demand of the executive Authority of the State from which he fled, be delivered up, to be removed to the State having Jurisdiction of the crime." In *Biddinger v. Commissioner of Police of City of New York* (1917), the Supreme Court said that the Rendition Clause was intended "to provide a summary executive proceeding by the use of which the closely associated states of the Union could promptly aid one another in bringing to trial persons accused of crime by preventing their finding in one state an asylum against the processes of justice of another."

Although the Rendition Clause does not explicitly grant Congress legislative authority in this field, Congress in 1793 adopted legislation governing interstate extradition. The current form of the statute, codified at 18 U.S.C.A. § 3182, provides:

Whenever the executive authority of any State or Territory demands any person as a fugitive from justice, of the executive authority of any State, District, or Territory to which such person has fled, and produces a copy of an indictment found or an affidavit made before a magistrate of any State or Territory, charging the person demanded with having committed treason, felony, or other crime, certified as authentic by the governor or chief magistrate of the State or Territory from whence the person so charged has fled, the executive authority of the State, District, or Territory to which such person has fled shall cause him to be arrested and secured, and notify the executive authority making such demand, or the agent of such authority appointed to receive the fugitive, and shall cause the fugitive to be delivered to such agent when he shall appear. If no such agent appears within thirty days from the time of the arrest, the prisoner may be discharged.

From the outset, the constitutional and statutory provisions were presumed to cover any and all violations of a state's criminal law. Thus the governor of an asylum state was required to deliver a fugitive to the requesting state, even if the fugitive's acts would not have been criminal in the asylum state. In *Kentucky v. Dennison* (1861), the Supreme Court upheld this interpretation but also held that the federal courts lacked authority to compel extradition. The case stemmed from Ohio governor William Dennison's refusal to comply with Kentucky's demand that he surrender a black defendant charged in Kentucky with aiding the escape of slaves. The Supreme Court unanimously held that although Governor Dennison had a duty to comply with Kentucky's demand, the federal courts could not enforce this duty.

In *Puerto Rico v. Branstad* (1987), the Supreme Court finally overturned the *Dennison* holding that federal courts lacked authority to compel governors to comply with extradition requests from sister states. Writing for the Court, Justice Thurgood Marshall concluded that "there is no justification for distinguishing the duty to deliver fugitives from the many other species of constitutional duty enforceable in the federal courts."

Every offense punishable by law of a jurisdiction where it was committed can be subject to extradition, but extradition is usually sought only in serious offenses. Frequently it is used to regain custody of parole violators, prison escapees, or those persons who have jumped bail.

Most states have adopted the Uniform Criminal Extradition Law, which sets out procedural rules for handling interstate extradition. The governor of the demanding state issues a requisition warrant seeking return of the fugitive. This is presented to the governor of the asylum state (that is, the state in which the fugitive is located). After investigation, the governor of the asylum state issues a warrant for the fugitive's arrest. An opportunity exists for the person sought as a fugitive to contest the extradition in a court of law in the asylum state. Often this challenge takes the form of a petition for a writ of habeas corpus challenging whether the petitioner is in fact the person charged or attacking the regularity of the proceedings. Such proceedings seek the release of the prisoner who is to be extradited but do not focus on the issue of the prisoner's guilt or innocence.

See also Accused, Rights of the; Death Penalty and the Supreme Court; Extradition, International; Human Rights Watch; International Law

John M. Scheb II and Otis H. Stephens, Jr.

F

FACE. *See* Freedom of Access to Clinic Entrances Act

FAIR HOUSING ACT (1968)

In the 1960s, the federal government took steps to combat long-standing racial discrimination in the housing market. On November 20, 1962, President John F. Kennedy issued Executive Order 11063, which prohibited discrimination in the sale, leasing, and renting of properties owned or operated by the federal government. Kennedy's order furnished the impetus for continuing federal involvement in this area, most notably the adoption of the Fair Housing Act in 1968.

Shortly after the establishment of the U.S. Department of Housing and Urban Development in 1965, President Lyndon Johnson proposed a law that would radically update and improve the U.S. Housing Act of 1937. That law, referred to as the Fair Housing Act, became Title VIII of the 1968 Civil Rights Act. Although the Fair Housing Act had been introduced in Congress in 1966, it was not until the occurrence of three significant events in 1968 that enough momentum existed for Johnson to push the legislation through Congress. The first event was Senate Minority Leader Everett Dirksen's reversal of his opposition to the bill. Dirksen's quest for reelection played a noteworthy role in this decision. The second event was the March 1, 1968, release of the Kerner Commission report on civil disorder during the 1960s. This report found a link between housing segregation and urban violence and school desegregation; therefore, the commission recommended federal fair housing legislation to alleviate societal tensions. The third event was the assassination of Dr. Martin Luther King, Jr. Johnson was able to parlay sympathy for the slain civil rights leader into support for the Fair Housing Act. Johnson signed the act into law on April 21, 1968.

The 1968 Fair Housing Act prohibits discrimination in the sale, rental, and financing of dwellings based on race, color, or national origin. The act also extends to denial of real estate services based on those factors and prohibits advertising that expresses a racial preference, limitation, or discrimination. These restrictions apply to all housing in the United States. However, the law was not immediately successful in eliminating housing discrimination due to various weaknesses inherent in the legislation as well as the manner in which it has been interpreted and enforced. According to Lamb (2005), the most serious flaw of the Fair Housing Act was its weak and unenforceable provisions. The Department of Housing and Urban Development (HUD) had no power to require compliance with the law. The department was limited to asking the parties of a fair housing dispute to meet and attempt to resolve the complaint with HUD's help. There were other weaknesses in the law as well. For instance, three types of housing were not covered by the legislation. This included single-family homes sold or rented without the employment of a real estate agent, or the use of discriminatory advertising by someone owning or receiving income from up to three such dwellings. It also included what is known as Mrs. Murphy's boardinghouse exemption, which means that the law does not apply to homes with up to four separate living units in which the owner also resides. A third exemption applied to housing owned by private clubs and religious organizations. The law's ambiguity led to several problems. Many key terms of the legislation, including "fair housing" and "discriminatory housing practice," were not defined. Moreover, this ambiguity allowed presidents wide discretion in interpreting how the provisions of the act should be enforced (Lamb 2005, 47–50).

The law was amended in 1988 to prevent discrimination in housing based on disability or familial status. The 1988 amendments also established new enforcement mechanisms within HUD and expanded the jurisdiction of the Justice Department to allow suits to be brought in federal district courts. HUD's new enforcement power put teeth into the Fair Housing Act by authorizing the department to initiate investigations rather than passively wait for a claim to be brought. Additionally, the department was authorized to establish an administrative law procedure to adjudicate disputes. This has allowed HUD to pursue remedies other than asking the parties to resolve disputes themselves. For instance, administrative law judges have the authority to award "damages, civil penalties to the government, injunctive relief, and attorney's fees" (Sidney 2003, 57). Collectively, these provisions prohibit actions against target populations in housing or rental transactions, mortgage loans, property appraisals, and in advertising about housing.

The Fair Housing Act was likewise strengthened by other actions of the federal government. The HCD Acts of 1987 and 1992 implemented the Fair Housing Initiatives Program, which furnished funding to organizations seeking to prevent discriminatory housing practices. During 1994, President Bill Clinton issued Executive Order 12892, which established the President's Fair Housing Council and required federal agencies to promote fair housing in programs and activities. Finally, in June 2001 President George W. Bush released Executive Order 13217, which mandated that federal agencies evaluate existing programs to determine whether improvements in the availability of community-based living arrangements for persons with disabilities could be made.

Despite the aforementioned laws and programs, there is still evidence that discrimination in housing has continued nationally. A 2002 study by the U.S. Department of Housing and Urban Development encompassing 20 metropolitan markets over the 1989 to 2000 period found that 17 percent of African Americans and 20 percent of Hispanic Americans experienced discrimination in home sales transactions. In renting, those groups suffered even higher rates of discrimination, according to the HUD report. On the other hand, groups such as the National Fair Housing Alliance together with a plethora of state-based entities have displayed effectiveness in advancing the goals of the Fair Housing Act.

See also Housing, Discrimination in; King, Martin Luther, Jr.; Restrictive Covenants; U.S. Department of Justice

Bibliography

Bristo, Marca, ed. 2003. *Reconstructing Fair Housing.* Collingdale, PA: Diane Publishing.

Department of Housing and Urban Development. 2005. *Fair Housing Act Design Manual: A Manual to Assist Designers and Builders in Meeting the Accessibility Requirements of the Fair Housing Act.* Books for Business.

Lamb, Charles M. 2005. *Housing Segregation in Suburban America since 1960: Presidential and Judicial Politics.* New York: Cambridge University Press.

National Affordable Housing Management Association. 2000. *Fair Housing: A Guidebook for Owners and Managers of Apartments.* n.p.: Compass Group.

Sidney, Mara S. 2003. *Unfair Housing: How National Policy Shapes Community Action.* Lawrence: University Press of Kansas.

Samuel B. Hoff

FAIR LABOR STANDARDS ACT. *See Alden v. Maine;*

FAMILY MEDICAL LEAVE ACT OF 1993. *See* Employment Discrimination

FARRAKHAN, LOUIS. *See* Nation of Islam

FBI. *See* Federal Bureau of Investigation

FCC. *See* Federal Communications Commission

FCC V. PACIFICA FOUNDATION (1978)

In passing the Communications Act of 1934, Congress delegated to the Federal Communications Commission (FCC) the power to regulate broadcast media "in the public interest." In 1948 Congress enacted a prohibition against uttering "obscene, indecent, or profane language by means of radio communication." However, prior to the Supreme Court's decision in *FCC v. Pacifica Foundation* (1978), the FCC had no formal rules effectuating that prohibition. Prior to the 1970s, television and radio stations throughout the country engaged in a high level of self-censorship, and there were few controversies over the broadcasting of allegedly indecent material.

The controversy that led to the *Pacifica* decision began on an October afternoon in 1973 when a New York radio station aired a satirical monologue by the comedian George Carlin. The 12-minute sketch discussed in some detail the etymology of "the seven dirty words you can't say on the radio." Before airing the recording, the station warned listeners that it contained "sensitive language which might be regarded as offensive to some."

Although the station received no complaints directly from listeners, a man who claimed that he had heard the monologue while driving in his car with his young son filed a complaint with the Federal Communications Commission. While it imposed no formal sanctions, the FCC indicated that the

complaint would be "associated with the station's license file, and in the event that subsequent complaints are received, the commission will then decide whether it should utilize any of the available sanctions it has been granted by Congress."

Pacifica Foundation, the station's parent company, appealed the agency's action to the United States Court of Appeals for the District of Columbia. Attorneys for Pacifica argued that the Carlin monologue did not meet the legal test of obscenity and therefore could not be banned from the radio by the FCC. In a two-to-one decision, the court agreed, which prompted the FCC to seek review in the Supreme Court.

In a five-to-four decision, the Supreme Court reversed the D.C. circuit. Writing for the majority, Justice John Paul Stevens stressed the unique nature of the broadcast medium and, in particular, its accessibility to children. Stevens also discounted the value of warnings that stations might issue to protect unwilling listeners from offensive material: "Because the broadcast audience is constantly tuning in and out, prior warnings cannot completely protect the listener or viewer from unexpected program content." Stevens concluded his opinion by invoking a colorful metaphor, writing that "when the Commission finds that a pig has entered the parlor, the exercise of its regulatory power does not depend on proof that the pig is obscene."

In dissent, Justice Potter Stewart (joined by Justices William Brennan and Byron White and Thurgood Marshall) stressed that because the Carlin monologue did not rise to the level of obscenity, it was speech protected by the First Amendment. Stewart concluded, "Since the Carlin monologue concededly was not 'obscene,' I believe that the Commission lacked statutory authority to ban it."

In the wake of the *Pacifica* decision the FCC established formal rules prohibiting obscenity and indecency in broadcasting and defining those terms in light of relevant Supreme Court jurisprudence. The significance of the *Pacifica* decision became apparent in recent years as public controversy erupted over allegedly indecent programming on radio and television and the FCC's enforcement actions against various media entities charged with violating the decency rules.

See also Brennan, William J., Jr.; Federal Communications Commission; First Amendment; Internet, Free Speech on; Marshall, Thurgood; Obscenity and Pornography; Press, Freedom of the; Speech, Freedom of; Stevens, John Paul; Stewart, Potter; White, Byron R.

John M. Scheb II and Otis H. Stephens, Jr.

FDR. *See* Roosevelt, Franklin D.

FEDERAL BUREAU OF INVESTIGATION (FBI)

The Federal Bureau of Investigation (FBI) is the primary law enforcement agency in the United States Department of Justice. The formation of the FBI dates back to the late nineteenth century, when special investigators in the Justice Department were assigned to enforce federal criminal statutes. In 1907, President Theodore Roosevelt requested U.S. Congress to create a new law enforcement agency in the Justice Department. When Congress opposed, Roosevelt in 1908 created the Bureau of Investigation by executive order. The word "Federal" was added in 1935.

Initially, the bureau's jurisdiction included only a limited number of federal offenses that related to interstate commerce. Yet the bureau would rapidly rise to become the most important federal law enforcement organization in the United States, especially as it was assigned to enforce new federal criminal statutes, such as the 1912 Mann Act, which prohibited the interstate transportation of women for prostitution or other immoral purposes, and the National Motor Vehicle Theft Act of 1919.

By the early 1920s, the bureau was riddled with scandal and incompetence due to a lack of professionalism. In order to turn the bureau into a more accountable and professional organization, J. Edgar Hoover was appointed in 1924 as the bureau's new director, a position he would hold until his death in 1972.

During his nearly five decades as FBI director, Hoover was one of the most powerful public officials in the United States. Under his direction, the FBI became a modern law enforcement agency that acquired world fame. However, it was also rumored that politicians and other leaders feared Hoover because of the information that the FBI collected about them. Not until several years after Hoover's death was it was uncovered that the FBI under Hoover's direction had collected vast amounts of personal information about political leaders and community activists, among them Dr. Martin Luther King, Jr., whom Hoover accused of having ties with the Communist Party.

The gangster era of the 1930s provided an important impetus for the bureau's public image as a top law enforcement organization. The bureau's involvement in some heavily publicized criminal cases captured the public's imagination and garnered political support as well. The bureau also became increasingly responsible for cross-border and international crimes, such as violations of immigration laws and the prostitution trade. To successfully accomplish its broadened functions, the FBI acquired additional personnel; an ever-growing budget; and advanced technological means, such as the Uniform Crime Reports, the Scientific Crime Detection Laboratory, and an elaborate fingerprint system.

The events surrounding World War II were critical in the development of the FBI. In 1934, President Roosevelt had issued a secret order for the bureau to investigate the American Nazi movement, and shortly after the outbreak of war in Europe in 1939, the FBI was formally charged to investigate violations of neutrality laws as well as espionage, sabotage, and subversive activities. During the Second World War, the FBI would drastically expand its powers, as the bureau's budget and personnel increased more than fivefold.

After World War II, the FBI further solidified its position. The FBI became responsible for the enforcement of hundreds of federal criminal statutes pertaining to such issues as gambling, racketeering, and civil rights violations. The bureau was also very actively involved in government actions against the Communist threat in the United States during the 1950s and the violent excesses of the anti-Vietnam War movement in the 1960s and 1970s.

With its ever-broadening powers, FBI activities would occasionally also touch on legitimate forms of dissent, but the abuses of the FBI would not be exposed until several years after Hoover's death. Since then, the FBI's activities in matters of domestic security and counterintelligence have often been questioned as a result of their potential to harm constitutional rights.

Traditionally, the FBI has also been heavily involved in international police work. In 1938, the FBI became the official U.S. representative on the International Criminal Police Commission, the organization today known as Interpol. In the late 1950s, the FBI left Interpol and from then on pursued a more independent international course. The bureau became responsible for investigating violations of federal law with international dimensions, such as terrorism and drug trafficking. The FBI also maintains an extensive system of agents abroad, the so-called legal attachés, and oversees training programs of foreign police.

Besides its usual federal duties, the FBI, beginning in the late 1980s, turned its attention to the rising crime problems in the former Communist countries in Eastern Europe, when suddenly new domestic issues emerged. In 1992, the FBI was involved in a stand-off with a criminal suspect in Ruby Ridge, Idaho, that left a woman, child, and law enforcement agent dead. Less than a year later, the FBI could not prevent the deaths of some 80 members of the Branch Davidians, a religious sect in Waco, Texas, whose compound burned down after a 51-day standoff. These events led to congressional inquiries about the FBI's ability to respond to emergencies. During the 1990s, the FBI was further exposed to public criticisms because of mistakes that had been made in investigations involving the bureau's crime laboratory.

Although the FBI had begun to accord higher priority to the challenges of terrorism during the 1990s, the tragic events of September 11, 2001, launched a new phase in the bureau's development. In the months following 9/11, the FBI assigned some 4,000 of its 11,500 special agents to counterterrorist activities, and since June 2002, the FBI has been reformed as the leading counterterrorism agency in the United States. The FBI, in collaboration with local and state agencies, oversees various joint terrorism task forces across the United States. Independent from the Department of Homeland Security, the FBI has also been given increased intelligence and investigative powers by the USA PATRIOT Act. The FBI budget request for fiscal year 2006 amounts to $5.7 billion to support 31,475 positions, of which 12,140 are special agents and 2,745 are intelligence analysts. Thus, as was the case during other momentous social disturbances, such as World War II and the Cold War, the events of 9/11 have brought about important changes for the FBI, the impact of which may last for a considerable time to come.

See also American Nazi Party; Communist Party USA; Homeland Security, Department of; Roosevelt, Franklin D.; Terrorism, War on; USA PATRIOT Act; U.S. Department of Justice

Bibliography

Cunningham, David. 2004. *There's Something Happening Here: The New Left, the Klan, and FBI Counterintelligence.* Berkeley and Los Angeles: University of California Press.

Deflem, Mathieu. 2002. *Policing World Society: Historical Foundations of International Police Cooperation.* Oxford: Oxford University Press.

Powers, Richard Gid. 2004. *Broken: The Troubled Past and Uncertain Future of the FBI.* New York: Free Press.

Theoharis, Athan G. 2004. *The FBI and American Democracy: A Brief Critical History.* Lawrence: University Press of Kansas.

Ungar, Sanford J. 1976. *FBI.* Boston: Little, Brown.

Mathieu Deflem

FEDERAL COMMUNICATIONS COMMISSION (FCC)

An independent agency located within the executive branch of the federal government, the Federal Communications Commission (FCC) regulates a wide array of communications media and technologies, including radio and television stations, telephones, and communications satellites. Like other regulatory agencies, the FCC performs executive, quasi-legislative, and quasi-judicial functions (Krasnow, Longley, and Terry 1982). The agency is headed by five commissioners appointed to five-year terms by the president subject to confirmation by the Senate. The president also appoints the chairman of the FCC from among the sitting commissioners.

A key element of the regulatory rationale for broadcast radio and television is the public ownership of the airwaves; therefore, broadcasters should operate in the "public interest, convenience, and necessity" (Communications Act, 1934, § 307 and 309). Of course, the "public interest, convenience and necessity" is an imprecise notion, but one that vests considerable discretion in the FCC. However, the FCC rarely acts alone. Rather, its policies are the result of interactions among the agency and the industries it regulates, various interest groups, the courts, and Congress.

Because broadcasters must obtain licenses from the FCC, the agency can enforce its regulations through suspension or revocation of licenses. Alternatively, the FCC can deny an application for a renewal of license if it determines that the licensee is not operating in the public interest. The agency is also empowered to issue cease-and-desist orders and impose monetary fines on entities that violate FCC rules.

In *FCC v. Pacifica Foundation* (1978), the Supreme Court upheld an FCC enforcement action against a radio station for broadcasting content the FCC determined to be indecent. The Court held that the FCC was empowered by Congress to restrict indecent broadcasting and that such restrictions do not offend the First Amendment.

The FCC defines indecent speech as "language or material that, in context, depicts or describes sexual or excretory activities or organs in terms patently offensive as measured by contemporary community standards for the broadcast medium." The FCC does not independently screen broadcasts for indecent material. Complaints must first be submitted to the commission before an investigation is launched or deemed necessary.

In recent years, the FCC has become the center of controversy as it has enforced its decency rule against numerous radio and television networks and stations. Large fines have been imposed on, among other corporate entities, CBS, Fox, Clear Channel Communications, Viacom, and Infinity Broadcasting for violating FCC decency rules. Some believe that the FCC should not act as the "decency police" and that its enforcement actions threaten First Amendment values. But others demand action from the FCC to stem what they perceive to be increasingly indecent programming on radio and television. After Janet Jackson's infamous "wardrobe malfunction" during the halftime show of the 2005 Super Bowl, the FCC received more than half a million complaints. Several months later, the FCC imposed a $550,000 fine on CBS, the network that aired the Super Bowl.

In April 2004 the FCC fined Clear Channel Communications $495,000 for 18 decency rule violations committed by so-called shock jock Howard Stern during one of his radio shows. This prompted Clear Channel to cease carrying the Stern program on its radio stations. Stern, a vocal critic of the FCC, announced shortly thereafter that he was moving his program to satellite radio, which is currently not within the FCC's jurisdiction.

See also *FCC v. Pacifica Foundation;* First Amendment; Internet, Free Speech on; Obscenity and Pornography; Speech, Freedom of

Bibliography

Coase, Ronald H. 1959. "The Federal Communications Commission." *Journal of Law and Economics* 2:1–40.

Creech, Kenneth C. 2003. *Electronic Media Law And Regulation.* 4th ed. Oxford: Focal Press.

Krasnow, Erwin G., Lawrence D. Longley, and Herbert A. Terry. 1982. *Politics of Broadcast Regulation.* New York: St. Martin's Press.

Krattenmaker, Thomas G., and Lucas A. Powe, Jr. 1994. *Regulating Broadcast Programming.* Cambridge, MA: MIT Press.

Krugman, Dean M., and Leonard N. Reid. 1980. "The 'Public Interest' as Defined by FCC Policy Makers." *Journal of Broadcasting* 24 (3): 311–25.

Wollenberg, J. R. 1989. "The FCC: Arbiter of 'the Public Interest, Convenience, and Necessity.'" In *A Legislative History of the Communications Act of 1934,* ed. M. D. Paglin. New York: Oxford University Press.

Maria Fontenot

FEDERALISM AND CIVIL RIGHTS AND LIBERTIES

When most people think about civil rights and liberties today, they usually think of a court enforcing the rights enumerated in our Bill of Rights, such as those of free speech, press, and religion under the First Amendment or the rights to due process and equal protection of the law under the Fourteenth Amendment. This view, however, did not become prominent until the 1950s, when the U.S. Supreme Court threw its weight behind the Civil Rights Movement. For most of American history, rights were protected through the structure of government. This view was endorsed by many of the Framers of the U.S. Constitution and is evidenced by the fact that the Constitution, as originally proposed, lacked a Bil of Rights.

The Framers of the Constitution dispersed the power of the federal government into three separate branches so as to impede the concentration of power. Additionally, they established a federal system of government that affirmed the independent sovereignty of the states. This new form of government, where the federal government and the states share responsibility in governing, has been called "our federalism."

A federal system of government can be contrasted to a unitary system of government, which has only one central government, and the subsidiary governments of which serve as agents of the central government. In the United States, the states are not mere agents of the federal government but exist independently of the federal government. States exert their own political control over the territory within their respective geographical boundaries.

Each state has its own laws, passed by its own legislature, administered by its own executive (the governor), and enforced by its own courts.

The relationship between federalism and the protection of rights has long been neglected (see Chen 2002; Katz and Tarr 1996). The Framers knew, however, that the way in which government was structured was just as important for the protection of rights as having a Bill of Rights. James Madison, who saw Bills of Rights as mere "parchment barriers," argued in *Federalist* no. 51 that federalism and the separation of powers, both of which were incorporated into the structure of the new government, provided a "double security" for the people's rights: "The different governments will control each other, at the same time that each will be controlled by itself." Alexander Hamilton in *Federalist* no. 28 also noted that each government could impose checks on the other governments' infringements of rights:

Power being almost always the rival of power, the general [i.e., federal] government will at all times stand ready to check the usurpations of the state governments, and these will have the same disposition toward the general government.... If [the people's] rights are invaded by either, they can make use of the other [government] as a means of redress.

In spite of the Framers' intent that federalism serve to protect rights, it has also been invoked by those opposed to rights protection. Because of the South's blighted association with slavery, racial segregation, and resistance to efforts to correct these discriminatory practices, people most frequently blamed the states for violating people's rights. Ultimately, it took federal action in the form of Supreme Court rulings and congressional legislation under the Fourteenth Amendment to end state-sponsored discrimination. The Supreme Court invalidated state laws in the areas of racial segregation (and later mandated busing), criminal rights, and legislative apportionment. Congress passed the Civil Rights Act of 1964 and the Voting Rights Act of 1965. Because Southern leaders appealed to federalism and states' rights to defend these social evils, federalism was perceived as an "enemy of rights and for that reason, not a very good thing" (Zuckert 1996, 75; See also Riker 1964). The recent history of the Civil Rights Movement, however, has obscured the fact that the political institutions of the states provided the primary means for protecting rights for the first 150 years or so of the Republic (Dinan 1998). Furthermore, the federal government has engaged in its share of restricting civil rights and liberties.

Shortly after the federal government was established, Congress passed the Fugitive Slave Act of 1793, which authorized the return of runaway slaves to their owners. Abolitionists in the Northern states invoked federalism and states' rights to advocate defiance of the federal law, while Southerners supported the law. Congress passed an even tougher Fugitive Slave Act in 1850, but similar opposition in Northern states made this law practically unenforceable.

Soon after that, Congress passed the Alien and Sedition Acts in 1798. Allegedly enacted in response to the immanence of war with France, the acts were in fact devised by the Federalists to silence Republican criticism of President John Adams. The Sedition Act, which prohibited written and oral criticism of the government, Congress, or the president, violated the First Amendment protections of freedom of speech and the press. Following the passage of these acts, the legislatures of Kentucky and Virginia adopted resolutions drafted by Thomas Jefferson and James Madison, respectively, challenging the legality of those acts.

In other eras, both the state and federal governments were guilty of restricting civil liberties. Following World War I, both state and federal laws were enacted prohibiting criticism of the government. Congress's passage of the USA PATRIOT Act following 9/11 created concern that civil rights would be (and already had been) violated in the name of fighting terrorism. In response to the PATRIOT Act, local governments have adopted resolutions opposing the legislation based on the demands of their citizens. This situation is similar to the resolutions adopted by the Kentucky and Virginia legislatures opposing the Alien and Sedition Acts.

In recent decades some state courts operating in the new judicial federalism (see Brennan 1977; Tarr 1994) have afforded greater protection of rights than that required by federal law. State judges have accomplished this by interpreting their own state constitutions more broadly than federal judges have interpreted the U.S. Constitution, even in cases where the language of the two constitutional provisions was identical.

These examples demonstrate that the historical relationship between federalism and the protection of rights in America has been complex: both the federal government and the states have in different periods defended as well as restricted civil rights and liberties. Katz and Tarr note that "[t]he division of responsibility between nation and state for protecting rights has varied throughout American history, and so too the willingness of nation and state to live up to that responsibility" (Katz and Tarr 1996, xii). Whether one concludes that federalism's relationship to the protection of rights has been positive or negative, one cannot deny that the federal structure of American government has had a significant impact on the protection of rights and liberties.

See also Abolitionist Movement; Alien and Sedition Acts; Bill of Rights (American); Brennan, William J., Jr.; Civil Rights Act of 1964; Civil Rights Movement; *Federalist Papers;* Fourteenth Amendment; Jefferson, Thomas; Kentucky and Virginia Resolutions; Madison, James; New Judicial Federalism; Segregation, De Facto and De Jure; Slavery; State Action Doctrine; USA PATRIOT Act; Voting Rights Act of 1965

Bibliography

Brennan, William J., Jr. 1977. "State Constitutions and the Protection of Individual Rights." *Harvard Law Review* 90:489–503.

Chen, Paul. 2002. "Federalism and Rights: A Neglected Relationship." In *Comparative Federalism in the Devolution Era,* ed. Neil C. McCabe. Lexington, MA: Lexington Books.

Dinan, John J. 1998. *Keeping the People's Liberties: Legislators, Citizens, and Judges as Guardians of Rights.* Lawrence: University Press of Kansas.

Katz, Ellis, and G. Alan Tarr. 1996. Introduction to *Federalism and Rights,* ed. Ellis Katz and G. Alan Tarr. Lanham, MD: Rowman & Littlefield.

Riker, William H. 1964. *Federalism: Origin, Operations, Significance.* Boston: Little, Brown.

Tarr, G. Alan. 1994. "New Judicial Federalism in Perspective." *Notre Dame Law Review* 72:1097–118.

Zuckert, Michael. 1996. "Toward a Corrective Federalism: The United States Constitution, Federalism, and Rights." In *Federalism and Rights,* ed. Ellis Katz and G. Alan Tarr. Lanham, MD: Rowman & Littlefield.

Paul Chen

FEDERALIST PAPERS (1788)

The Federalist Papers is a collection of brilliant essays authored by Alexander Hamilton, John Jay, and James Madison in support of the new Constitution. Published in New York newspapers during the winter of 1788, these essays certainly helped to secure ratification of the Constitution in that crucial state. Yet *The Federalist Papers* is much more than a compendium of political tracts. Because it represents a clear exposition of the Constitution, *The Federalist* continues to be employed by judges in addressing questions of constitutional interpretation. Scholars also regard *The Federalist* as an important work in the history of political theory.

See also Articles of Confederation; Bill of Rights (American); Bill of Rights, Incorporation of; Bills of Attainder; Clemency, Executive; Common-Law Background of American Civil Rights and Liberties; Ex Post Facto Laws; Federalism and Civil Rights and Liberties; Madison, James; Police Power; Property Rights; Tyranny of the Majority; United States Constitution

Bibliography

Hamilton, Alexander, James Madison, and John Jay. [1787–1788] 1961. *The Federalist Papers.* New York: Mentor.

John M. Scheb II and Otis H. Stephens, Jr.

FEDERAL TORT CLAIMS ACT. *See* Sovereign Immunity

FEMINIST MOVEMENT

Historically the women's movement has been concerned with "equality and justice for all women, and [the elimination of] systems of inequality and injustice in all aspects of women's lives" (Shaw and Lee 2001, 9). Often the term "feminism" is used synonymously with the women's movement; it is employed more precisely to refer to the ideology of the women's movement. Yet contemporary Americans often distinguish between the two, tending to view feminism as something more extreme than the women's movement. Although in 1999 "two-thirds of Americans surveyed say they support the 'women's movement' only 26% consider themselves 'feminists'" (Huddy et al. 2000, as reprinted in McGlen et al. 2005, 11).

Most scholars date the origins of the first wave of feminism to either the eighteenth-century writings of Mary Wollstonecraft, who advocated equal education for both girls and boys, or the Seneca Falls Convention of 1848, which had the primary goal of citizenship for women. However, scholars had advocated for women's equality even earlier. Indeed, Christine de Pizan argued in favor of both equal education and the right of inheritance for women in *Book of the City of Ladies* (1405). One could even argue that Plato's *Republic* proposes equality for women, at least in the guardian class. The focus on education, citizenship, and some financial freedoms emphasized the need for protection from de jure (by law) or legal discrimination. Pioneers in women's history, including Elizabeth Cady Stanton, Sojourner Truth, Lucretia Mott, Susan B. Anthony, Lucy Stone, Alice Stone Blackwell, Ida B. Wells, and Alice Paul, worked tirelessly for these rights during the first wave. Unfortunately, not all of them lived to see the first wave conclude with a significant victory: women's suffrage was attained with the ratification of the Nineteenth Amendment in 1920.

The second wave of feminism dates from 1920 until the beginning of the 1980s. In reality, though, with the Great Depression, World War II, and the relatively quiescent 1950s, the apex of the second wave was during the 1960s and 1970s. Two key themes dominated the second wave: continuing to overturn de jure barriers to women's equality, and exploring de facto (in point of fact, customary, or by tradition) discrimination that women faced.

The legal barriers that women faced were complex. Women were typically only hired for clerical, child-care, or housekeeping jobs, and they were not entering college in large numbers. Most women felt the pressure to be stay-at-home wives and mothers. This push came during the 1950s after World War II veterans returned from the war and did not want women competing for jobs or their spots in college—which young men could now afford due to the GI Bill.

Women became so frustrated with these legal constraints that they began mobilizing in the 1960s and 1970s. Numerous aspects of legal discrimination were overturned through the 1972 amendments to Title VII of the Civil Rights Act of 1964 (preventing hiring discrimination on the basis of gender), the addition of Title IX to the Education Amendments Act (prohibiting discrimination in education, including sports), and key Supreme Court decisions like *Reed v. Reed* in 1971 (which established that the Fourteenth Amendment protects women against unreasonable discrimination). Also, *Roe v. Wade* (1973) gave women the freedom of reproductive choice. Additionally, women were provided affirmative action and given de jure protection against sexual harassment.

The second wave went beyond prohibiting de jure discrimination to addressing de facto discrimination. A key impetus for this shift came with the publication of Betty Friedan's *The Feminine Mystique* in 1963. Addressing the "problem with no name," which she labeled the feminine mystique, Friedan argued that millions of women were quietly miserable in the media-projected image of what they were supposed to be: "perfect mothers to perfect children, … perfect lovers for their perfect husbands … and women who derived enormous pleasure from cooking and housecleaning (especially when they used sponsors' products)" (Friedan 1963, 18).

Efforts to end de jure and de facto discrimination against women began to coalesce after 1963—the same year that President Kennedy appointed the Commission on the Status of Women (CSW), after which every governor followed his lead at the state level (McGlen et al. 2005, 13). The national CSW recommended the Equal Pay Act, which became law in 1963. Women realized, however, that neither the Equal Pay Act nor the Civil Rights Act was being enforced, and Betty Freidan, along with Gloria Steinem and others, wanted to seek action "now" (Harrison 2002, 25). This led to the formation of the National Organization for Women (NOW), the goal of which was the passage of an Equal Rights Amendment (ERA) to the Constitution, an objective that ultimately failed when the deadline for ratification expired in 1982. The major reason for the defeat of the ERA was the efforts of Phyllis Schlafly, who predicted that passage would result in women being drafted, the creation of unisex restrooms, and even forced abortions. These scare tactics also helped inaugurate the backlash of the 1980s, which in turn fueled the third wave of feminism.

The third wave includes both young women and men born into the freedoms provided by the second wave who may have never experienced discrimination on the basis of gender, and those who are older but ideologically aligned with current tenets. It gained momentum during the backlash against women's rights that occurred during the Reagan years. Accordingly, Susan Faludi's book of the same name, *Backlash* (1991), maintained that the conservative ideological tenor of the 1980s fostered a sense of resentment against women who had made both de facto and de jure strides during the 1960s and 1970s. When some limited research came out suggesting both that juvenile crime was rising and that women were working longer hours, many conservatives, including Schlafly, blamed working moms. These women, they suggested, had abandoned their children during after-school hours while they worked, creating so-called latch-key children who were home alone and had the opportunity to commit crime. Faludi asserted that the conservatives failed to account for the rising divorce rate that resulted in single mothers who were forced to work or the economy as other factors explaining the rising crime rate.

Now that the backlash has passed, what are the parameters of the third wave of feminism? This is a question more simply asked than answered. It is almost a penumbral collection of opinions on gender issues. Amy Richards argues:

To unite today's young women, we need to focus on a particular issue and then bring together the diverse feminist opinions on the matter to create a rich, complex dialogue. Better to disagree than to be silent. (Quoted in Shaw and Lee 220)

Moreover, Michelle Sidler notes that important questions must be asked post-second wave. She suggests that possibly the second wave only benefited upper-class white women, and that the third wave must focus on all races and all classes (Shaw and Lee 2001, 353). Inclusion seems to be the key theme of the third wave.

Accordingly, the chosen medium for third-wave participation varies widely. A common theme is college participation in Take Back the Night rallies, but other outlets include zines or e-zines (online publications to promote so-called girl power), all-girl bands like Riot Grrls, and alternative dressing. Other methods of third wave participation, however, are much more traditional and focus on academic and economic research.

In conclusion, feminism, or more specifically, the three waves of the women's movement, has "come a long way baby" from its nascent stages, when women sought only to be taught and to vote. It evolved through the second wave, when women obtained working rights, educational opportunities, freedom of choice, civil rights, and other constitutional freedoms; to now, when many girls born in the United States may not ever experience overt government-sponsored gender discrimination; Women can be proud of their accomplishments while still realizing that there is much work left to be completed.

See also Anthony, Susan B.; Equal Protection Clause; Equal Rights Amendment; Fourteenth Amendment; Seneca Falls Declaration; Stanton, Elizabeth Cady; Title IX, Education Amendments Act; Truth, Sojourner; Women's Suffrage

Bibliography

Faludi, Susan. 1991. *Backlash: The Undeclared War Against American Women.* New York: Crown.

Friedan, Betty. 1963. *The Feminine Mystique.* New York: WW Norton.

Harrison, Brigid. 2002. *Women in American Politics: An Introduction.* Belmont, CA: Wadsworth.

McGlen, Nancy, Karen O'Connor, Laura van Assendelft, and Wendy Gunther-Canada. 2005. *Women, Politics, and American Society.* 4th ed. New York: Pearson.

Shaw, Susan, and Janet Lee. 2001. *Women's Voices, Feminist Visions: Classic and Contemporary Readings.* New York: McGraw-Hill.

Lori Maxwell

FIELD SOBRIETY TESTS. *See* DUI Field Tests and Breath Tests; Implied Consent Statutes

FIFTEENTH AMENDMENT (1870)

Like the Thirteenth and Fourteenth amendments, the Fifteenth Amendment was adopted in the aftermath of the Civil War to protect the rights of the newly freed former slaves and other persons of African descent. The Thirteenth Amendment abolished slavery; the Fourteenth Amendment conferred federal and state citizenship on all persons born or naturalized in the United States and prohibited states from denying persons within their respective jurisdictions due process or equal protection of the law. Neither of those amendments mentioned the right to vote.

In 1866, Congress enacted a statute extending to persons of African descent the right to vote in elections in the District of Columbia and the federal territories. The first Reconstruction Act also readmitted to the Union those states that had seceded, but only on the condition that they recognize the right of suffrage for all their citizens. However, because the Constitution gives to the states the power to set qualifications for voting, another constitutional amendment was needed to ensure that all states extended the right to vote to African Americans. Thus Section 1 of the Fifteenth Amendment (ratified in 1870) provides: "The right of citizens of the United States to vote shall not be denied or abridged by the United States or by any State on account of race, color, or previous condition of servitude." In addition, Section 2 states: "The Congress shall have power to enforce this article by appropriate legislation."

Shortly after the Fifteenth Amendment was ratified, Congress enacted the Civil Rights Act of 1870, which made it a federal crime to interfere with the right to vote, and the Force Act of 1871, which provided for federal oversight of elections. In *Ex parte Yarbrough* (1884), a case where a member of the Ku Klux Klan was prosecuted for interfering with an African American citizen's right to vote, the Supreme Court upheld the Civil Rights Act of 1870 as "appropriate legislation" under Section 2 of the Fifteenth Amendment. In his opinion for Court, Justice Samuel F. Miller expounded on the meaning of the Fifteenth Amendment, saying in part:

In all cases where the former slave-holding states had not removed from their constitutions the words 'white man' as a qualification for voting, this provision did, in effect, confer on him the right to vote, because, being paramount to the state law, and a part of the state law, it annulled the discriminating word 'white,' and thus left him in the enjoyment of the same right as white persons. And such would be the effect of any future constitutional provision of a state which should give the right of voting exclusively to white people, whether they be men or women.... In such cases this fifteenth article of amendment does ... substantially confer on the Negro the right to vote, and Congress has the power to protect and enforce that right.

During the Reconstruction Era, African Americans voted freely in the South, turning out to vote at rates comparable to those of white citizens. After Reconstruction ended, the situation changed. Beginning in the late nineteenth century and continuing until well past the middle of the twentieth century, Southern states employed a variety of means to prevent their African American citizens from exercising the right to vote. These devices included grandfather clauses, which were invalidated by the Supreme Court in *Guinn v. United States* (1915); the infamous white primary, which was struck down in *Smith v. Allwright*

(1944); and racial gerrymandering, an extreme instance of which was declared unconstitutional in *Gomillion v. Lightfoot* (1960). States also employed literacy tests and poll taxes to discourage African American participation in elections. Poll taxes as conditions for voting in federal elections were abolished by the ratification of the Twenty-fourth Amendment in 1964. Two years later, in *Harper v. Virginia Board of Elections* (1966), the Supreme Court declared poll taxes in state elections unconstitutional under the Fourteenth Amendment. Although in *Lassiter v. Northampton County Board of Elections* (1960) the Supreme Court held that requiring citizens to pass literacy tests as a precondition for voting was not unconstitutional on its face, Congress effectively abolished literacy tests by enacting the Voting Rights Act of 1965.

See also Civil Rights Act of 1870; Civil Rights Act of 1957; Fourteenth Amendment; Free And Fair Elections; Grandfather Clause; Literacy Tests; Poll Tax; Racial Gerrymandering; Reconstruction; *South Carolina v. Katzenbach;* Thirteenth Amendment; Twenty-fourth Amendment; Universal Suffrage; Vote, Right to; Voting Rights Act of 1965; White Primary

Bibliography

Gillette, William. 1969. *The Right to Vote: Politics and the Passage of the Fifteenth Amendment.* Baltimore: Johns Hopkins University Press.

Keyssar, Alexander. 2000. *The Right to Vote: The Contested History of Democracy in the United States.* New York: Basic Books.

Maltz, Earl M. 1990. *Civil Rights, the Constitution, and Congress, 1863–1869.* Lawrence: University Press of Kansas.

John M. Scheb II and Otis H. Stephens, Jr.

FIFTH AMENDMENT (1791)

The Fifth Amendment to the United States Constitution, adopted in 1789 and ratified in 1791 as part of the Bill of Rights, contains a number of provisions that are of crucial importance in the field of civil rights and liberties. To guard against arbitrary prosecution, the amendment provides: "No person shall be held to answer for a capital, or otherwise infamous crime, unless on a presentment or indictment of a Grand Jury, except in cases arising in the land or naval forces, or in the Militia, when in actual service in time of War or public danger." The Double Jeopardy Clause states that "nor shall any person be subject for the same offence to be twice put in jeopardy of life or limb." The Self-Incrimination Clause provides that no person "shall be compelled in any criminal case to be a witness against himself." Indeed this is the clause that is invoked when one "takes the Fifth." Without question, the most important provision of the Fifth Amendment, and perhaps the entire Bill of Rights, is the Due Process Clause, which guarantees that no person shall "be deprived of life, liberty, or property, without due process of law." Finally, the Fifth Amendment limits the exercise of eminent domain by providing that "nor shall private property be taken for public use, without just compensation."

See also Accused, Rights of the; Bill of Rights, Incorporation of; Double Jeopardy, Prohibition of; Due Process, Procedural; Due Process, Substantive; Due Process Clauses; Grand Jury; Indictment; Just Compensation Clause; Liberty; Property Rights; Public Use Clause; Self-Incrimination Clause

John M. Scheb II and Otis H. Stephens, Jr.

FIGHTING WORDS DOCTRINE

Fighting words, speech that is likely to bring about a breach of peace or that is insulting by its very nature, are generally not considered protected speech. This includes personal epithets and other words intended for causing harm rather than communicating. However, forceful speech is generally protected, even when it is potentially insulting, and particularly when it constitutes political speech. The question of fighting words is highly controversial because of the diverse nature of our society, but also because traditionally, political speech has been the most protected type of speech both in terms of the right of a speaker to speak and the right of a listener to hear.

In *Cantwell v. Connecticut* (1940), a Jehovah's Witness was arrested under a breach of peace law for playing a record that listeners found offensive. While the Court overturned his conviction, it was not particularly solicitous of forceful speech by today's standards. Cantwell's phonograph record was not classified as unprotected fighting words, in part because of his conduct toward listeners—his words were general rather than specifically directed toward a person, and he was deferential to listeners' requests for him to stop. Additionally, he did not use obscenity or other low-level speech.

In contrast, in *Chaplinsky v. New Hampshire* (1942) the Court examined a situation in which the alleged fighting words were much more forceful, and it upheld the conviction. Chaplinsky directed his words toward a specific listener, calling a police officer a fascist and a racketeer. Although the statements were not necessarily a direct threat, they did represent threatening speech of a character not found in *Cantwell*. Here, the directionality of the words at a specific person rather than a generalized group made the speech fighting words.

Today, even when speech is directed at specific groups, the government may not regulate fighting words when the law in question targets specific content or viewpoints. In *RAV v. St. Paul* (1992), the Court addressed cross burning and the use of other symbols that might be considered fighting words. St. Paul, Minnesota's Bias-Motivated Crime Ordinance banned the burning of crosses and the use of swastikas and similar symbols to arouse fear or anger "on the basis of race, color, creed, religion, or gender." St. Paul argued that the law prohibited the use of fighting words, which are not protected by the First Amendment. However, the Supreme Court disagreed because the ordinance banned the offensive symbols only when used by the proponents of racial and religious hatred. If a speaker had other intentions, such as fighting intolerance, he or she could use the symbols as he or she pleased. St. Paul prevented the use of these fighting words only by specific groups, therefore making an unconstitutional content-based restriction.

The Court again dealt with cross burning in *Virginia v. Black* (2003). Here, the Court allowed laws banning cross burning only when the action is "carried out with an attempt to intimidate." The ruling was not inconsistent with *RAV* because it ruled specifically on cross burning, noting that this particular act has a long history in the United States and that in certain circumstances burning a cross becomes a truly threatening action rather than being simply speech. When used in situations of intimidation, where the perpetrator is using the symbol to cause fear, the state may regulate it because it is a "true threat," a threat in which the speaker is "communicat[ing] a serious expression of an intent to commit an act of unlawful violence to a particular individual or group of individuals." Because the Ku Klux Klan often used the burning of crosses to relay this message, it still holds the same threat today and is therefore not protected when used to intimidate in this manner. Here, the act of burning a cross becomes fighting words that are directed toward a specific individual for the purpose of intimidation, and therefore the act is unprotected.

The Court has found that per se fighting words, that is, words offensive by their very nature, do not exist. In *Cohen v. California* (1971), the Court overturned the conviction of a California man who entered a public courthouse wearing a jacket displaying the words "Fuck the Draft." In overturning his conviction, the Court noted that there was no directionality in Cohen's message; additionally, it had a political purpose. His audience was not captive—viewers could avert their eyes if they wished. Cohen's jacket was ruled to be essentially speech and not action. Though the jacket was not a traditional method of speaking, it was not accompanied by any violent action, either by Cohen or by others. The Court said that the "emotive force" of the words justified their use. In some contexts, offensive words might constitute fighting words—words yelled at a specific person on the street, for example—but they are not on their own classified as per se fighting words. In certain contexts, they represent protected First Amendment speech.

On a similar note, flag burning has also been viewed by some as per se fighting words—an act so offensive that it should not receive constitutional protection. However, here too, the Court has ruled that laws prohibiting flag burning and desecration are inherently content-based and thus constitutionally invalid. Because they punish flag burning only when it is intended to protest the government and not, for example, when one disposes of a flag by burning it, these laws unconstitutionally discriminate against certain viewpoints.

In *Texas v. Johnson* (1989), the Court permitted flag burning by striking down a Texas law that prohibited defacing or damaging the flag when one knew that such action would "seriously offend one or more persons likely to observe or discover his action." In overturning Johnson's conviction, the Court found that the statute turned typical symbolic speech thinking on its head. Instead of permitting the conduct because of its political or otherwise expressive content, the law banned the burning of a flag *because* it was expressive. Texas argued that its interest in the law was in "preserving the flag as a symbol of nationhood and national unity;" the Court replied that this interest was directly related to suppressing free expression, since the only reason this would be a concern would be if, in fact, the speaker were communicating some message contrary to this belief in burning the flag. Though many find flag burning and the message it communicates to be offensive, the Court wrote that this concern was not important enough to permit the government to prohibit such behavior. Rather, the First Amendment was designed to protect especially that speech with which others disagree.

Today, fighting words remain a highly controversial aspect of First Amendment law, particularly when they involve some of the most heinous segments of society. In 1977, a group of neo-Nazis decided to protest in Skokie, Illinois, a Chicago suburb with a large Jewish population, including approximately 5,000 concentration camp survivors. The group intended to wear Nazi uniforms and swastika armbands. In attempting to bar what they viewed as the most harmful aspects of the march, city officials attempted to prohibit the wearing of Nazi uniforms, the displaying of swastikas, and the distribution of anti-Semitic literature.

City officials argued that the protest was unprotected under First Amendment free speech rights because, in this context, actions such as the display of the swastika were an intentional attempt to harm others and would cause real harm to the citizens of Skokie. Additionally, threats of violence and planned counterprotests made the protest too dangerous to hold. However, both state and federal appeals courts ruled that such restrictions, as well as others that Skokie attempted to put into place, violated the First Amendment. The Court refused to acknowledge that speech could be considered fighting words just because others might be offended, or even become violent, upon hearing the speech. The protest lacked the sort of directionality present in *Chaplinsky*—marchers did not plan to accost individuals on the sidewalk, for example. Although the march was voluntarily cancelled by the protesters, the free speech doctrine introduced in this case remains alive today.

See also American Nazi Party; *Cantwell v. Connecticut; Cohen v. California;* Flag Burning; Profanity; Speech, Freedom of; Symbolic Speech; *Texas v. Johnson*

Bibliography

Delgado, Richard, and Kean Stefancic. 1996. *Must We Defend the Nazis? Hate Speech, Pornography, and the First Amendment.* New York: New York University Press.

Goldstein, Robert Justin. 2000. *Flag Burning and Free Speech: The Case of Texas v. Johnson.* Lawrence: University Press of Kansas.

Greenawalt, Kent. 1995. *Fighting Words: Individuals, Communities, and the Liberties of Speech.* Princeton, NJ: Princeton University Press.

Strum, Philippa. 1999. *When the Nazis Came to Skokie: Freedom for Speech We Hate.* Lawrence: University Press of Kansas.

Ronald Kahn

FINES. *See* Excessive Fines, Prohibition of

FIRST AMENDMENT (1791)

The First Amendment to the United States Constitution, adopted by Congress in 1789 and ratified by the states in 1791, explicitly recognizes the freedoms of religion, speech, press, and assembly as well as the right to petition government for a redress of grievances. The courts have also recognized that the First Amendment implicitly protects freedom of association as well as freedom of conscience.

See also *Abington School District v. Schempp;* Academic Freedom; Alien and Sedition Acts; Assembly, Freedom of; Association, Freedom of; Bad Tendency Test; Bill of Rights (American); Black, Hugo L.; *Bob Jones University v. United States; Boy Scouts of America v. Dale; Brandenburg v. Ohio;* Campaign Finance Reform; *Cantwell v. Connecticut;* Child Pornography; Clear and Present Danger Doctrine; Clear and Probable Danger Doctrine; *Cohen v. California;* Commercial Speech; Conscience, Freedom of; Defamation; Draft Cards, Burning of; *Edwards v. South Carolina; Employment Division, Department of Human Resources of Oregon v. Smith; Epperson v. Arkansas;* Establishment Clause; *Everson v. Board of Education;* Evolution/Creationism Controversy; *FCC v. Pacifica Foundation;* Fighting Words Doctrine; First Amendment, Approaches to; Flag Burning; Flag Salute Controversy; Freedom from Religion Foundation; Free Exercise Clause; Free Marketplace of Ideas; Free Press/Fair Trial Problem; *Gitlow v. New York; Hamilton v. Regents of the University of California;* Hate Speech; Holmes, Oliver Wendell, Jr.; Internet, Free Speech on; *Lemon v. Kurtzman;* Military Service, Civil Rights and Liberties in; *Miller v. California;* Moment of Silence Laws; *NAACP v. Alabama; Near v. Minnesota ex rel. Olson; New York Times v. Sullivan; New York Times v. United States;* Obscenity and Pornography; Overbreadth, Doctrine of; Petition, Right of; Picketing; Preferred Freedoms Doctrine; Press, Freedom of the; Prior Restraint, Doctrine of; Profanity; Public Employees, Constitutional Rights of; Public Forum; Religion, Freedom of; Religion, Official Endorsements of; Religious Displays on Public Property; Religious Schools, Government Aid to; Religious Tests, Prohibition of; *Reno v.*

American Civil Liberties Union; Reynolds v. United States; Schenck v. United States; School Choice Programs; School Prayer Decisions; Separation of Church and State; Speech, Freedom of; Speech/ Conduct Distinction; Sunday Closing Laws; Symbolic Speech; Tax Exemptions for Religious Organizations; Ten Commandments, Public Display of the; *Texas v. Johnson;* Time, Place, and Manner Restrictions; *Tinker v. Des Moines Independent Community School District; United States v. Virginia; West Virginia Board of Education v. Barnette*

John M. Scheb II and Otis H. Stephens, Jr.

FIRST AMENDMENT, APPROACHES TO

Freedom of expression is an essential element of democracy. The political importance of free expression is reflected in the fact that it is the first of the 10 amendments constituting the Bill of Rights, and it is guaranteed in absolutist language. The First Amendment provides that Congress shall make no law "respecting an establishment of religion, or prohibiting the free exercise thereof; or abridging the freedom of speech, or of the press." The First Amendment's absolutist language is unusual compared to freedom of expression in most constitutional democracies, which typically provide for qualified or conditional freedom of expression. In most modern constitutions, the declaration of the right to freedom of religion, speech, and press is accompanied by explicit statements limiting freedom of expression. The absolutist language of the First Amendment is problematic insofar as it is hard to reconcile with the fact that there are restrictions of free expression in the United States. Judges, members of Congress, and other government officials have never read the First Amendment literally to mean there can be no law restricting freedom of expression. In the United States, freedom of expression is actually a complex system of thinking about individual freedom and government control (Emerson 1971) that includes the First Amendment, statutory law, administrative regulations, and an extensive body of case law interpreting the Constitution. Understanding the First Amendment requires examining (1) the different areas of First Amendment jurisprudence (freedom of religion, speech, and press) and (2) the methods, doctrines, and tests that judges have used to determine the meaning of the words in the First Amendment.

The need for judicial interpretation of the text of the Constitution is usually attributed to the fact that someone has to provide concrete meaning for ambiguous phrases such as "unreasonable search and seizure," "cruel and unusual punishment," and "due process of law." The First Amendment requires interpretation not because of ambiguity but because of clarity. The absolutist language prohibiting Congress from making any law restricting freedom of expression is the primary reason why the First Amendment is not read literally to mean what it says. Instead, there are various approaches to determining what kinds of expression are not protected by the First Amendment and therefore can be prohibited, what kinds of expression are protected and therefore cannot be restricted, and what kinds of expression are protected but can nonetheless be regulated.

The Supreme Court rejected the literal or plain meaning of the words approach in its earliest First Amendment cases. In *Reynolds v. United States* (1879), Mormons argued that a federal statute providing that bigamy "shall be punished by a fine of not more than $500, and by imprisonment of not more than five years," was unconstitutional because it restricted their religious freedom to practice polygamy. The Court upheld the law by concluding that the Framers never intended to protect polygamy, which all Western nations considered "odious," and which England considered an offense against society. This case established the principle that Congress could restrict certain religious practices despite the First Amendment language providing that Congress shall make no law restricting the free exercise of religion. The *Reynolds* majority provided an approach that continues to be used today in First Amendment cases: "Laws are made for the government of actions, and while they cannot interfere with religious belief and opinions, they may with practices." The distinction between religious beliefs, which cannot be restricted, and religious practices, which can be restricted, became the conceptual framework for determining the boundaries of expression generally. For example, the distinction between thought, which cannot be restricted, and action, which can be restricted, is essential for understanding freedom of speech.

Freedom of Speech

The Court's first important free speech cases arose during the World War I era. In *Schenck v. United States* (1919), Justice Oliver Wendell Holmes, Jr., wrote for a unanimous Court upholding the Espionage Act of 1917 prosecution of individuals who opposed U.S. participation in World War I and urged men eligible for the military draft to oppose conscription. Holmes asserted that not even the strongest advocate of freedom of expression would allow an individual to falsely shout fire in a crowded theater and cause a panic. The fire analogy is still widely used as an argument against reading the First Amendment literally to mean absolute freedom of expression. In his dissenting opinion in the Pentagon Papers case (*New York Times v. United States*, 1971), where the government tried to prevent a newspaper from publishing a study of Vietnam War decision making, Chief Justice Warren E. Burger cited the Holmes fire analogy to support the argument that the government can restrict freedom of the press because the First Amendment does not give newspapers an absolute right to publish. The *Schenck* Court reasoned that the First Amendment does not protect words that create a "clear and present danger" that they will bring about "substantive evils" that Congress has a right to prevent, such as harming the war effort. Consequently, the government does not have to wait until political speech actually undermines its policies, creates public disorder, promotes imminent lawlessness, or foments revolution.

The logic of the clear and present danger test allowed the government to act only when there was a cognizable (clear) and proximate (imminent) threat. In *Abrams v. United States* (1919) Holmes dissented from a majority opinion upholding the Sedition Act of 1918 prosecutions of war critics

because he thought the clear and present danger test was being applied to allow the government to punish speech that might be harmful or merely had a "bad tendency." Holmes's dissent advocated a more libertarian reading of the First Amendment, one that was based on a free-market model of freedom of expression. The market model assumes that "the ultimate good desired is better reached by free trade in ideas." It also asserts that "the best test of truth is the power of the thought to get itself accepted in the competition of the market." The market is a culturally powerful concept in a nation committed to the ideals of democratic capitalism, and the logic of the free marketplace of *goods* has been applied to the free marketplace of *ideas*, where it is assumed that individual choice prevails unless the government has a good reason for intervening for or against ideas.

Beginning in the 1920s, on a case-by-case basis, the Court expanded the scope of freedom of expression by nationalizing the First Amendment, applying the First Amendment to state and local government officials as well as Congress. But during the World War II and Cold War eras, the Court used the distinction between thought and action to uphold national and state laws that restricted freedom of speech in order to maintain public order or protect national security. However, the Court did become more protective of civil liberties by requiring the government to meet the burden of proof to justify laws that restricted freedom of speech, press, or religion. In effect, the Court applied the harm principle to civil liberties cases. As articulated by Thomas Jefferson and the English political philosopher John Stuart Mill, the harm principle provides that government power can only be used to protect an individual from being harmed by another person, and laws cannot be legitimately used primarily or exclusively to regulate morality or to protect individuals from harming themselves.

The concept of fighting words illustrates how the harm principle has been applied to cases. In *Chaplinsky v. New Hampshire* (1942) the Court held that a person could be arrested for creating a public disturbance by calling the arresting police office "a Goddamned racketeer" and a "damned Fascist" because the First Amendment did not protect fighting words. The Court reasoned that some words, including "the lewd and the obscene, the profane, the libelous, and the insulting or 'fighting words,'" have little or no expressive value and "by their very utterance inflict injury or tend to incite an immediate breach of the peace." The government's power to maintain social order justifies laws that prohibit insults, which make the blood boil and provoke immediate physical retaliation. During the 1950s and 1960s, the liberal justices on the Warren Court used the harm principle as a libertarian doctrine that limited traditional government power to restrict freedom of religion, speech, and press. The harm principle effectively undermined the traditional police power to legislate morality by requiring the government to provide evidence that a law that restricted freedom of expression had a secular legislative purpose such as the prevention of physical or social harm.

Beginning in the 1940s, justices who believed that the clear and present danger test was being used to rationalize government restrictions on free speech began to search for alternative approaches. Justice John M. Harlan (the younger) advocated a balancing approach in which an individual's claim right to free speech was balanced against the government-claimed power to limit it. Although balancing seems like a reasonable, even Solomonic, approach to deciding civil liberties cases, it is controversial because balancing produces rulings that are not based on clearly identified principles or are not generally applicable because they are case-specific decisions. Balancing also is a method that has an important substantive impact on the outcome of civil liberties cases. The practical effect of weighing an (often unpopular) individual's rights against the (usually popular) majority's, community's, society's, or government's interests in decency, morality, national security, or good moral order is that First Amendment rights are tried in the court of popular opinion.

The fear that individual rights would be balanced away produced two alternative approaches

to the First Amendment. The first approach was to return to a literal-absolutist reading of the First Amendment. Justice Hugo L. Black, who served from 1937 to 1971, was the Court's foremost advocate of a literal-absolutist reading of the First Amendment as prohibiting any law restricting freedom of speech. But Black achieved this clear, simple rule for reading the First Amendment to mean there could be no laws restricting freedom of speech by narrowly defining speech. Black maintained that the First Amendment protected only political speech, not commercial speech such as advertising, and only pure speech, not symbolic speech or expressive conduct such as demonstrations, nude dancing, flag burning, or campaign contributions. Black's approach has never been accepted by a majority of the Court, which considers expressive conduct protected by the First Amendment but subject to a variety of time, place, and manner restrictions. There is no absolute First Amendment right to demonstrate. In many cases the question is not always whether expression is protected by the First Amendment, but how much protection the Constitution provides.

The second approach, which remains the dominant approach of the Court, is fundamental rights analysis. Fundamental rights analysis is based on the distinction between ordinary *interests,* which democracies can determine by majoritarian political processes, and basic, preferred, or fundamental *rights,* which constitutional democracies protect from majoritarian politics. Fundamental rights such as freedom of expression can be restricted only if the government demonstrates that it has a compelling interest in doing so and there is no less restrictive means to achieve that compelling end. The fundamental rights approach has generally been libertarian insofar as it has put the burden of proof on the government to provide evidence of the need to restrict fundamental rights.

The widespread acceptance of fundamental rights analysis has not solved the problem of determining the boundaries of free speech. The Court has recognized that advertising is a kind of commercial speech with some First Amendment protection, but there remains controversy about how much protection is provided for advertising for goods (e.g., tobacco or alcohol) or services. And in recent years the Court's acceptance of campaign contributions as a form of political speech has raised questions about the constitutionality of campaign finance laws.

The political correctness movement has also been controversial. The conservatives on the Court have been most skeptical of the constitutionality of speech codes and hate crime laws. In *RAV v. City of St. Paul* (1992), the Court struck down a city ordinance that made it a crime to put on public or private property a burning cross, swastika, or other symbol likely to arouse "anger, alarm, or resentment in others on the basis of race, color, creed, religion, or gender." Justice Antonin Scalia's majority opinion concluded that the hate crime ordinance violated the judicial doctrine of content neutrality, which requires the government to remain neutral toward the ideas it regulates, because the ordinance specifically listed some hate crimes but not others. The Court considers content-based restrictions on speech "presumptively invalid." The government could justify a hate crime law where there was evidence that the ordinary criminal statutes were insufficient. But when the government regulates free speech by requiring demonstrators to obtain permits, for example, it cannot take sides by granting permits to those whose ideas it supports while denying permits to those ideas it opposes. Taking sides constitutes viewpoint discrimination. The content-neutrality doctrine does not require the government to treat all ideas as though they were equally valid, but it does limit the government's ability to regulate the marketplace of ideas by promoting certain ideas and prohibiting others. With the notable exception of political correctness, the liberals on the Court have been more supportive of content neutrality than the conservatives on the Court, who are more skeptical of a doctrine that treats all political ideas as relatively equal without distinguishing between freedom and fascism or artistic expression and pornography. Conservatives are likely to consider content neutrality akin

to value relativism. In a case where the majority upheld a state law prohibiting totally nude dancing, Justice Scalia's concurring opinion emphasized that the Framers intended the First Amendment to protect political expression, not nude dancing, and therefore the government could regulate nude dancing and other behavior both to protect against harm and to promote traditional moral values (*City of Erie v. Pap's A. M.*, 2000). Chief Justice William H. Rehnquist took a similar position in dissent in *Texas v. Johnson* (1989), where the majority struck down the Texas flag desecration law that was used to convict Gregory Johnson of burning an American flag at a political demonstration during the 1984 Republican National Convention in Dallas. Rehnquist argued that the government could protect the flag, which is a unique symbol of the nation. This view is articulated even more clearly in conservative interpretations of the Establishment Clause.

Freedom of Religion

The end of the Cold War and the rise of the culture wars are reflected in the Supreme Court's agenda. Radical political speech cases have been replaced by cases raising questions about religion and values. The main freedom of religion issue has been the conflict between the Wall of Separation and the Accommodation understandings of the Establishment Clause of the First Amendment. The liberal Warren Court Justices generally read the Establishment Clause to have created a wall of separation between church and state. The conservative Burger and Rehnquist Court Justices generally read the Establishment Clause to allow government to support religion as long as it does not officially establish a church, support a particular denomination, or inhibit a particular religion. The Court still uses the *Lemon* test, first developed in the 1971 case *Lemon v. Kurtzman*, for determining whether government support violates the Establishment Clause. The *Lemon* test has three parts. First, the law must have a secular legislative purpose; its intent must be secular, not religious. Second, the law must neither advance nor inhibit religion; its results must be neutral.

Third, the law cannot foster excessive entanglement of government and religion. The justices who support the wall of separation approach generally do so because they believe that the Framers desired government neutrality between belief and nonbelief as a way to avoid the historical tendency of religious group to use political power to establish orthodoxy and use law to compel certain religious beliefs and practices. Justice Tom Clark's opinion in *Abington v. Schempp,* the 1963 case where the Court struck down Bible reading and recitation of the Lord's Prayer in public schools, reflects this view of the separation of church and state as a solution to the historical experience with religion as a source of political conflict. Justice Clark described the government's official position between the people and religion as "wholesome neutrality." Justice Stephen G. Breyer's opinions in cases challenging the display of the Ten Commandments on public property are based on his reading of the establishment clause as intended to avoid religious conflict as a political issue.

The Court's reading of the Free Exercise Clause of the First Amendment is informed by the distinction between belief and practice. The former is absolute; the latter is not. Religious conduct is subject to regulation (*Cantwell v. Connecticut,* 1940), but because the free exercise of religion is a fundamental right, the government must have a compelling interest in order to restrict it. Historically, state and local governments had wide latitude to use their police powers—traditionally defined as the power to pass laws for the public health, welfare, safety, and morals—to legislate morality. The mid-twentieth-century civil rights revolutions undermined this traditional power by reading the Constitution to require that laws regulating freedom of expression have a secular legislative purpose such as the prevention of harm. There often is no bright line between moral and secular regulatory policy, but the Court does use the distinction to limit government power. The liberal justices are more willing to strike down a law whose primary purpose is the promotion of virtue or the prevention of vice, while the conservatives justices have been more willing

to allow the political branches of government to determine how much promotion of virtue and prevention of vice is appropriate. Conservatives generally read the Constitution to allow government to enact moral regulatory policies concerning obscenity and indecency, school prayer, abortion, patriotism, and sexual behavior.

Freedom of the Press

The passage of the Alien and Sedition Acts in 1798 is early evidence that Congress did not read the First Amendment literally to mean there could be no law restricting freedom of the press. The Sedition Act made seditious libel, defined broadly to include strong or intemperate criticism of the government, a criminal offense. Although the acts were repealed before the Supreme Court ruled on their constitutionality, the Court's First Amendment rulings allow restrictions on freedom of the press. The general rule concerning freedom of the press is that the Framers intended the First Amendment to prohibit prior restraint (or censorship) but to allow subsequent punishment for publishing certain materials, such as defamatory articles, or broadcasting certain programming, such as indecent broadcasts. The rule against prior restraint does have notable exceptions, including the protection of national security. Furthermore, unlike the print press, the broadcast media are licensed by the government. Congress has delegated to the Federal Communications Commission the authority to consider whether it is in the public interest to grant a broadcast license application or renewal. So the government does have some power to regulate the content of broadcast programming. Some press advocates have claimed that the First Amendment gives the institutional press special status as the "fourth estate," checking the "three official branches" of government (quoting Justice Potter Stewart, dissenting *Branzburg v. Hayes,* 1972), and shielding reporters from subpoenas, search warrants, and compelled grand juries, but the Court has never accepted the argument. The emergence of new electronic media, particularly the Internet, has challenged established First Amendment law.

Obscenity and Indecency

Obscenity is not protected by the First Amendment, but defining obscenity has been difficult. Until the middle of the twentieth century, the courts upheld the government's broad power to suppress obscene materials by applying an old English common-law test that defined obscenity as materials that tended to corrupt those whose minds were open to such influences. This definition was so broad that it limited adults to reading materials fit for children and the mentally depraved. Consequently, in *Roth v. United States* (1957), the Court defined obscenity as material in which "the average person, applying contemporary community standards," found that the "dominant theme of the material taken as a whole" appealed to prurient interests. This definition has been modified since then, but it remains the basic framework for identifying obscenity. Indecency has been even harder to define than obscenity, and indecent materials have some First Amendment protection. When deciding whether a law regulating indecency is constitutional, the Court considers the harm that the government is trying to prevent. Congress passed the Communications Decency Act of 1996 to protect minors from harmful material on the Internet. The act, which made it a felony to knowingly transmit obscene or indecent materials to a person under 19 years old, was declared unconstitutional in *Reno v. American Civil Liberties Union* (1997), because (1) the word "indecency" could be defined so broadly that it included protected materials, (2) existing filtering technology did not adequately differentiate between materials that the government could restrict and materials that adults had a right to access, and (3) there were less restrictive ways (i.e., fines rather than felony charges) to achieve the compelling government interest in protecting minors. Congress then passed the Children's Online Protection Act (1998), which addressed some of the Court's concerns by (1) subjecting individuals to fines rather than criminal prosecution and (2) providing that the use of screening devices such as a credit card was an affirmative defense for an individual subject to the act. Nevertheless,

the Court struck down the law because its definition of prohibited material was still too broad, and the screening was of questionable effectiveness. Congress responded with the Children's Internet Protection Act of 2001, which required libraries receiving federal funding to use Internet filtering technology, and the Court upheld the act.

These cases illustrate how the modern Court judges laws restricting freedom of expression. The justices generally require the government to provide some empirical evidence of the need to restrict fundamental freedoms, and the justices assess the effectiveness of the means the government has chosen to achieve its ends. Consequently, today's First Amendment cases are not about first principles, such as the role of freedom of expression in a democratic society, as much as they are about the secondary rules that define the boundaries of free expression: the drawing of buffer zones around abortion clinics; Federal Communications Commission investigations of viewer complaints about broadcast indecency; or congressional debates about the effectiveness of Internet filtering technology in an age of globalization. As a result, these essentially administrative approaches to the First Amendment are likely to become even more important in defining freedom of expression.

See also *Abington v. Schempp;* Abortion, Right to; Academic Freedom; Alien and Sedition Acts; Assembly, Freedom of; Association, Freedom of; Bad Tendency Test; Bill of Rights (American); Bill of Rights, Incorporation of; Black, Hugo L.; Breyer, Stephen G.; Burger, Warren E.; Campaign Finance Reform; *Cantwell v. Connecticut;* Child Pornography; Civil Rights Movement; Clark, Tom C.; Clear and Present Danger Doctrine; Clear and Probable Danger Doctrine; Commercial Speech; Common-Law Background of American Civil Rights and Liberties; Conscience, Freedom of; Conservatism; Constitutional Democracy; Defamation; Douglas, William O.; Draft Cards, Burning of; Espionage Act of 1917; Establishment Clause; Evolution/Creationism Controversy; Federal Communications Commission; Fighting Words Doctrine; First

Amendment; Flag Burning; Flag Salute Controversy; Free Exercise Clause; Free Marketplace of Ideas; Free Press/Fair Trial Problem; Fundamental Rights; Hand, Learned; Harlan, John M., II; Hate Crimes; Hate Speech; Holmes, Oliver Wendell, Jr.; Internet, Free Speech on; Jefferson, Thomas; *Lemon* Test; Liberalism; Libertarianism; Military Service, Civil Rights and; Moment of Silence Laws; *Near v. Minnesota ex rel. Olson; New York Times v. United States;* Obscenity and Pornography; Overbreadth, Doctrine of; Picketing; Police Power; Preferred Freedoms Doctrine; Press, Freedom of the; Prior Restraint, Doctrine of; Profanity; Public Forum; Public Nudity; Rehnquist, William H.; Religion, Freedom of; Religion, Official Endorsements of; Religious Displays on Public Property; Religious Schools, Government Aid to; *Reno v. American Civil Liberties Union;* Representative Democracy; *Reynolds v. United States;* Scalia, Antonin; School Prayer Decisions; Sedition; Separation of Church and State; Speech, Freedom of; Speech/Conduct Distinction; Strict Scrutiny; Sunday Closing Laws; Symbolic Speech; Tax Exemptions for Religious Organizations; Ten Commandments, Public Display of the; Time, Place, and Manner Restrictions; Warren Court; Zenger, John Peter

Bibliography

Alley, Robert. 1988. *The Supreme Court on Church and State.* New York: Oxford University Press.

Baker, C. Edwin. 1989. *Human Liberty and Freedom of Speech.* New York: Oxford University Press.

Bollinger, Lee C., and Geoffrey R. Stone, eds. 2002. *Eternally Vigilant: Free Speech in the Modern Era.* Chicago: University of Chicago Press.

Emerson, Thomas I. 1971. *The System of Freedom of Expression.* New York: Vintage Books.

Kelly, Alfred H., and Winfred A. Harbison. 1976. *The American Constitution: Its Origins and Development.* New York: W. W. Norton.

Kersch, Ken I. 2003. *Freedom of Speech: Rights and Liberties under the Law.* Santa Barbara, CA: ABC-CLIO.

Levy, Leonard. 1986. *The Establishment Clause: Religion and the First Amendment.* New York: Macmillan.

O'Brien, David M. 2003. *Constitutional Law and Politics.* 5th ed. New York: W. W. Norton.

Powe, Lucas A. Jr. 1991. *The Fourth Estate and the Constitution: Freedom of the Press in America.* Berkeley and Los Angeles: University of California Press.

Schweber, Howard. 2003. *Speech, Conduct, and the First Amendment.* New York: Peter Lang.

Tedford, Thomas L. 1985. *Freedom of Speech in the United States.* New York: Random House.

Timothy O. Lenz

FIRST APPEARANCE. *See* Initial Appearance in Criminal Cases

FISA. *See* Foreign Intelligence Surveillance Act

FLAG BURNING

Because it is a meaningful symbol to so many Americans, the flag has become a battleground for free speech rights. Those who wish to protect the flag argue that as a symbol of national unity, it ought to be the one area where unlimited speech may not take place, and the physical integrity of the flag should be respected. Opponents, however, argue that it is precisely because the flag is such a powerful symbol that symbolic speech, speech that does not use traditional means, should be allowed. The Court has agreed that the burning of flags must be permitted by the Constitution.

For years, the Court avoided dealing directly with flag burning. In *Street v. New York* (1969), the Court overturned a flag burning conviction but refused to comment on flag burning itself. It ruled on a New York law that prohibited both the desecration of flags and derogatory words spoken about the flag. Because Street could have been convicted merely for speaking badly about the flag, the law was struck down, and his conviction was overturned.

In *Smith v. Goguen* (1974), the Court dealt with a related issue, contemptuous treatment of the flag. Here, a man was convicted for wearing an American flag sewn to the seat of his pants. Again, the Court refused to deal with the portions of the statute that dealt with the physical integrity of the flag and instead ruled that the statute was too vague, since the flag is treated casually and worn on clothing by many.

That same year, the Court decided *Spence v. Washington* (1974), again on the narrow grounds that the specific case did not deal with the physical integrity of the flag. Here, Spence had affixed a peace sign to a flag with removable tape and displayed the flag in his window. While the Court still avoided discussing flag burning directly, it did rule that issues of flag desecration did not fall under the *O'Brien* test. This test was established in *United States v. O'Brien* (1968), a case involving the burning of draft cards, and addressed situations of symbolic speech, or speech through nontraditional means. Because flag burning is nonverbal, nonwritten communication, it is symbolic speech. According to *O'Brien,* the state may regulate symbolic speech only under certain circumstances: (1) Is the law within the Constitutional power of the government? (2) Does the law further a substantial or important government interest? (3) Is the interest unrelated to the suppression of free expression? (4) Is this the least restrictive means with regard to free speech?

The Court wrote that laws regulating flag desecration and burning are automatically related to the suppression of free expression, and that the *O'Brien* test therefore does not apply. This set the stage for future cases involving flag burning.

In *Texas v. Johnson* (1989), the Court addressed flag burning directly for the first time. Johnson burned a flag during the Republican National Convention in 1984 in order to protest actions of the Reagan administration. He was arrested under a Texas law that made it a crime to "deface, damage or otherwise physically mistreat" the American flag "in a way that the actor knows will seriously offend one or more persons likely to discover his action."

In overturning Johnson's conviction, the Court found that the statute turned typical symbolic speech thinking on its head. Instead of permitting the conduct because of its political or otherwise expressive content, the law banned the burning of a flag *because* it was expressive. Texas argued that its interest in the law was in "preserving the flag as a symbol of nationhood and national unity." The Court replied that this interest was related to suppressing free expression, because any reason that the government might have to ban this form of symbolic speech would necessarily be based on the content of that speech and therefore constitutionally invalid. Though many find flag burning and the message it communicates to be offensive, the Court wrote that this is not enough to permit the government to prohibit the behavior. Rather, the First Amendment was designed to protect especially that speech with which others disagree.

After *Johnson* was decided, Congress passed the Flag Protection Act of 1989, which was designed to prohibit flag burning while avoiding the problems that cause the Supreme Court to overturn the Texas law. According to its authors, this act protected the physical integrity of the flag while "not target[ing] expressive conduct on the basis of the content of its message." Therefore, it prohibited damaging the flag whatever the motive or intention of the actor in all cases except for disposal of the flag.

In *United States v. Eichmann* (1990), the Court ruled that the act was unconstitutional for many of the same reasons that the Texas statute proved invalid. Despite the fact that the act did not specifically refer to content-based restrictions, the Court found that the intent behind the law was nonetheless to restrict free expression. The Court wrote that because the act "suppress[ed] expression out of concern for its likely communicative impact," it created an unjustifiable infringement on free speech rights under the First Amendment. The government's stated purpose for the law was preserving a symbol of national unity and ideals, a purpose that would only be compromised when a speaker was communicating a message contrary to those ideals through damaging the physical integrity of the flag.

See also First Amendment; Speech, Freedom of; Symbolic Speech

Bibliography

Goldstein, Robert Justin. 2000. *Flag Burning and Free Speech: The Case of Texas v. Johnson.* Lawrence: University Press of Kansas.

Greenawalt, Kent.1995. *Fighting Words: Individuals, Communities, and the Liberties of Speech.* Princeton, NJ: Princeton University Press.

Ronald Kahn

FLAG SALUTE CONTROVERSY

Although the American flag commands respect as the official emblem of the nation, it has on occasion become the center of controversy. It was not until 1942 that Congress formalized appropriate treatment of the flag in the U.S. Flag Code, dictating rules that the flag must never be displayed upside down (except to signal great distress), dipped to any person or thing, carried flat or horizontally, or used as a covering (except on a casket under certain circumstances). While highly detailed, the U.S. Flag Code relies on voluntary compliance, as it contains no enforcement provisions. Flag regulations exist in every state, however, and those regulations are enforceable by law.

The manner of saluting the flag is part of the Flag Code: civilians are directed to face the flag and stand with the right hand over the heart, while military personnel are expected to stand at attention. Reciting the Pledge of Allegiance is often part of a flag salute ceremony, as is singing the Star Spangled Banner, the designated national anthem of the United States. The Pledge of Allegiance originated with Frances Bellamy in 1892, when he wrote the short statement for school children to recite on the four hundredth anniversary of Columbus reaching America. Millions of copies of the pledge were distributed to schools, starting a daily ritual for children across the United States. Although changes were made in the pledge over the years, Congress did not officially recognize it until 1942. The most recent modification came in 1954, when the words "under God" were added.

By tradition, many school children salute the flag each day, usually at a flagpole or in their classroom. The ceremony ordinarily includes facing the flag, placing the right hand over the heart, and reciting the pledge. While the activity may be a positive one for many students, others take exception to participation. Controversy over saluting the flag developed in Minersville, Pennsylvania, in 1935, when two children who were Jehovah's Witnesses, Lillian and Walter Gobitas (although their name is spelled Gobitis in the court case), refused to participate in saluting the flag and pledging allegiance. Saluting the flag was a daily requirement for students and teachers, and when the Gobitas children refused to comply, they were expelled from school.

Attorneys argued that the state's requirement inhibited the free exercise of religion of the Gobitas children as Jehovah's Witnesses and violated their liberty under the Due Process Clause of the Fourteenth Amendment. The Supreme Court rejected that contention and ruled eight-to-one for the school district in *Minersville School District* v. *Gobitis* (1940). Justice Felix Frankfurter, writing for the Court, said, "Conscientious scruples have not, in the course of the long struggle for religious toleration, relieved the individual from obedience to a general law not aimed at the promotion or restriction of religious beliefs." In dissent, Justice Harlan F. Stone said, "History teaches us that there have been but few infringements of personal liberty by the state which have not been justified, as they are here, in the name of righteousness and the public good, and few which have not been directed, as they are now, at politically helpless minorities." The Court's ruling in this case is viewed as favoring judicial restraint and the importance of patriotic training for the common good.

The Supreme Court's ruling in the *Gobitis* case surprised many observers and was quite unpopular. Most law review articles published immediately thereafter disagreed with the ruling. The flag salute issue quickly returned to the Supreme Court, not only because of the unpopularity of the *Gobitis* ruling, but also for other reasons. In Germany, there were frightening images of Nazis saluting the swastika, and reports of Jehovah's Witnesses being condemned for refusing to do so. In addition, several members of the Supreme Court were uncomfortable with the ruling. Dissenting in *Jones v. City of Opelika* (1942), three justices wrote, "Since we joined in the opinion in the *Gobitis* case, we think this is an appropriate occasion to state that we now believe that it also was wrongly decided."

In 1943 the Court revisited the flag salute issue. *West Virginia Board of Education v. Barnette* (1943) arose out of a disputed regulation adopted by the state board of education requiring all teachers and school children to salute the flag. Children who refused were subject to expulsion, after which they were considered delinquents subject to criminal prosecution. On Flag Day, the Supreme Court reversed the *Gobitis* ruling, declaring per Justice Robert Jackson, "If there is any fixed star in our constitutional constellation, it is that no official ... can prescribe what shall be orthodox in politics, nationalism, religion, or other matters of opinion."

The flag salute controversy emerges from time to time, typically in public schools, as students refuse to stand or participate in the ritual. The American Civil Liberties Union frequently intervenes in such disputes. Recent questions have included those of whether schools can require permission slips from parents of students who wish to sit out the pledge and whether students who do not wish to participate in the pledge can be required to stand for the ceremony. The ACLU takes the position that the act of standing is itself part of the pledge.

See also American Civil Liberties Union; Due Process Clauses; Fourteenth Amendment; Frankfurter, Felix; Jackson, Robert H.; Jehovah's Witnesses; Stone, Harlan Fiske; Symbolic Speech; *West Virginia Board of Education v. Barnette*

Bibliography

Curtis, Michael Kent. 1993. *The Constitution and the Flag: The Flag Salute Cases.* New York: Garland.

Gloria Cox

FOIA. *See* Freedom of Information Act

FOOTNOTE FOUR. *See United States v. Carolene Products*

FORCE, USE OF BY LAW ENFORCEMENT

Today's concept of law enforcement originated with the early police departments of the mid-1800s that formed in the major metropolitan areas of New York City, Philadelphia, Boston, Chicago, and Detroit. As the public's notion of law enforcement developed, so did the public's concerns for the amount of force it was willing to authorize to be used against other citizens. By the early 1930s use of force by police officers was being questioned at various levels of government. In fact, the Wickersham Commission, which was appointed by President Herbert Hoover to review the criminal justice system, in its 1931 Report on Lawlessness in Law Enforcement said there was "extensive evidence of police misconduct and violence throughout major urban departments" (Gilles 2000, 18).

Shortly after the Wickersham Report was released, the Supreme Court in *Brown et al. v. Mississippi* (1936) examined whether the use of force by officers in securing a confession by "brutality and violence" was consistent with the Due Process Clause of the Fourteenth Amendment. In overturning the defendant's murder conviction and death sentence as a "clear denial of due process," the Court said, "It would be difficult to conceive of methods more revolting to the sense of justice than those taken to procure the confessions of these petitioners."

Four years later in *Chambers et al. v. Florida* (1940), the Court again overturned a defendant's conviction and death sentence by virtue of the Due Process Clause of the Fourteenth Amendment. In *Chambers,* the Court again stated its unwillingness to accept this type of use of force to obtain a confession; the Court made it clear that it was not impressed "by the argument that law enforcement methods such as those under review are necessary to uphold our laws. The Constitution proscribes such lawless means irrespective of the end." While the Court stated its displeasure with the actions of the officers involved in these cases, it failed to indicate what action could be taken against the officers involved.

In *Screws v. United States* (1945), a five-to-four Court upheld the constitutionality of 18 U.S.C.S. § 52, a federal criminal statute that criminalized willful deprivations of a citizen's rights under color of law. The statute had formed the basis for charges against three Georgia officers accused of beating to death an arrestee in their custody. However, while the Court upheld the constitutionality of the statute, the Court reversed the trial court verdict and ordered a new trial for the officers on the grounds that the jury was not properly instructed on the proper standard guilt, willingness, as required by the statute. Dissenting, Justice Frank Murphy argued that the facts of the case were so clear that the judgment against the officers should be upheld. In their dissent, Justices Owen Roberts, Felix Frankfurter, and Robert Jackson were cautious of federal involvement in state issues:

We are told local authorities cannot be relied upon for courageous and prompt action, that often they have personal or political reasons for refusing to prosecute…. In any event, the cure is a reinvigoration of State responsibility. It is not an undue incursion of remote federal authority into local duties with consequent debilitation of local responsibility.

Later in *Williams v. United States* (1951), the Court, applying its holding from the *Screws* case, upheld, under 18 U.S.C.S. § 52, the conviction of the defendant, who operated a detective agency and held the status of a special police officer with the city of Miami. The Court found the defendant had been acting under color of law, and the authority of the state of Florida, when he used "brutal methods" in obtaining confessions from four men who were accused of theft by the company that had hired him. The Court noted, "[W]here police take matters in their own hands, seize victims, beat and pound them until they confess, there cannot be the slightest doubt that the police have deprived the victim of a right under the Constitution."

The following year, in *Rochin v. California* (1952), the Court expanded its prohibition against the physical abuse of persons to obtain confessions to police efforts in gathering evidence from a person. The *Rochin* case began on July 1, 1949, when officers of the Los Angeles County sheriff's office, based on some evidence that Rochin was selling drugs, forcibly entered Rochin's residence, where he lived with his common-law wife, mother, and siblings. When the officers' entered Rochin's room, he swallowed two capsules that were located on a nightstand next to his bed. The officers proceeded to wrestle with Rochin as they attempted to handcuff him and force him to expel the capsules he had swallowed. When the officers' actions failed to force the expulsion of the capsules, the officers transported Rochin to a hospital. At the hospital the officers ordered a doctor to pump Rochin's stomach to recover the capsules. The capsules were recovered and used as evidence to convict Rochin for possession of morphine. In reversing the conviction, as a violation of the Due Process Clause of the Fourteenth Amendment, the Court stated:

[W]e are compelled to conclude that the proceedings by which this conviction was obtained do more than offend some fastidious squeamishness or private sentimentalism about combating crime too energetically. This is conduct that shocks the conscience … this course of proceeding by agents of government to obtain evidence is bound to offend even hardened sensibilities. They are methods too close to the rack and the screw to permit of constitutional differentiation.

These early cases establish the Court's intention to prevent physical abuse by law enforcement by allowing federal criminal action against the officers involved; reversal of convictions; remand of cases; and, later, exclusion of evidence under the exclusionary rule. However, while the courts were given great legal recourse to deal with law enforcement misconduct, there remained the underlying issue of what recourse, if any, was available to victims of law enforcement abuse.

On October 29, 1958, at 5:45 A.M., 13 Chicago police officers under the direction of Deputy Chief of Detectives Frank Pape forcibly entered the residence of James Monroe, without either a search or arrest warrant. Monroe was struck several times with a flashlight while racial slurs were yelled at him. Other officers ransacked the residence and assaulted both Monroe's wife and his children. Ultimately, Monroe was taken to the police station, where he was held, placed in lineups, and finally released ten hours later without being charged. In seeking recourse Monroe filed a lawsuit under 42 U.S.C.S. § 1983, which provides:

Every person who, under color of any statute, ordinance, regulation, custom, or usage, of any State or Territory, subjects, or causes to be subjected, any citizen of the United States or other person within the jurisdiction thereof to the deprivation of any rights, privileges, or immunities secured by the Constitution and laws, shall be liable to the party injured in an action at law, suit in equity, or other proper proceeding for redress.

The district court dismissed the complaint, and the court of appeals affirmed the dismissal, contending that Monroe did not state a claim under the federal civil rights laws for which relief could be granted. In *Monroe v. Pape* (1961) the Supreme Court held that the intent of the legislation enacted by Congress was to provide a "remedy to parties deprived of constitutional rights, privileges and immunities by an official's abuse of his position." Furthermore the Court noted this federal remedy is supplementary to any state remedy that may be available. Regarding the argument that "under color of" meant that the actions of officers outside the scope of any "authority under state law, state custom, or state usage" were exempt from the statute, the Court said there was no doubt that "Congress has the power to enforce provisions of the Fourteenth Amendment against those who carry a badge of authority of a State and represent it in some capacity, whether they act in accordance with their authority or misuse it." The Court reversed the dismissal and allowed the action against the officials to proceed. However, the Court held that the municipality was not a person for purposes of the statute; therefore it was exempt from its application.

As litigation developed in the area of excessive use of force by law enforcement, 42 U.S.C.S. § 1983 became the basis for civil action in use of force cases. As a consequence, these civil actions

have led to the development of case law that has served to guide law enforcement in developing policy and training. Use of force litigation pursuant to 42 U.S.C.S. § 1983 generally follows the legal theory that a person detained, arrested, or otherwise has his freedom limited by law enforcement officers is considered seized under the Fourth Amendment and thus must be afforded the protection of the Fourth Amendment that such use of force against them be reasonable (see *United States v. Brignoni-Ponce,* 1975).

In 1985 the Supreme Court regarding seizure under the Fourth Amendment examined the highest level of force available to law enforcement, lethal or deadly force. In *Tennessee v. Garner* (1985) the Court considered the constitutionality of using deadly force to prevent the escape of an apparently unarmed 15 year old for the crime of burglary, in which it was later discovered $10 and a purse had been taken. At the time of the shooting the actions of the officers were authorized by both departmental policy and a Tennessee statute that provided: "[If], after notice of the intention to arrest the defendant, he either flees or forcibly resists, the officer may use *all the necessary means* to effect the arrest" (emphasis added). The Court noted that while the statute did not say it, Tennessee case law did forbid the use of deadly force in order to arrest a misdemeanant.

The Court began by stating, "Whenever an officer restrains the freedom of a person to walk away, he has seized that person," and "While it is not always clear just when minimal police interference becomes a seizure, … there can be no question that apprehension by the use of deadly force is a seizure subject to the reasonableness requirement of the Fourth Amendment." The Court noted that in determining the reasonableness of a seizure under the Fourth Amendment, a court must balance the nature and quality of the intrusion on the individual's Fourth Amendment interests against the countervailing governmental interests. The Court went on to state that given the extreme level of intrusion by the use of deadly force, there was little doubt that such seizure could be justified by anything less than probable cause. The Court said:

Where the officer has probable cause to believe that the suspect poses a threat of serious physical harm, either to the officer or to others, it is not constitutionally unreasonable to prevent escape by using deadly force. Thus, if the suspect threatens the officer with a weapon or there is probable cause to believe that he has committed a crime involving the infliction or threatened infliction of serious physical harm, deadly force may be used if necessary to prevent escape, and if, where feasible, some warning has been given.

Justice Sandra Day O'Connor, joined by Chief Justice Warren E. Burger and Justice William H. Rehnquist, in her dissent criticized the Court for ignoring the long-standing common-law rule allowing the use of deadly force, if needed, to apprehend a fleeing felon, which was still accepted in many states. According to O'Connor, the Court in effect created "a Fourth Amendment right allowing a burglary suspect to flee unimpeded from a police officer who has probable cause to arrest, who has ordered the suspect to halt, and who has no means short of firing his weapon to prevent escape." While the dissenters agreed that Garner was seized for the purposes of the Fourth Amendment analysis, and that circumstances of the case were unfortunate, they contended that "clarity of hindsight cannot provide the standard for judging the reasonableness of police decisions made in uncertain and often dangerous circumstances." Furthermore, the reasonableness of an officer's actions should not be subject to evaluation based on what afterwards "appears to have been a preferable course of police action." As to the constitutionality of the Tennessee statute, the dissenters noted that the statute provides for the interests of a suspect by allowing him or her to avoid the use of deadly force and subsequent risk of life by simply obeying a "valid order to halt."

Four years later in *Graham v. Connor* (1989), the Court stated that all claims of excessive force by a free citizen, whether deadly or not, "in the course of an arrest, investigatory stop, or other 'seizure' of a free citizen should be analyzed under the Fourth Amendment and its 'reasonableness' standard, rather than under a 'substantive due process' approach." Furthermore, the Court said reasonableness in excessive force cases is a question of "whether the officers' actions are 'objectively reasonable' in light of the facts and circumstances confronting them, without regard to their underlying intent or motivation." Furthermore the Court stressed that "[t]he 'reasonableness' of a particular use of force must be judged from the perspective of a reasonable officer on the scene, rather than with the 20/20 vision of hindsight." The Court acknowledged that in determining reasonableness, allowance must be made "for the fact that police officers are often forced to make split-second judgments—in circumstances that are tense, uncertain, and rapidly evolving—about the amount of force that is necessary in a particular situation."

In *Graham,* the petitioner, a diabetic, had asked his friend to drive him to a convenience store to buy some orange juice to counteract the onset of an insulin reaction. At the store, Graham encountered a number of people ahead of him in line, so he changed his mind. He hurried out and asked his friend to drive him to another friend's house instead. A police officer, who had observed Graham's actions, considered the actions suspicious and proceeded to follow the vehicle. The officer then made an investigative stop of the vehicle. The officer ordered Graham and the driver to wait while he found out what had happened in the store. When backup police officers arrived on the scene, Graham was handcuffed. The officers ignored Graham's attempts to explain his condition or and refused to provide him any treatment. Once the officers learned that nothing had happened in the store, Graham and the driver were released. During the encounter Graham sustained multiple injuries. After examining the facts of the case and the standard used by the lower courts, the Court remanded the case to the trial court with instructions to reconsider it under the proper Fourth Amendment standard of analysis of "objective reasonableness."

Today, *Garner* and *Graham* still set the standards by which law enforcement's use of force is to be evaluated under the Fourth Amendment. In addition there is continuing research into the physiological and physical aspects of use of force on both the officers and the recipients of its use. This research has provided the courts with a better understanding of the difficulty facing officers who must make split-second decisions regarding the use of force. However, even with modern training and research, law enforcement still struggles with excessive use of force and abuse of prisoners. Additionally, technology such as chemical weapons (i.e., mace and pepper spray), electronic shocking devices (i.e., stun guns/tasers), and nonlethal projectiles (i.e. bean bag rounds, rubber bullets, and wooden projectiles) designed to allow officers to control persons more easily are all subject to abuse or misuse by officers. Consequently, just as when the Wickersham Commission released its now famous report, we continue to have concerns about the amount and abuse of force that law enforcement uses to control persons. Given the media exposure of excessive force incidents that continue to plague the profession, the question that remains is whether courts will have to increase their oversight of law enforcement in order to alleviate these concerns.

See also Accused, Rights of the; Arrest, Constitutional Limits on; Burger, Warren E.; Common-Law Background of American Civil Rights and Liberties; Due Process, Procedural; Due Process, Substantive; Due Process Clauses; Fourteenth Amendment; Fourth Amendment; Frankfurter, Felix; Interrogation and Confessions; Jackson, Robert H.; O'Connor, Sandra Day; Rehnquist, William H.; Section 1983 Actions

Bibliography

Avery, Michael. 2003. "Unreasonable Seizures of Unreasonable People: Defining the Totality of Circumstances Relevant to Assessing the Police Use of Force Against Emotionally Disturbed People." *Columbia Human Rights Law Review* 34:261.

DuCharme, Seth D. 2002. "The Search for Reasonableness in Use-of-Force Cases: Understanding the Effects of Stress on Perception and Performance." *Fordham Law Review* 70 (6): 2515–60.

Gilles, Myriam E. 2000. "Breaking the Code of Silence: Rediscovering 'Custom' in Section 1983 Municipal Liability." *Boston University Law Review* 80:17–92.

McGuinness, J. Michael. 2002. "Law Enforcement Use of Force: The Objective Reasonableness Standards Under North Carolina and Federal Law." *Campbell Law Review* 24:201.

Fermin De La Torre

FOREIGN INTELLIGENCE SURVEILLANCE ACT (FISA)

In passing the Foreign Intelligence Surveillance Act (FISA) of 1978, Congress created special rules and procedures affecting foreign intelligence surveillance in the United States. Foreign intelligence surveillance, or counterintelligence, consists of activities designed to protect the United States against espionage, sabotage, assassinations, and terrorism conducted by or on behalf of foreign governments or organizations. Frequently, these activities include electronic eavesdropping and other means of covert surveillance. Ever since *Katz v. United States* (1967), electronic eavesdropping by law enforcement agents has required prior judicial authorization. In *Katz,* the Supreme Court recognized that the Fourth Amendment protects personal privacy from any means of intrusion by law enforcement. In *Berger v. New York* (1967), the Court recognized that "eavesdropping involves an intrusion on privacy that is broad in scope," and its "indiscriminate use ... in law enforcement raises grave constitutional questions."

In 1968, Congress enacted the Omnibus Crime Control and Safe Streets Act. Title III of the act, adopted largely in response to the *Berger* and *Katz* decisions, authorized the use of electronic surveillance by federal law enforcement officers but required prior judicial authorization and otherwise limited the conditions for its use. However, Congress included language in the statute making clear that Title III was not intended to limit "the constitutional power of the President to take such measures as he deems necessary to protect the Nation against actual or potential attack or other hostile acts of a foreign power, to obtain foreign intelligence information deemed essential to the security of the United States, or to protect national security information against foreign intelligence activities."

Invoking this exception and asserting inherent executive power, the Nixon administration conducted extensive wiretapping and other forms of electronic surveillance of U.S. citizens without probable cause or prior judicial approval. In 1973, the Senate Select Committee to Study Governmental Operations with Respect to Intelligence Activities, better known as the Church Committee, conducted a far-reaching investigation of the activities of intelligence agencies from the early 1960s through the end of the Nixon administration. The committee's reports, published in 1975 and 1976, documented the extent to which foreign intelligence agencies conducted unauthorized surveillance of domestic groups perceived as security risks. Among them were civil rights, antiwar, and various New Left organizations.

In *United States v. U.S. District Court* (1972), the Supreme Court held that these activities offended the Fourth Amendment prohibition against unreasonable searches and seizures. Writing for the Court, Justice Lewis Powell recognized that:

domestic security surveillance may involve different policy and practical considerations from the surveillance of "ordinary crime." The gathering of security intelligence is often long range and involves the interrelation of various sources and types of information. The exact targets of such surveillance may be more difficult to identify than in surveillance operations against many types of crimes specified in Title III. Often, too, the emphasis of domestic intelligence gathering is on the prevention of unlawful activity or the enhancement of the Government's preparedness for some possible future crisis or emergency. Thus, the focus of domestic surveillance may be less precise than that directed against more conventional types of crime.

In light of these considerations, Powell suggested that Congress consider enacting protective standards for the conduct of foreign intelligence surveillance separate and apart from those applicable to

domestic law enforcement. The decision in *United States v. U.S. District Court,* as well as the Church Committee reports of 1975 and 1976, prompted Congress to enact the FISA in 1978. The act established the Foreign Intelligence Surveillance Court (FISC) consisting of seven federal district court judges appointed by the Chief Justice of the United States Supreme Court. The USA PATRIOT Act of 2001 expanded the number of judges to 11.

FISC judges are from different federal judicial circuits and serve staggered terms of seven years. Individual judges review applications to conduct surveillance aimed at obtaining information on foreign intelligence activities. Surveillance includes electronic eavesdropping, physical entries, and the use of pen registers and trap-and-trace devices, as well as access to certain business records.

The FISC conducts its business in a secret windowless courtroom located inside the Department of Justice building in Washington, D.C. Applications for surveillance are prepared by the Justice Department's Office of Intelligence and are submitted to the FISC on the authority of the attorney general. The procedure for obtaining a FISA warrant is nonadversarial, much like the procedure by which law enforcement officers obtain search warrants. Surveillance is authorized if a FISC judge finds there is probable cause that the target of the surveillance is a foreign power or an agent of a foreign power. There is no requirement that the target be engaged in any unlawful activity.

A foreign power is defined by the statute as "a foreign government or a component thereof," "a faction of a foreign nation or nations," "an entity that is openly acknowledged by a foreign government or governments to be directed and controlled by such foreign government or governments," "a group engaged in international terrorism or activities in preparation therefore," "a foreign-based political organization," or "an entity that is directed and controlled by a foreign government." Denials of surveillance orders are reviewable by a Foreign Intelligence Surveillance Court of Review consisting of three federal district or appeals court judges designated by the chief justice.

The passage of the USA PATRIOT Act in 2001 brought about significant changes in the operation of the Foreign Intelligence Surveillance Act. FISA envisioned a clear distinction between the areas of criminal investigation and foreign intelligence gathering, as well as a patent separation of the agencies and departments responsible for performing these tasks. The PATRIOT Act eliminated this distinction. After 2001 the institutions of law enforcement and intelligence gathering would engage in the sharing of information. Many situations presented the opportunity for both criminal investigation and intelligence gathering. If the government characterized its actions as the investigation of crime, then more stringent notions of probable cause would dictate their options and set the rules that would be applied by the courts. However, if the government could justify its actions as the gathering of foreign intelligence, the much more accommodating world of FISA would offer greater freedom for agents and fewer procedural restrictions. With the passage of the PATRIOT Act the government has been given much greater opportunity to proceed under the guise of intelligence gathering and the less restrictive FISA while simultaneously gaining information to be used in criminal proceedings, without having to concern itself with the inconvenience of matters such as probable cause.

It was this blurring of the lines between the realm of criminal investigation and foreign intelligence gathering that resulted in the Court of Review's first meeting. Prior to 2002 the Court of Review never met because no application for surveillance had ever been denied. In 2002 the FISC rejected the Justice Department's effort to use evidence obtained pursuant to FISA warrants in criminal cases. The court ruled that FISA was intended to create something of a firewall between foreign intelligence surveillance and ordinary law enforcement. The Justice Department appealed to the Court of Review, which vacated the judgment of the FISC in August 2002 and ordered it to approve the Justice Department's request. No doubt influenced by the horrendous terrorist attacks of September 11, 2001, the Court of Review held that FISC may be used to obtain evidence for a criminal prosecution as long as the government also has a "significant non-law enforcement foreign intelligence purpose" in making application for the surveillance warrant.

However, even this modified FISA failed to provide enough power in the eyes of many within the executive branch. In late 2005 the *New York Times* revealed that President George W. Bush authorized the National Security Agency to bypass the Foreign Intelligence Surveillance Court entirely and engage in warrantless eavesdropping on American citizens who were suspected of having ties to Al-Qaeda.

When the Foreign Intelligence Surveillance Act was passed, it was criticized by those who opposed governmental secrecy and objected to the secretive nature of the FISA court. Civil libertarians objected to the relative ease with which government agents were able to obtain surveillance warrants from that body. However, FISA was ultimately accepted as an effort to bring legal standards and procedures to an area that has historically operated outside the law. After the terrorist attacks of 2001, Congress saw a need to revise FISA and expand the power of the government. While some saw the changes brought about in the Foreign Intelligence Surveillance Act by the PATRIOT Act as a dangerous erosion of Fourth Amendment principles, others viewed it as a much-needed enhancement of the ability of the government to identify and act upon threats to our national security in a world that is more perilous than ever. The revelation of the Bush administration's program for secret and warrantless electronic surveillance demonstrates the reality of governmental authority. The more it is expanded, the more it seeks to expand. The Foreign Intelligence Surveillance Act was initially accepted as a necessary tool in our country's quest to survive in a dangerous world. After 9/11, we decided that FISA did not go far enough and we had to give even more power to government in this realm with the passage of the PATRIOT Act. The final days of 2005 demonstrated that the Bush administration did not regard the PATRIOT Act as going far enough and its belief that the executive branch would not be bound even by laws intended to expand the power of the presidency. If the Foreign Intelligence Surveillance Act was designed to allow the protection of national security interests within a framework of the rule of law and checks and balances, then it must be regarded as yet another casualty of the terrorist attacks of September 11, 2001.

See also Electronic Surveillance; Fourth Amendment; *Katz v. United States;* Privacy, Constitutional Right of; Probable Cause; USA PATRIOT Act

Bibliography

Bazan, Elizabeth B. 2002. *The Foreign Intelligence Surveillance Act.* New York: Novinka Books.

Risen, James. 2006. *State of War: The Secret History of the CIA and the Bush Administration.* New York: Simon & Schuster.

Anthony Simones and John M. Scheb II

FOREIGN INTELLIGENCE SURVEILLANCE COURT. *See* Foreign Intelligence Surveillance Act

FORTAS, ABE (1910–1982)

Described by Justice John Marshall Harlan (the younger) "as the most brilliant advocate to appear before the High Court in his time" (qtd. in Shogan 1972), Abe Fortas was a wealthy, highly successful lawyer when he became an associate justice of the Supreme Court in 1965. With Chief Justice Earl Warren's announcement in 1968 that he would retire, President Lyndon Johnson nominated Fortas to be chief justice. Political opposition, however, doomed Fortas's nomination. Not long afterward, disclosure of ethically questionable financial arrangements forced Fortas's resignation from the Court.

Born in Memphis, Tennessee, Fortas attended Southwestern University in Memphis and Yale Law School. He became a faculty member at Yale and worked in President Franklin Roosevelt's New Deal. After he met Lyndon Johnson in 1939, they developed close ties over the years, and Fortas successfully represented Johnson in 1948 when his 84-vote victory in the Democratic primary for U.S. Senate was challenged (Shogan 1972).

Working with Thurman Arnold and later Paul Porter, Fortas formed Arnold, Fortas and Porter, a law firm that grew to be one of the most successful Washington firms. Primarily representing the interests of large corporations, the firm also represented on a pro bono basis a number of individuals accused of disloyalty. Appointed by the U.S. Supreme Court to represent an indigent appellant, Fortas successfully argued *Gideon v. Wainwright* (1963), which held that there is a federal constitutional right to counsel in state criminal cases involving serious offenses (Kalman 1990).

As a justice, Fortas generally voted with the liberal wing of the Court. One of his most important majority opinions is *In re Gault* (1967), which established that juveniles have at least some due process rights in juvenile court hearings. Fortas also wrote the majority opinion in *Tinker v. Des Moines Independent Community School District* (1969), which helped develop the doctrine that symbolic speech is protected by the First Amendment.

Working closely as an advisor to Lyndon Johnson while serving on the Court, Fortas was Johnson's clear choice when Chief Justice Warren announced his retirement. It was, however, late in the 1968 presidential election cycle, and there was considerable reaction to Fortas's liberalism and the liberalism of the Warren Court. Johnson's effort to appoint his friend to the chief justiceship failed (Murphy 1988). During this controversy, critics charged that Fortas had improperly accepted a $15,000 fee from American University for lecturing in a summer course.

After Fortas's name was withdrawn from consideration for chief justice, *Life* magazine disclosed that Fortas had obtained $20,000 from a foundation established by a wealthy financier who had significant criminal law problems. Later, it was discovered that Fortas was to get regular payments from the foundation and that the payments would continue to his wife even after his death. (Fortas received the first check in January of 1966. He returned the money in December of that same year and severed his relationship with the foundation.) There was nothing proved illegal in Fortas's actions, but there was ethical impropriety. Facing a political outcry for his impeachment or resignation, Fortas resigned from the Court. Not even his old firm would allow him to return, although he continued to practice law until his death (Shogan 1972; Kalman 1990).

Abe Fortas demonstrated a strong commitment to civil liberties during his brief tenure as an associate justice. This commitment, unfortunately, has been overlooked due to the circumstances surrounding his resignation.

See also Counsel, Right to; Due Process, Procedural; First Amendment; *Gault, In re; Gideon v. Wainwright;* Harlan, John Marshall, II; Juvenile Justice; Liberalism; New Deal; Roosevelt, Franklin D.; *Tinker v. Des Moines Independent Community School District;* Warren, Earl; Warren Court

Bibliography

Kalman, Laura. 1990. *Abe Fortas: A Biography.* New Haven, CT: Yale University Press.

Murphy, Bruce Allen. 1988. *Fortas: The Rise and Ruin of a Supreme Court Justice.* New York: William Morrow.

Shogan, Robert. 1972. *A Question of Judgment.* Indianapolis, IN: Bobbs-Merrill.

Anthony Champagne

FOURTEENTH AMENDMENT (1868)

The Fourteenth Amendment, proposed in 1866 and ratified in 1868, fundamentally altered the constitutional relationship between the states and the national government. The amendment consists of five sections, but only sections 1 and 5 have had a lasting impact on the development of American civil rights and liberties. Section 1 provides:

All persons born or naturalized in the United States and subject to the jurisdiction thereof, are citizens of the United States and of the state wherein they reside. No state shall make or enforce any law which shall abridge the privileges or immunities of citizens of the United States; nor shall any state deprive any person of life, liberty, or property, without due process of law; nor deny to any person within its jurisdiction the equal protection of the laws.

Section 5 declares that: "[t]he Congress shall have power to enforce, by appropriate legislation, the provisions of this article." Section 1 placed specific restraints on the states, and Section 5 empowered Congress to enforce the provisions of the amendment. By its blanket extension of citizenship, the Fourteenth Amendment, together with the Thirteenth Amendment's abolition of slavery, overruled the Dred Scott decision of 1857.

The Supreme Court first interpreted the scope of the Fourteenth Amendment in the *Slaughterhouse Cases* of 1873. While acknowledging that the primary purpose of the amendment was to protect the rights of former slaves, the Court did not confine the amendment to this objective alone. In this initial Fourteenth Amendment decision, the Supreme Court greatly narrowed the scope of the privileges or immunities clause by holding that it applied only to national, as distinguished from state, citizenship. Because most privileges and immunities were guaranteed by state citizenship, the practical effect of the Court's conclusion was to read Privileges or Immunities Clause out of the Fourteenth Amendment, leaving only the Due Process and Equal Protection Clauses as significant limitations on state power.

In attempting to define the scope of the Fourteenth Amendment, the Supreme Court emphasized that its restrictions applied only to *state action* and did not extend to questions of private discrimination. Citing this distinction between state and private action, the Court invalidated the Civil Rights Act of 1875, the last major Reconstruction statute that Congress enacted. This law provided that "[a]ll persons within the United States shall be entitled to the full and equal enjoyment of the accommodations, advantages, facilities, and privileges of inns, public conveyances on land or water, theaters, and other places of public amusement; subject only to the conditions and limitations established by law and applicable alike to citizens of every race and color, regardless of any previous condition of servitude." In striking down the key provisions of this statute, the Court held that the Fourteenth Amendment limited congressional action to the prohibition of official state-sponsored discrimination, as distinguished from discrimination practiced by privately owned places of public accommodation.

The Supreme Court has never repudiated the state action limitation on the scope of the Fourteenth Amendment, but it has had great difficulty over the years determining the degree of state involvement that converts private action into state action. The existence of state action in support of discrimination depends on whether the Supreme Court perceives a "close nexus" between the functions of the state and the practice of private discrimination at issue. For example, the Court found state action where a state agency leased property to a coffee shop that did not serve black patrons. The fact that the business was privately owned did not insulate it from the nondiscrimination requirements of the Fourteenth Amendment (*Burton v. Wilmington Parking Authority,* 1961). By contrast, in *Moose Lodge v. Irvis* (1972) the Court determined that the grant of a liquor license did not convert the club's racially discriminatory policy of refusing to serve the black guest of a white member into state action under the Fourteenth amendment.

Not surprisingly, the Fourteenth Amendment figured prominently in a number of early cases involving racial discrimination. The Supreme Court, for instance, ruled in 1880 that the Equal Protection Clause was violated by the systematic exclusion of members of a criminal defendant's race from the trial jury (*Strauder v. West Virginia*). On the other hand, the Court ruled in the landmark case of *Plessy v. Ferguson* (1896) that Louisiana did not violate the Equal Protection Clause by enacting and enforcing a statute requiring that blacks and whites occupy separate coaches on passenger trains traveling through the state. It was in this case that the Court crafted its infamous separate but equal doctrine. Not until the historic 1954 decision of *Brown v. Board of Education* did the Court formally repudiate this doctrine—first in the field of public education and later in other areas of American life.

Prior to the mid-1930s, Fourteenth Amendment interpretation was of great importance in the broad field of state economic regulation. From

about 1890 until the judicial revolution of 1937, a majority of Supreme Court justices interpreted the Due Process Clause as embodying a substantive, as distinguished from a procedural, limitation on the power of the states to regulate business enterprises. If the Court found that a challenged law restricting or forbidding particular business practices was arbitrary or unreasonable, it would declare the law unconstitutional, not because it violated any procedural safeguard (the usual requirement of due process), but because a majority of the justices deemed it incompatible with the content—the substance—of due process of law. Applying this subjective rationale, the Court invalidated, for example, a New York statute restricting the working hours of employees in bakeries (*Lochner v. New York,* 1905). In *Adkins v. Children's Hospital* (1923) the Court declared that a federal minimum-wage law was unconstitutional as a substantive violation of the Due Process Clause of the Fifth Amendment and applied the same reasoning 13 years later in striking down New York's minimum-wage statute as a Fourteenth Amendment violation (*Morehead v. New York ex rel. Tipaldo,* 1936). On the same substantive due process grounds, the Court struck down separate federal and state efforts to prevent employers from requiring employees to sign yellow-dog contracts (preemployment agreements not to join labor unions) (see *Adair v. United States,* 1908; *Coppage v. Kansas,* 1915). While the Court upheld many state and federal economic measures during this period of American history, it frequently invoked substantive due process to place significant checks on the growth of legislative regulation of business.

The Great Depression of the 1930s brought increasing popular demands for government at all levels to play a more active role in economic affairs. Matters came to a head early in 1937 when President Franklin D. Roosevelt, many of whose congressionally enacted New Deal programs had recently been declared unconstitutional, initiated his Court-packing proposal to add six new members to the high bench. With the landmark decision in *West Coast Hotel v. Parrish* (1937), a five-to-four majority of the justices abruptly abandoned the economic substantive due process approach and began routinely to uphold governmental regulation of business. By the same narrow margin the Court also upheld the National Labor Relations Act and the Social Security program (see *National Labor Relations Board v. Jones and Laughlin Steel*, 1937; *Steward Machine Company v. Davis*, 1937). Since 1937, substantive Fourteenth Amendment due process challenges to state economic legislation have been uniformly unsuccessful (see, for example, *Ferguson v. Skrupa*, 1963). Nevertheless, substantive due process reemerged in the 1960s and 1970s as a basis for protecting the right of privacy under the Fourteenth Amendment (see *Griswold v. Connecticut*, 1965; *Roe v. Wade*, 1973).

Long before the adoption of the Fourteenth Amendment, the Supreme Court had ruled that the just compensation clause of the Fifth Amendment and, by analogy, all other provisions of the federal Bill of Rights applied only to the national government and placed no limitations on the states (*Barron v. Baltimore*, 1833). After ratification of the Fourteenth Amendment in 1868, however, this important question was reopened. Did the Fourteenth Amendment's due process guarantee of individual liberty and property rights against state deprivation encompass the specific safeguards contained in the Bill of Rights? In the century that followed, the Supreme Court, incrementally and selectively, incorporated most of the provisions of the Bill of Rights into the Fourteenth Amendment, thereby making them applicable to the states. The ultimate choice of a process of selective incorporation represented a compromise among three theories of Fourteenth Amendment interpretation. These theories have been labeled due process, total incorporation, and incorporation plus (Abraham and Perry 2003).

The due process approach was first articulated by Justice Stanley Mathews in the 1884 decision of *Hurtado v. California*. There the Supreme Court refused to apply the grand jury requirement of the Fifth Amendment to the states. Justice Mathews concluded that since the Fifth Amendment itself contained a due process clause virtually identical to that found in the Fourteenth Amendment, the omission of a grand jury provision from the latter clearly indicated that it was distinct from the due process requirement. Justice Felix Frankfurter, the most prominent of the recent proponents of a due process theory, maintained that this concept referred to "those canons of decency and fairness which express the notions of justice of English-speaking peoples" (*Adamson v. California* 1947, concurring opinion). For him the question was not whether the provision under consideration was listed in the Bill of Rights, but whether it embodied basic notions of justice.

By contrast, Justice Hugo L. Black, who ranks with Justice John M. Harlan (the elder) as the leading proponent of total incorporation, asserted that the Due Process Clause of the Fourteenth Amendment was shorthand for the Bill of Rights. According to Justice Black's reading of history, the framers of the Fourteenth Amendment intended to apply the entire Bill of Rights to the states—nothing more and nothing less (*Adamson v. California*, 1947, dissenting opinion).

For a few other justices, including Frank Murphy, Wiley Rutledge, and, on occasion William O. Douglas, the Fourteenth Amendment not only incorporated all the provisions of the Bill of Rights but other fundamental rights as well (*Adamson v. California*, 1947, dissenting opinion of Justice Murphy). This approach seems to combine elements of the due process and total incorporation approaches. The middle ground of selective incorporation was perhaps best stated by Justice Benjamin N. Cardozo in *Palko v. Connecticut* (1937). If a provision of the Bill of Rights was "not of the very essence of a scheme of ordered liberty," it would not be "absorbed," or incorporated, into the Fourteenth Amendment. Through use of the selective incorporation approach, the Supreme Court by 1969 had applied almost all the guarantees of the Bill of Rights to the states. This piecemeal process began in 1897 with the Court's incorporation of the just compensation provision of the Fifth Amendment, thereby implicitly rejecting Justice Mathews's rationale in the *Hurtado* case decided only 13 years earlier. Then, between 1927 and 1947, the Court incorporated the First Amendment provisions on speech, press, assembly, and religion, as well as the right of indigent, young, and uneducated black defendants to the timely appointment of defense counsel to represent them in their racially charged prosecutions for the capital offense of rape (see *Chicago, Burlington and Quincy Railroad v. Chicago,* 1897; *Fiske v. Kansas,* 1927; *Near v. Minnesota ex rel. Olson,* 1931; *DeJonge v. Oregon,* 1937; *Cantwell v. Connecticut,* 1940; *Everson v. Board of Education,* 1947; and *Powell v. Alabama,* 1932). Between 1949 and 1969 most of the criminal procedure guarantees of the Bill of Rights were incorporated into the Fourteenth Amendment (see, especially, *Wolf v. Colorado,* 1949; *Mapp v. Ohio,* 1961; *Gideon v. Wainwright,* 1963; *Malloy v. Hogan,* 1964; *Duncan v. Louisiana,* 1968; and *Benton v. Maryland,* 1969). Only the Fifth Amendment provision for grand jury indictment, the Seventh Amendment right to a jury trial in civil cases, and the Eighth Amendment provisions regarding fines and excessive bail have not been incorporated and made binding on the states.

The process of selective incorporation of the Bill of Rights into the Fourteenth Amendment means, in effect, that a uniform system of basic constitutional rights is guaranteed to Americans, regardless of the state in which they reside. It is important to recognize, however, that state judges are free to give even greater protection to individual rights by interpreting the civil rights and liberties enumerated in state constitutions. To a large extent these state constitutional safeguards parallel those of the federal Constitution, but state judges, especially since the early 1970s, have in some instances gone beyond the rulings of the U.S. Supreme Court in protecting the procedural rights of criminal defendants as well as the substantive right of privacy.

In conclusion, the Supreme Court's interpretation of the Fourteenth Amendment, and in particular its Due Process and Equal Protection Clauses, has contributed enormously to the expansion and unification of constitutional rights against encroachment by the states. This enlargement of rights has been particularly important in the fields of First Amendment freedoms of speech, press, and religion; protections afforded criminal defendants under the Fourth, Fifth, Sixth, and Eighth amendments; personal privacy and autonomy; and nondiscrimination on the basis of race, ethnicity, religion, and gender.

See also Abortion, Right to; Abolitionist Movement; Accused, Rights of the; Assembly, Freedom of; *Barron v. Baltimore;* Bill of Rights (American); Bill of Rights, Incorporation of; Black, Hugo L.; Black Codes; *Brown v. Board of Education; Cantwell v. Connecticut;* Cardozo, Benjamin N.; *Chicago, Burlington and Quincy Railroad v. Chicago;* Citizenship; Civil Rights Act of 1866; Civil Rights Act of 1870; Civil Rights Act of 1871; Civil Rights Act of 1875; Civil Rights Cases; Civil Rights Movement; Counsel, Right to; Discrimination; Double Jeopardy, Prohibition of; Douglas, William O.; Dred Scott Case; Due Process, Procedural; Due Process, Substantive; Due Process Clauses; *Duncan v. Louisiana;* Economic Freedom; Eighth Amendment; Equality; Equal Protection Clause; Equal Protection Jurisprudence; Establishment Clause; *Everson v. Board of Education;* Excessive Bail, Prohibition of; Excessive Fines, Prohibition of; Federalism and Civil Rights and Liberties; Fifteenth Amendment; Fifth Amendment; First Amendment; Fourteenth Amendment, Section 5 of the; Fourth Amendment; Frankfurter, Felix; Free Exercise Clause; Fundamental Rights; Gender-Based Discrimination; *Gideon v. Wainwright; Gitlow v. New York;* Grand Jury; *Griswold v. Connecticut; Hamilton v. Regents of the University of California;* Harlan, John Marshall; Jim Crow Laws; Jury, Trial by; Just Compensation Clause; Liberty; *Lochner v. New York; Mapp v. Ohio; Near v. Minnesota ex rel. Olson;* New Deal; Ninth Amendment; *Palko v. Connecticut; Plessy v. Ferguson; Powell v. Alabama;* Press, Freedom of the; Privacy, Constitutional Right of; Privileges or Immunities Clause; Property Rights; Public Accommodation, Places of; Public Use Clause; Reconstruction; Religion, Freedom of; Restrictive Covenants; *Robinson v. California; Roe v. Wade;* Roosevelt, Franklin D.;

Second Amendment; Segregation, De Facto and De Jure; Segregation in Public Education; Self-Incrimination Clause; Separation of Church and State; Seventh Amendment; Sexual Orientation, Discrimination Based on; *Shelley v. Kraemer;* Sixth Amendment; *Slaughterhouse Cases;* Slavery; Speech, Freedom of; State Action Doctrine; States' Rights, Doctrine of; Third Amendment; Thirteenth Amendment

Bibliography

Abraham, Henry J., and Barbara A. Perry. 2003. *Freedom and the Court.* 7th ed. New York: Oxford University Press.

Berger, Raoul. 1977. *Government by Judiciary: The Transformation of the Fourteenth Amendment.* Cambridge, MA: Harvard University Press.

Braveman, Daan, William C. Banks, and Rodney A. Smolla. 2000. *Constitutional Law: Structure and Rights in Our Federal System.* 4th ed. New York: Lexis Publishing.

Cortner, Richard C. 1981. *The Supreme Court and the Second Bill of Rights: The Fourteenth Amendment and the Nationalization of Civil Liberties.* Madison: University of Wisconsin Press.

Curtis, Michael Kent. 1990. *No State Shall Abridge: The Fourteenth Amendment and the Bill of Rights.* Durham, NC: Duke University Press.

Mendelson, Wallace. 1960. *Capitalism, Democracy, and the Supreme Court.* New York: Appleton-Century-Crofts.

Meyer, Howard N. 2000. *The Amendment That Refused to Die (Equality and Justice Deferred): A History of the Fourteenth Amendment.* Lanham, MD: Madison Books.

Otis H. Stephens, Jr., and Glenn L. Starks

FOURTEENTH AMENDMENT, SECTION 5 OF THE

After President Abraham Lincoln's assassination, his successor, President Andrew Johnson, commenced a Reconstruction program that encouraged state resistance to black suffrage. Congress responded by passing the Civil Rights Act of 1866 over President Johnson's veto. This legislation granted citizenship to African Americans and stated that citizens had certain rights that could not be abridged by the government, including rights related to contracts, litigation, and property ownership. It also guaranteed the full and equal benefit of the law to all citizens. Until this point, the protection of individual rights had been a state function. Due to the possibility that this legislation could be repealed, Congress proposed the Fourteenth Amendment, which was ratified in 1868 to make these guarantees permanent and to counter repressive legislation like the Southern Black Codes. Section 1 of the Fourteenth Amendment guaranteed rights of citizenship, privileges or immunities, due process, and equal protection. Section 5 gave Congress the power to enforce, by appropriate legislation, the amendment's provisions, including Section 1. Section 5 also gave Congress the authority to make national laws pursuant to Section 1 that affected a vast range of state conduct and individual liberty.

The Fourteenth Amendment's legislative history is ambiguous, and scholars cannot agree on the critical question of framing intent, which clouds the meaning of sections 1 and 5. The constitutional debate concerns federalism: does the Fourteenth Amendment grant Congress unfettered power over the states in protecting individual rights? Before the Civil War, states enjoyed the prerogative to safeguard citizen liberty without national interference. Yet, in spite of the Civil War and slavery's demise, the states were not ready to cede to the national government unlimited authority to create civil rights legislation. Determining the scope of Congress's Section 5 power has been an ongoing process of constitutional interpretation.

The *Civil Rights Cases* (1883) invalidated the 1875 Civil Rights Act's public accommodations provisions, thereby limiting Congress's power to create an antidiscrimination law based on Section 5. The provision only authorized appropriate laws correcting the effects of prohibited state laws compromising state citizen rights. The state action principle is the cornerstone of subsequent judicial interpretations preventing the amendment from applying to private discriminatory acts. The onus was put on Congress to write laws responding to specific state law violations, a characteristic of restrictive Section 5 cases.

The New Deal, the U.S. Supreme Court's Footnote Four in *United States v. Carolene Products* (1938), and the doctrine of incorporation all helped to nationalize enforcement of the Fourteenth Amendment and select rights in the states, including rights pertaining to voting, criminal procedure, public accommodations, and higher education. The aggrandizement of national power peaked with the Warren Court (1953–1969) due process and egalitarian revolutions, and Section 5 became the focus for testing the limits of national power in the political struggle to enact the Voting Rights Act of 1965. In *Katzenbach v. Morgan* (1966), which represents the outer limits of enforcement power, the Court held that Section 4(e) of the Voting Rights Act was a valid exercise of legislative power under Section 5. Under Section 4(e), no person completing the sixth grade in an accredited non-English-language Puerto Rican school could be denied voting rights regardless of whether he or she could read English. This provision was challenged by two registered voters in New York City who argued that this section would bar the enforcement of a New York state literacy test as applied to Puerto Rican residents of New York, an action that could not be undertaken, it was argued, unless the courts held that the law was unconstitutional. Justice William Brennan's majority opinion disagreed. He wrote that the Court's role was to determine whether 4(e) was "appropriate legislation" to enforce the Equal Protection Clause. Brennan asserted that Section 5 was a powerful grant of delegated power akin to *McCulloch v. Maryland*'s (1819) implied necessary and proper principle. Moreover, in footnote 10 of his opinion, Brennan stated that Congress's Section 5 power must only enhance, and never limit, Fourteenth Amendment liberty, a construction suggesting the judiciary should defer to Congress when it legislated to preserve Section 1 liberty. That view did not command a majority or the court, however, and Justice Harlan's dissent countered that it was the province of the Court, not Congress, to deter-

mine the scope of Fourteenth Amendment rights. Harlan also insisted that the legislative record demonstrate Congress was acting to remedy a state law violating constitutional rights.

Harlan's narrow construction prevailed as the country and Court became more politically conservative with the elections and judicial appointments of presidents Ronald Reagan and George H. W. Bush. The Rehnquist Court interpreted Section 5 to constrain national power, often asserting that the judiciary must protect the states against national domination. In *City of Boerne v. Flores* (1997), Congress relied on Section 5 to enact the Religious Freedom Restoration Act of 1993, which reversed the ruling in *Employment Division v. Smith* (1990), a case that jettisoned the compelling governmental interest standard that had previously characterized judicial review of free exercise cases involving religious exemptions. The new law reinstated the old approach, a policy judgment negated by *Boerne.* After noting that there was little evidence of widespread national religious discrimination, the justices in *Boerne* held that legislation altering the meaning of a constitutional right is improper. Only laws that are congruent and proportionate to their remedial purpose are constitutionally valid, since a different interpretation would let Congress, and not the Court, determine the Constitution's substantive meaning.

After *Boerne,* achieving congruence and proportionality in Section 5 cases requires that federal law must be remedial and a deterrent to future constitutional violations. Congress must also create a legislative record that satisfactorily documents the existence of state discrimination, a key finding that shows that Congress has authority to use Section 5 to correct state law violations. These principles also have been applied in testing the limits of Eleventh Amendment sovereign immunity. In *College Savings Bank v. Florida Prepaid Postsecondary Education Expense Board* (1999) and *Florida Prepaid Postsecondary Education Expense Board v. College Savings Bank* (1999), the Court held that the 1992 Trademark Remedy Clarification Act and the 1992 Patent and Plant Variety Protection Remedy Clarification

Act did not validly abrogate state sovereign immunity under Section 5, thus insulating the states from federal lawsuits raising false advertising and patent infringement claims. *Kimel v. Florida Board of Regents* (2000) rejected Section 5 as a basis for subjecting nonconsenting states to private federal lawsuits alleging equal protection violations under the Age Discrimination in Employment Act.

In *United States v. Morrison* (2000), the Court held that a victim of gender-based violence could not sustain a private action for civil damages under the federal Violence Against Women Act, which otherwise would have allowed the victim to sue her attackers in federal court. Since the Court held that there was no state action, permitting the federal lawsuit would have been an invalid exercise of Congress's Section 5 power. Similarly in *Board of Trustees of the University of Alabama v. Garrett* (2001), two state employees could not sue in federal court under Title I of the Americans with Disabilities Act for allegedly discriminating against the disabled because Congress did not have Section 5 power to abrogate state immunity. But in *Nevada Department of Human Resources v. Hibbs* (2003), the Court ruled Congress had Section 5 power to abrogate Nevada's Eleventh Amendment immunity in a private lawsuit claming damages under the Family and Medical Leave Act of 1993 because claims of gender discrimination are reviewed under a standard of heightened scrutiny instead of rational basis review. In *Hibbs,* Nevada could not rebut the presumption that it engaged in unconstitutional gender bias when it decided to fire the claimant. Finally, in *Tennessee v. Lane* (2004), the Court distinguished *Garrett* by ruling that Congress had Section 5 power to abrogate Tennessee's Eleventh Amendment immunity, a holding that permitted the state to be sued under Title II of the Americans with Disabilities Act when it denied a disabled person public access to a courthouse.

The extent to which the Section 5 enforcement power should be interpreted broadly or narrowly has been a key question in the Supreme Court's federalism jurisprudence. A central component underlying these rulings concerns the scope of congressional power. Most recently, under a conservative Rehnquist Court, rulings have tended to limit the power of Congress when it impedes state sovereignty.

See also Bill of Rights, Incorporation of; Black Codes; Brennan, William J., Jr.; Civil Rights Act of 1866; Eleventh Amendment; *Employment Division, Department of Human Resources of Oregon v. Smith*; Equal Protection Clause; Fourteenth Amendment; Free Exercise Clause; New Deal; Rehnquist Court; Religious Freedom Restoration Act; Slavery; Sovereign Immunity; State Action Doctrine; *Civil Rights Cases;* Warren Court

Bibliography

Aynes, Richard L. 1993. "On Misreading John Bingham and the Fourteenth Amendment." *Yale Law Journal* 103 (October): 57–104.

Caminker, Evan H. 2001. "'Appropriate' Means-End Constraints on Section 5 Powers." *Stanford Law Review* 53 (May): 1127–99.

Gressman, Eugene. 1952. "The Unhappy History of Civil Rights Legislation." *Michigan Law Review* 50: 1323–58.

Post. Robert C. 2003. "Fashioning the Legal Constitution: Culture, Courts, and Law." *Harvard Law Review* 117 (November): 4–112.

Christopher Banks

FOURTH AMENDMENT (1791)

Adopted in 1789 and ratified by the states in 1791 as part of the Bill of Rights, the Fourth Amendment to the United States Constitution provides:

The right of the people to be secure in their persons, houses, papers and effects, against unreasonable searches and seizures, shall not be violated, and no Warrants shall issue but upon probable cause, supported by Oath or affirmation, and particularly describing the place to be searched and the persons or things to be seized.

Limiting the government's powers of search and seizure was a major concern of the founding generation. One of the main grievances of the American colonists in the decades preceding the American

Revolution was the power afforded British customs officials under the infamous writs of assistance, which "authorized customs officers to search any houses or businesses at their whim" and "permitted virtually unlimited invasions of privacy" (Stephens and Glenn 2006, 35). Arguing before a Boston court in the Writs of Assistance Case of 1761, James Otis called the writs "the worst instrument of arbitrary power, the most destructive of English liberty and the fundamental principles of law, that ever was found in an English law book" (Stephens and Glenn 2006, 32).

The Fourth Amendment was adopted to ensure that officials of the United States government would never be able to exercise such unlimited powers of search and seizure. In his dissenting opinion in *United States v. Rabinowitz* (1950), Justice Felix Frankfurter characterized the adoption of the Fourth Amendment as "a safeguard against recurrence of abuses so deeply felt by the Colonies as to be one of the potent causes of the Revolution."

A profound distaste for general warrants (those authorizing searches of unspecified persons and places) led the framers of the Bill of Rights to write the particularity requirement into the Fourth Amendment. Courts tend to enforce vigorously the Fourth Amendment requirement that search warrants be issued only "upon probable cause, supported by Oath or affirmation" and are specific as to "the place to be searched and the persons or things to be seized." In *Maryland v. Garrison* (1987), the Supreme Court recognized that "limiting the authorization to search to the specific areas and things for which there is probable cause to search ... ensures that the search will be carefully tailored to its justifications, and will not take on the character of the wide-ranging exploratory searches the Framers intended to prohibit."

The Fourth Amendment, like all the protections of the Bill of Rights, was originally conceived as a limitation on the powers of the newly created national government. However, the protection of the Fourth Amendment, along with most of the protections contained in the Bill of Rights, has been extended to state criminal defendants on the basis of the Fourteenth Amendment's broad limitations on state action. In *Wolf v. Colorado* (1949) the Supreme Court held that the freedom from unreasonable searches and seizures is "implicit in 'the concept of ordered liberty' and as such enforceable against the States through the Due Process Clause [of the Fourteenth Amendment]." Clearly, unrestricted powers of search and seizure are anathema to the classical liberal ideals of individual liberty and limited government on which this country was founded. Consequently, the Fourth Amendment limits search and seizure activities by law enforcement agencies at all levels of government, whether federal, state, or local.

When searches are challenged as being unreasonable, courts must first determine if the Fourth Amendment is applicable. Because the Constitution limits government action, the Fourth Amendment protects a person's rights against the police and other government agents, but not against searches and seizures conducted by private individuals. In *United States v. Jacobsen* (1984), the Supreme Court said that the Fourth Amendment "is wholly inapplicable to a search or seizure, even an unreasonable one, effected by a private individual not acting as an agent of the Government or with the participation or knowledge of any government official." Thus, a search by a privately employed security guard or a search of a package by an employee of a common carrier is not considered a violation of the Fourth Amendment unless the search was instigated by government action. Moreover, the Fourth Amendment does not apply to searches at the national border, searches conducted outside the United States, searches of "open fields," or searches of abandoned property. Indeed, the Fourth Amendment does not apply to any situation where a person lacks a "reasonable expectation of privacy."

Where it does apply, the Fourth Amendment expresses a decided preference for searches and seizures to be conducted pursuant to a warrant. The warrant requirement is designed to ensure that the impartial judgment of a judge or a magistrate is interposed between the citizen and the state. As the Supreme Court recognized in *McDonald v. United*

States (1948), the rights enshrined in the Fourth Amendment are "too precious to entrust to the discretion of those whose job is the detection of crime and the arrest of criminals."

Searches and seizures often entail serious intrusions into the private spheres of individuals, sometimes resulting in personal injury and/or property damage. Law enforcement officers are not permitted to conduct searches and seizures arbitrarily, or even based on their hunches about criminal activity. For a search to be reasonable under the Fourth Amendment, police generally must have probable cause to believe that a search will produce evidence of a crime. Yet there are certain instances, for example, stop-and-frisk situations, airport searches, and school searches—where police may conduct limited searches based on the lesser standard of reasonable suspicion. In addition to searches based on consent or conducted incident to a lawful arrest, a number of exceptions to the warrant requirement are based on the doctrine of exigent circumstances, evanescent evidence, and emergencies that qualify as exigent circumstances allowing warrantless searches.

To enforce the Fourth Amendment, courts have adopted an exclusionary rule that provides that evidence obtained through unreasonable searches and seizures is not admissible in criminal prosecutions. As the Supreme Court recognized in *Weeks v. United States* (1914), if illegally obtained evidence "can thus be seized and held and used in evidence against a citizen accused of an offense, the protection of the 4th Amendment, declaring his right to be secure against such searches and seizures, is of no value, and, so far as those thus placed are concerned, might as well be stricken from the Constitution." As Stephens and Glenn point out, "[t]he federal exclusionary rule, barring the admission of evidence obtained in violation of the Fourth Amendment, departed sharply from the old common law rule that determined the admissibility of evidence based on its reliability without regard to how it was obtained" (Stephens and Glenn 2006, 3).

In its landmark decision in *Mapp v. Ohio* (1961), the Supreme Court extended the exclusionary rule to the state courts by way of the Due Process Clause

of the Fourteenth Amendment. In recent years, a more conservative Court has limited the scope of the exclusionary rule somewhat. For example, in *United States v. Leon* (1984), the Court recognized a limited "good-faith exception" exempting from the exclusionary rule evidence secured by a law enforcement officer pursuant to a presumably valid search warrant that is subsequently invalidated.

The Fourth Amendment has applicability beyond the seizure of evidence. Because the arrest of a suspect is considered a seizure, the Fourth Amendment applies to arrests and various lesser police-citizen encounters, as well as to the use of force by police in making arrests. Writing for the Supreme Court in *Tennessee v. Garner* (1985), Justice Byron White observed, "[I]t is not always clear just when minimal police interference becomes a seizure" but concluded that "apprehension by the use of deadly force is a seizure subject to the reasonableness requirement of the Fourth Amendment."

Although the Fourth Amendment sets national standards for search and seizure, state constitutions can afford their citizens more protection than the federal constitution. For example, in some states courts do not recognize the good-faith exception adopted by the U.S. Supreme Court in *United States v. Leon*. Another illustration involves the issue of standing to challenge a Fourth Amendment violation. In *Minnesota v. Carter* (1998), the Supreme Court held that a nonovernight visitor has no legitimate expectation of privacy in an apartment, thus no standing to challenge a police search that yields contraband. In contrast, some state supreme courts hold that in such an instance a defendant has automatic standing to challenge a search on state constitutional grounds. Yet, in an attempt to prevent state courts from granting more protection to defendants than the federal Constitution allows, voters in a few states have adopted constitutional amendments requiring their courts to follow the interpretations of the Supreme Court on search and seizure issues.

Technological advances have afforded law enforcement new means to ferret out crime; the use of helicopters and such high-tech devices as infrared sensors, super-sensitive microphones, and miniature radio transmitters challenges the traditional right of privacy enjoyed by citizens in a free country. The current war on terrorism creates new demands for law enforcement agencies to conduct surveillance as well as considerable pressures on courts to allow such activities. In turn, these new means of ferreting out crime present new challenges to the courts in interpreting what constitutes an unreasonable search under the Fourth Amendment.

See also Administrative Searches; Arrest, Constitutional Limits on; Automobile Stops and Searches; *Bivens v. Six Unknown Named Federal Narcotics Agents;* Border Searches; Castle Doctrine; Consent Searches; Dogs, Use of by Police; Drug Courier Profiles; Drug Testing; Due Process Clauses; Electronic Surveillance; Emergency Searches; Field Sobriety Test; Force, Use of by Law Enforcement; Fourteenth Amendment; Fourth Amendment Exclusionary Rule; Frankfurter, Felix; Fruit of the Poisonous Tree Doctrine; Good-Faith Exception; Hot Pursuit, Doctrine of; Implied Consent Statutes; Informants, Anonymous and Confidential; Inventory Searches; *Katz v. United States; Mapp v. Ohio;* Open Fields Doctrine; Plain View Doctrine; Privacy, Reasonable Expectations of; Probable Cause; Public Schools, Searches and Seizures in; Roadblocks and Sobriety Checkpoints; Search Incident to a Lawful Arrest; Search Warrants; Stop and Frisk; Warrantless Searches; White, Byron R.; Writs of Assistance and General Warrants

Bibliography

Amar, Akhil Reed. 1994. "Fourth Amendment First Principles." *Harvard Law Review* 107:757.
Amsterdam, Anthony. 1974. "Perspectives on the Fourth Amendment." *Minnesota Law Review* 58:349–477.
Davies, Thomas Y. 1999. "Recovering the Original Fourth Amendment." *Michigan Law Review* 98:547.
Franklin, Paula A. 1991. *The Fourth Amendment.* Englewood Cliffs, NJ: Silver Burdett Press.
Greenhalgh, William. 2003. *The Fourth Amendment Handbook.* Chicago: American Bar Association.
Landynski, Jacob W. 1966. *Search and Seizure and the Supreme Court: A Study in Constitutional Interpretation.* Baltimore: Johns Hopkins Press.
———. 1978. *Search and Seizure and the Supreme Court.* Baltimore: Johns Hopkins University Press.
Lasson, Nelson B. 1937. *The History and Development of the Fourth Amendment to the United States Constitution.* Baltimore: Johns Hopkins Press.
Maclin, Tracey. 1997. "The Complexity of the Fourth Amendment: A Historical Review." *Boston University Law Review* 77:925.
Scheb, John M., and John M. Scheb II. 2005. *Criminal Law and Procedure.* 5th ed. Belmont, CA: Wadsworth/Thomson.
Stephens, Otis H., Jr., and Richard A. Glenn. 2006. *Unreasonable Searches and Seizures: Rights and Liberties under the Law.* Santa Barbara, CA: ABC-CLIO.
Wetterer, Charles M. 1998. *The Fourth Amendment: Search and Seizure.* Springfield, NJ: Enslow.

Hon. John M. Scheb, John M. Scheb II, and Otis H. Stephens, Jr.

FOURTH AMENDMENT EXCLUSIONARY RULE

The Fourth Amendment to the U.S. Constitution protects persons from unreasonable searches and seizures. The amendment is silent, however, as to how this right is to be enforced. In *Weeks v. United States* (1914), the U.S. Supreme Court adopted the so-called exclusionary rule, which held that evidence obtained by police in violation of the Fourth Amendment could not be used against a criminal defendant in a federal trial. In short, because the police had no authority to seize the evidence, the prosecution had no right to introduce the evidence at trial. The *Weeks* decision clearly marked the start of a suppression of evidence doctrine that had not previously existed in the common law.

The exact scope and significance of the decision in *Weeks* have been subjects of much discussion and controversy. This is in large part because the opinion in *Weeks,* though unanimous, was ambiguous about whether the exclusionary rule was a constitutional requirement or simply a judicially created remedy to deter constitutional violations. On one hand, the opinion written by Justice William Day observed that to allow the use of illegally seized evidence would be to affirm "a manifest neglect if not an open defiance … of the Constitution." Yet the opinion also noted that the exclusion of illegally seized evidence was necessary to deter further police misconduct. Since the case against the defendant would be harmed by the exclusion of relevant evidence, police would be less likely to violate the prohibition against unreasonable searches and seizures. Justice Day further noted that the integrity of trial courts would be undermined if they permitted the introduction of illegally obtained evidence. He emphasized this point by stating that "[t]he efforts of the courts and their officials to bring the guilty to punishment, praise-worthy as they are, are not to be aided by the sacrifice of those great principles established by years of endeavor and suffering which have resulted in their embodiment in the fundamental law of the land."

Almost a century after its adoption, scholars are divided. Some maintain that the Fourth Amendment implicitly requires the exclusion of all illegally seized evidence. Others insist that the exclusionary rule is simply a judicially created remedy applicable only in those situations in which the exclusion of evidence would deter further police misconduct. If the latter interpretation is true, of course, then exceptions to the rule are possible.

The *Weeks* decision explicitly stated that the exclusionary rule did not apply to searches conducted by state police officers. As a result, states were not required to exclude evidence obtained by an unreasonable search and seizure. Some states chose to do so; most did not.

In *Wolf v. Colorado* (1949), the Supreme Court faced the question of whether the Fourth Amendment, and by extension the exclusionary rule, should be applied to the states through the Due Process Clause of the Fourteenth Amendment. While making the Fourth Amendment applicable to the states, the justices specifically rejected the notion that the exclusionary rule should be binding

upon the states. In a five-to-four opinion, Justice Felix Frankfurter noted that the rule was a "judicial implication" without foundation in the Fourth Amendment. Accordingly, states remained free to adopt or ignore the exclusionary rule in state criminal proceedings.

Twelve years later, in *Mapp v. Ohio* (1961), the Supreme Court, again dividing five to four, overruled this aspect of the *Wolf* decision and extended the federal exclusionary rule to state criminal prosecutions. Justice Tom Clark's opinion for the majority emphasized both the constitutional foundations and the practical necessities of the rule. Reiterating *Weeks,* the opinion called the exclusion doctrine an "essential ingredient" of the Fourth Amendment and declared it necessary to discourage police misconduct and maintain judicial integrity. As such, all evidence obtained by searches in violation of the Fourth Amendment was inadmissible in state criminal proceedings.

Mapp formally linked the exclusionary rule to the Fourth Amendment. Subsequent decisions of the Supreme Court, however, have deconstitutionalized the rule, redefined its purpose, and limited its application. In *United States v. Calandra* (1974), for example, the Court, per Justice Lewis Powell, rejected the notion that the rule was a personal constitutional right. Instead, the six-member majority declared that the exclusionary rule was merely a prophylactic measure designed to deter future unlawful police misconduct. The justices then adopted a "cost-benefit approach," concluding that the rule was only to be applied in those settings where the exclusion of evidence would result in the significant deterrence of future police misconduct. In all other settings, the social costs of excluding relevant evidence far outweighed any potential benefits from its application.

This cost-benefit approach of the past quarter century has resulted in the curtailment of the operation of the exclusionary rule. In addition, the Supreme Court has formally adopted several exceptions to this rule. The first exception, announced in *Nix v. Williams* (1984), does not require the suppression of evidence that has been seized illegally if the prosecution can establish that the evidence inevitably would have been discovered by lawful means in the course of a continuing investigation. In a companion ruling, *Segura v. United States* (1984), the justices held that the exclusionary rule does not prohibit the use of illegally obtained evidence if the prosecution can establish that the evidence later would have been found as a result of other independent sources. The most controversial exception was adopted in *United States v. Leon* (1984). The good-faith exception permits the use of illegally seized evidence where police have a search warrant and in "good faith" conduct the search on the assumption that the warrant is valid, though the warrant is later found to be unsupported by probable cause. The justices extended this exception in *Illinois v. Krull* (1987), holding that the exclusionary rule does not apply to evidence obtained by police who acted in objectively reasonable reliance upon a state statute authorizing warrantless searches, but that is subsequently found to violate the Fourth Amendment. Finally, *Arizona v. Evans* (1995) held that the exclusionary rule does not require the suppression of evidence seized in violation of the Fourth Amendment where the mistaken information upon which the investigating authorities based their actions resulted from clerical errors of court employees. In each of the aforementioned cases, the Court concluded that no basis existed for believing that the exclusion of evidence would have any deterrent effect upon police (or judicial) misconduct.

Almost a century after its adoption, the exclusionary rule continues to generate controversy. Supporters of the exclusionary rule argue that without the rule, the protection of the Fourth Amendment is of no value. In the words of Justice Frank Murphy in dissent in *Wolf,* the rule is the only means of "giving content to the commands of the Fourth Amendment." Without it, nothing will deter the police from heavy-handed tactics and clear violations of individual constitutional rights. Opponents assert that the rule is contrary to justice and leads to the withholding of valuable evidence that could help establish truth in judicial proceedings. Much of the opposition to the exclusion of relevant evidence

was distilled in a single sentence in *People v. Defore* (1926), where Judge (later Justice) Benjamin N. Cardozo critically observed the undeniable consequence of the exclusionary rule: "The criminal is to go free because the Constable has blundered."

See also Accused, Rights of the; Burger Court; Cardozo, Benjamin N.; Clark, Tom C.; Due Process Clauses; Fourteenth Amendment; Fourth Amendment; Frankfurter, Felix; Good-Faith Exception; *Mapp v. Ohio;* Powell, Lewis F., Jr.; Rehnquist Court; Warren Court

Bibliography

Stephens, Otis H, Jr., and Richard Glenn. 2005. *Unreasonable Searches and Seizures: Rights and Liberties under the Law.* Santa Barbara, CA: ABC-CLIO.

                                                                    Richard Glenn

FRANK, LEO (1884–1915)

The lynching of Leo Frank marked a turning point in the American experience of racism and anti-Semitism. Frank, who was Jewish, moved from New York City to Atlanta, Georgia, in 1908 to manage the National Pencil Factory. Mary Phagan, an employee of the pencil factory, was two months short of her thirteenth birthday when she was murdered shortly after picking up her wages on April 26, 1913. Initially, suspicion focused on Newt Lee, a night watchman at the factory, and Arthur Mullinax, an ex-streetcar driver. Although Frank initially assisted in the investigation of the crime, for reasons that have never been fully explained, police attention soon turned to him. On May 8, 1913, a coroner's jury ordered that Frank and another man be charged in the murder.

Frank was convicted of the murder on August 25, 1913, despite serious questions about the evidence pointing to him. The circumstances of his case directly inspired both a revival of the dormant Ku Klux Klan and the founding of the Anti-Defamation League.

Frank was born on April 17, 1884, and earned a degree in mechanical engineering from Cornell University. He was 29 years old in 1913 and had been managing the National Pencil Factory for nearly five years. Leo Frank had become prominent in the Jewish community, and at the time of the murder was serving as president of the Atlanta chapter of B'nai Brith. Mary Phagan was born on June 1, 1900. She worked at the National Pencil Factory fitting metal tips on pencils. When a shipment of metal to make the tips failed to arrive on time in April 1913, Mary was temporarily laid off. She was owed $1.20 in back wages, which she went to collect from the factory on April 26, the Confederate Memorial Day then recognized in Georgia as an official holiday.

When Mary arrived at the factory around noon, she sought her pay from Leo Frank, who was working alone in his office on the fourth floor. Mary's body was discovered in the basement of the factory at about 3:00 the next morning by the night watchman. She had been strangled, and two handwritten notes were found with her body.

Mary Phagan's murder evoked public outrage, and the police investigation was extensively covered in the newspapers. Such intense scrutiny, in combination with the threat of mob vengeance, placed great pressure on law enforcement to solve the case quickly.

This pervasive coverage has been likened to that of the O. J. Simpson case of the 1990s. Papers initially reported that superintendent Leo Frank had been routinely questioned and eliminated as a suspect. One article mentioned that, unhappy with the investigation's progress, Frank had personally hired a private investigator to assist.

Most suspicion continued to fall on the night watchman after a bloody shirt was discovered in his home, although he insisted the blood was his own from an injury. After a friend of Mary's testified at an inquest into her death on April 30 that Mary had told him she had been afraid of Leo Frank because he had flirted with and made advances toward her, suspicion began to shift toward Frank, and he was arrested. The next day Jim Conley, an African American employed as a janitor, who had been working at the factory on the day of Mary's death, was discovered trying to rinse a soiled shirt in the

basement of the factory. When closer inspection revealed the stains to be blood, he was arrested and questioned at great length.

Meanwhile, the attention focused on the case spawned numerous hoaxes and rumors, which were reported in the papers and grew in credibility by virtue of being in print. Supposed witnesses claimed to have seen Frank acting oddly on the day of the murder, and others alleged knowledge of previous "immoral acts" by Frank. Some of these witnesses, including Frank's cook, were improperly pressured by police into giving stories later proved false. Despite being later discredited, these reports played a significant role in focusing suspicion on Frank, as did Jim Conley's story.

When it became clear that the notes found with Mary's body matched Conley's handwriting, Conley claimed that he had written the notes only at Frank's request after Mary's murder. Shortly after this revelation and despite inconsistencies in Conley's story, Frank was indicted for murder.

Police and attorneys missed or ignored significant problems with Conley's version of events. First, they disregarded the fact that Conley initially claimed to have written the notes before Mary's death, changing his story after several days to say he had written them after her death. Even more incriminating was the fact that when Conley was first taken to the factory to walk detectives through the events of his day, he claimed to have defecated in the elevator shaft early on the morning of Mary's murder. However, when the detectives first arrived at the factory to investigate on April 27, the feces had not been flattened. This fact was significant because Conley claimed he had taken Mary's body down the elevator with Frank, which would have flattened the feces. The fact that they were intact should have indicated to detectives that Mary's body was there before Conley relieved himself, but no one noticed the error.

Frank's trial began on July 28, 1913. Jim Conley was the star witness, testifying falsely that he had often stood watch while Frank entertained young women in his office. He said he had stood watch outside Frank's office while Mary collected her check and was murdered. He also alleged that Frank paid him to help move her body to the basement.

Among the witnesses for Frank in the 25-day trial was 13-year-old Alonzo Mann, an employee at the factory, whose brief testimony about Frank's good character went almost unnoticed. Not until 1982, when he signed an affidavit and told his story to the *Tennessean*, would he publicly reveal that he had seen Jim Conley carrying Mary's body at the factory on the day of her death. Conley had threatened Alonzo with death if he ever reported what he had seen, and Alonzo's mother advised him to keep quiet even after Frank's conviction.

On August 26, 1913, the day following his conviction, Frank was sentenced to hang. After rejection of their motion for a new trial, Frank's attorneys succeeded in bringing the case before the Georgia Supreme Court on a writ of error, alleging, among other things, the unfairness of the trial as a result of "disorder in and about the court room." On February 17, 1914, this court affirmed Frank's conviction (*Frank v. State*, 1914). After the exhaustion of legal remedies at the state level, Frank's counsel filed a petition for habeas corpus in the United States District Court for the Northern District of Georgia.

On April 19, 1915, the United States Supreme Court, dividing seven-to-two, affirmed the district court's denial of this petition (*Frank v. Mangum*, 1915). Justice Oliver Wendell Holmes, joined by Justice Charles Evans Hughes, filed a powerful dissenting opinion, asserting that "[m]ob law does not become due process of law by securing the assent of a terrorized jury." He noted that "[w]hatever disagreement there may be as to the scope of the phrase 'due process of law,' there can be no doubt that it embraces the fundamental conception of a fair trial, with opportunity to be heard." Holmes went on to explain that "[w]e are not speaking of a mere disorder, or mere irregularities in procedure, but of a case where the processes of justice are actually subverted.... It is our duty ... to declare lynch law as little valid when practiced by a regularly drawn jury as when administered by one elected by a mob intent on death." A few years later a majority

of the Supreme Court relied heavily on Holmes's classic dissent in applying the fair trial doctrine as a basis for overturning mob-dominated verdicts and convictions based on coerced confessions (see for example *Moore v. Dempsey*, 1923; *Powell v. Alabama*, 1932; *Brown v. Mississippi*, 1936; and *Chambers v. Florida*, 1940).

Following Frank's unsuccessful judicial challenges, the governor of Georgia commuted Frank's sentence from death to life in prison on his last day in office in June 1915. Among the evidence he considered was a letter from Conley's attorney saying he had become convinced that his client was guilty, and one from the trial judge claiming he seriously doubted Frank's guilt. Knowing the decision would be unpopular, and fearing for Frank's safety, the governor arranged for Frank's transfer from the Atlanta jail to a more secure state prison in Milledgeville.

Two months later, a group of men calling themselves the Knights of Mary Phagan did indeed break into the jail and abduct Leo Frank. They drove him around for most of the night until they arrived in Marietta and hanged him. No one was ever prosecuted for his murder, although one researcher (Goldfarb) has claimed to have identified some of the men involved based on photographs taken at the lynching.

In November 1915, the Knights of Mary Phagan met again at Stone Mountain, Georgia. There they burned a cross and initiated a new invisible order of the Ku Klux Klan. Only days later, the Anti-Defamation League of the B'nai Brith was founded in New York to combat anti-Semitism, citing Frank's case as a direct cause for its creation. It was at the Anti-Defamation League's urging that the Georgia Board of Pardons and Paroles issued a posthumous pardon to Leo Frank in 1986, not on the basis that he was innocent of Phagan's murder, but because of the state's failure to protect him while in custody.

See also Anti-Defamation League; Habeas Corpus; Habeas Corpus, Federal; Holmes, Oliver Wendell, Jr.; Interrogation and Confessions; Ku Klux Klan; *Powell v. Alabama*

Bibliography

Frey, Robert S. 1988. *The Silent and the Damned: The Murder of Mary Phagan and the Lynching of Leo Frank.* New York: Madison Books.

Goldfarb, Stephen. "Leo Frank Lynchers: Identifying the Lynchers of Leo Frank." www.leofranklynchers.com.

Melnick, Jeffrey Paul. 2000. *Black-Jewish Relations on Trial: Leo Frank and Jim Conley in the New South.* Jackson: University Press of Mississippi.

Moseley, Clement Charlton. 1967. "The Case of Leo M. Frank, 1913–1915." *Georgia Historical Quarterly* 51:1.

Oney, Steve. 2003. *And the Dead Shall Rise: The Murder of Mary Phagan and the Lynching of Leo Frank.* New York: Random House.

Phagan, Mary. 1987. *The Murder of Little Mary Phagan.* Far Hills, NJ: Horizon Press.

Pou, Charles. "The Leo Frank Case." www.cviog.uga.edu/Projects/gainfo/leofrank.htm.

Amy M. Lighter and Otis H. Stephens, Jr.

FRANKFURTER, FELIX (1882–1965)

Felix Frankfurter was born to a lower-middle-class Jewish tradesman's family in the ghetto of Vienna, Austria, on November 15, 1882. In 1894, the Frankfurters immigrated to America and settled on Manhattan's Lower East Side. There, Frankfurter developed early loves of learning, law, and socially progressive causes. He attended public schools and the City College of New York, then a free institution, and earned his way to Harvard Law School, graduating first in his class in 1906.

Frankfurter was soon recruited by the progressive Republican Henry Stimson to help fight corruption through the office of the U.S. Attorney for the Southern District of New York. Stimson became a mentor to Frankfurter, and, through his support, the future Supreme Court justice subsequently was promoted to posts in the Bureau of Insular Affairs, then part of the Department of War, in the Taft and Wilson administrations. Frankfurter seemed to enjoy the work of crafting and enforcing regulations aimed at enhancing public welfare. While in Washington, Frankfurter spent considerable time with another mentor, Supreme Court Justice Oliver Wendell Holmes, Jr., for whom the young man had almost unqualified admiration.

In 1914 Frankfurter joined the faculty of Harvard Law School. He taught for three years before returning to Washington. During this first residence at Harvard, Frankfurter met another great influence, attorney and later Supreme Court Justice Louis D. Brandeis. When Brandeis ascended to the high court in 1916, Frankfurter succeeded him as unpaid counsel for the National Consumer's League. In this role Frankfurter argued a small number of cases before the high court, defending the necessity and constitutionality of state limited-work-day laws and minimum-wage laws. In doing so, Frankfurter made use of the so-called Brandeis brief, a fact-rich sort of treatise designed to give the Court an understanding of the social realities affected by the law in question. Before World War I, the Court upheld the validity of two such state laws; after the Great War, Frankfurter faced a more conservative Court and lost a similar battle.

During World War I, Frankfurter served at the request of President Woodrow Wilson on a fact-finding and mediation commission devoted to calming labor unrest in the west. As part of his work on this commission, Frankfurter concluded that labor should have power and influence in the industrial world adequate to create a "just equilibrium" between labor and management.

After the War Frankfurter returned to Harvard, where, in addition to teaching, publishing, and devoting a large amount of time to cultivating and advancing the careers of his brightest students, he also remained actively involved in matters outside the ivory tower. The professor was an early advisor to the NAACP, active in the early days of the ACLU, an advocate for the cause of Zionism, and a public voice in defense of Sacco and Vanzetti. Frankfurter also served as an informal but deeply involved advisor to President Franklin D. Roosevelt (a role that he continued to fill after he became a Supreme Court justice), drafted the National Securities Act of 1933, and remained involved with the National Consumers League. Partly due to these activities, Frankfurter attained a celebrity rare for law professors, although it was a celebrity tainted (or bolstered) by controversy. Nonetheless, when Roosevelt nominated Frankfurter to the Supreme Court in 1939, the Senate confirmed his appointment by unanimous vote.

Despite his lack of prior judicial experience, Frankfurter approached the Supreme Court expecting to assume a leadership role. His attempts to instruct his fellow justices on the proper role of the judiciary contributed to the long-standing and now famous discord between Frankfurter and the Court's liberals, most notably Justices Hugo Black and William Douglas. The short, energetic Frankfurter was warmly intense about most things: his friendships, his disputes (he was prone to take even intellectual differences personally), his egotism, his espousal of progressivism, his patriotism, and his esteem for the virtue of judicial restraint. To Frankfurter, broad exercise of judicial review in overturning legislation threatened to lead to rule by judges.

Frankfurter believed that the substantive due process approach used by the Court prior to 1937 in striking down economic regulations posed just as much threat to the health of the nation and the integrity of the judiciary when used to strike down laws that burdened individual liberty interests. In applying due process principles, he seemed to be searching for a set of constraints within which to act. In his opinion for the Court in *Rochin v. California* (1952), Frankfurter expressed dismay that a man had been convicted of drug use based on the forcibly extracted contents of his stomach and wrote: "[D]ue process of law [is not] a matter of judicial caprice…. In each case 'due process of law' requires an evaluation based on a disinterested inquiry pursued in the spirit of science, on a balanced order of facts exactly and fairly stated, on the detached consideration of conflicting claims, on a judgment … duly mindful of reconciling the needs both of continuity and of change in a progressive society."

This balancing approach is evident in Frankfurter's eloquent opinions but, as his critics point out, often led to a refusal to expand the reach or content of Bill of Rights protections. In one of the first and most notable opinions authored by Frankfurter, the

majority upheld a Pennsylvania law under which two Jehovah's Witness children were expelled for refusing to salute the United States flag. The children's parents argued that because their religion prohibited veneration of any nondivine symbol, the law burdened their free exercise of religion (*Minersville School District v. Gobitis,* 1940). Frankfurter wrote that "[t]he mere possession of religious convictions which contradict the relevant concerns of a political society does not relieve the citizen from the discharge of political responsibilities [such as expressing loyalty to the nation's symbol, the flag]." Three years later, when the Court reversed its stance on the flag salute issue (*West Virginia Board of Education v. Barnette,* 1943), Frankfurter held firm to his *Gobitis* opinion. In *Adamson v. California* (1947), the Court held the Fifth Amendment's self-incrimination prohibition to be inapplicable to the states, and Frankfurter wrote a strongly worded concurrence in opposition to the idea that all provisions of the Bill of Rights were made applicable to the states through the passage of the Fourteenth Amendment. In a notable line of cases dealing with apportionment of legislative districts, Frankfurter, ultimately in the minority, refused to apply constitutional provisions to curtail the discretion of legislatures in reapportionment. In all these cases, Frankfurter was balancing not individual interests against arbitrary dictates of the state but rather the interests of individuals against the needs of the whole citizenry as expressed through its laws.

Some critics believe this balancing act led to unjustified curtailment of civil liberties. After all, Frankfurter joined the majority in *Korematsu v. United States* (1944), upholding the constitutionality of an order excluding Japanese Americans from parts of California and thereby also upholding their removal to interment camps. On the other hand, Frankfurter was one of the architects of constitutionally mandated desegregation; he joined the unanimous opinion in *Brown v. Board of Education* (1954) and contributed the most famous phrase in *Brown*'s 1955 reaffirmation, prescribing the manner in which desegregation was to proceed: "with all deliberate speed."

Despite never becoming the Court's intellectual leader, as he wished and expected to be, Frankfurter was nonetheless highly influential through his teaching, his writing, his audiences with presidents, his ability to place his students in government positions, and his tireless proselytizing of those around him. He retired from the Court in 1962 after suffering a stroke and died three years later. Writings left behind by the justice include: *The Case of Sacco and Vanzetti* (1927); *The Business of the Supreme Court* (1928); *The Commerce Clause under Marshall, Taney and Waite* (1937); *Mr. Justice Holmes and the Constitution* (1938); and *The Public and Its Constitution* (1964).

See also American Civil Liberties Union; Bill of Rights, Incorporation of; Black, Hugo L.; Brandeis, Louis D.; *Brown v. Board of Education;* Douglas, William O.; Due Process, Substantive; Due Process Clauses; Fourteenth Amendment; Holmes, Oliver Wendell, Jr.; Jehovah's Witnesses; Judicial Restraint; *Korematsu v. United States;* National Association for the Advancement of Colored People; Reapportionment; Roosevelt, Franklin D.; Warren Court; *West Virginia Board of Education v. Barnette*

Bibliography

Baker, Liva. 1969. *Felix Frankfurter.* New York: Coward-McCann.

Hirsch, H. N. 1981. *The Enigma of Felix Frankfurter.* New York: Basic Books.

Mendelson, Wallace. 1966. *Justices Black and Frankfurter: Conflict in the Court.* Chicago: University of Chicago Press.

Rachel Pearsall

FREE AND FAIR ELECTIONS

In any democracy, one of the central tenets is ensuring that all citizens have a just and equal voice when choosing the elected officials who will represent them. In American democracy, the Constitution's framers chose those twin emphases of representative democracy and consent of the governed to form the core of the philosophy of free and fair elections and manifested in the principle one person, one vote. Without an equal voice, republican democracy would be worthless. In the original Constitution, there was little mention of the principle of one person, one vote, but that principle has been evoked by the Supreme Court's interpretation of the Constitution's original text as seen through the Fourteenth Amendment.

"One person, one vote" implies that votes will be counted equally in such fashion that each person's electoral voice is no greater than any other person's. Free and fair elections also imply that the populace has adequate access to the ballot box. For an election to be free and fair, access to the ballot must be available to all, and the votes must count in an equitable fashion.

Early elections were more freewheeling affairs than they are today, with parties printing up slates of candidates that could be used in place of regular ballots. The different colors and sizes of ballots made it easy to tell which party and candidates a voter had chosen. In many parts of the country, this led to intimidation and physical violence. To minimize the fraudulent practices of the interested parties, in 1889 New York adopted Australia's system of uniform ballots printed by the election authority, and the process spread nationwide quickly thereafter. While paper has been replaced by punch cards and now electronic voting systems, the intent of keeping ballots secret and therefore fair has remained a guiding principle.

Over time, the Supreme Court has struck down the more onerous methods of disenfranchisement to ensure equal ballot access. One of the most appalling forms of disenfranchisement was the white primary, where parties (as private bodies free from government regulation) would restrict black citizens from ballot access. In *Smith v. Allwright* (1944), the Supreme Court invalidated the white primary, but more was to come. Restrictive and unevenly enforced literacy tests were also invalidated by the courts, as was the grandfather clause. The Twenty-Fourth Amendment, ratified in 1964, ended the poll tax in federal elections.

With the intentional methods of disenfranchisement null and void, the Court turned to making sure that votes were counted equally. *Baker v. Carr*

(1962) showed how Tennessee's state legislative district apportionment plan denied people the right to a fair election, since urban voters had roughly half the representation of their rural counterparts. Tennessee's method of apportioning districts based on county meant some representatives had nearly one million constituents, while others had fewer than ten thousand, thus amplifying the votes of those constituents in smaller areas. The *Baker* decision required legislative districts at all levels to be redrawn decennially according to the census to ensure that the ratio of citizen to legislator was close in all districts.

In the 1980s, the U.S. Justice Department began requiring states to present redistricting plans that would amplify the votes of African American voters to correct for the inequities of past elections. North Carolina's plan for the 1990 census round was particularly curious, with extraordinarily shaped districts resembling straight lines and ink blots. The oddly shaped districts contained African American voters in such concentration that they represented more than half of the district's population and hence were titled majority-minority districts. A white citizen filed suit to enjoin the district, and in *Shaw v. Hunt* (1996) invalidated the majority-minority district as a violation of the one-person, one-vote doctrine.

The most recent challenge to the concept of free and fair elections came in the 2000 presidential election. Nationwide electoral vote tallies pointed to Florida as the state whose votes would decide the election's outcome. Florida voters were evenly split between Republican nominee George W. Bush and Democratic nominee Albert Gore, Jr. The final tally showed a thin 527-vote victory margin for Bush, which triggered a statewide recount. During the recount procedure, numerous groups (particularly African American leaders) claimed to have had their votes discarded, which, had evidence been uncovered, would have shown a violation of free and fair elections. The Gore and Bush campaigns sought help from the courts, and eventually the U.S. Supreme Court decided in *Bush v. Gore* (2000) that while the lack of unified vote-counting procedures

in Florida was likely a violation of free and fair elections, inadequate time remained to impose such a standard, and the original results of a 527-vote Bush win were validated.

See also *Baker v. Carr;* Constitutional Democracy; Fourteenth Amendment; Grandfather Clause; Reapportionment; Representative Democracy; Twenty-fourth Amendment; U.S. Department of Justice; Voting Rights; White Primary

Bibliography

Caesar, Richard, and Andrew Busch. 2001. *The Perfect Tie.* New York: Rowman & Littlefield.

Goldman, Robert 2001. *A Free Ballot and a Fair Count: The Department of Justice and the Enforcement of Voting Rights in the South, 1877–1893.* New York: Fordham University Press.

McGill Arlinton, Karen. 1992. *Voting Rights in America: Continuing the Quest for Full Participation.* Washington, DC: University Press of America.

Posner, Richard. 2001. *Breaking the Deadlock: The 2000 Election, the Constitution, and the Courts.* Princeton, NJ: Princeton University Press

Sabato, Larry J. 2001. *Overtime: The Election Thriller of 2000.* New York: Longman.

Chapman Rackaway

FREEDOM. *See* Liberty

FREEDOM FROM RELIGION FOUNDATION

Established in 1978, the Freedom from Religion Foundation describes itself as "a national membership association of freethinkers: atheists, agnostics and skeptics of any pedigree." The group's Web site (www.ffrf.org) states, "Our Constitution was very purposefully written to be a godless document, whose only references to religion are exclusionary." Since its inception, the organization has brought more than 20 lawsuits challenging government practices it deems in violation of the Establishment Clause of the First Amendment. Through litigation, the Freedom from Religion Foundation has succeeded in forcing the removal of crosses and religious monuments from public buildings and lands across the country, preventing faith-based organizations from receiving public funds, halting government subsidies of religious schools, and even preventing the U.S. Postal Service from issuing religious cancellations of used postage stamps.

In 1996, the Foundation went so far as to challenge the constitutionality of inscribing the national motto, In God We Trust, on the currency. In support of its complaint, the Foundation cited a national survey that found that an overwhelming majority of American citizens regard the national motto as a religious statement. Nevertheless, in *Gaylor v. United States* (1996), the U.S. Court of Appeals for the Tenth Circuit rejected the Foundation's challenge. That court found that "a reasonable observer, aware of the purpose, context, and history of the phrase 'In God we trust,' would not consider its use or its reproduction on U.S. currency to be an endorsement of religion." While some saw the litigation as frivolous, Anne Nicol Gaylor, lead plaintiff in the lawsuit and president of the Freedom from Religion Foundation, indicated that the national motto is one of the chief concerns of her organization. Gaylor was quoted in the Foundation's publication *Freethought Today* as saying that the national motto "is constantly cited by the religious right as verification that this is a 'Christian nation,' and as grounds for further state/church entanglement. The religious right needs to be reminded that ours is a godless Constitution, and was very purposefully and deliberately written that way" (Freedom from Religion Foundation 1994).

Bibliography

Freedom from Religion Foundation. 1994. "Foundation Lawsuit Challenges 'In God We Trust' Motto." *Freethought Today,* June/July.

John M. Scheb II and Otis H. Stephens, Jr.

FREEDOM OF ACCESS TO CLINIC ENTRANCES ACT (FACE)

The Freedom of Access to Clinic Entrances Act (FACE) is a federal statute that was enacted in 1994 to prohibit the intimidation of or interference with, by force or threat of force or by use of physical obstruction or intentional injury, anyone who is obtaining or providing reproductive health services. Obstructive conduct is prohibited at locations that provide abortion services as well as at locations where alternatives to abortion are supported. In addition to providing criminal penalties, FACE allows the Attorney General as well as any person offended by prohibiting conduct to bring a civil action to obtain injunctive relief and/or compensatory and punitive damages.

Pressure on Congress to enact laws regulating abortion protests mounted after individuals and groups associated with the pro-life movement had begun resorting to more intrusive and extreme methods, such as obstructing clinics, vandalizing property, intimidating clinic patients and personnel, trespassing, bombing clinics, and even murdering doctors who performed abortions. Prior to the adoption of FACE, the U.S. Supreme Court had ruled that other existing statutes were not applicable to control anti-abortion protest. In 1993, the Court decided in *Bray v. Alexandria Women's Health Clinic* that an 1871 statute prohibiting the deprivation of civil rights by private groups (the so-called Ku Klux Klan Act) could not be applied to prevent abortion clinic blockades. In 1994, the Court ruled that abortion clinics need not show an economic interest to bring RICO action against anti-abortionists should they engage in racketeering activity. Yet in 2003, the Supreme Court decided that anti-abortion protest did not fit the definition of extortion in the Hobbs Act, which requires the obtaining of someone's property under threat of force (see *National Organization for Women v. Scheidler,* 1994; *Scheidler v. National Organization for Women,* 2003).

Originally introduced in 1993 as two separate bills in both the U.S. Senate and House of Representatives, FACE was presented in the form of the Senate Bill to President Clinton and signed into law on May 26, 1994. While the House version of the bill was primarily oriented toward the prevention of violence against employees and patients of abortion clinics, the Senate bill was based on recognition of the need to protect a woman's right to seek an abortion and the need to safeguard civil rights. The Senate version discussed the extremist tactics of anti-abortion demonstrators and the fact that these protests often overburden local law enforcement. The Senate concluded that such unlawful conduct interfered with the exercise of a woman's constitutional right to have an abortion, which has been guaranteed since the Supreme Court's ruling in *Roe v. Wade* in 1973.

FACE was designed to prohibit only unlawful conduct, such as assault, trespassing, and vandalism, while not infringing on the free speech rights of abortion protesters. The statute may be distinguished from the contemporaneous case of *Madsen v. Women's Health Center* (1994) in that *Madsen* went so far as to uphold prohibitions on conduct that was obstructive and hostile, but not otherwise illegal. Insofar as the statute provides protection to counseling centers that provide alternatives to abortions as well as to clinics that provide abortions, it is not meant to discriminate on the basis of content or one's viewpoint on the morality of abortion. FACE is also meant to apply to anyone engaging in the prohibited conduct irrespective of motive or purpose.

Some critics raised concerns that FACE would be overbroad and not content neutral, as it was written in view of anti-abortion activism. However, while the majority of people arrested under the provisions of FACE have been anti-abortion protestors, FACE has also been applied to pro-choice activists who had resorted to similar violent or threatening acts.

The constitutionality of FACE might also be challenged on the grounds that clinic blockades and intimidation could be considered expressive conduct protected by the First Amendment. Some legal scholars have argued this to be the case because such forms of abortion protest are not primarily meant to prevent abortions from taking place, so much as they are meant to be very noticeable expressions of personal opinion on the morality and legality of abortion.

The courts that have examined the provisions of FACE have upheld the statute. Specifically, the courts have stated that the FACE statute is content neutral because it prohibits all threats of force or physical obstructions, not just those of anti-abortion protestors. FACE was also held to be narrowly tailored to serve an important government interest and to provide sufficient alternative means of communication because protestors retain the right to engage in free speech activities that do not violate the provisions of the statute. The U.S. Supreme Court has not ruled specifically on the constitutionality of FACE. Nevertheless, this statute appears to be consistent with the Supreme Court's 2000 decision in *Hill v. Colorado,* holding that a narrowly tailored, content-neutral restriction on speech within 8 feet of another person without consent, or within 100 feet of the entrance to any health-care facility, does not violate the First Amendment.

See also Abortion, Right to; Assembly, Freedom of; First Amendment; Fundamental Rights; Overbreadth, Doctrine of; Reproductive Freedom; *Roe v. Wade;* Speech, Freedom of; Symbolic Speech; Women's Rights

Bibliography

Bauer, Rebecca. 2002. "Abortion Protesting." *Georgetown Journal of Gender and the Law* 4:179–95.

Franco, Helen R. 1995. "Freedom of Access to Clinic Entrances Act of 1994: The Face of Things to Come?" *Nova Law Review* 19:1083–119.

Hoang, Lan. 1996. "Freedom of Access to Clinic Entrances Act, 18 U.S.C. 248: The Controversy Behind the Remedy." *Seton Hall Legislative Journal* 20:128–68.

Rose, Jill W., and Osborn, Chris. 1995. "Face-ial Neutrality: A Free Speech Challenge to the Freedom of Access to Clinic Entrances Act." *Virginia Law Review* 81:1505–60.

Tepper, Arianne K. 1997. "In Your F.A.C.E.: Federal Enforcement of the Freedom of Access to Clinic Entrances Act of 1993." *Pace Law Review* 17:489–551.

Mathieu Deflem and Brian Hudak

FREEDOM OF ASSOCIATION. *See* Association, Freedom of

FREEDOM OF INFORMATION ACT (FOIA)

The founders of the United States believed that self-governing people must have information in order to arm themselves with the power that knowledge gives. The founders could not have envisioned, however, the sprawling growth and complexity of the federal government, especially after the Great Depression of the 1930s. As Congress delegated authority to administrative agencies to handle specialized activities affecting the daily lives of citizens, fear of government secrecy and impenetrability grew. Shortly after World War II, Congress passed the Administrative Procedure Act, which helped standardize how agencies performed their work. While this act helped the public better understand the workings of the federal government, it did not produce the openness that journalists, public interest groups, and scholars thought necessary for informed public participation in civil life. After years of intense lobbying from these groups and others, Congress amended the Administrative Procedure Act in 1966 by passing the Freedom of Information Act (FOIA).

Amended several times in subsequent years, the act provides that all records in the possession of agencies of the federal government must be available for inspection and copying unless the records fall into one of nine specifically exempt categories. The FOIA defines agency as "each authority of the Government of the United States, whether or not it is within or subject to review by another agency." This includes any executive department; military department; government corporation; government-controlled corporation; or other establishment in the executive branch of the government, including the Executive Office of the President, cabinet offices, and independent regulatory agencies. The act does not include the president and his immediate White House staff, Congress, the courts, governments of the territories or possessions of the United States or the District of Columbia, courts-martial, or military commissions or military authority exercised in the field in time of war or in occupied territory. Receiving federal funding does not automatically subject an entity to the FOIA. The Corporation for Public Broadcasting and the American Red Cross, for example, receive federal funds but are neither chartered nor controlled by the federal government. In addition, the Supreme Court has held that a private organization established for the sole purpose of conducting government research and totally funded by the federal government is not automatically an "agency" subject to the act.

As computer databases replaced file cabinets in government offices, the FOIA was amended in 1996 to cover electronic information, including e-mail messages. The Electronic Freedom of Information Act also lengthened the time in which an agency must respond to FOIA requests to 20 business days from the previous 10-day requirement and required agencies to include a FOIA section on their Web sites to facilitate requests. In practice, most agencies simply acknowledge receipt of the request within the time limits, as backlogs and sometimes intentional stalling delay delivery of records.

The issue of exactly what records the act encompasses has been addressed in numerous court cases. Generally, the term "record" is defined expansively to include all types of documentary information, such as papers, reports, letters, films, computer tapes, photographs, and sound recordings. It does not include physical items, such as evidence collected in space disasters or crimes. The act does not apply to records of state or local governments; however, information submitted to a federal agency by a state or local agency or by the courts or Congress becomes subject to the FOIA if a federal agency has control over the records and if the record does not fall into one of the nine exempt categories. Note, however, that not all records in the possession of a federal executive branch agency, such as those from state or local governments or Congress, are necessarily under the control of the federal agency and thus subject to disclosure under the FOIA.

The statute provides for access to "any person," interpreted to mean organizations, corporations, and foreign nations, among others. A person's citizenship or purpose for wanting the information is immaterial. Persons seeking to gain access to a particular record must be able to "reasonably describe" the material they want, and they must know what agency has the material. Information on agency Web sites and in the Federal Register and the United States Government Manual help pinpoint which agency may have the documents sought.

If an agency denies a request for information, it must notify the requester and specify the reason for the denial. The requester has the right to appeal the decision to the agency, which then must act on the appeal within 20 working days. If the request is again denied in whole or in part, the agency must notify the requester of the provisions for judicial review. The notice should also indicate the names and titles or positions of each person responsible for the denial. Once administrative remedies are exhausted, the requester has the right to file suit with a federal district court in his or her home district, where the agency records are situated, or in the District of Columbia. The defendant agency then has 30 days to file an answer with the court. The district court has the authority to examine the contents of the record privately to determine whether it falls into one of the exempt categories. The burden of proof is on the agency.

Any reasonable portion of a record shall be provided after exempt portions are deleted. The Freedom of Information Act exempts from disclosure the following categories of matters:

(1) (A) specifically authorized under criteria established by an Executive order to be kept secret in the interest of national defense or foreign policy and

(B) are in fact properly classified pursuant to such Executive order;

(2) related solely to the internal personnel rules and practices of an agency;

(3) specifically exempted from disclosure by statute, provided that such statute

(A) requires that the matters be withheld from the public in such a manner as to leave no discretion on the issue, or

(B) establishes particular criteria for withholding or refers to particular types of matters to be withheld;

(4) trade secrets and commercial or financial information obtained from a person and which is privileged or confidential;

(5) inter-agency or intra-agency memorandums or letters which would not be available by law to a party other than an agency in litigation with the agency;

(6) personnel and medical files and similar files the disclosure of which would constitute a clearly unwarranted invasion of personal privacy;

(7) records or information compiled for law enforcement purposes, but only to the extent that the production of such law enforcement records or information

(A) could reasonably be expected to interfere with enforcement proceedings,

(If the investigation or proceeding involves a possible violation of criminal law; and there is reason to believe that (i) the subject of the investigation or proceeding is not aware of its pendency, and (ii) disclosure of the existence of the records could reasonably be expected to interfere with enforcement proceedings, the agency may, during only such time as that circumstance continues, treat the records as not subject to the FOIA.)

(B) would deprive a person of a right to a fair trial or an impartial adjudication,

(C) could reasonably be expected to constitute an unwarranted invasion of personal privacy,

(D) could reasonably be expected to disclose the identity of a confidential source, including a state, local, or foreign agency or authority or any private institution which furnished information on a confidential basis, and, in the case of a record or information compiled by criminal law enforcement authority in the course of a criminal investigation or by an agency conducting a lawful national security intelligence investigation, information furnished by a confidential source,

(E) would disclose techniques and procedures for law enforcement investigations or prosecutions, or would disclose guidelines for law enforcement investigations or prosecutions if such disclosure could reasonably be expected to risk circumvention of the law, or

(F) could reasonably be expected to endanger the life or physical safety of any individual;

(8) contained in or related to examination, operating, or condition reports prepared by, on behalf of, or for the use of an agency responsible for the regulation or supervision of financial institutions; or

(9) geological and geophysical information and data, including maps, concerning wells.

Whenever a request involves access to records maintained by the Federal Bureau of Investigation pertaining to foreign intelligence or counterintelligence, or international terrorism, and the existence of the records is classified information, the bureau may, as long as the existence of the records remains classified information, treat the records as exempt from the requirements of this section. The exemptions in the FOIA do not give agencies the authority to withhold information from Congress.

At the time of this writing, it is too early to know the full impact on openness of the Critical Infrastructure Information Act of 2002, one part of the Homeland Security Act, passed in response to the terrorist attacks on September 11, 2001. The act codifies a new category of restricted information by instructing the president to "identify and safeguard homeland security information that is sensitive but unclassified." The law does not define the word "sensitive."

"FOIA makes government work better," said Senator Patrick Leahy (D-VT), chairman of the Senate Judiciary Committee, in a September 25, 2002, statement expressing concern about secrecy provisions of the Homeland Security Act. "In times of heightened security, the tendency to close doors and conduct the government's business in secret is natural. Secrecy can become addictive, and that is a danger we have to guard against. The nation needs a robust FOIA in times of peace, but also in times of war. The Freedom of Information Act is the people's window on their government, showing where it is doing things right, but also where it can do better."

See also Homeland Security, Department of; Press, Freedom of the; Reporters Committee for Freedom of the Press

Bibliography

Bowles, Dorothy. 2001. *Media Law in Tennessee*. Stillwater, OK: New Forums Press.

Communication Law Writers Group. 2004. *Communication and the Law*. Northport, AL: Vision Press.

Daugherty, Rebecca, ed. 2004. *How to Use the Federal FOI Act*. 9th ed. Arlington, VA: Reporters Committee for Freedom of the Press.

Dorothy Bowles

FREEDOM OF RELIGION. *See* Religion, Freedom of

FREEDOM RIDES

In *Morgan v. Virginia* (1946), the United States Supreme Court struck down racial segregation on interstate buses, saying it was an "undue burden on interstate commerce." The Congress of Racial Equality (CORE), a New York-based civil rights activist organization, developed the idea of Freedom Rides to prove that desegregated buses would not wreak havoc on society. In April 1947, 16 Freedom Riders, including 8 African Americans and 8 whites, boarded a bus to begin a tour of cities in Virginia, North Carolina, Tennessee, and Kentucky. In North Carolina, the Freedom Riders encountered resistance from bus drivers and police, and several riders were arrested. One of them was Bayard Rustin, who went on to play a leading role in the Civil Rights Movement.

In *Boynton v. Virginia* (1960), the Supreme Court interpreted the Interstate Commerce Act to prohibit racial segregation of bus terminals, waiting rooms, restaurants, restrooms, and other interstate travel facilities. Two young African Americans, John Lewis and Bernard Lafayette, decided to test this decision by sitting in the "whites only" section of a bus and refusing to give up their seats to white passengers. Subsequently, CORE asked Lewis and Bernard to participate in a second CORE-sponsored Freedom Ride. John Lewis agreed to join the ride, but Lafayette's parents refused to allow their son to participate.

CORE coordinated this new Freedom Ride with the Student Nonviolent Coordinating Committee (SNCC). They began the ride in Washington,

D.C., on May 4, 1961, and it was scheduled to end in New Orleans on May 17, the seventh anniversary of the landmark *Brown v. Board of Education* decision. Thirteen people, seven African Americans and six whites, who were trained in nonviolent action, including John Lewis, took two buses, a Trailways and a Greyhound, through the South in order to challenge segregated public facilities. Some riders left, while others joined throughout the trip.

It was not until the riders reached Rock Hill, South Carolina, that the group encountered the first episode of violence. As the riders entered a "whites only" waiting room, 20 people attacked the group, and John Lewis was the first to be hit. Police interference was necessary before the group could enter the waiting room. The riders then passed through Georgia without a major incident.

On May 14, Mother's Day, the buses entered Anniston, Alabama. Anniston authorities permitted the Ku Klux Klan to strike against the Freedom Riders without fear of repercussion. A mob of 200 attacked the Greyhound bus and left one man permanently paralyzed. Not only did the mob slash the tires of the bus, but they also stoned and firebombed it. The group found another bus and continued their journey. The Trailways bus driver refused to continue the journey with the second group until the bus was segregated. The mob enforced this by beating the African Americans until they moved to the back of the bus. In Birmingham, they overwhelmed the group again with iron pipes. Police Chief Eugene "Bull" Conner stated that there were no officers at the scene due to the holiday. However, the FBI knew about the attack, and law enforcement intentionally avoided the scene. Alabama governor John Patterson did not apologize for the incident. The following day, the riders desired to continue their trip, but they could not locate a bus company willing to transport them. While in the bus terminal, a mob attacked the group once again. The riders decided to complete the trip by flying to New Orleans, which they deemed to be safer. The first SNCC/CORE Freedom Ride had come to an end.

Three days later, Diane Nash, a SNCC member, attempted another Freedom Ride. The goal of this ride was to demonstrate that violence and intimidation would not prevent them from reaching their destination. The SNCC, along with the Nashville Student Movement, began the ride in Nashville, Tennessee. Their first objective was to go to Birmingham and Montgomery, Alabama, and then finish the ride in Mississippi and Louisiana. This ride consisted of eight African-Americans and two whites, including some of the original riders and John Lewis.

On May 17, U.S. Attorney General Robert Kennedy ordered the Birmingham police to place the Freedom Riders in "protective custody." At 2:00 A.M., Police Chief Conner and the Birmingham Police arrested the group and transported them to the state line of Tennessee. The riders were able to receive a ride for the 100-mile trip back to Nashville. Upon arrival, they returned to Birmingham and sang freedom songs in the bus terminal.

President John F. Kennedy feared violence would occur once again in Alabama. He ordered Alabama's governor to secure the safety of the riders. Floyd Mann, head of the Alabama highway patrol, agreed to protect the riders, and Attorney General Robert Kennedy coerced a Greyhound bus company to transport them. A Justice Department representative, John Seigenthaler, met with Governor Patterson and agreed to accompany the Freedom Riders. The riders left Birmingham on May 20 accompanied by a police and helicopter escort. When they arrived in Montgomery, the escorts vanished. A crowd of 300 had gathered in Montgomery. The media covering the ride was beaten by 25 members of this mob. The riders decided to exit the bus through the back entrance, because it appeared to be the safest way. However, James Zwerg, a white rider, bravely exited the bus through the front. The mob beat Zwerg severely, but he never attempted to defend himself. During the attack, some riders were able to exit the bus safely. Mann and Seigenthaler attempted to stop the mob, but Seigenthaler was beaten until he was unconscious and left in the street for 30 minutes. Mann finally ordered the state troopers to end the violence, but it was too late. Attorney General Robert Kennedy sent federal marshals to stop the attack. Due to the increasing size of the crowd, which eventually grew to 1,000, tear gas was necessary to end the conflict.

That night, the riders spent the night in Ralph Abernathy's First Baptist Church in Montgomery. Martin Luther King, Jr., went to Montgomery in support of the Freedom Riders. A white mob of thousands conducted an all-night siege in the church. King contacted Robert Kennedy to assist the riders once again. Kennedy ordered Governor Patterson to declare martial law. The state police and National Guard dispersed the mob and helped the riders exit the church. Kennedy hoped that the riders would allow for a cooling off period, but the riders continued their journey.

King did not participate in the Freedom Rides. He supported the ideal the ride represented but questioned if it was worth the danger. King did not believe the riders would make it out of Alabama. Because he only supported the rides morally and financially, some activists criticized King. His speech at the Montgomery Baptist Church was the only time that King was ever present at a ride. King publicly stated that he could not participate in the rides due to his previous arrest record and probation. Student participants rejected King's reasoning, and Ella Baker said that King lost some of his demagogue status because of his failure to participate.

The Freedom Riders, escorted by the National Guard, continued their journey and arrived safely in Jackson, Mississippi. Jackson law enforcement moved the riders through the bus terminal without the presence of a mob. However, they served the riders with an injunction that stated they could not proceed with their journey in Alabama. When some of the riders used "whites only" waiting rooms and restrooms, the police arrested them, and they were taken to jail in an awaiting paddy wagon.

Robert Kennedy made an agreement with Mississippi Senator James Eastland wherein Kennedy would not send federal troops to Mississippi if Eastland protected the riders. However, the riders were now subject to the judicial system because

of their arrest. On May 25, the riders were tried. While the defense presented its case, the judge ignored them and turned his back. At the conclusion of the defense case, the judge turned around and sentenced all the riders to 60 days in jail.

By the end of summer of 1961, more than 300 Freedom Riders had been arrested in Jackson and spent more than a month in prison. Not one Freedom Rider was able to make it to New Orleans by bus, and many were injured trying. However, the national publicity received by the Freedom Rides forced the Kennedy administration to reconsider civil rights. On May 29, the Interstate Commerce Commission adopted its own rules prohibiting segregation in interstate bus travel. However, the greatest victory for the Freedom Riders, and the Civil Rights Movement in general, came with the passage of the Civil Rights Act of 1964 and the Voting Rights Act of 1965.

See also *Brown v. Board of Education;* Civil Rights Act of 1964; Civil Rights Movement; Congress of Racial Equality; Jim Crow Laws; Kennedy, Robert F.; King, Martin Luther, Jr.; Ku Klux Klan; Student Nonviolent Coordinating Committee; U.S. Department of Justice; Voting Rights Act of 1965

Bibliography

Arsenault, Raymond. 2005. *Freedom Riders: 1961 and the Struggle for Racial Justice.* New York: Oxford University Press.

Houser, George, and Bayard Rustin. 1947. *We Challenged Jim Crow! A Report on the Journey of Reconciliation, April 9–23, 1947.* New York: Congress of Racial Equality.

Ann M. Bennett

FREEDOM SCHOOLS. *See* Freedom Summer

FREEDOM SUMMER (1964)

In the summer of 1964, more than 1,000 civil rights activists, many of whom were white college students from the North and west, came to the South to work toward the enfranchisement of African Americans. Efforts focused on Mississippi, where only about 7 percent of black adults were registered to vote. In that state the campaign was organized by the Mississippi Council of Federated Organizations, which included the National Association for the Advancement of Colored People (NAACP), the Congress of Racial Equality (CORE), and the recently formed Student Nonviolent Coordinating Committee (SNCC). In addition to registering more than 1,600 black voters, activists also taught in 30 Freedom Schools established across Mississippi. More than 3,000 young African Americans attended the Freedom Schools that summer, where they received instruction not only in reading and math but in black history and leadership development.

In Mississippi the summer of 1964 was also a time of violent reaction by forces that opposed civil rights for blacks. More than 100 African American houses, businesses, and churches were bombed or burned. Many of the civil rights workers were harassed; some were even beaten by police or angry white mobs. By far the most notorious act of reactionary violence was the murder of three workers, James Chaney, Andrew Goodman, and Michael Schwerner. The three had ventured to Philadelphia, Mississippi, to investigate the bombing of an African American church. They were arrested and held for several hours, ostensibly for speeding. No one, other than their murderers, is known to have seen Chaney, Goodman, and Schwerner alive following their release from police custody. Their bodies were discovered six weeks later on a nearby farm. Two had been shot; one had been beaten to death. After an investigation by the FBI, seven men including a deputy sheriff, were convicted in federal court of civil rights violations and sentenced to prison terms ranging from 3 to 10 years. None actually served more than 6 years in prison. At that time Mississippi authorities declined to pursue the murder investigation. It was not until January 2005 that a reputed member of the Ku Klux Klan, Edgar Ray Killen, was arrested for the murders. Killen was convicted of manslaughter by a Mississippi jury on June 21, 2005. Two days later he was given the maximum total sentence of 60 years (consecutive sentences of 20 years on each of the three charges).

Referring to Chaney, Goodman, and Schwerner, trial judge Marcus Gordon said, just before imposing sentence: "[E]ach life has value … and the three lives should absolutely be respected and treated equally."

Freedom Summer was an extremely important event in the development of the Civil Rights Movement . The Movement achieved significantly higher levels of participation, organization, coordination, and recognition. The violence that plagued Freedom Summer helped to stir the national conscience and thus created more favorable political conditions for the enactment of landmark voting rights legislation in 1965 (see Voting Rights Act of 1965).

See also Civil Rights Movement; Congress of Racial Equality; Federal Bureau of Investigation; Ku Klux Klan; National Association for the Advancement of Colored People; Student Nonviolent Coordinating Committee; Voting Rights Act of 1965

Bibliography

Belfrage, Sally, and Robert P. Moses. 1990. *Freedom Summer*. Carter G. Woodson Institute Series in Black Studies. Charlottesville: University Press of Virginia.

Martinez, Elizabeth. 2002. *Letters from Mississippi*. Brookline, MA: Zephyr Press.

McAdam, Doug. 1990. *Freedom Summer*. New York: Oxford University Press.

John M. Scheb II and Otis H. Stephens, Jr.

FREE EXERCISE CLAUSE

The Bill of Rights protects religious liberty through the First Amendment's provision that "Congress shall make no law respecting an establishment of religion, or prohibiting the free exercise thereof." This language is divided into two clauses, each with its own separate significance: the establishment clause and the free exercise clause. The Supreme Court compartmentalizes its religion clause jurisprudence into these categories, and this, of course, compels lawyers bringing religious liberty cases to do the same.

Historical records show that the Framers worried that the new federal government would constrict the religious liberty of individual citizens and that it would interfere with churches established by other institutions, including the official churches that were recognized in several states at the time. Without the First Amendment, Congress could have interfered with these churches in either of two ways: by setting up a Church of the United States, which would have nullified the state churches, or by passing laws forcing individuals to attend, or to refrain from attending, particular churches. The Establishment Clause addressed the first of these fears; the Free Exercise Clause addressed the second.

In the Supreme Court's religious liberty cases, the sharp separation between the Establishment Clause and the Free Exercise Clause has raised numerous problems. The tendency in the Supreme Court has been to read the Establishment Clause as sharply limiting all government contacts with religion, and the Free Exercise Clause as a source of protection for religious conduct. But the two types of cases are not always neatly distinguishable.

If a public school has a clergyman give a blessing at the beginning of a high school graduation, is the government accommodating the Free Exercise rights of the students and parents who want to have the benediction? Or should it instead protect the Free Exercise rights of students and parents who object to the benediction? Neither: when this fact pattern reached the Supreme Court in *Lee v. Weisman* (1992), it did so under the rubric of the Establishment Clause, and the majority opinion by Justice Anthony Kennedy held that the benediction was an establishment of religion and hence unconstitutional.

If the Free Exercise Clause is not implicated in this kind of case, what strength does it have? The Supreme Court's cases construing the clause can shed some light. The Free Exercise Clause flared briefly into constitutional litigation in 1878 and then lay dormant until the 1940s. This is because it was not until the 1940s that the Court began to accept the idea that the First Amendment, which is specifically addressed to Congress, could also be applied to state government actions. The Free Exercise Clause's 1878 appearance was in *Reynolds v. United States*.

The case arose in Utah, which at that time was still a territory, not a state. As such, Utah was governed directly by Congress, so the Free Exercise Clause applied. Even so, the Court held that the clause did not allow the Mormons to practice polygamy, although it was beyond dispute that this practice was, for them, religiously motivated. The Court adopted a stark distinction between belief and action. Belief, it said, was absolutely protected, but action was open to regulation. The Mormons were free to believe in polygamy (and, under the speech clause of the First Amendment, to advocate it), but not to practice it.

The Free Exercise Clause was first applied to the states in *Cantwell v. Connecticut* (1940), which struck down a local ordinance requiring a permit before one could solicit for religious purposes. The ordinance gave city officials too much latitude to decide what constituted religious purposes. *Cantwell* sounded three themes that have echoed throughout free exercise jurisprudence: The clause applies to the states; It disfavors any arrangement that has government officials determining what is religious and what is not; And it generally bars any statute, ordinance, or regulation that singles out religious conduct for unfavorable treatment.

In 1963, the Supreme Court's free exercise jurisprudence took a dramatic turn. Perhaps in response to the growing number of laws that could have unintended yet severe impacts on individual religious liberty, the Court, speaking through Justice William J. Brennan, held in *Sherbert v. Verner* (1963) that any government action that "burdens" religion—even if that burden is only a side effect of a law that in no way singles out religion for disfavored treatment—must yield to an individual's religiously based need to act otherwise, unless the government can show that the application of the rule to the religious objector is "narrowly tailored" to serve a "compelling state interest."

In *Sherbert,* the plaintiff had to leave her job because, as a convert to the Seventh-Day Adventist faith, she could no longer work on Saturdays. The state denied her unemployment benefits because, under its rules, she was eligible only as long as she could not find "suitable work." Jobs were available, but they all involved Saturday hours. The state's denial of unemployment benefits, she argued, unconstitutionally burdened her free exercise of religion—and the Court agreed.

Sherbert continued to be applied in unemployment benefit cases, such as *Thomas v. Review Board* (1981), *Hobbie v. Unemployment Appeals Commission* (1987), and *Frazee v. Illinois Department of Employment Security* (1989). But outside of that area, *Sherbert* proved difficult to apply in any way that reliably protected religious liberty. In particular, the range of interests that the Supreme Court was willing to consider compelling, for purposes of applying *Sherbert,* tended to grow. For example, an Orthodox Jewish officer in the U.S. Army argued that under *Sherbert* he was entitled to a free exercise exemption from the Army's rule banning nonstandard headgear. He wanted, of course, to wear his yarmulke and had been doing so, without incident, during several years of Army service. But the Supreme Court deferred to the Army's interest in headgear uniformity (*Goldman v. Weinberger,* 1986).

Another sign that the *Sherbert* rule had ceased to operate as an effective tool for protection of religious liberty, at least in fully litigated cases, emerged in *United States v. Lee* (1982), in which the Court held that federal government's interest in "assuring mandatory and continuous participation in and contribution to the social security system is very high"—high enough to constitute a compelling state interest and thus sufficient to allow the government to force the Old Order Amish to obtain Social Security numbers, to which they objected on religious grounds. This is essentially an argument from administrative convenience, which, in other contexts, the Court has held to be much less than a compelling interest, in fact, not even an "important" one (see, e.g., *Reed v. Reed,* 1971; and *Frontiero v. Richardson,* 1973).

In another important case involving the Old Order Amish, *Wisconsin v. Yoder* (1972), the Court held in effect that freedom of religion in combination with parents' rights to direct the education of their children trumped the state's power to compel children to attend school beyond the eighth grade.

Although the continuing effectiveness of *Sherbert* was in doubt in the 1980s, no one expected it to be significantly changed. So religious liberty litigators were taken by surprise in 1990 when the Court, in *Employment Division v. Smith,* announced that when a statute is "religiously neutral" and "generally applicable" (i.e., it does not single out religion or religiously grounded conduct for unfavorable treatment), then the Free Exercise Clause alone does not provide an exemption for individuals who wish, on religious grounds, to violate the statute. Distinguishing *Yoder,* which involved parental rights as well as religious liberty, the Court concluded that the Free Exercise Clause bars laws that overtly discriminate against religion but is not a source of individual exemptions from law in general.

The *Smith* decision was extremely controversial. In particular, religious liberty litigators were afraid that government could begin to regulate religious conduct at will merely by passing laws that gave the appearance of neutrality. Religious freedom advocates were given some reassurance in the case of *Church of Lukumi Babalu Aye v. Hialeah* (1993). Here, a city ordinance banned animal slaughter—but only when done for ritual purposes. So drafted, the ordinance was not neutral and generally applicable, even under the lenient test of *Smith.* Consequently, the compelling governmental interest test was applied, resulting in the invalidation of the ordinance.

Congress also reacted strongly against *Smith.* In 1994, it passed a statute called the Religious Freedom Restoration Act (RFRA), which explicitly condemned *Smith* and sought to impose the *Sherbert* compelling government interest rule in its place. Unsurprisingly, the Court eventually struck RFRA down, for reasons that go beyond the scope of this entry. The case in which RFRA was struck down (*City of Boerne v. Flores,* 1997) also serves to clarify *Smith* through a concurrence written by Justice Antonin Scalia, in which he argued the historical case for the *Smith* rule in much more detail than he had done in *Smith* itself.

The state and colonial constitutional provisions on which the Free Exercise Clause was based, Scalia argued, all contain reservation clauses stipulating that persons, in exercising their religious liberty, shall not disturb the peace, violate good order, or cause a "breach of the King's peace." These reservations may look like modern compelling state interest analysis: free exercise prevails unless the contrary would cause violence. But, Justice Scalia argued, to the common-law mind, all violations of law are "against the peace." Consequently, individual exemptions from law itself, for the benefit of personal conscience, cannot have been the original meaning of the Free Exercise Clause.

States remain free to enact religious exemptions; *Smith* encourages them to do so, and numerous decisions, including *Smith,* hold that such legislatively granted exemptions do not violate the Establishment Clause. The question is only whether the Free Exercise Clause *compels* states to grant such exemptions; under presently prevailing case law, it does not. Nor does *Smith* mean that the Free Exercise Clause is without effect or impact. As discussed at the outset of this entry, it prevents government from either compelling or prohibiting attendance at any religious worship. It also means that laws that impede religious practice in any way must be rigorously neutral toward religion; *Lukumi* affirms this principle.

In February of 2004 the Court, in *Locke v. Davey,* reaffirmed its commitment to *Smith*'s principles by upholding a state scholarship program that funded all fields of study except those leading to a career in the clergy. The majority, led by Chief Justice William H. Rehnquist, found that the plaintiff's free exercise of religion was not seriously burdened by the nonavailability of a grant that the state had no obligation to provide anyway.

The Establishment and Free Exercise Clauses together mean that government cannot set up a religion, nor can it favor or disfavor already existing religions by encouraging or penalizing participation in them.

See also Bill of Rights (American); Bill of Rights, Incorporation of; Brennan, William J., Jr.; *Cantwell v. Connecticut;* Church of Jesus Christ of Latter-Day Saints; Conscience, Freedom of; *Employment Division, Department of Human Resources of Oregon v. Smith;* Establishment Clause; First Amendment; First Amendment, Approaches to; Fundamental Rights; *Hamilton v. Regents of the University of California;* Jefferson, Thomas; Jehovah's Witnesses; Kennedy, Anthony; Madison, James; Military Service, Civil Rights and Liberties in; Native American Church; Religion, Freedom of; Religious Freedom Restoration Act; Scalia, Antonin; School Prayer Decisions; Separation of Church and State; Seventh-Day Adventists; Strict Scrutiny; Sunday Closing Laws; Virginia Statute for Religious Freedom; Williams, Roger; *Wisconsin v. Yoder*

Bibliography

Amar, Akhil Reed. 2000. *The Bill of Rights: Creation and Reconstruction.* New Haven, CT: Yale University Press.

Hamburger, Philip. 2004. *Separation of Church and State.* Cambridge, MA: Harvard University Press.

McConnell, Michael, John Garvey, and Thomas Berg. 2002. *Religion and the Constitution.* New York: Aspen Law and Business.

McDonald, Forrest. 1979. *E Pluribus Unum: The Formation of the American Republic, 1776–1790.* 2nd ed. Indianapolis, IN: Liberty Fund.

Rutland, Robert Allen. 1983. *The Ordeal of the Constitution.* Boston: Northeastern University Press.

David M. Wagner

FREE MARKETPLACE OF IDEAS

The metaphor of a free marketplace of ideas reflects the theory that all ideas should be placed before the public, whereupon citizens will accept or reject these ideas much as consumers choose among products arrayed on the grocery store shelf. The notion derives both from democratic theory, which emphasizes citizen knowledge, informed decision making, and effective self-regulation, and economic theory, which emphasizes efficiency, competition, and consumer satisfaction (Napoli 1999).

The marketplace of ideas extends the shelter of constitutional protection to speech so citizens can better understand the world in which they live. Robert Post writes that "at a minimum, the Constitution ought to be concerned with all communication conveying ideas relevant to our understanding the world, whether or not those ideas are political in nature" (Post 2000, 2363).

The marketplace of ideas, in relation to democratic theory, has been traced to the seventeenth-century work of John Milton. During the concept's early development phase, the main ideas were those of truth being reached via the free exchange of ideas and the importance of individual rights of self-expression and freedom of thought (Napoli 1999). In his landmark essay *On Liberty*, John Stuart Mill offered a threefold defense of free speech. Mill first proposed that the idea suppressed as false may really be true, since to challenge otherwise is to assume the infallibility of the individuals who adhere to the dominant opinion. Second, Mill argued that the suppressed opinion may be at least somewhat true, since one view hardly ever contains all of truth in a given area. Third, he suggested that even if the suppressed idea were entirely false, the suppression would tend to result in the true idea's becoming a sterile and unchallenged belief that would lack the vital force necessary for a living truth.

The economic aspect of the marketplace of ideas concept dates back to Justice Oliver Wendell Holmes, Jr.'s dissent in *Abrams v. United States* (1919). Justice Holmes disagreed with the majority's decision to uphold the conviction of five Russian immigrants for disseminating anti-American leaflets. Holmes said, "The ultimate good desired is better reached by free trade in ideas—that the best test of truth is the power of thought to get itself accepted in the competition of the market....That at any rate is the theory of our Constitution."

Justice Holmes's dissent in *Abrams* was the first time the marketplace of ideas was introduced into Supreme Court decisions. Holmes's use of the metaphor was the first of many by the justices. Between 1919 and 1995, 24 of the 49 Supreme Court justices used the metaphor (Hopkins 1996). Justices have also used the metaphor to strengthen free expression in nearly every area of First Amendment jurisprudence—prior restraint, libel, privacy, pornography, media access to criminal proceedings, advertising, picketing, expressive conduct, broadcasting, and cable regulations (Hopkins 1996). The Supreme Court's embracing of the linkage between free speech and truth is seen in *Red Lion Broadcasting v. FCC* (1969): "It is the purpose of the First Amendment to preserve an uninhibited marketplace of ideas in which truth will ultimately prevail."

Though the Supreme Court accepted the link between free speech and truth, some constitutional scholars have rejected the linkage. Professor C. Edwin Baker suggested that the linkage between free speech and truth is hardly possible. He thought the marketplace of ideas might lead to the wrong person's or group's truth being accepted (Baker 1978). Stanley Ingber rejects the marketplace of ideas theory, arguing that citizens must be capable of making determinations that are sophisticated and rational if they are to separate truth from fiction. Ingber (1984) also believes that the market is insufficiently competitive—that new ideas do not receive a fair chance to compete against more established ideas for the public's adherence. Frederick Schauer has argued that people are not very rational, as assumed by the theory. But, he also written, "Just as we are properly skeptical about our own power always to distinguish truth from falsity, so should we be even more skeptical of the power of any governmental authority to do it for us" (Schauer 1982, 34). The marketplace of ideas is perhaps the most enduring image invoked by jurists and scholars to legitimate the First Amendment freedoms (Horwitz 1991).

See also Clear and Present Danger Doctrine; Commercial Speech; Defamation; First Amendment; Internet, Free Speech on; Holmes, Oliver Wendell, Jr.; Liberalism; Obscenity and Pornography; Press, Freedom of the; Prior Restraint, Doctrine of; Speech, Freedom of

Bibliography

Hopkins, Wat W. 1996. "The Supreme Court Defines the Marketplace of Ideas." *Journalism Mass Communication Quarterly* 73:40–53.

Ingber, Stanley. 1984. "The Marketplace of Ideas: A Legitimizing Myth." *Duke Law Journal*, 1:1–91.

Napoli, Philip M. 1999. "The Marketplace of Ideas Metaphor in Communications Regulation." *Journal of Communication* 49 (4): 151–69.

Post, Robert. 2000. "Reconciling Theory and Doctrine in First Amendment Jurisprudence." *California Law Review* 88:2353–74.

Wonnell, Christopher T. 1986. "Truth and the Marketplace of Ideas." *University of California Davis Law Review* 19:669–776.

Maria Fontenot

FREE PRESS/FAIR TRIAL PROBLEM

The debate that pits the First Amendment guarantee of free press against the Sixth Amendment guarantee of a fair trial generally focuses on two related questions—whether government can regulate what the media can print or broadcast about criminal matters, and whether government can limit public and press access to trials and pretrial proceedings.

The question regarding restraint of the media generally has been resolved in favor of press freedom, and the U.S. Supreme Court has looked to other methods—within the direct control of trial courts—to try to provide impartial juries. The question of media access to criminal proceedings has an evolving history, and the Supreme Court has distinguished between pretrial and trial proceedings and among different types of media.

The free press/fair trial debate has its origins in the tension between two fundamental constitutional principles. The First Amendment says government "shall make no law ... abridging the freedom of speech, or of the press." The Sixth Amendment says that in a criminal prosecution, the accused "shall enjoy the right to a speedy and public trial, by an impartial jury." The difficulty, of course, is in selecting unbiased jurors when a criminal case has been the subject of widespread pretrial coverage.

The most prominent—some might say notorious—court case involving media impact on fair trial was *Sheppard v. Maxwell* (1966), in which the Supreme Court overturned the second-degree murder conviction of Dr. Sam Sheppard on the grounds that his trial was tainted by "massive, pervasive and prejudicial publicity."

Sheppard's pregnant wife, Marilyn, was bludgeoned to death on July 4, 1954, in the upstairs bedroom of the couple's home in suburban Cleveland. Sam Sheppard told police he was asleep on a couch and rushed upstairs when he heard his wife's screams, only to be knocked unconscious by a "form" he saw standing next to his wife's bed. When he came to, he told police, he pursued the form out of the house to the lakeshore but was again knocked out.

Police immediately focused on the doctor as prime suspect, and the developing case was widely reported in newspapers and on radio and television. Stories accused Sheppard of refusing to cooperate with police and emphasized that he refused to submit to a lie detector test. Prior to Sheppard's August 17 indictment, front-page newspaper editorials charged that someone was getting away with murder and asked, "Why Don't Police Quiz Top Suspect?" and "Why Isn't Sam Sheppard in Jail?"

The case came to trial two weeks before the November 1954 elections, in which the chief prosecutor was a candidate for judge and the trial judge was on the ballot for reelection. The names and addresses of jurors were published in all three Cleveland newspapers, and jurors received phone calls and letters, some of them sent anonymously. As a result of numerous media requests to cover the trial, the court set up a long table inside the bar to accommodate 20 newspaper and wire service reporters, making it difficult for Sheppard and his lawyer to talk in confidence. Although jurors were sequestered during deliberations, they were allowed to make phone calls, and no record was kept of who did so.

Writing for an eight-to-one majority, Justice Tom C. Clark criticized the trial judge for failing to protect Sheppard from prejudicial publicity:

Much of the material printed or broadcast during the trial was never heard from the witness stand, such as the charges that Sheppard had purposely impeded the murder investigation and must be guilty because he had hired a prominent criminal lawyer; that Sheppard was a perjurer; that he had sexual relations with numerous women; that his slain wife had characterized him as a "Jekyll-Hyde"; that he was "a bare-faced liar" because of his testimony as to police treatment; and, finally, that a woman convict claimed Sheppard to be the father of her illegitimate child.

A responsible press, Clark wrote, has always been the "handmaiden" of an effective criminal justice system: "The press does not simply publish information about trials but guards against the miscarriage of justice by subjecting the police, prosecutors, and judicial processes to extensive public scrutiny and criticism." But in the Sheppard case, he said, the judge should have taken steps to prevent the "carnival atmosphere" that prevailed at the trial. The judge should have adopted stricter rules governing the seating of reporters, insulated witnesses from news accounts of the ongoing trial, and put an end to the spread of groundless rumors and inaccurate information by directing police, witnesses, and lawyers not to talk about the case.

Sheppard, who was represented before the Supreme Court and in the subsequent retrial by famed criminal defense attorney F. Lee Bailey, was found not guilty when he was retried in late 1966, almost 12 years after his first trial. The sensational coverage of the Sheppard case and the Supreme Court's ruling gave impetus to efforts to establish guidelines on pretrial coverage of crimes and criminal suspects in order to insulate potential jurors from prejudicial information. In 1968, the American Bar Association adopted its *Standards Relating to Fair Trial and Free Press*. While some media representatives were distressed by some of the recommendations in the so-called Reardon Report, the report did persuade many states to set up voluntary bar-press guidelines. One of the states that did so was Nebraska, whose guidelines cautioned against reporting the existence or contents of a confession, the results or

refusal of a suspect to submit to any examination or test, opinions on the guilt or innocence of a suspect, and other statements that might influence the outcome of a trial.

Those guidelines provided the focus of another important free press/fair trial debate when a Nebraska trial judge entered an order making them mandatory until a jury was impaneled in a murder case, effectively imposing a gag order on news coverage of certain aspects of the case, including matters that already were in the public record. *Nebraska Press Association v. Stuart* (1976) involved the October 18, 1975, slaying of six members of a family in Sutherland, Nebraska, a community of about 850. At the request of the prosecutor and defense attorney, the trial judge imposed the order, not only enumerating what could *not* be reported about the case but also preventing the press from reporting on the content of the restrictive order itself. The U.S. Supreme Court unanimously ruled that the restrictive order was an unlawful prior restraint. Writing for the court, Chief Justice Warren E. Burger said the trial court had not met its "heavy burden" for justifying prior restraint. The trial court could have considered other methods of ensuring an unbiased jury, Burger said, including changing the venue to a location where news coverage had not been as intense, delaying the trial until public attention subsided, questioning prospective jurors closely, instructing jurors to consider only evidence presented in court, and sequestering the jury. The trial judge also could have ordered the lawyers, police, and witnesses not to comment on the case prior to trial, the opinion said.

In a concurring opinion, Justice William J. Brennan, Jr., went even further than the majority in criticizing the gag order: "The right to a fair trial by a jury of one peer's is unquestionably one of the most precious and sacred safeguards enshrined in the Bill of Rights. I would hold, however, that resort to prior restraints on the freedom of the press is a constitutionally impermissible method for enforcing that right." He encouraged continued efforts at voluntary guidelines. The press can sometimes be abusive and sensational and it can sometimes be incisive and informative, he said, "[b]ut at least in the context of prior restraints on publication, the decision of what, when, and how to publish is for editors, not judges."

After the *Nebraska Press Association* decision, the focus of the free press/fair trial debate shifted from one of prior restraint to one of public access to judicial proceedings. A sharply divided Supreme Court ruled five-to-four in *Gannett v. De-Pasquale* (1979) that the public and press have no constitutional right to attend pretrial suppression hearings. Exactly a year later, however, the Court held, in *Richmond Newspapers v. Virginia* (1980), that the public and press do have a constitutional right to observe criminal trials. And in subsequent decisions, the Supreme Court chipped away at its *Gannett* holding by ruling for openness in pretrial proceedings as well.

The victim in the *Gannett* case was robbed and killed, and his body was dumped in Seneca Lake in New York. Two defendants, charged with second-degree murder, moved to suppress statements they gave to police, contending they were given involuntarily. The trial judge ruled that the defendant's right to a fair trial outweighed the right of the press and public to an open proceeding.

The Supreme Court considered the closed proceeding in the context of the Sixth Amendment's guarantee of a public trial. Justice Potter Stewart's majority opinion held that a public trial was a right exclusive to the defendant that could be waived, not a right of the public and press. "Publicity concerning pretrial suppression hearings such as the one involved in the present case pose special risks of unfairness," he wrote. "The whole purpose of such hearings is to screen out unreliable and illegally obtained evidence and insure that this evidence does not become known to the jury."

But the dissenting justices contended that news coverage of the case wasn't at all sensational, and they asserted that the right to a public trial does not belong solely to the defendant. Writing for the four dissenters, Justice Harry A. Blackmun characterized the coverage as "placid, routine, and innocuous," with no coverage at all in the 90 days preceding the suppression hearing. Society has an interest in a public trial that exists separate from, and in some cases in opposition to, the interests of the defendant, Blackmun said.

The broad language in *Gannett* raised concerns that the high court might deny the public and press access to a trial itself. The court addressed that question in *Richmond Newspapers v. Virginia* (1980), holding that, in fact, the public does have a constitutional right of access to criminal trials. The decision was based on the First Amendment, as made applicable to the states by the Fourteenth Amendment. Although seven justices agreed with the decision, they wrote six opinions explaining their reasoning—none of which was signed by more than three justices. The case involved the fourth trial of a defendant accused of murder in the December 2, 1975, stabbing death of a Virginia hotel manager. The defendant asked that the fourth trial be closed to the public. The prosecutor did not object, and the court granted the request. During the closed proceeding, in the absence of the jury, the defense successfully moved to strike the prosecution's evidence. The judge granted the motion and then found the defendant not guilty.

The plurality opinion, written by Chief Justice Burger, drew a distinction between closing the pretrial proceeding in *Gannett* and closing the trial itself in the *Richmond* case, noting that trials have a long-standing tradition of openness under English and American law: "People in an open society do not demand infallibility from their institutions, but it is difficult for them to accept what they are prohibited from observing. When a criminal trial is conducted in the open, there is at least an opportunity both for understanding the system in general and its workings in a particular case." The opinion faulted the trial court judge for failing to make any findings that would support closure and overcome the presumption of openness and also for failing to explore alternative means of ensuring a fair trial. The vigor with which various justices supported open courts seemed to be in sharp contrast to the earlier ruling in *Gannett* and suggested the possibility that the Court might be backing away from the earlier decision.

That proved to be the case. In *Globe Newspaper v. Superior Court* (1982), the court ruled that a Massachusetts law violated the First Amendment in requiring, under all circumstances, that the public and press be banned from a rape trial in which the victim was a minor. In *Press-Enterprise Company v. Superior Court* (1984), it held that voir dire examination of potential jurors is presumptively open. In another case involving the same parties, popularly known as *Press Enterprise II* (1986), the Court seemed to abandon *Gannett,* ruling that there is a qualified First Amendment right of public access to a preliminary hearing in a criminal case.

Press Enterprise II was a California case involving a nurse who was charged with murdering 12 patients with massive doses of a heart medicine. The trial court closed the preliminary hearing, which took 41 days, and refused to release a transcript. Writing for a seven-to-two majority, Chief Justice Burger said that free press and fair trial are not necessarily inconsistent: "Plainly, the defendant has a right to a fair trial but, as we have repeatedly recognized, one of the important means of assuring a fair trial is that the process be open to neutral observers." Noting that the preliminary hearing is often the most important step in a criminal proceeding, Burger said such hearings can be closed only when specific on-the-record findings show that closure is essential to preserve fairness.

The development of communication tools other than the printed word raised additional complexities in the free press/fair trial debate. The sensational coverage of the 1935 trial of Bruno Richard Hauptmann, who was convicted of kidnapping and killing the 19-month-old son of American aviation hero Charles Lindbergh, prompted the American Bar Association to adopt a canon of ethics forbidding photographic coverage of trials. That canon later was extended to radio and television coverage as well.

In one of the Supreme Court's first important rulings on televising a criminal trial, a five-to-four majority concluded that televising a notorious case was inherently unfair to the accused and in violation of the Sixth Amendment right to a fair trial. In *Estes v. Texas* (1965), the Court reversed the conviction of accused Texas swindler Billie Sol Estes because the trial judge permitted portions of the proceeding to be televised.

The majority opinion by Justice Clark said the potential impact of TV on jurors is of greatest significance: "From the moment the trial judge announces that a case will be televised it becomes a *cause celebre.* The whole community, including prospective jurors, becomes interested in the morbid details surrounding it." The presence of TV cameras also could frighten witnesses or induce them to overstatement, distract the trial judge with the additional duty of supervising camera crews, and subject the defendant to a form of harassment resembling a police lineup or the third degree, the court said.

As television technology improved—reducing the noise level, the need for lighting, and the use of bulky equipment, for example—the ban on electronic coverage was reexamined. In 1978, the Conference of State Chief Justices approved a resolution to allow the highest court in each state to write guidelines permitting radio, television, and photographic coverage of court proceedings, under the control of the trial court judge.

Florida already had initiated a pilot program along those lines. When the program was challenged on constitutional grounds, the Supreme Court held that such coverage was permissible, absent a showing that the coverage resulted in an unfair trial. The 8–0 decision came in the case of *Chandler v. Florida* (1981).

The case involved the burglary conviction of some Miami Beach police officers who were inadvertently overheard and recorded by an amateur radio operator as the officers conversed on police walkie-talkie radios while they were burglarizing a restaurant. Over the objections of the defendants, the court permitted a television camera in the courtroom. A news segment of less than three minutes was broadcast, and that segment reported only on the prosecution's side of the case. In an opinion by Chief Justice Burger, the Supreme Court rejected the idea that the defendants were harmed by the coverage: "The appellants have offered no evidence that any participant in this case was affected by the presence of cameras. In short, there is no showing that the trial was compromised by television coverage, as was the case in *Estes."* In the years following *Chandler,* all 50 states developed rules on allowing cameras and microphones in some courtrooms. While cameras have not become commonplace, they have increasingly become a presence—sufficiently so to facilitate development of a cable channel, Court TV, devoted to covering legal proceedings. The extensive TV coverage of the 1995 trial of former football star O. J. Simpson, who was acquitted of killing his ex-wife and her male companion, renewed the debate over the impact of cameras in the courtroom. Some states give the trial judge broad discretion to permit coverage. Others limit coverage to appellate courts or impose such tight restrictions as to effectively ban trial coverage. Federal courts have experimented with cameras in the courtroom, but federal judges generally have resisted that effort, and the Supreme Court has thus far been adamantly opposed to televising its proceedings.

Tensions involving free press and fair trial rose following the September 11, 2001, terrorist attacks on the United States when the focus shifted to whether national security might trump *both* free press and fair trial guarantees. Within weeks of the attacks on the World Trade Center and the Pentagon, Congress passed the USA PATRIOT Act, which gave the government broadened surveillance powers and, under certain circumstances, the right to use secret search warrants. And in the aftermath of 9/11, federal officials considered whether to try some of the suspected Al-Qaeda terrorists before military tribunals, where proceedings could be cloaked in secrecy and defendants would not be afforded the full protections of traditional criminal proceedings.

See also First Amendment; Press, Freedom of the; Prior Restraint, Doctrine of; Public Trial, Right to; Sixth Amendment; USA PATRIOT Act

Bibliography

Hopkins, W. Wat, ed. 2003. *Communication and the Law.* Northport, AL: Vision Press.

Teeter, Dwight L. Jr., and Bill Loving. 2004. *Law of Mass Communications: Freedom and Control of Print and Broadcast Media.* 10th ed. New York: Fountain Press.

Daniel J. Foley

FREE SPEECH MOVEMENT

The Free Speech Movement does not refer to a broadly based social movement but rather to a series of events that took place in Berkeley, California, during the fall of 1964. However, these events helped spark protests on college campuses across the country and, ultimately, a virtual cultural revolution in the United States in the 1960s.

The Free Speech Movement was a series of protests at the University of California, Berkeley, in which students demanded and ultimately won the right to engage in political activism on campus. University rules promulgated in response to political unrest in the 1930s barred students from engaging in political advocacy or activism on behalf of candidates or causes. When the university attempted to enforce these regulations against student activists in the fall of 1964, it touched off a protest that would forever change not only the political culture of Berkeley but that of the entire nation.

With an explosion of new students in the social sciences and humanities, the Berkeley campus in the early 1960s was a fertile field for recruiting supporters of the Civil Rights Movement . In September 1964, after students active in the movement began to engage in political activity and solicit funds on campus, the university administration announced that its ban on political advocacy would be strictly enforced. Various student organizations, including Student Friends of SNCC (Student Nonviolent Coordinating Committee), Campus CORE (Congress of Racial Equality), Students for a Democratic Society, and the Young Socialist Alliance, formed the United Front to oppose the restrictions. In late September, 5 students were suspended for violating the anti-activism regulations, leading to a sit-in by some 500 students at Sproul Hall, the University administration building. Three students identified as leaders of the sit-in were also suspended by the university. Student groups continued to defy the University by setting up tables outside Sproul Hall to solicit support and disseminate materials.

On October 1, 1964, Jack Weinberg, a recent Berkeley graduate who was manning Campus CORE's table outside Sproul Hall, was arrested for trespassing on the campus. The arrest touched off a massive protest. A crowd of students surrounded the police car in which Weinberg was being transported and prevented it from moving. Students climbed atop the police car and made impromptu speeches. The crowd of protesters outside Sproul Hall swelled, although accounts vary as to how many students were involved. The demonstration continued for more than 30 hours but ended peacefully after the president of the university signed a pact with leaders of the protest. Under the pact the university agreed to drop charges against Weinberg and submit the student suspensions for review by the faculty senate. Within days, the United Front renamed itself the Free Speech Movement.

In December, university officials announced that they would take action against the students who organized the sit-in, resulting in an even larger student protest that effectively shut down the university. Students and many faculty members refused to attend their classes. A large crowd gathered outside Sproul Hall to demonstrate their opposition to the university's position. On December 2, Mario Savio, a philosophy student who had emerged as leader of the Free Speech Movement, urged the crowd to take more dramatic action:

There is a time when the operation of the machine becomes so odious, makes you so sick at heart, that you can't take part; and you've got to put your bodies upon the gears and upon the wheels, upon the levers, upon all the apparatus and you've got to make it stop. And you've got to indicate to the people who run it, to the people who own it, that unless you're free, the machine will be prevented from working at all.

Inspired by Savio's speech, protesters poured into Sproul Hall and occupied the building for several days. Many faculty members expressed support for the students' grievances, although some did not approve of their methods. The occupation ended with the arrest of nearly 800 students. Mario Savio dropped out of Berkeley and pursued his political activism, drawing the attention of J. Edgar Hoover's FBI, which at that time was pursuing its COINTELPRO program to disrupt the New Left. Savio made news again in 1994 when he became a vocal opponent of efforts to eliminate affirmative action in California's institutions of higher education. Savio died in 1996 after suffering a heart attack.

The protests at Berkeley in the fall of 1964 made national news. More importantly they spawned a wave of student activism and protest that swept across college campuses in the mid-1960s. Ultimately, the Berkeley protesters succeeded with the support of the faculty in liberalizing university policies regarding political activism and communication. Berkeley emerged as the leading center of political radicalism in the United States. In 1997, the University of California at Berkeley officially named the steps outside Sproul Hall the Mario Savio Steps in commemoration of Savio's famous speech there in December 1964. The university that once did battle with the Free Speech Movement now celebrates what happened there in 1964 as a great victory for civil rights and liberties.

See also Civil Disobedience; Civil Rights Movement; Congress of Racial Equality; Federal Bureau of Investigation; Liberalism; Student Nonviolent Coordinating Committee; Students for a Democratic Society

Bibliography

Cohen, Robert, and Reginald E. Zelnick. 2002. *The Free Speech Movement: Reflections on Berkeley in the 1960s.* Berkeley and Los Angeles: University of California Press.

Goines, David Lance. 1993. *The Free Speech Movement: Coming of Age in the 1960s.* Berkeley, CA: Ten Speed Press.

Steffens, Bradley. 2004. *The Free Speech Movement.* San Diego, CA: Greenhaven Press.

John M. Scheb II and Otis H. Stephens, Jr.

FRONTIERO V. RICHARDSON (1973)

In this landmark sex discrimination case, the Supreme Court divided eight-to-one in upholding Lt. Sharron Frontiero's claim against the U.S. Secretary of Defense. The Court concluded that the Air Force violated the implicit equal protection component of the Fifth Amendment in requiring women, but not men, to demonstrate that their spouses were in fact dependents for the purpose of receiving medical and dental benefits. Supporting Frontiero in this litigation was the American Civil Liberties Union, which was represented by Ruth Bader Ginsburg, a future member of the Supreme Court.

Despite the strong majority in support of the judgment (only Justice William Rehnquist dissented), it was unable to produce a majority opinion. The justices split over the question of whether sex should be treated as an inherently suspect classification. Expressing the views of four members of the Court, Justice William Brennan's plurality opinion was unequivocal in declaring gender-based discrimination to be inherently suspect and thus presumptively unconstitutional:

[S]ince sex, like race and national origin, is an immutable characteristic determined solely by the accident of birth, the imposition of special disabilities upon the members of a particular sex because of their sex would seem to violate "the basic concept of our system that legal burdens should bear some relationship to individual responsibility."

The remaining four members of the majority were not prepared to go so far. In an opinion concurring in the judgment only, Justice Lewis Powell wrote that "[i]t is unnecessary for the Court in this case to characterize sex as a suspect classification, with all of the far-reaching implications of such a holding." Moreover, Powell believed that to declare sex a suspect classification would render superfluous the Equal Rights Amendment, which was then pending before the state legislatures: "It seems to me that this reaching out to pre-empt by judicial action a major political decision which is currently in process of resolution does not reflect appropriate respect for duly prescribed legislative processes." Of course, the Equal Rights Amendment ultimately failed to win ratification.

In the two decades since *Frontiero,* the Court has still not declared gender-based discrimination to be inherently suspect, though its recent decisions have come close by demanding that government articulate "an exceedingly persuasive justification" to sustain any policy that confers unequal status on the basis of sex.

See also American Civil Liberties Union; Brennan, William J., Jr.; Due Process, Substantive; Equal Protection Clause; Equal Protection Jurisprudence; Equal Rights Amendment; Fifth Amendment; Fundamental Rights; Gender-Based Discrimination; Ginsburg, Ruth Bader; Strict Scrutiny; Powell, Lewis F., Jr.; Rational Basis Test

John M. Scheb II and Otis H. Stephens, Jr.

FRUIT OF THE POISONOUS TREE DOCTRINE

The fruit of the poisonous tree is a judicial doctrine that provides for exclusion of evidence derived from information obtained in violation of the Fourth or Fifth amendments to the U.S. Constitution. The doctrine is an extension of the exclusionary rule first announced by the Supreme Court in *Weeks v. United States* (1914). In *Weeks* the Court held that evidence obtained in violation of the Fourth Amendment (which proscribes unreasonable searches and seizures) is inadmissible in a federal criminal trial. The fruit of the poisonous tree doctrine stems from the Supreme Court's opinion in *Silverthorne Lumber v. United States* (1920). Speaking for the Court in that case, Justice Oliver Wendell Holmes opined:

The essence of a provision forbidding the acquisition of evidence in a certain way is that not merely evidence so acquired shall not be used before the Court but that it shall not be used at all. Of course this does not mean that the facts thus obtained become sacred and inaccessible. If knowledge of them is gained from an independent source they may be proved like any others, but the knowledge gained by the Government's own wrong cannot be used by it in the way proposed.

During the 1960s the Supreme Court forged new doctrines enhancing the constitutional rights of criminal defendants. In *Mapp v. Ohio* (1961), the Court extended the Fourth Amendment exclusionary rule to the state courts via the Fourteenth Amendment. In *Escobedo v. Illinois* (1964) and *Miranda v. Arizona* (1966), the Supreme Court fashioned a new exclusionary rule to enforce the Fifth Amendment protection against compulsory self-incrimination in the context of police interrogation of criminal suspects. As a result of *Mapp, Escobedo,* and *Miranda,* evidence obtained in violation of either the Fourth or Fifth Amendment may not be used in state criminal trials. Under the fruit of the poisonous tree doctrine, neither may information derived from tainted evidence be used. For example, if police interrogate a suspect in custody without first warning the suspect of his or her right to counsel and right to remain silent as required by *Miranda v. Arizona,* statements made by the suspect are inadmissible in court. If those statements contain information that allows the police to locate physical evidence they would not have located otherwise, the physical evidence is likewise suppressed as the fruit of the poisonous tree.

In *Wong Sun v. United States* (1963), the Supreme Court held that statements made by a suspect who was unlawfully arrested, as well as heroin recovered from a third party as the result of these statements, was the "fruit of the poisonous tree" and therefore could not be used in evidence. Writing for the Court in *Wong Sun,* Justice William Brennan concluded:

We need not hold that all evidence is "fruit of the poisonous tree" simply because it would not have come to light but for the illegal actions of the police. Rather, the more apt question in such a case is "whether, granting establishment of the primary illegality, the evidence to which instant objection is made has been come at by exploitation of that illegality or instead by means sufficiently distinguishable to be purged of the primary taint." … We think it clear that the narcotics were "come at by the exploitation of that illegality" and hence that they may not be used [in evidence].

During the 1980s a more conservative Supreme Court announced some refinements to the fruit of the poisonous tree doctrine. Under the independent source doctrine, first recognized by Justice Holmes in the *Silverthorne* case, derivative evidence obtained on the basis of independently and lawfully obtained information may be admissible in court. In *Segura v. United States* (1984), Chief Justice Warren E. Burger pointed out that "evidence is not to be excluded if the connection between the illegal police conduct and the discovery and seizure of the evidence is 'so attenuated as to dissipate the taint.'" According to Burger, such attenuation occurs "if police had an 'independent source' for discovery of the evidence." A variation on the independent source doctrine is what is termed the inevitable discovery doctrine, under which derivative evidence that would otherwise be excluded is admissible because it inevitably would have been retrieved through lawful means. Speaking for the Court in *Nix v. Williams* (1984), Chief Justice Burger observed, "Exclusion of physical evidence that would inevitably have been discovered adds nothing to either the integrity or fairness of a criminal trial."

Refinements of the exclusionary rule have lessened somewhat the application of the fruit of the poisonous tree doctrine. Yet criminal defendants continue to invoke its benefits by filing a motion to suppress evidence derived directly or indirectly from physical evidence and witness testimony obtained in violation of the Fourth and Fifth amendments to the U.S. Constitution.

See also Accused, Rights of the; Brennan, William J., Jr.; Burger, Warren E.; Fifth Amendment; Fourteenth Amendment; Fourth Amendment; Fourth Amendment Exclusionary Rule; Holmes, Oliver Wendell, Jr.; Interrogation and Confessions; *Mapp v. Ohio; Miranda v. Arizona;* Self-Incrimination Clause

Bibliography

Bradley, Craig M. 2003. "The 'Fruits' of *Miranda* Violations." *Trial* 39:56–.

Pitler, Robert M. 1968. "'The Fruit of the Poisonous Tree' Revisited and Shepardized." *California Law Review* 56:579.Scheb, John M., and John M. Scheb II. 2005. *Criminal Law and Procedure.* 5th ed. Belmont, CA: Thomson/Wadsworth.

John M. Scheb II and Otis H. Stephens, Jr.

FULL FAITH AND CREDIT CLAUSE

Article IV, Section 1, of the United States Constitution provides that "Full Faith and Credit shall be given in each State to the public Acts, Records, and judicial Proceedings of every other State." The section goes on to provide that "the Congress may by general Law prescribe the Manner in which such Acts, Records, and Proceedings shall be proved, *and the Effect thereof.*" Acting pursuant to the power conferred by the Full Faith and Credit Clause, Congress enacted the full faith and credit statute, which provides, in part, that the "[a]cts, records and judicial proceedings" of a state "shall have the same full faith and credit in every court within the United States and its Territories and Possessions as they have by law or usage in the courts of such State, Territory or Possession from which they are taken."

The Full Faith and Credit Clause and its implementing statute have had their greatest impact in defining the effects judicial proceedings in one state have on subsequent judicial proceedings brought in another state. A judgment rendered in one state is entitled to recognition in the other states of the United States. A foreign judgment is recognized when the forum state gives the judgment the same conclusive effect that it has in the state that rendered it with respect to the persons bound by the judgment and the claims and issues that no longer are open to litigation. A judgment also may be entitled to enforcement in another state. A foreign judgment is enforced when, in addition to being recognized, the prevailing party is given the affirmative relief in the forum to which the foreign judgment entitles him or her. When a state enforces a foreign judgment, the constitutional obligation of full faith and credit means that the forum enforces the foreign judgment the same way it would enforce one of its own judgments.

A fundamental limitation on the obligation of a state to give full faith and credit to a foreign judgment is that only a *valid* judgment is entitled to full faith and credit. A judgment is valid if the court that rendered it had subject matter jurisdiction over the dispute, and territorial jurisdiction over the person or property of the defendant or the status being adjudicated, and the defendant was given constitutionally adequate notice of the proceedings. Valid judgments are entitled to recognition and enforcement even if the court that rendered the judgment made an error of fact or law and even if the underlying claim giving rise to the judgment violates the public policy of the state in which enforcement is sought (see *Fauntleroy v. Lum,* 1980).

Outside the area of foreign judgments, the Full Faith and Credit Clause has played a more modest role. At one time, the clause was interpreted to place more stringent restraints on a state's ability to choose its own substantive law to decide cases than the restraints imposed by the Due Process Clause of the Fourteenth Amendment. Today, however, the Full Faith and Credit Clause has been interpreted to require nothing more than the Due Process Clause in the choice-of-law context (*Allstate Insurance v. Hague,* 1981). Full faith and credit does prohibit a state from refusing to adjudicate a case it otherwise is empowered to decide solely because the plaintiff's claim is based on the law of another state (*Hughes v. Fetter,* 1951). But full faith and credit does not require a state to refuse to adjudicate a case because a foreign state wishes to concentrate litigation in its own courts (*Tennessee Coal, Iron and Railroad v. George,* 1914; *Crider v. Zurich Insurance,* 1965).

See also Due Process Clauses; Fourteenth Amendment

Bibliography

American Law Institute. 1971. *Restatement, Second, Conflict of Laws.* Philadelphia: American Law Institute.

Leflar, Robert A., Luther L. McDougal III, and Robert L. Felix. 1986. *American Conflicts Law.* Charlottesville, VA: Michie.

Scoles, Eugene F., Peter Hay, Patrick J. Borchers, and Symeon C. Symeonides. 2004. *Conflict of Laws.* 4th ed. St. Paul, MN: West.

John L. Sobieski, Jr.

FUNDAMENTAL RIGHTS

The term "fundamental rights" suggests that certain rights are foundational or essential in character. The adjective "fundamental" has been applied to various rights over the course of American constitutional history. Often the term has been used to refer to the rights of life, liberty, and property as formulated by John Locke and enshrined in the Due Process Clauses of the Fifth and Fourteenth Amendments to the United States Constitution. In the late nineteenth and early twentieth centuries, the Supreme Court most often used the term "fundamental rights" in connection with its protection of private property, contracts, and the free enterprise system. After the constitutional revolution of 1937, the Court shifted its emphasis to the protection of First Amendment freedoms. Writing for the Supreme Court in *Palko v. Connecticut* (1937), Justice Benjamin Cardozo characterized freedom of speech as "the matrix, the indispensable condition, of nearly every other form of freedom." Six years later, in *Murdock v. Pennsylvania* (1943), Justice William O. Douglas's opinion for the Court went so far as to suggest that the First Amendment freedoms of speech and press enjoy a "preferred position" in relation to other constitutional rights.

Although the Court no longer uses the language of preferred freedoms, it often refers to the First Amendment freedoms—speech, press, assembly, and religion—as fundamental rights that require a higher level of judicial protection. In recent decades, the Court has also characterized as fundamental the right to counsel (see *Gideon v. Wainwright,* 1963), the right to vote (see *Bush v. Gore,* 2000), and the due process right of access to the courts (see *Tennessee v. Lane,* 2004).

The term "fundamental rights" has also been used to refer to certain unenumerated constitutional rights, notably the right to privacy and personal autonomy, and in particular reproductive freedom. These unenumerated rights have been recognized as implicit in the broad term "liberty" found in the Due Process Clauses of the Fifth and Fourteenth amendments. In *Washington v. Glucksberg* (1997), the Supreme Court summarized the fundamental rights recognized via the doctrine of substantive due process:

The Due Process Clause guarantees more than fair process, and the "liberty" it protects includes more than the absence of physical restraint.... The Clause also provides heightened protection against government interference with certain fundamental rights and liberty interests.... In a long line of cases, we have held that, in addition to the specific freedoms protected by the Bill of Rights, the "liberty" specially protected by the Due Process Clause includes the rights to marry, ... to have children, ... to direct the education and upbringing of one's children, ... to marital privacy, ... to use contraception, ... to bodily integrity, ... and to abortion.... We have also assumed, and strongly suggested, that the Due Process Clause protects the traditional right to refuse unwanted lifesaving medical treatment.

Under a doctrine emanating from *United States v. Carolene Products* (1938) and developed extensively by the Warren Court in decisions such as *Shapiro v. Thompson* (1969), courts must strictly scrutinize any alleged abridgment of fundamental rights by the government. The burden is on the government to justify any infringement on a fundamental right by showing that it is necessary to achieve a compelling governmental interest and is narrowly tailored to that end. In *Roe v. Wade* (1973), the Court put it this way: "Where certain 'fundamental rights' are involved, the Court has held that regulation limiting these rights may be justified only by a 'compelling state interest,' ... and that legislative enactments must be narrowly drawn to express only the legitimate state interests at stake."

The notion of fundamental rights is a controversial one. What empowers the courts, critics will ask, to play favorites with constitutional rights? Why, for example, is the Second Amendment right to keep and bear arms not viewed as deserving the same level of judicial protection as the free exercise of religion? To some Americans, gun ownership is almost a religious commitment. And certainly those who wrote the Bill of Rights placed tremendous importance on the right to keep and bear arms as a means of preventing tyranny.

Today, however, the larger controversy involves the unenumerated rights recognized by the courts as fundamental, thus triggering strict judicial scrutiny when they are infringed upon. Prior to *Roe v. Wade,* the Supreme Court limited its recognition of unenumerated rights to those "so rooted in the traditions and conscience of our people as to be ranked as fundamental." In his dissenting opinion in *Lawrence v. Texas* (2003), Justice Antonin Scalia observed that *Roe v. Wade* "subjected the restriction of abortion to heightened scrutiny without even attempting to establish that the freedom to abort was rooted in this Nation's tradition."

Concurring in *Griswold v. Connecticut* (1965), Justice Arthur Goldberg insisted that:

[i]n determining which rights are fundamental, judges are not left at large to decide cases in light of their personal and private notions. Rather, they must look to the "traditions and [collective] conscience of our people" to determine whether a principle is "so rooted [there] ... as to be ranked as fundamental." ... The inquiry is whether a right involved "is of such a character that it cannot be denied without violating those 'fundamental principles of liberty and justice which lie at the base of all our civil and political institutions.'"

See also Abortion, Right to; Assembly, Freedom of; Counsel, Right to; Douglas, William O.; Due Process, Substantive; Due Process Clauses; Equal Protection Jurisprudence; First Amendment; Fourteenth Amendment; *Gideon v. Wainwright;* Goldberg, Arthur; *Griswold v. Connecticut; Korematsu v. United States; Lawrence v. Texas;* Liberty; Locke, John; Ninth Amendment; Press, Freedom of the; Privacy, Constitutional Right of; Religion, Freedom of; Reproductive Freedom; *Roe v. Wade;* Scalia, Antonin; Speech, Freedom of; Strict Scrutiny; Travel, Right to; Vote, Right to; Warren Court

Bibliography

Brest, Paul. 1981. "The Fundamental Rights Controversy: The Essential Contradictions of Normative Constitutional Scholarship." *Yale Law Journal* 90:1063.

Licht, Robert A., ed. 1992. *The Framers and Fundamental Rights.* Washington, DC: American Enterprise Institute.

John M. Scheb II and Otis H. Stephens, Jr.

FURMAN V. GEORGIA (1972)

By the mid-1960s, it was clear that public support for the death penalty had diminished substantially. As a reflection of this change in societal attitudes, only two persons were executed in the United States between 1967 and the Supreme Court's decision in *Furman v. Georgia* (1972), which struck down the Georgia death penalty law and effectively instituted a national moratorium on capital punishment.

The *Furman* decision involved appeals by two African American males, Furman and Jackson, sentenced to death by Georgia courts, and one African American male, Branch, sentenced to die by a Texas court. Furman shot a homeowner while committing burglary. Jackson and Branch were both convicted of raping white women.

Dividing five-to-four, the Supreme Court reversed all three death sentences and struck down the statutes on which they were based. Because the Court produced only a brief per curiam opinion announcing its judgment in the case, one had to examine five separate concurring opinions to discern the reasons for the Court's decision. Two of the five justices—William J. Brennan and Thurgood Marshall—expressed the view that the death penalty itself was cruel and unusual punishment, given the "evolving standards of decency." The others in the majority focused their concerns on procedural aspects of capital sentencing, suggesting that if certain defects were corrected, the death penalty might well be reinstated in a future case.

Of the five justices who voted to invalidate the death penalty in *Furman,* Justice Potter Stewart's opinion seems to have been the most influential. For Stewart the problem with the death penalty was not the punishment itself but the fact that trial juries were being left with virtually unfettered discretion in deciding when to impose capital punishment, not only for murder, but for rape, armed robbery, and kidnapping as well. It was difficult to discern any principle by which some defendants convicted of death-eligible crimes were being sent to prison while others were being sentenced to death. Justice Stewart noted that "if any basis can be discerned for the selection of these few to be sentenced to die, it is the constitutionally impermissible basis of race." In Stewart's view, "the Eighth and Fourteenth Amendments cannot tolerate the infliction of a sentence of death under legal systems that permit this unique penalty to be so wantonly and so freakishly imposed."

The four dissenters in the case, Chief Justice Burger and associate justices Rehnquist, Blackmun, and Powell, accused the majority of imposing their own policy preferences on the Constitution. Pulling no punches, Justice William H. Rehnquist asserted that the "decision holding unconstitutional capital punishment is not an act of judgment, but rather an act of will." Stressing that "judicial self-restraint is surely an implied, if not an expressed, condition of the grant of authority of judicial review," Rehnquist accused the majority of ignoring that maxim and imposing its "own views of goodness, truth, and justice upon others."

In an unusually personal opinion, Justice Harry Blackmun confessed that death penalty cases produced in him "an excruciating agony of the spirit." "Were I a legislator," wrote Blackmun, "I would vote against the death penalty." But judges, Blackmun insisted, "should not allow our personal preferences … guide our judicial decision in cases such as these." He concluded that the Court's decision was "difficult to accept or to justify as a matter of history, of law, or of constitutional pronouncement."

In the wake of the *Furman* decision, Georgia and most other states revised their death penalty laws to address the concerns raised by Justice Stewart. Four years later, the Supreme Court would revisit this issue in *Gregg v. Georgia* (1976).

See also Bifurcated Trial; Brennan, William J., Jr.; Cruel and Unusual Punishments Clause; Death Penalty, Crimes Punishable by the; Death Penalty and the Supreme Court; Death-Qualified Jury; Eighth Amendment; Fourteenth Amendment; *Gregg v. Georgia;* Marshall, Thurgood; Stewart, Potter; Warren, Earl

John M. Scheb II and Otis H. Stephens, Jr.

G

GAG ORDERS

Gag order is the preferred term for American journalists when referring to a restrictive order issued by a court of law to regulate the news media's pretrial coverage of a particular criminal case. Under free speech jurisprudence, gag orders exemplify prior restraint. American constitutional law prefers subsequent punishment in balancing freedom of the press with other conflicting societal interests because, as a famous United States Supreme Court decision noted, prior restraint "freezes" speech, while punishment after publication merely "chills" it (*Nebraska Press Assn. v. Stuart*, 1976). Thus, prior restraint is permitted only in exceptional circumstances, such as protection of national security in time of war, prohibition of obscenity, and safeguarding society against imminent lawless action.

In *Sheppard v. Maxwell* (1966), the Supreme Court noted several methods that trial judges could employ to protect a defendant's right to a fair trial. Among the remedial methods that have evolved from *Sheppard* and its progeny in mitigating prejudicial media coverage are:

- Limiting in-court activities of journalists;
- Moving the trial to a new location where there has been less prejudicial publicity (change of venue);
- Changing the pool of potential jurors (change of venire);

- Postponing the trial until initial publicity of the trial subsides (continuance);
- Rigorous questioning of potential jurors (voir dire);
- Ordering jurors to avoid exposure to media coverage of the trial and to forgo communication with others beyond their fellow jurors (admonition to the jury);
- Keeping jurors from prejudicial publicity by sheltering them from the public (sequestration).

But the Court in *Sheppard* never suggested that trial courts use gag orders aimed directly at the media. The current judicial standard for gag orders is derived from the three-prong test the Supreme Court enunciated in *Nebraska Press Association v. Stuart* (1976). The test requires trial judges, before issuing gag orders, to demonstrate sufficient evidence that:

- There must be intense and pervasive publicity about the trial at issue;
- No other alternative measures—such as a change of venue or continuance or extensive voir dire process—will likely lessen the effects of the pretrial publicity; and
- The gag order will effectively prevent prejudicial publicity from reaching potential jurors.

Largely because of its nearly absolute prohibition on prior restraints on the press, *Nebraska Press Association* has resulted in fewer gag orders directed at the news media. However, courts have turned their attention to trial participants. They impose gag orders on the sources of information about trials. Therefore, lawyers, prosecutors, witnesses, and law enforcement officials may be prohibited from talking to the press without violation of the First Amendment guarantee of a free press.

The Supreme Court in *Gentile v. State Bar of Nevada* (1991) held that penalizing extrajudicial speech by lawyers involved in criminal cases is not as serious a violation of the First Amendment as punishing speech by the media and the public. Gag orders against trial participants are rarely challenged by the news media. But they pose a significant threat to the First Amendment right of a free press.

Regardless, the benchmark for issuing gag orders against trial participants does not necessarily hinge on the identity of the trial participants. It should consider other variables such as the nature of the statements restrained and the actual or perceived degree of threat to the administration of justice created by those statements.

No gag order will survive First Amendment scrutiny if it is solely to preserve the dignity of the bench. In *Bridges v. California* (1941), Justice Felix Frankfurter stated that the First Amendment forbids the state "to protect the court as a mystical entity or the judges as individuals or as anointed priests set apart from the community and spared the criticism to which in a democracy other public servants are exposed."

On the other hand, the news media can be prohibited from publishing material they have obtained through discovery. The Supreme Court in *Seattle Times Co. v. Rhinehart* (1984) held that a gag order does not violate the First Amendment "if it is entered on a showing of good cause, is limited to the context of pretrial civil discovery, and does not restrict the dissemination of the information gained from other sources."

In this light, singularly instructive is the Sixth Circuit Court of Appeals' invalidation of the gag order issued against *Business Week* in the mid-1990s. A *Business Week* reporter obtained copies of sealed documents in a civil case. Three hours before the *Business Week* story based on the documents was to roll off the presses, a trial judge ordered McGraw-Hill, publisher of *Business Week*, not to publish the story. The judge unsealed the documents three weeks later, but he refused to lift his gag order barring *Business Week* from publishing its original article.

In *Procter & Gamble Co. v. Bankers Trust Co., BT Securities Corp.* (1996), the Sixth Circuit found the gag order patently invalid. The federal appeals court reasoned that the order did not fall into "that 'single, extremely narrow class of cases' where publication would be so dangerous to fundamental governmental interests as to justify a prior restraint." The documents, the court pointed out, were sealed for the litigants "in protecting their vanity or their commercial self-interest."

One of the still evolving First Amendment issues for the news media confronting gag orders is: What would have happened to McGraw-Hill if it had ignored the trial judge's order not to publish the *Business Week* story? Under the "collateral bar rule," McGraw-Hill would most certainly have been guilty of contempt of court.

The collateral bar rule disallows a person who disobeys a court order to collaterally challenge the constitutionality of the order as a defense to the contempt of court charge. The U.S. Court of Appeals for the Fifth Circuit in *United States v. Dickinson* (1972) stated that journalists have to obey a gag order until it is reversed or set aside "in an orderly fashion."

More recently, the collateral bar rule was made more flexible by one federal appeals court to accommodate the press's unique needs in covering news in a timely manner. The First Circuit Court of Appeals in *In re Providence Journal* (1986) held that a "transparently invalid" gag order could be violated insofar as the news media first made "a good faith effort" to have the order reversed on appeal.

Gag orders against American news media remain an option to trial courts in balancing freedom of the press with the defendant's right to a fair trial. But the courts rarely resort to the gag orders because they fail to meet the strict prior restraint test, as set forth in the *Nebraska Press Association* case.

Bibliography

Smolla, Rodney A. 2004. *Smolla and Nimmer on Freedom of Speech*. St. Paul, MN: Thomson/West.

Kyu Ho Youm

GARRISON, WILLIAM LLOYD. *See* Abolitionist Movement

GAULT, IN RE (1967)

Beginning in the late nineteenth century, public concern about the maltreatment of juveniles by the criminal justice system led to the establishment of separate courts for juvenile offenders. These courts were usually separate from the regular tribunals; often the judges or referees that presided over these courts did not have formal legal training. There was little procedural regularity or even opportunity for the juvenile offender to confront his or her accusers.

The abuses that came to be associated with juvenile courts were addressed by the Supreme Court in the landmark 1967 case *In re Gault*. The case began when 15-year-old Gerald Francis Gault and another teenage boy were taken into police custody in Gila County, Arizona. The arrest resulted from a complaint filed by a neighbor who accused Gerald and the other boy of making obscene phone calls to her. Gerald's parents were not notified of the arrest, nor was Gerald advised of his right to remain silent or his right to counsel. After being arrested, Gerald was held in detention without judicial authorization for several days and then released without official explanation. At the delinquency hearing several days later, the complainant did not appear in court to testify. However, the judge and probation officer assigned to the case stated that Gerald had admitted making lewd remarks to the complainant over the telephone. On that basis, the court committed Gerald to a juvenile detention facility "for the period of his minority," that is, six years.

Gerald's family sought relief via a writ of habeas corpus filed in the Gila County Superior Court. That court dismissed their petition, whereupon the Gaults sought review in the Arizona Supreme Court. Failing to obtain relief there, the Gaults petitioned the U.S. Supreme Court for a writ of certiorari. The Supreme Court granted review and ruled in Gault's favor, holding that he had been denied due process of law. Writing for a nearly unanimous bench, Justice Abe Fortas observed that "under our Constitution, the condition of being a boy does not justify a kangaroo court."

In *Gault*, the Supreme Court essentially required that juvenile courts adhere to elementary standards of due process, applying most of the basic procedural safeguards enjoyed by adults accused of crimes. Specifically, the Court held that juvenile courts must respect the right to counsel, the freedom from compulsory self-incrimination, and the right to confront (cross-examine) hostile witnesses.

Despite *In re Gault* and subsequent efforts to make the juvenile courts conform to due process requirements, juvenile delinquency proceedings are still, strictly speaking, civil matters, although they now possess many of the accoutrements of criminal cases.

See also Accused, Rights of the; Confrontation, Right of; Counsel, Right to; Due Process, Procedural; Fourteenth Amendment (1868); Habeas Corpus; Juvenile Justice; Self-Incrimination Clause

Cases Cited

In re Gault, 387 U.S. 1 (1967).

John M. Scheb II and Otis H. Stephens, Jr.

GAY RIGHTS MOVEMENT

One of the hallmarks of the 1960s was the sexual revolution, a broad cultural revolt against traditional sexual values and mores. Out of the sexual revolution emerged a new openness with regard to homosexuality, which had long been taboo in Western culture. In the 1970s, people who were homosexual began to "come out of the closet" (i.e., stop keeping their homosexuality secret), and heterosexuals began to express sympathy or tolerance rather than revulsion and condemnation. A new term, *gay* was coined to replace more negative terms for being homosexual.

The origin of the gay rights movement is often linked to an event that took place in New York City on June 28, 1969. When police raided the Stonewall Inn, a gay bar in Sheridan Square, patrons resisted arrest and a riot erupted (D'Emilio 1983; Duberman 1993). Although raids on gay bars had been common in big cities for years, this was the first time that patrons resisted en masse. Within a month a new organization, the Gay Liberation Front (GLF), appeared in New York City and soon spread to cities and college campuses throughout the country. A year after the Stonewall riot, nearly 10,000 people joined a GLF-sponsored gay rights march from Greenwich Village to Central Park. Today, gay pride marches are held in many cities in June to commemorate the Stonewall riot of 1969.

The first national gay rights march was held in Washington, D.C. in October 1979 and as many as 100,000 people participated. With strong media coverage of the event, the gay rights movement finally achieved national recognition.

By the 1980s, gay men and lesbians had become politically aware and activated. They had even organized a number of interest groups to push for policy changes in the legislative and judicial branches of government at the local, state, and national levels. Among the more prominent gay rights interest groups are the National Gay and Lesbian Task Force, the Lambda Legal Defense and Education Fund, and the Gay and Lesbian Alliance against Defamation.

In particular, gays sought the repeal of sodomy laws that, although seldom enforced, technically made their sexual practices illegal. In the 1960s, 1970s, and 1980s, many states did repeal these types of laws, not so much as a result of political activity by gays, but rather because these statutes were widely regarded as outmoded. In a setback to the gay rights movement, however, in *Bowers v. Hardwick* (1986), the U.S. Supreme Court ruled that state sodomy laws, as applied to homosexual

conduct, did not violate the U.S. Constitution. In what gay rights activists regarded as an affront, the High Court said that gays have no right under the Constitution to engage in homosexual sodomy. Subsequently, however, many state courts invalidated their own state sodomy laws based on state constitutional privacy protections. In *Lawrence v. Texas* (2003), the Supreme Court, likely influenced by state court decisions as well as changing public attitudes, overturned its 1986 decision and declared unconstitutional a Texas law criminalizing homosexual conduct.

More important than the demise of sodomy laws, however, is the effort by gay men and lesbians to acquire specific protection under civil rights laws. In 1992, voters in Colorado adopted an amendment to the state constitution prohibiting the state legislature and courts from extending civil rights protection to gays. In *Romer v. Evans* (1996), however, in a major victory for gay rights, the U.S. Supreme Court struck down the amendment on the basis of the Equal Protection Clause of the Fourteenth Amendment.

A number of cities have adopted ordinances prohibiting discrimination on the basis of sexual orientation in housing, employment, and public accommodations. Sixteen states have enacted statutes prohibiting various forms of sexual orientation discrimination and 19 states now permit gay and lesbian couples to adopt children. Gay rights activists have been less successful at the national level. Congress has been reluctant to designate sexual orientation as a protected category covered by federal civil rights legislation.

By 2004, the agenda of the gay rights movement focused on the issue of marriage. Gay rights activists saw the legalization of homosexual marriage as a critical test of public acceptance of gays and lesbians. In November 2003, the Massachusetts Supreme Court ruled that the Massachusetts state constitution required that the legislature rewrite its statutes to provide marriage rights for gay couples. This set off a national discussion of gay marriage that led some local officials to perform weddings for gay couples. While these marriages were later overturned, the right to marry a person of the same sex further widened the discussion of rights for gay and lesbian couples. Although at the end of 2005, the issue of gay marriage was still very much in flux, it was clear that there had been tremendous cultural change in this area over the preceding three decades. The gay rights movement certainly is responsible for much of that change.

See also *Boy Scouts of America v. Dale* (2000); Civil Rights Movement; Discrimination; Equality; Interest Groups; *Lawrence v. Texas* (2003); Privacy, Constitutional Right of; *Romer v. Evans* (1996); Same-Sex Marriage and Civil Unions; Sexual Orientation, Discrimination Based on

Bibliography

D'Emilio, John. 1983. *Sexual Politics, Sexual Communities.* Chicago: University of Chicago Press.

Duberman, Martin. 1993. *Stonewall.* New York: Dutton.

Gerstmann, Evan. 1999. *The Constitutional Underclass: Gays, Lesbians, and the Failure of Class-Based Equal Protection.* Chicago: University of Chicago Press.

Rimmerman, Craig A., Kenneth D. Wald, and Clyde M. Wilcox, eds. 2000. *The Politics of Gay Rights.* Chicago: University of Chicago Press.

Otis H. Stephens, Jr., and John M. Scheb II

GENDER-BASED DISCRIMINATION

"No state shall ... deny to any person within its jurisdiction the equal protection of the laws." The authors of this clause included it in the Fourteenth Amendment to the United States Constitution primarily to help secure the rights of four million men, women, and children who had been freed from slavery by the Union's victory in the Civil War. But, in contrast to the two other "Civil War Amendments," the language of the Fourteenth Amendment is neutral. Unlike the Thirteenth and Fifteenth Amendments, it does not specify what governmental practices it forbids. The Fourteenth Amendment is also silent on the question of gender. However, during congressional debate over the Fourteenth Amendment, speakers who were challenged to provide an example of a group not covered by this amendment usually mentioned women or children (Baer, 1983).

The first Supreme Court decisions interpreting the Equal Protection Clause hewed closely to its original intent. *The Slaughterhouse Cases* (1873) declared, "We doubt very much whether any action of a State not directed against the negroes as a class" would "ever come within the purview of this provision." The same day, the Court upheld a state's refusal to admit a woman to the bar (*Bradwell v. Illinois*). Fifty years later, a Supreme Court decision accurately described the Equal Protection Clause as "the traditional last resort of constitutional arguments" (*Buck v. Bell*, 1927). But the Court had used the Due Process Clause of the Fourteenth Amendment to frustrate and alleviate some of the ill effects of the Industrial Revolution and to permit gender discrimination.

Lochner v. New York (1905) invalidated a state law limiting the working hours of bakers on the grounds that it arbitrarily interfered with freedom of contract, a right mentioned nowhere in the Constitution. *Muller v. Oregon* (1908), however, sustained a similar law applying only to women laundry workers. Limitations on women's freedom of contract were viewed as legitimate because physical differences between the sexes such as women's relative lack of muscle strength and their childbearing capacity made them more vulnerable to exploitation. "Differentiated by these matters from the other sex," woman "is properly placed in a class by herself." Since laundry work was a woman's occupation, *Muller* did not encourage employers to hire men who could work longer hours. Subsequent decisions (e.g., *Radice v. New York*, 1924) relied on *Muller* to uphold "protective" labor legislation that limited women workers' opportunities to compete with men for jobs, while *Adkins v. Children's Hospital* (1923) invalidated a minimum wage for women as an arbitrary determination that a certain income was necessary for health and safety.

The reversal of *Adkins* in *West Coast Hotel Co. v. Parrish* (1937) signaled the Court's retreat from economic activism in response to the threat of Franklin Roosevelt's effort to increase the number of justices. This "Court-packing" bill failed partly because of "the switch in time that saved nine" of which this ruling was a part (Leuchtenberg, 1995). This abandonment of judicial scrutiny in economic cases extended to gender discrimination. *Goesaert v. Cleary* (1948) upheld a Michigan law prohibiting women from tending bar. Ignoring strong evidence that the law was designed to create job vacancies for men, the justices accepted the state's protective rationales for banning women from doing a job they had been doing safely since the United States' entry into World War II had sent men into military service.

Traditional due process and equal protection doctrine divides constitutional claims into two tiers. Every law must bear some rational relationship to a legitimate governmental purpose. When this "rational basis" is lacking, the law is arbitrary and, therefore, unconstitutional. Most laws survive this test because courts presume that they are constitutional. But there are instances in which the presumption of constitutionality does not hold. Laws that appear to invade constitutional rights, to frustrate access to the political process, or to be directed against disadvantaged minorities are suspect and receive strict scrutiny; they will be upheld only upon showing that a compelling justification for them exists (*United States v. Carolene Products*, 1938; *Korematsu v. United States*, 1944).

The tenure of Chief Justice Earl Warren (1953–69) was notable for cases that used strict scrutiny to invalidate laws. Warren and several associate justices believed that the protection of the disadvantaged was the special responsibility of the Supreme Court. The landmark case of *Brown v. Board of Education* (1954) ordered racial integration of the public schools because "separate schools are inherently unequal." The Warren Court also curbed the government's power to punish suspected Communists and uncooperative witnesses in loyalty-security cases and also broadened the rights of criminal suspects. But this solicitude for the underdog did not extend to cases involving women. The most important women's rights case during Warren's tenure, *Hoyt v. Florida* (1961), used the rational basis test to uphold a law restricting women's eligibility for jury service. Evangeline Hoyt had been convicted of the murder of her husband. She argued that she had been denied equal protection because the pool from which her jury was chosen was all-male. The Court sustained the law on the grounds that it was a reasonable accommodation of women's role as "the center of home and family life."

Gender discrimination would remain on the lower tier of constitutional classifications until after Warren was replaced by a less activist chief justice. Warren Burger did not share his predecessor's view of the role of the Court as the protector of the oppressed. However, when it came to interpreting the law, Burger displayed no great deference to legislatures. *Reed v. Reed* (1971) was the first equal protection case to invalidate a gender-based discrimination under the rational basis test. The Court ruled that Idaho's automatic preference for males over equally qualified females in selecting the administrator of a dead person's estate was "the very kind of arbitrary legislative choice" forbidden by the Fourteenth Amendment.

The impact of *Reed* as precedent was problematic for two reasons: (1) the factual situation involved could occur only rarely, and (2) because there were two vacancies on the Court when it was decided. Two years later, *Frontiero v. Richardson* (1973) came within one vote of ranking sex with race as a suspect classification. Three justices relied on *Reed* to invalidate a law that made it harder for women military personnel than for men to get dependency benefits for their spouses. The other four members of the majority found sex discrimination inherently suspect and, therefore, subject to strict scrutiny. "Sex, like race or national origin," wrote Justice William Brennan, is "determined solely by the accident of birth" and "frequently bears no relation to the ability to perform or contribute to society."

This plurality opinion represents the high point in the Court's commitment to gender equality. One more vote on the side of strict scrutiny would have rendered the Equal Rights Amendment, then before the states, superfluous. The dwindling support for the ERA over the next several years and its eventual defeat probably contributed to the Court's refusal to assign sex to the top tier of inherently suspect classifications. But a majority of the justices were equally reluctant to continue using the rational basis test. A 1976 case became the basis for a permanent reconstruction of the two-tier model (rational basis/strict scrutiny).

Craig v. Boren overturned an Oklahoma law that allowed females to buy 3.2 percent beer (but no other alcoholic beverage) at eighteen, while men had to wait to buy it (but not to drink it) until they were twenty-one. Seven justices rejected the state's argument that this law was an acceptable means of reducing the number of alcohol-related automobile accidents. The opinion represented a compromise between *Reed*'s minimal scrutiny and *Frontiero*'s strict scrutiny, adding a middle tier in the process. "To withstand constitutional scrutiny, previous cases established that classifications by gender must serve *important* governmental objectives and be *substantially* related to these objectives." This "intermediate scrutiny" standard remains the prevailing test for gender-based discrimination.

Craig left equal protection doctrine in a complex state. The revised schema requires judges to discriminate among nonsuspect classifications, semisuspect classifications, and inherently suspect classifications and to apply the appropriate level of scrutiny: minimal ("rational basis"), intermediate ("substantial relationship to important objectives"), or strict ("compelling justification").

Between 1976 and 1984, the Supreme Court decided a series of gender discrimination cases that fell into no clear pattern. They involved subjects as diverse as alimony, fathers' rights, and sexual assault. The Court's resolution of these cases brought order and clarity to intermediate scrutiny by distinguishing between permissible and impermissible justifications for gender discrimination. Laws that were based on traditional or stereotyped notions about gender roles did not survive scrutiny. *Orr v. Orr* (1979) invalidated an Alabama statute that restricted eligibility for alimony to women. Neither the state's preference for "an allocation of family responsibilities in which the wife plays a dependent role" nor "a legislative purpose to provide help for a needy spouse "that used "sex as a proxy for need" counted as an important legislative objective. *Kirchberg v. Feenstra* (1981) effectively erased traditional marriage law by overturning Louisiana's "head and master" statute giving husbands exclusive control over marital property.

On the other hand, women's reproductive role may still provide an acceptable rationale for gender discrimination. When the Court is persuaded that the policy in question is related to the unique mother-child relationship, however flimsy the argument, scrutiny is minimal. A series of cases in the 1970s and 1980s involved the constitutionality of statutes that gave single fathers more limited rights than single mothers in such areas as custody, adoption, and immigration. These fathers won if they could show they had an ongoing relationship with their children (e.g., *Caban v Mohammed* [1979]), but a father who had not seen his daughter in several years lost his bid to prevent her adoption by her stepfather, even though he had made efforts to see the child (which the mother had rebuffed) (*Lehr v. Robertson* [1983]). *Michael M. v. Superior Court of Sonoma County* (1981) revealed how far the Court would go to accept a rationale based on reproductive functions. *Michael M.* upheld California's statutory rape law, which made it a crime for men to have sexual intercourse with women under 18 but not vice versa. Six justices concluded that the law was substantially related to the state's efforts to discourage teenage pregnancy. The dissenters found this rationale tenuous at best.

Rostker v. Goldberg (1981) was an outlier in this series of cases. It involved one of the most controversial of all gender issues, military service: to be precise, draft registration. No military draft has existed in the United States since 1973. But in 1980, in the aftermath of the Soviet invasion of Afghanistan, Congress enacted a law requiring men to register for the nonexistent draft when they reached 18. A young man challenged the constitutionality of this gender discrimination. The Court upheld the law, but not on the basis of sex stereotype or biological function; instead, the opinion stressed the fact that Congress and the Armed Forces prohibited women from serving in combat. By the late 1990s, women routinely filled combat positions even though the rules against such service remain on the books. If and when another young man brings a lawsuit, single-sex registration may not survive judicial scrutiny.

Craig v. Boren remains binding precedent. But the number of constitutional cases involving gender discrimination has dwindled to the extent that only three cases in the last 10 years have used the intermediate scrutiny doctrine. These cases show, however, that the *Craig* doctrine remains a powerful tool for achieving equality between the sexes. *J.E. B. v. Alabama ex rel. T.B.* (1994) prohibited the use of peremptory challenges to exclude jurors on the basis of sex. In *United States v. Virginia* (1996), the Court ruled that the Virginia Military Institute (VMI) had violated the Constitution by refusing to admit women. VMI, a state college, boasted that it was even tougher than the federal service academies. VMI's "adversative" training "sought "to instill mental and physical discipline in its cadets and impart to them a strong moral code." Students, faculty, administration, and alumni argued vehemently that a single-sex environment was necessary for this training.

The state had established a Virginia Women's Institute for Leadership at Mary Washington College. VWIL struck women would-be VMI students as no better a substitute for VMI than the hastily established law school at the Texas State University for Negroes had been an alternative to the University of Texas Law School (*Sweatt v. Painter*, 1951.) The Supreme Court agreed. Justice Ruth Bader Ginsburg, who had won several landmark sex discrimination cases in the 1970s, declared, "Virginia has shown no exceedingly persuasive justification for excluding women from VMI." In the absence of such a justification, the state could not "afford a unique educational opportunity only to males. However 'liberally' this plan serves the State's sons, it makes no provision for her daughters. That is not *equal* protection."

Some commentators (e.g., Karst, 1998; Merritt, 1998) argued that this ruling represented Ginsburg's attempt to do what as a lawyer she had urged the Court to do: declare gender an inherently suspect classification (Baer, 2002.) "An exceedingly persuasive justification" reads less like "substantial" than it does like the "compelling justification" standard that suspect classifications must meet. But the Court's most recent ruling, *Nguyen v. Immigration and Naturalization Service* (2001), made it clear that the *Craig* standard prevailed.

Tuan Anh Nguyen, born to a Vietnamese mother and an American G.I. father, arrived in the United States with his father, Joseph Boulais, in 1975 and became a lawful permanent resident. The Immigration and Naturalization Service ordered Nguyen deported as an alien felon in 1995, after he pled guilty to sexual assault on a child. Nguyen and Boulais appealed the deportation order on the grounds that Nguyen would have been a U.S. citizen had he been born abroad to an unmarried American mother, and that this discrimination between mothers and fathers was unconstitutional. They lost by one vote. Writing for the majority, Justice Anthony Kennedy found the law justified by its substantial relationship to Congress's important "objective of ensuring a blood tie between parent and child"—although DNA testing had proved that Boulais was Nguyen's biological father.

The courts have refused to rule that gender discrimination, like its racial counterpart, is inherently suspect. Gender cases receive intermediate scrutiny, not strict scrutiny. But there are three types of cases where the justices have treated gender-based classifications exactly as they have racial classifications.

Majority opinions speak, not in terms of sexism or racism or of discrimination against women or African Americans, but of discrimination on the basis of race or gender. Decisions refer not to "white supremacy" or "male dominance," but to the neutral concepts of "classification" and "discrimination." These word choices imply a premise, sometimes made explicit, that there is no difference between invidious and "reverse" discrimination; policies that impose inferior treatment on a dominant group, are "just as bad as" policies that disadvantage the out-group (*Regents of the University of California v. Bakke,* 1978; *Gratz v. Bollinger,* 2003.) Neither legislative history nor constitutional language commands a neutral interpretation. And yet the justices have adopted the premise that the amendment is aimed, not at laws that oppress, but at laws that make certain classifications. Judges ask not whom a law hurts, but on what basis it classifies. If the central idea is that law must concern itself with the disadvantaged (the idea of *Brown I*), decisions may well disturb the patterns of domination and subjection that prevail in society. But if the central idea is that race or sex discrimination is unacceptable (the idea of *Bakke* and *Gratz*), sooner or later the doctrine will lose its power to initiate change.

The effect of this neutral approach is revealed when we recall that the last equal protection case brought and won by a woman, *Kirchberg v. Feenstra,* was decided in 1981. Between 1971 and 2001, the Court decided 29 cases involving the constitutionality of gender discrimination cases. Ten of these cases were brought by or on behalf of women. The remaining 19 were brought by men. The appellant in *Taylor v. Louisiana* (1975), for example, the case that overturned *Hoyt v. Florida,* was Billy Taylor, who argued that an all-male jury pool deprived him of the right to be tried by a cross-section of the community.

Male plaintiffs initiated eight of the nine most recent cases. The one exception, the VMI case, was brought by the U.S. government. Part of the explanation for this discrepancy is the fact that men predominate in the pool of cases available for review. The number of male appellants far exceeds the number of women, even when criminal cases are excluded from the total (Baer, 1991). But the even-handed language of equal protection doctrine is receptive to men's claims. Women win more of their cases than men do, but men have won more cases than women. Some of the cases won by men also benefit women, but rulings like *Orr v. Orr* and *Caban v. Mohammed* benefit men at women's expense. Despite the important gains made in women's rights under constitutional law, the numbers suggest that contemporary doctrine

has served primarily as a way for men to vindicate their interests.

The second area in which gender discrimination is treated like race discrimination is what is called facially neutral discrimination: laws that do not mention race or gender but have a disproportionate impact on one group. The Burger Court reversed two decisions that had invalidated neutral laws with a disproportionate racial impact. *Washington v. Davis* (1976) upheld a verbal aptitude test for police recruits even though four times as many black applicants failed the test as did whites. *Arlington Heights v. Metropolitan Housing Development Corporation* (1977) rejected a claim that a local zoning regulation that discouraged multifamily dwellings unconstitutionally kept lower-income African American families out. Both cases insisted that the Equal Protection Clause forbade only intentional discrimination; disparate impact by itself was unaffected by the clause. Since the Court held no racial discrimination existed, the policies were evaluated under, and easily survived, minimal scrutiny.

The same nine justices who had decided *Davis* and *Arlington Heights* heard *Personnel Administrator v. Feeney* in 1979. At issue here was a provision for veterans' preference in civil service jobs. The national government and all but a few states had such a rule. The state of Massachusetts, Helen Feeney's employer for most of her working life, had an "absolute lifetime preference": any veteran who passed the relevant Civil Service test could bump any nonveteran on the eligibility list. This rule applied equally to male and female veterans; however, 98 percent of veterans living in Massachusetts were male. This statistic was almost a mirror image of an Armed Forces rule which remained in effect until 1967: no more than 2 percent of its members could be women. Even with this rule, the state had some management-level jobs open to women through the merit system. Feeney, the age of many World War II veterans, held several of these until 1975, when her position was abolished because of statewide budget cuts. Feeney took several examinations, placing high on the list each time, but she was consistently bumped by veterans. No nonclerical state job seemed open to her any longer.

Seven justices found no intentional discrimination. Following the line of the two racial cases, Potter Stewart insisted that "the distinction made by [the law] is, as it seems to be, quite simply between veterans and nonveterans, not between men and women." He defended the law as a reasonable method of rewarding patriotism and attracting responsible employees to government work. Only Justices Thurgood Marshall and William Brennan dissented. Although they had also dissented in *Davis,* they now treated the necessity of discriminatory intent as a closed issue. They characterized the veteran's preference as "purposeful gender based discrimination" because "this consequence [the virtual exclusion of women] followed foreseeably, indeed inexorably, from the long history of policies severely limiting women's participation in the military." They mentioned a fact ignored by the majority: until 1971, the regulations had exempted from veterans' preference any job "especially calling for women," which meant clerical work. The Court's insistence on evidence of a discriminatory purpose before a neutral statute with a disparate impact can be overturned drastically limits the use of the Equal Protection Clause as a vehicle for getting rid of policies that reinforce race and gender inequality. No racist or sexist intent is necessary to sustain this status quo. It sustains itself.

Whether or not gender discrimination exists is a threshold decision courts must make in cases where the sex bias is not explicit. Another necessary threshold decision in equal protection cases is whether the discrimination at issue is the result of public or private action. The *Civil Rights Cases* (1883) stipulated that state action was necessary for an equal protection violation to exist; therefore, the Fourteenth Amendment did not give Congress the power to forbid racial discrimination in privately owned public accommodations. Subsequent decisions have weakened this precedent. *Shelley v. Krae-mer* (1948) ruled that a "restrictive covenant"—an agreement among property owners not to sell to African Americans—could not be enforced in court.

Heart of Atlanta Motel v. United States (1964) sustained the public accommodations section of the Civil Rights Act of 1964 under the Commerce Clause. Congress has not prohibited private gender discrimination, but many state and local governments have. *Roberts v. United States Jaycees* (1984) upheld a Minnesota court's ruling that the state antidiscrimination law forced the Junior Chamber of Commerce to admit women. *Roberts* had no effect outside Minnesota, but the national organization behaved as though it had and directed all chapters to admit women.

The three doctrines of evenhanded application, discriminatory intent, and state action limit the utility of the Equal Protection Clause as a tool for ending male supremacy. None of these doctrines is commanded by the language of the history of the Fourteenth Amendment. Its authors did not clearly distinguish between racial discrimination and discrimination against a racial group (Baer, 1983). The provision forbids denial of equality, not the intent to do so. Section 1 does refer to "no state," but a plausible reading of "no state shall deny" is "every state shall grant." The Equal Protection Clause does not even provide interpreters with any useful guidance on how, if at all, to apply the guarantee to cases involving women. The historical fact that the primary concern of the authors of the three Civil War amendments was the status of the former slaves does not compel the interpreter to limit the amendments' scope to laws affecting African Americans. The legislative history of the Fourteenth Amendment does not suggest that the Framers meant it to apply to gender discrimination. In fact, the evidence is more negative than positive. However, the record contains no categorical statement that gender discrimination lies outside the scope of the guarantee.

The language of Section 1 is loose, if not lavish. There is no mention of race or any other kind of classification, and only the most general specification of categories of rights. This inclusive language gains significance when compared to its two neighbors. The Thirteenth Amendment mentions only one prohibition—against slavery or involuntary servitude—while the Fifteenth confines itself to one right, voting, and one set of classifications, racial. These differences in wording suggest that the choices of broad or narrow language may have been intentional. But arguments that the scope of Section 1 need not be confined to race alone do not resolve disputes about what specific areas are covered and what standards of review should be used when.

In the years following *Brown v. Board of Education*, constitutional doctrine jumped ahead of public policy and social consensus with regard to racial equality. The rest of the country had to catch up. Appellate courts have not shown similar boldness with respect to women's rights. Judges seem to find it necessary not to be too far ahead of society. In fact, the Supreme Court was behind the curve in decisions like *Goesaert* and *Hoyt*. Then, at about the same time the Equal Rights Amendment became a viable issue, Supreme Court decisions began to show the influence of the second wave of feminism. Participants in the ERA controversy considered the relationship of the proposed amendment to the revised doctrine, while at times judges indicated wariness to expand individual rights in the absence of a clear national consensus. The two developments peaked at about the same time. In the courts as in society, a long period of stasis preceded several years of active doctrinal change, which have been followed by two and a half decades of stasis. The Supreme Court heard no equal protection cases on gender discrimination between 1984 and 1994 and has heard only three since: *J.E.B.*, *Virginia*, and *Nguyen*. The important victories that women have won in courts have typically involved either statutory construction or some other constitutional provision than the Equal Protection Clause. The intermediate scrutiny standard has not lost its value, but fewer and fewer occasions arise where the rule is applicable.

However, the Supreme Court's ruling in *Nevada Department of Human Resources v. Hibbs* (2003) indicates that change may be coming. By a 6–3 vote, the Court uncharacteristically ruled that the Family and Medical Leave Act of 1993 was binding on state governments. Chief Justice William H. Rehnquist wrote that the FMLA was a valid exercise of Congress's Fourteenth Amendment power to prevent gender discrimination in the workplace. Since Rehnquist had never before held that the Fourteenth Amendment prohibited gender discrimination *per se*, his concession was a significant development.

Constitutional doctrine has often seemed to be searching for a compromise between tradition and modernity that mirrors the present societal consensus. This approach to gender discrimination accords with the familiar idea that law is the product of consensus among political actors. Law does not oppress; it simply makes errors in expressing this consensus. But a competing conception of law, less popular but equally tenable, is that law is an instrument of domination of some by others. According to this view, the law's purpose is to subjugate some people to others. To the extent that equal protection doctrine presumes a polity built on consensus rather than on subjection and domination, constitutional interpretation will not be a sufficient means to achieve gender equality.

See also *Brown v. Board of Education* (1954, 1955); Burger Court; Burger, Warren E.; The Civil Rights Cases (1883); Due Process Clauses; Equal Protection Clause; Equal Rights Amendment; Family and Medical Leave Act; Feminist Movement; Fifteenth Amendment; Fourteenth Amendment (1868); Fourteenth Amendment, Section 5 of the; *Frontiero v. Richardson* (1973); Ginsburg, Ruth Bader; *Heart of Atlanta Motel v. United States* (1964); Intermediate Scrutiny; *Korematsu v. United States* (1944); *Lochner v. New York* (1905); Rational Basis Test; Rehnquist Court; Rehnquist, William H.; Roosevelt, Franklin D.; *Shelley v. Kraemer* (1948); State Action Doctrine; *Slaughter-House Cases* (1873); Thirteenth Amendment; *United States v. Carolene Products* (Footnote 4); *United States v. Virginia* (1996); Warren Court; Warren, Earl

Bibliography

Baer, Judith A. 1983. *Equality Under the Constitution: Reclaiming the Fourteenth Amendment*. Ithaca, NY: Cornell University Press.

———. 1991. "Women's Rights and the Limits of Constitutional Doctrine." *Western Political Quarterly* 42 (December): 821.

———. 2002. "Advocate on the Court: Ruth Bader Ginsburg and the Limits of Formal Equality." *Rehnquist Justice" Understanding the Court Dynamic.* Ed. Earl M. Maltz. Lawrence, Kans.: University Press of Kansas: 216.

Karst, Kenneth L. 1998. "'The Way Women Are': Some Notes in the Margin for Ruth Bader Ginsburg." *Hawaii Law Review* 20: 619.

Leuchtenberg, William E. 1995. *The Supreme Court Reborn: The Constitutional Revolution in the Age of Roosevelt.* New York: Oxford University Press.

Merritt, Deborah Jones. 1998. "Hearing the Voices of Individual Women and Men: Justice Ruth Bader Ginsburg." *Hawaii Law Review* 20: 635.

Judith Baer

GENERAL WARRANTS. *See* Writs of Assistance and General Warrants

GERRYMANDERING. *See* Racial Gerrymandering; Reapportionment

GIDEON V. WAINWRIGHT (1963)

The Sixth Amendment to the U.S. Constitution stipulates that "[i]n all criminal prosecutions, the accused shall enjoy the right ... to have the assistance of counsel for his defence." The amendment, however, makes no reference to the provision of counsel at governmental expense. Nevertheless, in *Powell v. Alabama* (1932), the U.S. Supreme Court noted that, "in a capital case, where the defendant ... [is] incapable adequately of making his own defense ... , it is the duty of the [state] court, whether requested or not, to assign counsel for him as a necessary requisite of due process of law." Shortly thereafter, the justices held in *Johnson v. Zerbst* (1938) that the Sixth Amendment required the appointment of counsel for all federal criminal defendants charged with felonies. Four years later, *Betts v. Brady* (1942) held that the same rule did not apply to state prosecutions. Instead, the Court required the appointment of counsel only in those "special circumstances" where the absence of

counsel rendered the criminal proceedings "fundamentally unfair."

The special circumstances rule in state criminal proceedings prevailed until *Gideon v. Wainwright.* Clarence Earl Gideon, a middle-aged drifter who had been in and out of prisons most of his life, was charged in a Florida state court with breaking and entering into the Bar Harbor Poolroom in Panama City, Florida, and stealing beer, wine, and some change from a vending machine. At his trial, Gideon, claiming indigency, requested that the judge appoint a lawyer to represent him. The judge refused, noting that under Florida law, indigent defendants were entitled to appointed counsel only in capital cases. Gideon represented himself in a jury trial, where he was convicted and sentenced to five years in the state penitentiary for petty larceny. Gideon requested a writ of habeas corpus in the Florida Supreme Court, alleging that the trial court had abridged his Sixth Amendment rights. After that court denied him relief, Gideon, from his prison cell and on paper borrowed from a prison guard, hand-wrote a petition for certiorari to the U.S. Supreme Court.

Because Gideon had petitioned *in forma pauperis* ("in the manner of pauper"), the Supreme Court appointed Abe Fortas, a prominent Washington lawyer who later became an associate justice, to argue Gideon's case. Specifically, the Court instructed Fortas to address the question, "Should this Court's holding in *Betts v. Brady* be reconsidered?" In a three-hour oral argument, Fortas contended forcefully that a criminal court was not properly constituted unless there was counsel for the defense. Without such counsel, he said, a civilized nation cannot "pretend that it is having a fair trial." Twenty-two states agreed with Fortas, filing amicus briefs encouraging the Court to reverse *Betts;* only two states other than Florida argued that *Betts* should be upheld.

On March 18, 1963, the Supreme Court overruled *Betts,* holding that the Sixth Amendment's guarantee of counsel, as applied to the states through the Due Process Clause of the Fourteenth Amendment, required that a state appoint counsel to all indigent defendants charged with serious offenses. Writing for the unanimous Court, Justice Hugo L. Black noted:

[R]eason and reflection require us to recognize that in our adversary system of criminal justice, any person haled into court, who is too poor to hire a lawyer, cannot be assured a fair trial unless counsel is provided for him. This seems to us to be an obvious truth.... [L]awyers in criminal courts are necessities, not luxuries. The right of one charged with a crime to counsel may not be deemed fundamental and essential to fair trials in some countries, but it is in ours.

Gideon's conviction was thus overturned. At his retrial, and with the assistance of appointed counsel, Gideon was acquitted by a jury.

Gideon v. Wainwright recognized the necessity of legal representation in securing a fair trial. Subsequently, the Supreme Court extended the right to counsel. *Gideon,* to recall, had required that a state appoint counsel to all indigent defendants charged with *serious* offenses. In *Argersinger v. Hamlin* (1972), the justices declared that no person could be imprisoned for *any* offense—whether classified as petty, misdemeanor, or felony—unless that person had the opportunity to be represented by counsel at trial. Seven years later, in *Scott v. Illinois* (1979), the Court clarified this extension, holding that individuals charged with offenses where imprisonment was statutorily authorized but not judicially imposed did not enjoy a Sixth Amendment right to state-appointed counsel.

See also Accused, Rights of the; Bill of Rights, Incorporation of; Black, Hugo L.; Counsel, Right to; Due Process, Procedural; Fortas, Abe; *Powell v. Alabama* (1932); Sixth Amendment

Bibliography
Lewis, Anthony. *Gideon's Trumpet.* New York: Vintage Books, 1964.

Richard Glenn

GINSBURG, RUTH BADER (1933–)

During the Senate hearings preceding her confirmation as the nation's 107th Supreme Court Justice, Ruth Bader Ginsburg surmised that, as the daughter of Jewish immigrants, "[w]hat has become of me could happen only in America" (Senate Judiciary Committee 1993, 50).

Joan Ruth Bader was born on March 15, 1933, in Brooklyn, New York. Her father, Nathan, emigrated from Russia at the age of 13. Her maternal grandparents emigrated from Poland four months before her mother, Celia, was born. Nathan Bader worked at a men's clothing store. Celia Amster Bader was a homemaker who instilled in her daughter an independence of spirit and thought. Celia also insisted that her daughter obtain a good education. Justice Ginsburg's earliest memories include accompanying her mother to the library and her mother shopping for bargains to save money for Ruth's college education (Halberstam 1998).

In June 1950, Ruth Bader graduated sixth in her high school class. She attended Cornell University on scholarship and graduated first in her class in 1954. Shortly thereafter, Ruth Bader married Martin Ginsburg, a first-year law student at Harvard, whom she had dated as an undergraduate at Cornell. Following their marriage, the Ginsburgs moved to Oklahoma for two years so that Martin Ginsburg could fulfill his obligation to the United States Army (Halberstam 1998).

In 1956 Ruth Ginsburg began her first year of study at Harvard Law School while Martin Ginsburg returned to Harvard to begin his second year. Ruth Ginsburg excelled academically and was elected to the *Harvard Law Review.* In 1958 her husband graduated from Harvard and accepted a position with a law firm in New York. Seeking to balance her family life with her educational pursuits, Ginsburg transferred from Harvard to Columbia Law School for her third year. She was elected to the *Columbia Law Review* and, in 1959, graduated at the top of her class (Halberstam 1998).

Following graduation, Ginsburg encountered gender discrimination as she sought employment. The relatively tolerant atmosphere she enjoyed in law school was not representative of the climate women faced in the job market. For example, Harvard Law School Dean Albert Sachs and Columbia

Law Professor Gerald Gunther both recommended that Justice Felix Frankfurter hire Ginsburg as a law clerk. Although Frankfurter acknowledged that her credentials were impeccable, he declined to offer Ginsburg a clerkship, admitting that he was not prepared to hire a female in that capacity (Gunther 1998).

Ginsburg ultimately obtained a clerkship with U.S. District Court Judge Edmund L. Palmieri in 1959 (Gunther 1998). Ginsburg became a research associate for the Project on International Procedure at Columbia Law School in 1961 (Halberstam 1988). Two years later she joined the faculty at Rutgers Law School, becoming the second woman ever to teach there (Ginsburg 1997).

In 1971, Ginsburg participated in her first case before the United States Supreme Court by coauthoring the brief with the American Civil Liberties Union (ACLU) legal director, Melvin Wulf, challenging the constitutionality of sex-based classifications. Following that victory, the ACLU established the Women's Rights Project, which Ginsburg codirected, to wage a comprehensive legal battle against sex discrimination (Gilbert and Moore 1981). Throughout the 1970s, Ginsburg wrote briefs on behalf of litigants in nine cases and presented oral argument before the Supreme Court in six of those cases, prevailing on five occasions (Morris 2002).

In 1972, Ginsburg joined the faculty at Columbia Law School, becoming the first woman on its faculty to obtain tenure (Ginsburg 1997). Professor Ginsburg was a productive scholar at Columbia, simultaneously participating in an historic litigation campaign. The success of this litigation campaign was dramatic: the Supreme Court reversed nearly one hundred years of precedent, striking down gender-based classifications as violative of the Equal Protection Clause of the Fourteenth Amendment. Initially, the Court found that such classifications failed even the permissive rational basis standard. Ginsburg's ultimate goal was to persuade the Court to apply the most demanding legal standard, strict scrutiny, to gender discrimination claims, arguing that gender was comparable to race: both are visible, immutable characteristics unrelated to one's

ability to contribute to society (Morris 2002). Discrimination based on either characteristic was equally invidious. Although declining to adopt the strict scrutiny standard, the Court was ultimately persuaded to apply "intermediate scrutiny" to gender discrimination cases. Although less stringent than strict scrutiny, the intermediate or heightened scrutiny standard is more demanding than the rational basis test.

President Jimmy Carter appointed Ruth Bader Ginsburg to the Court of Appeals for the District of Columbia Circuit in 1980. During her 13-year tenure, Ginsburg established a reputation as a consensus-building, moderate judge. On June 14, 1993, President Bill Clinton nominated Judge Ginsburg to the United States Supreme Court. Her selection was not controversial, and she was easily confirmed. Ideologically, Ginsburg is a left-leaning centrist. Justice Ginsburg adheres to a limited view of the role of judges and is not considered an outcome-oriented activist (Morris 2002).

Over the course of her professional life Ruth Bader Ginsburg has made significant contributions to the development of equal protection jurisprudence. As a lawyer, Ginsburg persuaded the Supreme Court to extend the Constitution's equal protection guarantee to sex-based classifications. She gradually persuaded the Court to raise the standard of review applied in cases presenting sex discrimination claims. As a Supreme Court justice, Ginsburg authored the majority opinion in *United States v. Virginia* (1996) in which the Court held that Virginia Military Institute's male-only admissions policy violated the Equal Protection Clause of the Fourteenth Amendment. The Court further held that the state's proposed remedy of a separate women's college did not cure the constitutional violation. This ruling emphasized that state-funded schools could not discriminate on the basis of sex. This ruling also required a more rigorous remedy to cure the constitutional violation than the Court had imposed in the past. Her majority opinion in *United States v. Virginia* is evidence that Ruth Bader Ginsburg remains a faithful defender of equality as a United States Supreme Court Justice.

See also American Civil Liberties Union; Equal Protection Clause; Equal Protection Jurisprudence; Feminist Movement; Fourteenth Amendment (1868); Gender-Based Discrimination; Rational Basis Test; Strict Scrutiny; *United States v. Virginia* (1996)

Bibliography

Gilbert, Lynn, and Gaylen Moore. 1981. *Particular Passions: Talks With Women Who Have Shaped Our Times.* New York: Clarkson N. Potter.

Ginsburg, Ruth Bader. 1997. "Remarks On Women's Progress in The Legal Profession in The United States." *Tulsa Law Journal* 33 (1): 13–21.

Gunther, Gerald. 1998. "Ruth Bader Ginsburg: A Personal, Very Fond Tribute." *Hawaii Law Review* 20 (2): 583–601.

Halberstam, Malvina. 1998. "Ruth Bader Ginsburg: The First Jewish Woman on the United States Supreme Court." *Cardozo Law Review* 19 (4): 1441–54.

Morris, Melanie K. 2002. "Ruth Bader Ginsburg and Gender Equality: A Reassessment of Her Contribution." *Cardozo Women's Law Journal* 9 (1): 1–25.

Senate Judiciary Committee. *A Nomination Of Ruth Bader Ginsburg, To Be Associate Justice Of The Supreme Court Of The United States.* 103d Cong., 1st sess., 1993; 50.

Melanie Morris

GITLOW V. NEW YORK (1925)

Gitlow v. New York was the first Supreme Court decision to hold that the Bill of Rights limits the states' power to regulate free speech and press. The case arose in the context of the Red Scare (1919–1920) that followed World War I and the triumph of the communist revolution in the Soviet Union. Public fear of communism and anarchy led a number of states to pass new laws or begin enforcing older laws aimed in part at suppressing alleged subversive speech.

Benjamin Gitlow was indicted for the felony of advocating criminal anarchy, defined in a 1902 New York statute as "the doctrine that organized government should be overthrown by force or violence … or by any unlawful means." Gitlow, a member of the revolutionary wing of the American Socialist Party and former member of the New York legislature, arranged for the printing and distribution of the party's "The Left Wing Manifesto." The manifesto advocated "proletarian revolutionary struggle" and a "mass political strike" directed at "the overthrow of the political organization upon which capitalistic exploitation depends."

The Fourteenth Amendment to the Constitution prohibits states from denying anyone "life, liberty or property without due process of law." Gitlow's lawyers argued that the statute was therefore unconstitutional. One of the elements of the liberty protected by the Fourteenth Amendment's Due Process Clause, Gitlow contended, was the liberty of speech and press referred to in the First Amendment ("Congress shall make no law … abridging the freedom of speech, or of the press"). Speech was a right that could be restrained only when its exercise was likely to cause a substantive evil. As the statute did not require a showing of such a connection between speech and an illegal result, it was unconstitutional.

The argument was rejected by the courts of New York. The case reached a Supreme Court that had adopted Justice Oliver Wendell Holmes' formulation in *Schenck v. United States* (1919) that Congress could punish speech if it constituted a "clear and present danger." Justice Edward T. Sanford, writing for the Court, relied on *Schenck* in rejecting Gitlow's appeal. It was up to the legislature to decide if the articulation of particular ideas constituted a clear and present danger, he declared, and by passing the statute, New York had declared speech like Gitlow's to be such a danger.

More importantly, however, all the justices agreed that the Due Process Clause did protect the rights of speech and press from state action—even though in this instance, they upheld Gitlow's prison sentence on the grounds that the manifesto was meant to incite unlawful acts. Until *Gitlow*, the Supreme Court had held that the First Amendment limited the powers only of Congress, not the states. The new interpretation would be drawn upon in the coming years to minimize state restrictions on speech, and the Gitlow decision would later be understood as the case that began the incorporation into the Fourteenth Amendment of most of the liberties in the Bill of Rights. That meant the Bill of Rights would provide protection against abridgement of civil liberties by the states as well as the federal government.

An additional aspect of *Gitlow* was the dissent by Justice Holmes for himself and Justice Louis Dembitz Brandeis, arguing that Gitlow's speech was mere advocacy of an idea and did not constitute a clear and present danger. "Every idea is an incitement," Holmes wrote, because it is offered in the hope that the listener will accept and act upon it. Holmes denied that the state could punish speech because of its content, for the First Amendment required Gitlow's speech to be allowed in the absence of a "present danger of an attempt to overthrow the government by force." In keeping with his notion that a democracy should be a free marketplace of ideas, Holmes added, "If in the long run the beliefs expressed in proletarian dictatorship are destined to be accepted by the dominant forces of the community, the only meaning of free speech is that they should be given their chance and have their way."

Gitlow had served three years in Sing Sing prison before the Supreme Court decision was handed down. He was pardoned a few months later by Governor Al Smith, who cited the Holmes/Brandeis dissent. By the time he died in 1965, Gitlow had renounced communism, but the case that bears his name had become an important part of American constitutional law. As Justice Felix Frankfurter wrote in 1951, "It would be disingenuous to deny that the dissent in *Gitlow* has been treated with the respect usually accorded to a decision," and the precept that the mere advocacy of an idea should not be punished would soon be enshrined in American law.

See also Bill of Rights; Bill of Rights, Incorporation of; Brandeis, Louis D.; *Brandenburg v. Ohio* (1969); Clear and Present Danger Doctrine; Due Process Clauses; Due Process, Substantive; First Amendment; Fourteenth Amendment (1868); Frankfurter, Felix; Fundamental Rights; Holmes, Oliver Wendell, Jr.; Liberty; Press, Freedom of the; Red Scare; Sanford, Edward T.; *Schenck v. United States* (1919); Speech, Freedom of

Bibliography

Stone, Geoffrey R. 2004. *Perilous Times: Free Speech in Wartime From the Sedition Act of 1798 to the War on Terrorism.* New York: W. W. Norton.

Wermiel, Stephen J. 1992. "Rights in the Modern Era: Applying the Bill of Rights to the States," 1 *William & Mary Bill of Rights Journal* 121.

Philippa Strum

GOLDBERG, ARTHUR (1908–1990)

Associate Justice Arthur Goldberg's story mirrors the American dream. He was the son of immigrants who faced poverty and prejudice that forced him to take nontraditional routes to success. His experiences fostered unmistakable views on salient issues, particularly labor relations; however, these views assisted Goldberg in obtaining a position on the U.S. Supreme Court.

Goldberg's parents, Joseph and Rebecca, were from the Ukraine, immigrating to the United States to escape virulent anti-Semitism and violent pogroms. The Goldbergs settled on the west side of Chicago and raised a large family. Arthur was born on August 8, 1908, the last of eight surviving children. When Goldberg's father died in 1916, Arthur worked odd jobs to assist the family; as the youngest, he was also able to continue his education. At age 16 he graduated from high school with distinction—the only child of the Goldberg family to receive a diploma.

Goldberg continued his education by attending a junior college (Crane) during the day and De Paul University in the evening, defraying the costs of tuition through scholarships. In 1926, Goldberg transferred to prestigious Northwestern University, again obtaining a scholarship, and graduated a year later in 1927 when he was 19.

During this period, Goldberg witnessed the sensational trial of Nathan Leopold and Richard Loeb, who had murdered a Chicago boy, and Clarence Darrow's orchestration of their defense in order to spare them the death penalty. Inspired, Goldberg pursued a career in law. He received a scholarship from Northwestern University Law School and supplemented his income by working part-time in the construction industry. Indeed, it was here, as well as during his childhood on the west side of Chicago, that Goldberg saw firsthand the plight of the worker. Such experiences would heavily influence Goldberg's future career choices.

In law school, as elsewhere, Goldberg excelled despite his arduous work schedule. He graduated in two and a half years at the age of 21. Ironically, his first case was his own, as he sued for admittance to the Illinois state bar, fighting against an age limitation. He won and received a court order admitting him to practice.

Goldberg began his career with a prominent law firm, Pritzger and Pritzger, practicing legal finance. Though Goldberg excelled, he became dissatisfied with working for "big business," as his sympathies lay with workers. Following his principles, he left Pritzger and Pritzger in 1933 to start his own practice and joined the Civil Liberties Committee (soon to merge with the ACLU). During this same period, Goldberg became acquainted with many future members of Congress and future heads of labor. Throughout the 1930s, Goldberg gained a reputation for his liberal beliefs and his considerable legal skills, but also revealed a strong opposition to communist influence in labor.

In 1938 Goldberg took the position as advisor to the American Newspaper Guild during a major strike, and by 1939 he had extracted major victories for labor at the expense of the Hearst newspaper empire. This success led to other major roles in representing labor in both the prewar and postwar periods, including serving as counsel to the Steelworkers Organizing Committee in 1940, and crafting the merger of the American Federation of Labor (AFL) and the Congress of Industrial Organizations (CIO) in 1955.

As the conflict in Europe erupted, Goldberg recognized early on that Hitler represented a threat to humanity. He actively lobbied for U.S. intervention in the war, joining a council of intellectuals in Chicago, and serving on the White Committee. The attack on Pearl Harbor piqued Goldberg's patriotism and he joined the war effort first as a civilian and then as an officer in the Office of Strategic Services, an intelligence gathering agency; Goldberg's labor contacts proved instrumental in his efforts to gather intelligence abroad.

While Goldberg was involved in many major labor strikes, disputes, and lobbying efforts, his work in 1959, fighting the anti-union Landrum-Griffin bill, certainly affected the course of his life. During this battle, Goldberg met and befriended a young Senator named John Kennedy. Also in 1959, Goldberg spent three weeks presenting labor's case regarding a Taft-Hartley injunction before the Supreme Court (*United Steelworkers v. United States*); he lost, but his performance garnered high praise.

As the 1960 election loomed, Goldberg threw his support, and that of labor, behind Senator Kennedy. This support, and their ongoing friendship, landed Goldberg a seat in the cabinet as Secretary of Labor. This appointment was not Goldberg's first choice. His preferred position, the position of Attorney General, was filled by the president's brother Robert. Ultimately, Goldberg served as Secretary of Labor for two years.

During the summer of 1962, Justice Felix Frankfurter retired and President Kennedy immediately turned to Goldberg to fill the so-called "Jewish" seat. This appointment solidified an already liberal court by replacing the restrained Frankfurter with a more activist Goldberg. Goldberg believed that the Court could and should address current social problems. He also viewed the Constitution as a living document.

Goldberg had spent three years on the Supreme Court when Adlai Stevenson, Ambassador to the United Nations for the United States, died suddenly. President Johnson sought someone of similar stature and prestige to replace Stevenson, as well as someone who could handle tough negotiations. Johnson requested Goldberg's service, and Goldberg felt compelled to accept. As he said in 1965, "In all candor, I would rather the President had not asked me to undertake this duty. But it appears perhaps I can at this stage of our national life make a contribution, I hope, in this area of foreign affairs" (Cushman 1995, 469.) He did not do so without conditions; Goldberg sought and received assurances from Johnson that the president was willing to negotiate a settlement to the Vietnam conflict and that as ambassador to the United Nations Goldberg would be the primary advisor to the president.

While Goldberg was able to secure many successes in this position, including negotiating a ceasefire between India and Pakistan in 1965, he was unable to significantly affect Johnson's policies in Vietnam. Goldberg argued for de-escalation while the United States became more mired in the conflict. Goldberg became increasingly dissatisfied with his post. He resigned from his position with the United Nations in April, 1968. after Johnson passed him over for as chief negotiator for peace talks with North Vietnam.

Goldberg returned to private practice as the senior partner in the prestigious New York law firm of Paul, Weiss, Goldberg, Rifkind, Wharton, and Garrison. In 1969, Goldberg entered electoral politics and attempted to oust the incumbent governor of New York, Nelson Rockefeller. After this defeat, Goldberg retreated from public life and moved to Washington. During this time Goldberg continued to practice law, to teach law, and to serve on various international commissions. Goldberg even returned to the Supreme Court as a party in 1972, arguing against Major League Baseball in *Flood v. Kuhn, et al.* (1972). President Jimmy Carter appointed Goldberg ambassador to the Belgrade Conference on Human Rights in 1977. In 1978 Goldberg received the Medal of Freedom for his service to the nation.

Given his attitudes and experiences, had Goldberg spent more time on the Court, his contributions to the civil liberties jurisprudence would likely be considerable. However, Goldberg spent only three years on the Court. Perhaps, it is easier to characterize Goldberg by referring to justices with longer tenures and more well-known reputations for liberalism and support of civil liberties. During this time period on cases dealing with the

First Amendment, Goldberg generally agreed with Justices Brennan, Douglas, Warren, and Black; his interagreement scores with these justices ranged from a low of 85 percent (Black) to a high of 93 percent (Douglas and Brennan). In the areas of civil rights or privacy, his interagreement scores with the same four justices are even higher. Clearly, the appointment of Arthur Goldberg strengthened the liberal activist bloc on the Court.

It would be hard to claim a strong legacy for Arthur Goldberg; he only authored 36 opinions during his short tenure. However, the list includes several significant civil liberties cases. It is clear from these few cases that Goldberg strongly supported the rights of the individual. He willingly utilized the Court's power to safeguard liberties and applied the highest levels of scrutiny to any attempt by the state to infringe upon preferred freedoms.

Aptheker v. Secretary of State (1964) is among his more prominent opinions. In this case, the Court struck down part of the Subversive Activities Control Act that restricted the ability of some individuals to obtain passports. Goldberg recognized that the right to travel cannot be denied indiscriminately without violating the Fifth Amendment. In *Gibson v. Florida Legislative Investigation Committee* (1963), Goldberg again supported the cause of the individual, prohibiting the state of Florida from using its power to compel groups to provide the names of their members. The right of association, according to the Justice, could only be infringed if the state "convincingly" showed a "compelling interest."

His sense of equal justice for all was offended by the slow pace of desegregation, and he made his contempt clear in *Watson v. City of Memphis* (1963) by explaining, "[t]he rights to desegregation of public parks and other public recreational facilities are, like all such rights, present rights, and not merely hopes to some future enjoyment of some formalistic constitutional promise; the basic guaranties of the Federal Constitution are warrants for the here and now, and, unless there is an overwhelmingly compelling reason, they are to be promptly fulfilled."

Goldberg's greatest contribution, in terms of civil liberties, stems from his concurrence in *Griswold v. Connecticut* (1965). It should not be surprising that Goldberg envisioned a Constitution that protected a right to privacy, and to Goldberg the promise of privacy was fulfilled by the Ninth Amendment. Goldberg wrote:

I do agree that the concept of liberty protects those personal rights that are fundamental, and is not confined to the specific terms of the Bill of Rights. My conclusion that the concept of liberty is not so restricted and that it embraces the right of marital privacy though that right is not mentioned explicitly in the Constitution is supported both by numerous decisions of this Court, referred to in the Court's opinion, and by the language and history of the Ninth Amendment.

This statement of the right to privacy was utilized by the justices of the Court when handing down the landmark decision of *Roe v. Wade* (1973). Clearly, Goldberg's definition of privacy is a key part of his legacy.

Arthur Goldberg suffered a fatal heart attack on January 19, 1990. His wife of 51 years, Dorothy Kurgans Goldberg, had passed away in 1988. Goldberg was buried with full military honors in Arlington National Cemetery. He was inducted into the Labor Hall of Fame posthumously in 1995.

See also American Civil Liberties Union; Black, Hugo L.; Brennan, William J., Jr.; Douglas, William O.; *Griswold v. Connecticut* (1965); Ninth Amendment; Privacy, Constitutional Rights of; *Roe v. Wade* (1973); Warren, Earl; Warren Court

Bibliography

Cushman, Clare, ed. 1995. *The Supreme Court Justices.* 2nd ed. Washington, D.C.: Congressional Quarterly.

Goldberg, Dorothy Kurgans. 1975. *A Public View of a Private Life.* New York: Charterhouse.

Shils, Edward B. 1997. "Arthur Goldberg: Proof of the American Dream." *Monthly Labor Review* (January).

Stebenne, David L. 1996. *Arthur J. Goldberg: New Deal Liberal.* New York: Oxford University Press.

Rorie Spill Solberg

GONZALES V. RAICH (2005)

This case involved two California women, Angel Raich and Diane Monson, who used marijuana in their homes as treatment for several illnesses on their doctors' recommendation. Such medicinal use is expressly protected under the Compassionate Use Act, enacted into California law in 1996 through Proposition 215, a citizens' ballot initiative. Federal law, however, makes the possession or use of marijuana for any purpose a crime. The 1970 Controlled Substances Act (CSA), that is, classifies marijuana as a Schedule I controlled substance, meaning that in Congress's view, it has a high potential for abuse, no officially accepted medicinal use, and no safe level of use under medical supervision. When agents of the U.S. Drug Enforcement Administration learned that Monson was cultivating six marijuana plants in her home, they obtained a warrant, entered her home, and seized and destroyed her plants.

Ordinarily, federal law preempts contrary state law, but the federal law must be one that Congress has power to enact in the first place. Monson and Raich thus brought a civil suit in federal court, claiming that application of the CSA to them exceeded Congress's power to regulate interstate commerce, and seeking a declaratory judgment and injunction against future DEA raids. While the District Court denied such relief, a divided panel of the Ninth U.S. Circuit Court of Appeals reversed, holding that application of the CSA to Monson was beyond Congress's power. The Supreme Court granted review, and Justice John Paul Stevens, writing for a six-to-three majority, reversed the Ninth Circuit, holding that Congress can constitutionally criminalize the possession and medicinal use of marijuana, even on a licensed physician's recommendation and under the express protection of state law. While early cases like *McCulloch v. Maryland* (1819) and *Gibbons v. Ogden* (1824) cast a long shadow in *Raich*, the three key Commerce Clause rulings directly involved were *Wickard v. Filburn* (1942), *United States v. Lopez* (1995), and *United States v. Morrison* (2000). In *Wickard*, the Court took an expansive view of Congressional power under the Commerce Clause, but in *Lopez* and *Morrison* the more conservative Rehnquist Court sought to limit federal power over matters not truly involving interstate commerce. While Justice Stevens argued that *Raich* is indistinguishable from *Wickard* and distinguishable from *Lopez* and *Morrison,* Justice Sandra Day O'Connor argued just the opposite in a powerful dissent. Justice Clarence Thomas also added a powerful dissent based on textual, structural, and originalist considerations.

Though *Raich* is a moderately complex case, the upshot was that the judges simply had to choose which of two basic, powerful principles would prevail—deference to federal power or limits on federal power—and six of them chose the former. It remains to be seen what real impact this ruling will have, as it does not invalidate state medical marijuana laws, but rather only affirms that the federal government can raid, prosecute, and incarcerate the likes of Monson and Raich under the CSA. Ninety-nine percent of marijuana prosecutions take place in state court under state law. Law enforcement officials in most of the 12 states with medical marijuana laws announced that *Raich* would be largely irrelevant to their daily operations.

See also Drug Enforcement Administration; Drugs, War on; Federalism and Civil Rights and Liberties; O'Connor, Sandra Day; Drugs, Private Use of; Rehnquist Court; Stevens, John Paul; Thomas, Clarence; *United States v. Lopez* (1995)

Martin Carcieri

GOOD-FAITH EXCEPTION

The exclusionary rule requires courts to suppress illegally obtained evidence in criminal cases. In *Weeks v. United States* (1914), the United States Supreme Court created the rule to enforce the Fourth Amendment guarantee against unreasonable search and seizure. Under the Court's decision in *Mapp v. Ohio* (1961), the rule became binding on state as well as federal courts. The rule has always been controversial. Conservative critics of the rule believe it hampers law enforcement. Others object

to excluding probative evidence on the ground that it impedes the truth-finding function of courts. In the 1980s, a more conservative Supreme Court under Chief Justice Warren E. Burger, a long-time critic of the exclusionary rule, carved out a "good-faith exception" to the rule.

Under the good-faith exception, evidence obtained on the basis of a search warrant that is subsequently invalidated may be admitted in evidence at trial if the officers who conducted the search relied on the warrant in good faith. The doctrine emerged from two 1984 decisions of the U.S. Supreme Court: *United States v. Leon* and *Massachusetts v. Sheppard.* In *Leon,* police officers, acting on a tip from a confidential informant of unproven reliability, obtained a search warrant from a magistrate. In executing the warrant at a residence, the officers seized a substantial quantity of illicit drugs. The investigation led eventually to Leon, who was turned over to federal authorities for prosecution. Responding to Leon's motion to suppress this evidence, the federal district court ruled that the state magistrate had erred in issuing the initial search warrant because at that time police lacked sufficient information to constitute probable cause. The error was made by the magistrate who issued the warrant, not by the police, who were deemed to be acting in good faith. Nevertheless, under existing Fourth Amendment law, the evidence had to be suppressed.

The Supreme Court ultimately held that the evidence could be admitted because to exclude such evidence would have no deterrent effect on police misconduct. Writing for the Court, Justice Byron White concluded that that "the marginal or nonexistent benefits produced by suppressing evidence obtained in objectively reasonable reliance on a subsequently invalidated search warrant cannot justify the substantial costs of exclusion." Dissenting, Justice William Brennan asserted that "it is clear that we have not been treated to an honest assessment of the merits of the exclusionary rule but have instead been drawn into a curious world where the 'costs' of excluding illegally obtained evidence loom to exaggerated heights and where the 'benefits' of such exclusion are made to disappear with a mere wave of the hand."

Justice White's majority opinion in *United States v. Leon* identified four situations involving police reliance on a warrant where the good-faith exception to the exclusionary rule does not apply: (1) if the magistrate was misled by an affidavit that the affiant knew was false or would have known was false except for reckless disregard for the truth; (2) if the magistrate wholly abandons his or her judicial role; (3) if the affidavit is so lacking in indicia of probable cause as to render belief in its existence unreasonable; and (4) if the warrant is so facially deficient that the executing officer cannot reasonably presume its validity.

It is important to note that the good-faith exception developed in *Leon* applies only to cases where police officers rely on warrants that are later held to be invalid; it does not apply to warrantless searches. In *Illinois v. Krull* (1987), the Supreme Court extended the logic of *Leon* by ruling that the good-faith exception permits the introduction of evidence obtained by an officer in reliance upon a statute authorizing warrantless administrative searches where the statute is later declared unconstitutional. Writing for the majority in a five-to-four decision, Justice Harry Blackmun concluded, "The application of the exclusionary rule to suppress evidence obtained by an officer acting in objectively reasonable reliance on a statute would have as little deterrent effect on the officer's actions as would the exclusion of evidence when an officer acts in objectively reasonable reliance on a warrant."

Critics of the good-faith exception object to the underlying assumption as to the scope and purpose of the Fourth Amendment exclusionary rule. In their view, the rule is not merely a judicially created device to safeguard Fourth Amendment values by deterring police misconduct. It is rather a remedy to which anyone whose Fourth Amendment rights have been violated, whether by the police or by a magistrate, is entitled. As Justice Brennan argued in his *Leon* dissent, "[I]f the [Fourth] Amendment is to have any meaning, police and the courts cannot be regarded as constitutional strangers to each other;

because the evidence-gathering role of the police is directly linked to the evidence-admitting function of the courts, an individual's Fourth Amendment rights may be undermined as completely by one as by the other."

As with other provisions of the Bill of Rights, the Fourth Amendment sets a minimal national standard. Under our system of judicial federalism, state courts are free to interpret counterpart provisions of their respective state constitutions to provide their citizens with greater protection than is required by the federal Constitution. Most states have adopted the good-faith exception; a significant number have not. For example, in *State v. Novembrino* (1987), the New Jersey Supreme Court refused to follow the good-faith exception as a matter of state law. The court concluded that a good-faith exception would "ultimately reduce respect for and compliance with the probable cause standard."

See also Accused, Rights of the; Blackmun, Harry A.; Brennan, William J., Jr.; Burger Court; Burger, Warren E.; Fourth Amendment; *Mapp v. Ohio* (1961); White, Byron R.

Bibliography

Bernardi, Frederick A. 1980. "The Exclusionary Rule: Is a Good Faith Standard Needed to Preserve a Liberal Interpretation of the Fourth Amendment?" 30 *De Paul Law Review* 51.

del Carmen, Rolando V. 2003. *Criminal Procedure, Law and Practice.* 6th ed. Belmont, CA: Wadsworth Publishing Co.

Kamisar, Yale. 1984. "Gates, 'Probable Cause,' 'Good Faith,' and Beyond." 69 *Iowa Law Review* 551.

Scheb, John M., and John M. Scheb II. 2006. *Criminal Procedure.* Belmont, CA: Thomson/Wadsworth.

Stephens, Otis H., Jr., and Richard A. Glenn. 2006. *Unreasonable Searches and Seizures: Rights and Liberties under the Law.* Santa Barbara, CA: ABC-CLIO.

John M. Scheb II and Otis H. Stephens, Jr.

GRANDFATHER CLAUSE

Slavery in the United States, "except as a punishment for crime whereof the party shall have been duly convicted," was abolished by the ratification of the Thirteenth Amendment in 1865. The Four-teenth Amendment, ratified in 1868, guaranteed equal protection of the laws and due process rights to all citizens, including the former slaves. The Fifteenth Amendment, which followed in 1870, made it illegal to deny a citizen the right to vote based on "race, color, or previous condition of servitude." One result of the Fourteenth and Fifteenth Amendments was the creation of a vast pool of new black voters. These new voters of course began exercising the franchise in opposition to the Southern whites, who had held political power prior to and during the Civil War (Schmidt, Jr. 1982).

Shortly after the end of Reconstruction in 1877, the white majority in the South and border states regained its political dominance. Many states soon adopted constitutional or statutory provisions requiring literacy tests and/or poll taxes as a precondition for voting. These measures, in combination with outright violence and intimidation, had the effect of preventing most African Americans from exercising the franchise.

The new legal restrictions on voting also had the unintended effect of disenfranchising many poor and uneducated white citizens as well (Schmidt, Jr. 1982; Wechsler 2002). As a means of reinstating disqualified white voters, "grandfather clauses" were instituted in seven Southern states, beginning with Mississippi in 1890. Six other states followed suit: Alabama, Georgia, Louisiana, Maryland, North Carolina, and Oklahoma.

These provisions generally exempted illiterate whites from literacy test requirements if they could establish that they or one of their ancestors had been qualified to vote or had performed military service at some date prior to adoption of the Fourteenth Amendment. For example, Oklahoma's Grandfather Clause, adopted as an amendment to the state constitution in 1910, read:

No person shall be registered as an elector of this state or be allowed to vote in any election held herein, unless he be able to read and write any section of the Constitution of the state of Oklahoma; but no person who was, on January 1st, 1866, or any time prior thereto, entitled to vote under any form of government, or who at that time

resided in some foreign nation, and no lineal descendant of such person, shall be denied the right to register and vote because of his inability to so read and write sections of such Constitution. Precinct election inspectors having in charge the registration of electors shall enforce the provisions of this section at the time of registration, provided registration be required. Should registration be dispensed with, the provisions of this section shall be enforced by the precinct election officers when electors apply for ballots to vote.

Few African American men in the South qualified to be "grandfathered in" and so were subject to any literacy or property requirements (Wechsler 2002). Registrars charged with enforcing and administering literacy requirements had almost unlimited discretion. As a result, these registrars typically found African American applicants to be illiterate. The registrars could easily construct a literacy test consisting of questions that even the most educated person would be unable to answer. Using these techniques, registrars had no difficulty in finding, for example, that African Americans holding doctoral degrees from Booker T. Washington's Tuskegee Institute were "illiterate" (Klarman 1998). The goal was to create a "totally white male electorate" (Wechsler 2002, 40) without violating the Fifteenth Amendment.

Southern states that chose not to adopt grandfather clauses, including Arkansas, Florida, Tennessee, and Texas, used such devices as poll taxes and secret ballot laws to disenfranchise African American voters. The grandfather clause, combined with these disenfranchisement techniques and the ever-present threat of violence, kept most African Americans throughout the South and the border states away from the polls.

Even before grandfather clauses were enacted, the Supreme Court had indicated its reluctance to protect the rights of black voters. As early as 1870, Congress, acting pursuant to its power to enforce the Fifteenth Amendment, had passed legislation designed to ensure the voting rights of African Americans by punishing officers who interfered with the exercise of such rights. The Court, in *United States v. Reese* (1875), declared that

Congress violated the Constitution by legislating beyond the scope of its enforcement power.

During the 1880s and 1890s the Supreme Court rejected other efforts to combat racial discrimination. For example, in the Civil Rights Cases (1883), the Court struck down the Civil Rights Act of 1875 in which Congress had banned discrimination in places of public accommodation, and in *Plessy v. Ferguson* (1896) the Court endorsed the legal segregation of the races by enunciating the "separate but equal" doctrine.

The grandfather clause remained intact until well into the twentieth century. The National Association for the Advancement of Colored People (NAACP), founded in 1909, launched an active campaign to restore voting rights to African Americans. This campaign was ultimately successful when the Supreme Court invalidated Oklahoma's grandfather clause in the 1915 case of *Guinn v. United States* (1915). In this case, Chief Justice Edward D. White, writing for a unanimous Court (Justice McReynolds not participating) asserted:

It is true it [the grandfather clause] contains no express words of an exclusion from the standard which it establishes of any person on account of race, color, or previous condition of servitude, prohibited by the 15th Amendment, but the standard itself inherently brings that result into existence since it is based purely upon a period of time before the enactment of the 15th Amendment.

The elimination of grandfather clauses did not end the disenfranchisement of African Americans. For a number of years the Supreme Court was reluctant to overturn other laws that had the effect of denying voting rights to African Americans, including secret ballot laws, literacy requirements, white primaries, and poll taxes. The Court's position finally began to change with its invalidation of the white primary in 1944 (*Smith v. Allwright*). The continuing efforts of civil rights activists, culminating with the passage of the Voting Rights Act of 1965, effectively ended legal restrictions on the voting rights of African Americans.

See also Civil Rights Act of 1870; Civil Rights Act of 1875; The Civil Rights Cases; Civil Rights Movement; Due Process Clauses; Equal Protection Clause; Fifteenth Amendment; Fourteenth Amendment (1868); Jim Crow Laws; Literacy Tests; National Association for the Advancement of Colored People; Poll Tax; Public Accommodation, Places of; Reconstruction; Slavery; Thirteenth Amendment; Tyranny of the Majority; Vote, Right to; Voting Rights Act of 1965; Washington, Booker T.; White Primary

Bibliography

Klarman, Michael J. 1998. "Race and the Court in the Progressive Era." 1 *Vanderbilt Law Review* 881.

Schmidt, Jr., and C. Benno. 1982. "Principle and Prejudice: The Supreme Court and Race in the Progressive Era, Part 3: Black Disfranchisement from the KKK to the Grandfather Clause." 82 *Columbia Law Review* 835.

Wechsler, Burton D. 2002. "Black and White Disenfranchisement: Populism, Race, and Class." 52*American University Law Review* 23.

Rosalie R. Young and Otis H. Stephens, Jr.

GRAND JURY

A grand jury is a body composed of a group of citizens convened for the purpose of determining whether there is sufficient evidence to warrant criminal prosecution of a particular person. The institution is deeply rooted in the English common law. The Assize of Clarendon promulgated by King Henry II in 1166 required 12 "good and lawful men" to come together to act as an investigative agent of the Crown. Eventually, the grand jury at common law comprised 23 persons, at least 12 of whom had to agree in order to hand down an indictment. It then began to function as a check against arbitrary and unwarranted prosecution.

The Fifth Amendment to the U.S. Constitution provides, "No person shall be held to answer for a capital, or otherwise infamous crime, unless on a presentment or indictment of a Grand Jury, except in cases arising in the land or naval forces, or in the Militia, when in actual service in time of War or public danger…." In *United States v. Mandujano* (1976), the Supreme Court reflected on the intentions of the authors of the Bill of Rights with respect to the Grand Jury Clause:

The grand jury is an integral part of our constitutional heritage which was brought to this country with the common law. The Framers, most of them trained in the English law and traditions, accepted the grand jury as a basic guarantee of individual liberty; notwithstanding periodic criticism, much of which is superficial, overlooking relevant history, the grand jury continues to function as a barrier to reckless or unfounded charges.

A grand jury has unique characteristics. Grand jurors often serve for months. After a judge administers their oath, charges them as to their duties, and admonishes them to maintain secrecy of their proceedings, grand jurors meet in closed session with only the prosecutor, witnesses, court reporter and, if necessary, interpreters present. Witnesses are not allowed to have counsel present, but often are allowed to consult with counsel outside the hearing chambers. Testimony is not always transcribed, and if it is, access to transcripts is either limited or nonexistent. While controversial, grand jury secrecy is designed to encourage uninhibited testimony by witnesses and to prevent the circulation of derogatory statements about persons who are investigated but ultimately not indicted. The prosecutor is the key figure who presents the evidence in support of an indictment. After the prosecutor has presented testimony and physical evidence, the members of the grand jury vote whether to hand down an indictment.

A federal grand jury comprises 16 to 23 persons, but the 12-votes-for-indictment rule applies in every case. In keeping with the Fifth Amendment, federal law requires that prosecution for an offense punishable by death or by imprisonment for more than one year must be based on a grand jury indictment, but the Federal Rules of Criminal Procedure make provision for a defendant to waive the grand jury process in open court. Trial of a misdemeanor may be by indictment or by an "information," an accusatorial document filed by a prosecutor.

In *Hurtado v. California* (1884), the U.S. Supreme Court held that the Fourteenth Amendment, which demands that states provide due process of law to persons within their jurisdictions, does not require states to follow the grand jury system. As long as a court of law conducts a preliminary hearing on the evidentiary sufficiency of the information, due process is satisfied.

Most state constitutions have provisions concerning grand juries. In a few, for example, Tennessee, an indictment by a grand jury is required for prosecution of all crimes beyond petty offenses; in most other states it is required only for prosecution of felonies. In Florida and a few other states, a grand jury indictment is required only for charging a capital crime. Where indictment by a grand jury is not required, as is the case in most Midwestern and Western states, the grand jury is seldom used to charge persons with crimes. Where a grand jury indictment is not required, states permit prosecutors to charge defendants by filing a charging document under oath known as an information (or, in some states, an accusation). In these jurisdictions, courts hold preliminary hearings to determine whether there is probable cause, that is, sufficient evidence, to formally charge a defendant with a crime.

States vary in regard to the size of grand juries, but in every state at least a majority of grand jurors must agree that there is probable cause for trial in order to hand down an indictment against the accused. The grand jury, like the magistrate presiding over the preliminary hearing, examines the evidence and testimony the prosecution has collected against the accused. Unlike the preliminary hearing, the grand jury proceeding is normally closed—the defendant is not represented by counsel or even present at the proceeding. There is some variation among jurisdictions in the rules that determine grand jury indictments, but in no case can a grand jury return a "true bill" (another term for an indictment) unless a majority of grand jurors votes to indict. Normally, an indictment is a public document from the time it is handed down by the grand jury. However, to facilitate the arrest of persons who are still at large, grand juries are empowered to issue sealed indictments, which are made public only after those named in the indictments are taken into custody.

Grand juries possess the authority to compel the appearance of witnesses, to subpoena documents, to hold individuals in contempt, and to grant immunity from prosecution in exchange for testimony. Many of the rules of evidence that apply to the criminal trial do not apply to the grand jury. For example, hearsay evidence is generally admissible, whereas at trial, except in certain instances, it is not admitted over the defendant's objection. In *United States v. Calandra* (1974), the U.S. Supreme Court upheld the use in grand jury proceedings of illegally obtained evidence, stating that "allowing a grand jury witness to invoke the exclusionary rule would unduly interfere with the effective and expeditious discharge of the grand jury's duties." Similarly, in *United States v. Williams* (1992), the Supreme Court found that the prosecution does not have a duty to disclose exculpatory evidence to the grand jury. The theory underlying these rulings is that the grand jury is an investigative body and that any infringement of the rights of the accused can be corrected in subsequent adversary court proceedings. Despite the fact that a grand jury may consider evidence that is inadmissible at trial, it may not violate a valid evidentiary privilege (for example, the attorney-client or spousal privilege) established by the Constitution, statutes, or the common law.

Supporters of the grand jury system argue that it represents democracy in action and enhances the public confidence in the criminal justice system. On the other hand, because grand juries seldom refuse to hand down indictments sought by prosecutors, critics contend grand juries become a rubber stamp for the prosecutor. They point out that it is unfair to exclude potential defendants and their lawyers from the process and they question the utility of the institution as a safeguard for the rights of the accused. They sometimes cite an old adage, quoted frequently by defense lawyers, that "a grand jury would indict a ham sandwich if the prosecutor asked it to do so." These criticisms may explain why a number of states have adopted the information/ preliminary hearing mechanism in place of the grand jury.

See also Accused, Rights of the; Assize of Clarendon; Bill of Rights, Incorporation of; Common Law Background of American Civil Rights and Liberties; Due Process Clauses; Due Process, Procedural; Exculpatory Evidence, Disclosure of; Fifth Amendment; Fourteenth Amendment; Fourth Amendment; Indictment

Bibliography

Kadish, Mark. 1996. "Behind the Locked Door of an American Grand Jury: Its History, Its Secrecy, and Its Process." 24 *Florida State University Law Review* 1.

Morse, Wayne. 1931. "A Survey of the Grand Jury System." 10 *Oregon Law Review* 101.

Scheb, John M., and John M. Scheb II. 2006. *Criminal Procedure*. Belmont, CA: Thomson/Wadsworth.

Schwartz, Bernard. 1971. *The Bill of Rights: A Documentary History*. New York: Chelsea House.

Schwartz, Helene E. 1972. "Demythologizing the Historic Role of the Grand Jury." 10 *American Criminal Law Review* 701.

Hon. John M. Scheb and John M. Scheb II

GREGG V. GEORGIA (1976)

In the wake of the Supreme Court's decision in *Furman v. Georgia* (1972), which invalidated the death penalty as it was being administered by the state courts, state legislatures around the country rewrote their death penalty laws. Georgia's revamped death penalty statute was before the Supreme Court in the *Gregg* case of 1976. The revised Georgia Law requires a bifurcated trial for capital crimes: In the first stage guilt is determined in the usual manner; the second stage deals with the appropriate sentence. For the jury to impose the death penalty, it has to find at least one of several statutorily prescribed aggravating factors. Automatic appeal to the state supreme court is also provided. The appellate review must consider not only the procedural regularity of the trial, but whether the evidence supports the finding of the aggravating factor and whether the death sentence is disproportionate to the penalty imposed in similar cases.

Troy Gregg was convicted of armed robbery and murder and was sentenced to death under Georgia's revised death penalty statute. In reviewing the sentence, the Supreme Court upheld the revamped capital punishment law, with only Justices William Brennan and Thurgood Marshall dissenting. These justices took the view, as they would for the rest of their careers on the Court, that the death penalty is inherently cruel and unusual punishment, regardless of any procedural changes designed to enhance its fairness or predictability.

Justice Potter Stewart's opinion announcing the judgment of the Court made clear that he believed that the state of Georgia had addressed adequately his concerns over the administration of the death penalty:

The new Georgia sentencing procedures … focus the jury's attention on the particularized nature of the crime and the particularized characteristics of the individual defendant.… In this way the jury's discretion is channeled. No longer can a jury wantonly and freakishly impose the death sentence, it is always circumscribed by the legislative guidelines.

In Stewart's view, Georgia (and, by implication, the other states that followed the same model) had done what was necessary to make the death penalty more rational, fair, and just. Thus, after a hiatus of only four years, the death penalty was effectively reinstated by the Supreme Court in 1976.

See also Bifurcated Trial; Brennan, William J., Jr.; Cruel and Unusual Punishments Clause; Death Penalty, Crimes Punishable by the; Death-Qualified Juries; Eighth Amendment; *Furman v. Georgia* (1972); Marshall, Thurgood; Stewart, Potter

John M. Scheb, II and Otis H. Stephens, Jr.

GRISWOLD V. CONNECTICUT (1965)

In *Griswold v. Connecticut,* the Supreme Court held for the first time that privacy is a constitutional right and thereby set off a national debate on the subject. The Court's decision later became the basis for holdings in areas such as abortion and homosexual rights.

The case began when Estelle Griswold, the executive director of the Planned Parenthood League of Connecticut, opened a birth control clinic in New Haven. She and Dr. C. Lee Buxton, the center medical director who gave birth control advice and devices to married couples, were convicted under a previously unenforced 1879 Connecticut statute that forbade both the use of contraceptives to prevent conception and the giving of advice about them.

The word *privacy* does not appear in the Constitution. The Supreme Court had nonetheless found such a right as it applied to governmental intrusion in specific, limited circumstances. It had, for example, described the Fourth and Fifth Amendments, which ban unreasonable searches and seizures and forbid forced self-incrimination, as safeguarding "the sanctity of a man's home and the privacies of life" (*Boyd v. United States,* 1886) and protecting an individual's expectation of privacy for calls made from a public telephone booth (*Katz v. United States,* 1967). The Court had similarly spoken of a privacy right in conjunction with such First Amendment rights as the right to join organizations (*NAACP v. Alabama,* 1958). While in the past it had specifically rejected a "general constitutional 'right to privacy'" (*Katz v. United States*), Justice William O. Douglas, writing for the Court in *Griswold,* drew on precedents such as those cited above to proclaim that "specific guarantees in the Bill of Rights" do indeed create such a generalized right. He pointed not only to the First, Fourth, and Fifth Amendments but to the Third, with its prohibition against the quartering of soldiers in private homes during peacetime, and the Ninth Amendment, which reserves rights that are unenumerated in the Constitution to the people. Together, Douglas asserted, the "penumbras" (shadows or emanations) of these Amendments created a constitutional right that applied to many areas of life.

That constitutional privacy right, he continued, was particularly important when applied to married couples such as those counseled by Griswold's center. Marriage involved "a right of privacy older than the Bill of Rights," and the Connecticut law regulating the use of contraceptives by married couple "seeks to achieve its goals by means having a maximum destructive impact upon that relationship." The law could not stand. While the amendments which Douglas listed were written as limitations only on the federal government, the word "liberty" in the Fourteenth Amendment's Due Process Clause ("No State shall … deprive any person of life, liberty, or property, without due process of law") made them applicable to the states as well.

Concerned about what he saw as the vagueness of the "penumbras" argument, Justice Arthur Goldberg wrote for himself and two other justices that the only relevant section of the Constitution was the Ninth Amendment's reservation of unenumerated rights to the people. "The entire fabric of the Constitution," Goldberg said in his concurring opinion, made it clear that "the rights to marital privacy and to marry and raise a family" had the status of fundamental rights. Justices Hugo L. Black and Potter Stewart, while calling the statute "offensive" and "an uncommonly silly law," nonetheless voted to uphold it because the Constitution did not specifically mention privacy.

In 1972, the Court held that states could not deny unmarried people the same privacy right held by those who were married (*Eisenstadt v. Baird*), and in 1973, it drew upon the right set out in *Griswold* when it enunciated a right to legal abortion (*Roe v. Wade*). Thirty years later, the Court referred to *Griswold* and *Eisenstadt* when it decided, in *Lawrence v. Texas* (2003), that laws outlawing sex between adult homosexuals were unconstitutional because homosexuals "are equally entitled to respect for their private lives."

See also Abortion, Right to; Bill of Rights (American) (1789); Bill of Rights, Incorporation of; Black, Hugo L.; Douglas, William O.; Due Process, Substantive; Fourteenth Amendment; Goldberg, Arthur; Judicial Activism; *Katz v. United States* (1967); *Lawrence v. Texas* (2003); Liberty; Marriage, Rights Pertaining to; Ninth Amendment; Planned Parenthood; Privacy, Constitutional Right

of; Reproductive Freedom; *Roe v. Wade;* Stewart, Potter; Surrogate Motherhood

Bibliography

Garrow, David J. 1994. *Liberty & Sexuality: The Right to Privacy and the Making of Roe v. Wade.* New York: Macmillan Publishing Co.

Johnson, John W. 2005. *Griswold v. Connecticut: Birth Control and the Constitutional Rights of Privacy.* Lawrence: University Press of Kansas.

Philippa Strum

GROTIUS, HUGO. *See* Natural Law and Natural Rights

GROUP RIGHTS

In recent years there has been a renewed interest in the idea of group rights. For many people this is a dangerous development evoking memories of "the folk" and "chosen people" beliefs that have wrought so much damage through the centuries. For others it is a welcome alternative to the increasingly radical individualism that seems to pervade American culture, and which is invading other cultures as well. One might reasonably ask why interest in group rights has arisen at the beginning of the twenty-first century. There are several reasons. First, in the United States the issue of affirmative action based on racial identity has stimulated the most interest and controversy in the context of group rights as it is perceived by many to constitute reverse discrimination. Second, globalization, abetted by low transportation costs, has made mass migration of workers a worldwide phenomenon, with the majority of migrants coming from developing nations. The idea of group rights develops when these migrants are minority groups. Third, inexpensive communications has made it much easier for migrants to maintain frequent contacts with their countries of origin, families, and villages, thereby making assimilation a less urgent necessity and maintaining the mother tongue and village customs much more easily. Finally, an enhanced consciousness of human rights and group identity, even among migrants, makes it easier for groups to insist upon maintaining their own identities.

Historical Roots of Group and Individual Rights

Before the advent of Christianity there was hardly a conception of a "self" with rights apart from and outside of one's group. In Greek culture the city was considered the locus of identity, while in the rest of the world the tribe provided a meaning system and, indeed, the parameters of one's world. A person traveling abroad would likely be identified as "the Athenian," or "the man from Corinth." In tribal societies, names usually reflected family or tribe: "son of Abram," "son of Eric," and so on. Banishment from city or tribe was a fate worse than death. In *The Republic* and *The Laws,* Plato focused on how to train individuals to be good citizens of individual cities. Ancient literature records the differences between Athens and Sparta in their conceptions of what this virtue might encompass, but in each case the focus was on how to train the individual to submit to the ethos of the city.

Christianity added a radical new dimension: Every person has a soul and may look forward to eternal life *as an individual;* God loves even women and slaves. Still, group identity remained enormously strong, and it was difficult to conceive of a new religion created by Jews developing outside of Judaism. As a result there were centuries of conflicts as Jews and Christians developed separate group identities and cultures. Nevertheless, the seeds of individualism had been planted and continued to flourish.

The Protestant Reformation in the sixteenth century had a mixed impact on the development of individualism. Catholicism had a sense of community ("outside the church there is no salvation") that was broken by Luther's priesthood of all believers, as well as his teaching that each person could interpret Scriptures. This promoted the interests of the individual over the group, inadvertently leading to a major splintering of Protestants into a multitude of sects. It also left individuals at the mercy of secular rulers.

Americans like to consider their Constitution, and particularly the Bill of Rights, ratified in 1791, as the epitome of protection for individual freedoms and rejection of group rights. The reality is more complex. The Constitution does provide a legal foundation for individual rights, but it treats "Indians not taxed" as a group in order to exclude them from representation (Art. I, Sec. 2). It gives Congress power to regulate commerce "with the Indian tribes" (Art. I, Sec. 8). It also establishes the infamous "three-fifths of all other Persons" standard for counting slaves for purposes of representation without giving them any individual rights (Art. I., Sec. 2). The Fourteenth Amendment changed this provision.

The most significant concession to group interests, however, was establishing a federalist system. The Founders recognized that citizens had a stronger loyalty to their geographical entities, now called states, than to any national entity, so the Constitution established a federal structure based on states. Individuals were given national representation through their state legislatures, or in the instance of presidential elections, through the electoral college, which itself provided representation by states.

As the system has worked for more than two centuries, American federalism has managed to keep groups in check without rendering them irrelevant. There are subtleties that allow some under-represented groups to have a voice, or at least a presence, in government. For example, states with small populations elect the same number of senators as more heavily populated states. As a result 16 percent of the American people elect 50 percent of the senators. Also, American presidents have used their power to appoint federal judges and Supreme Court justices as a means to appeal to various groups. President Washington carefully appointed justices from the Northeast, the Middle States, and the South. Later presidents provided religious representation of Catholics and Jews. In recent years both Republicans and Democrats considered it important to appoint women and racial minorities to the Supreme Court. In brief, while Americans tout their commitment to individual rights, the reality of American practice is much more nuanced. Groups are sometimes recognized as such.

The American Racial Dilemma

The United States is a multiracial society. Over 30 percent of its population is nonwhite. Twelve percent are of African-American heritage. They are descendants of slaves and freed blacks who suffered decades of discrimination, exclusion, and violence. Through a remarkable series of court decisions and legislative efforts, legal discrimination and segregation ended. Informal and subtle discrimination was harder to eradicate. Certainly the effects of discrimination and exclusion show up in statistics of lower wages, lower levels of education, and less wealth accumulation, as well as higher rates of poverty, single-parent families, unemployment, health problems, and incarceration of African Americans. Similar statistics apply to Hispanics and Native Americans. How can these problems be addressed? Should they be?

Affirmative action, that is, making special efforts to attract, employ or admit, African Americans, Hispanics, and Native Americans in preference to similarly qualified whites, has been one successful tactic, at least in the eyes of its supporters. The question, however, is whether this preferential treatment creates a group right giving these minorities an advantage over whites based on group identity rather than individual merit. The Supreme Court has stated emphatically that it does not. Justice Sandra Day O'Connor wrote in *Adarand Constructors, Inc. v Pena* (1995) that "the basic principle [is] that the Fifth and Fourteenth Amendments to the Constitution protect persons, not groups." Rather than outlawing affirmative action, however, she and the Court have required that it be subject to heightened judicial scrutiny to determine whether there is indeed a compelling state interest. A Supreme Court majority reiterated this position in *Grutter v. Bollinger* (2003), upholding the University of Michigan law school's affirmative action admissions policy. The court stated that student diversity is a compelling interest of the law school, but insisted that each applicant be given individualized consideration. In short, group rights have a somewhat tenuous existence in American law.

See also Affirmative Action; Bill of Rights (American); Diversity; Equality; Equal Protection Clause; Federalism and Civil Rights and Liberties; Fifth Amendment; Fourteenth Amendment (1868); Gender-Based Discrimination; Individual Rights; Latino Americans, Civil Rights of; Native Americans, Civil Rights of; O'Connor, Sandra Day; Plato

Bibliography

Ingram, David. 2000. *Group Rights: Reconciling Equality and Difference.* Lawrence: University Press of Kansas.

Sistare, Christine, Larry May, and Leslie Francis, eds. 2001. *Groups and Group Rights.* Lawrence: University Press of Kansas.

Paul Weber